JOURNEYS OF THE PERSIAN BOUNDARY COMMISSION,

1870–71–72.

GEOGRAPHY

OF

EASTERN PERSIA.

BREAKFAST WITH THE AMIR OF KAÍN.

EASTERN PERSIA

AN ACCOUNT OF THE

JOURNEYS OF THE PERSIAN BOUNDARY COMMISSION
1870 – 71 – 72

VOL. I

THE GEOGRAPHY

WITH

NARRATIVES

BY

MAJORS ST. JOHN, LOVETT, AND EUAN SMITH

AND AN

INTRODUCTION

BY MAJOR-GENERAL

SIR FREDERIC JOHN GOLDSMID, C.B., K.C.S.I.

British Commissioner and Arbitrator

Published by the Authority of the Government of India

London
MACMILLAN AND CO.
1876

[All rights reserved]

OXFORD:
BY E. PICKARD HALL AND J. H. STACY,
PRINTERS TO THE UNIVERSITY.

CONTENTS.

By Major-General Sir Frederic J. Goldsmid, C.B., K.C.S.I.

	PAGE
INTRODUCTION	ix

By Major Oliver B. St. John, R.E.

THE PHYSICAL GEOGRAPHY OF PERSIA	1
NARRATIVE OF A JOURNEY THROUGH BALUCHISTAN AND SOUTHERN PERSIA, 1872	18

By Major Beresford Lovett, R.E., C.S.I.

NARRATIVE OF A JOURNEY IN BALUCHISTAN, 1870–71	117

By Major Euan Smith, C.S.I.

THE PERSO-BALUCH FRONTIER MISSION, 1870–71	143
THE PERSO-AFGHAN MISSION, 1871–72	225

APPENDICES:

A.—The Sistán Arbitration—Summary of evidence, conclusions, information, &c. 395

B.—The Sistán Arbitration—General summary and arbitral opinion 410

C.—Genealogical Trees, with notes, for the Sistán chiefs of the Káiyáni, Sarbandi, and Shahraki Families; as also the Nharui and Sanjaráni (Toki) Baluchis of Sistán . . 415

D.—Itineraries 428

INDEX 431

MAPS AND ILLUSTRATIONS.

Breakfast with the Amir of Káin	*Frontispiece to Volume.*
Castle of Aibí in the district of Kalagán	„ to *Physical Geography.*
Map descriptive of Hydrography of Persia	*To face page* 3.
„ of Orography of Persia	„ *page* 6.
„ of Routes traversed by Authors	„ *page* 18.

EXPLANATORY NOTICE.

The system of spelling Indian words now commonly accepted in official correspondence has been here applied to the transliteration of Persian. The accents have not always been repeated, as they will scarcely be always needed for the reader's guidance. Names such as 'Isfahan' and 'Karman,' for instance, once written 'Isfahán' and 'Karmán,' will, it is hoped, be readily understood to carry the accent on the second 'a' only. A few words have been selected for separate interpretation, and are arranged in alphabetical order :—

Ab-ambár, p. 166, &c.; reservoir of water; usually, a covered tank.

Abdár, p. 239, &c.; a servant who looks after the cups and saucers, and drinking department.

Ahwál-pursí, p. 310, &c.; enquiry after health.

A'kásh-báshi, p. 361; photographer-in-chief.

Atak, p. 5; a Turkish word, 'skirt' (of the hills).

Azán, p. 332; the call to prayers.

Bád-i-bistróz, p. 287; literally, the 'wind of twenty days.'

Band, p. 272, &c. &c.; a dam, or embankment.

Bhúta, p. 165, &c.; *bhutta* in Hindustání; Indian corn or maize.

Chapáti, p. 45; in Hindustání, a thin bread cake.

Chars, p. 317; an intoxicating drug, prepared, like *bang*, from hemp.

Chinár, p. 108, &c.; the plane-tree.

Dák, p. 324; in Hindustání, 'posting;' vulgarly, *dawk*.

Faráhí, p. 323; inhabitant of Farah or Farrah.

Farangi, p. 44, &c., *Faringi*, p. 155; Frank or European.

Farásh, p. 22, &c.; more strictly *farrásh*, a tent-pitcher or carpet-spreader; with *báshi*, p. 220, the head *farrásh*.

Farsakh, p. 88, &c. (parasang); a measure of distance, varying from three to four miles.

Gabr, p. 59; vulgarly *guebre*, a fire-worshipper.

Ghí, p. 31; vulgarly *ghee*, 'clarified butter' (Sanskrit).

Hákim, p. 99; a governor.

Hámún, p. 254, &c.; a lake or swamp.

Iliát, p. 80, &c.; wandering tribes.

Imámzádah, p. 90, &c.; literally, 'descendant of an Imám;' a tomb or shrine.

Júlgah, p. 320, note; a plain between mountains.

Kahur, p. 234, or *Kuhar*, p. 247; a tree common to the tracts south of the Sistán desert.

Kalián, p. 73, or *kaliún*; the Persian pipe.

Kásid, p. 22; commonly 'cossid,' a messenger.

Kirbás, p. 336; fine linen.

Kúrk, p. 337; fine short wool of the goat, nearest the skin.

Majlis, p. 291; conclave or council.

Mann, p. 172; vulgarly *mann* or *maund*; a weight varying from 6¼ to 9 lbs., according to locality.

Masjíd, p. 347; a mosque; literally, a 'place of prostration' for prayer.

Mihmándár, p. 186, &c.; one whose office is to attend to guests.

viii   EXPLANATORY NOTICE.

Mihmán-khánah, p. 90; a 'guest-house,' or caravanserai.

Mihráb, p. 315; that part of the mosque where the priest prays, with his face towards Makkah.

Múazzin, p. 299; the caller of the *azán* above explained.

Múnshi, p. 150, &c.; scribe or secretary: with *báshi*, p. 183, head secretary.

Múshtahid, p. 189; should rather, perhaps, be *mújtahid*, learned Doctor of Divinity, a title well described by Chardin.

Náib, p. 257; a deputy, a lieutenant.

Nauroz, p. 272; Persian New-year's Day.

Náushirwán, p. 384 (*Núshirwán*, p. 46); an ancient monarch famed for justice.

Názir, p. 213; steward, overseer, superintendent of household.

Pish-khidmat, p. 357; valet or body-servant, waiter, one 'serving in the presence.'

Ramadhán, p. 175, *Ramazán*, p. 163; the Muhammadan Fast.

Rúd-khánah, p. 197; river; strictly river-bed.

Shia'h, p. 98, note; Persian Muslims, i.e. Muslims whose tenets differ from the orthodox *Súnnis* of Turkey, Arabia, and India.

Shúr, with *jungle*, p. 296 (correctly *jangal*); salt-vegetation.

Sowár, p. 36, &c.; a horseman.

Trat, &c., p. 314; Sistán vegetation.

Túfangchi, p. 375; a matchlock-bearer.

Wakíl-ul-múlk, p. 86; a title meaning 'Agent' or 'Vice-gerent of the kingdom.'

Wazír, p. 61; the Turkish *Vizier*; a minister.

Zábit, p. 346; a village functionary, a collector of revenue.

Zamín-i-kavír, p. 370; land of *kavír*, or salt-swamp.

Ziárat-gáh, p. 321; place of pilgrimage, shrine.

Here and there a discrepancy of spelling, such as in 'Daharzin,' page 86, and 'Dárzin,' page 195, has been caused by the existence of reasonable grounds for each of two conflicting versions.

The maps accompanying this work are necessarily on a reduced scale. The large map of Persia prepared by Major St. John for the India Office is, indeed, the only one obtainable which would fairly illustrate the journeys recorded. The geological map illustrative of Mr. Blanford's memoir will be deposited in the India Office, and a copy placed at the disposal of the Director-General of the Museum for Geology, for reference.

F. J. G.

ERRATA.

Page 124, line 14 from bottom, *for* 'Khákhi' *read* 'Kháki.'

„ 145, line 10, *for* 1837 *read* 1857.

„ 146 to 162 *passim*, *for* 'Sir F.' *read* 'Major-General Goldsmid.'

„ 165, line 3 from bottom, *for* 'whence' *read* 'where.'

„ 208, line 9 from bottom, *for* 'at' *read* 'of.'

„ 212, line 4, *for* 'are' *read* 'were.'

„ 244, line 7, *for* 'then' *read* 'than.'

„ 248, line 14, *for* 'shows' *read* 'show.'

„ 257, line 16, *after* 'graveyard' *insert* 'the possessors of.'

„ 319, line 2, *for* 'Hisám-i-' *read* 'Hisámu-s-.'

„ 366, after line 17, insert heading: 'V. *Mash-had to Tehrán*.'

INTRODUCTION.

Indian Frontier from Peshāwar to Karāchi.—Afghānistán.—Balúchistan.—Abstract Narrative of Perso-Makrán Boundary Commission—of Sistán Arbitration.—Consideration of Results.—Explanatory Notice of Papers contained in the present Work: Official Duties of the Authors.

THE origin of the Travels and Researches which form the groundwork of the present volumes may be traced to the interest aroused of late years in India by political revolutions in the lands of immediate neighbours on the West; an interest naturally heightened by progressive encroachment from without, affecting all faith in those frontiers which, next to our own, it is of the greatest importance to us to keep inviolate. Hence it was that arose anxiety to recognise a more settled state of things; but as annexation and enlargement of territory were no longer contemplated by Indian statesmen, already overworked in the internal administration of the vast Empire committed to their charge, the desired object could only be attained by a process which might be determinate but must be peaceful. Such innovation in the ways of Asiatic policy was beset with difficulties; and its dangers were at least as great, if not as palpable and immediate, as those of hostile armies. The main question was how to bring about a reign of order for the bordering population, and at the same time strengthen and secure the attachment to ourselves of normally turbulent border allies, without armed or abrupt interference. Added to this consideration was the grave fact that whatever line of policy were chosen or whatever step taken, a move would unavoidably be made, on the Central-Asian board, towards completion of the game in which our play had become characterised by a discretion so tardy, and a deliberation so excessive, that it was hardly clear to the outer world whether we were playing at all.

The battles of Miáni (1843) and Guzerat (1849) were significant political events as well as mere military successes. For the conquest of Sind and annexation of the Panjáb carried our whole frontier beyond the Indus, or to a line reaching from Persháwar on the north to Karáchi on the south. Afghánistán and Balúchistán thus became contiguous States to British India; and this contiguity of territorial possession could not fail to provoke, at least in some material respects, identity of interests. If mistrust, fear and aversion, on one side, and patient conciliation, on the other, have not hitherto favoured the happy development of geographical position or smoothed off the rough edges of accidental affinity, the cause is far from exceptional. Time may have been insufficient, and circumstances contrary. The second quarter of a century may be more propitious than the first. Before coming to recent facts and results, a brief retrospect of some twenty to thirty years will perhaps be appropriate. Let us commence with Afghánistán, the more familiar to English ears of the two States above-named.

Had there never been an Anglo-Hindustáni Expedition of 1839, and its consequent chapters of disaster, we should no doubt have taken advantage of a common frontier to inaugurate a policy of mutual benefit, and sought by friendly offices and conciliatory missions to make the Afgháns forget that Persháwar and Shikárpur were once their own. But our extension and rectification of boundary occurred at a time when the Kábul tragedy had weakened our prestige, and the retaliating policy had embittered the feeling of hostility against the invaders however notably it had reasserted their power. We could negotiate; because negotiation may be carried on in the East under all circumstances: but we could not send our agents freely into the country of our Afghán neighbours, nor could we have an Envoy at Kábul as at Tehrán or Constantinople. The residence of a British officer at Kandahár, rendered especially hazardous though opportune by the critical accident of the Indian mutinies, was of too temporary a character to be cited in evidence of genuine amicable relations. Nor can the Treaty with Dost Muhammad Khán, signed 'on his own part and on the part of his heirs and successors,' two years before, be considered more significant or binding, as an international agreement, than any other which we may have made and ratified with individual chiefs now dead and gone. The 'heirship' involved a question, and exception might be taken, in the eyes of the law, to the mode of solution accepted by our politicians.

INTRODUCTION. xi

Very important facts to be remembered, in unravelling the complex knot of Afghán politics, are these. The prestige of an Afghán sovereign such as Ahmad Shah Duráni, who reigned from 1747 to 1773, was won and maintained by possession of a kingdom represented by the three cities of Herát, Kábul, and Kandahár in the West, North, and South respectively. Pesháwar in the East, and even Lahor might be added; but they are not required for present illustration. In the dawn of the present century this power was fairly broken up, and re-integration was never perhaps again successfully or thoroughly effected until Herát fell to Dost Muhammad Khán on the 27th May, 1863[1]. The Dost died in a fortnight from the date of that event—an important one, to judge from Persian protestations and special missions, but little regarded in England; and later in the year, when his power to make good his nomination had been tested, Sher Ali was acknowledged by the British Government as his successor. The normal state of revolution, however, so far re-asserted its influence in Kábul, the head-quarters of substantial Government, that, on the 21st May 1866, we find Afzal Khán, elder half-brother of Sher Ali, there installed in room of the latter; and he so remained, virtual Amír and lord of the capital, until his death in October, 1867, when Azím Khán, another elder half-brother, succeeded. Sher Ali, meanwhile,

---

[1] I quote from a brief abstract of Afghán history for the years 1801-3, prepared by myself in the course of official duty on the Sind frontier (1854), and printed by the Bombay Government:—'Shortly after the demise of Taimur Shah, the solid monarchy of the great Ahmad had weakened into a broken and divided state, the principal cities in which, such as Kábul, Kandahár, Herát, Ghazni, and Pesháwar, would mark, as it were, separate chiefdoms, held by the more successful pretenders to supremacy. The prestige was for Kábul above all others. It had become synonymous with the seat of royalty; and its Bála Hisár was perhaps more eagerly sought after than the whole beautiful province of Kashmir. Fath Khán Barakzai won this important stronghold for Prince Mahmúd, who had, according to some authorities, become the legitimate heir to the crown after the death of his elder brother Humáiyún in 1798; for Shah Zamán can only be considered in the light of an usurper. The Shahzádah was equally successful at Pesháwar and Herát; and Kandahár had long since acknowledged his power. There was almost a prospect of consolidated government being restored to Afghánistán. But Mahmúd was little more than a weak sensualist, and knew better how to lose than consolidate an empire. His former opponent, Shuja', on the other hand, while reduced to vagrancy and destitution, had consoled himself with the conviction that opportunity was the richest jewel he could possess, and only required a steady search to be found. The expected moment arrived ere long. The conduct of Mahmúd had produced intestine disorder at the capital. Fath Khán made a defence for his master; but the popular tide had turned: the king was a prisoner in the hands of his people, and in July, 1803, Shah Shuja' was paramount.'—Selection from the Records of the Bombay Government, No. xvii. New Series.

accepting the precarious share of dominion left him by circumstances, patiently bided his time amid the disquiet of an erratic life till, in September, 1868, having gathered sufficient strength to make a bold move when the fitting occasion offered, he advanced northward to the reconquest of his sovereignty from Kandahár.

From this period it became not only the desire but the expressed policy of the Indian Government to cement an Anglo-Afghán alliance, by any measures short of open interference in the internal administration of the country. It would be foreign to the purpose of the present Introduction to explain the causes or discuss the propriety of the course pursued. The writer has only to deal with facts. On Sher Ali's return to Kábul, a correspondence was opened on the part of its chief with the Indian Government, which resulted in the grant by the latter of twelve lacs of rupees and arms, and the Viceroy's intimation, on leaving India in January, 1869, that periodical aid, in similar shape, might be anticipated for future years. A proposed visit of the Amir to British territory was in no way set aside by the change of Governors-General. Lord Lawrence's departure was soon followed by Lord Mayo's arrival on the scene. And the *darbár* held at Ambála, in the dawn of the new personal *régime*, gave unmistakable testimony that the offer of substantial friendship made by Her Majesty's Indian Government to Sher Ali Khán would be recognised so long as his appreciation of the boon was such as could, in common honesty, be expected. Nor did after events afford indications of any change in the relations between the Viceroy of India and the Amir of Afghánistán, up to the sudden date of the calamity which deprived India of one of her noblest of statesmen. During that interval Sher Ali had not rested upon a bed of roses. But he had been upon the whole successful; he had maintained his essential power; and our moral and material aid had, no doubt, served him well in subduing his enemies and consolidating his chiefdom.

He had had relations with Bukhára and Russia, with Kalát and with Persia, the nature of which could not fail to interest the Indian Foreign Office: for in the progress of these cropped up questions of great political importance. So far as could be judged under circumstances which involved a marked geographical separation and permitted no interchange of resident diplomatists, his loyalty to the British had been fairly true. According to common custom in Oriental States, and invariable practice in Afghánistán, his most formidable opponents had been his own relatives. Of these, his deposed brother, Azim Khán, had died at Shahrud, in Northern Persia, in October, 1869. Two of Azim's sons, Sarwar and Izhák, and their cousin, Abdul Rahman, son of Afzal Khán, had carried their ambition and intrigues across the Oxus; the second having been fairly defeated in the field in the neighbourhood of Balkh. The more obnoxious of his half-brothers, Ahmad, Zamán, and Umar Khán, were located in British territory. Last, but not least in a list sufficiently long for the present purpose, remains Muhammad Ya'kub Khán, the Amir's own son, Governor of Herát, who appears to have exercised a more general than divisional control on the occasion of his father's absence at Ambála. We shall revert to him further on in the course of the present Introduction.

Among other questions which attracted the serious attention of Lord Mayo during his Indian Viceroyalty, was that of Sistán, a province on the Eastern Frontier of Persia, which had become comprehended in Afghánistán on its first conversion into a consolidated monarchy by Ahmad Shah Duráni, but which, by a common process of intrigue and encroachment, had lapsed almost imperceptibly to her stronger neighbour on the West. Sher Ali, as Amir of Afghánistán, aimed at recovery of a province, the loss of which he could see in no other light than that of territorial disintegration. Persia, on the other hand, laid claim to Sistán by virtue of a more ancient sovereignty than that of Ahmad Shah; and justified recent conquest and annexation, within its limits, as the mere assertion of dormant rights. In England, or indeed in Europe, few people knew anything of the particular tract in dispute, or of the arguments of the litigants respectively claiming ownership; and of these few the greater part were rather scholars and geographers than politicians. It had been described, more or less in detail, by Conolly, Ferrier, and Khanikoff; but, with rare exceptions, the descriptions had been serviceable to *savants* and societies, not to Ministers and Governments. The Asiatic department of the Russian Foreign Office did not fail to note the information conveyed, for its mere political bearing on one branch of the Eastern question; and as acquaintance with its history and geography was considered essential to a due comprehension of the whole matter, it may be presumed that St. Petersburg was not much behind Calcutta in arriving at a respectable appreciation of the situation. But there were intricacies that could only be mastered by local enquiry and inspection. Persia had complained to the Court of St. James's of Afghánistán; and Afghánistán had complained to the British Indian Government of Persia. It was eventually determined that the knot should be untied, or, at least, severed by Arbitration. On the 9th August, 1870, the present writer was honoured by the instructions of Her Majesty's principal Secretary of State for India for guidance in carrying out the duties of Arbitrator, a post to which he had been nominated by the Duke of Argyll with the concurrence and approval of the late Lord Clarendon.

Our more modern and immediate relations with Balúchistán may be said to date from the march of British troops into that country, *en route* to Afghánistán. This movement, part of the before-mentioned Anglo-Hindustáni Expedition, had been preceded by Lieutenant Leech's Mission in 1838, and the conclusion of a treaty with Mihráb Khán, ruler of Kalát, the conduct of which, on the part of England, had been confided to Sir Alexander Burnes. Whether or no the chief's failure to fulfil the terms of his agreement warranted the severe punishment it received is a question for history. So far as opinion may now be formed, the intrigues of an ambitious Minister had much to do in misleading the Khán, and enthusiasm in a cause of 'king-making' had something to do in blinding ourselves. But it is quite certain that Mihráb Khán's capital was stormed and taken by our soldiers, he himself killed in fight, his territory partitioned, and the succession of his son ignored for a more convenient pretender; moreover, that an insurrection ensued, resulting in the deposition of the new Khán, the imprisonment and murder of the British agent, and the eventual recognition and restoration to his father's territory, by the Governor-General of India in 1841, of Mihráb Khán's own son and heir, Nasír Khán. Shortly after this last event Sind was conquered and annexed, and the politics of Balúchistán became a question of permanent interest to the authorities of British India.

Nasír Khán ruled for some sixteen years. During this period the British alliance may be said to have exercised a direct as well as healthful influence upon Kalát affairs; and the energy and spirit of the Frontier Administration, illustrated by a *personnel* of exceptionally single-minded type, gave truer evidence than history or tradition that loyalty would be met with loyalty, truth with truth, and honour with honour. The formal annexation of Sind in 1843 was followed by hostilities with certain Balúch tribes on its north-western borders. These marauders, finally subdued by the frontier troops into comparative quiescence, were both troublesome neighbours and refractory subjects. It was essential to the maintenance of amicable relations and the development of commerce that their misdoings should be checked, and that the passes leading through Kalát and Afghánistán should be cleared of banditti. At one time Sir Charles Napier, at another Major Jacob and Mr. Frere, met the Khán in a formal but friendly manner. In 1856 an English political agent (Major Henry Green) was accredited to Nasír Khán's court. The Persian war broke out in the same year, and the services of this officer were required with the Expeditionary Force despatched from India to Bushahr. Very soon after his departure, the Khán died, under the influence, it is credibly affirmed, of poison administered by intriguing and ambitious counsellors whose advice he had learned to disregard.

Khudadád Khán, who succeeded his half-brother Nasir II eighteen years ago, is the ruler of Kalát at the present day. A narrative of his career of chiefdom would offer to the readers of civilised Europe a good example of the normal distractions of a petty Oriental State without an Oriental despotism. On the present occasion space will not admit of more than a rough summary. Chosen at sixteen years of age from among other claimants, according to a rule of inheritance which, setting aside an episode of foreign interference, had been fairly respected for three generations, he at once became initiated in the cares as in the gratifications attendant on his position. His accession to power was the signal for action on the part of intriguing advisers and jealous, turbulent feudatories. While the latter were his co-religionists, if not all of his kith or kin, the former were of less uniform composition; and in the administration of State affairs, the slow craft of the Hindu was made available, at one time to temper, at another time to whet the vindictive impulses of the Muhammadan. We learn that the first notable act of the new reign was a *coup-d'état* brought about by the Darogha Gul Muhammad, an old man of 75, one-eyed, of 'a tall, spare nervous figure with stern deeply-marked features, high narrow forehead, and long white hair [1].' The young Khán's artillery was ordered to open fire on certain of the principal Kalát

---

[1] Major (now Major-General Sir) Henry Green, to Political Superintendent of the Frontier, Upper Sind.

chiefs who, whatever their aims or objects, were encamped outside the walls of the capital, wholly unsuspicious of such rough treatment. In the absence of the British resident, this bold, unjustifiable act was naturally followed by complications which culminated in an appeal to British mediation. The request was responded to by the despatch of an officer with a small escort, who remained with the Khán until the Political Agent's return in November, 1857. At this period Major Green found matters in a somewhat critical state. One especially obnoxious adviser, whom he had observed in Nasír Khán's *entourage* on the occasion of his previous brief sojourn at Kalát, was still in the official foreground: the same elements of confusion and discord as before were in full operation; but there was also a new Khán.

Kalát is composed of several territorial divisions, or petty chiefdoms, of which Sarawán and Jalawán are, as it were, the true national centre, the former hemming in the capital from the north, the latter on the south. Further south again, west and east, are the outlying provinces of Las Baila, Makrán, and Kachi or Kach Gundáva, respectively. Of the minor divisions, or subdivisions, Panjgúr and Kej have the greatest political importance from geographical position. The more northerly Khárán is claimed as an offshoot of Afghánistán, rather than of Kalát. Among the Khán's opponents, Múlla Muhammad, chief of Sarawán, Táj Muhammad, chief of Jalawán, and Azád Khán of Khárán, were foremost. The last had possessions within Kalát territory, which gave to his open opposition the character of rebellion; and no more dangerous or determined rebel has in late years disturbed the peace of Balúchistán. To these names may be added Núrúdin, chief of the Mingals—feudatories, who in Pottinger's day had the credit of numbering more fighting men than could be mustered by any Brahúi tribe; Mir Khán, designated the 'Jám,' or hereditary ruler, of Las Baila; and Fakír Muhammad, 'Náib' or Deputy of Kej.

Major Green's work for the three years 1858, 1859, and 1860 affords material for a most valuable chapter of Oriental experience. Neither in point of display, of ease or of remuneration, was the post he held that which would be coveted by an aspirant to Indian Residencies. His home was his tent; his frugal board was not always cheered by the presence of a single countryman; his daily duties were to keep in a straight path a semi-barbarian chief, beset with crooked counsels from without, and a wayward will from within. If with a high hand he upheld the sovereign rights and authority of his *protégé* against the turbulent barons and intriguing officials leagued against him, he had also to advise concession, where the ruler had manifestly erred or trampled on national precedent and individual privilege. The main difficulty was to create and organise authority, so that a sovereign centre should be acknowledged and obeyed. Could this point have been gained, the reward of loyalty or suppression of treason, the encouragement of industry and punishment of lawlessness, would have been comparatively plain sailing to the British Political Agent. But the arm of the reigning law did not reach far beyond the walls of Kalát, the capital; and it was manifest that one of the first steps to be taken by the new Khán was to show himself to his feudatories in their homes, and make himself personally acquainted with their condition and wants, as well as with the lands they cultivated and occupied. A tour of inspection towards Makrán was warmly proposed by the British adviser, and eventually carried out; but although the Khán was led to undertake this, in addition to an expedition against the Marís, during the incumbency of Major Green, he did not persevere in progressive policy; and lack of perseverance, while proving the absence of any fixed principle of action, fairly neutralised the good produced by spasmodic energy.

Captain Dickenson, who succeeded Major Henry Green as Political Agent at Kalát in 1861, and Major Malcolm Green, who succeeded Captain Dickenson in 1862, continued, under considerable difficulties, to support the Khán, on the part of the British Government, by tendering honest advice and open sympathy, by mediating with his refractory chiefs where mediation appeared expedient, and by general endeavours to secure for him the homage and regard of his subjects, and a fair and legitimate revenue.

In 1854, a yearly grant of £5000, subject to certain conditions, had been made by the Government of India to the then chief of Kalát, 'his heirs and successors,' under treaty negotiated by Major Jacob with Mír Nasír Khán. The latter bound himself, 'his heirs and successors, to prevent all plundering or other outrage by his subjects within or near British territory; to protect the passage of merchants to and fro between the British dominions and Afghanistan, whether by way of Sindh, or by the seaport of Sonmeeanee, or other seaports of Mekran[1];' and to permit no undue exactions. On the death of

---

[1] Aitcheson's Treaties, vol. vii. pp. 77, 78.

Nasír Khán the amount was continued to Khudadád; and in 1859 and the two following years, it was doubled at the request of the Political Agent.

In March 1863 a rebellion broke out, and Khudadád was temporarily deprived of the chiefdom by his cousin, Sher Dil. The usurper, aided by his disaffected chiefs, managed to seize the capital, and was proclaimed ruler. Major Malcolm Green was absent on the Sind frontier at the time of the insurrection; but his office was not ignored by the rebels, who communicated to him the story of their grievances, real or imaginary, and asked him to recognise their nominee. It was naturally impossible to accede to their wishes. At the same time any direct interference in a contrary sense would have been unwise; and the attitude of the Indian Government was one rather of watchfulness than of action. The reign of Sher Dil Khán was short: for in little more than a year from his accession he was shot by an Afghán officer in his own service, whose men despatched him with their swords. In June 1864, by a reactionary movement, Khudadád Khán was restored to power. Later in the same year, the Indian Government, advised of stability in the existing order of things, formally recognised the restoration. The subsidy of £5000, suspended pending the success of the revolutionists, was revived, *pur et simple*, in accordance with the letter of the treaty; but it was judged prudent to keep in abeyance the despatch of a permanent British Agent to Kalát.

In 1865, the Jám of Baila, the chief of the Mingals, and Azád Khán of Khárán, rebelled against the Khán, and were defeated. In 1866, the Sardár of Jalawán, attempting to create a revolt among the Khán's troops, was captured and imprisoned. At the same time the Sardár of Sarawán fled to Kandahár, and his property was confiscated. Some months afterwards Táj Muhammad died in confinement. In 1868 Mulla Muhammad, through the intervention of Sir Henry Green, then Political Superintendent of the Sind frontier, was permitted to return to his home. During this year Colonel Green took leave of absence to England, and was succeeded in charge of the border by Colonel Phayre, late Quartermaster-General in the Abyssinian campaign. In 1869, Captain Harrison was appointed Political Agent at the Khán's court.

The renewal, at this time, of direct diplomatic relations with the Kalát State, may have had a good effect in checking rebellion and strengthening the sovereign position of the Khán; but the result was neither permanent, nor could it be said to have satisfied the wishes or fulfilled the hopes of the Indian Government in creating and maintaining a Political Agency of exceptional stamp. Kalát—strange as it may appear, when proximity to India, together with the great importance of geographical position generally, is borne in mind—implies something which, as a rule, has been rather committed to the charge of the Sind or frontier officers immediately concerned in its progress, than anything intelligible or interesting in detail to higher and more distant authority. It is one of those minor divisions of Muhammadan Asia, west of the Indus, which, unless violently thrown forward, is barely noticed, and which needs a crisis to be interesting. Hence few have known or cared for its history. Hence, also, have arisen difficulties of a serious nature; for the politics of Kalát, like those of more civilised lands, are illustrated by turbulent tribes and fighting factions, and are open to many points of view, especially for outside observers. There long have been, and indeed now are, in that Khanate, two great parties; one, more or less despotic; the other, more or less republican. One, in favour of a sovereign head, of which the nod is a command to the masses; one, requiring a President, who should himself bow to the will of feudal majorities. It is easier for England to uphold the despotism; and alliance with despotism would undoubtedly serve her interests better: but it is a question whether we ourselves have not unwittingly rendered impossible, by our extreme liberal policy in India, the regeneration or existence of Asiatic despotism in a territory contiguous to our own. As for limited sovereignty and representative government, in the Western acceptation of the terms, our Political Agents have work enough to make such theories intelligible to independent Nawábs and Rajahs within the circle of India Proper, without attempting to break hard ground across the border.

Captain Harrison's appearance on the scene was a signal for a new line of action on the part of the dissatisfied chiefs of Kalát. Some poured out their grievances to the British Agent, and he did his best to mediate on their behalf, and reconcile them to the Khán. Others took up a more decidedly adverse position. Conspicuous among the first was the Sardár of Sarawán; but he soon threw up his allegiance, and joined the ever-restless Jám of Baila in open hostility. Defeated by the loyal troops, Múlla Muhammad fled to Kábul, and the Jám took refuge in Sind. The result of these movements might have been foreseen by those acquainted with the inner history of Kalát, and the several influences brought to bear upon its development from British India. Anarchy and confusion prevailed throughout the Khán's dominions. England sought to mediate, but was required to protect and support. Loth to take an active part in the affairs of a territory beyond her extreme frontier, she pursued a course of passive vigilance; and such was, perhaps, on the present occasion, the most expedient policy, for, had it been her wish to interfere, it was not quite clear to the Indian Council whether the Khán or his recusant nobles deserved most her favour. A change had come over the natural advisers and reporters in this particular business. The Government local officers in 1869-70 were not altogether those of previous years; and although the Chief Commissioner in Sind was a staunch upholder of the original programme, the views of the first Political Superintendent and Commandant of the Sind Frontier were not those of *his* third successor, who now occupied the post. Be this as it may, Sir William Merewether was enabled to state, on the 18th October, 1870, that 'Balúchistán was never more quiet; and in better order than ever known before;' and the time was considered fitting to carry out the settlement of the Khán's western frontier, with a view of limiting those insidious encroachments upon his outlying territory which Persia had allowed and encouraged her unscrupulous vicegerents to effectuate for more than twenty years.

The following brief narrative of the proceedings of the Sistán and Makrán Boundary Commissions is more or less adapted from the official reports already submitted to Government. As it is proposed to supply some statement of causes and objects in the review of results before the close of the present Introduction, no apology is offered that allusion to, rather than detailed explanation of, these, has been attempted in the foregoing prefatory remarks.

Perso-Makrán Boundary.

In August 1870 Major-General Goldsmid left England, with instructions to proceed to Tehrán, and thence set out, accompanied by a Persian Commissioner, to Sistán, there to investigate the claims to the territory of Persia and Afghánistán respectively, and arbitrate as to a future permanent boundary line between the two States. He was apprized that a Commission to adjust the frontier between Persia and the Kalát State would follow that on which he was to be more immediately engaged, but no detailed instructions on this head were supplied. Reaching Enzeli, on the Caspian, the 27th September, he was at the Persian capital on the 3rd October. The Commissioner who was to accompany him had been named, and was in readiness to join his camp so soon as formed. The Sháh had just quitted Tehrán, on a pilgrimage to Karbala, in Turkish Arabia.

The day after his arrival at Tehrán, General Goldsmid telegraphed to the Government of India reporting his proposed proceedings; and two days later added the suggestion that, as the Persian Commissioner wished to enter Sistán by Mash-had and Káin, he could meet the Afghán Commissioner at Káin or Juwain. A reply to the first telegram showed that the Amir's acceptance of arbitration had not been received by the Viceroy, that his son Muhammad Ya'kub Khán was in open rebellion, and that the state of affairs might seriously affect the project for a meeting on the border. In answer to the second telegram, General Goldsmid was informed that the Arbitration could hardly go on without the consent of the Amir, and that this could not be received within three weeks at least. Hereupon, the General, feeling that so much depended on an early movement from the capital, immediately submitted a proposal to the Viceroy, by telegraph, that, to save time, he should commence with the Makrán boundary, unless affairs changed in Sistán. By marching to Karmán, in the south-east, instead of to Mash-had, in the north-east of Persia, he would reach a point equally convenient for the two routes, and this modification of programme seemed, at least, desirable. The Viceroy's consent to the arrangement proposed was telegraphed on the 10th October, and on the 21st idem General Goldsmid received by telegram authority to the same effect from Her Majesty's Secretary of State for India, with instructions to be guided by the circumstances of the time, and advice of the Viceroy, in communication with Mr. Alison. The British Commissioner moved out of Tehrán on the 22nd October, was joined by the Persian Commissioner on the 25th, and the Commission fairly took its departure *en route* to Karmán on the 26th October.

A difficulty, however, now arose in respect of the Persian Commissioner. This officer would accompany the Mission to Karmán as being on the way to Sistán, but was not authorised to commence proceedings with Makrán, nor could he obtain such authority except from his own Government. The Sháh was far on the road to Baghdad and Karbala, and the Minister of Foreign Affairs was in attendance on His Majesty. And what made this difficulty the more serious was the circumstance that while Persia was especially anxious to dispose of the Sistán question through the mediation of England, she did not evince the same interest to limit her encroachments on Makrán by the declaration of a fixed boundary line.

The dilemma resulted in the Mission remaining at Isfahán from the 10th to 26th November, for General Goldsmid did not feel authorised to move without securing the required authority for the Persian Commissioner; nor did he like leaving the line of telegraph at Isfahán, to continue his journey to Karmán eastward, until some definite understanding had been attained. A long Persian correspondence between the Governments, and a long telegraphic correspondence between Her Majesty's Minister, the Government of India, and General Goldsmid, at length closed with a telegram from Mr. Alison, notifying the assent of the Persian Government to the change in operations provided the Sistán expedition were not found feasible. The Commissioners moved from Isfahán towards Yazd and Karmán on the 26th November, the date of the British Minister's telegram last noted. On the 6th December they reached Yazd, and Karmán on the 23rd idem. Here fresh obstacles again presented themselves to the prosecution of the journey. It had become evident by telegrams from the Government of India that the Sistán arbitration could not take place during the winter season then commenced; but the Persian Commissioner awaited further instructions for the affairs of the Perso-Makrán Frontier, and other excuses for delay were put forward at Karmán. The Mission was detained in that city from the 23rd December till the 5th January, when the march was resumed. On the 10th January they reached Bam, where it became necessary to make several modifications in the marching establishment. Not only was a reduction expedient on account of the scarcity of provisions eastward of Persia Proper, but it was considered politic to leave a certain number of tents and horses at a point near which the road diverged to Sistán, as a guarantee that the question of the latter province had been merely deferred, and not abandoned by the Commissioner of Her Majesty's Government. The two Commissioners moved from Bam on the 14th, and reached Bampúr in Balúchistán on the 28th January.

INTRODUCTION.

General Goldsmid had at this time received no special instructions to guide him in his proceedings in Makrán, but feeling sure that the Government would wish him to make the best use of his time in obtaining a settlement of boundary where the early recognition of *some* definite line was important, he determined on moving in accordance with the views he had long before submitted in official form. He proposed therefore to leave Bampúr as soon as he could get the Persian Commissioner to accompany him, to take the direction of Jálk and the northernmost points of the Perso-Kalát Frontier, and pass down thence along the whole line to the sea in Gwatar Bay. Prior to entering Balúchistán he had expressed his wish to meet the Kalát Commissioner in the neighbourhood of the Northern Frontier aforesaid, so that the Joint Commission might be complete and work in an orthodox manner.

But his intentions were in this respect frustrated. During the night preceding his arrival at Bampúr, a messenger brought him letters reporting that Major Harrison, political agent at Kalát; Major Ross, political assistant at Gwádar; Captain Lovett, R.E.; Dr. Bowman, together with the Kalát Commissioner and nearly 900 followers, were on their way to join him at once, and had already reached Kasarkand, a village in the heart of the Perso-Baluch territory and midway between Bampúr and the sea. Such a report necessitated a change of proposed arrangements. In the first place, the arrival of the Kalát Commissioner and party must be awaited; and, secondly, it was more than probable that they would meet with no welcome reception from the local chief, Ibrahim Khán, whose guests General Goldsmid and Staff had necessarily become on entering his immediate territory.

The position was embarrassing. General Goldsmid had notified the probability that Major Ross would join him at Bampúr, and the Governor of Karmán had promised that an honourable reception would be accorded to that officer. The General had also informed the Persian Commissioner that Captain Lovett had been sent to the actual frontier for purposes of preliminary survey; but he had never hinted at the arrival of a deputation such as that reported. Not unnaturally the Persians took advantage of the occasion to raise obstacles in the way of a fair discussion, by assuming that the British Commissioner had concealed his preliminary dispositions, and complaining of the procedure which had been adopted. Formal accusations, or material for the same, were forwarded to the Foreign Minister at Tehrán; and to such extent did the ill-feeling display itself towards the Kalát Delegate and his companion chiefs, that the General was finally compelled to adjourn the meeting of the Commissioners to the actual frontier.

Here, too, he failed to secure the attendance and co-operation of his Persian colleague, who would not admit any existing boundary line unless including places claimed by his Government, and who wished to be attended on his mission by companies of regular infantry and bodies of Baluch horsemen. Finally, in default of definite instructions (the despatch of which from Calcutta had been intimated by telegraph), and to get the benefit of immediate telegraphic communication with Tehrán and Calcutta, General Goldsmid moved down to Gwádar on the sea coast. In so doing, however, he made arrangements to survey and map out the existing Perso-Kalát Boundary Line from personal knowledge, enquiry, and observation, and by despatching Captain Lovett, R.E., northward on the Kalát side of the frontier.

It was on the 16th February, and after a stay of 19 days, that General Goldsmid left Bampúr, crossing the Perso-Kalát Frontier below Píshín on the 3rd March, and reaching Gwádar on the 6th idem. Two days prior to this last date, he received his instructions from the Government of India, and was gratified to perceive they were quite in accordance with his preconceived notions. He was authorised by telegram to proceed in his work on the basis he had himself recommended for adoption when reviewing the whole question in 1869[1]. Captain Lovett rejoined his camp at Gwádar on the 21st March. The information acquired on the actual Frontier was not as full as might have been wished, in respect of Jálk and Kohak[2], but was held upon the whole sufficiently reliable to form the groundwork of practical negotiation. Where personal observation had been wanting it was sought to supply the deficiency by examination and cross-examination of disinterested persons acquainted with the localities. Below Kohak the data were surer and more readily available.

Mirza Ma'súm Khán, the Persian Commissioner, could not, for

[1] See 'Correspondence on the Progress of Persia, in Makrán and Western Balúchistán, from A.D. 1860 to A.D. 1869 inclusive;' compiled for Government. Bombay, 1869.

[2] Singularly enough, a place of similar name is prominently brought forward in the geography of the Sistán Arbitration. I have distinguished the two localities by writing *the latter* after the more approved Persian pronunciation, i. e. Kúha'.

a long time, be persuaded to rejoin General Goldsmid, though he had to a certain extent pledged himself to come to Gwádar. But every endeavour was made, by letter and other means, to induce him to renew negotiations; and the Government of India was in active telegraphic communication on the subject with Mr. Alison. At length, on the 9th April, having already found his way to the coast, he agreed to embark on board the 'Hugh Rose' gunboat at Cháhbár, and Captain Euan Smith escorted him to Gwádar, where they disembarked on the 11th idem. He remained as a guest of the British Commissioner, at Gwádar, from this date until the 24th April, when the 'Hugh Rose' conveyed him back to Cháhbár. On each occasion of embarkation and disembarkation, his official position was recognised in a manner which he did not fail to appreciate.

Although the residence of the Persian Commissioner at Gwádar did not seem to forward the progress of negotiations, or indeed to present any features of negotiation at all, certain results obtained thereby could not but give material aid in bringing the whole question to an issue. Mirza Ma'súm Khán had, in the first place, clearly verified the circumstance that Gwádar was not, as he had before alleged, in the possession of Persia. He must have ascertained, moreover, that the same status applied to neighbouring places even more to the eastward. Secondly, he had admitted that Kej was the only given locality he was required by his government to visit with the British Commissioner; and as Kej was the recognised centre of Kalát authority in Eastern Makrán, the proposal could not be accepted. The Persian Commissioner would not confer with the Kalát Commissioner, nor did they exchange visits as at Bampúr; but he did not disguise the possibility of a fair discussion of the case at Tehrán, on the data to be brought there; and while urging the necessity of despatching his surveyor to make a survey of his own for future guidance, he did not scruple to ask for a copy of Captain Lovett's map.

The Persian Government had expressed a strong desire that the question should be eventually referred to Tehrán for final settlement, and not disposed of on the Frontier itself. Her Majesty's Government was inclined to permit such procedure to have effect, however opposed to the original intention. Her Majesty's Minister at Tehrán had, moreover, received a memorandum from the Persian Minister of Foreign Affairs in July, 1870, indicating the Shah's wishes in the above respect; and the purport of this paper, while never officially accepted, had at the same time never been officially rejected by Mr. Alison. Under these circumstances, General Goldsmid was ordered to repair again to the Persian capital, and there, in conjunction with Her Majesty's Minister, endeavour to bring the matter of the Perso-Kalát Boundary to a satisfactory termination. General Goldsmid left Gwádar for Karáchi on the 30th April, left Karáchi again on his return to Gwádar on the 16th May, re-embarked for Persia on the 20th May, and landed at Bushahr on the 28th idem. From Bushahr he proceeded, by Shiráz and Isfahán, to Tehrán, arriving at the capital on the 10th July.

General Goldsmid's orders at this time from the Viceroy in India were that he should lay before Her Majesty's Minister at Tehrán the map which Captain Lovett had prepared under his instructions, and the information he himself had collected, with the object of enabling Mr. Alison 'to settle, in consultation with the Persian Government, their Eastern boundary in accordance with the proposals made by the Persian Government . . . and agreed to by the Secretary of State and His Excellency in Council.' He accordingly, on arrival at Tehrán, put Mr. Alison in possession of the details which the Indian Government had approved as expressing the boundary between Persian Balúchistán and Kalát, attaching a tracing of Captain Lovett's map. A few days later he added a fuller statement for translation into Persian, with explanatory remarks for Mr. Alison's own guidance. The British Commissioner further replied, *seriatim* and *singulatim*, to the charges which had been made against him orally or by letter to Her Majesty's Minister, and supplied every data which His Excellency would seem to require in communicating on the subject under discussion with the Shah and his Ministers. Mirza Ma'súm Khán returned to Tehrán on the 25th July, fifteen days after the British Commissioner. On the 1st August, General Goldsmid, accompanied by Mr. W. Dickson, of the Persian Legation, and Captain Euan Smith, met him at the residence and in the presence of Mirza Sa'íd Khán, the Persian Minister of Foreign Affairs. The interview lasted some two hours or more. The proceedings of the Commission were generally reviewed, and the Persian Minister, notwithstanding the charges that he himself had imparted to Mr. Alison, felicitated General Goldsmid on the cordiality and good feeling which had prevailed between the Commissioners! Much desultory talk ensued, and a promise was given that the Shah's orders would be taken as to future procedure.

On the 3rd August, Her Majesty's Minister, acting on a telegram he had received from the Foreign Office, addressed a memorandum to the Persian Minister urging attention to a speedy settlement of the Makrán question. On the 6th idem Mr. Alison took General Goldsmid and Staff to call upon the Shah. His Majesty, who had only just returned from the hill country, spoke to the General about his mission, and asked many questions on the countries he had visited. On the day following, the detailed statement of the actual Frontier, as translated into Persian, and Captain Lovett's map in illustration, were forwarded for the Shah's examination. A second map on a smaller scale, but comprising Afghánistán and other countries bordering on Persia, was also sent, in compliance with Mirza Sa'íd Khán's request. On the 13th August, Mr. Alison, accompanied by General Goldsmid, attended on the Foreign Minister to hear the royal decision. His Majesty had abandoned Kej and Gwádar, but wished certain tracts included within the windings of the Dasht river, as well as the Kohak district which had been placed on the Kalát side. General Goldsmid pointed out that such a modification was simply impossible, and contrary to the spirit of his duty as a mediating or arbitrating Commissioner. Next day he addressed Her Majesty's Minister in writing with a view of supplying a detailed reply to the Shah's proposition and arguments. On the 16th August General Goldsmid was visited by Mirza Ma'súm Khán, and on the 18th idem the visit was returned. Other visits were paid to the British Commissioner with the evident intention of eliciting his views and arguments, the most significant of which was perhaps that of Mahmúd Khán, formerly Minister in London.

On the 20th August, agreeably to a summons from the Shah, General Goldsmid attended on His Majesty. There was no one present at the audience but the Persian Minister of Foreign Affairs and Captain Euan Smith. The Shah used his endeavours to make the General agree to his proposed modifications of boundary, but the British Commissioner could only regret inability to meet the Royal wishes. Nothing could be more courteous and affable than the Shah's manner and behaviour from first to last; yet the result did not appear satisfactory. An essential reference to some expressions said to have been used by the Shah caused General Goldsmid on leaving the palace to ask a second and separate interview with the Minister. A long discussion ensued, the Persian Commissioner and the King's aide-de-camp joining; but no point was conceded. It was arranged, however, that a communication should shortly be made to Mr. Alison.

On the 22nd August, Her Majesty's Minister met the Persian Minister to learn the Shah's determination on the interview granted two days before to General Goldsmid. His Excellency considered the meeting so far satisfactory and conclusive of the acceptance by Persia of the line contemplated by Her Majesty's Indian Government, that he telegraphed to the Foreign Office for permission to draw up a final paper, and so dispose of this long-pending question. General Goldsmid, accompanied by Mr. Dickson, held one further interview with the Minister of Foreign Affairs on the 27th August, when the Kohak discussion was revived, this district remaining as the one solitary bone of contention. No concession in this respect was made by the British Commissioner, but a suggestion was offered that if the King considered the possession of Kohak would make a better geographical boundary for Persia, such opinion might be stated *after* the unconditional acceptance of the line proposed. Finally, on the 4th September, the boundary as originally defined by General Goldsmid, and approved by the Indian Government, was accepted *pur et simple;* the acceptance was notified in writing, and maps were interchanged.

Sistán Boundary.

We now advert to the later proceedings of the Sistán Arbitration, which forms, as it were, the second part of the Special Persian Mission of Major-General Goldsmid. This officer left Tehrán on the conclusion of the Perso-Makrán Treaty, and reached London on the 26th September, 1871. Here he was enabled to make personal report of past occurrences, and receive oral instructions for future guidance. After some weeks of discussion and delay caused by the want of a clear preliminary understanding with the Persian Government on the precise scope of the proposed Arbitration, he again set out for Persia on the 10th November. He was accompanied by Captain Euan Smith, as before, and by Mr. Gerard Thomas, who had been permitted to join the Mission as an unpaid *attaché*. On the eve of departure he was honoured by a gazetted knighthood, with admission to the Order of the Star of India.

Major-General (now Sir Richard) Pollock was an outward passenger on the same occasion. It had been proposed to associate him with the

Mission, as delegated by the Viceroy, to join the representative of the Amir of Afghánistán on his journey from Kandahár to Sistán; and in such light he was to proceed at once to Calcutta for instructions. General Goldsmid was to have left the Indian mail-steamer at Aden, making his way thence by gunboat to the Persian Gulf. Owing to unforeseen circumstances, and contrary to original arrangement, the two officers continued the voyage together to Bombay, and did not separate until arrival in Calcutta, on the 7th December. There it was arranged, with the approval of the late Lord Mayo, that while Sir Frederic Goldsmid and Staff moved up to Sistán and Western Afghánistán in a tolerably direct line from Bandar-Abbas, General Pollock, accompanied by Surgeon Henry Bellew of the Bengal army, should journey to the same goal by direct land route from the Indus. The programme was carried out to the letter. General Goldsmid left Calcutta within twenty-four hours after arrival there, returned to Bombay for re-embarkation; and landed, on the 21st December, at Bandar-Abbas, where he was joined by Mr. Apothecary Rosario, of the Medical Department of the Bombay Presidency, who had been waiting his arrival. Leaving Bandar-Abbas for the interior of Persia on the 23rd December, they reached Bam on the 7th January, 1872. Here they were met by the Persian Commissioner, Mirza Ma'súm Khán, and joined by Captain Lovett and Quartermaster-Sergeant Bower, R.E. From Bam the whole party moved across the Eastern skirt of the Karmán desert to Sistán, a journey which, inclusive of halts, occupied nineteen days, or from the 12th to the 31st January. On the 1st February, they encamped at Sekuha, the capital of the Sarbandi Sistánis.

The British officers had scarcely been a day at Sekuha when the Persian Commissioner commenced to show himself virtually hostile. In a retrospect of this character, it is distasteful to the narrator, and immaterial to the narration, to 'harp on' behaviour the impropriety of which has been practically admitted by the principal, and professedly visited on the agent. And the counter-experience of much courtesy goes far to efface the less pleasing record. Still something more than mere allusion must be made to the Mirza's Sistán tactics. His first overt act of obstructiveness took the form of complaint against an old native guide in the pay of the British Mission, whom he accused of inciting the inhabitants of Sekuha to riot, by threats of English aggression upon their lands and homes.

This charge was quickly followed by objections to the use of the Mission flag; and an unproven querulous statement reflecting on the temper of an officer in camp. On arrival at Nasirabád, the headquarters of Persian Sistán, the opposition was strengthened and, as it were, organised by the accession of the Amir of Káïn. It would have been absurd to expect actual assistance from a man whose acts were to become the subject of investigation by an alien Power: but the British Commissioner had not contemplated the very severe trial of patience to which he became subjected by this ruler's virtual disregard of the orders and assumed wishes of his Sovereign. Whether the matter be considered in a public or personal sense, the local authorities laid themselves open to serious blame. They failed in honourable dealing towards the British Mission, as towards the Afgháns, whom they had practically invited: the letter of diplomatic agreement acknowledged by the Shah and his Ministers was virtually considered waste paper: attention was not even duly given to the conventional letter of courtesy which in Persia is an official study of no secondary character.

The ten days' halt at Nasirabád, to allow time for the arrival in the province of Major-General Pollock and the Afghán Commissioner, was productive of annoyance and embarrassment. If there was no open insult, there was no want of inclination to offend. The withholding of asked-for evidence, the veto to free intercourse with the inhabitants, the hollow and superficial character of every attention paid to the wants and comfort of the English officers; in any of these things might have been found sufficient cause for disruption of relations, had not procedure been fettered by circumstances over which Sir Frederic Goldsmid had no control. As much of the daily occurrences of this period are recorded in the later pages of the present volume, the reader will be spared the infliction of wholesale repetition; but a brief detail of the actual business of the Sistán Mission from the date of leaving Nasirabád till the final breaking up of their camp in Sistán may be here appropriate.

On the 15th February, the camp, reduced to bell tents and the lightest of light marching order, and accompanied by the Persian Commissioner in like unconspicuous array, moved out of the walled arcana in which it had been too long confined, with the professed intention of visiting and mapping out places in actual possession of Persia. Ma'súm Khán had, however, been informed that although such proceeding *might* effectually forestall the necessity of further inspection, General Goldsmid could not promise that the Afghán Commissioner would be satisfied with their joint labours in this respect[1]. It was agreed that the flag difficulty should remain in abeyance during the tour; and that as they were to move in a quasi non-official way, without large tents or heavy baggage of any kind, the flag-staff should be relinquished and even the practice of using led horses discontinued. The first day's march was to the large village of Deshtak, outside the walls of which the General encamped, receiving a deputation headed by the Mayor, who delivered himself of a set speech expressive of loyalty to the Shah. On the following day they made a short march to Búrj-i-Alam Khan, crossing to the left bank of the main canal during the afternoon. The 'Búrj' or tower was held by a Baluch chief, Sher Dil Khan, whose son came out to see the strangers. He was a lad of about 19 or 20, and of prepossessing appearance; and had only recently returned from Tehrán. It is certain that many of these chiefs are taken in boyhood or early manhood to the latter capital, and trained there, returning, in semi-Persian guise and with Persian habits of thought, to their own country only when their presence at home is held safe and politic. In the present instance the schooling did not seem to have destroyed an open ingenuous disposition, or brought about the purely artificial address so prevalent in Persia and necessarily part of the education of Persian youth.

From the next day's encampment at Kala'h-i-Dost Muhammad Khan, the two Commissioners and suite made an excursion to Kimak, a flourishing and wall-enclosed village on the main canal. The inhabitants had a rough and uncivilised exterior. No sooner had the visitors crossed the water and entered the precincts of the place, than the gates were closed violently upon the crowds struggling for admittance. But there was a numerous population within, bewildered and not over-respectful: and every act of the stranger was subject to the scrutiny and criticism of man, woman and child. The return

[1] The terms of acceptance of British Arbitration by the Shah of Persia were thus expressed in the late Mr. Alison's telegram to the Viceroy dated 23rd October, 1871: 'When the British, Persian, and Afghán Commissioners are all assembled together in Sistán, the Persian and the Afghán Commissioners respectively will state and substantiate their claims. If local enquiry be necessary, the Commissioners will proceed to any point for that purpose, and make a map of any districts without let or hindrance. When the British Commissioner considers that there is nothing further to be done on the spot, the Commissioners will then return to Tehrán,' &c. &c.

to the gates was better organised than the entrance; and a kind of narrow rampart or banquette near the upper wall became available for those who preferred quiet to crowds. The Persian Commissioner, when clear of the town, examined a rough-looking fellow who had been pointed out to him as a fitting referee on the condition and opinions of the inhabitants, and put a few pertinent questions clearly intended for the hearing of his English colleague, with whom he had held some previous discussion on the difficulties of distinguishing Súnni from Shia'h. 'Are you all Musalmáns?' may have been his way of ascertaining whether the townspeople were of his own (the Shia'h) way of thinking; or it may have been a mere evasion of the point at issue. At all events, the reply was in the affirmative. 'Do you intermarry?' was, perhaps, equally ambiguous; for it was difficult to understand from the responsive statement that 'they *did* intermarry,' whether the application was to Persians and Balúchis or to Súnnis and Shia'hs. There was a cool impudence in the way of giving these answers which might either have been assumed for the occasion, or provoked by the not very pleasant or conciliatory tone of the questioner.

From Kala'h-i-Dost Muhammad Khan the camp moved to Kúhak on the Helmand. Here it is that the Amir holds possession of his great 'band' or dam across the river, whereby the main body of the water is turned to the westward, through a canal of sufficient importance to have been considered by modern travellers the Helmand itself. It might indeed be appropriately termed the 'artificial Helmand.' Quartermaster-Sergeant David Bower made a minute and careful examination of this work, the result of which was communicated to the Government of India[1]. On the 19th February a long and tedious march, at one time over high stony ground, at another over low sandy soil, and again amid dwarf jungle, hillocks and mud ruins, brought the Commissioners to Dak-i-Dehla, a crumbling watch-tower, twenty-eight miles along the left bank of the Helmand. The next day they encamped twelve miles further, at Kamál Bandar, a village and fort held by Sardár Kamál Khán, Sanjaráni, a Baluch chief in Persian pay. The British officers arriving first, they were met and escorted to their ground by a respectable *istikbál*; the Sardár's tent was placed

---

[1] Par. 24 of Sir F. Goldsmid's Letter to the Foreign Secretary, Calcutta, No. 17, of the 11th of March, 1872, the purport of which will be found in fuller detail at pages 281, 282 of Major Euan Smith's narrative in this volume.

at their disposal for breakfast; and they were otherwise civilly treated by the local magnates. On the following day they crossed the river to the right bank and pitched at the fort and village of Chahár Búrjak, belonging to Sardár Kamal Khán's brother, Imám Khan. Here it was that Mirza Ma'súm Khán began to be troublesome in earnest.

He had proposed that Sir Frederic Goldsmid should visit, with him, all places possessed by Persia in Sistán; and this arrangement had been accepted as the safest and least objectionable mode of utilising time until the full Commission could meet. To have visited *claimed* places as well as those *in actual possession* might naturally have caused complications: and to have demurred, before starting, to the Persian interpretation of 'possession' in certain cases, might have been tantamount to cancelling the tour proposed. But when, at the Amir's Band, the Helmand had been fairly reached, and subsequent progress would be *up the bank of the river* in a direction where possession was, to General Goldsmid's mind, of a far more dubious character than in Central Sistán, it became a question to what extent Ma'súm Khán would use the fact of association with the future Arbitrator for purposes of his own. Captain Smith was, therefore, sent to the Persian Commissioner at Kuhak, to represent that the General's consent to accompany him southward of that fort must not be held to imply any acknowledgment which could have bearing on the coming arbitration. For certain reasons it was judged necessary to repeat the purport of this communication in writing, two days later at Kamál Bandar; but the letter calling attention to the matter, referred at the same time to the happy circumstance that in continuing the journey up the Helmand the writer would be enabled to fall in with General Pollock and the Afgháns, whose advent in that quarter was daily expected. Further correspondence ensued, the result of which was so far unsatisfactory, that Mirza Ma'súm Khán on reaching Chahár Búrjak expressed officially his determination to return to Nasirabád, there to await the coming of the Afghán Commissioner! General Goldsmid remonstrated; but in vain[1]. It was evident that the tour

---

[1] He received a letter to the effect that the proceedings of the two camps were not in accordance with the agreement drawn up between the British and Persian Governments. Had the British Commissioner, it was urged, after certifying present Persian possessions, *prevented future discussion thereon by the Afghán Commissioner, the arrangement would have been an excellent one.* But on learning that the joint progress up the Helmand would not necessarily admit Persian possession in that quarter, Ma'súm Khán had quite

in Sistán had not been to certify that such and such places were Persian by right of possession; but to ratify their concession to Persia by virtue of passing through them with a Persian escort. Independent witnesses were to be kept out of sight: and the admission of the Shah's sovereignty by certain subsidised and otherwise interested chiefs was to be accepted without reserve in proof of the validity of Persian pretensions. Failing this, the object of joint progress was nullified. It were better to strike tents and return to head-quarters. Such, at least, was the view taken by Ma'súm Khán; and in this spirit it can well be understood that he neither cared to await the arrival of the Afgháns nor to facilitate the work of investigation entered upon by Sir Frederic Goldsmid.

Consequently the two camps, which had left Nasirabád under more favourable circumstances than could have been anticipated by the first reception of the Mission and subsequent treatment of the British officers at the Amir's Sistán stronghold, separated after an eight days' experience of joint survey and inspection. The Persian Commissioner, agreeably to his expressed resolution, made his first return march on the 23rd February; and General Goldsmid was thrown upon his own resources for the rest of the tour. The latter officer felt that so long as the local authorities evinced no opposition, so long could he continue to inspect and map out the undoubted possessions of Persia, or such places as Persians were strong enough to hold in subjection; and in so doing he need not commit himself to any arbitral opinion, or violate in any way the principles of arbitration. Under these impressions, he still contemplated the advantages of an onward march to Rúdbar, a point about forty miles further up the Helmand. But mature consideration resulted in a change of procedure; and he finally determined that no independent action on his part should give his wayward colleague any handle whereby he could break off or paralyse the business of the Commission. Moreover it was authoritatively affirmed that no provisions or fodder were procurable to suffice the camp for a three days' journey; and however false and groundless may have been the statement, it would have been inconvenient to have provoked further antagonism from the authorities by measures involving open or secret interference with the inhabitants. It was therefore resolved, on Mirza Ma'súm Khán's departure, to halt only for one more day at

changed his opinion. He would return to Nasirabád on the succeeding day, and await his new colleague's arrival.

Chahár Búrjak, and that Captain Lovett should make the most of the time thus placed at his disposal in determining the course of the river towards Rúdbar, and, if possible, the position of Rúdbar itself[1].

These preliminaries having been arranged and carried into effect, and guided by no trustworthy accounts of the movements of the Afghán Mission, General Goldsmid's party retraced their steps by the opposite bank of the river to that which they had chosen on the upward move. Their first march was to Kala'h-i-Fath, the 'Fort of Victory,' a collection of extensive ruins said to mark a former city of the Káiyánis; but evidently of no great antiquity. The story is that the Káiyánis abandoned this bank of the Helmand after offering resistance to Nádir Shah, and fled to the Kuh-i-Khwájah in the west: and as Fath Ali Káiyáni was one of the conqueror's chief opponents it is not improbable that the 'Kala'h,' or fort, owed its name to this prince. The local garrison was reported to consist of a number of men, from 50 to 100, the lower being the more probable figure: and there was good reason to suppose any armed occupation at all to have been effected at a very recent date.

On February 25th, after riding some twenty miles over a generally barren tract, but covered with ruins as of large towns or villages, tents were again pitched at the Amir's 'Band.' This time, however, the encampment was on the right bank of the river, at the water's edge, and close to the mud tower constructed for the soldiers who guard the dam from pilferers of wood or more formidable enemies. Contradictory reports had been received on General Pollock's progress: and one account represented that he had arrived at Chakhansúr, and would enter Sistán by the upper route, avoiding the Helmand. From the Amir's Band the bank of the river was followed to Agha Ján. The crossing to the left bank was effected at about 200 yards below the starting-point, where the water was up to the horses' girths as at

---

[1] Dr. Bellew, in his interesting volume designated *From the Indus to the Tigris* (Trübner, 1874), has described the country between Rúdbar and Chahár Burjak, and so supplied any deficiency of information on these points noticeable in the survey made by the officers of General Goldsmid's Mission. Within a week of the departure of the latter, in fact, Major-General Pollock, Dr. Bellew, and the Afghán Commissioner had arrived in the immediate vicinity of Chahár Burjak, having left Rudbár on the 27th February. They had marched 28 miles due west along the course of the river to Kala'h Ján Beg, passing the bed of 'a great canal called Juí Gúrshasp;' and a second march of 14 miles west by north had brought them to a sandy spot in the wide channel of the Helmand, directly opposite Chahár Burjak.

Kamál Bandar, but in a narrower channel. A second crossing and recrossing followed at Agha Ján, to admit of an inspection of the fort of Nad Ali held for the Persians on the right bank, by a son of Sardár Sharif Khan Nharui[1]. The remainder of February was passed in visiting places of local repute sufficiently close together to be reached by a succession of short easy marches; but the inhabitants, high and low, showed little disposition to cultivate the friendship or to forward the objects of the British officers; and the minor wearers of 'brief authority' were positively inimical. On March 1st the want of courtesy shown at the town of Jalálabád was so marked that tents were struck and a move made to the neighbouring village of Búrj-i-Afghán. The next morning the ground of encampment was chosen at Banjár, about five miles distant from Nasirabád; and here were spent the last days of the Mission in Sistán.

On the 6th March the light-marching order of the camp was changed, and attention again given to strict official requirements, preparatory to commencing business on the appearance of the Afghán Commissioner, whose coming was imminent. The flag-staff was reared, as it had been customary to rear it before the discussion raised at Sekúha, and the colours were once more conspicuously exhibited, in token of the presence of the arbitrating power. When this state of things was inaugurated, and the British Commissioner passed over to the larger tents, Captain Lovett, Mr. Thomas, Quartermaster-Sergeant Bower, and Mr. Rosario were present with him in camp. Captain Smith had been detached on duty to Nasirabád, whence he was to ride out in quest of General Pollock and his companions; but this officer had before arranged in personal communication with the Persian Commissioner that there was to be no longer any difficulty started on the use of the flag, and Ma'súm Khán had been informed in writing that its resumption would be carried into effect. General Goldsmid had not been long, however, in his new quarters, when a

---

[1] Nád Ali is the locality of some really remarkable ruins, which bear evidence of great antiquity. The *Damdamaks*, or mounds, are suggestive of hidden treasures for the excavators, and the octagonal tower is almost indicative of a bygone local Hinduism. Between these prominent points is a vast extent of ground, from which crop out solid brick foundations of former tenements, or on which are strewed detached baked bricks of large size and broken specimens of painted tiles and earthenware of past generations. Here, if anywhere in Sistán, are visible traces of age and substantial structure, which may belong, as tradition affirms, to the period of Darius or other monarchs of the House of Kái, or the Shiwasthán of Lieut. Leech.

letter reached him from the 'Yáwar' affected to his service by the local authorities, to the effect that the Sáiyids, Mullahs and other inhabitants of Banjár sought an explanation of the, to them, novel display! Signs of commotion, real or assumed, were moreover reported from the town by a trustworthy native attendant. The reply was naturally brief; but it more or less closed the door to further paper controversy. Nor did the outer excitement, if it existed, show itself in any definite shape, or by any overt act.

On the 8th March the camp was strengthened by the arrival of General Pollock, Dr. Bellew, and the Afghán Commissioner, Sáiyid Núr Muhammad. The force of circumstances had prevented a junction at an earlier date or elsewhere. More than once, and long before the coming of this particular Mission, Sir Frederic Goldsmid had expressed his hope, in writing as by word of mouth, that all necessary arrangements would be made for its fitting reception. But by one chief on the banks of the Helmand they were refused supplies, and at a village within twenty miles of Nasirabád (where the Amir and Persian Commissioner were both residing) the same treatment was repeated. It can be understood how, under such circumstances, the Afghán Sáiyid declined to make the first ceremonious call on the Amir of Káïn and Persian Commissioner; and although General Goldsmid felt it his duty to urge conciliation, and might have rejoiced had a less determined attitude been approved, the delegate's statement that a different course would have been inconsistent with his position was intelligible, and could not be disregarded. General Pollock and Sáiyid Nur Muhammad Shah pitched their tents for a reasonable time outside the walls of Nasirabád, and received and returned the usual ceremonious enquiries about health; but there the courtesies ended. No visits were paid, nor were the official intercommunications more frequent or felicitous than the exchanges of social compliment.

Negative hostility was followed by complaint and indications of mischief. The presence of certain chiefs in the Afghán camp was considered offensive to Persia. Something like a threat of collision was expressed in writing and outward action by Ma'súm Khán and his associates. Nor was recrimination wanting on the part of the Afgháns and those whom they had identified with their cause. The Amir of Káïn was charged with inveigling a follower of the Juwain chief into his power, and hints of darker dealing were freely given. In fine, scarcely two days had passed since the junction of the two

Missions when Sir Frederic Goldsmid, acting upon the refusal of the Persian Commissioner to meet his Afghán colleague anywhere but at Nasirabád, a locality of all others most fatal to fair hearing and discussion, decided upon quitting the province and adjourning all further procedure on the business of his mission until return to Tehrán.

The duties of the Arbitrator were to hear each side of a disputed question, and judge upon pleadings laid before him. It was natural that he should seek to make himself acquainted with the truth of the general story by the opportunities at his disposal: it was essential that he should strive to conciliate the litigants, and allay as much as possible an irritation which, among Orientals, is far more likely to impede than assist justice: but it would have been inconsistent with his office to have exercised an out-of-Court interference tending to demonstrate that the arbitrator was more desirous of arbitrating than plaintiff or defendant to entrust a case for arbitration. And when antagonism began to show itself in outward action, between the followers of two distinct forms of faith at the dawn of a month (Muharram) especially celebrated by both, a hesitating course might have produced bad results.

To sum up the whole story: during the full month of February, and for several days in March, the Mission remained in Sistán; in the first instance within the walls of Nasirabád, the Persian headquarters; afterwards on a tour of general survey and enquiry; and, lastly, in camp at Banjár, a considerable village within five miles of Nasirabád. On the 11th March, tents were struck and advanced a short stage towards the Afghán district of Lásh Juwain: on the 15th, the camp was pitched below the hill fort of Lásh, from which it was separated by the Farah river. The northern frontier of Sistán had then been crossed; and the British delegates were on their way to Tehrán, to endeavour by all available means to attain such a settlement of the Perso-Afghán boundary dispute as, if not in the letter, would at least be in the spirit of the instructions communicated to the Arbitrator. It may appear strange that although General Pollock's party did not join the Mission camp until the 8th March, all were moving together, three days later, towards the Persian capital. But so it was. The measure was a well-considered one; rather the result of a continuous experience than of a hastily formed conclusion; inevitable to the preservation of the dignity of the British officers; perhaps of peace in the respective camps; indispensable for carrying into effect in any shape the objects of the so-called joint Commission. The cause of this hasty termination of the proposed enquiry, so soon as the representatives of the litigating powers had met in the presence of the Arbitrator, must be looked for in the action of the Persian Commissioner, who, failing to secure a procedure in accordance with his own views or confidential instructions, used every effort to defeat the aim of the British Mission, and inhibit the production of all trustworthy local evidence.

Before leaving Sistán, Sir Frederic Goldsmid reported to the Government of India the difficulties he had had to encounter there, and the causes which had led him to precipitate his departure, on being joined by Major-General Pollock and the Afghán Commissioner. As he himself subsequently represented, had it not been that the presence of the last-named was absolutely essential to the completion of a case, under the Agreement signed in the previous year at Tehrán[1], he would, in all likelihood, have made the behaviour of the Persian authorities a reason for still earlier withdrawal from the scene of litigation. He had been detained for ten days on worthless pleas and pretexts in a walled military cantonment; had been left by his Persian colleague in the course of a supposed friendly tour, because he declined to admit the Persian view of the *uti possidetis* principle in its local application, and so to forestall a material part of his arbitral opinion, then necessarily in embryo; had been annoyed by strained notions of *étiquette*, by unfounded objections to the display of the Mission flag, by petty complaints against one or other of the members of his Staff, by *espionage* and retention of important or honest evidence, by obstacles in procuring carriage, cattle, money—in short by constantly recurring proof that a jealous and antagonistic agency was actively engaged in opposition to the legitimate progress of the arbitration. And whatever forbearing power the arbitrating officer might still have possessed, he felt that a sufficient amount of patience had been exercised to make a close of proceedings the only fitting course to be pursued under the circumstances. Major-General Pollock, on his part, was well convinced that no good was to be gained by delay; and the treatment that he himself and the Afghán Commissioner had experienced was but a new incentive to speedy departure[2].

[1] See the Shah's autograph quoted in note, *ante* page xxxi.
[2] Major-General Goldsmid addressed the Secretary of State for India to this effect on the 21st October, 1872. The Government of India, in a despatch of the 18th November

Passing through Lásh Juwain, Káïn and Mash-had, the British camp reached Tehrán, by the Khurasán high road so well known to readers of Persian travel, early in June, after a journey of nearly three months. The passage through the Káïn districts, or Káïnát, had a geographical as well as political interest; and the visit to Káïn, the ancient capital—found some 60 miles north, instead of a like distance south of Birjand[1], the modern capital—was of itself an important novelty. There was little to complain of in the treatment of the Mission on its march north and west from Sistán. His Royal Highness the Prince Governor of Khurasán was especially friendly and courteous; and other functionaries of less note might be named who did the English officers more than conventional honour. The proceedings at Tehrán need not be here closely scrutinised, having been the subject of ordinary diplomatic report. Suffice it to say that they culminated in the delivery of the Arbitral award; in appeal on the part of both litigants to His Majesty's Principal Secretary of State for Foreign Affairs; and in a confirmation of the award on appeal. Readers who desire to look closer into the case, and become acquainted with its full merits, will find the Arbitrator's statement and summary in an Appendix to this volume; but the voluminous correspondence supplying the details, in this as well as the Perso-Kalát question, could only become legitimately public in a Blue-book.

It yet remains to be considered whether the results of the two Boundary Commissions have been commensurate with the outlay which they have occasioned, and—far more important still—with the political expectations raised regarding them? Although the two proceedings are distinct, and have been treated politically, as they are geographically apart one from the other, no reasonable man can doubt that they are really phases of one great question—the peace and protection of our Indian frontier. If not so regarded by statesmen, it is difficult to know in what light to place them. In no case should they be misunderstood, or confused by ignorance of detail—a contingency almost unavoidable where public interest is wanting to support vitality. Nor is this interpretation the expression of any narrow,

following, were pleased to consider their thanks due to this officer 'for the tact and good judgment . . . displayed through these negotiations under circumstances of no ordinary difficulty.'

[1] See some of our best maps before 1872.

selfish policy—the advocacy of any measures by which England will benefit, regardless of independent neighbouring states. Far from it. In defining a frontier beyond our own Indian frontier, we better and strengthen ourselves only by the increased prosperity of our neighbours. If we do not create friendly and prosperous states between our proper border and the further line, it should be our misfortune but not our fault. We should strive by all fair means and processes to achieve this end; we should meddle as little as possible with our neighbours' domestic affairs, but where interference *is* exercised on our part it should be respected; and whatever anarchy or revolution may prevail in Afghánistán and Balúchistán, Persia should understand that she is pledged to us to take no advantage of either condition for purposes of territorial encroachment to the Eastward.

As to the positive, matter-of-fact value of results, how is this question to be solved for Balúchistán? According to time-honoured precedents, the Boundary Commissioner should be the last man to decide: so that in one sense his reply must be accepted *cum grano*. At the same time, he pleads conscientious discharge of duty; knowledge of the work he has had to perform from a study and practice of many years; and the fact that he is acting under instructions in putting forward his views. Let us first examine the advantages or necessities of a fixed territorial *status* in Balúchistán; and then see what end has been attained by the Perso-Kalát Boundary Commission of 1870–71. The reader is solicited to consult the map, if he be not *au fait* in respect of all places noted, for many of these are comparatively obscure.

Shortly after the suppression of the Sipáhi revolt, an event of serious warning and import—whatever view may be taken of its scope and origin—the attention of the Indian Government was drawn to the establishment of a line of overland telegraph to connect Basrah with Karáchi: a measure rendered urgent by the intention to make the former place the terminus of the proposed Turkish line from the Bosphorus to the Persian Gulf. To lay a cable was the obvious course for avoiding political complications: but cables are expensive, and plain-sailing diplomacy does not always anchor in the safest ports. It was well to know to what extent a land telegraph was feasible in the localities indicated, even if such were needed for no other purpose than a mere alternative means of communication.

From Bandar-Abbas to Karáchi, the Shah of Persia, the Sultan of

Maskat, the Khan of Kalát, all had territorial claims, of which the precise nature was rather suspected than understood. It was, however, evident that if the British authorities wished to engage the local chiefs to the protection of posts and wires in Makrán, they must more or less acknowledge some special suzerainty, under the shadow of which these chiefs were contented to reside. Persia was encroaching to the east: Kalát was retreating from the west: Maskat was a settler or a farmer here and there on the coast, in lands possessed or claimed by either power. This state of things had been known and reported for some years: but details had been wanting, and reports were now prepared and transmitted by various officers with intent to supply deficiencies.

Eventually (1862–3) a cable was laid, and communication opened between the ports mentioned. A land line of telegraph was also constructed to Gwádar, and prolonged at a latter date (1869–70) to Jásk. But the political difficulty still remained. It had been explained and made intelligible; but it could only be removed by diplomatic action. The following exposition of the abstract right of Persia to Balúchistán in 1863[1] is extracted from a report of the present writer, employed, in the first instance, to negotiate the passage of the telegraph from Karáchi for some 400 miles beyond the Indian border: afterwards to ascertain the territorial *status* west of Gwádar, and arrange for extension of the line; more recently to define a permanent political boundary. The third of these duties was the result of the two former: and its accomplishment, it is believed, could not but be desired in the interests of peace and progress :—

'As to her right, I know of none but of the strong over the weak; of the *prestige* of a high-sounding monarchy over the obscurity of a small chiefdom. More than one hundred years ago Nádir Shah appointed Násir Khán Brahúi the Beylerbey or Governor of the whole

---

[1] Nearly two years before, when referring to the then actual Perso-Kalát frontier, he had reported :—'This boundary, so far as the question has become intelligible to me in its detail, is very nearly defined by the tract of country called the "Dasht," and the river known as "Dasht Khaur," which may be said now to mark the south-westerly independent possessions of the Khan of Kalát in Kej.' And he had suggested that a line drawn from the Northern frontier, east of Jálk, Síb, Kasarkand and such districts as had to all intents and purposes fairly thrown off the Khan's authority, to the sea-board east of Gwádar, would not only ensure the common and therefore unknown advantages of a recognised frontier, but afford that security to the telegraphic scheme then under consideration which the existing *status* did not promise.

of Balúchistán, inclusive of Makrán, and in such capacity he was no doubt to some extent a feudatory of Persia, but it is also more than one hundred years ago that he exchanged the *quasi* service of the Shah for that of the Afghán King. His allegiance to Kandahár was no less binding than to Persia. It was the allegiance exacted by a stronger arm than his own. When the Afghán monarchy fell to pieces the service ceased; but Balúchistán also fell to pieces, and its chiefs set up claims of independence for themselves. Then came the opportunity for Persia to regain what she had lost. She had, however, in this case, no great prize to recover, and could allow her Governor of Karmán or a subordinate at Bampúr to proceed leisurely in the work of oppression, and set forth, as occasion served, obsolete claims. Of late years she has, perhaps, been more than usually active in this re-assertion of Makrán sovereignty. The present state of affairs in Kalát must be specially favourable to her views. Anarchy in that quarter cannot but afford occasion for intrigue, if not for the actual advance of troops. . . . . . If possession for a period of years must necessarily imply acknowledgment by the local rulers, it is the acknowledgment of helplessness. I do not for a moment believe that the Persian yoke is acceptable to the Sardárs of Makrán west of Kalát. A petition was presented to me when at Gwádar in February last year, from one of the neighbouring chiefs, and others had been forwarded to the Commissioner at Karáchi before my departure from that place, praying generally for British interference against the tyranny of the Gajars[1] collecting the revenue. None of these could be noticed at the time, and that addressed to myself was, if I rightly remember, returned to the bearer unread, so soon as its purport was ascertained. And yet, if we acknowledge the right of prior conquest, in the wide sense of the word, whether for Nádir Shah on behalf of Persia, Ahmád Shah of Kandahár, or Násir Khán of Balúchistán, it is not clear how exception can be taken to any description of past territorial aggression and encroachment by the same, or any of the same powers involving no stronger claim upon our interference than direct and open warfare. Moreover, the results with which we have to do are those of a state of things in which we could not legitimately have exercised interference at any time. At the present moment the case

[1] The way of pronouncing Kajars on the Makrán coast, where the name of the ruling *Túrki* family is ignorantly applied to the whole Persian race.

xliv   INTRODUCTION.

is different. Kalát is our close ally. Though not bound by existing treaty to protect her frontier by force, we have treated with her as an independent state, to protect our telegraph up to a certain point within her limits, and there is now a legitimate opening for taking exception at any unauthorised aggression from without upon such boundary line.'

Persia's position in Balúchistán had been clearly of a different kind in the beginning of the century. In the year 1810 not only was the Shah's authority disavowed in Bampúr, which, it should always be borne in mind, if Makrán at all, is the most westerly, that is, the district nearest to Persia of that province; but we are told of the existence of a feeling there decidedly hostile to Persian influence. In talking to Lieutenant Pottinger, Mihrab Khán spoke of the Persians in terms of little measured abuse, wondering why the Faringi did not exterminate them. On his side, the distinguished English traveller, then a passing guest of this robber chief, was desirous of ascertaining the terms on which the Persians and Balúchis stood with each other, and enquired from Mihráb if the intercourse was frequent between him and the Government of Karmán? 'Intercourse,' rejoined he, laughing, 'no! we have had none for these last two years, nor is it likely to be again renewed. A few months anterior to that period, Shah Mihrab Khán, Káim Khán, and myself sent our collective armies on a *chapao* into Láristán, and laid waste that province. . . . . The consequence was that there were no revenues forthcoming, and the Hákim of Mináb was called to Karmán, to be made answerable for the defalcation; but when he represented the true statement of the business to the Shahzádah, he was released from confinement, and two messengers were forthwith despatched with threatening *firmans* to us. . . . . We transmitted these letters to the Prince, setting him and his threats at defiance. Such,' the narrator continues, 'being the state of affairs in the extreme west, it is but natural to infer that at this period the more easterly parts of Balúchistán, as the more remote from the Shah's influence, were wholly independent of Persia from 1810 to 1843[1].'

---

[1] History of Balúchistán, chapter xii. pages 173-4. In 1843 or 1844, a brother of H. H. Agha Khán Mehlati, who then resided in Sind, left Karáchi for Makrán at the head of a party of horsemen. In a few weeks they reached Gwádar, where they made a short halt. Hence it is said they advanced to Cháhbár, which was found a convenient spot for remaining in, owing to the number of Khojas residing there, who pay tribute to

Captain Grant's journal of a route through Western Makrán gives further evidence of the divisions of the country, geographical and political, about the same period as Pottinger. This officer, not finding a favourable state of things at Gwádar, proceeded a few miles further up the coast, to disembark at Gwatar; but failed to observe at either place any sign whatever of the exercise of power or pretensions on the part of Persia. The present writer visited Gwatar in 1864, and found it a poor village of about 70 mat houses and 250 inhabitants, situated near the north-west corner of the bay of the same name, and hidden to the south-west by rocky projections, separating it from the sea-beach. Arriving in a fishing-boat at about 3 P.M. on February 5th, he had landed, and held some conversation with the hereditary heads of the community. Three respectable old men, named Hájji Murád, Basol, and Mithano, appeared to him as patriarchs in this cluster of hovels. They received Hájji Abdu, his guide, as an old acquaintance; and his own reception was as cordial and friendly as could have been expected. One of the three brothers spoke Persian and Hindustáni fluently, so they had no difficulty in becoming mutually intelligible. He learnt that Hájji Murád paid 400 rupees per annum (£40) as farmer of the Gwatar revenues; but that there was scarcely a *banya*, or Hindu dealer, in the town, nor a shop or store-house. The inhabitants were called Méds, Durzádas, and Ráises. The fisheries might be considered to be the only true source of revenue, and he noticed some boats in the mouth of the little Gwatar river below the village. Some also were sailing about the bay. No wish was apparent to conceal from him the politics of the country. While sitting together in conclave on the mat outside their door, the old men spoke to their visitor with freedom, and heedless of the many listeners grouped

the Agha. At Cháhbár communication was opened, and systematically kept up with the inland town of Bampúr. Sardár Khán made friends and partisans of the Balúchis in the vicinity, besides getting a footing for his own immediate followers, and eventually succeeded in obtaining possession of the place from the hands of the independent Balúch chief. In these head-quarters he applied himself to collect a force, and may have succeeded in drawing together some thousand men. On the report of occupation of this town by the party from Sind, made to his Government by the Governor of Karmán, it is not surprising that a royal mandate was issued for its investment. It was besieged, and in course of time reduced. Sardár Khán was taken prisoner, and sent to Tehrán. From this period the Persian hold of Bampúr has been more or less maintained. Some three or four years later the *employés* of Persia moved still further to the eastward, encroaching upon the Balúch chiefdoms of Gaíh and Kasarkand.

around. They assured him that, until that time, never within the memory of man had Persian claims been urged upon Báhú. They had formerly paid tribute to Kalát, but had since been independent.

The village was both dirty and desolate, and stay there was not prolonged. An hour or so seemed sufficient to collect all requisite information, without giving rise to unnecessary suspicions. There was an unmistakeable dread and dislike of the Gajar in the place, and that not so much for himself, as that he brought the Balúch marauder behind him. 'You pay 400 rupees as farmer,' said the stranger guest to his host, 'whether the Gajar come or not; of what consequence, then, is it to whom it is given by Muhammad Ali?' The reply was to the effect that this was Muhammad Ali's own legitimate revenue, but having to give up his right to the Gajars, he allowed his Balúchís to make up his losses for him by unlawful means. They were victims to this kind of robbery.

The old men accompanied their questioner to the beach, and sheep and *dahi*[1] were brought for his acceptance on departure. Prior to leave-taking, and while rambling alone about the place, he had heard a voice crying 'Welcome to the country,' in a language which might have been idiomatic Persian but that there was something of Balúchí in the substitution of *khúb hasti* for *khésh ámadi*. He had turned round to ascertain whence the sound proceeded, and observed at about fifty yards off, an ill-clad woman, with a child in her arms, following his track; and though she moved away, and called no further on his looking towards her, the movement and her very silence at such a time had seemed to give a deeper meaning to her former cry. The story of the boatmen, that Hájji Murád's family were preparing to remove to Gwádar, might have been quite true: oppression might well cause the whole population to migrate thither.

The opinions formed in 1863 were strengthened rather than modified by later consideration, and it became tolerably certain—

1st. That the claims of Persia to Makrán generally were based upon somewhat traditionary conquests of former years, more or less substantiated by the formal disposal of the province to Mohbut Khán Brahúi, in the middle of the last century; that the later rise of a new government, and enterprise of a new chief in Balúchistán, virtually dispossessed Persia of her never well-defined Makrán territories; but that forcible re-assertion of the Shah's sovereignty over certain parts

---

[1] *Dahi* or *dhai*, coagulated milk: the *mást* of Persia; Turkish, *yoghúrt*.

of Makrán, so far as hitherto carried out, however unwarrantable in accordance with the rule of European politics, was not a matter for foreign interference, upon a bare principle of justice and equity. In this view, such Makrán territories as Persia held in tribute were hers by mere right of possession.

2ndly. That those portions of Makrán obeying the authority of the Khán of Kalát were that chief's by possession, as also by acknowledgment of the local rulers. They were part of an inherited Balúchistán state, held, at first, in a sort of feudal tenure from Persia, subsequently from Kandahár, but in reality on a basis of independence. The revolutions which distracted the province after the death of Násir Khán in 1795 could only be said to affect such petty chiefdoms as had been successful in permanently throwing off their allegiance. Those which had revolted and were afterwards subdued, still remained component parts of the inheritance of the Kháns.

In June, 1865, under instructions from the Right Honourable the Secretary of State for India, the Chief Director of the Government Indo-European Telegraph was deputed to Tehrán to assist Her Majesty's Minister at the Court of Persia in negotiating a Telegraph Treaty. During the stay of that officer in Tehrán, the question was brought formally to his notice, and it became his duty to consider what was 'the extreme limit to which the aerial line could be extended westward from Gwádar without opposition or reasonable objection from the Persian Government?'

There was not much difficulty in coming to a conclusion on either head. The question of 'opposition' was found to differ from that of 'reasonable objection.' Reference to former proceedings and former correspondence showed that opposition of some kind had distinctly been made by the Persian Government to an advance along the coast west of Gwádar, without their consent obtained. The statement of the Minister for Foreign Affairs to this effect in May, 1863, was on record; and Mr. Thomson, then *Chargé d'Affaires* at Tehrán, had explained that Persia wanted to have assured the coast from Cháhbár to frontier of Bandar-Abbas. The Directors' reading of their objections was, that they bore also upon the coast from Gwádar to Cháhbár.

As to 'reasonable objection,' the case was tolerably clear. In point of fact, they had really none to urge as regards the coast from Karáchi to the eastern limit of Bandar-Abbas and adjacent lands farmed by the Imam of Muscat. But the question was one of which it was recommended to discuss the merits with Persia herself. Such discussion could not, it was urged, have any retrograde tendency. Rather would its result serve to place the acts of the Indian Government on a securer basis than if they moved blindfolded. Besides, by such procedure, successive politicians would not be hampered with the defence of a line of policy or proceeding on which there was no record, but that Englishmen came, saw, and planted their telegraph posts.

But some time before this reference was made, Persia had asked for British interference in adjusting her eastern boundary. The request had been declined in the form approved by her diplomatists; and perhaps, upon the whole, on valid grounds. It was quite another thing, however, in the instance now presented. There might be both wisdom and justice in accepting a settlement of boundary on behalf of the Kalát state of Balúchistán, so very recently invaded by Persian troops. The chief of that State, who really owed no allegiance, nor acknowledged any to the Shah—the inheritor, moreover, of an independent dominion—had proved himself our faithful ally, and was desirous of consolidating his power. In aiding him to define his western frontier, the British authorities need not care to define which were Persian and which not Persian territories. All that they would require was a guarantee from Persia that she would not permit her soldiers or subjects to pass a certain line of frontier considered to mark the Kalát boundary.

On completion of the Telegraph Convention at Tehrán, Lieutenant-Colonel Goldsmid and Major Smith, R.E., Director Persian Telegraph, proceeded together from Tehrán to Isfahán, Yazd, and Karmán. At a hundred miles eastward of the last-named place they parted. Major Smith explored the route to Bandar-Abbas, and to some extent along the coast; and Colonel Goldsmid went on to Bampúr, in Balúchistán, and thence through the Makrán passes to the sea at Cháhbár. A report of this exploration was forwarded to Government. Two passages are here extracted:—

'The question of Persian occupation in Balúchistán has, I think, been fairly solved by the present journey. In modern maps we are accustomed to find a red line drawn in about long. 59°, and coming westward to long. 54° 50″, as defining the eastern boundary of Persia from Sistán to the Indian Ocean. The state of the case is, however, very different in reality. We should be much nearer the truth were the line to curve to the eastward before reaching the sea, taking in from the Bampúr district southwards a tract in extent nearly four degrees of longitude. The Wazír of Karmán, Muhammad Ismail Khán, *de facto* Governor of the province, has lately received from his sovereign the title of Sardár of Balúchistán, and the honour is not in this instance mere sound and emptiness. Attached to Karmán, and forming its Balúchistán division, are the two large districts of Bampúr and Makrán. The first, which lies to the north, is about as much Persia as Karmán proper. It is governed by a Persian, and garrisoned by Persian regular troops, as well as irregulars and Balúchís. The second, Makrán on the south, is immediately under Bampúr, but is governed by a Balúch; and there are, as a rule, no Persian troops to garrison its towns or forts. The system of government prevailing here is to acknowledge every legitimate chief who, on his side, acknowledges the Persian supremacy, or to set up an obedient competitor who is not likely to be wanting. . . . . .

'The Persian tenure of the sea-coast is not like that of Bampúr. The Minister of Karmán frankly told us he would give no passports for landing there. Ibrahim Khán said he would take no responsibility for the telegraph along the shores west of Gwádar and Jeoni. The country is theirs, inasmuch as tribute is paid to Persia by Mír Abdullah, Chief of Gaih, and he repays himself by levies from his neighbours. Din Muhammad, Jadgál, who has immediate control of the coast from Cháhbár to the frontier of Kej, is married to Mir Abdullah's sister, and may therefore be supposed in some way attached to his interests. There is no mistake about the line of boundary with Kej, which is clearly defined. It is just as I formerly surmised and reported. A point in Gwatar Bay, the mouth of the Dasht Khaur, is the termination, on the sea-board, of a line drawn east of Jálk and Dízak from Sistán. . . . . Sarbáz and Píshín are on the Persian side; Túmp and Jeoni belong to Kej of Kalát. My opinion is that if we wish to set up a line of telegraph from Gwádar to Bandar-Abbas, or elsewhere, to join the present Persian line, we must treat with Persia for permission to do so. . . .'

Much more correspondence followed on the same subject; and at the end of 1866 the Director of the Telegraph was despatched from London to Tehrán to negotiate, under the superintendence of Her Majesty's Minister, an extension of the coast wires to the west.

INTRODUCTION.

There was, however, to be no definition of political boundaries. Negotiations commenced accordingly, interviews and messages passed, but the occasion was unfavourable; and the Shah's departure for Mashhad rendered imperative a postponement of the question. About a year later it was re-opened, and a short Convention of three Articles between the British and Persian Governments agreed upon and ratified [1]. Under this authority the British land line of telegraph was prolonged westward, from Gwádar to Jásk: but the want of territorial definition gave rise to serious troubles, and threatened to perpetuate a state of restlessness and revolution distressing to our *employés*, embarrassing to the Indian Government, and most detrimental to the inhabitants of Balúchistán, whether in the interior or on the Makrán coast.

Inroads were made on Panjgúr, in the north of Kalát territory; immediately below it, the district of Kej was threatened; Gwádar was claimed by Persia on the coast; and the more especially because of its mention in the first Article of the Convention! Finally, in 1870, Her Majesty's *Chargé d'Affaires* in Tehrán had become so encumbered with references on Persian encroachments that he could suggest no remedy but a formal investigation; and to such procedure he was enabled to obtain the king's consent. The good sense of His Majesty and His Majesty's Ministers prevailed in accepting a joint Commission, representing England, Persia, and Kalát. 'Let them,' said the Shah, 'settle the boundary line. Otherwise, if the frontier be not defined, these difficulties will be daily recurring.'

The Commission was appointed, and the narrative of its proceedings is told in these pages. Should illustration of the unsettled condition

---

ARTICLE I.
[1] In order to provide against any accident to the Persian Gulf Cable, it is agreed that the British Government shall make arrangements in regard to the construction and efficient working of a line of telegraph between Gwádar and a point between Jask and Bandar-Abbas.

ARTICLE II.
The Persian Government will employ her good offices and authority for facilitating its construction, maintenance, and protection; and the English Government will pay annually to the Persian Government the sum of 3000 tomans for leave to lay down a line of telegraph on those parts of coasts and places which are under the sovereignty of Persia, the payment of the above sum being made from the day upon which the work of laying the wire is commenced.

ARTICLE III.
The present Convention to remain in force for twenty years.

of Makrán, and consequent misery, prior to the settlement of 1871, be needed in support of the latter measure, viewed in a purely philanthropic light, the present writer could supply it from his own experience. Rebellion, division, and discord in the Kalát country have unfortunately been too rife, within the last three years, to give opportunity for material improvement in any portion of the Khán's dominions. Yet, about a year after the Boundary Commission had visited Bampúr, notwithstanding the stormy nature of its work there, the vicinity of the newly declared frontier was reported to have enjoyed an unusual quiet; and the President of the Royal Geographical Society took public cognizance of the fact in addressing a meeting in 1872. If attention be given to the due fulfilment of the ratified international agreement, and if the Persian Government check their ambitious lieutenants with the firmness they can exhibit when roused, and in the spirit of true civilisation, the inhabitants of both sides of the border should benefit incalculably from the combined action of England, Persia, and the Kalát State in seeking to close a political breach. On the other hand, if Kalát be allowed to drift into anarchy, and her rulers, in a narrow, selfish regard to personal objects, ignore the importance of the outer territorial limits, to look after more immediate inner interests, or if the spirit of the short but significant note of 1871[1] be lost sight of in the

---

[1] The undersigned, Her Britannic Majesty's Envoy Extraordinary and Minister Plenipotentiary at the Court of Persia, acting on the part of his Government, has the honour to submit, for the approval of His Majesty the Shah, a map in which the boundary line between the territories possessed in Balúchistán by Persia and the territories forming the exclusive property of the independent state of Kalát is delineated.

This line may be described:—Commencing from the northernmost point, or that which is furthest from the sea, the territory of Kalát is bounded to the west by the large Persian district of Dizak, which is composed of many *dehs* or minor districts, those on the frontier being Jálk and Kalagán. Below these two last-named is the small district of Kohak, which, together with Panjgúr, comprising Parom and other dependencies, is on the Kalát side.

Below Panjgúr, the frontier possessions of Kalát to the sea are Bolaida, including Zamirán and other dependencies, Mund and Dasht. Within the Persian line of frontier are the villages or tracts belonging to Sarbáz and Bahu Dastyári. The boundary of Dasht is marked by a long line drawn through the Drabol hill, situated between the rivers Bahu and Dasht, to the sea in the bay of Gwatar.

To summarize,—Panjgúr and Parom, and other dependencies, with Kohak, Bolaida, including Zamirán and other dependencies; Mund, including Tump, Nusrabad, Kej, and all districts, *dehs*, and dependencies to the eastward; Dasht with its dependencies as far as the sea. These names exhibit the line of actual possession of Kalát, that is to say, all tracts to the east of the frontier of actual Persian possession, which frontier comprises Dizak and Bampusht, Sarbáz and Pishín, Bahu and Dastyári.

discussion of comparatively minor points, then very much labour will have been expended and a certain cost incurred in vain.

One word in explanation of the allusion just made to minor heads of discussion. When the Persians accepted at Tehrán the British Commissioner's decision on the Perso-Makrán line of boundary, an endeavour was made in the most distinguished quarter to transfer Kohak, a district in the northern part of the frontier, from the Kalát to the Persian side. This request was further pressed by the Persian Minister in London; and it is probably one which may not have been officially disposed of at the present hour. The British Commissioner could not, in justice, make over the bone of contention to Persia: nor had he the power, in expediency, to treat the matter on its geographical merits. Whatever views, however, may be entertained on the rights to Kohak, there can be no doubt that the original decision, making it over to Kalát, was accepted *pur et simple*, and, therefore, that for Persia to reject any modification of that decision short of the full, unreserved grant of the district, must be construed as a virtual return to the first award. If, eventually, any concession to Persia be made, it should certainly be conveyed in such particular form that, without involving Her Majesty's Government in responsibilities inconvenient as to the issue, the future independence of the district should as well as possible be secured. For all evidence goes to prove that it *is*, more or less, independent.

Cháhbár is a port west of Gwatar and Gwádar, which at the period of the Perso-Kalát settlement was in the hands of the Arabs, and had been so for nearly a century. As it was not considered in the British Commissioner's province to discuss the question of its ownership when the line of boundary was drawn, there was no provision made regarding it. Persia has thought fit to supersede the Arab rule there by her own. We do not acknowledge the justice of the act: but, independently of right and wrong, Persia seems to have done unwisely in expelling from the place a thriving commercial community. She might in this, as in similar instances, have reaped material benefit from toleration and generosity: whereas the law of might may have been exercised to her detriment both in purse and prestige.

Little need be said on the results of the Sistán Arbitration. Recourse had been had by both Persia and Afghánistán to British mediation; the former under Article VI of the Anglo-Persian Treaty of March 1857, promising the 'friendly offices' of the British Government when required; the latter on the plea that arms were not

INTRODUCTION.

taken up in defence of Sistán, out of deference to the wishes of the Viceroy of India. Intervention was considered advisable, and a Commissioner instructed accordingly by Her Majesty's Secretary of State. This officer would accompany the Persian Boundary Commissioner to Sistán, there to be met by the Viceroy's Delegate accompanying the Afghán Commissioner to the same place. The meeting was so far held, that all parties arrived at the place appointed, and within easy distance of each other: but discussion was reserved for Tehrán, where a decision was publicly given.

Exception was taken on both sides, and appeals duly forwarded to Her Majesty's Secretary of State for Foreign Affairs. Perhaps the double appeal bore testimony that the award was, at least, impartial. In any case, two of the main objections may here be noted. They were on the Persian side:—

1st. That the oblique line drawn across the Sistán desert, by cutting off the Persians from the left bank of the Helmand above Kuhak, endangered the needed supply of water to the tract called 'Sistán Proper.'

2nd. That the limitation of 'Sistán Proper' to the line of the 'Náizár,' or reed-beds on the north, deprived the Persian villages in the vicinity of their legitimate lands and revenues.

Reasons for this disposition of territory have been fully given, independently of the abstract justice of the case as explained in the recorded Arbitration. The question of water-supply is one of a local detail into which it would be tedious now to enter[1]; but it has been

---

[1] On this subject I quote the opinion of Major Lovett, R.E.:—

'The Helmand flows between high banks from Rúdbár to Kohak, and the only places where canal works would be practicable, and where it is at all feasible to lead off the water, is at the bend of the river at Bandar Kamál Khan, and lower down below Kala'h Fath on the right bank, where formerly, according to tradition, a canal started and irrigated the country near Chakhansúr. As to the objection that the Afgháns, by reconstructing the canal heads at Bandar Kamál Khan, might deprive the Persians in Sistán Proper of water for irrigation, I would observe that beyond works of irrigation in the bed of the Helmand itself, which would not decrease the water-supply at Kohak, the Afgháns would have no object in the reconstruction of the old Bandar Kamál canal, originally intended for irrigating the low lands lying to the east of the lake where now are the ruins of Hanz-i-Dar, Kandar, &c., all to the west of the line of delimitation, and therefore any resuscitation of these works would be for the benefit of the Persians. Between these low lands and the valley of the Helmand there is a tract of land too high for river irrigation. To the statement that water may be led off from Kala'h Fath to Chakhansúr, I reply that, however physically possible such a work might be, its accomplishment by the Afgháns is most unlikely. Moreover, Chakhansúr itself, the only village of note east of this section of the Helmand, is already irrigated by the Khásh river.'

referred to in the award, and any evil result contemplated by Persia from the possession by Afghánistán of the left bank of the Helmand above Sistán Proper, would be as much in contravention of the spirit of the settlement as a forcible attempt to recover Nasirabád or Sekúha. In other respects the boundary line to the south has its advantages.

Personal experience, combined with a study of the declared experience of others, led the Arbitrator to the conclusion that fixed and understood boundaries between restless and antagonistic nations, guided rather by circumstances than principles, and not amenable to strict laws of civilisation, afford the best guarantee for peace and progress within the territorial limits of those nations, especially in the neighbourhood of the frontier defined. But it is almost as essential to the due adjustment of frontier disputes such as the Perso-Kalát and Perso-Afghán, to secure the lasting integrity of a defined frontier, as to define it acceptably in the first instance. And while the opinion is held that, both in a geographical and political sense, the best boundary between semi-civilised Oriental States is a desert, or barren mountain range through or along which an arbitrary line offers no inducement to transgression from either side; a river is, on the other hand, believed to possess, in this respect, simply geographical advantages. Politically, as it is the cause of rendering land fertile and valuable, so must it be the cause of envy and dissension to a nomadic population equally ready to find means of livelihood in cultivating the right or the left bank; and therefore, politically, is it all the more necessary that these nomads, or their representative chiefs, should be subject to one sovereign power, whichever side they may select for the transfer of their labours.

As regards the second objection by Persia, the Arbitral award states that 'North of Sistán the Southern limit of the Náizár should be the frontier towards Lásh Juwain. Persia should not cross the "Hámún" in that direction.' But it is not contrary to the spirit of this ruling to allow Persia the benefit of any reeds or cultivation within the Náizár which fairly belong to places assigned to her in Sistán Proper, such as Jalálabád and Jahánabád, provided they do not equally belong to places North of the Náizár and on the Western side of the Helmand. The general line of the Náizár, or broad bed of reeds, should not, under any circumstances, be transgressed, as all territory *to its North* must be held to belong to Lásh Juwain. There seems, in fine, to be no real obstacle to the perpetuation of the settlement, if only the spirit of discord will allow of a mutual understanding for mutual advantage.

The authors of the papers comprised in these volumes on Eastern Persia are Majors St. John and Lovett of the Royal Engineers, Major Euan Smith[1] of the Madras Army, and Mr. W. T. Blanford of the Geological Survey of India. A few concluding words are necessary to show the circumstances under which the *matériel* and data have been collected.

Captain Oliver St. John, an officer of much practical experience in Persia, had been originally named to carry out the survey and scientific objects of General Goldsmid's Mission in 1870; but the urgency of his duties in the Telegraph Department at Tehrán had stood in the way of acceptance. Captain W. H. Pierson, also an officer of local knowledge and varied ability, was next offered the post; but his temporary employment under the Lords of Her Majesty's Treasury being ruled as of greater importance, the work eventually fell to the lot of Captain Beresford Lovett, a junior officer to both the above on the Staff of the Persian Telegraph. The want of honest co-operation on the part of the Shah's authorities in Makrán had compelled the British Commissioner to precipitate a settlement, based on sufficient knowledge but somewhat incomplete geographical details; so that, when negotiating a permanent boundary line at Tehrán, to which the royal fiat was eventually given, General Goldsmid suggested that 'for the prevention of future disputes, and to ensure accuracy in mapping,' a newly-deputed engineer officer should certify, by careful observation and in company with an emissary from Persia and Kalát respectively, the frontier already sketched by Captain Lovett. This suggestion was adopted both by the Home and Indian Governments, and Captain St. John's nomination to the duty approved: General Goldsmid, in anticipation of such adoption and approval, had left provisional written instructions for Captain St. John's guidance, when himself returning to England[2]; and about the time that the General's Mission had again

---

[1] Local rank of Major was given to these officers for special duties.

[2] The following is an extract of his letter to the India Office dated 7th May, 1873: 'When first appointed to the Boundary Commission, I was permitted to select an Engineer officer for the practical and scientific duties of survey. A superintendence of nearly five years of the Indo-European Telegraph had made me well acquainted with its officers and *employés*, and I had, on more than one occasion, brought to the notice of the Government of India, and Public Works Department of the Home Government, their good and efficient

started for Sistán, Captain St. John was on his way to Gwádar to execute the minute survey required at his hands.

Detained by severe sickness before embarkation at Bushahr, and again by Government orders on arrival in Makrán, owing to the disturbed state of the interior, it was not until the 22nd January, 1872, that the upward journey was commenced from the sea-board. On the 13th March he had reached Jálk, in the tracts due south of the Sistán desert; too late in the season for independent action. This was, moreover, the very day that General Goldsmid's Mission crossed the Sistán frontier *en route* to Tehrán. Had it been otherwise, it would have been desirable to attempt a junction of the camps. Such a measure might have been accomplished two months earlier, with due regard to heat, scarcity, and want of carriage, by crossing the desert along the Mashkid river, and through Pir Kaisar; or by a western track *viâ* Sarhad. As it was, returning through Bampúr, Bam, Karmán and Shíráz, Captain St. John was again in the Persian capital on the 1st July.

The detailed account of this officer's journey will be found not the least interesting portion of the following pages; and he has prefaced

---

services, laying stress especially on the names of Major Bateman Champain, Captains St. John and Pierson, and the late Quartermaster-Sergeant Bower. The nature and sphere of my coming work induced me naturally to turn towards those whom I had long had reason to esteem as coadjutors in the Telegraph—particularly the Persian section. For Major Champain's services I could not well ask, as he had just succeeded me in the Chief Directorship of the Government lines: Captain St. John could not be spared by Major Champain, and I was informed at the Foreign Office that the then employment of Captain Pierson under the Treasury, for a special duty in Persia, rendered impossible his transfer to my Mission. I had, therefore, to look elsewhere for a scientific assistant, and eventually selected Captain Lovett. About a year later I had completed the actual negotiations for the acknowledgment of a Perso-Balúch frontier, but the difficulties encountered by the Mission in the neighbourhood of the tracts to be mapped, rendered advisable a revision of the geographical boundary under discussion. Captain St. John's services being at this time available, I recommended his nomination for the duty, both to the Home and Indian Governments: but as I was myself called away to the settlement of a new question in Sistán, I could not personally superintend Captain St. John's work. The written instructions which I gave him, and which had been duly submitted, before delivery, to Government approval, were consequently of a character to leave him much responsibility in details and a free exercise of judgment hardly applicable to the case of any member of the Staff accompanying myself; and I felt it but a proper suggestion to make, in the interests of the Public Service, that Captain St. John be allowed to correspond directly, while employed in Makrán, with the Foreign Secretary in Calcutta. Thus the Survey Mission, though not invested with any actual political authority, became, as it were, a separate service, and its conduct and result were not without political importance.'

the narrative with a thoughtful and instructive chapter on the Physical Geography of Persia, the result of long residence and intelligent observation. The official value of his reports has nowhere been more conspicuous than in the confirmation of the views first expressed on the independence of Kohak, a district which could not be visited by the Boundary Commission, owing to the objections put forward by the Persian authorities[1].

Captain Beresford Lovett, R.E., accompanied General Goldsmid during both his Missions. On the first occasion, to enable him to obtain some preliminary acquaintance with the frontier to be surveyed, he was despatched from camp east of Isfahán to Bushahr and Gwádar, rejoining at Bampúr by the Kasrkand valley and Chámp south-east of that place. From Bampúr he was detached on a survey to the northward; when, after visiting Panjgúr and Kej, he was enabled to collect many material data, rejoining the Mission Camp at Gwádar. His experience, acquired in these particular expeditions, will be found under the head of 'Narrative of a Journey in Balúchistán,' immediately following Captain St. John's papers. On the occasion of the Perso-Afghán Arbitration, he joined Sir Frederic Goldsmid at Bam, having reached that station from Tehrán, by the Karmán road, a course which enabled him to effect an interesting exploration of Khabis and the neighbouring country, elsewhere described. He was then accompanied by the late Quartermaster-Sergeant David Bower, a non-commissioned officer of engineers, whose subsequent death, in the discharge of the noblest of duties[2], will have been deplored, not alone by relatives, but by the many who could give personal testimony to his worth, zeal, and ability. Captain Lovett's labours, during the rough period of the Sistán difficulty, comprised an expedition to the Kuh-i-Khwája[3] and a brief mission to Chakhansúr.

Captain C. Bean Euan Smith was Personal Assistant to Major-General Goldsmid, and present with him throughout the two Missions with which that officer was entrusted. He has now completed a narrative of both expeditions; worked out in considerable detail, yet not incautiously infringing on secret and political archives. In justice to the narrator it should be stated that, owing to his absence in India

---

[1] Captain St. John's services in the Persian telegraph have been already recorded in Part I. of Telegraph and Travel, published by Messrs. Macmillan and Co. (1874); more especially in the Appendix to that volume, p. 641.

[2] See note, p. 77.   [3] See Geographical Magazine for October 1873.

and delay in receipt of manuscripts, an adaptation from his diaries, rather prepared for official record than public circulation, fills up a *vacuum* from pages 164 to 211 in a manner not originally contemplated; and other modifications or curtailments of text, which might have been more satisfactorily effected by the author himself, have been necessitated in the course of publication. Apology must, moreover, be made that the order in which the pages came to hand interfered with the due division of the story into chapters; a method suggesting itself to the editor, but set aside in favour of headings originally given by Captain Smith to certain sections.

Mr. Blanford's reputation as a naturalist and geologist will be a sufficient introduction to his highly valuable contribution to the second of these volumes. His presence in England fortunately enabled him to see the pages on Zoology through the Press, and to leave little to be done by editorial hands in respect of the remainder. How he came to be associated in these Boundary Commissions may be easily explained. When Captain St. John was about proceeding to Makrán in accordance with the British Commissioner's recommendation, the Government of India appointed Mr. Blanford to accompany him. The wisdom and uses of such an appointment could hardly find better illustration, or better warrant for precedent, than in the results obtained from the combination of duties in this particular instance.

F. J. GOLDSMID.

LONDON,
11*th May*, 1876.

ON THE

PHYSICAL GEOGRAPHY OF PERSIA

AND

NARRATIVE

OF A

JOURNEY THROUGH BALUCHISTAN
AND SOUTHERN PERSIA

BY

MAJOR OLIVER B. ST. JOHN, R.E.

ON THE

PHYSICAL GEOGRAPHY OF PERSIA.

By Major OLIVER B. ST. JOHN, R.E.

Necessity for the chapter — The Iranian plateau generally described — The Caucasus a part of it — Its area, elevation, and drainage — Extent and drainage of Persia — Oceanic basin — Caspian basin — Helmand basin — Interior drainage area — Rainfall — Prevailing winds — Absence of great rivers — The Safíd-Rúd — The Atrak — Rivers of Western Persia — Of Fars — Of Balúchistán — Of Central Persia — Oreography of Persia — Errors in older maps — Discoveries of M. Khanikoff — Of Major Lovett — Of the Author — Uniform direction of Persian mountains — Elevation of ditto — Valleys and plains of Persia — KAVIR — The great salt desert — The desert of Lút — Political frontier of Persia.

I HAVE undertaken, with much diffidence, to attempt a description of the physical geography of Persia as a whole. It would have been an easier task, and one less likely to provoke criticism, to have confined it to those parts which have been surveyed by myself and other officers of the recent frontier commissions. But a work giving so full an account of the zoology of the country, would be incomplete without a general sketch of the external features which play so large a part in modifying the nature and distribution of the fauna; and a description of the geology must necessarily contain, if it does not supplement, an outline of the physical geography. Moreover, the journey of Mr. Blanford and myself was performed under circumstances which enabled us, not only to examine the nature of the country we traversed with a completeness rare in the annals of Persian travel, but to throw a considerable amount of light on the accounts of other explorers in proximate fields, which from want of scientific basis to go upon have been imperfectly, and often quite incorrectly, generalised by geographers. The study of the works of all modern travellers in Persia, while engaged in compiling a map of the country for the India Office, has familiarised me, as far as reading by the light of experience can do so, with those districts I have not myself visited. In the following pages I will therefore attempt to place before the reader a sketch in outline of the outward appearance of that section of the earth's surface which owns the sway of the Sháh, emphasising, and filling up in more detail, here and in the course of the succeeding narrative, those portions of the picture which have been either changed in form, or brought from shadow into light by our recent researches and other material unknown to or unused by geographers.

Modern Persia occupies the western and larger half of the great elevated plateau, rising between the valleys of the Indus and the Tigris. This plateau, generally termed the *Iranian*, may be described in relation to the general mountain system of the old world, as a section and southern spur of that great dividing range, which forms the backbone of the Europeo-Asiatic continent. On the west the highlands of Armenia unite the Iranian plateau with the mountains of Asia Minor; and on the east the Paropamisus and the Hindú Kúsh connect it with the Himalayas and the highlands of Tibet. Between the two it is bounded on the north by the vast desert steppes of South Russia, Khiva, and Bukhára, with the intervening depression which forms the Caspian Sea.

The Caucasus range and the highlands between it and Adarbaiján present no features sufficiently distinctive to entitle the geographer to separate them from the Iranian plateau; from which they are divided by no well-marked physical boundary. The opposite sides of the valley of the Araxes, a mere mountain torrent on a large scale, which forms the political frontier, are alike in character. The same may be said of the valley of the Kúr; and the great Caucasian range itself is but a prolongation of the Kúren and Kopet ranges[1], the undoubted northern scarp of the Iranian plateau, east of the Caspian. At best the Caucasian provinces of Russia are but an excrescence of the great elevated mass to the south-east; differing from it only in characteristics produced by the more bounteous rainfall, which has scooped out the valleys to a greater depth.

On the south-west, the valley of the Tigris, with its continuation the Persian Gulf; on the south the Arabian Sea; and the Indus

[1] This fact was unknown until the publication of surveys made by the officers of the recent Russian expeditions from forts Krasnovodsk and Chikishlar against the Túrkman nomads, and is not therefore shown in any existing general maps.

HYDROGRAPHICAL Map of PERSIA

valley on the east, form the other limits of the Iranian plateau, which covers, in round numbers, somewhat over a million square miles. Its average height above the sea may be about four thousand feet, varying from eight thousand or higher in certain of the outer valleys, to not more than five hundred in the most depressed portions of the centre. This greater elevation towards the edge gives an indication of the true basin-like character of the plateau. Less than one-half its surface drains outwards to the ocean, or to the Caspian and Aral lakes. The river Kúr rises upwards of 300 miles as the crow flies, and the Kizil-Uzún or Safíd-Rúd over 200 miles, from the nearest shore of the Caspian, into which they flow. But with these exceptions, no river on the Iranian plateau has a source more than 150 miles in a straight line from the foot of the scarp; and the average breadth of the lip of the basin hardly exceeds one hundred miles.

A glance at the accompanying sketch map (No. 1) will bring this prominent feature more clearly home to the reader than any mere description. He will also notice at once that the inward draining part of the plateau is divided into two sections. Of these the eastern, coloured yellow, drains into a single central depression the Hámún, or lake of Sistán, and is usually termed, from the name of its principal river, the Helmand basin. The western and larger half is as it were honeycombed into many depressions, each receiving the drainage of an area of more or less magnitude. The number of these depressions is quite uncertain, but the extent and character of the principal will be separately described hereafter. This natural separation of the central area into two parts, is nearly followed in the political division of the plateau. The whole of the western division, with the exception of a small corner near Herát, belongs to Persia, as does the narrow belt of country draining into the Sistán Lake from the west, with the greater part of the lake itself, and the fertile plain on its east bank. The rest of the Helmand, with a large part of the Oceanic and Caspio-Aral basins, belongs to the states of Afghánistán and Kalát, and their details are therefore beyond my limits.

The drainage areas of the whole Iranian plateau are approximately as follows:—

The ocean drains	230,000 square miles
The Aral and Caspian	250,000 ,, ,,

Leaving 550,000 to the interior drainage, of which surface the Helmand basin covers over 200,000.

The 610,000 square miles included in Persia proper are drained as follows:—

Into the ocean	130,000
„ the Caspian and Aral seas	100,000
„ the Sistán lake	40,000
„ Urmía lake	20,000
Interior drainage	320,000
Total	610,000

Referring to the map it will be seen that the area draining into the ocean consists of a long strip, nearly parallel to the Tigris and the sea-coast, and without a single protrusion inland. It should be noticed here, that there is no certainty as to whether an outlet exists from the Bampúr plain to the sea, by which the water of the Bampúr river might escape in extraordinary floods. Native evidence on the subject differs, and the country south-west of Bampúr has not yet been visited by an European. It is possible, therefore, that the line of the water-parting should be continued eastwards, a little north of the 28th parallel, as far as the Helmand watershed.

A narrow strip of land not more than thirty to fifty miles wide, along the southern coast of the Caspian, drains into that sea. On the west it suddenly widens out to a depth of 250 miles, meeting the watershed of the Tigris on the one side, and that of the Euphrates and Lake Van on the other, and embracing between the two the basin of Lake Urmía or Urúmíyah, which is thus completely shut off from the rest of the inward draining area of Persia, forming, with the basin of Lake Van, what may be termed the supplementary plateau of Armenia, which differs only from the Persian and Helmand basins in its superior altitude and smaller area. The basin of Lake Gokcha, in the mountains, between the Kúr and the Araxes, might be considered as forming another distinct drainage area; but though it has no external outlet, the perfect freshness of its waters would seem to point with a probability amounting to conviction to its having subterranean communication with one or other of these rivers.

On the east the watershed of the Caspian gradually increases in breadth, the foot of the scarp extending considerably to the north of the south-east angle of that sea, three degrees east of which it turns to the south-east parallel to the axis of the Kúren and Kopet ranges, which, as before stated, are a prolongation of the Caucasus. A short distance south of Herát the Caspian water-parting turns eastwards, separating the valleys of the Hari-Rúd and Hárút Rivers. West of Herát, the desert plateau of Kháf divides the Caspian from the Helmand basin.

It may be noticed here that the Tajand River, as the united waters of the Hari-Rúd and Mash-had rivers are called, does not, as represented in some recent maps, end in the desert close to Sarakhs, but forms a swamp in the *Atak* about the fifty-eighth meridian. Had its waters sufficient volume they would doubtless find a channel to the Caspian in Hájji Bugár Bay, or to the old bed of the Oxus, between the Lesser Balkan and the Kopet range. This point will probably be cleared up by the Russian expeditions against the Tekeh Túrkmans, which, as these lines are written, are said to be starting from the Caspian. As far south as latitude 30°, the eastern slopes of the ranges which shut off the valley of the Helmand from the deserts of Eastern Persia drain directly towards the Sistán Lake. But south of that parallel the surplus water flows by several channels in a south-east direction, or away from the lake. About latitude 29°, the water-parting of the Balúchistán mountain system, running east and west, changes the direction of these streams, and collects them into a single channel, which, under the name of the Máshkíd River, bursts through the northern scarp of the Balúch hills into the Khárán desert. Here it takes a north-westerly course, thus reversing the original direction of its waters, which are lost in the desert not far from their most northern sources. It is very probable that they find a subterranean channel some distance further to the north, and aid to fill the Zirreh swamp, the southern of the three depressions which, united by flood waters, form the Hamún or Sistán Lake.

The great central area of Persia, included in the watersheds described above, forms a figure nearly triangular, with a base running south-west about 1000 miles long, and nearly equal sides north and east of 700 miles. The subdivision of this vast area into different drainage basins will be treated when we come to describe the hill ranges by which they are divided.

It will be readily believed that the rainfall on the Oceanic and Caspian watersheds is far in excess of that on the interior. Wherever the water-parting is formed, as it is in most parts, by a lofty mountain ridge, it intercepts the moisture-bearing clouds from the sea, which are discharged on its outer slopes. The Albúrz chain, which shuts off the plateau from the Caspian, may be taken as the typical instance of this. Its northern face is furrowed into deep valleys by the constant and heavy showers which have clothed them in forests of almost tropical luxuriance, while the southern generally presents a single abrupt scarp, rising above long gravel slopes, unchannelled by anything worthy the name of a river, and bare of any vegetation rising to the dignity of a tree. At the most moderate estimate the rainfall of Gilán and Mazandarán may be taken as five times that of the adjoining districts across the ridges to the south.

In other parts, however, we find the water-parting considerably below the level of the summits further inland; and here the interior has a more plenteous rainfall than the coast. This is particularly the case in south-eastern Persia, where the Khurasán, Sarhad, and Dízak hills, far exceeding in altitude the ranges to the south, attract to themselves the major portion of the scanty supply of moisture borne inland from the sea.

Again, the rainfall differs very much in different parts of the country, under apparently similar conditions as regards mountains and distance from the sea; the east and south being far drier than the north and west, while the dampest parts of the Tigris valley have not half the rainfall of the southern and south-eastern shores of the Caspian.

Two palpable causes unite to produce the prevailing winds throughout Persia and the Persian Gulf. These are, with an extraordinary uniformity, north-west or south-east. The first cause is the position of the Black Sea and Mediterranean on the north-west, and of the Arabian Sea on the south-east. The second is the bearing of the axes of the great mountain chains, which lie mainly in the same direction (vide diagram II), and thus tend to guide the currents of air in a uniform course. The south-west, moreover, is not felt, except as moderating the temperature of the Makrán coast, inside a line from Rás-al-Hadd, south of Maskat, to Karáchi.

The effect of the sun on the great Iranian plateau is to produce a heated stratum of air; which, when it rises, is succeeded by a current from the colder atmospheres above the seas to the south-east or north-west. Naturally the latter is the colder, and therefore, as might be expected, north-west winds are most prevalent. But in southern Persia and the Gulf it often occurs that the two currents meet, and that a north-westerly gale is raging at Bushahr, while a south-easter is blowing at

DIAGRAM No. 2

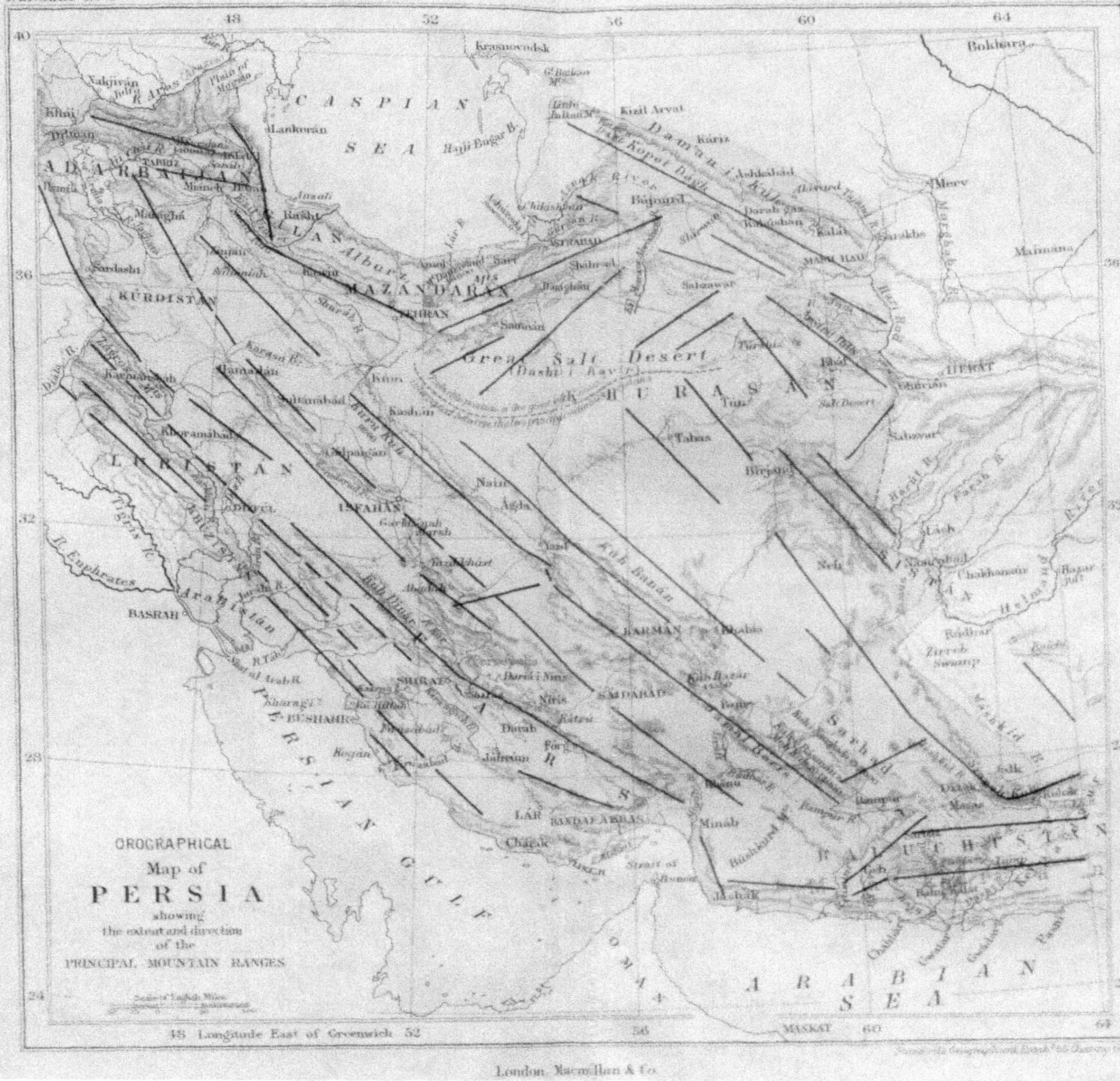

London, Macmillan & Co.

Bandar-Abbas. This latter wind is the rain-bearer throughout the greater part of Persia, the exception being the north-west, where occasional rain-clouds from the Black Sea and the Caspian find their way across the Kúrdish mountains or the Albúrz. It is true that it often rains even on the Gulf during a north-wester, but only when this has followed a succession of south-easterly gales, the moisture borne by which is returned from the opposite quarter.

In the absence of statistics extending over even a single year (and an average of fifteen years at least would, I think, be requisite), it is impossible to give more than an opinion as to the amount of rainfall in Persia. But I believe I am well within the mark in stating that no part of the country, with the exception of the Caspian watershed, and that of the Persian Gulf north of the twenty-eighth parallel, and their immediate reverse slopes, with perhaps the Urmía basin, has an average yearly rainfall of ten inches, taking mountain and valley together. Throughout the greater part of central and south-eastern Persia, and Balúchistán, the annual rainfall cannot be much more than five inches. On most parts of the plateau the rainfall is divided as follows: A little rain is hoped for, but not always expected, in November, to sow the early crops. In December there is generally a tolerably heavy fall of snow, and another in February, followed by showers in March and the beginning of April, after which there is nothing but an occasional thunderstorm in the mountains till the next winter. Were it not that the lofty hills store the moisture in the shape of snow, nine-tenths of Persia would be the arid desert that half of it is now. As it is, cultivation over the greater part of the country is only possible by artificial irrigation, either by canals, or by the system of wells connected by underground channels called *kanát* or *kariz*, and peculiar, I believe, to the Iranian plateau.

With so scanty a rainfall, great rivers are not to be expected, and we accordingly fail to find a single stream unfordable during the dry months throughout the whole of the interior plateau. The Caspian watershed, besides the Kúr and the Araxes, presents three considerable streams in Persian territory. The first is the Kizil-Uzún or Safid-Rúd, which drains about 25,000 square miles of country east and south of the Urmía basin. On the south-west of the Caspian the streams, though often of considerable volume, are of small length. The most important is the Lár, which rises north of Mount Damávand, and flows round its southern foot, thus nearly encircling it before completing its course to the sea.

The other two are the Atrak and the Gúrgán, of which the former and larger is very incorrectly laid down on existing maps of Persia, being shown as rising near Abivard, about longitude 60°, flowing due west through four degrees of longitude before turning southwest to the Caspian, and receiving many affluents from either side in its course.

The recent Russian explorations and the travels of Colonel Valentine Baker and Lieutenant Gill, R.E., last year, have largely modified this view. It appears that the true Atrak is the same stream as that shown on maps as the Germeh Khaneh or Germe Rúd. This has its origin in a dry torrent near Kabúshán or Kúshán, and flows through Shírván and Bújnúrd in a north-westerly direction, receiving several considerable streams from the Kúren Dágh on the north, but none of importance from the hills to the south. As the Atrak river is supposed in certain quarters to form the frontier of Persia throughout its course, this modification is one of considerable importance, as it places the Persian town of Shírván and the flourishing Persian district of Darah-gaz outside the limits of the kingdom. In describing the present state of the political frontier of Persia at the close of this chapter, I shall advert to this subject again.

The streams draining southern and western Persia into the sea, diminish regularly in importance from north-west to south-east. The slopes of the mountains of Kúrdistán and the Zágros pour their waters into the great river Tigris through the Diála and Karkhah rivers. Further south the Diz and Kárún, or Kúrán, unite their waters in the plain of Khúzistán, to form a river navigable from the sea to the first range of hills. It is worthy of remark that this stream, which formerly discharged its whole volume direct into the sea, now parts with the larger half through an artificial channel into the Shat-ul-Arb, the common outlet of the Tigris and Euphrates. South of the Kárún the Jaráhi and Táb rivers have with it formed the delta of Persian Arabistán, the most extensive and fertile plain in Persia.

After this, not a single stream unfordable at all seasons bars the passage of the traveller along the coast till he reaches the Indus, eighteen degrees of longitude to the east, and five degrees of latitude further south, a stretch of riverless waste perhaps unequalled save on the neighbouring shores of Arabia and the Red Sea. The lofty hills south and west of Shíráz originate several streams, which are discharged into the Gulf by two mouths; one at Rú-hilleh, north of Bushahr; and the other formed by the Kár-agach and Fírúzábád rivers a little south of Kogán.

There appears to be no valid authority for the extent and direction of any streams delineated on the maps between the last-named and the Mináb river, which again is of far more importance than the maps would lead the observer to suppose. So little is known of the quadrilateral between the Shíráz and Karmán road on the north, the sea on the south, and the Shíráz-Firúzábád and Karmán-Bandar-Abbas roads west and east, that we can pronounce nothing with certainty about its streams except that all are quite insignificant. On the other hand, the Mináb creek receives the drainage of all the wide plain across the hills north of Bandar-Abbas.

In Persian Balúchistán the Aimini and Kír torrents drain very narrow valleys. The former is remarkable as being the only watercourse in Balúchistán which pierces the plateau, rising amid low hills on the plain of Bampúr. The uncertainty whether this latter has an outlet to the sea has already been adverted to. It is possible that the flood-waters of its stream, after joining the Jírúft or Rúdbár torrents, find a way along the north of the Búshkúrd hills to the Mináb. For my own part I incline to the belief that no such outlet exists.

The Dashtiárí river is more considerable than either the Kír or the Aimini, but is less than the Dasht or Nihing, whose course has been fully described in the narrative portion of this work. Its erroneous connection by geographers with the Máshkíd and Rakshán torrents has also been mentioned elsewhere.

We now come to the streams which have no outlet to the sea. Where all are so inconsiderable, and moreover vary so much at different seasons, and have as much as possible of their water drained off in canals, it is difficult to signalise the most prominent. The general character is everywhere much the same, and may be described as follows. Before the brooks have left the hills, part of their water is taken off to irrigate the mountain sides, and when they unite in the wider valleys larger canals lead from the channel. As long as the slope is rapid and the bed stony, a great deal of the precious liquid manages to escape, but when the open alluvial plain between the ranges is reached it is soon exhausted in irrigating the banks; and, but for constant affluents from the never far distant hills would soon present an empty bed. As it is, many rivers struggle on for a considerable distance from their sources, till they end in salt swamps or lakes. Nearly all are brackish in the latter part of their course, being tainted by the salt common in the gypseous strata so universally occurring throughout Persia.

The principal of these inland streams are the Aji-Chái and Jaghatú flowing into the salt lake of Urmía; the Hamadán Rúd, or Kárasu, and the Shúráb flowing eastwards to the salt desert; the Zaindarúd, fertilising the neighbourhood of Isfahán, and lost in the unexplored swamp or salt marsh of Gávkhánah, and the Kúr, commonly known in Europe as the Bendameer, which forms the salt lake of Nírís, miscalled Bakhtegán on our maps.

The Shíráz lake receives little or no water from influent streams, being apparently mainly fed by springs, as is the smaller lake of Kazrán.

Having thus completed a brief account of the hydrography of Persia, let us turn to the consideration of its oreography, to illustrate which I have prepared a diagram showing the direction and extent of the axes of the principal ranges, (vide fig. II)[1]. This is the more necessary, as it is here that the largest modifications in maps have been made by recent travellers. A glance at the diagram will show that the most prominent characteristic of the mountain system of Persia is the uniform direction of its ranges, which lie, with few exceptions, nearly north-west and south-east, a feature I have already referred to as influencing the prevailing winds. That part of the Albúrz which lies east of Damávand, and the ranges

---

[1] I should have wished to have included the eastern half of the Iranian plateau in this diagram as in that of the drainage areas. But I find that, with the exception of the main valley of the Helmand, and that of the Hari-Rúd, near Herat, we have little exact information regarding the axes of the ranges which make up the mountain system of Afghanistán, west of the Indus basin. Taking into consideration the known direction of the Ghazní ridges (N.E. and S.W.), and that of the chains bounding the Herat valley (E. and W.), and supposing the water-parting of the Paropamisus to be correctly shown on our maps, it would appear probable that we have a formation in the outline of the axes of the hills identical with that found between eastern and western Balúchistán, where the Persian mountains, coming from the north-west, are connected with the Khivan hills from the north-east, by a series of parallel ridges running east and west.

parallel to it on the south, with the ridges intersecting the Balúch plateau, form the only remarkable exceptions to the rule.

A comparison between the hydrographic and oreographic diagrams will show that the disposition of the hills affords little indication of that of the watersheds. There is nothing in the latter to show which of the many parallel ridges form the water-partings of the plateau. Indeed the general outline would seem to point rather to a great river flowing to the sea in the south-east, than to a series of depressions receiving the surplus drainage.

The view generally taken by geographers of the mountain system of Persia, is that of an offshoot of the Hindú Kúsh, connecting that chain with the Caucasus and the Taurus. If there be any necessity for establishing such an origin (apart from the fact that the Iranian plateau is a link in the chain of high land running through Europe and Asia), the affinities of the Persian mountains would seem rather to lie westwards than eastwards: but in the absence of any accurate information regarding the geography or geology of northern Afghánistán, the points cannot be finally settled. To me it appears probable that the Harí-Rúd valley, the political frontier of Persia and Afghánistán, is also the point of contact of their respective mountain systems.

The idea of the continuity of the Persian ranges with those of the eastern watershed of the Helmand was borne out by all maps engraved previous to the publication of the results of the travels of M. Khanikoff in eastern Persia.

A reference to any atlas published before 1860, and indeed many of later date, will show all ranges east of the main road from Shíráz, through Isfahán to Tehrán (about the fifty-second meridian), running east and west, i.e. parallel to the coast ranges of the Arabian Sea, and the valley of Herát, THE ONLY SURVEYED PORTIONS. M. Khanikoff was the first to show that not only the mountains of Khurasán lie in ridges nearly parallel to those of western Persia, north-west and south-east, but that central Persia is intersected by more than one continuous range, with its axis in the same direction. This fact, which is strongly insisted on in his text, is rather ignored in the unworthy little map attached to it, in which minor spurs are exaggerated to equal dimensions with the main ridges, a defect increased rather than diminished by his English copyists.

However, his journey made a revolution in the prevailing ideas regarding the oreography of eastern Persia, and the surveys of Major Lovett and myself have done as much for the south. Major Lovett's first journey in 1870-71 established the facts of a water-parting in Balúchistán, about 100 miles from the coast, dividing the Helmand valley from the oceanic basin; and of a singular south-western deflection of the axes of the ranges south of Bampúr. The following year we proved the continuity of the great plateau west of Sistán with the Sarhad and Siáneh mountains; ascertained that Pottinger's text was right in distinguishing between the two extinct or dormant volcanos, the Kúh-i-Naushada, and the Kúh-i-Basmán; and his maps wrong in making but one: further west we traced Khanikoff's great central range west of Yazd, as far south as latitude 27° 30'; and found the other minor ridges between Karmán and Shíráz to lie in the same uniform direction, a parallelism I had previously found to occur in the ranges on all the roads between Bushahr and Shíráz, and that city and Isfahán.

On returning to England the new data obtained by ourselves and M. Khanikoff have enabled me to interpolate with them the observations of older travellers, to which, from want of solid base to work upon, justice had not been done by geographers. Thus the travels of Christie and Truilhier between Tabas and Yazd, and of Keith Abbott[1] between Yazd and Karmán, conclusively demonstrated the existence of three parallel ranges between the two former towns, and of a lofty and fertile plateau (Kúh-Banán), east of the road between the two latter, in a situation marked on the maps as part of the Karmán desert.

The ranges on the coasts of the Caspian and of the Arabian Sea,

---

[1] It is a matter of regret that this most painstaking and conscientious of non-scientific travellers has not survived to see justice done to his labours. No general map that I know of contains the results of his travels in Persia (published in the journal of the Geographical Society), which remained unnoticed by geographers till their value was pointed out by Colonel Yule in his 'Marco Polo.' Without pretending to aught but a most rudimentary knowledge of surveying, Mr. Abbott, in addition to a great amount of political and topographical information, kept a careful road-book by compass and watch, through twelve hundred miles of travel over a country then quite unexplored, and but little of which has been since seen by an European. Having myself followed part of Mr. Abbott's route, and having plotted the whole of the remainder from the astronomically fixed points since laid down, I can bear testimony to the skill and perseverance with which he carried out his self-imposed task. Had his labours been properly utilised by map-makers, many of the gross errors which still disfigure maps of Persia would long ago have disappeared.

and the neighbouring part of the Persian Gulf, are thus well nigh conclusively shown to form the only important exceptions to the general rule of a north-west and south-easterly direction to the ridges. It seems far from improbable that the same phenomenon will be found to be repeated in the neighbouring peninsula of Arabia, when that country is opened to fuller scientific exploration.

The general elevation of the mountains of Persia is far greater than has been generally supposed. The volcanic peak of Damávand, whose fires are still slumbering, marked upon our maps as 14,700 feet above the sea, has been fixed by the Russian Caspian Survey at 18,600 feet. Mount Savalán, in Adarbaiján, is declared by the same authorities to be 14,000 feet in height. I found the Kúh Hazár, south of Karmán, to exceed the latter altitude; and the summits of the neighbouring Jamal-Báris range are not inferior. But I believe the highest continuous range in Persia to be the Kúh Dinár, an unvisited chain of mountains in Fars, (the southern peak is marked on our maps as Daena 11,000?). These are visible from the sea near Bushahr, a distance of 130 miles over ridges known to be 10,000 feet in altitude. I myself have seen them from the hills near Yazdikhást in August, presenting an appearance both as to outline and extent not unlike the Bernese Alps, and hardly inferior in extent of snow-covered surface. As the snow-line at that season is certainly not below 14,000 feet, I am inclined to estimate the average height of the Dinár peaks at 17 to 18,000 feet above the sea. Many other summits in Armenia, Kúrdistán, and Lúristán never totally lose their snow, and can therefore be little less than 15,000 feet. The peaks in the water-parting of the Albúrz do not exceed 13,000 feet, but when these were snowless in the summer of 1871, I observed a snow-clad ridge north of the watershed, about the western frontier of Mazandarán. In central and eastern Persia there are no such lofty mountains, but the higher summits of the Kúrú range, between Isfahán and Kashán, exceed 11,000 feet; and the Khurasán mountains probably attain an equal elevation.

Absence of prominent spurs is the main characteristic of all Persian ranges except the Albúrz, and to a lesser extent the Khurasán hills. Inconsiderable rainfall has of course much to do with this, but the primary reason is to be sought in the geological formation. The extraordinary gravel slopes extending for many miles from the foot of the interior hills present a phenomenon fully treated of by Mr. Blanford in his account of the geology, and I will not, therefore, enlarge upon it here.

It remains to notice the valleys and plains between and beyond the ranges. The Khúzistán delta is the only plain of extent and importance at the sea-level. The strip of land between the outer hills and the sea is generally narrow and barren, but occasionally, as north of Bushahr, and north and east of Bandar-Abbas, expands into respectable dimensions. Part of the plain of Mogán, at the mouth of the Araxes, belongs to Persia, and the delta of the Safíd-Rúd has considerable extent and extraordinary fertility. Inland the long and narrow plains between the ridges rise gradually from 1000 feet to eight times that height in the valleys between the ridges on the east side of the western water-parting, and 4, 5, and 6000 further south and east. The plains of Isfahán, Shíráz, and Persepolis are about 5000 feet; that of Karmán somewhat higher. The valleys of Adarbaiján present alluvial slopes furrowed by torrents, and the only extensive tableland in Persia, that of Sultániah.

As they recede from the east and north, the intervals between the ridges are wider, and the rainfall smaller, till grassy valleys are replaced by gravelly deserts, which culminate in wastes of shifting sand. The valley between Abádah and Yazd, a prolongation of the Zaindarúd valley, contains the first of these sandy wastes, which, under the influence of the strong south-easterly winds, occasionally invade the neighbouring cultivated tracts. The original city of Rhages, south-east of Tehrán, is said to have been abandoned on this account.

The most remarkable feature, however, in the plains of Persia is the salt swamp called Kavír or Kafeh.

The universal condition of the alluvial soil of the Persian plateau appears to be that wherever it is exposed to sufficient moisture, either by the overflow of rivers, surface-drainage from the hills, or want of sufficient slope to carry off desert rainfall, a saline efflorescence is produced, which, forming a thin whitish crust on the surface, retains the moisture beneath for a considerable time, and thus creates, in winter and spring, a treacherous and impassable bog.

Where the supply of water is constant, but insufficient to form salt lakes such as those of Urmía and Nírízⁿ, a bog of slimy mud is formed in the lowest depression, covered with brine in winter, and in summer by a thick crust of salt. These salt swamps are termed Kavír in the north, and Kafeh in the south. The principal is that shown on our maps as the Great Salt Desert, the Dasht-i-Kuweer, or Daria-i-Kabír[1]. This is the eastern part of what is probably the most extensive plain in Persia, that intercepted between the Albúrz and its parallel ridges and the heads of the ranges of the central plateau which run south-east. Westward it is divided into two valleys, originating, one in the Sultániah plateau, and the other north of and near Hamadán. Each of these is drained by a river named respectively the Shúráb and the Kárasú, which with another considerable affluent from Túrshíz on the east, unite to form the great Kavír. It has only once been seen by an European, Dr. Bühsé, a Russian, who crossed it about latitude 34°, when travelling from Damghán to Yazd. He describes it as about nine versts or about six miles wide. The patches of ordinary *Kavír* seen by travellers on the Mash-had road may possibly communicate with the great *Kavír* through gaps in the intervening range; but Clark, who travelled from Túrshíz to Samnán, does not mention any *Kavír*, though he crossed the Abrisham river, which was supposed by travellers on the northern road to end in one of these smaller *Kavírs*. This stream, therefore, at least would appear to be a contributor to the great Kavír.

The altitude of the latter cannot be fixed with any certainty. It *may be* below the level of the sea; and is certainly not far above it, as the town of Tabas, on the edge of the hills to the south, was determined by Khanikoff at 1500 feet. The same traveller crossed a part of the Karmán desert, not more than 500 to 600 feet above the sea, and the lowest point of the northern waste is probably not much, if at all, in excess of this measurement.

Other *kavírs*, with constant mud and salt incrustations, are found in the Sarján or Saidábád plain, west of Karmán; and in the neighbouring valley of Kútrú. The ordinary *kavírs* are innumerable. That south of Kháf is one of the largest. Another receives the water of a small stream flowing north-west, from near Karmán. The banks of the 'Gavkhánah' marsh, formed by the Zaindarúd, are also 'kavír;' and a *kavír*, perhaps the same, was crossed by Trézel, between Abádah and Yazd. Abbott records another in the valley between the Kúh-Banán and the ridges east of Yazd. The best known is that north of

[1] I have never myself heard this last term used, nor have Persians from whom I have enquired; but it has the authority of the author of Hajji Baba to back it. The meaning would be not 'the great sea' as usually supposed, but the 'Lake of Salt Mud.'

Kúm, which is a bay, as it were, of the great Kavír; but it is by no means formidable in the worst of weathers, compared with the 'Kafehs' of Karmán.

The desert of Karmán, called by Khanikoff the desert of Lút or Lot[1], that of Kharán, which bounds Persian territory on the south-east, and the smaller waste of Bampúr, are drier, and therefore more sandy than the northern desert. Perhaps also the soil is less favourable to the formation of *kavír*. The great depression of the Karmán desert has been noticed. It should be mentioned that though no *kavír* was crossed by Truilhier, between Tabas and Yazd, and though there is an undoubted water-parting between the Great Salt Desert and that of Lút, the wastes of shifting sand passed by the traveller just mentioned may very possibly form a communication between the two.

As the object of the missions which have resulted in these volumes was to fix certain portions of the frontier of Persia, a few lines on the subject may not be amiss.

A glance at the outline of the dominions of the Sháh, with the Gulf in either of the diagrams, will show the general line of frontier to be nearly as like that of a cat on a footstool, as the coasts of Italy and Sicily are to the proverbial boot. If Persia is famous for anything, it is for cats, so that the fitness of the similitude is undeniable.

On the north-west, the frontier adjoining Russian territory is fixed by treaty. The same may now be said of the Balúch frontier, from the sea to the Máshkíd, and that in Sistán. Between the two, and further north, all is uncertain, save the names of the frontier towns. On the west the common frontier of Persia and Turkey, from Ararat to Basrah, is still undefined, though it was fixed within certain limits by the Anglo-Russian Commission of 1851-54. Recent maps emanating from Russian sources give the Atrak, from its mouth to the point where its most northern affluent joins it, as the western boundary of the new Russian district east of the Caspian, and this is probably the interpretation placed in St. Petersburg on the so-called and oft-denied Atrak frontier treaty. Further east all is as yet uncertain, but can hardly remain so for long. Sarakhs is held by

---

[1] I cannot help doubting this derivation, as I more than once heard the word 'lút' used in Balúchistán as equivalent to waterless. A Rigi camel-driver at Jalk, describing the route across the Kharán desert, said, that seven marches to Pír-i-kasr had water, but the remaining three to the Helmand were 'lút.'

Persia; the Dáman-i-Kúh, or Atak, by the Tekeh Túrkmans. The southern slopes of the Kúren hills are held as far west as Darah-gaz by the Kúrdish vassals of the Shah, transplanted there three centuries ago: thence to the Russian frontier they are probably occupied by the Goklán Túrkmans. Even if the Russian columns now marching eastwards from the Caspian do not settle this part of the frontier of Persia satisfactorily, they will assuredly obtain the geographical information necessary for doing so.

NARRATIVE

OF A

JOURNEY THROUGH BALUCHISTAN AND SOUTHERN PERSIA.

By Major OLIVER B. ST. JOHN, R.E.

CHAPTER I.

Gwádar to Píshín.

On the 7th of January, 1872, I landed from the British India Steam Navigation Company's ship 'India,' in Gwádar Bay. Orders from England to proceed to Balúchistán to survey the recently determined frontier had found me early in October at Tehrán, where I was acting as director of the Anglo-Persian Telegraph. By the 20th of the month all preparations for the long journey before me were made, and I started for Bushahr, expecting to reach that port, whence fortnightly steamers run down the Persian and Makrán coasts to Bombay, towards the end of November. Unfortunately, when only two days' march on the road southwards, I was struck down by a sudden attack of acute dysentery, which, with typhoid and typhus fever, was very prevalent in the neighbourhood of the capital, in consequence of the famine, then in its second year. Good nursing, and the skilful attendance of Dr. Baker, the medical officer of the telegraph staff, enabled me to reach Isfahán in a mule litter, after a fortnight's delay at Kúm and Kashán; another fortnight at Isfahán so far set me up that I was able to sit on a horse again, though at first for an hour or two a day only; and before long I had dispensed altogether with my *takht-i-rawán*, or portable bed, as the Persians call that most uncomfortable of conveyances, a mule litter. Bushahr was reached on the 30th of December, just a month later than anticipated. Here I felt doubtful for a moment whether I ought not to turn my steps towards England instead of to the wilds of Balúchistán. I was still far from having recovered my normal strength, and the doctors

ROUTE Map of PERSIA

London: Macmillan & Co.

advised me not to risk another hot season in Persia. But the winter was too far advanced for the government of India to replace me; the large outlay that had been made in preparations would have been thrown away; and to have deferred the survey for a year might have caused inconvenience. Moreover, I was naturally unwilling to relinquish my first chance of geographical discovery; so the hesitation was of short duration, and I took passage for myself, ten horses, and fifteen servants, to Gwádar, for which we embarked the next day.

A week's sail, broken by a few hours' stay at Lingah and Bandar-Abbás, and a night at Maskat, brought us to Gwádar Bay, where, almost before the anchor dropped, I was welcomed by my friend Mr. W. T. Blanford of the Geological Survey of India, who, at my suggestion, had asked and obtained leave from the Viceroy to be my companion in the approaching journey. After superintending the deposit of horses, baggage, and Persian servants in a clumsy native boat, in which the unfortunate quadrupeds were packed as close as sardines in a tin, we bade adieu to the 'India,' and pulled on shore. A strong wind off the land sprung up shortly afterwards, and the *impedimenta* remained in their uncomfortable conveyance all night, tossing at anchor in the Bay. The Persian servants were awfully sick, and the horses a good deal cut and bruised, in spite of tight packing. However, they all turned up the next morning without serious damage, though it is a mystery to me to this day how, in the absence of any mechanical contrivance whatever, the horses were got out of the deep native craft, whose bulwarks were high over their heads. In the meantime I had been hospitably welcomed by Captain Miles, then the Political Resident on the Makrán coast, whose headquarters are at Gwádar.

The next few days were busily employed in making preparations for a start. Stores and instruments had to be unpacked and repacked, provisions purchased, and money provided. Besides Blanford and his servants, the party was increased at Gwádar by an apothecary, Mr. Roane, a native surveyor from the quarter-master-general's department of the Bombay army, with six assistant peons, and a couple of bird-skinners from the Calcutta Museum. Tents for all had been sent from the Bombay Arsenal, and were ready pitched on my arrival. Fifty camels had been engaged beforehand by Captain Miles, and were now eating the bread, or rather browsing the thorns, of idleness at sixpence each per diem; and more were promised if required.

All was ready in four or five days, when a telegram reached me from Calcutta, ordering us to delay starting on account of disturbances at Kej, a dependency of Kalát, some seventy miles inland. This little province, inhabited by men of the turbulent and warlike tribe of Rinds, had enjoyed a long quasi-independence under a governor whose authority was only limited by the necessity of paying a small yearly tribute to the Khan of Kalát. The latter had lately been ill advised enough to replace him by a nominee of his own. The former governor made no resistance, but retired to a neighbouring village. The Rinds, however, whose opinion had not been consulted in the matter, not only declined to submit to their new master, but besieged him in his fort. It was supposed that this fighting in the immediate vicinity of the frontier we had come to survey might endanger the safety of our party. But a day or two later tidings arrived that peace was restored at Kej, and on the 19th I received leave from Calcutta to proceed, but with the greatest caution.

It had been arranged at Tehrán that the subordinate commission, the occasion for which has been explained by Sir Frederic Goldsmid in the preface to these volumes, should consist besides myself of deputies from Kalát and Persia. The former never turned up at all, and his absence, as will be seen further on, was rather detrimental to the completeness of the map.

The representative of His Majesty the Sháh was a lanky young man, *ancien élève* of the College at Tehrán, where he had picked up a fair knowledge of plan and map drawing, but whose acquaintance with surveying was of the slenderest. His name was Mírza Ashraf Ali, which appellation he had dignified on his own account with the affix of Khán, and had further had the rank of Sarhang, or Lieut.-Colonel, bestowed on him by his government for the occasion. His full title therefore was Mírza Ashraf Ali Khán Sarhang, but by the last he was known in the camp, and 'Sarhang,' therefore, we will call him for the future. He had marched down from Tehrán nearly at the same time as myself, but with a delicacy rare in his countrymen had avoided intruding himself upon my party, so that I had hardly seen him till the day after we left Bushahr in the 'India,' when I found him sitting on a couple of big trunks in the waist of the ship. On entering into conversation, he soon communicated the reason of his occupying so undignified a position. The authorities at Tehrán had furnished him with a sum of money, little more than sufficient to defray his expenses as far as

Bushahr. The delay on the road caused by my illness had left him quite 'au sec' when he reached the sea, and the price he got for his own and his servant's horse only served to take their deck passages to Bandar-Abbás and buy provisions for the three days' voyage. He had an order from the Minister for Foreign Affairs on the Governor of Karmán for the equipment necessary for the expedition, and therefore intended landing at Bandar-Abbás, marching thence to Karmán, obtaining there tents, horses, and escort, and eventually joining me on the frontier, via Bam and Bampúr. This little detour of 750 miles would have involved two months' delay at least. I therefore at once offered to lend him money and fit him out completely, if he would only come on to Gwádar at once, and begin operations without delay. This the Sarhang would not hear of; in fact from his manner it was easy to see that he had orders not to go to Gwádar at all. At Bandar-Abbás we fortunately heard that the Governor of Karmán had left the latter town for Balúchistán. This decided the Sarhang to come on to Maskat, where I left him with a couple of hundred rupees to hire a native boat to Gwatar, the nearest port in Persian Balúchistán to Gwádar. After some little delay he arrived at the former place a week after I reached the latter, and finding the governor at Sarbáz, got a fit out from him and met my party at Píshín.

Late in the afternoon of the 22nd of January, we got finally under weigh, after the usual scene of confusion and quarrelling, grunting and groaning of camels, and objurgations in a variety of tongues. The Balúch camel-driver is not a handy animal like the Persian muleteer, part of whose regular duty it is to find ropes and fit the most awkward-looking packages on his mules' saddles. Beyond making his camel kneel down to receive the load, and remonstrating in tones barely more melodious than those of his beast if he thinks the latter too heavily laden, the Balúch takes no interest or trouble in the transaction. Packing and loading had therefore all to be done by ourselves, and starting was thus a much slower business than in Persia. Our smaller packages were secured in huge baskets woven of the 'písh' leaf, a sort of dwarf palm found in torrent beds all over Balúchistán and part of Afghánistán as far north as Kábul. The same material supplied ropes, which, though they did not last long, had the advantage of being replaceable at every village. Before all the baggage was off the ground, the fifty camels originally provided had increased to eighty, which, with ten horses of mine and my Persian servants, and two of

Blanford's, formed the sum-total of our caravan. Blanford's Indian servants and the surveying party were on foot, my Persian grooms and *farashes* on the camels which carried the paraphernalia of their different departments.

Our first three stages led through dreary and desolate wastes along the line of telegraph to the banks of the Dasht river, at the village of Sirokí. Before reaching it we had not seen a vestige of human habitation, hardly of life. The road, a mere track a few inches wide, passed over plains of whitish clay, between distant ranges of barren hills, those on the south broken into the fantastic outlines which characterise the coast scenery of Makrán. At Falarí, the second halting-place, a few stunted bushes grew near a scanty stream better filled than usual by the recent heavy rains. Here a few miserable-looking sheep gave evidence of the proximity of some nomad Balúchís, who did not, however, honour us with a visit. Each day before noon a strong north wind raised clouds of sand which hid the landscape for hours, and added positive discomfort to the depressing influences of the scenery.

We were far from sorry, therefore, to see, on the third day, the belt of trees which marks the course of the Dasht river, and to find the tents pitched between the two clusters of eighty to a hundred huts which form the village of Sirokí. Here we stayed till the 27th, observing and collecting specimens and information. My original intention had been to go on to Sísád on the Dashtiárí river, two days' journey to the west, where I had appointed to meet the Mihmándár sent by Ibráhím Khán, deputy governor of Persian Balúchistán; but the country about Sísád being reported so swampy as to be impassable for camels, I sent a *kásid* to inform the Mihmándár of my change of plan, and determined to make direct for Báhú Kalát, a considerable place on the eastern or Sarbáz branch of the Dashtiárí river, and on the Persian side of the frontier, which had not been visited by either of the exploring parties the previous year.

At ten o'clock on the morning of the 27th we started, bidding adieu to our kind host, Captain Miles, who had accompanied us thus far from Gwádar; and, quitting the last relic of civilisation in the shape of the telegraph line, turned our horses' heads to the interior. For about a mile the road led through the tamarisk and acacia jungle bordering the river, which we then crossed at a ford. The stream was at that time about sixty or eighty yards wide, running between steep clay banks from a hundred to a hundred and fifty yards apart. The Dasht river is the most considerable of the torrents which carry off the scanty rainfall of southern Balúchistán. Its western branch, which forms the boundary of Kalát in the upper part of its course, rises in the highlands of Bampúsht and Zamirán, where it bears the name of Nihing or Nahang. After passing the escarpment of the main plateau, at a point which we afterwards visited, it turns eastward through the fertile valleys of Mand and Túmp, and at Kej joins its waters with those of its eastern affluent, which flows due west through the long valley lying at the foot of the escarpment, and forming a natural highway between Persia and the Indus valley. From the point of junction the united streams flow south-west through a wide alluvial expanse, known as *Dasht* or the 'plain,' whence the river in this part of its course takes its name. Storms in the hills make it occasionally impassable for days together, and it sometimes overflows its banks. The quantity of silt brought down has raised the bed above the surrounding country, and the torrents from the Jambkí and other hills bordering the southern part of the Dasht, instead of finding their way to the river, spread themselves over the level plain. A belt of jungle and cultivation, principally of millet (*jowar*), from a couple of hundred yards to half-a-mile in width, borders the stream on either side.

Passing this we turned northwards over a level desert towards the foot hills of the Jambkí range, whose conical peaks, though not more than 2,500 feet high, towered far above the lesser ranges. A short march of thirteen miles brought us to our camp, pitched in the wide shallow bed of a torrent issuing from a gap in the hills a mile to the north. A chain of muddy pools showed the course of a subterranean stream, and nourished a few scanty shrubs, amongst which a flock of sheep were grazing.

A small hamlet called Sáman, from the name of the torrent, existed here up to the last few years, when it was plundered by the Sarbáz people, and all the male inhabitants killed. The territory is considered to belong to Dasht, although the sheep we found were the property of Báhú Kalát people.

The next morning, two or three smart showers warned us to get out of the dangerous position in which the camp was pitched. Leaving the servants to strike the tents as fast as possible, Blanford and I walked up towards the hills. Before we got back to breakfast, a strong southerly wind rose, bringing clouds of dust. We loaded up the camels as fast as possible to move to higher ground in case of rain, or to go on to our next halting-place if the weather should clear. Hardly was the last load on, before the rain came on, slightly at first, but soon in veritable torrents. There being no shelter anywhere, we got up a tent on the gravelly bank opposite, on the highest ground we could find. Long before the tent was secure, there was a stream of muddy water a hundred yards wide and five or six feet deep, where our former encampment had been. About two the rain ceased, but the water continued to rise till within a foot of the lowest tents, causing us some little anxiety.

The next morning rose bright and clear, but the camel-drivers declined to move, on account of the slippery state of the ground after the rain. The camel's foot, admirably adapted for sand, is by no means so for mud, which it does not penetrate enough to get a firm hold of. The movements of a loaded camel on a muddy road are not unlike those of the proverbial cat in walnut-shells on the ice; but attended with more danger to the sufferer. The poor brutes not unfrequently break their legs in falling, and occasionally, it is said, get split up by their feet slipping in opposite directions. I cannot say that I have witnessed this latter catastrophe.

After some discussion we bargained with our camel-drivers that they should go to Báhú Kalát in two marches, instead of three as agreed on, we allowing them in return to halt for the day. Ascending the torrent bed for half-an-hour the next morning, we entered the hills through a narrow gorge in the sandstone rocks. A few puddles in places were all that remained of the boiling torrent of two days before; but the still slippery state of the ground showed that the camel-drivers were right in refusing to move till a day's sun had partially dried the surface. Our path led up the main ravine for a short distance, and then turned off to the left up a side channel among a bewildering congeries of low hills of sandstone and clay, with no vegetation to speak of. Here we saw for the first time the little desert partridge, *Ammo-Perdix Bouhami*, the *see-see* or, as the Persians call it, *tíhú*, which we hardly expected to find so far south. Before long we crossed a low water-parting into the Kalaki torrent, which here forms the frontier between Dasht and Dashtiárí, the outlying districts of Kalát and Persia respectively. A second inconsiderable ascent brought us into the Roghán ravine, down which we proceeded in a westerly direction to our halting-place, a wide open space in the hills. Abundance of the 'písh' palm, and many fairly grown acacia and jujube shrubs, the latter just coming into leaf, gave the encampment a somewhat less desert appearance than usual. Three cows were grazing in the valley, though there was no appearance of cultivation. In the afternoon I climbed a ridge a mile from the camp, to get an idea of the run of the hills, which it was not easy to see from the low ravines through which our road had passed.

The Jambkí hills, as they may be called from their central and highest peaks, are a spur of the range which forms the south wall of the long valley, lying all along the foot of the escarpment of the Balúchistán plateau, and interpose between the Dasht and Dashtiárí rivers. Unlike the general configuration of the elevated masses in Southern Balúchistán, which rather tend to long isolated ridges divided by wide valleys, these hills consist of three abrupt peaks, at each angle of a right-angled triangle, surrounded by innumerable short and irregular ranges, inconceivably distorted and broken up. The three main peaks rise to the height of 2000 to 2500 feet, but the ridges at their feet do not attain more than half that height. It is impossible to imagine more barren and desolate scenery. Except here and in the ravines not a speck of green is anywhere visible; nor does the clay and sandstone, of which the rocks are composed, take form or colour, which might by grandeur or brilliancy compensate for the lack of softer beauty. The strata generally dip at a very high angle, indeed are often absolutely perpendicular. This and the infrequent but violent storms of rain tend to divide the surface of the elevated masses into serrated ridges, between which are narrow ravines. Though the walls of these are mostly of small elevation, their steepness hides all view of the loftier masses beyond; and thus, though his path leads amid what, judging by height, would be considerable mountains in Great Britain, the traveller in Balúchistán rarely sees anything but petty ridges of rock. Further north the ranges are somewhat bolder in outline, but till we reached that called Siáneh Kúh, which overhangs the Kúhak plain and divides it from the Sistán desert, we saw nothing deserving the distinction of being called a mountain.

Another result of the configuration of Balúch hills affected me more seriously than their want of beauty. The tortuous and narrow ravines and the difficulty of recognising and fixing prominent points, made it by no means easy to carry on the survey. A brief description of the manner in which this was done may not be uninteresting to past and future travellers. At every halting-place, except in the rare instance of a cloudy night, I fixed the latitude with a reflecting circle or sextant, and artificial horizon, by meridian altitude of a star or by altitudes of the polestar out of the meridian. Wherever I halted for a day or more, this was supplemented by meridian altitudes of the sun with the reflecting circle, and repetitions of the night observations. I had several pocket chronometers with me, but could not get them carried on a litter or handbarrow, and soon found that carried in the pocket of a man on horseback they were more trouble than use. The mounted traveller who intends to get trustworthy results out of a chronometer carried by himself, must be content to be its slave. Putting all ideas of galloping out of the question, he must deny himself the quietest trot; not even a light spring from the saddle after the weary day's ride can be indulged in with safety to the precious charge. Shooting and hill-climbing are of course out of the question. If the chronometers are placed on a man on foot to accompany the horseman it is not much better. The latter must keep so constant an eye on his companion, that he might almost as well be carrying the chronometers himself. On a direct journey between two fixed points at a moderate distance and traversed without long halts, or on an expedition like that of the Turko-Persian frontier survey, where the surveyors had ample time to carry their chronometers backwards and forwards between their stations, they may be used with advantage; but for a long journey through unknown country I prefer good perambulating wheels. Of these I had four of the Indian pattern, two for use and two in case of accidents. The wheels of the latter, slung on each side of a camel, were generally considered by the Balúchís as belonging to some new and formidable piece of artillery, and added much, I have no doubt, to the impressive appearance of our party.

The two wheels in work were trundled along by the Indian peons accompanying the native surveyor, a Marhatta, who with a prismatic compass made a regular traverse of the path. This left me at liberty to move off the road to collect information and sketch the general features of the country. Every evening I plotted the surveyor's work on a large scale, and reduced it at once to that of my field map, four miles to the inch, which was mounted in cloth, projected and ruled in mile squares in England, and sent to me at Gwádar. This map I carried on as far as Dízak, where the Indian surveying party left for the coast to return to Bombay. From thence I had to do the traverse myself; but as the country throughout

Eastern Persia is generally open, this was less troublesome work than in the winding defiles of Balúchistán.

On arriving at Shíráz, twelve hundred miles from Gwádar, I found my error in longitude to be ten miles only.

To return to the record of our journey to Báhú Kalát. On leaving the camp in the Roghán ravine, we kept down the latter for five miles, when we crossed the low rocks bordering it to the north, and issued on the valley of the Dashtiárí river. To the south-west the low hills on the west coast were indistinctly visible; and north-east of us were the successive parallel ranges of central Balúchistán; while beyond the dark belt of jungle, crowned by an occasional tuft of date palms, which showed the course of the river, spread a wide and apparently boundless desert. After breakfasting by the side of a good-sized pool of water, Blanford and I plunged into the jungle to collect specimens, with results which, though not so barren as on many after occasions, strengthened us in the opinion we were gradually forming that the fauna of Balúchistán is as scanty as its human population. On this occasion I find in my journal that I saw a gazelle, shot at a fox, and killed a spotted woodpecker, 'Picus Sindianus.' We had some little difficulty in picking up the caravan, but found the tail of it at last crossing a deep and muddy watercourse close to the village.

As we rode in, the *farashes* were pitching the tents on a low gravel mound opposite a similar larger mound, on which stands the village of 'Báhú Kalát,' the great fort. This is the principal of a number of hamlets dotted along the course of the Dashtiárí or Sarbáz river. The whole district is generally called the 'Kúchah' (Anglicé, street), a name applied in Western Balúchistán to any river valley, as Rúdbár is in Persia proper.

Báhú Kalát has about 300 houses irregularly dotted about the low gravel bluffs overhanging the river. Half-a-dozen, perhaps, are of mud and stone with flat roofs, and capable of a certain amount of defence, the rest are mere reed huts. The surveyor, who was of an enquiring and statistical turn, noted in his field book that Báhú contained four shops, at one of which English calico was obtainable.

Some wayfarers, met the day before near Roghán, had informed our people that four Kajárs[1], as Persians are here called, with a 'Sáhib' and some soldiers had arrived at Báhú. At this earlier period of our sojourn in the land, we had an idea, derived I know not whence, that

[1] Pronounced by them like our word Cudgel.

Balúchís were truthful and honest compared to surrounding nations. Honesty of a certain kind they undoubtedly have, petty thieving and pilfering being nearly unknown. But camel lifting and highway robbery are common enough on the Kalát border, though rare on the Persian side, which is under the vigorous administration of Ibrahím Khán. But though the Balúch is a clumsier liar than a Persian or Hindú, he is as cynically indifferent to being found out after his object is attained as the former, while in magnitude his falsehoods are quite equal to the best performances of either.

In the present instance it need not be said that no vestige of Kajár, Sáhib, or soldier was to be found at Báhú Kalát, where the *venu* of their presence was shifted to Sarbáz, the capital of the district of the same name of which Báhú Kalát is a dependency. Ibrahím Khán, the governor of Bam-Narmashír, to which Balúchistán is attached, was now said to be there with a considerable force. Accompanying him were the Sáhib and Kajárs, the former of whom one man professed to have seen with his own eyes in the Persian camp. As it was just possible that Sir Frederic Goldsmid might have sent one of his party to meet me, I sent a messenger to Ibrahím Khán, with letters, enclosing a note for the unknown Sáhib, and for my colleague the Sarhang, if he should have reached Sarbáz, asking them to meet me at Píshín. The Sarhang turned out to be there, but the Sáhib was a pure figment of Balúch imagination.

Shortly after we were settled in the tents, a message arrived from Yár Muhammad Khán, the chief of the village, that he was too ill to pay us a visit, but would send his brother, who accordingly came over, but had not much to say for himself. After his departure he sent over a sheep and ten fowls as a present. In the course of the evening the camel-drivers, who had brought us so far, announced their intention of returning to their villages near Gwádar. This was an unexpected blow, as we had no previous reason to suppose they would not take us as far as the end of the frontier at least. However, the news did not affect us so severely as it would have done had we known the endless worry and delay the question of camel-hiring would cause on this and many subsequent occasions.

Although this place is not more than a hundred feet or so above the sea-level, the nights here are far colder than at Gwádar. The night after our arrival at Báhú Kalát, that of the 31st of January, the minimum thermometer, hung under the eaves of my tent, fell to 34°, rising to nearly 80° in the day. This, with one exception, was the greatest cold we experienced in Balúchistán, though we should of course have found severer weather on the plateau had we reached it before spring. Altogether the weather was very enjoyable at this time, forming a marked contrast to that on the coast with its gales and sandstorms. The Zodiacal light was visible every evening of our stay, and seemed more clearly defined than I have noticed it either in India or Persia.

While I was enjoying the traveller's regular luxury on a first day's halt, a good morning snooze, the chief Yár Muhammad Khán made his appearance with the notables of the village, and as soon as I was dressed we received him on a carpet spread on the shady side of the tent. Yár Muhammad was a very old man, feeble and emaciated, with apparently little life about him except in his cruel treacherous eye. Altogether he was as ill-looking an old scoundrel as any to be met with between the Indus and the Tigris, a region where age in combination with villany is far from uncommon. Without losing much time in compliments he came to the object of his visit, which was to enlist my sympathies to help him in regaining a small annual stipend formerly allowed him by the Bombay Government for protecting the line of telegraph in his district, but which for some, no doubt, excellent reason had been lately discontinued. The old gentleman was so eloquent on the subject of his wrongs, that I could get no opportunity of introducing the subject of camels before he left, which he did after a quarter-of-an-hour's visit. As soon as he had gone, I sent after him my 'názir,' or *homme d'affaires*, a Persian named Muhammad Husain Beg, who had been eight years in my service, to make arrangements for hiring the necessary number of camels at once. In an hour he returned boiling with indignation at the extortion and impudence of the Balúchís, who asked five rupees a camel for the journey to Píshín, which we supposed from our map to be not more than two short marches distant. In addition, Yár Muhammad asked for a Kashmír scarf which he had noticed round my waist as a preliminary present for himself. This I refused, but sent him a few rupees to buy a clean turban, of which he stated himself, apparently without reason, to be in want.

The day was passed in fruitless negotiation and attempts to persuade the Gwádar camel-drivers to continue the journey. One man, the owner of nine camels, consented to proceed; the rest were obdurate.

The next morning, early, Yár Muhammad made his appearance again, and after a little public conversation about the frontier and the date of the annexation of the village to Persia, which he informed me took place six years previously, I referred to the subject of camels, which he declared his inability to supply. He then asked for a private interview, and came with me into the tent, when he stated that there were plenty of camels, but not more than two or three were his own property; that the camel-owners were all relations, combined together to keep up the price; and finally that he would undertake to give as many as I liked for four and a half rupees each to Píshín, three long days' march distant. This was rank extortion, as we had paid only half a rupee per diem per camel from Gwádar, and the map led me to believe the distance to Píshín exaggerated by a day at least; so I declined to give more than two and a half rupees, and the old rascal went away pretending to be in a very bad temper.

An hour afterwards he sent over to say that if I would give him a present he would supply camels for four rupees each. To this, as time was valuable, the provisions we had brought with us rapidly disappearing, and little grain or flour to be bought, I agreed, sent Yár Muhammad twenty rupees as a present, and sixty camels were promised for the next morning.

The day was spent by the servants in readjusting the loads, which were reduced from eighty-one to seventy, but the next morning, instead of camels, a message was brought that news had arrived that Ibráhím Khán, the governor, was on his way to Báhú Kalát, and that all the owners of camels had driven them into the jungle, afraid of their being pressed for the carriage of the Persian. This was a plausible excuse, so I answered that the Khán must know very well that the Sháh himself dare not touch camels hired by an English officer; but that if the people were foolish enough to be afraid, I would wait for Ibráhím Khán's arrival, and trust to him to obtain camels at a reasonable rate. This caused a change of ground, the reply being that unless we took eighty-one camels, the full number brought from Gwádar, not one would be supplied. This was too much, especially as three or four loads of fodder had been consumed since we left the coast, so I positively refused to take more than sixty-one, which, with the nine Gwádar camels that remained, made up the full complement required. After much argument and expostulation these terms were at last agreed to, but the day, the third of our stay, was too far spent to think of moving. The next morning the camels were brought in twos and threes, and after the usual squabbling about the loads we got off at noon. The fiction of the ownership of the beasts was by this time quite dropped by our venerable friend Yár Muhammad, to whom the majority, if not all, belonged, and he sent his son in charge. At the last moment, when half the caravan was across the river, he made a final attempt to squeeze out another present by stopping the last camels under pretext of fresh news of the arrival of Ibráhím Khán. But it was too late. We were fairly off; even his own son laughed at him, and we shook off the dust of Báhú Kalát from our feet. This was the first, but by no means the last, of our camel-hiring difficulties. The same vexatious delay occurred in every district; and the Mand people, a fortnight later, proved so troublesome and impracticable that we came to remember Yár Muhammad Khán of Báhú Kalát as a comparatively pleasant and accommodating old man.

What we should have done was to have bought a nucleus of twenty or five and twenty camels at Gwádar, hiring drivers to attend them. This would have made us dependent on local carriage for the heavy baggage only, which might have been sent from point to point direct instead of wandering over the country as necessitated by the exigences of the survey. Moreover, the Balúchís could not have starved us into submitting to their extortionate charges as they invariably attempted. Supplies were rarely produced on our arrival at a halting-place, and extravagant prices always asked till the camels were obtained and the caravan just starting, when rice, corn, and *ghee* were generally offered in abundance where only handsful had been previously forthcoming. Our own camels might have been sent to purchase supplies from other villages, and we should have had it in our own power to regulate the length of our day's journey, instead of being at the mercy of the hired camel-drivers, who halted when and where they liked.

The experiences of the mission of the year before gave us no idea of the difficulty and delay to be expected in obtaining carriage, and of the invincible repugnance of the Balúch villagers to travelling out of their own district. Sir Frederic Goldsmid's and Major Harrison's parties had not gone off the high-roads between Bampúr and Gwádar; and Major Lovett, who travelled from Bampúr to Panjgúr, and thence to the sea, had but a slender following. Ours was the first numerous party that had thrown itself on the resources of the country, and it was therefore hardly to be expected that we should get along without difficulties of some sort.

To return to our journey from Báhú Kalát. The Dashtiárí river, which we crossed by a ford opposite the village immediately on leaving the encamping ground, is here from sixty to eighty yards wide, and not more than three feet deep, with a slow current and muddy water. The bottom is treacherous in places, and crossing on horseback is therefore unsafe without a guide. The actual banks are low, ten feet or so above the stream, and the water in high floods evidently overflows them. On the side opposite the village are many extensive clearings, flooded at the time of our visit with water retained on them by embankments. Rice and millet are the principal, if not the only grains cultivated. Garden vegetables, even onions, seemed unknown, and the date groves are far from extensive.

The road for the first march cut across a bend of the stream to a point where the spurs of the Petteh Hills, an isolated range running east and west ten miles north of Báhú, come down to the river bank, forming with the Jambkí ridges a rather pretty gorge. The road lay through scattered acacia jungle and shallow ravines. This was one of the few places in Balúchistán where game seemed at all abundant, and we got several sand-grouse and *tihú* partridge, besides wounding a gazelle. The day was moreover memorable as that on which we first procured the new 'Nectarinia,' which Blanford has named *brevirostris*, and which is figured on page 221. It was then of course in the dull winter plumage. Crossing the stream we camped amid some fine tamarisks in the river bed, which is here confined by cliffs sixty or eighty feet high.

Our road the next morning turned abruptly to the eastward up a narrow valley between low hills. These got higher as we advanced, and the valley became a ravine which turned north again, and about the twelfth mile ended in a short and not difficult pass. Mounting this we emerged on the water-parting between the Dasht and Dashtiárí rivers, which, except in this spot, forms the boundary of Persia and Kalát. A mile or two in front was a steep black hill, the Síáh Kúh, rising nearly a thousand feet above the general level; and from its shape and colour a capital landmark, standing a few miles west of the frontier. To the east, wide valleys separated by narrow sandstone ridges, and covered in patches with low *pish* and acacia jungle, sloped gently down to the Dasht. Dismounting at the foot of the hill we climbed half-way up, where Blanford pronounced the rock to be amygdaloid. Leaving him to ascend to the summit, a feat which he successfully accomplished, ascertaining the height of the Síáh Kúh to be 1500 feet above the sea, I rode on to Kastag, a halting-place in the neighbourhood of a few acres of cultivation at the head of one of the wide valleys. This and a neighbouring valley to the south named Ghistán, though drained into the Dashtiárí river, are cultivated by people from Píshín, and therefore belong to Persia, though on the Kalát side of the watershed.

The next day's march was comparatively short, the road winding through narrow ravines till it emerged on the great valley which lies at the foot of the Balúch plateau throughout its extent.

A mile from the village we were met by a small party of mounted men, at the head of whom was the officer sent to escort me. He was a fat jovial-looking young Persian, and introduced himself as Ibráhím Súltán, a captain in the infantry, and nephew of the governor. With him was a solemn-looking personage clad in a bright scarlet cloak and white turban. This was Mústafa Khán, the agent of Diláwar Khán the chief of Dízak, whose territory marches with that of Kalát along the frontier north of Píshín. In their train were half-a-dozen horsemen and a motley rabble on foot, who escorted us to our camping-ground.

CHAPTER II.

Píshín to Jálk.

As we rode in, our tents were being pitched on a bare piece of ground midway between the two forts, each surrounded by a cluster of mat huts, which compose the village, or, as the Balúchís pompously term it, the 'Shahr,' or city of Píshín. This is the latest acquisition of the Persians in Balúchistán, having been annexed only two years before our visit. The majority of the population, like that of most villages in Southern Balúchistán, are slaves; apparently mostly of pure Balúch blood, but with many mulattos, and a few negros. Their masters are *Rinds*, members of a widely-spread tribe, extending even into Sind, which boasts its pure Arab descent. We noticed that the long greasy locks floating over the shoulders, which in India and the Gulf mark the Balúch among the motley crowds of the bazaar, are here worn only by the young bucks. The slaves have their heads shaved as a mark of servitude, or perhaps, as Pottinger says, to prevent their running away; and the older men use the razor to their polls, and don the turban, from motives of real or feigned piety. All alike wear the Arab shirt, a few putting on in addition a pair of cotton trousers and the sleeved cloak, or coat woven of brown worsted and worked at the seams with crimson silk, which, with the red skull cap, seems the characteristic garment of the country. The women, though not particularly shy, rather avoided, than came to gaze at the strangers. The few we saw were most unprepossessing in appearance. Like most of the men the Arab shirt was their sole garment, generally unbleached, but occasionally dark blue.

The village forts of Balúchistán are far more solidly built and picturesque in outline than those of Persia, though inferior to them in a military point of view. From one end of Persia to the other a

'Kala'h' or fort, from the citadel of the Sháh at Tehrán to the tiniest mountain hamlet of Fars or Karmán, presents the same level line of mud wall crowned with elliptically crenellated battlements, above which nothing rises to break the sky-line. At the angles, and, if the enclosure be large, at regular intervals along the sides, are semi-circular towers narrowing towards the top. Apart from the intrinsic ugliness of the structure, the constant reiteration of the same type lends in many cases an additional, and quite unnecessary, feature of gloom to the dismal monotony of a Persian landscape. When embosomed in trees, however, the effect is not so bad.

The Balúch fort on the other hand is more like the castle of a Rhenish robber-knight of old, consisting of a square central tower of rough stone, surrounded by lower walled courts and minor buildings, and surmounted by a watch turret peering over the surrounding date-groves, from which incessant watch is kept for the ever possible enemy. Round the little castle are clustered the huts of the villagers; here in the south mere screens of date-leaf mats, but in the colder districts to the north, solid buildings of mud and sun-dried brick.

Each of the forts of Pishín is built on the banks of a watercourse flowing from the hills to the north. Their beds unite half a mile to the south, and flow through low hills to the Báhú river. The water of the western and larger of the two is confined by an artificial dam, forming a reservoir four or five hundred yards long and thirty wide. On the banks of this and of the eastern watercourse are a few acres of cultivation and a considerable grove of date palms. Here, for the first time, I found that mark of rudimentary civilisation, the onion, but rarely, and in small quantities, as if it were hardly as yet fully appreciated. Beyond the date-groves stretched a wide expanse of acacia jungle, not yet green with spring. Here and there lines of darker tamarisks showed the course of a torrent from the hills, dry, save after rain. To the north the jungle got more scanty till it failed altogether in the gravel slopes at the foot of the long scarp which seemed to rise like a wall some two thousand feet above the plain, and ten miles or so distant.

This is the southern face of the plateau of Balúchistán, which shuts off the waters of the Helmand from the sea. To the west its continuity is broken by the rapidly ascending valley between the Rúndú and Bagarband hills, the latter of which, seen in profile from Pishín, forms the outer wall of the plateau; the valley to its north being a thousand feet or more higher than that to the south. Next to the Rúndú hills, the Talár range stretches away to the eastward, succeeded by the more prominent limestone peaks of Shairas, which rise to a height of four thousand feet above the sea.

Two days after our arrival at Píshín my colleague the 'Sarhang' made his appearance. He had crossed over from Maskat to Gwatar in a native boat, and ridden on a camel to Sarbáz, where he found the Wakíl-ul-Múlk, governor of Karmán, to whom he had letters from the Foreign Office at Tehrán. From him he obtained a horse, tents, and baggage camels, with an escort in the shape of the old 'Yáwar' who had accompanied Sir Frederic Goldsmid from Karmán to Píshín the year before, and a couple of *sowars*. The next evening I asked the Sarhang and Yáwar with my own escort Ibrahím Súltán to dinner, and settled with the first the method of conducting the survey. We agreed that it would be quite a useless labour to carry on work simultaneously; so the 'Sarhang,' assuring me at the same time that he had no want of confidence in his own ability, and gave way solely on account of the superior appliances I possessed in the shape of wheels, &c., consented to accept the result of my survey, which he would copy as occasion should offer. This arrangement proved equally satisfactory to both parties. It enabled the Sarhang to obtain credit with his superiors by producing at Tehrán a correct and finished map as his own performance, which indeed, as far as handiwork goes, it was. On my side, it gave me a hold on him I should not have otherwise had, and, what was much more important, prevented any possible discrepancy which might afford the Persian government a handle for prolonging discussion by disputing the accuracy of my map.

During the next three days negotiations went on with the villagers for the supply of camels to take us along the frontier, but they were frustrated by the machinations of Mústafa Khán, the agent of the Dízak chief, who for some reason, probably by his master's orders, wished us to go straight across the hills to that place. I have little doubt that he was aided by the Yáwar and Súltán, who, even if they had no positive instructions to the effect, thought, and probably with reason, that the Wakíl-ul-Múlk would be by no means sorry to see the party return with its object unfulfilled. It was not till the afternoon of the fourth day after the Sarhang's arrival, the sixth of our sojourn in Píshín, that we got off, and then only to march to Kalakí, a village of the little independent district of Mand, twenty miles off.

On one of the intervening days Blanford and I made an excursion into the neighbouring country to pick up game and specimens, and ascertain the whereabouts of a little bit of Mand territory which encroaches on the Báhú watershed. Four or five miles from Píshín are two little 'Mazra'hs,' or plots of cultivation away from habitation, situated on two watercourses flowing into the Píshín river. They are denominated respectively Bok and Mazamband. The former, which is nearer to Píshín, belongs to that village, the latter to Mand. It is thus the only place on the watershed of the Báhú or Sarbáz river which does not belong to Persia. During the day we saw numerous 'houbareh' bustard, *Otis houbara*, and many gazelle, probably *G. Bennetii*, but failed to get within shot of either. In the case of the former this is the more curious, as there was ample cover, whereas in the desert plains of South Persia, where there is none, it is by no means difficult to approach 'houbareh.' About Shíráz it is easy enough to get within shot of them on horseback, either by riding round them in diminishing circles, or by galloping straight on, thus preventing their resting for more than a few seconds on the ground. About Bushahr it is only necessary to approach the bustard obliquely, to get within forty yards or even nearer. In this way I have killed half a dozen in the course of a couple of hours. In Persia, moreover, like all other game, they are constantly shot at and hawked, whereas in Balúchistán, the gun is seldom used for feathered game, and hawking, little, if at all practised. Yet we were unable to get within a hundred yards of a houbareh all day, though we saw scores of them. It is possible that they were birds of passage unfamiliar with the comparatively thick cover, which thus made them unusually wary; or, if residents, they were aware of the facilities for ambush and had abandoned the characteristic tactics of their race, squatting on the ground and trusting to similarity of colour for concealment, for the safer policy of keeping well out of the way of suspicious objects. Besides bustard and gazelles no game was visible; indeed animal life altogether was scarcer than the aspect of the country would seem to indicate. A few small birds and a large buzzard, *Buteo ferox*, formed our only prizes. It is worth noting that Píshín was the only place in Balúchistán where we found the common brown 'maina' of India. An ibex was one day brought in from the neighbouring hills by a Shikári. It proved to be *Capra ægagrus*, the supposed ancestor of the domestic goat. This species extends over the whole of the Iranian plateau.

Our present camel-drivers were more unaccommodating than the last. The hire was fixed at one rupee per beast per diem, and not a man would start till the silver coin was actually placed in his palm; and then they took three days to go twenty miles. From one of the chiefs I bought for rs. 132 a very beautiful riding camel or dromedary, called here 'jambáz.' I never had occasion to ride it, but it was most useful in carrying our breakfasts on the road, from being able to keep up with the horses, which the baggage camels could not do. It was evidently a great pet, for the owner, an old man, kissed and fondled its nose repeatedly before parting with it, and it was certainly a very handsome and docile creature, as different from the ordinary pack camel as an Arab from a cart horse. The climate of Upper Persia proved too severe, and it died soon after we reached Tehrán. It is curious that riding camels are never used in Persia proper, though all the eastern and central parts of the country seem peculiarly adapted for them.

It was not till the third day of our march from Píshín that we reached Kalakí, where the camel-hunting process had to be reiterated. Our road had been nearly east, skirting the base of the hills bounding the valley to the south. At first these consist of a line of irregular and precipitous peaks, known as the 'Ná-kúh,' possibly a corruption of 'Neh,' a reed or spear, which might well be used for a pointed summit. Further north I found the same designation in the 'Sianeh Kúh,' above Kúhak. South of Mand the hills are called Jhal, or 'lower,' a word which reappears in 'Jhal Zamirán,' and further east in Jhalawán, the 'low country;' the converse being Sarawán, the 'upper country,' equivalent terms to the 'Sarhad' and 'Garmsír' of Fars.

The character of the country was much the same as about Píshín. Patches of acacia and tamarisk jungle intervened between broad gravelly slopes and alluvial flats. The villages we passed were smaller than Píshín, but nearly all had a central keep of more or less pretentious aspect, and each nestled in a grove of date-palms.

The little independent district of Mand occupies that part of the great Kej valley lying between Píshín and the Nihing river, which, till it turns abruptly eastward through Túmp, forms the frontier of the country acknowledging the supremacy of the Khán of Kalát. To the north Mand is bounded by the Shairas hills and the Hamzai torrent. To the south it is separated by the Jhal Kúb from the Dasht district. Its average extent in each direction is about twenty miles. It has no recognised head, each village being governed by its own chief. The dominant tribe are Rinds; and the Mand people have the reputation of being the most thieving and murderous set of ruffians in Balúchistán.

The day after reaching Kalakí we enlisted the services of Mír Akhírdád[1], the *ráis* or head of the village, to conduct the party to Múrtí, the chief place of Bampúsht, which Major Lovett, from native information, had placed not far north of the frontier. He engaged to supply us with the necessary camels, and guide the party to, and as far as possible along, the Nihing river, which here forms the boundary. Lovett's map showed, and as it afterwards turned out correctly, a place called Gishtigán as the point where the river rises; but both Mír Akhírdád and Mústafa Khán denied all knowledge of such a spot.

On the 16th February we left Kalakí or Kalarí, and marched five miles over an open gravelly plain, with occasional patches of low jungle, to the Nihing river, in the bed of which we camped, at a spot called 'Taradár-i-narm,' at the extremity of a low range which here turns the course of the river from south-west to south-east. The stream has cut itself a bed about 300 yards wide, and 30 feet deep, in the gravel and alluvium of the plain. Of flowing water there was but a rivulet a few yards wide, and about six inches deep.

Our road the next morning led up the bed of the Nihing for nine miles, to a place named 'Shírpachár,' where two torrents from the north-west debouch from the hills. The path was in parts rather bad, over ledges of sandstone and shale, behind which, in places, the water had collected in deep pools of considerable depth, and a beautiful green colour. We passed on the right a well-wooded valley, with many date trees and a small fort called Kala'h-i-Aspikán. Old Mír Akhírdád here gave us a first insight into his character by

---

[1] 'The last given.' Balúchis, even those boasting their Arab descent, seem very fond of these Persian compound names, which are uncommon in Persia itself. Besides 'Akhírdád,' I met more than one 'Allahdád' and 'Khudadád.' The days of the week are also used as names. Juma 'Friday,' and Shamba 'Saturday,' I have heard elsewhere; but 'Ek-Shamba,' 'Do Shamba,' 'Monday,' 'Tuesday,' &c., are perhaps peculiar to Balúchistán in being utilised as names.

wanting to halt after five miles, at a place where there was good grazing for camels. Fortunately many of the loads were in front of him, and he could not call them back, so was obliged to come on, grumbling and cursing, and threatening to take his beasts back to Kalakí.

The river here runs between precipitous hills of the same monotonous sandstone and shale, than which we had seen nothing else since leaving Gwádar. The vegetation was of the scantiest, and there was no level ground on either side. Our tents were pitched on a high bank between the two torrents, close to a solitary tamarisk tree. In the course of the afternoon we were told by Mír Akhírdád that the road up the river was impracticable, and that a detour of several miles must be made through Húng before we should hit it again at Bogán.

Our road for the next day, and part of the following, lay up the Hamzai torrent, which here marks the frontier. The ravine is bounded by lofty and precipitous rocks, and when we passed held no running water. Occasional patches of high grass and of the 'písh' palm formed the only vegetation.

At noon on the second day we emerged on the plateau of Húng, 2500 feet above the sea. The difference of temperature was not such as might have been expected from the great increase of altitude, but possibly this was attributable to the weather, which from clear had become overcast and threatened rain. On reaching the plateau we turned north, and camped on the bank of the Húng torrent, not far from the deserted village of that name. Two small huts sheltered a couple of families of wandering Balúchís, the first people we had met for three days.

In the course of the evening Mír Akhírdád declared his intention of returning to Kalakí, to which, it now appeared, there was a direct road through the Shairas hills. We had therefore taken four days to do what we might have done in one; but my object being to see as much as possible of the country in the vicinity of the frontier, and not to get from point to point by the nearest road, I was rather pleased at the deception which had been practised. Mústafa Khán had probably something to do with Mír Akhírdád's breach of contract, as he at once proposed that we should send for camels to Irafshán, a place about twenty miles to the north, belonging to his master, the Khán of Dízak. To this I assented, provided that the Irafshán camels would take us along the Nihing. This he said was impossible, there being no water or provisions, and no one knowing the road; his object, as before, being to force us to go to Dízak direct. There was therefore nothing to be done but to fall back upon Mír Akhírdád, and after bribing him, giving him a sheep for a feast, and allowing him to charge for the camel on which he rode, he engaged to conduct us to Múrtí for seven rupees a camel, the distance taking, as he declared, the same number of days. This was, I knew, at least too much by two days, but there was no resource but to submit. Our supply of provisions was daily lessening, and we could not hope to replenish them before reaching Múrtí. Moreover, the warm weather was approaching, and an overcharge of a hundred rupees or so to save time was of small consequence to a party which was costing Government somewhere about 300 rupees a day. I was therefore only too glad to be taken in with my eyes open, and the policy was rewarded by an offer of Mír Akhírdád, before we started, to convey us to Gishtigán, the place whose existence he had previously denied, for two rupees a camel extra. To this, of course, I gladly assented.

The plateau of Húng forms the water parting between the Nihing basin and that branch of the Báhú river draining the unexplored district of Múrtí. It is a waste of dark-coloured gravel, seamed with many nullahs, to which the scanty vegetation was confined, and intersected by many steep flat-topped ranges, running a little south of west. The hills to the north are called the Kúh Salai, and their stratification being nearer horizontal than usual, have more picturesque rounded outlines than is often seen in Balúchistán. Through them lies the direct road to Irafshán, said by Mústafa Khán to be impassable for loaded camels.

On the 21st February we struck our camp at Húng, and reached the Nihing again on the second day, its bed being here 800 feet below the level of the Húng plateau. The road skirted the base of the Salai, and afterwards of the Súrok hills, whose summits decreased considerably in altitude as we proceeded, those abutting on the river being of insignificant height.

The last part of the road to the Nihing lay between some low hills and the south bank of a wide torrent bed. Whilst riding in front of the caravan a shout of 'Shikár' from one of the servants behind called our attention to a ram and two ewes of the wild sheep, which were descending the rocks on our right not fifty yards distant.

I was unfortunately carrying a shot gun, and before the man who carried my rifle could give it to me, and I could load it, the game had crossed the road into the ravine, and I only got a long running shot, which I missed. I mention this, as it was the only occasion on which we saw hill game, i. e. sheep or ibex, in Balúchistán. Moreover, though we offered considerable rewards we failed to get good specimens of either. From this it would seem that mountain game is as scarce in Balúchistán[1] as are other forms of animal life.

The bed of the Nihing river, where we came upon it at a point where it abruptly changes its course from west to south, a little above the hamlet of Bogán, is about half a mile wide, though the stream of water is but scanty. Below Bogán, which lies a little way south of the road, the channel is narrowed to less than a hundred yards by precipitous rocks, enclosing many deep pools of beautifully clear and fresh water. The open part of the bed was pretty thickly grown with tamarisk and mimosa. A mile further on the Sháhrí river, a considerable affluent of the Nihing, enters the latter from the north-west, after irrigating the district of Irafshán. It flows in a narrow channel between high banks, and when we passed had far more running water than the Nihing.

A quarter of an hour after passing the Sháhrí, we found the loads, which had passed us while at breakfast, thrown down in confusion in the lowest part of the river bed, exposing us to the danger of losing all our property by a sudden flood. On asking the first servants we met, why the baggage had not been placed in a safe place, we were told that it was Mír Akhírdad's doing. Seeing that worthy a little way off, busily engaged in unloading camels in the deepest hollow he could find, I galloped up to him, and remonstrated in no measured tones on the risk to which he was exposing us. He replied with a volley of abuse, drawing his sword, and swearing he would slaughter us all, Farangis and Kajárs too, ordering at the same time his men to load their matchlocks. As an effective threat this was ridiculous, as I at once pointed out to him. For Blanford and myself, with our breech-loading arms, could have shot down the old rascal, and the half dozen of his men who had firearms, in half the time they would have taken to get their clumsy weapons into fighting order. However it was only a piece of theatrical bravado, and Ibráhím Súltán, coming up, explained the matter, and pacified Mír Akhírdád.

[1] Vide vol. ii. p. 87.

It appeared that that worthy, who had been, as usual, in rear of the caravan, had ordered his men to halt for the night at the mouth of the Sháhrí river; but the Sarhang, who was in front, had prevented their doing so. As soon as Mír Akhírdád reached the spot, and found his camels gone on, he had pushed on, caught them up, and thrown down the loads then and there in a rage, swearing he would go back to his village and leave us in the lurch. My coming up had added fuel to the flame, and produced the explosion of wrath just described.

After a little negotiation the baggage was moved to higher ground, and Mír Akhírdád pacified by the promise of a short march the next day. Any concession was better than being abandoned in that desert country without a guide, and three days' march from any place where provisions were procurable.

The following morning Mír Akhírdád made to a small extent the *amende honorable*, by riding up to me on the road and pointing out the surrounding hills and districts by name.

For the next four days the road lay up the bed of the Nihing, which here, as before mentioned, forms the frontier of Persia and Kalát. The scenery was monotonous in the extreme. Soon after leaving our last halting-place the wide jungly bed contracted to a narrow channel between precipitous banks. The water soon ceased to be a continuous stream. Steep rocks of sandstone and shale, running east and west, at first bordered the bed on either side, but were further apart as we advanced. In places, where their nearly vertical strata showed through the boulders and sand which covered the channel, they formed natural dams, collecting the waters, elsewhere flowing beneath the surface, into deep and clear pools. About these were patches of high reedy grass, and occasionally a few stunted tamarisk trees. At such places we pitched our camp. Not a vestige of human habitation was seen. In one or two spots, sheep tracks crossing the river-bed showed that the country was sometimes trodden by the foot of man, but either the season was not that during which the shepherds graze their flocks here, or perhaps fear of our approach induced them to flee, and we met not a solitary human being during our four days' march. Of birds we saw hardly any, of beasts none; a few lizards on the rocks, and small fish in the pools, with an occasional harmless snake, represented the animal life of this desolate region.

Cheerless as was the prospect between the banks, that from above them was no better. To the north an arid brown plain stretched away to the Bampúsht hills, rising like a wall in naked ugliness, some ten miles off. The few scanty desert plants were hardly fresher in colour than the stony waste from which they sprung. To the south, range after range of insignificant flat-topped hills stretched away in the distance. Between them we were told are many flourishing villages and fertile spots belonging to Zamirán, but none lay within sight, and wherever the eye turned nothing but a burnt-up wilderness met our gaze. For a mountainous country I cannot conceive a more desolate scene. Even my Persians, well enough accustomed to dreary wildernesses in their own land, were affected by it, and lost their usual spirits till one of them suggested that the Sháh ought to confer the country in 'tuyúl' (i. e. make them pay themselves out of its revenue) on those of his ministers who had, by their advice, given us the trouble of coming there.

Nobody was sorry, therefore, when on the fourth day the river-bed ended in a maze of ravines; and after crossing the plain for a short distance, we saw the palm trees and tiny fort of Gishtigán. The latter was manned by half-a-dozen matchlock men, who made ready for action when the head of the caravan drew near, but the presence of Mústafa Khán, the agent of their chief, at once allayed their apprehensions. Exaggerated reports of our approach had, we heard, caused much alarm throughout the country. On the Persian side it was supposed that a combined army of Farangis and Kalátis were coming to transfer the recent acquisitions of the Sháh to the Khán of Kalát; and on the other side a rumour had spread that we were on our way to annex Kúhak to Persia. This little district occupies a somewhat similar position on the north of the Balúch plateau to that of Mand on the south, its chief being completely independent of both his neighbours, Persian and Brahúi. This gentleman, Mír Múrád by name, on hearing of our vicinity, had sent his women to a village he owned in Panjgúr, and placed his fort in a state of defence. This was serious, as I wished if possible to go to Kúhak, or at all events to the neighbouring dependent village of Kunárbastah.

As soon as possible, therefore, a messenger was dispatched to Mír Múrád with a letter acquainting him with the purport of my journey, and an offer to visit him at Kúhak, or to meet him at Kunárbastah. Another man was sent off to Panjgúr for fresh camels, to replace those of our friend Mír Akhírdád, who, being too close to an enemy's country to stay longer than necessary, departed directly he got his money, grumbling and swearing at not receiving a handsome present in addition to the three days' hire, amounting to 225 rupees, out of which he had cheated us by exaggerating the distance. Every one was glad to see the last of him and his crew, with whom the camp was an incessant scene of wrangling and contention. However, it was a matter of congratulation to have got along the most difficult part of the frontier at any price.

We had been led by Mústafá Khán to expect ample supplies of provisions at Gishtigán, but little or nothing was forthcoming, and for that little outrageous prices were asked. A rupee, or, as it is here called, a 'kaladár[1],' was demanded for a lump of butter the size of a walnut, or for a handful of rice or barley. This was annoying, as our provisions were well nigh exhausted by the long march through the desert, and we had not more than a couple of days' supply of rice and flour in camp, and were two or three days' march at least from the nearest place where it was supposed provisions were obtainable. In this, too, I might be deceived, as Mústafá Khán's information was clearly not to be trusted. Dates of course were procurable in plenty, and the Persians, accustomed to scanty and irregular food, could get along on them; but the Indian servants and the Survey party were already grumbling at the absence of *ghee*, and persisted in half poisoning themselves with stinking dried fish they had brought from the coast, in preference to eating dates with their 'chapátís,' or investing part of their ample wages and food-money in a kid or lamb.

I was therefore anxious to be off as soon as possible, but four days passed without the promised camels arriving from Panjgúr. In the mean time we had collected about five and twenty in the vicinity of Gishtigán, and obtained half a dozen more from the Persian escort, from whom I also purchased some of their spare rice and flour for the use of the Survey party. With these we made a start on the fifth day, leaving all but two of the lightest tents and the major part of the baggage in charge of a couple of *farashes* and two of the Yáwar's men.

The messenger to Mír Múrád Khán had previously returned with an answer to my letter, alleging illness as an excuse for not coming to meet me, but saying that he would send his nephew to the camp. With the messenger came one of Mír Múrád's own men, sent, as he at once avowed, to see whether there was actually a Farangi in the

[1] Kaladár: Anglicè, *bearing a head*, from the profile of the Queen on the obverse.

country, as his master feared that the whole story might be a ruse of Ibrahim Khán to get him (Mír Múrád) into his power. Satisfied on this point the spy returned at once to Kúhak.

Gishtigán is a miserable little place, inhabited by Rinds and Balúchís. These latter, from whose tribal appellation Nádir Sháh, after conquering the country, gave it the name of Balúchistán, are apparently of Iranian origin, mostly nomads, and scattered all through Balúchistán and Karmán, as far as longitude 56°. They seem a quiet and inoffensive race, disinclined to fight unless attacked, and generally living under the protection of some more warlike tribe, Kúrd, Rind, or Núshírwáni. The name of Nharoes, more properly Narahúis, which Pottinger gives to the tribes of Western Balúchistán, is unknown to, or unrecognised by them now. As most of his information seems to have been derived from his Brahúi guide, it is possible that, like Makráni, the term Narahúi is used in a contemptuous sense by the Kalát people; or perhaps the true Narahúi Balúchís are now confined to the Helmand valley. At all events the Arbábís, about whom he makes a blunder, which will be noticed hereafter, are certainly not Narahúis.

The appellation 'Balúch' is thus applied in two senses throughout the country; in the restricted sense, as a member of the Balúch tribe, in the general sense, as an inhabitant of Balúchistán. For instance, a Rind or a Núshírwáni, excusing himself for poverty or bad manners, will say, 'What would you have, *má Balúch hastim* (we are Balúchís)'; while the same man, if asked if he is a Balúch, will indignantly repudiate the idea, and answer, with all the pride of superior race, 'No, I am a Rind,' or Núshírwáni, as the case may be.

The Rinds take Balúch wives, but do not give their own daughters in return. This mixture of blood perhaps accounts for the fact that the Rinds of Gishtigán are finer and handsomer men than the Mand people, who seemed mostly of the lowest Arab type, with small eyes, bulbous noses, and thick lips. Two brothers, relations of the chief of Gishtigán, Khán Muhammad and Yár Muhammad by names, who obtained some camels for us, and afterwards accompanied the party to Jálk, were two of the best-looking specimens of humanity I have ever seen, and their manners were as great a contrast as their features to those of Mír Akhírdád and his crew.

During our halt at Gishtigán, I rode out one day with the Sarhang some miles to the eastward, to ascertain the position of the boundary in that direction, and connect my survey with that of Major Lovett the previous year. Five or six miles from Gishtigán we reached the summit of the plateau, 3000 feet above the sea.

This appears to be the most elevated plain south of the water-parting. It is an alluvial expanse, so level that there are no perceptible watercourses draining in either direction. At one place, an embankment, called Sar-i-sham, a few inches high, had been made at some period to retain the rainfall for cultivation; and a few pomegranate trees marked the site of a former garden, but all was now desolate, and there was no sign of habitation. About fifteen miles due east, over a level plain, lies the village of Diz, the chief place of the Kalát district of Párúm, visited by Major Lovett.

To the south the parallel ridges of upper Zamirán show a bolder outline and greater height than they do further west. The most considerable was named to me the Kúh Manjián, and another of serrated outline, here so rare, the Kúh-i-Miánúk. To the north the Bampúsht hills continue their bold scarp, under the name of Kúh-i-Mazampúsht, in the same even west to east direction, until they end in a loftier and bolder peak called the Kúh-i-Sagarkand. Beyond this, which marks the frontier, the hills diminish rapidly in height, changing the direction of their ridges from E. to E.N.E.

In the Mazampúsht hills the water-parting between the oceanic and central basins turns abruptly south over the Sar-i-Sham plateau, after which it resumes its eastward direction along the northern scarp of the prolongation of the Zamirán hills.

Leaving Gishtigán on the 2nd of March, we camped in a ravine only three miles distant, hearing a rumour that the camels coming from Panjgúr to bring on the rest of our baggage were not far off. The next day we crossed a wide gravelly plain to the foot of the hills, behind the first ridge of which we found a slender stream flowing westwards to the Nihing. Turning due north up a branch of this we camped amid dismal precipices at the foot of the Hindúwán pass. Here we were overtaken by Yár Muhammad, with the welcome intelligence that the camels had arrived. He was accompanied by their owner, a splendid-looking Balúch from Panjgúr, nearly six feet and a half high, and stout in proportion, with long curling locks floating over his shoulders. I could not help thinking what a model he would make for one of the heroes of the Sháh-námah.

Without much difficulty a bargain was struck with this worthy, and he started back to Gishtigán, promising to catch us up in a couple of days.

On reaching the summit of the pass, 4100 feet above the sea, the next day, the finest view we had seen in Balúchistán burst upon us. Some five-and-twenty miles to the north an imposing range of mountains, with bold peaks and rugged sides, stretched along the horizon. In front of them, and partially hidden by the lesser ranges parallel to that on which we stood, lay a wide valley sloping up towards the more distant hills. This was the Kúhak valley, and the hills beyond it the Siáneh Kúh[1] and the Kúh-i-Sabz[2], between which the Máshkíd river finds its way to the great desert which stretches away to the Helmand. In our atlases this river is shown under the name of the Boodoor, as rising in the desert and the Sarawán hills to the east, and flowing southward to the Niháng.

Some maps indeed indicate it as a possible ancient outlet of the Helmand to the sea. This southern course of the Máshkíd or Boodoor rested on the authority of Sir Henry Pottinger, who crossed the desert from Sarawán to Kalagán in 1810. When sixty miles from the latter place we camped on the bank of a 'dry river, five hundred yards in width, running S.S.E. towards the west.' Up this river-bed he proceeded five miles in a north-westerly direction, to the site of a ruined village called Regán.

In the second part of his book Sir Henry Pottinger states that he was informed that the 'Boodoor' extended to the Garmsíl, as the valley of the Helmand is termed in the great bend which it takes to the south. The improbability of a torrent five hundred yards wide, having its origin on the banks of a great river, in an almost waterless desert, presumably led to Pottinger's supposition that the Boodoor was an old outlet of the Helmand to the ocean[3].

Of course a knowledge of the altitude of the Khárán desert would at once have disposed of this theory, but Pottinger had no instruments for measuring heights. On Major Lovett's journey to Panjgúr in 1871, he was informed that the 'Rakshán' and other streams draining the Panjgúr valley to the westwards fell into a stream called the Máshkíd, which flowed north and north-west through the Siáneh-Kúh and Kúh-i-Sabz, to the desert in which it was stated to disappear, several days' march distant. This information, which, if true, amounted to a revolution in the recognised geography of Balúchistán, was borne

[1] Black peak hills. [2] Green hills. [3] See his Travels, p. 303.

out by the levels as far as known. Major Lovett found Panjgúr to be over 3000 feet above the sea, and the Garmsíl valley, considering the height of the Sistán lake, calculated by Khánikoff at 1500, could hardly exceed 2000[1].

Still it was possible that the Rakshán might have a rapid fall to the Máshkíd, and that the latter might, as described by Pottinger, join the Dasht either by the Nihing or the Sháhrí rivers. Of the first possibility our journey up the Nihing had disposed.

To remove the last shadow of doubt from Lovett's theory, which was, I need not say, the true one, it was only necessary to see whether the Máshkíd, which we could see in the distance, flowed east or west. If east, it could not possibly reach the Sháhrí, and Pottinger, who had seen it, was wrong; and Lovett, who had not, right; if west, the older traveller was correct. Thus, though I had little doubt as to the result, I was anxious to get to the stream as soon as possible.

[1] Dr. Bellew, in the appendix to 'The Indus to the Tigris,' gives the height of Rúdbár as 1830 feet.

CHAPTER III.

Píshín to Jálk (continued).

The travels of Sir Henry Pottinger will of necessity be so frequently referred to in the course of this and the following chapter, describing a part of Balúchistán where he was our only European predecessor, that a brief sketch of his journey will hardly be out of place.

When Sir John Malcolm was setting out from Bombay on his second mission to Tehrán, Captain Christie[1] and Lieut. Pottinger of the Bombay army volunteered to find a route overland to Persia through the unexplored wastes of Balúchistán.

Their offer being accepted, Christie and Pottinger sailed to Sonmiání, a small port not far west of Karáchí, and travelled thence through Las Baila to Kalát. At this time they passed as European servants of a Hindú horse-dealer of Bombay. From Kalát they made their way to Núshki, on the borders of the Helmand desert. Here they separated, Christie striking north-west across the desert to the Helmand, whence he passed through Sistán and Herát to Yazd and Isfahán; while Pottinger turned southwards to complete his investigation of the geography of Balúchistán. After traversing the Sarawán district, he attempted to obtain a guide to Sarhad, even now unvisited by a European; but he was unable to do so, and found himself unwillingly compelled to take the route we afterwards traversed through Kalagán and Dízak to Bampúr. During this stage of his travels he was forced to assume the character of a Musalmán pilgrim. From Bampúr he followed the direct road through Basmán to Rigán in Narmashir, and so on to Bam and Karmán, whence he reached Shíráz through Shahr-i-Bábak and Arsinján, a route not since described.

In 1816, Sir Henry Pottinger published an account of his journey through Balúchistán and South Persia, accompanied by a geographical and historical account of the former country and Sind, with a map

[1] Killed at the battle of Aslandúz in 1812.

compiled from his own observations, those of Captain Grant, who had visited Bampúr in 1809, and from native information.

Careful study of this work on the spot made it impossible for me to avoid the conclusion, already drawn by an eminent foreign critic [1], that Sir Henry Pottinger, though a most daring and successful traveller, was neither a competent surveyor nor a careful observer. Even allowing the widest margin for miscalculation of distance while travelling by night, and rough bearings hastily taken by pocket compass, it is difficult to understand how he could have fallen into some of the blunders found on his map. It is perhaps unfair to blame him for placing the whole of north-western Balúchistán three quarters of a degree too far north; but his error in the direction of the Búdúr or Máshkíd, noticed in the last chapter, is inexplicable, as he followed its bed for five miles by daylight; and that there are two such rivers in the Khárán desert, close together but flowing opposite ways, the second of which Pottinger passed without noticing it, seems more than improbable. Again, a comparison of his map with that at the beginning of this volume will show that some of the hill ranges passed by him are drawn at right-angles to the real bearing of their axes; e. g. the Kúh-i-Bírg close to Magas or Mughsee. Either his pocket compass must have been utterly untrustworthy, or he must have been far from careful in noting it. For instance, the true bearing of Bampúr from Púhrá is exactly west. Pottinger gives it in text and map as south-west by south. Another defect is the fondness, shared by him with some more recent geographers, for tracing all the hills in a country to a common source; often true enough as regards the great elevated masses, or plateaux, but utterly incorrect with respect to the ridges rising above the general level, which throughout the plateaux of Persia and Balúchistán are often remarkable for their isolated character. To carry out this pet theory he takes unwarrantable liberties with the oreography. For instance, from the high hill near Dízak, called by him the Kúh-i-Guebre (a name I was unable to identify, but which is no doubt one of the lofty isolated limestone mountains west of that village), he draws a prominent range due south for more than seventy miles, and a second south-west to meet the hills south of Bampúr. Both are figments of imagination. The country on which they are shown is a vast plain, drained by several affluents of the Máshkíd, flowing south-east, and diversified only by insignificant

[1] Khánikoff.

ridges running in the same direction. The errors in names of districts, and in the identification of natural objects, will be mentioned as occasion arises.

The task of calling attention to the mistakes of a predecessor is an invidious one; the more so that his journey was successfully pursued in the teeth of difficulties, dangers, and hardships which would have turned back many a traveller, and with which the petty troubles and annoyances experienced by Mr. Blanford and myself cannot bear the shadow of a comparison. It seemed, however, better to do so at once and openly, than to be constantly contradicting him page after page, or to ignore his blunders altogether, and leave the work of comparison to critics.

With all its faults, moreover, Sir Henry Pottinger's volume was invaluable as a handbook; and I know that much of the information I obtained is due to questions prompted by its pages. On many points its accuracy is wonderful; and more than one Balúch chief was astonished by my knowledge of his pedigree and family history, due to the details on such subjects which Pottinger delighted to collect. The contrast between the manner of our journeys was often brought vividly to my mind in perusing his daily experiences by the light of my own, to corroborate or correct his observations. The traveller of 1810 flitted hastily and cautiously through a country swarming with cut-throats. Obliged at first to disguise himself as the servant of a Hindú, and afterwards as a Musalmán pilgrim, accompanied by a single Indian attendant, and mounted on a worn-out camel, he was often dependent on hospitality for food, and on the sand of the desert for a couch. His rough notes and sketches could be made only at the risk of discovery which might probably mean a cruel death. His successors of 1872 followed nearly the same road, with little more risk than on British soil. They were provided with horses, tents, servants, and all the appliances of Anglo-Indian travelling; and though accompanied by a merely nominal escort, used theodolite and sextant, measuring-wheel and note-book, as freely and openly as in their own land.

Most of the change is doubtless due to the vast increase of prestige enjoyed by the conquerors of the Panjáb and Sind; but we could not shut our eyes to the fact that much of the security and safety of our travelling was attributable to the substitution of Persian rule for that of the independent barbarians of Pottinger's time.

To return to the narrative. Descending the Hindúwán pass we entered the Askán torrent-bed, now quite dry. A couple of miles further we halted for the night (March 4th) at a tiny spot of cultivation in the mouth of a ravine from the eastward. A wall of loose stone built across the entrance served as escarpment to retain a platform of flood-debris and made-soil, perhaps a tenth of an acre in extent. This was planted with a few date-palms, beneath which were little patches of several different seeds: cotton, barley, onions, and radishes among the number. Habitation there was none, the little garden belonging to a tribe of nomad Balúchís encamped further up the ravine. We had seen ruins of similar walls on the Húng plateau; but this was the first met with in working order. Afterwards such gardens were not uncommon; and it appears that these ravine mouths are the only cultivated spots through a wide extent of country from Bampúsht to Panjgúr, in which there are no settled villages. The inhabitants are exclusively Balúchís, owning allegiance to one or other of the powerful chiefs in the neighbourhood, often quite irrespective of the district over which they wander. Thus we found on the Askán ravine, in close proximity to each other, camps of Balúchís belonging to Persian Bampúsht, to Kalátí Panjgúr, and to independent Kúbak.

This may hereafter prove as fertile a source of frontier disputes on a small scale as do on a larger the loose allegiance and wandering propensities of the Kúrds and Arabs on the Turko-Persian frontier.

The next day we made a short march down the ravine to Tashkúk, a date-grove without habitation. Here the rest of the baggage caught us up. We had now passed two considerable ranges parallel to the Bampúsht scarp, and the country in front was more open, sloping rapidly down towards the Máshkíd, but still intersected by numerous minor ridges. Leaving the Askán ravine the next morning we turned westward behind one of these, and by a narrow and rocky path crossed to a parallel torrent called Kodání, where we halted near a camp of nomad Balúchís. We were now only a day's journey from the villages of Múrtí and Barúi, the principal places of Bampúsht. The head men came down to the camp. One of them, a pleasant-looking old man, told me he was among the defenders of Kalát when it was stormed by the British army in 1839.

Here occurred the only episode of excitement which varied the even tenor of our march through Balúchistán. After dinner Mústafa Khán came to my tent in a state of unusual excitement, and reported that a hostile army was somewhere in the neighbourhood. Outlying shepherds had reported a strong-armed force to be halting on the Máshkíd at the mouth of the Kodání ravine, five or six miles below our camp. It was supposed that they were Mamasanís from Nál, a district south of Kalát, who were known to have a blood-feud to avenge on the people of Isfandak; in which case it was unlikely that they would meddle with our party. On the other hand, Mústafa Khán thought it by no means improbable that they were Helmand Balúchís from Rúdbár on a general plundering expedition, who would certainly attack us, if they got scent of so rich a prize in their vicinity.

Balúchís neither march nor fight after dark, so there was nothing to be done till the morning. In the meantime I wrote a letter to the Mamasaní chief, Yúsúf Khán, pointing out the impropriety of his proceedings in disturbing the peace of the frontier at the very time when the British Government had sent an officer to settle its position in the interests of his master, the Khán of Kalát. This missive was to be despatched at daybreak, or as soon as tidings confirmatory of the marauders being Mamasanís should arrive.

Early the next morning we heard the sounds of distant firing; and on turning out found the nomads camped near us hard at work packing their goods and chattels on camels, and driving them as soon as loaded up the ravine in the direction of Múrtí. Our own people were taking it quietly; but the Persian escort were making the hastiest of preparations for a start. The Sarhang, the Yáwar and Súltán, with the Bampúsht chiefs, were on a hill looking in the direction from which the report of dropping shots came at intervals. On joining them we found the fat Súltán green with terror, and counselling immediate flight. The Sarhang was evidently nervous, but kept a good face on it; while the old Yáwar counted his beads and muttered prayers incessantly without offering an opinion. We learnt that it was still uncertain who the enemy were; but as the Balúchís, with whom they were then exchanging shots, belonged to Kúhak, and were therefore allies of the Mamasanís, it was supposed by the Súltán that they must be the much dreaded Helmand robbers. This amiable people have the reputation of being the most blood-thirsty villains in Western Asia, and that, too, under the cloak of religion. Nothing will induce them to violate the precepts of the Korán by plundering a living man; but stripping a dead one appears to their tender consciences a laudable act, or at most a venial sin. They therefore always murder travellers before annexing their belongings.

Mústafa Khán had not been able to find a messenger to carry my letter, and though both he and the Bampúsht chiefs had little doubt that the raiders were Yúsúf Khán's people, the mere possibility of their proving Helmand Balúchís made them counsel our sending off the baggage into the hills. Whilst we were discussing the matter, a man armed with a matchlock, half naked and streaming with perspiration, appeared running up the ravine. He proved to be a Balúch from the camp below; and said that they had been attacked at daybreak by a dismounted detachment of the Mamasanís, who had wounded a man and a woman and carried off several others with some sheep. He had come to ask assistance from the Bampúsht people in recovering the captives. The Mamasanís had retreated to their main body, who had gone off westwards in the direction of Isfandak before sunrise.

All apprehension of the marauders being Helmand people was now at an end; but neither the Persians nor our camel-drivers would listen to any proposal for a move towards Isfandak. However, after a couple of hours, during which the wounded woman was brought in, and her wound dressed by Mr. Roane, Mústafa Khán found a messenger to carry my letter to the Mamasaní chief, to which I added a postscript, requesting the release of his prisoners. The messenger returned the next morning with intelligence that the Mamasanís had killed two Isfandak Balúchís, who were grazing their flocks outside the village, about the same time that their dismounted men had attacked the camp near us. On the receipt of my letter, to which no reply was returned, they released their captives, and started eastwards for Nál at once.

In the course of the following week I learnt the whole story, which, as an example of the manners and customs of Balúchistán, is perhaps worthy of record.

The district of Jálk, on the other side of the Siáneh Hills, is famous for its dates, and caravans from Eastern Balúchistán resort to it yearly to buy them. Their road lies through the village of Isfandak, which was last year in the hands of a certain Balúch Khán, not a Balúchí, as his name would seem to denote, but a Núshírwání[1], and

[1] These Núshírwánís appear to be the most warlike tribe in Balúchistán. They are of Persian origin, having emigrated from Núshírwán, a district, and former town, on the

cousin of Azád Khán of Khárán, the chief of that powerful clan. This man had taken forcible possession of Isfandak, and levied blackmail on all passing caravans.

A large caravan from Nál, on its way back from Jálk with dates, refused to pay, and was accordingly attacked by Balúch Khán—two men, Balúchís, not Mamasanís, being killed, and a large number of camels seized. Yúsúf Khán, the Mamasaní chief, complained to Azád Khán of this proceeding of his relative; and he, after obtaining the restoration of the camels, gave Yúsúf Khán permission to purge the blood-feud—no noble blood, Mamasaní or Núshírwání, having been spilt—by the slaughter of two Isfandak Balúchís, in return for the two Nál Balúchís slain by Balúch Khán. This was the object of the raid, and as the programme was exactly carried out, honour was fully satisfied. The attack on our neighbours on the Kodání ravine was a mistake, the sufferers being supposed to belong to Isfandak, and not Kúhak.

It is very possible that this error, when discovered, had just as much to do with the release of the captives, as any remonstrance: however, we met them on our road the next day, on their way to our camp. They expressed much gratitude, and begged for rupees.

The Persians, though now boasting that only our pacific mission on the frontier had prevented their attacking and slaughtering the Mamasanís, kept their horses saddled all night in readiness for bolting in case of a night attack. The precaution was unnecessary, all was quiet, and neither Ibráhím Súltán nor the camel-drivers objected to a start the following morning, though they kept in the hills, instead of going straight to the Máshkíd.

After a longer march than usual, crossing several small dry torrents, and one large one, the Shaitáb, higher up on which lie Múrtí and Barúi, we emerged on the river-bed, down which an insignificant stream was trickling eastwards, thus proving its identity with Pottinger's Búdúr.

The next morning the bodies of the slain Balúchís were brought

Zaindarúd, a few miles above Isfahán. As they claim kindred with the Mamasanís of Nál, an offshoot of the well-known Lúr tribe of the same name, the Núshírwánís are probably also Lúrs. I could not learn any tradition as to the date of their emigration into Balúchistán; but it seems not improbable that they were found troublesome neighbours by Sháh Abbas, when he established his court at Isfahán, and turned out by him to make room for the Armenian colonists brought from the north, whose descendants are still numerous in the neighbourhood.

to the camp by their relatives; not, as might be supposed, to ask for justice against the murderers, but to beg for contributions towards the funeral expenses. One, a fine young man of five-and-twenty, had been killed by sabre cuts. He had refused to take shelter in the village, preferring to run the chance of death to abandoning his flocks, which he had not had time to drive off into the hills.

The Máshkíd river here runs along the southern edge of the plain, which is a vast glacis of gravel, sloping gently upwards to the foot of the Siáneh range, here about ten miles distant, and parallel to the Bampúsht hills. To the left the mountains appeared to trend northwards, and nothing broke the horizon-line in the westward direction but three abrupt peaks, which Mústafá Khán stated to be the hills of Dízak.

Three miles from the halting-place we passed the village of Isfandak, the first permanent habitation since leaving Mand, three weeks before. It lies on the edge of extensive date-groves, among which flourishing crops of young corn were springing. The buildings were of mud and stone; and the whole place had an air of greater prosperity and civilisation than anything seen in Southern Balúchistán.

Our road lay across the plain in a north-westerly direction to the hills, which we entered by an easy pass, called the Godar-i-Bonsir. The summit is about 4500 feet above the sea, 1250 feet higher than our halting-place on the Máshkíd.

Seen from the other side of the valley, the Siáneh hills had bolder and more varied outlines than the southern ranges, of whose monotonous ridges of sandstone and shale our eyes had long been weary. But any hopes of something new in geological formations were disappointed, and the only novelty was a welcome increase of vegetation. In an hour's stroll after reaching the camping-ground, a knoll near the path, a mile from the summit of the pass, I found asafœtida in abundance, maiden-hair fern growing round springs in the gullies, wild pistachio, and the two most characteristic plants of the lower ranges of South Persia, the broom-like wild almond, and a shrubby heath, which has a curious resemblance to a gooseberry-bush covered with fruit.

The asafœtida was just coming into flower, and some of the stalks were five feet high at least. Unlike the other plants of the same family in Persia, which seem to prefer barren plains or arid and exposed hills, the asafœtida is found in sheltered and comparatively damp spots among the mountains. Pottinger found it in the vicinity of Núshki, where it is collected by the Balúchis both for export and their own use. As far as I could learn, its value either as a condiment, or as an article of commerce, is unknown in Western Balúchistán.

The day had been cloudy, and before the baggage camels could get in, it came on to rain heavily. Fortunately our tents got in before dark, but the greater part of the caravan was overtaken by darkness, and did not reach the camp till morning. We had in consequence to go nearly dinnerless to sleep, though not to bed, for beds and bedding were with the missing camels.

The morning was bright and clear; and, after breakfast, we descended a narrow path into the broad shingly bed of the Kalagán ravine. Following this for five miles in a northerly direction, we came upon a copious spring of water, bubbling out of the stones, and flowing briskly down the valley through green turf and rushes, the pleasantest sight we had yet seen. Soon afterwards the ravine turned abruptly to the eastwards, and a mile further we halted in a date-grove below the castle of Aibí. This is a picturesque building, perched on an isolated rock [1], and is the first place in the flourishing little district of Kalagán.

A mile further down the valley is the village of Pahúrá or Púhrá. Between the two, palm-groves and gardens skirt the edge of the hills. At the time of Pottinger's visit the cultivation was much more extensive; but a heavy flood, about ten years ago, not only carried away all the trees from the middle of the valley, but left a deposit of shingle, which has prevented the re-cultivation of much of the land. Nevertheless, what remains made Kalagán by far the most inviting spot we had seen in Balúchistán, added to which the rivulet and gardens promised unwonted additions to the natural history collections. We therefore, not unwillingly, consented to give the camels a day's rest.

Rice, flour, barley, and ghee were brought in in quantities considerable compared to the supplies produced in Mand, and at prices comparatively reasonable, and not before it was time, for the commissariat was at the lowest ebb. The vendors attracted our attention by their unvarying low stature, ugly but good-humoured faces, and the constant chatter they kept up, so unlike the sulky taciturn people of Makrán. On enquiry I found them to be members of the tribe

[1] *Vide Frontispiece.*

called 'Arbábí,' supposed, as the name would denote, to be the aboriginal inhabitants[1]. They are admirable cultivators, resembling in this respect the Gabrs of Yazd, and the inhabitants of Karmán generally. They have no distinctive dialect, but do not intermarry with other village-dwelling tribes, or with the nomad Balúchís, like whom they invariably occupy a subject position. The villages owned and tilled by them are always under the protection of some more warlike tribe. The districts of Súrán, Gosht, Paskúh, Náhú, and Sinúkán, much of Dízak and Jálk, besides Kalagán, are inhabited by Arbábís.

Pottinger's description of the Dehwárs of Kalát would serve equally well for the Arbábís of Western Balúchistán, and both are perhaps identical with the Tájiks of Afghánistán and Central Asia. These latter are, however, if I remember rightly, described as a handsome race of pure Iranian origin. The Arbábís are, on the other hand, extraordinarily short, hardly, I should think, averaging five feet two inches, with blunt features, straight brows, and sturdy clumsy limbs, bearing a far stronger likeness to Turks of Adarbaiján than to any Persian-speaking people of modern Irán. It is worth noticing that both Dehwárs and Arbábís are found only on the higher plateaux of Balúchistán.

The day after our arrival at Kalagán, the nephew and cousin of Mír Múrád of Kúhak came to the camp, having been sent by that

[1] Sir Henry Pottinger's account of this singular people differs so entirely from my experience, and from the information I gathered, that I annex his remarks on the subject. He says (pp. 169-70), 'Mihráb Khán is the most powerful chief in this quarter . . . and he is acknowledged to be the paramount authority from Dízak to Basman . . . His tribe is that branch of the Nharoes called Urbabees, who are stated to have been of no note whatever, and had dwelt in obscurity in a sterile and elevated tract near Surbud, whence the progenitors of the present Khan emigrated with a body of followers to Dízak, in which district they acquired a footing by a donation of soil from some of the Mukrance chiefs . . . his revenues (Mihráb Khán's) are now computed at four and a half lacs of rupees annually (£56,250).

'The Urbabees are the fairest tribe of Beloochees I met with, and there is a peculiar elevation in their countenances that pre-eminently distinguishes them among their countrymen. They are, without almost an exception, tall handsome men, with great indications of activity. Their predatory character, on which they pride themselves, is sufficiently proved by their deeds,' &c.

Pottinger is here probably describing the Bárakzai Afgháns, to which tribe the ruling family of Dízak, who own all the districts inhabited by 'Arbábís,' state themselves to belong, having emigrated at no very recent date from the Helmand. He passed very hurriedly through this part of the country; and must have confused the tribe cultivating the soil with that of their lords paramount.

chief to meet me at Isfandak, from which place they had followed our caravan to Kalagán.

The nephew was a truculent-looking young man of two or three and twenty, clad in a striped red stuff, with a large turban of the same colour, and the cousin, Mirza Khán, an intelligent youth speaking good Persian, learnt at Tehrán where he was educated. His paternal relatives were formerly chiefs of Irafshán; and his connection with Kúhak is through his mother, a relation of Mír Múrád. A few months only before I saw him, the head of his father's family, a certain Juma Khán, had been put to death by Ibráhím Khán of Bampúr, when Mirza Khán had taken refuge with his mother's people at Kúhak.

From him I obtained all the information required about Kúhak, and the neighbouring villages of Kunár-bastah and Isfandak. Only the two first are subject to Mír Múrád, Isfandak belonging half to a child, Sháh-nawáz Khán, nephew to Mír Múrád, and half to his cousin Rústam Khán, the chief of an Afghán family recently settled in Dízak.

Kúhak, which is from all accounts one of the strongest forts in Balúchistán, was conquered early in the present century by a Núshírwání chief from Khárán, who married the daughter of the rightful owner after putting the latter to death. Since that time Kúhak, which had been dependent on Dízak, has paid tribute or allegiance to no one, though its Núshírwání chiefs seem to acknowledge the head of their tribe, the Khán of Khárán, as their feudal superior.

Mirza Khán declared that Mír Múrád, though willing to acknowledge himself a vassal of the English government, declined to have anything to do with either Persians or Barahúis. He added that Mír Múrád lived in constant expectation of being attacked by Ibráhím Khán of Bampúr; but had made every preparation to resist him, and had received a promise of assistance from Azád Khán of Khárán.

I had a tent pitched for the Núshírwánís, and provided them with food. Being on Persian soil they were under my protection and my guests. Early the next morning they started on their return to Kúhak, the two chiefs riding on the same camel. At mid-day we rode six and a half miles down the valley, passing the villages of Lají and Balá Kalát, about four miles from Aibí.

Opposite the first named, half-a-dozen extra-dirty-looking Balúchís were standing in a row, headed by a man in a white turban. As I rode past, one of them came forward and addressed me in Hindustáni, which he said he had learnt whilst working as a day labourer in Bombay. On being asked who his friend in the turban was, he replied, '*Hamára shahr ka padisháh hai*' (He is the king of my city).

Balá Kalát is the largest village of Kalagán, and may contain some hundred or a hundred and twenty houses. It is famous for its greyhounds; but not one was to be seen when we passed, as it had leaked out that Ibráhím Khán had ordered his nephew the Súltán to bring him a pair or two of good dogs. Every one in the place had been carried off to the hills. I succeeded in getting one on our return, but lost her a few days afterwards. They are of the Arab breed; similar to the English greyhound, but smaller. The dogs with silky ears and feathered tails, known as Persian greyhounds, are bred among the wandering tribes of Western Persia.

Our camp was pitched behind the last range of hills, on ascending which the desert, stretching without interruption to the Helmand, lay before us. Crossing a bay in this the next morning, March 13th, over a firm gravelly soil, with rocks protruding here and there above the surface, we reached the goal of our frontier journey, the district of Jálk, unvisited till then by a European.

A mile from the town we were met by the eldest son of Diláwar Khán of Dizak, who though only twelve years old is supposed to govern Jálk and Kalagán for his father. With him was a crowd of ragged matchlock-men and other tagrag and bobtail, dignified by Mústafa Khán, who proudly pointed them out, with the titles of *sarbáz, ghulám*, &c. The young Khán was a lively and intelligent youth, and chattered incessantly to the Sarhang and myself, between whom he rode into the town. His loquacity and the straightforward way in which he asked questions and proffered opinions, drew down on him several reproofs from a dignified, but very dirty, old gentleman who called himself *wazír*, and was, I suppose, the virtual ruler of the district.

Jálk consists of a group of half-a-dozen villages scattered along the last two miles of a wide ravine opening between low hills on the desert. A subterranean conduit, called *kanát* in Persia, and *káríz* here and in Afghánistán, affords an ample supply of water; and the whole width of the ravine is filled with the date-groves whose fruit is celebrated in Balúchistán. Beneath the trees fine crops of wheat and barley were already as high as the knee. The villages have the usual form of a cluster of huts round a central fort, in the principal of which lived the young Khán with his mother. So closely is the valley cultivated that it was difficult to find a spot large enough to pitch our tents. Altogether Jálk was by far the most flourishing and cheerful place we had seen; though Mústafa Khán declared that Kalagán before the great flood was even more prosperous. Until the last few years Jálk had been regularly plundered by Azád Khán of Khárán twice a year, once after the corn and once after the date harvest. Six years before our visit, Ibráhím Khán of Bampúr had defeated Azád Khán's men, and captured and destroyed a fort the latter had built on the Máshkíd, two days' march to the east.

Since then the peasants of Jálk and Kalagán have enjoyed peace and tranquillity, tempered however by increased taxation. Indeed it is a question whether most of the people of Balúchistán would not gladly return to their old state of anarchy and insecurity of life and property, in preference to having to pay their taxes regularly. Probably the upper classes preferred the old state of things; while the actual cultivators, though they may have more of their produce to give up than of old, appreciate the benefit of protection which enables them to enjoy the remainder in quiet, without fear of their winter stock of provisions being plundered, and their wives and children carried off into slavery.

A solitary Hindú was settled in Jálk, where he had been since childhood. Hearing that there were fellow-countrymen in our camp, he daubed some red and white caste marks on his face, and paid us a visit. He said he carried on a small trade in cotton goods, but did not make much money; and though he strenuously denied having become a Musalmán, admitted that he had a Balúch wife. He asked permission to see the inside of my tent, a very old and ragged hill-tent from the Bombay arsenal, and was overwhelmed at its magnificence, being only up to exclaiming under his breadth '*padisháhí*,' '*padisháhí*,' royal, royal. The standard of regal state is not very high in Balúchistán.

Another visitor to the camp was a Kábuli pilgrim on his way to Makkah (Mecca), a ruffian who, though he begged for alms, looked as if he would like to have stuck his knife into the Farangis who gave them.

We halted five days at Jálk to obtain camels from the Rígí[1] Balúchís, who graze their flocks and herds along the banks of the Máshkíd. It was now too late in the year to join Sir Frederic Goldsmid in Sistán, which indeed would at any time have involved the return of all our baggage and camp equipage to the coast, from the difficulty of transport across the desert to the Garmsíl. From a Rígí chief, who contracted

[1] From *rig*, sand, i.e. inhabitants of deserts.

to furnish our camels, I obtained particulars of the road, which he had traversed several times. Its distance to the Helmand is ten marches, of which the last three are *lút*, a word which was explained as waterless[1]. The halting-place of Pirikaiser, shown on our maps, should be Pirikasr, the old fort.

Some twenty miles north-east of Jálk is an extensive tract of marsh, caused apparently by the drainage from the hills flowing under the gravelly glacis which here, as in so many places in Persia, stretches a long distance from the base of the ranges. At the southern end of the marsh, which is called Dehgwar, are two villages, Ladgasht and Kalag, belonging to Jálk. Immense date-groves cover the marsh throughout its extent. These are the property of various tribes, Panjgúrís and Kháránís as well as men from Jálk and Kalagán. The proprietors visit the groves twice a year only, when the female blossom requires fertilisation by the pollen of the male, and when the fruit is ripening. A day's march beyond Dehgwar is the Máshkíd river, which ceases to afford water not far to the north.

My informant in the preceding particulars accompanied the Sarhang and myself one morning to the point where the Jálk ravine opens on the desert. Here on an isolated rock are some deep shapeless marks in the stone, said to be hoof-prints of Ali's horse, though I could not ascertain that there was any legend current explaining what the prophet's son-in-law was doing there. Besides their settlements on the Máshkíd, the Rígís own two villages in Jálk. They are fine handsome men, proud of their valour, which enables them to hold their own against the dreaded Helmand Balúchís. In features and manners they strongly reminded me of the Persian Iliáts of Fars.

I tried to persuade the Rígí chief to take us to Sarhad, six or eight marches from Jálk, but he declared it impossible, and we had to resign ourselves to going to Dízak, whence we might forward the superfluous camp equipage and Indian servants to Gwádar.

---

[1] Khanikoff calls the great desert north of Karmán the desert of Lút, or Lot, supposed to derive its appellation from the patriarch of that name. Probably the meaning given to me is the true one, and *lút* no more a proper name than 'Sahra' or 'Kavir,' designations applied by geographers to the great deserts of North Africa and Khúrasán.

CHAPTER IV.

Jálk to Bampúr.

On the 18th of March we broke up our camp at Jálk, and turned our steps towards Dízak, whence it was intended to send Blanford's Indian domestics and the surveying party back to Gwádar. Endeavours to obtain a responsible person at Jálk to take charge of them to the coast had failed, and I had therefore to take them on to Dízak. On our journey westward they would have been more trouble than use. Indian servants, useful and uncomplaining as they doubtless are in their own country, are too much the slaves of custom to adapt themselves with any readiness to strange surroundings. Moreover, the prejudices of caste, which influence Indian Musalmáns nearly as strongly as Hindús, are a constant source of annoyance to their masters in foreign countries. A Turk, a Persian, even an Arab, soon learns to fit in his ways with those of the people among whom he finds himself; but an Indian out of India, with rare exceptions, is, in my experience, a square man in a round hole.

The first halting-place on the Dízak road was that in the Kalagán valley, which we had left on the 12th. So, leaving the caravan to find its way thither by the regular path, Blanford and I indulged in the unwonted luxury of a wandering ride across the desert in search of game and specimens. Our particular object was to obtain a male of the gazelle, which Blanford, from a female procured in Jálk, suspected, and as it afterwards turned out with reason, to belong to a hitherto undescribed species[1].

During the day we saw but one, a fine male, walking leisurely along a quarter of a mile ahead, and crossing our path at right angles towards a low ridge of rock which presently concealed him from view. As soon as he disappeared I galloped straight towards the rock, and on nearing it jumped off and crept to the top, rifle in hand. There was the gazelle,

[1] *Gazella fuscifrons.* See pages 192, 193.

walking quietly along, utterly unconscious of the presence of an enemy, and not fifty yards off. Of course I looked upon his head as good as in the British Museum, and resting the rifle, a double breech-loading express, on the rock, took a deliberate shot. Horrible to relate, the cap did not explode; the snap of the lock startled the antelope, which set off at a canter; and the bullet from the second barrel, as it always does in such cases, whistled harmlessly over his head. That the only Boxer cartridge I have had miss fire should have been aimed at the only male *Gazella fuscifrons* I or any other collector have seen within shooting distance, was a coincidence that I cannot yet think of with any feeling of resignation. At the time the disappointment was less keenly felt, for we hoped to find more gazelles of the same kind on that or subsequent days; but alas! we saw no more that afternoon, and the gazelle of the deserts further west proved to be of another and well-known species.

After crossing the desert we entered the Kalagán torrent-bed, here a mere nullah in the desert, some four miles below our former halting-place, and close to the lowest village Kal'ah-ad-din. The date-groves here are fertilised by a spring of beautifully clear and sweet water, welling out of the east side of the ravine, and conducted in an artificial channel along its steep face. Spring and channel were alike fringed with a mass of maiden-hair fern I have never, save in Abyssinia, seen equalled in luxuriance, and whose vivid green, contrasted with the sunny tints of the rocks amid which it grew, formed a picture refreshing to the eye to a degree unknown to those who have never experienced the wearying monotony of the arid landscapes of Western Asia.

A little further on an almost equally pleasing sight was the poplar willow, of which many small groves were scattered along the valley. In early spring, when we saw it, the foliage of this tree assumes every variety of tender hue from pink to green. The Persians call it 'Pádár-bíd' (foot-bearing willow), probably from the long narrow point in which the heart-shaped leaf terminates. It is found, I believe, in all suitable localities throughout Western Asia from the Indus to the Mediterranean. In Persia, where it is not very common, I have seen it as far north as the valley of the Safíd-Rúd in Ghílán, about latitude 37°[1].

[1] This must be the tree called by Pottinger the 'peepul' (*ficus religiosa*), to the leaf of which well-known Indian species that of the Pádár-bíd bears considerable resemblance.

The next morning we breakfasted under the palm-trees of Aibí, close to our old camping-ground. Here I had the misfortune to leave, unread, the last number of the 'Westminster Review,' a serious loss in a bookless land, where posts were few and far between. I consoled myself with the reflection that it might have been left in a worse place. There are no weak brethren to have their faith shaken in Balúchistán.

We camped that night in a pleasant spot, a mile or so up a branch turning westward from the main ravine down which we had come in the journey northward. Here it was that Pottinger, sleeping *à la belle étoile*, had one of his only pair of shoes carried off by a fox; a loss even more deplorable than that of my 'Westminster Review.'

The next day's march led for some fifteen miles up the same ravine, which is wide and easy. It is formed by the dislocation of the axes of the ridges of the Siáneh Kúh, which here change their east and west bearing to north-west, marking the commencement of the mountain system of Persia proper. Although of the same geological formation, the change of direction to the west was also emphasised by a difference in the form assumed by the hills. On our left were numerous steep short parallel ridges, on our right three well-marked chains of somewhat rounded outline. The road through this pass, called Godár-i-Brinjínán, had evidently been improved in several places to admit the passage of guns; and we were told that Ibráhím Khán had more than once taken artillery to Jálk by this route, which presents no difficulty of importance. Only in one place, where the path had been washed away by the recent heavy rain, did it require serious repair.

The water-parting, 4500 feet above the level of the sea, lies in the last chain. Two miles further on, the road emerged on the Dízak plain, crossed by us ten days before through Isfandak. The Dízak hills, whose tops had just been visible that day, now loomed high to the west; and to the south the Bampúsht plateau showed a gradual slope upwards from the Máshkíd, varied by numerous low parallel ridges. Many date-groves dotted the plain on both sides of the road, which led south-west to the little fort of Kalpúrakán[1], which seems to

---

[1] This, according to the Sarhang, who was fond of etymology, means 'head full of itching.' Pottinger says 'full of spirits or fairies.' The 'fort full of sands,' *púr rigán*, would seem the most obvious derivation, but the plain is stony, not sandy. Perhaps it is the fort of Púra Khán from the name and title of the first owner; though I cannot say I ever heard such a name.

have given its name to the district in Pottinger's time. It is now called Dehak, from a much larger village to the east.

Our road the next morning (the 27th of March, new year's day in Persia) lay north-west across a barren plain, passing some low ridges of limestone rock, one of which, called Gwánkúh, has the echo mentioned by Pottinger. A few miles further we halted for breakfast at a garden containing, besides the usual date-palms, rose bushes, apple, apricot, and pomegranate trees. The sight of the roses was hailed by the Persians as a happy omen on this their great national fête day, presaging a fortunate issue to the journey, and a safe return to Irán. In the afternoon we continued our march, passing the villages of Ziárat, Aspích, and Muhammadi, before arriving at the principal place, and residence of the chief, called simply Kala'h[1], 'the fort,' opposite the gate of which the tents were pitched.

Dízak consists of a group of half a dozen villages scattered along the north bank of an affluent of the Máshkíd, flowing from the lofty plateau of Sarhad, whose only permanently inhabited spot, Washt, is said to be six days' journey from Dízak. Considerable groves of palm-trees lie between the villages of Dízak and the river, interspersed with carefully-tended fields neatly fenced with stone. This district, the richest in north-western Balúchistán, has been paying tribute to Persia for upwards of thirty years, but had not been brought thoroughly under subjection till some six or seven years before our visit, when Ibráhím Khán reduced the chiefs to submission, freeing them in return from the attacks of their enemies, the Khárán Núshírwánís. Besides Kalagán and Jálk, personal appanages of the chief, Sib, Magas, Bampúsht, and Irafshán are subject to his authority, which thus extends over a third of Persian Balúchistán.

The land-tax, levied on the whole district by the Persians, amounts, I was told, to no more than 1000 tomans of five rupees each. Of this Jálk and Kalagán contribute 200, Bampúsht, Irafshán, Sib, and Magas 100 each, leaving 400 as the contribution of Dízak and its dependent villages, Paskúh, Dehak, and others. Supposing the remaining two districts under their native chiefs, Geh and Sarbáz, each to produce an equal amount, we arrive at a total of £1500 a year as the land-tax of Balúchistán, excluding the Bampúr valley, farmed by

---

[1] Pottinger calls it Gull, evidently the same word as Kal'ah, which is twisted into many forms in Balúchistán. Besides Kalát and its diminutive Kalátak, we find Kalag, i.e. Kal'ahak, 'little fort,' whence Kalagén, the little forts.

the governor himself, where the produce is stored for the consumption of the troops. This is marvellously little considering the extent of the country, 50,000 square miles, and the apparently flourishing condition of some of it. It would amount to no more, according to such statistics of the population of individual places as I was able to collect, than one shilling per head per family. It must, however, be remembered that this tax is payable in coin, only obtainable by the sale of part of the scanty produce on the coast; also, that the Persians keep no permanent officials and no garrisons in these outlying districts, which are under the entire authority of their hereditary chiefs.

In Pottinger's time a certain Mihráb Khán held all the country from Dízak to Basmán, and his revenue was stated to amount to £56,250 a year, about the same amount as the whole land revenue of the wealthy province of Fars at the same period, as given by Macdonald Kinneir. Pottinger's informant must, I think, have multiplied by ten at least.

During our stay at Dízak I exchanged visits with Diláwar Khán, the chief, a dull heavy-looking man of forty. He received me in a wretched mud-plastered room over the gate of the fort. Trays of hot wheaten cakes fried in butter, very rich, but palatable, with spiced dates, were brought in. Contrary to custom on such missions, I had no presents to bestow, and paid for all services, past and future, in hard coin; in my opinion a better plan for both donor and recipient, except in cases where the rank of the latter would make the offer of money an insult. In this case, having travelled so long in Diláwar Khán's country, I thought it incumbent on me to give him something, so presented him with a silver hunting-watch of my own. He showed some anxiety about his inability to offer me anything of equal value in return, so I asked for one of the Balúch cloaks, woven in his own house, a very good specimen of which was accordingly sent to my tent.

On the occasion of the chief's visit to me I made particular enquiries as to the geographical extent and meaning of the name Makrán, applied by Pottinger to all Balúchistán west of the Khárán desert. The Dízak people scouted the idea of their country being in Makrán, which they said does not extend north of the water-parting along the crest of the Bampúsht hills. This would bring Irafshán and Sarbáz into Makrán; but men from the former place declared that Makrán is limited by the scarp of the plateau north of the Kej valley and its prolongation east and west. Diláwar Khán said that his country formed properly part of Sarawán, a term limited on maps to the elevation on the eastern side of the Khárán desert on the west, corresponding to the Dízak plateau.

As to the derivation of the term Makrán, no one seemed to know or care anything. Dean Vincent, in the 'Voyage of Nearchus,' says the word is derived from the Mehrán or Indus; and rightly adds that it is confined to the country near the coast. The most obvious derivation, and one that appears to have the authority of history to back it, is 'Máhi-khorán,' fish-eaters—'Ichthyophagi,' as the historians of Alexander's march tell us the people of the coast were called. Against this view philologists, I believe, state that the guttural *kh* never degenerates into the simple *k*. Possibly not; but the modern Balúch is as incapable of pronouncing the guttural Arabic *kh* as is the Turk of Constantinople, though the inability takes a different form. One leaves out the *h*, the other the *k*. Thus the common words, *khánúm*, a lady, *khúrmá*, a date, become *hánúm*, *húrmá* in Turkey, and *kánúm*, *kúrmá* in Balúchistán. This peculiarity of pronunciation struck me forcibly at the time, many years passed in Persia having habituated my ear to the full force of the guttural; and on returning to England, I was glad to find the same observation had been made by an intelligent native traveller, Hajji Abdun Nabi, sent by Major Leach, resident at Kalát, to explore Balúchistán in 1839, and whose experiences were published by that officer in the Journal of the Asiatic Society.

Rústam Khán, the part owner of Isfandak, came in one day from his village of Sarjo, a few miles off, and called to see me. His grandfather was an emigrant from Afghánistán, and he is descended, on the mother's side, from Mihráb Khán. Both in person and manner Rústam Khán was worthy of his name. His face was eminently handsome, and his manner as good as that of a well-bred Persian. Among other things he told me that all the chiefs, on both sides of the frontiers, north and east, are careful to connect themselves by marriage, so that if one chances to be slain in a foray, it may, if necessary, be treated as a mere family quarrel, not involving a blood-feud. I also asked him about the Loories, a tribe of gypsies mentioned by Pottinger as having murdered the chief of Magas and his family, under circumstances of peculiar atrocity, just before his arrival, and as being addicted to all sorts of evil-doing. Rústam Khán's head servant, an elderly man who had followed him into the tent, and stood, according to custom, by his master's chair, interrupted me with an exclamation of astonishment at the accuracy of my information. It appeared that his grandfather was chief of the Loories on the occasion of the murder of the Magas chief; since which some of the tribe had returned to Persia, and the rest become absorbed in the population of Dízak, by whom the eccentricities of their forefathers had been forgotten. The old man was evidently much displeased at my raking up old stories, and his indignation gave rise to a good deal of chaff among the others.

On the 24th we started off the Indians to Gwádar, their baggage and our superfluous tents accompanying them on donkeys, the whole caravan being in charge of a trustworthy servant of Diláwar Khán, who undertook to hand them over safe and sound to Captain Miles. They travelled by the direct road through Irafshán, and reached Gwádar in safety in twelve days. The next day we started for Bampúr. For two miles the road lay west across a sandy plain to the village of Sarjo, after leaving which we crossed the dry bed of the river and followed that of another torrent, smaller but with plenty of water, through dreary hills skirting the great limestone rocks of the Dízak range. Crossing the water-parting, we descended by a rather steep pass to a group of palms in some long grass at a gap in the limestone ridge, here very low. Below was a wide nullah, on whose bank we camped. The place, which has no permanent habitation, is called Áb-patán. Here, for the first time since leaving the banks of the Dashtiyari river at Báhú Kalát, we heard the well-known call of the francolin partridge. Our present camel-drivers, though in other respects their conduct was unexceptionable, had a habit of grazing their camels on the road, so that, even though we started early, the baggage rarely got in till dark. With former camel-drivers our tribulation had been the impossibility of getting them off in the morning till their camels had had a three hours' graze. Either arrangement involved spending the heat of the day in the sun, and making absurdly short marches. With every effort to push them on, we seldom got more than twelve miles a day out of the camel-drivers. Under these circumstances it was most provoking to be told, when enquiring the distance to any place, 'It would take you Farangís ten days to go, because you march so slowly: we Balúchís do it in four or five.'

Seven miles across a barren stony plain sloping to the south-west brought us the next morning to Súrán, a group of three villages built close together in thick groves of palms. The principal village gives its name to the whole place; the other two are called Pogí and Kalakí. The inhabitants are mostly Arbábís, undersized, ugly, and loquacious as usual. After breakfast, the sky being cloudy, we walked towards the stream which irrigates Súrán and the village of Sib, some half-a-dozen miles lower down. We found it half a mile from the villages, the intervening space being covered with magnificent crops of wheat and barley, manured I noticed with a compost of dry tamarisk leaves and camel dung. The stream was about thirty yards across, but only a few inches deep, running slowly between very low banks. We were told that it never entirely fails, in confirmation of which we shot a common water-hen, not previously seen in Balúchistán. Here too, for the first time, was noticed the true camel-thorn of Persia. I am no botanist, but I cannot help thinking that several plants are known by this name.

Our march the following day led through low hills, having the now regular direction north-west and south-east, over two insignificant passes, to the dry bed of a torrent called Khaur-i-chahár-rúkán. Water was obtained by digging holes a couple of feet deep in the torrent-bed, which was covered with pretty thick grass and tamarisk. The word Khaur seems universally applied in Balúchistán to any sort of water-course. Its proper meaning is creek, which word is, I believe, used in the same way in North America and Australia. The ravines called Khaur in upper Balúchistán would be called Wádí by Arabs.

The direction of the road the next day (March 28th) was 15° south of west, and it lay for the first four miles through low hills. After this was a steep descent, probably that mentioned by Pottinger as being hollowed out of the rock and defensible by a handful of men against an army. The road has been lately improved by Ibráhím Khán, and now presents no formidable difficulties. Below this pass was a good deal of tamarisk jungle, where we breakfasted. The tamarisk is here of two sorts, long and short leaved; the latter was in full flower. Three miles further we passed Koshán, a tiny square tower with a little cultivation, due to a pleasant brook running from the north-west. We were now on a wide plain sloping gently to the south-east, and better clothed with vegetation than usual. To our right front rose a lofty and imposing range of mountains with steep rugged sides and vividly tinted rocks. This was the Kúh-i-Birg[1]. Nearer us were low isolated hills.

[1] Possibly Kúh-i-burj, but more probably a contraction of Kúh-i-búzúrg.

A slight descent brought us opposite Kaimagár, a small date-grove half a mile to the east, after which the road gradually ascended towards Magas, a small fort surrounded by huts and extensive date-groves.

Pasand Khán the chief came out on foot to meet us, a fine-looking man over six feet high. He is one of the most noted warriors and thieves in Balúchistán, and told the Sarhang and myself that we had quite spoilt his trade by settling the frontier. He had been unable for some time to *chapáo*[1] villages on the Persian side for fear of Ibráhím Khán, but had hitherto been able to indulge his taste for murder and robbery at the expense of the outlying tribes across the border who were not recognised as belonging to any-one. This little game was now stopped by order.

The corn crops of Magas were the latest we had seen, the plain being 4200 feet above the sea, and the date-trees had suffered more severely from the frost than those of Súrán and Dízak. The past winter had been one of unexampled severity; snow having fallen for the first time in the memory of man all over the Máshkíd plateau. Numbers of date-trees had apparently perished, but the people said the greater number would revive the next spring. In the evening I took an altitude of the Kúh-i-Birg, and found the nearest high peak to be 4000 feet above Magas.

We crossed the plain the next morning, and after ten miles entered a dry torrent-bed among low hills, up which we rode for five miles. The plain was covered with low bushes, and here and there a few acacias and tamarisks. Our camp was pitched in a place called 'Sar-i-pahárú,' 'púhrá,' or 'fahraj,' marking the commencement of the Bampúr district of which Páharú, Púhrá, or Fahraj, is a sub-division. Immense quantities of asafœtida and wild rhubarb grew around. The use of neither seemed known to the natives. This was the last place where we saw asafœtida, and the first where we saw rhubarb. About Shíráz and Karmán the latter is extensively eaten as a relish raw with salt, never cooked with sugar as in England. It is not cultivated in gardens, but the rhubarb gatherers go to the hills as soon as the snow is off the ground, and heap up earth round the young plants, the stalks of which are thus properly blanched. The rhubarb of Shíráz is whiter and more tender than any I have tasted in England.

The night we spent at Sar-i-fahraj was bitterly cold, and the next morning a piercing north wind blew, which made us glad to walk the

---

[1] Anglicè, *harry*.

first few miles of the road. Three miles from camp we came upon the edge of the plateau. We were now exactly at the angle formed by the meeting of the plateau of Balúchistán with the great Khúrasán range, which divides the deserts of central Persia from the Helmand valley, and whose furthest extension south we had just crossed. All ranges on our right front had a north-west, all to our left front a west-south-west direction. The eastern angle, far less clearly defined, is in the Siáneh Kúh, where we crossed them by the Bringinán pass. Right and left of us were lofty limestone crags, and some twelve miles in front a high isolated conical peak was pointed out as the Kúh-i-Homand, marked by Lovett on his map of the year before. It does not, however, stand on, but quite clear of the scarp, and is drained entirely into the Bampúr river. The road now descended a ravine running west, with springs of water rising amid high and thick grass in many side clefts, but no running stream. Further on the ravine widened and turned north, having a stony bed with thick tamarisk jungle at intervals. The tents, which did not get in till dark, were pitched on a level plot of turf, at the foot of lofty limestone hills called the Kúh-i-Ispidán. These I climbed the next morning while the camels were being loaded, in the hope of seeing the Basmán mountain, a high conical peak beyond Bampúr. It was not visible, though it ought to be in clear weather. The sides of the hills were clad with the many aromatic plants characteristic of the Persian mountain Flora.

For seventeen miles the road lay down the bed of the Ispidán ravine, which varied from a mile to a quarter of a mile in width, and was filled with pretty thick jungle of tamarisk and acacia. The path then turned southwards through low igneous rocks, joining the ravine again a couple of miles further on. The latter here separates into many arms, one of which we followed to Haftar, or Aptar, a neat fort and village with large date-groves and corn-fields. None of our camels being up we accepted the Sarhang's offer of tea and *kaliáns*, while waiting for dinner. Here I found, to my great grief, that a small bull-terrier, the faithful companion of many thousand miles of travel, was missing. He had stopped to rest in the shade, or to drink, and had not been seen since. I rode back twenty miles the next day, and offered a large reward to any one who would bring the dog to Bampúr, but without effect. He was probably carried off by a leopard, said to be very numerous in the Isfidán ravine.

The next day's march was twelve miles only, over a shingly plain to Púhrá, a large village with abundance of water. This is the place supposed by geographers to have been the identical Púra mentioned by the historians of Alexander as the capital of Gadrosia, and the spot in which he was joined by Stasanor and Phrataphernes from the upper provinces with a convoy of provisions, when the army proceeded to Karmania, where they met Nearchus, who had left the fleet at the mouth of the Mináb river. The locality of this last meeting is identified by Dean Vincent, on very clear evidence, with Jírúft, which is not however, as he supposes, a town, but a district.

He therefore places Púra, which had then never been visited, a degree due east of Jírúft, that being the distance travelled by Alexander between the two places. But actually they are three degrees of longitude and one of latitude apart, or two hundred miles instead of a little over sixty, a fact which would seem to dispose at once of the claim of Púhrá to have been the site of the ancient capital of Gadrosia. Moreover, there are no ruins in the neighbourhood.

A clue to the real site of Alexander's halting-place is found in Dean Vincent's pages, which, added to a piece of geographical information obtained by Sir Frederic Goldsmid's party on their march to Sistán, places the question to my mind beyond a doubt.

The Dean says, 'One circumstance, however, must not be omitted, which is, that the position of Géroft depending on the Gadrosian Púra or Phoreg, it is remarkable that the Nubian geographer places Phoreg at the commencement of the great desert which extends to Segestán, and at 210 miles from the capital of that province.' In another place he says that he 'cannot account for the sixty days attributed to this march through Gadrosia, viz. 480 miles.' Again, he notices that D'Anville writes 'Fahrag, Fohreg, Pohreg, Puhreg, Puregh, and Pureh,' a variety of spelling which agrees with my own experience.

Now Sir Frederic Goldsmid, marching from Bam to Sistán, passed, about twenty miles north of Rigán in Narmashír, extensive ruins, called Fahraj. This is clearly the place referred to by the Nubian geographer, being on the edge of the great Karmán desert, and about 200 miles from Sistán. It is also 160 miles further from India than Púhrá near Bampúr, and therefore gets over the Dean's sixty days' difficulty; and, finally, is exactly at the right distance from the Jírúft plain. The only difficulty, if difficulty it be, in identifying this Fahraj as the Púra of the Greeks, is the consequent extension of the limits of ancient Gadrosia beyond Balúchistán over Narmashír.

In the early part of his march through Balúchistán, Alexander must, I think, have been deceived by his guides, who seem to have kept him exactly at that distance from the coast where there is least water. Had he followed the Kej valley, the natural road from the Indus to western Balúchistán, he would have found abundant water. It would certainly puzzle a Craterus now-a-days to march his elephants and heavy baggage from the Helmand to Narmashír; but there is every reason to suppose that part of Persia to have been far better populated and better watered than it is at present; and if the canal from the Helmand to Zirreh was then opened, he could have crossed the desert much lower down than Sir Frederic Goldsmid's party, where it is comparatively narrow.

To return to our journey. We were now 2000 feet below the Magas plain, and about the same altitude above the sea-level. Though the nights were still cool, the sun was getting too powerful to make midday marching pleasant. This morning (April 2) we started early, intending to breakfast half-way and halt till the evening, both to avoid the heat and make a formal entry into Bampúr, where the governor, Ibráhím Khán, had lately returned from a successful attack on the Arab port of Cháhbár, the last spot on the southern coast of Persia to retain its independence of the authority of the Sháh.

A couple of hours' ride brought us to Ab-band (the dam), a few huts by the side of a delightful stream fringed with thick wood, where a weir has been thrown across to supply the first irrigation channel. At four we started again. The road lay through sparse jungle over a sandy plain. Two miles out of Bampúr we met Ibráhím Khán's *mírakhor*[1], with a led horse for my use. A little further the governor's nephew, with an escort of thirty or forty horsemen, forming the usual *istikbál*, came in sight and accompanied us to the fort, under which we found our tents pitched in a walled garden.

The usual difficulty in obtaining camels detained us five days at Bampúr, a delay which would not have been unpleasant but for the climate, the most disagreeable I have ever felt. The highly-irrigated land to the south and the burning sandy desert to the north cause sudden changes of temperature, and alternations from intense dryness to complete saturation, that make Bampúr a by-word for unhealthiness

---

[1] Anglicè, *master of the horse;* literally, *head of the manger,* perhaps the most honourable position in a Persian household.

even in Balúchistán. The first night of our stay the thermometer did not fall below 58°; the next night it was 50°; the third 60°; the fourth 62°; and the fifth 48°. Until a year or two before our visit the garrison consisted of a battalion of infantry from northern Persia. Although relieved every year, half the strength died of fever each season. The consequence was something very like mutiny; and the governor of Karmán at last obtained permission from the Sháh to raise a local regiment of two battalions in Bam-Narmashír to garrison that province and Balúchistán. Though physically inferior to the sturdy Turk of Adarbaiján, as good material for infantry as any in Asia, the men seemed a hardy lot; and though they dislike military service, do not suffer much from the Bampúr climate.

Bampúr (Bam-putr, the son of, or lesser Bam) consists at present of a small fort on the first of a line of sand-hills stretching parallel to the river, and sheltering the fertile strip in its vicinity from the sand of the desert. These hills are caused by a bed of clay which here crops out and intercepts the sand carried before the prevailing north-west wind. No offer of visiting the fort was made to me, but the Sarhang drew a plan of it which he showed me: of the wonderful interior staircase, mentioned by Pottinger, he saw no trace. It has possibly fallen in, as the whole fort has been recently rebuilt, but without flanking defences. At one side of the fort stretch the gardens in which our tents were pitched, and on the other eighty or a hundred palm-leaf huts, occupied by the soldiers and a few Balúchís levied from the neighbouring tribes for military duty. From the fort to the river a couple of miles south, and for many miles on either hand, stretched a vast sheet of wheat and barley now just in ear. This is cultivated by Balúchís, who receive a per-centage for their labour, the rest being stored for the food of the troops.

The morning after our arrival the old Yáwar and Ibráhím Súltán called, nominally to congratulate us and themselves on the successful termination of our frontier labours. I saw that there was something else on their minds, and remarked to Blanford that they had come to find out diplomatically whether I was going to call on Ibráhím Khán the governor (or, as he is generally called here, the Sartip, from his military rank), or whether I expected him to call on me first. Actually I did not care who made the first visit, not being perhaps so particular in these matters as the traditions of European diplomacy in Persia would insist on. A minute observance of every detail of Oriental etiquette, all important, no doubt, at the beginning of the century, is now rather out of date. Persians themselves are not so careful on these points as they were (for instance, the use of an elaborate scale of turgid compliments in correspondence has quite ceased). Although it does not do to put up with an impertinence, I know that I lost more than I gained in my early days in Persia by being always on the look out for covert insults. Such, when they occur, are generally better parried by a joke or by absolutely ignoring them and waiting an opportunity of a return in kind, than by taking angry notice of them. Success with Orientals depends a great deal more upon how you treat them, than how they treat you. The great thing is to hit the happy medium between over familiarity and restraint. Frenchmen, who perhaps are more successful in gaining the confidence of Orientals than any other nation, incline too much to the first error, we Englishmen to the last[1]. But this is a digression. Just as I anticipated, Ibráhím Súltán, on getting up to take leave, said that his uncle, the Sartip, proposed to call on me in the afternoon.

About half-past five he made his appearance, and we sat outside in the shade and drank tea. The redoubtable ruler of Bam-Narmashír and Balúchistán is a short punchy man, of any age from forty-five to sixty, with a full and well-dyed beard, and small sharp eye. He speaks Persian with the broad southern twang, and uses provincialisms not very easy to understand by any one accustomed only to the conversation of educated men. My experience in out-of-the-way parts of Fars, however, enabled me to get on with him pretty well, but our conversation was confined to generalities, and the examination of fire-arms. To our breechloaders he made the usual objection of the difficulty of obtaining cartridges. There seemed nothing in his talk or in his face to indicate the really superior man he must be, not only as having risen to his present position by sheer merit, unaided by money or

[1] The most successful European I have ever seen in obtaining the respect and friendship of Persians was the late Quarter-Master-Sergeant David Bower of the Royal Engineers. In spite of the disadvantages of social position, for they knew perfectly well that he was but a non-commissioned officer, added to a somewhat quick temper, his genial manners gained him the heart of every Persian he came in contact with, from the royal princes who governed Shíráz and the haughty chiefs of the wandering tribes of Fars, to the humble *sarbáz* and villagers who formed our working parties on the telegraph. After ten years of admirable service in Persia he died, a victim to his own philanthropy, of typhus fever, caught while he was voluntarily engaged in the distribution of alms, collected among the European community of Tehrán, to the sufferers from the famine of 1870-72.

interest, but as having reduced one of the most turbulent countries in Asia to a state of order and tranquillity, comparing favourably not only with most of his own country but with many native states further east. Lucky would it be for his people and ours on the Sind frontier, if His Highness Khúdadád of Kalát had Ibráhím Khán's head on his shoulders.

Nevertheless this doughty warrior caught a Tartar some few months before our arrival. Having received intelligence of a raid of Helmand Balúchís on some outlying villages of Narmashír, Ibráhím Khán made a forced march to intercept them on their retreat in a well-known pass in the mountains between the desert and Sistán. Unluckily they were beforehand with him, occupied the pass in force, and, after firing a volley, fell on the Persians sword in hand, killed twelve *sarbáz*[1] and the Sartip's horse, and wounded twenty more men. The rest got on a hill and beat them off, but the Balúchís carried off 150 camels, with all the Persian baggage and spare ammunition.

The next day I paid the Sartip a return visit. He would not let me into the fort where he lives, but received me in a miserable little room on one side of a stable, underneath it. Our conversation was mostly on camels, which he could not promise us for four days more.

These we spent not unpleasantly, but for the heat, in collecting specimens, principally about the river, where the shade and water offered attractions to birds which considerably increased our collections. More unpleasant animals, too, were disagreeably common; tarantulas and scorpions of all sizes and colours were constantly found about the tents, and more than one of the servants was stung by the latter.

---

[1] Infantry soldiers.

CHAPTER V.

Bampúr to Karmán.

THE road from Bampúr to Rigán, the first village of Narmashír, presents little of interest. For the first five marches it continues in the Bampúr valley, which forms one with that of Rúdbár and Jirúft. The northern side of this is clad with acacia jungle, the south is a sandy desert intervening between the mountains of Bashakird and the Bampúr and Rúdbár rivers. These meet at a place called, according to Keith Abbott, Jaz-morián, but whether their flood-waters escape thence to the sea or are lost in the sand is uncertain. Major Lovett heard the former; my informants stated the latter.

Our first halting-place was near Kúcháhgardán, a small village belonging to Bampúr, a mile north of the river, whose waters are here nearly exhausted by the sandy bed and by irrigation. Immense quantities of drift-wood showed the force and frequency of floods. Here, for the first time, we saw the high conical peak of the Básmán hill, miscalled on maps the Kúh-i-Nausháda, or mountain of Salammoniac, the name of a much loftier hill further east covered with constant snow, and abounding in sulphur, as well as the mineral from which it takes its name, and having hot springs. It is probably, like Damávand, a dormant volcano, and the Básmán hill an extinct one. The proper name of this latter is the Meh-kúh, or Mehzárkúh, the misty or cloud-producing.

The next day's march led away from the river across a level plain of hard sand, bearing a few scattered tamarisks and acacias, and many thorn-bushes, like what is called the milk-bush in India, but here almost a tree, bearing a dull scarlet blossom. We passed a large flight of the European bee-eater feeding on yellow locusts, of which multitudes were about, apparently breeding. Twenty miles from Kúcháhgardán we camped at a group of wells called Cháh-shúr, the 'bitter well,' but the water, though undrinkably foul till the well was cleared, was better than might have been expected from the name. The following morning brought us to Kalánzao after a five-and-twenty mile ride through similar country. Here the road to Rúdbár turns off, and that from Geh through the Fanoch pass joins in. On the road we met a family of Balúchís journeying westwards, the two women riding on a single bullock, an uncommon sight in western Asia. In south Persia Iliáts of Kurdish descent are the only ox-riders.

This sandy valley abounds in reptiles and noxious insects. Our lights at night attracted winged creatures innumerable; among them, one of singular appearance, a delicate pale-green ephemerio, whose posterior wings were lengthened into the form of a racket, like the tail of the curious Drongo shrike of the sub-Himalayan forests. I had once seen the same insect in the oak forests of Fars. At Kalánzao the servants caught a tarantula of enormous size, two and one-eighth inches in length from the tip of the jaws to the end of the body, a hideous brute. Echis vipers were frequently found about the tents. Persians believe the flesh of an animal killed by snake-poison to possess equally deadly qualities with the original venom. We had experimented with an echis on a fowl, which died, if I remember rightly, in about five minutes. Muhammad Husain Beg, my old steward, told one of the *farashes* to bury it, that no other creature might come to harm by eating it; but immediately changed his mind and said, 'No! throw it out in the plain, that one of those sons of burntfathers, the jackals'—which were numerous and bold—'may find it and get his business in this world finished.'

The fourth halting-place on the Bam road is Ladi, a well in a thick jungle. To-day we saw far away in the north-west the snowy peaks of the Persian hills.

The next day we turned northwards in the direction of the low hills which had skirted our road from Bampúr at a considerable distance. Sixteen miles across a stony plain of limestone and trap pebbles brought us to Khúsrín, a marshy spring in a torrent-bed, elsewhere dry, but filled with thick tamarisk jungle. We were now at the entrance of a wilderness of barren hills of every conceivable form and colour, but of inconsiderable height. Beyond them lay the plain of Narmashír, to which it took us four days to cross. South of the sacred city of Kúm, ninety miles from Tehrán, a chain of lofty hills rises ten thousand feet above the desert, and stretches south-east right across Persia, dividing the narrower valleys of the west from the vast deserts of the central plateau. The continuous character of this range as far as Karmán was first pointed out by Khanikoff, though indistinctly shown on *his* map, and not at all on others. It is crossed by the traveller from Isfahán to Tehrán, near the pretty village of Kohrúd, by a pass 9000 feet above the sea. On the Yazd Isfahán road an easier passage traverses it near Kúhpá. West of Yazd its peaks are very lofty. Further south it diminishes in height. Where we crossed it a month later, by the Khán-i-Surkh pass between Mashísh and Saidábád, there are no high peaks, though the water-parting is 8500 feet above the sea. South of Karmán this long range attains its greatest elevation, many summits being from fourteen to fifteen thousand feet high, and covered with eternal snow. It is singular that this, the best defined chain in Persia, with the exception of the Albúrz, should have so long escaped recognition. So well marked indeed is it, that the road from Kúm through Yazd and Karmán to Narmashír, a distance of 600 miles, lies in a single valley along its eastern declivity.

The mass of volcanic hills that we were now about to cross connects the southern extremity of the chain just described (which, for want of a better name, may be called the Kohrúd range) with the great Khúrasán plateau, whose lower end we had crossed between Jálk and Bampúr. Though both have a direction east of south, their axes are inclined at a considerable angle, being 400 miles apart at their northern and 100 only at their southern ends. Between them and the Albúrz to the north is included that central depression of the Persian plateau, called on maps the great eastern desert of Persia, or the Dariá-i-Kabír and desert of Lút. Barren and inhospitable as this region doubtless is, it contains many pleasant oases, and is, moreover, furrowed by many minor ridges parallel to the great outer ranges.

Our first march after quitting the Bampúr plain at Khusrín led through low hills of trap and trachyte for fifteen miles to Gwám-i-Talab Kháni, the lote-tree of Talab Khán, passing Garambigáh, the usual halting-place at the tenth mile. The road was tolerably easy, and passable for guns. The next day (April 14th) brought us to Giranríg, the heavy sand, after fifteen miles of very stony road leading up and across torrents flowing south-west between high flat-topped hills. The most prominent is called the Takht-i-Nádír. Our third march brought us to Cháh Kambar, the first place in Narmashír, and therefore out of Balúchistán, on which no one in camp regretted having turned his back. A valley without outlet, covering some twenty square miles, and 3850 feet above the sea, occupies the summit of the pass. Its drainage collects in a sandy depression at the north-western end, called the Dag-i-Farhád. It was dry when we crossed it. Just beyond, an easy pass, named Saifu-d-dín, marks the frontier of Persia proper. From the summit of this we had a magnificent view of the snow-clad peaks to the west.

Descending the pass by a good road we crossed a plain, terminating in a narrow valley leading north. The tents were pitched by a well of tolerable water named Cháh Kambar. Near us was a camp of Balúchís, the first people, except travellers, seen since Kúchahgardán.

The usual halting-place further on is Ab-i-garm, ten miles from Cháh Kambar, the road leading through a marshy valley bounded by low hills of volcanic ash, more than one of whose peaks contained a small crater. But the unusual copiousness of winter rains enabled us to find water five miles further on in the bed of the little river Konar-nái, a clear stream running over granite pebbles along the skirt of the hills from the Sháh-Sowárán range to the west. The march throughout from Cháh Kambar was most disagreeable from the innumerable swarms of gadflies, sandflies, and mosquitos that rose from the swamp. We were now clear of the hills, and before us stretched the great desert of Eastern Persia. To the west rose the rounded hills of Sháh-Sowárán, beyond which rose peak after peak of the snow-clad mountains of Jamal-báriz[1]. Behind us to the south lay the irregular hills we had passed, which were continued, as far as the eye could reach, in a north-easterly direction.

The next morning was dull and overcast, threatening rain. The road lay due north across a stony plain. Sandflies and other insect pests annoyed men and horses terribly till eight o'clock, when a breeze sprang up and they disappeared. A few days before I had shot, on the other side of the hills near Khúsrín, a specimen of the rare and curious Uromastix lizard, described on page 337, vol. ii. To-day we saw another, sitting in a semi-erect posture outside its hole, looking not unlike and almost as big as a rabbit. On seeing us it scuttled into

[1] Corrupted from the Arabic, Jabal-bárida, 'the cold hills.'

the burrow, but Blanford, nothing daunted, set to work to dig it out, with no better implement than his geological hammer. After nearly an hour's labour, the lizard's retreat was so far laid open that the tip of his tail could be felt with the fingers. Being the smallest-handed of the party I then managed to slip a noose made with a leather shoe-string round the tail and to draw it tight over the spiny tubercles. A steady pull soon brought out our friend, a magnificent specimen. We might however have spared the labour, as further on we saw and shot several others. In spite of his formidable looks, which make him quite a miniature of the mighty saurians of antediluvian times, this lizard is quite harmless. The Persian name is Búz-míjí, or goatsucker, from a settled habit of bleating like a kid to attract the she-goats, whose teats it then sucks.

Fourteen miles from the Konar-nái the path entered a jungle of tamarisk and acacia, interspersed with magnificent crops of wheat and barley and occasional swamps. Here the Katkhuda (head man) of Rígán, with a Súltán (captain) commanding the little garrison, met us with a few horsemen, and led the way to the village. They stated that a courier from the Sistán Boundary Commission camp had passed Rígán six days before *en route* to Karmán, with information that Sir Frederic Goldsmid had left Sistán to return to Tehrán *viâ* Khúrasán; leaving Major Smith to complete the survey. This latter proved false.

Rígán is a neat little mud-built fort in the Persian style, enclosing the villagers' houses, not surrounded by them as in Balúchistán. The people, like all Narmashírís we saw, are thoroughly Persian in dress and manner. We particularly noticed that the women wore wide petticoat trousers instead of the loose Arab shirt universal further east. The direct road from Bampúr through Basmán, followed by Pottinger, joins the main road here. It is considerably shorter and less hilly than the one by which we came; but impracticable for large caravans from want of water. Either the site of the fort of Rígán has been changed or its dimensions contracted since Pottinger's time, as it is now less than half the size he describes.

A raid of Khárán Núshírwánís and Nál Mamasanís is said to be expected through Sarhad, and troops have been sent to the outlying villages of Narmashír. This turned out to be a false alarm, but Ibráhím Khán must have hard work to keep out his troublesome neighbours to the east.

The next morning (April 18th) we marched sixteen miles to Búrj-i-Muhammad Khán, or Búrj-i-Mírza Húsain, a small walled village with a neat round tower. On the way we passed two villages close together, Sangábád and Gumbokí. The country is generally cultivated, the crops principally wheat and barley, though much henna and tobacco is grown later on. The day was cloudy, with an occasional sprinkling of rain, very refreshing after the arid weather of the last week. A reminder of being on Persian soil was to-day furnished by the Katkhuda coming to the tents to ask for brandy for a sick woman—the usual excuse—and offering to sell a horse. Further evidences of civilisation were offered by the presence about the villages of darvishes and cats. The former have been driven into this out-of-the-way region by its comparative cheapness during the famine. The cats, I suppose, are aboriginal. It is curious that we saw none in Balúchistán. Apropos of cats it may be remarked that the long-haired variety, known in Europe as Persian, and in Persia as 'búrák,' is confined to particular parts of the country, notably to Isfahán, whence a considerable number are annually exported to India by horse-dealers, the cats travelling down to the coast on the horses' backs. Most of those seen in Europe come from Angora, in Asia Minor. As far as my experience goes, the Persian cat has a better tail and ruff, the Angora cat longer body-hair. I think too that the former has a longer pencil of hair on the ears than any other domestic breed. It is singular for its want of that fear of strange localities which is so marked a characteristic of the race generally. I have several times taken cats from Isfahán to other towns, and let them out of their cages at the daily halting-places, whether tent, post-house, or caravansarai, without their showing any signs of alarm at the strange place.

Seventeen miles the next morning along a good road, through cultivation and sparse jungle, brought us to Jamáli, a small village among several others on the south bank of a marshy river running between steep cliffs to the north-east. Further up this stream is Kúrúk, the largest village in Narmashír, and some miles down it Fahraj, mentioned in the last chapter as the ancient capital of Gadrosia. From Jamáli there was a magnificent view of the snowy hills, of which there are here two ranges, that nearest us being slightly lower than the other. The valley between the two is called Paskúh, i.e. 'behind the hills.' This fashion of naming districts from their position with reference to the neighbouring mountains has led to a very odd mistake occurring more than once in the best maps of Persia. Finding a district lying along the base of a range named by a traveller Púsht-i-Kúh, i.e. 'back of the hills,' the compiler in England, knowing that *kúh* means a hill, but knowing nothing more of Persian, imagines *púsht* to be the name of the hills, and transfers the title from their base to their summit. A second compiler, copying the first, improves upon his model by translating *kúh* into range; and we then have Púshtí Range, a misnomer that may be found in more than one place on any map of Persia.

From Jamáli the old Yáwar pointed out a distant snowy peak, barely visible above the horizon to the north-west, which he said was the Kúh Hazár, near which our route would lie six marches further, and which can be seen from the road to Shíráz, a long way on the other side of Karmán.

The next morning (April 20th) was cloudy and cool. The road, after passing the river, already nearly dry, led north-west across the plain for a couple of miles, and then traversed a swamp for four more; after which it lay through a gravelly desert sloping upwards to a range of low-peaked hills to the north. After eighteen miles' march we turned abruptly to the north along the base of a line of ragged sandstone cliffs, thirty or forty feet high, and through large gardens of date-palms and pomegranates, interspersed with barley crops.

Here we found the camp pitched opposite a little Imámzádah. A fresh fall of snow on the hills had made the weather delightfully cool, and as we had but a three-and-a-half miles ride into Bam we did not start the next morning until long after our usual time.

A mile from the camp the *istikbál* met us, composed of no very distinguished individuals, nearly all the military swells being with Ibráhím Khán at Bampúr. Bam had been left by him in charge of the Lieut.-Colonel of his regiment and brother-in-law, Sulimán Khán. The escort conducted us to a semi-ruined house of sunburnt brick, opening on a large garden of date-palms and rose-bushes, with abundance of lettuces, which formed a welcome addition to our breakfast.

The next two days were rainy and cold, though the spring was far advanced, and Bam is only 3000 feet above the sea. It can hardly be called a town, being a mere collection of isolated houses standing in gardens often sown with corn. The bazaar is small and poor. The fort, famous in Persian history, is a quadrangle about 500 by 400 yards, with a dry ditch, but no flanking defences. Within it is a citadel, crowned by a high narrow watch-tower. The population does not, I was told, exceed 2000 families. The neighbourhood is extremely fertile. A great deal of henna is exported from here, with a certain amount of indigo grown in Narmashír. It is however considered inferior in permanence to the Indian dye. We had the curiosity to visit a henna manufactory. The dried leaves and stems brought from the villages in bundles are ground to powder by a large stone roller driven by a camel.

After a couple of days' halt we left Bam on the 14th April. The road led north-west directly towards the Kúh Hazár, now a prominent object above the lower hills. The main range, of which the Kúh Hazár is an outlying spur, was nearly parallel to our course, which lay up a wide and gradually ascending valley between it and a nearer ridge of volcanic rocks, the Kúh Kafút, separating the Bam valley from the desert. On their further face is a district called Kashít. The valley, though even, is nowhere level, its surface being formed by the two gravel slopes at the bases of the bounding ranges, while the whole ascends gradually to the north-west. Ráyín, which we reached on the fifth day from Bam, is four thousand feet above that town, yet there is no perceptible rise between the two, except an insignificant cliff near Tahrúd.

The first halting-place was at Bídarán, six and a half miles off, a large village on the bank of the stream which, by the time it reaches Bam a mere torrent-bed, is here a respectable water-course. The next day we got over nine and a half miles only to Daharzin, a caravansarai, built in the desert by the late Wakíl-ul-Múlk, governor of Karmán, and supplied with water by a *kanát* from Sarbistán, sixteen miles off. It is difficult to admire too much the patient labour and ingenuity displayed in Persia in providing the first necessary of life in the most unlikely spots. The third march of seventeen miles brought us to Abárík (the slender rill), a small village on the bank of the Tahrúd river, which runs in many minute channels over a shingly bed. Near the village a rock of volcanic formation is crowned by a ruined fort, apparently of considerable antiquity, but about whose history I could learn nothing. One of the towers is square, an unusual construction in Persia. The hills to the right, hitherto irregular and of igneous rock, here give place to a lofty regular ridge of limestone running north-west and rising a couple of thousand feet above the plain. To the south-west, some five miles off, Sarbistán, doubtless a corruption of Sabzistán (the place of verdure), showed on the brown desert slope of the southern hills like an emerald on the neck of an Indian chief. From near it a spur of brightly-tinted cliffs projected northwards and contracted the valley in our front to its narrowest point.

Nine and a half miles the next morning brought us to the caravansarai of Khán-i-Khátún, a couple of miles north-east of the village of Tahrúd. Here the eastern road from Karmán to Bandar-Abbas branches off from the Bam road. This route—travelled throughout by Major Murdoch Smith in 1866, and partially by Mr. Keith Abbott before him, and Sir Frederic Goldsmid afterwards—leads through Sarbistán and the Deh Bakri pass over the Jamal-Báriz range to the plain of Jírúft. Colonel Yule, in a note to his 'Marco Polo,' thinks it probable that this was the road followed by that traveller from Karmán to the sea; but it will be seen that his description of the first five days from Karmán, through a *populous, fertile,* and *gradually ascending* country, does not at all answer to our experience of the road from Tahrúd to Karmán. I have little doubt that the ordinary caravan route from that city to the sea, which is open for ten months in every year, and often throughout the year, was the one followed by Marco Polo. No modern traveller is known to have traversed it; but the description I obtained of it from muleteers corresponds in every particular with that of the enterprising Venetian.

Heavy rain during the night soaked the tents, and made the ground slippery for camels, so that we did not get off the next morning (April 28th) till nearly noon. The distance to Ráyín was variously stated from five to ten farsakhs, which might be anything from twenty to forty miles. However, we were hard up for supplies, and determined to make a push for Ráyín in spite of the distance, our average marches from Bam having been hitherto ridiculously short.

The road soon quitted the little plain of Tahrúd, which is only an expansion of the bed of the river, and with a little more water would be a lake. It then ascended the bed of a little stream, here and there filled with tamarisk and jujube jungle. On the way we passed a small camp of wandering Balúchís, whose women ran out and offered us and the servants 'drík [1],' seeming quite astonished at being given a *krán*

[1] This is the common beverage of Persia, and is made by mixing sour curds with water.

or two in return. Immense numbers of sheep were being driven up to their summer pastures. They are much smaller than the sheep of Western Persia, and mostly white, the rarest colour elsewhere. Their wool is perhaps equal to any in the world, large quantities being exported to India for mixing with the down of the Kashmír goat, or perhaps for using alone, in the manufacture of the coarser kind of shawl. Their meat is remarkably fat and well flavoured, even for Persia, the land of good mutton. After riding eighteen miles we passed a small caravansarai, named Muhammadábád, in a patch of cultivation half a mile to the right of the road. Here we ought to have halted, but, seeing the trees of Ráyín on the horizon, we pushed on. A little way further we caught up a jovial-looking Persian on a donkey, accompanied by a boy on a pony. He announced himself as one of the *ghulams* (cavalry soldiers) quartered at Karmán, returning from collecting arrears of revenue, of which he had a considerable amount in specie in his saddlebags. This spoke volumes for the pacific character of the country, or the efficacy of the Wakíl-ul-Múlk's police. Further west or north he would have been robbed, probably by the people whom he had been squeezing, before he had gone ten miles. He declared we had three good *farsakhs* to ride to Ráyín, an estimate which was corroborated by the Yáwar and Súltán, who just then caught us up. This seemed incredible. The trees of the village were not only distinctly outlined against the now reddening western sky, but a fir-tree at one end and a clump of planes at the other were clearly distinguishable. Blanford, as good a judge of distance as I know, was convinced they could not possibly be more than four miles off, after making every allowance for the wonderful purity of the atmosphere. Nevertheless it took us three good hours' ride before we entered the village soon after dark. The march had been close upon thirty miles, and it seemed unlikely that the camels would be in till the morning, as indeed they were not. Fortunately Muhammad Husain Beg had strapped my bedding behind the grooms' saddles, and we had plenty to eat and drink, the cook and his pots and pans being with us.

Ráyín consists of a cluster of gardens with scattered houses some two hundred in number. It lies near the edge of a great gravel slope extending from the foot of the Kúh Hazár, the top of which is twelve miles off to the south-west. This slope is covered, as far as the eye can reach, with wild rhubarb. In the gardens, walnut, quince, apple and pear trees were abundant, with a few vines trained over masonry pillars. Near the village mosque is a group of the most magnificent plane-trees I ever saw, and a little way off a solitary one, if possible larger, which might well pass for the 'Arbre seul' of Marco Polo.

At the east end of the village rise a single fir-tree and a single cypress, visible from a great distance. The young wheat not more than six inches above the ground testified to the altitude we had attained, which I found to be between 7000 and 7500 feet, the Kúh Hazár being as much higher. Magpies were numerous about the gardens, and the carrion crow of Balúchistán was replaced by the raven.

The house allotted to us was large and well built, though unfinished and of sunbaked brick only. The courtyard was neatly paved with rubble stone, black basalt, and white limestone in patterns, divided by lines of burnt brick on edge. It belongs to the widow of a local magnate who died before he could finish it.

Owing to one of the camels straying, and the drivers positively refusing to start till it was found, we had to halt three days at Ráyín. On the 2nd May we started for Karmán, three marches distant by the road we took, but only two by a shorter path, still closed with snow. The road lay north-east for the first few miles to the south-western angle of the Askarúh hills, a precipitous range, north of Ráyín. Rounding this we turned north, and west of north, up a long easy slope till we reached an altitude of over 9000 feet between two subsidiary ranges at the foot of the lofty mountains of Júpá, of which the Askarúh ridge is the south-western prolongation. The direct road followed by Pottinger from Tahrúd to Máhún lies outside the range on our right, and is much shorter than that through Ráyín, but is rarely used, from the long distance, sixty miles, without water. Beyond the pass a more rapid descent brought us to the caravansarai of Hánaka, after a ride of twenty-three miles. Here a beautiful piece of turf by the side of a sparkling rivulet formed the pleasantest camping-ground we had seen for some time. A few Iliáts were about, and there were a few patches of barley further up the road, but no signs of permanent habitation.

The next morning I witnessed a phenomenon which enables me to bear testimony to the accuracy of one of Marco Polo's facts, without agreeing with him as to its cause. While measuring angles sometime after sunrise the next morning, I noticed that objects in the plain below were gradually becoming less distinct, and at last disappeared in a dull grey haze that seemed to form spontaneously, and gradually to rise until it hid all the surrounding hills from view. The air was still, and the sun was shining brightly. There had been no dew, and the fog rose from an arid plain; nor indeed had it in any way the colour or appearance of watery vapour rising from the earth under the influence of the morning sun. When it enveloped us it gave no marked sensation of damp; nor did it leave any deposit of dust. The darkness produced was about that of an ordinary London fog, a horseman being invisible at a short distance. As the day wore on it was less dense, and shortly before sunset cleared away as suddenly as it began.

It was no doubt such a mysterious fog as this that Marco Polo experienced, and attributed to the enchantments of the Caraunas, a tribe of freebooters, who used its gloom as a veil for carrying on their nefarious proceedings with impunity. Possibly they may have known by some signs when such a fog was likely to occur, and have timed their raids accordingly.

Under these circumstances we did not see much of the road to Máhún, except that it led down a gentle slope of desert for sixteen miles. Máhún is a large and flourishing place of the same character as Ráyín. We were conducted to an unfinished Mihmán-Khána, rebuilding by the Wakíl-ul-Múlk, opposite a large Imámzádah, with which it is connected by two flat pointed arches of no use or ornament. A stream of water ran under the pretty room in which we put up, and irrigated a neat garden in front. It is seldom one gets such good quarters in Persia.

The hills on the east side of the valley up which we had come all the way from Bam, hitherto far inferior to the great ranges to the west, rise suddenly to a nearly equal height opposite Máhún. M. Khanikoff's map, the only one that shows the mountain system of this part of Persia with any attempt at accuracy, incorrectly represents the two chains as joining behind Máhún.

Actually, as before mentioned, there is not a single hill on the road from Narmashír to Kúm, though there is more than one water-parting. But it is one of the vices of Russian cartography, this representation of every water-parting as a lofty ridge, and every water-course as a mighty river. The western range, named Júpá, from a district at its foot, is very steep and craggy, and ends abruptly twenty-five miles due south of Karmán. The eastern range diminishes in height towards Karmán, rising again further on into the lofty plateau of Dúrmánú and Banán. Beyond it is the desert, the beautiful district of Khabís lying in a valley at its edge.

The road from Máhún lies down a barren slope with traces of ruined *kanáts* on either hand. As we approached the city there was a little cultivation, but most of the irrigated land lies on the other side. Three miles from the town an *istikbál* from the Wakíl-ul-Múlk met us, with led horses, headed by the commanding officer of an Infantry battalion for me, and the Superintendent of the arsenal for my coadjutor the Sárhang. Entering the citadel we separated, our conductor leading Blanford and myself to a tolerably good house inside the Ark or citadel.

CHAPTER VI.

Karmán to Shíráz.

Of all the great cities of Persia, Karmán has perhaps been least visited by Europeans. In the present century Pottinger (1810), Keith Abbott (1845), Khanikoff (1859), Goldsmid and Murdoch Smith (1866), Goldsmid again in 1870, and Lovett in 1871, were our only predecessors, with the exception of a German named Mirheim in 1865.

The town is uninteresting even for Persia. It occupies but a portion of the site of the old city, razed to the ground in 1795 by Aghá Muhammad Khán, the barbarous founder of the Kajár dynasty. A mud wall and shallow ditch enclose about two-thirds of a square mile, closely filled with low mud-built houses. The prevalence of earthquakes renders it unadvisable to erect lofty buildings without solid and expensive masonry, which the dryness of the climate renders unnecessary for any other reason.

In Persia, as I believe elsewhere, the elegance and strength of domestic architecture varies regularly with the rainfall, as does the character of the roofs of the poorer class of houses. On the coast of the Caspian, where the rains are very heavy and constant, the roofs are tiled; a little further inland we find them thatched. In Fars and about Tehrán they are flat and terraced, and in Kúm, Kashán, and Isfahán, where the extreme of aridity is reached, mud domes afford sufficient protection.

In the older maps, on the authority of Sir Henry Pottinger, the position of Karmán was laid down in latitude 29° 56′ and longitude 56° 6′. This very erroneous position was corrected by Khanikoff's surveyor, Mr. Lentz, to latitude 30° 17′ 30″ and longitude 57° 13′; but this latter correction I find too great, and have therefore placed Karmán in longitude 56° 59″, for reasons given in the Appendix[1].

[1] Vide Appendix, Longitude of Karmán.

Its altitude above the sea is about 5700 feet, 700 feet higher than Isfahán or Shíráz. The summer heats of Karmán are, however, more intense than in either of those cities. The reason is probably to be sought in the arid and sandy valleys to the north-west, the direction of the prevailing wind, which becomes heated in blowing over them. Karmán enjoys an unenviable notoriety for unhealthiness of climate, occasioned by the sudden changes, caused by currents of cold air from the lofty mountains in the vicinity. Madrid, if I remember rightly, has a similar ill fame.

There is not a single building of beauty or importance in the town; but the ruins of the fort called Kala'h-i-Dukhtar, or Kala'h-i-Ardashír, on a limestone rock a few hundred yards from the eastern wall, are somewhat curious, showing traces of considerable antiquity. Unlike most Persian cities, there are but few gardens outside the walls, though the land is cultivated, where not occupied by ruins, up to the edge of the ditch. Quantities of fruit, however, are brought from Máhún and other villages in the Júpá district. This site was evidently selected for a city from its position at the confluence of four great valleys, and therefore roads. Two lead north-west on either side of the Badamán hills to Yazd and Kúh-Banán; the third, up which we had just come, communicates with Balúchistán; while the fourth, rising gently for several days' march due south through a fertile country, is the usual road to the coast at Bandar-Abbas. This route, which has never been described by a traveller since Marco Polo, traverses the Kíaratul-Aráb country to the water-parting of the great Kohrúd range, here at its greatest elevation; it then descends the mountains by an easy pass to the plain of Jirúft, reached by Murdoch Smith and Keith Abbott during severe winters by the roundabout route through the Deh Bakri pass.

The Kuh Hazár, so long a landmark on our road, is not visible from Karmán, being hidden by the almost equally lofty and more picturesque hills of Júpá, which seem to tower over the city, though twenty-five miles distant. Further west a long line of snow-covered peaks marks the main range of the Kohrúd mountains. The most prominent group is called the *Chahár Gúmbaz*, the four domes. Looking west the hills are insignificant and broken, but to the north a succession of terraces called Dúrmánú rises to a considerable height, and is said to be rich in minerals. A gap between them and the mountains north of Máhún gives access to the fertile low-lying district of Khabis.

The shortest road to Tehrán, that viâ Yazd and Kashán, was less likely, as lying at the foot of a single continuous range, to afford opportunity of geological research to Blanford, than the alternative route by Shíráz, which would cross several ranges at right angles. By this way too I ought to have reached a telegraph station sooner, and thus put myself in communication with my superiors earlier than by going viâ Yazd, on which road Kashán would have been the first telegraph station. We therefore decided on making for Shíráz, to which there are two roads from Karmán, about equal in length. The northern, described by Pottinger, and by no one since, passes through Shahr-i-Bábak and Arsinján to the Persepolis valley; the southern traverses the Sarján or Saiyidábád district to Níríz. As Lovett had travelled by the latter a few months before, we should have preferred Pottinger's route, but it proved impossible to persuade camel or mule drivers to risk their beasts on it for fear of robbers. We were therefore obliged to make up our minds to the Níríz road. Even for this it was a fortnight before we could make a start.

The famine which had been desolating Persia for two years was now nearly over. The bounteous rainfall of the past winter had given confident hopes of an abundant harvest; and the holders of corn all over the country were getting rid of their hoards as fast as possible. In Karmán the Wakíl-ul-Múlk proudly boasted to me that not a single native had died of hunger, though it is the driest province of Persia. At the first suspicion of famine he had taken a careful census of the grain resources of his province, prohibited exports without permission, fixed a regular standard of prices, and limited the amount to be sold in every market to the absolute necessities of the population, besides establishing relief centres for the absolutely indigent. By these wise precautions not only was famine averted from Karmán, but the Wakíl-ul-Múlk was able to send considerable quantities of food to the neighbouring province of Yazd, which suffered perhaps more terribly than any other part of the country. This shows what might have been done in other provinces by equally wise and honest governors, unmeddled with by the blundering central authorities at Tehrán. As it was, the few and tardy attempts at remedy only made matters worse.

The food resources of Persia, as a whole, are far in excess of the wants of the population. All cultivation on the plateau being entirely dependent on artificial irrigation, absolute failure of the harvest is unknown except in isolated spots, and then from preventible causes, such as neglect of the water-courses. Scarcity and high prices must naturally occur from time to time, but famine should be impossible under the present conditions of commerce. If the country is ever so penetrated by roads or rail as to enable the surplus stock of food to be exported at the close of each harvest, a famine like that anticipated in Bengal last year might be looked for. But here again facility for export means facility for import, and the cause of the disease would indicate the remedy.

The rise and progress of the recent famine in Persia were briefly as follows. From the winter of 1863-4, the rains, with a single exception, 1865-6, had been regularly below the average. Lakes, springs, and *kanats* all over the country got lower and lower every summer. The crops, nevertheless, had been generally good and abundant. During the sixth winter, that of 1869-70, hardly any snow or rain fell in the valleys. In the south particularly, the scanty showers produced little or no grass in the lower plains, frequented as cold-weather quarters by the nomads who form half the population of Fars. The consequence was the loss of the majority of the flocks and herds, upon which they depend for subsistence and for the carriage of their families and property in their half-yearly migrations. The camels and goats, hardier animals, survived, and the richer tribes, who alone possess the former, were thus able to get up to the elevated mountain plateau where snow had fallen, though to a less depth than usual. The poorer families, owners perhaps of a few sheep and goats with a mare or cow, on which their cooking pots and scanty tent are packed while travelling, saw their only means of transport to better pastures perish before their eyes; and either lay down and died or made their way to the towns and villages, prolonging their miserable existence with roots and herbs, or with the carcases of the dead animals that were unusually numerous on the great highways.

Towards the end of 1870 I marched down the road to Bushahr from Shíráz with Major Champain, Director-in-Chief of the Anglo-Persian Telegraph Department, of which I was then Officiating Director. At every halting-place crowds of famished half-naked men and boys (the women and children were nearly all dead) thronged around our camp, too weak to beg, but hoping, yet hardly expecting, succour from the bounty of the infidels. All that we could do was to give them a meal of rice for the day; and this we had no difficulty in procuring from the villagers at moderate prices, showing that there was no lack of food in the country. On my return, partly to avoid these terrible scenes and the contagion of disease—for typhus, cholera, and dysentery were adding their ravages to those of hunger—and partly for surveying purposes, I took the unfrequented eastern road to Shíráz. Even here my servants buried three corpses on one day's march of 35 miles, during which we did not meet a living soul, and I found disease, induced by bad and insufficient food, causing great mortality among the wealthier tribes of Iliáts, who had lost nearly all their horses, sheep, and cattle.

During this first season of distress, the villages suffered comparatively little, though a few places in the intermediate valleys from two to four thousand feet in altitude, notably the district of Kázrún, were nearly deserted on account of the failure of water in the *kanáts*. In the plains near the coast, where artificial irrigation is not used, the corn crops had totally failed; but the date harvest having been unusually plentiful, there was no want of food.

In Isfahán, Yazd, and Mashad, prices were very high through this first winter; and though the peasants generally had enough, the artizans and day labourers, who form a larger part of the population here than elsewhere, suffered terribly. Isfahán and Yazd are the principal manufacturing districts of Persia, and in the best of times dependent on Fars and Karmánsháh for a large proportion of their food. The rains of the second winter, 1870–71, fairly plentiful in the south, were again very scanty in the north and east of Persia. The harvest consequently failed entirely in many places, and was everywhere below the average. Still there was plenty of food in the country, the harvests in the south and west having been fairly good: but the great land-owners, who are also the great corn-dealers, instigated by love of filthy lucre, or perhaps, as they declared themselves, by fear of a third year of famine, held for a rise, utterly indifferent to the sufferings around them. A few feeble attempts were made at Tehrán to check the impending calamity, but without much effect.

The government granaries were emptied and grain imported to Tehrán from the fertile districts of the west, and sold at a loss to the bakers. The governor of Isfahán, a wealthy landed proprietor of Fars, who had been bringing food from his own estates to Isfahán, was recalled in obedience to popular clamour, and the distress in that city at once rapidly increased. Orders were sent to the authorities in the suffering towns, to register the amount of grain in the storehouses of private parties; but the order only served to enrich the men to whom its execution was entrusted, who were bribed to silence by the possessors of secret hoards of grain, who again were, strange to say—in Shíráz and Isfahán at all events—perfectly well known.

During the summer of 1871, the fruits and vegetables, so plentiful in Persia, kept the people alive, but as the autumn advanced, crowds of diseased and famished wretches, bringing pestilence in their train, thronged round the cities they were not permitted to enter, clamouring for food. Others beset the caravansarais on the great roads, to beg from travellers and feed on the dead bodies of camels and mules.

The winter rains of 1871 commenced early; and before the end of the year a heavy fall of snow covered the land, and cut off all communication between the capital and the villages, whence the landowners, in whose granaries all the corn of the country was collected, were doling out scanty supplies. This put the finishing stroke to the calamities of the country. The winter was the coldest and most prolonged ever known: thousands died of hunger, thousands more of cold and disease. But this was the end of the famine. With the return of spring, it became evident that the coming harvest would be most abundant. All motive for hoarding having ceased, food became comparatively cheap and plentiful at once, though strenuous efforts were made here and there to keep up the prices[1].

Passing through Kúm in June, I met endless files of camels taking last year's wheat and barley to Tehrán from a fertile district near Hamadán, belonging to one of the Sháh's near relations and ministers. Kúm is not on the direct road, but the harvest there was then being

---

[1] At Isfahán, in April 1872, a large quantity of corn was known to be on the way from Shíráz. The news caused all stores to be opened, and prices fell rapidly. This was taken advantage of by the Imám Juma, the head of the priesthood, and Rahím Khán the principal customs officer, the two most notable inhabitants to plan an operation. After proclaiming the advent of the corn from Shíráz, and pretending to dispose of the entire contents of their own granaries, while secretly buying up all the corn they could find through agents, Rahím Khán took advantage of his position to prevent the Shíráz caravan from passing the frontier; and the two worthies, having thus complete command of the market, raised the price of bread four hundred per cent in a single night. Unfortunately they reckoned without the English Telegraph Officer, who at once sent a message to his superior at Tehrán, by whom the man was reported to the Prime Minister. The latter wigged the Imám Juma severely, and ordered him to sell his grain at a reasonable price, but the other culprit got off scot free.

cut, while that of Hamadán is two months later. The caravan had come that way that the Prince might be able to evade the charge of having hoarded grain, by swearing that it was fresh grain brought from Kúm. Further from the capital people were less particular; and hoarded grain was produced without any shame. Altogether I have no doubt that, had timely measures been taken when the first warning was given by the distress among the Iliáts of Fars in 1870, most if not all of the subsequent distress would have been avoided.

The west and north-west did not suffer from anything beyond a rise of prices. Fars suffered severely only the first year, and almost entirely among the nomads, who could hardly have been helped in time. Karmán, thanks to the wise precautions of the Wakíl-ul-Múlk, escaped entirely. Yazd, Isfahán, and Khúrasán were the greatest sufferers, though Tehrán and its neighbourhood had a terrible time in the snows of the second winter. The population of Isfahán, Yazd, and Mash-had was diminished by a third at least, though not all of these died, numbers having emigrated west and south.

The population of Persia is variously estimated at from ten to four millions, or from six and a half to sixteen to the square mile. I myself am inclined to put it at the higher figure. Even then, taking into consideration that half the population at least were unaffected by the famine, I do not think that the actual deaths from disease and starvation can have exceeded half a million, though from the disproportionate mortality of women and children, the ultimate loss to the country will be far higher. One of the immediate effects of the famine was to let loose bands of robbers, generally half-starved Iliáts, all over the country.

At the time we were in Karmán, the road to Yazd had been held for some time by a chief of the Arab[1] tribe, whose grazing-grounds lie north-east of Shíráz. The last exploit of this worthy had been to murder and rob the messenger bringing the annual dress of honour from the Shah to the Wakíl-ul-Múlk. This was too much, and a price was put on his head. Shortly after we left, news was brought that the blood-money had been earned by one of his relations, who asked him to dinner, and shot him in the stomach at dessert.

Thus, as before mentioned, we were forced to take the southern road. Even here matters were not much better. What with the famine, and

---

[1] Originally emigrants from Bahrein. They have become Shia'hs and adopted the ordinary Iliát dress. They speak a patois compounded of Arabic and Persian.

a succession of incapable governors, Fars, at all times one of the most turbulent provinces, was in a very disturbed state, aggravated just then by an interregnum between the death of one governor and the arrival of his successor. Personally I was under no apprehension of danger, being well known among the tribes; but the difficulty was to persuade Karmáni muleteers or camel-drivers that they need be in no fear of losing their beasts. This seemed hopeless; and at last the Wakíl-ul-Múlk lent us fifteen mules of his own for our personal effects as far as Shíráz; and had seized in some outlying district a sufficiency of camels to take the tents and heavy baggage to Sarján, five marches on the road, where he sent orders to the governor to have carriage in readiness for us. All this took some time: and it was not till the fourteenth day that we turned our backs on Karmán. But for the annoyance of being detained, and losing all the best travelling weather, our time passed not unpleasantly.

Directly we entered the city, we were visited by the entire Hindú community. There were some dozen or fifteen of them, merchants from Sind engaged in the cotton trade. The more lucrative business of exporting wool they are not allowed to meddle with, it being the monopoly of the governor; though as British subjects, indirect means must be taken to prevent them. They have adopted the Persian dress, with even more outrageously high lambskin caps than usual; and their appearance therein showed that the Persian Aryan is a much better-looking man than his Hindú brother, and does himself woeful injustice in the matter of dress. Our friends from Sind looked nearly black compared to Persians, and in their dark under-garments and brown *a'bás*[1] were more like dressed-up monkeys than men. They seemed delighted to see representatives of their masters in India, and begged us to return their visit, that their dignity might be exalted in the eyes of the foreigners. Accordingly we went one afternoon to their caravansarai, a visit which, it is to be hoped, had the desired effect.

From the Wakíl-ul-Múlk we met with the greatest civility, and paid him several visits. He is a stout, pleasant-looking man of forty or a little over, and in his father's time, from commanding the local regiment, was known as the Sarhang. The old Wakíl-ul-Múlk held sway in Karmán, for about a dozen years, either as Wazír to a puppet governor, cousin of the Sháh, or as actual *hákim*. In this period he

---

[1] Long Arab cloaks, worn by all pious Muslims west of the Indus.

raised Karmán from the desolation it had been plunged in, since the siege, to its present position of the most orderly and one of the most prosperous divisions of the kingdom. The city has been rebuilt, caravansarais constructed, *kanáts* dug, and robbers put down. The major part of the Yazd trade with India, formerly carried on through Shíráz, has now been transferred to the more direct route through Karmán. The Wakíl-ul-Múlk found means to carry out these improvements and pay a yearly increased amount of taxation into the royal treasury, by assuming an absolute monopoly of the wool trade with India, which is very extensive, the Karmán sheep producing the only wool capable of being used to adulterate or represent the down of the Kashmír goat. Formerly the accounts of Karmán, like those of most other provinces, were audited in Tehrán; but the present Wakíl-ul-Múlk, who succeeded his father some three years before our visit, has obtained exemption from this arrangement, and pays a fixed sum of 200,000 tománs, about £80,000, to the Sháh yearly, besides an annual present of perhaps a fourth of that sum.

He is extremely anxious to develop the mineral resources of the country, which are doubtless considerable; and evinced great pleasure at hearing that Blanford was a geologist. He showed us some copper smelted from mines in the neighbourhood, and said he was instituting a search for coal. At his request Blanford one day took a long ride into the hills to the north to look at a supposed coal mine, which however turned out to be bituminous shale. Besides copper, lead and iron are known to exist, the latter in the ore called by Persians *fúlád*, or steel, from their being able to forge steel from it direct without passing through the intermediate state of wrought iron.

The conversation turning one day on snake poison, the Wakíl-ul-Múlk professed entire belief in the efficacy of bezoar as a remedy, and declared he had himself tried it successfully on a servant who had been bitten. He produced several bezoar-stones from his writing-desk, giving us each one. They are, as is well known, concretions formed in the intestines of various animals, most commonly in those of the wild goat of Persia, 'Capra ægagrus,' which, though found on every range of hills of any height, is said to contract the disease that produces the bezoar only on certain mountains of Eastern Fars. The stones vary much in size and form. That which I have is thirteen-sixteenths of an inch long, and three-eighths wide; an elongated oval in shape. Its surface is smooth and highly polished, and of an olive green colour, faintly marbled. Its gravity is about five-sixths that of water. Besides its attributes as an antidote to poison[1], bezoar has certain qualities as a talisman that make it much valued by ladies. It is usually enclosed in a little case of filigree gold, and worn round the neck.

The lieutenant-colonel of an Adarbaiján regiment quartered at Karmán called and invited us to dinner. He had been educated in Paris, and bitterly bewailed the dulness and savagery of his country quarters. A companion in misfortune is a doctor, also brought up in France, and called the Nawáb[2], being descended from some emigrant from Hindustán.

The curiosities of Karmán are the carpet and shawl manufactories. The former, once the most celebrated in the east, have much diminished in number since the fatal siege, from which date all the calamities of Karmán. In the governor's private factory alone are the finer qualities produced. The white wool of the Karmán sheep, added perhaps to some quality of the water, gives a brilliancy to the colouring unattainable elsewhere. In pattern the carpets are distinguishable from those of the north and west both by this purity of colour, and a greater boldness and originality of design, due probably to a slighter infusion of Arab prejudices on the subject of the representation of living forms. Not only flowers and trees, but birds, beasts, landscapes, and even human figures are found on the Karmán carpets. The Wakíl-ul-Múlk gave me two in return for a pair of double-barrelled breech-loading pistols of greater value that I presented him with; and I purchased a still finer one in the bazaar. The price varies from ten shillings to almost as many pounds for the square yard; but the ordinary price is about fifteen shillings. The costliness of Persian carpets, as well as their durability, is caused by the fact that each stitch is separately tied and finished off. The proof of a good carpet is that it should show no permanent mark of burning from a lighted coal being placed on it, left for a few seconds, and the place brushed smooth.

The best felt-carpets are also made in and about Karmán. A very beautiful one came into my possession at Bam, covered with an intricate geometrical pattern in blue, red, and green worsted. As

---

[1] In Persian 'Fa-zahr,' from Pád-zahr (or Bád-zahr), 'poison-expelling.'

[2] The title of Nawáb, so common in India, is reserved in Persia to the Royal Family, who are so addressed in writing only.

some curiosity was expressed by experts who saw this carpet in London, as to the manner in which the design was worked on to the felt, no apology is perhaps necessary for detailing the process.

In an inner room, carefully protected from the wind, is a polished plaster platform. On this pieces of coloured worsted are arranged in the desired pattern, with some sort of size. A very thin felt is then carefully pressed over them, and at once removed, carrying on its face the pieces of worsted in their proper places. This thin felt is laid on the thicker felt of the carpet, and the two incorporated with blows of a mallet.

The shawls of Karmán appear to differ from those of Kashmír in being of worsted instead of the under-down of wool. The term shawl, as we use it, is quite incorrect, *shál* meaning the stuff, not a particular article of dress. That most commonly made in Karmán is in pieces five or six yards long and three-quarters wide, which are cut up into outer coats for both sexes. It is also used by the rich for door hangings and tent linings, for caps, tray covers, and many other purposes. Long pieces of a single colour, embroidered with needlework at the ends, are used for turbans and waistcloths, and come nearer to the European idea of a shawl than anything else. The white turban shawls make an admirable material for ladies' dresses, and might be profitably exported to Europe, being no dearer than French merino.

On the 17th May we left Karmán shortly after sunrise and rode to Bághín. The distance is called seven *farsakhs*, but proved to be eighteen miles only. This stage being common to both the Yazd and Shíráz roads is shown on most maps in two places, north-west and south-east of Karmán. Several *kanáts* flowing N.N.W. from the Jupá hills crossed the path to irrigate the fertile valley leading to Kúh-Banán, in which many large villages were visible. At the twelfth mile we rounded the end of the Badamán or Dawirán hills and crossed a desert tract to Bághín, where we put up in the post-house, kept by a woman, a curious anomaly in a Musalmán country.

There is nothing remarkable about Bághín, which is a large and apparently flourishing village, rejoicing in bountiful crops of wheat and opium. We had the Wakíl-ul-Múlk's fifteen mules and ten camels with us; having left the tents and heavy baggage to be brought on by the impressed camel-drivers, under charge of Muhammad Husain Beg and Blanford's Portuguese butler.

During the day no one appeared, but towards morning the butler appeared with a doleful but somewhat confused tale, confirmed by Muhammad Husain the next morning. The impressed camels were unbroken, ringless as to their noses, and their backs unaccustomed to any loads but grain-bags. All efforts to make them keep our tents and boxes on their backs had proved ineffectual; and after every load had been thrown off a dozen times, the servants gave it up as a bad job, and came on to Bághín to tell the piteous tale. In the course of the day, the Wakíl-ul-Múlk's muleteer, a sturdy, quarrelsome, and energetic little Túrk, brought in twenty good camels he had found grazing in the neighbourhood; and with these Muhammad Husain Beg and the butler were sent back to Karmán to bring on the loads as best they could, and join us at Saiyidábád, for which we started with our fifteen mules and ten camels the next morning.

The road led south-west across the plain, here quite desert, and up the usual long gravel slope of a chain of low volcanic hills, named from two prominent cones, which may be supposed to stand for horns, Kúh Kal-i-gáv, the bull's-head hills. The pass, which is easy, is called the Godar-i-Dukhtar. A mile after entering the hills, we halted to breakfast at a small caravanserai named Kúnúkúh. Immense quantities of wild rhubarb, now in flower, grew in the valleys. Descending the hills by another long gravel slope, the road crossed a little river running north-west, and two miles further on reached Mashísh, a large village with many ruins and minor clusters of houses in the vicinity. In former times it possessed a strong fort, destroyed in the struggle between Zand and Kaján, at the end of the last century. The snowy hills were now prominent to the south and south-west, our old friend the Kúh Hazár being conspicuous some fifty miles off, with a still higher peak twenty miles south of it. The next two marches being eight *farsakhs* each, the first a very tiring one up hill, we halted a day at Mashísh, spent in specimen-hunting on the river, and idling in the shade of a magnificent double chinar-tree in a neighbouring garden.

The *ghulám* sent to escort us by the Wakíl-ul-Múlk was one of the most tremendous drawers of the long bow I ever met even in Persia. On the road from Bághín he showed me a *kanát*, which never requires repair. The villagers, he said, have only to kill a sheep on the spot, and let some of the blood trickle into the channel, to start the water with renewed vigour. Another object of interest in the neighbourhood is a spring in the high mountains south of Mashísh, whose water bubbles up to a great height with a noise that is audible a *farsakh* off, but which never overflows its basin. There was probably some substratum of truth in this latter story, but we had no time to verify it.

One of the direct roads to Bandar-Abbas from Yazd passes through Mashísh, whence it leads three long marches south to Baft, beyond which is the beginning of the gradual fall to the Garmsír or hot plain country. The Wakíl-ul-Múlk returned this way from Balúchistán last month. The Mashísh river unites with the stream irrigating Bághín to form a salt marsh at Kabútarkhána on the Yazd road. The hills we crossed on the way from Bághín are thus isolated.

For twelve miles the road from Mashísh traverses a gently rising plain in a westerly direction to a small river flowing among low hills to the Mashísh stream. For two miles we followed its bed in the hope of finding wild pigs among the thick tamarisk jungle with which it is filled, but without seeing any. Swarms of soft-bodied grey-flies tormented the horses, and we were glad to leave the river. We continued however in its vicinity, crossing and recrossing it more than once for the rest of the march of 29 miles. Many small canals are taken from the stream, irrigating extensive fields of wheat and grain. A large umbelliferous plant was very plentiful, not unlike asafœtida, but more closely resembling that found on the Yazdikhást plains, from which a drug is extracted. We halted for the night at the caravanserai of Khán-i-Súrkh, a mere stable with a couple of deep recesses on either side of the arched entrance. All around us were rolling green hills dotted here and there with bushes of the *arjan* or wild almond. The next morning was very cold, the halting-place being over 7000 feet above the sea. The road continued to follow the course of the stream. Here and there patches of wild asparagus and briar-roses in the hollows showed we were approaching less arid regions. At the end of the sixth mile an easy pass led to the water-parting some 8500 feet above the sea-level. Two short and easy descents about a mile apart brought us to a gentle slope for eight miles further, rounding the base of a prominent hill to the right, the Kúh-i-Panj.

We had now passed the great central chain which I have called elsewhere the Kohrúd range, and whose junction with the Khúrasán mountain system we had crossed between Bampúr and Narmashír. Before us lay the great valley stretching from the sources of the Zaindarúd near Gulpáigán to the ranges bordering the Persian Gulf. We breakfasted under some trees at a spot called Bádbíní, where is a little cultivation belonging to some semi-nomad Tájiks. Here I found a pair of the curious wormlike Typhlops snakes, which proved to be a new species. A mile and a half further, where the road leaves a secondary range of low hills, a curious cave was pointed out in a rock of volcanic conglomerate by the road side. I clambered into it with some little difficulty. It was evidently meant for habitation, having recesses for holding things cut in the walls, and a depression for a fire in the middle. On one side a hole served as a window. Below it is a large natural cavern on the ground-level which might serve for a stable. Such cave-dwellings are not uncommon in Persia; but whether they were originally tombs of great men like those of the kings at Persepolis, or not, is difficult to say. Perhaps not, as nowhere else have I noticed recesses hollowed out to receive the coffins or bodies as in the royal tombs at Persepolis.

Ten miles further down an even gravel slope brought us to Saadatá-bád, commonly contracted to Saatábád, the first village in the Sarján or Sirjún district. We lodged in a large empty house with a fine tank, bordered with pomegranate-trees, and full of immense carp. Hearing that the camels with the rest of the baggage were close behind, we halted the next day in preference to going on to Saiyidabád, a much hotter place.

The next morning the camels turned up all right, with the baggage less damaged than might have been expected. After breakfast we rode on to Saiyidabád down a long slope descending a thousand feet in sixteen miles. A short distance from the town, Zohráb Khan, brother of Yahia Khan the governor, met us with a dozen horsemen, who went through the usual feats of skill, firing off their long guns in all sorts of positions with their horses at a gallop. This escort led us to a little house in the middle of the town, which is unwalled and entirely of sunburnt bricks. The roofs are domed, and several wind-towers bear witness to the heat of the climate, though the plain is 5500 feet above the sea.

Hearing that camels were ready we hoped to start the next morning; but, alas! the drivers fled with their beasts in the night, and we were left lamenting. The governor, a bloated young man with coarser manners than any Persian I have met, came to see us and asked us to dinner. The Sultán (Captain) of the soldiers quartered here also paid us a visit—a mild, middle-aged gentleman, from Adarbaiján. He had orders to send thirty men with our caravan to Níris, and asked my leave to give the command to his son, a boy only ten years old, but nevertheless a sub-lieutenant in the regiment. He gave me some interesting details of the interior economy of the Persian service. A *sarhang* gets 500 *tumáns* a year; *yáwars*, equivalent to our majors, 150; *sultáns* 60; *náibs* or lieutenants 40; and sub-lieutenants 30; a *tumán* being worth about eight shillings. Each medal gives right to additional pay at the rate of ten *tumáns* to a *sultán*, five to a *náib*, and two to a private soldier.

The gardens in this part of Persia show signs of superior cultivation to any I have noticed elsewhere. They produce the finest pistachio nuts and pomegranates in the country, the former forming a considerable article of commerce. Potatoes too were abundant. Shahr-i-Bábak, the principal town of these parts when Pottinger passed, is now completely abandoned, though several flourishing villages have sprung up in the neighbourhood. It lies seventeen *farsakhs* to the north-west.

After a second disappointment about camels, nearly as many as we wanted were at last got together by means of threats and promises, and on the 28th of May we marched to the little village of Tarábád, twelve miles off on the edge of the Salt plain. The country passed through was rich with wheat and cotton. Two miles from Tarábád we reached the salt swamp, called here 'Kafeh,' and 'Kavír' in the north. It is about nine miles wide, the last four having a solid crust of white salt, through which the horses' feet did not break. In winter the whole is covered with water, and it is then very dangerous to cross, as the mud, pretty solid where we passed, liquifies everywhere off the beaten track. As it was, our mules, who carried heavier loads on smaller feet than the horses, came to considerable grief, and were not in till very late. This salt swamp extends to a considerable distance northwards, but it is not a continuation of that in which the Zaindarúd terminates, though in the same valley. This latter must be considerably below 5000 feet, the altitude of the river at Isfahán, while the Khairábád swamp slopes south-east, and is 5400 feet above the sea. The valley descends by a gentle slope to the Lár plain on the one hand, and the Jírúft plain on the other, the fall being probably between three and four thousand feet. Its western edge forms the boundary between Fars and Karmán; but Khairábád, where we halted, is now attached to the latter for revenue purposes. It is a wretched little walled village at the foot of the hills, with a good *kanát* of water, and a few fine Jordan willow-trees.

There are two roads from Khairábád to Nírís, one through Beshná, the other through Parpá, an abandoned iron mine, the two meeting at Kútrú or Kadarú. We took the latter, which was fortunate, as Lovett had gone by the Beshná road. The path lay up a long gentle slope between craggy limestone hills, prettily wooded with the wild pistachio. Fifteen miles from Khairábád the top of the pass was reached, 7300 feet in altitude; after which an easy descent led to Parpá, a spring near some deserted smelting-works. A short slope on leaving Parpá the next morning brought us to a wide desert plain, closed by hills to the west and north, but of apparently illimited extent to the south-east. It is famous for wild asses, but we were not lucky enough to see any. At the western end we crossed a small salt swamp to Kútrú, where we spent the day on a stone terrace built round the trunk of a magnificent plane-tree in a neat garden.

The hills we had crossed should be the continuation of those south of Isfahán, known as the Kúh Dúm ba-Lár, i.e. extending to Lár. Those in front of us are probably a prolongation of the chain of those south of Múrgháb. But all this very interesting country is entirely unknown, save from Pottinger's meagre description, and an unintelligible account by Serjeant Gibbons in the Geographical Society's Journal.

The next day (June 1) we crossed the hills to Nírís, or Níríz, often erroneously written Neyriz, a blunder that has led to its being twice inserted on many maps. Six and a half miles from Kútrú, the road entered the pass, which bears no more distinctive appellation than the Dahna-i-Nírís. The scenery was extremely pretty, and, to our eyes accustomed to the barest of hills, charmingly wooded. On the top is an open plateau three miles across, after which a steep descent leads to the plain. The day was misty, so that the lake was not clearly visible.

As Nírís was in charge of an old friend of mine, the Karaen-ul-Múlk, the principal nobleman of Shíráz, but at that time in Tehrán, I had sent a letter from Karmán, asking his son, who was looking after his father's affairs at Shíráz, to send some one to meet me there, Nírís having an evil reputation for inhospitality. Accordingly, at a distance of three miles from the town, a horseman appeared, sent from Shíráz by the Karaen's son to receive us, and bringing a welcome packet of letters. A little further on an extraordinary procession met us, as *istikbál* or cortége of welcome.

After the usual train of horsemen came a lot of men with kettle-drums and trumpets, headed by a professional jester. Then followed a band of singers, and then a miscellaneous crowd of ragamuffins. At every two or three hundred yards, an unfortunate sheep was brought forward, swiftly decapitated, and its head carried across the road. Tall glass vases of flowers with thin necks were held in the air at intervals, and broken with a sharp tap of a knife. All the time the drums were beating, the trumpets braying, as only Persian trumpets can, the jester making jokes, not always the most decent, while an unfortunate poet was trying to recite an ode in praise of somebody. At every turn more people were added to the crowd, till at last we were attended to the door of the house prepared for us by the whole male population of Níris, and a large proportion of the female. This is the good old-fashioned way of receiving a grandee, only now kept up in out-of-the-way parts. Before the Kajár times dancing-girls were added to the show; but this is strictly forbidden now-a-days.

Níris is chiefly remarkable from having been the head-quarters of Bábism, that extraordinary heresy which bade fair at one time to revolutionise Persia. The persecutions to which those suspected of participation in the forbidden mysteries of the Báb were subjected half depopulated Níris, and the famine, from which it suffered considerably the first year, drove many of the remaining inhabitants to seek their fortunes elsewhere. It has three parishes, surrounded by very pretty gardens of fruit, walnut, and chinar trees, with here and there a cypress or palm. The lake is distant about seven miles to the north-west.

After a day's halt to renew our extra carriage, we left in the evening of the 3rd June, with most of the spare baggage carried on asses. We spent the night twelve miles from Níris, on the borders of the lake, and went on the next morning early to Khír, a large village on a stream flowing from the hills. Here we breakfasted in a garden with a magnificent avenue of chinars: and after breakfast held a consultation with the elders of the place as to our onward movements.

The road usually followed to Shíráz leads along the south shore of the lake to the Kolvár or Kúrbár district. It is flat and safe, but in the summer is infested with gad-flies to such an extent as to render it dangerous to horses. Moreover, we were told that it would be difficult to find asses, which we were only able to hire from village to village. The other road passes over the hills to Sarbistán, in the Shíráz valley, and though comparatively free from flies, was said to be infested with thieves of the Baharlú and Kashkái tribes. After due consideration, I resolved to take the latter, and we started off with fresh asses the same afternoon for Rohnis, the first stage. The lake opposite Khír is at its narrowest, being barely a mile across. In summer a man can wade to the other side. The water is not so salt as that of the Shíráz lake, which receives several springs of brine, but is too much so for fish, which exist only at the mouth of the Bandani river, its main feeder. Passing a gap in the lofty limestone cliffs bordering the lake on its south side, we entered a wide valley running west, at the other extremity of which lies the town of Istabonat or Savonát, and the ancient fort of Irij or Ij. After a pleasant ride through a green valley bounded by high cliffs to the south, called the Kúh Túdah, we arrived at Rohnis, where the Katkhuda, a surly ruffian, would hardly take the trouble to get us a house.

Eleven miles the next morning over a desert plain covered with wild liquorice brought us to the pass of Tang-i-Karím, shortly after passing which we halted in a garden. A little way off under the hill is a deep clear pool in the rocks full of enormous carp. Its water is said to remain always at the same level. It is called the Atash Kadah, or 'place of fire,' presumably from a fire temple having existed there, though there are now no traces of it. Three *farsakhs* to the south of Tang-i-Karím lies the town of Fasá, one of the most prosperous towns in Fars, and the first place in the Garmsír or hot country, whose limit seems to be that of the date-palm bearing fruit.

The most dangerous stage of the journey was now before us. A reiving party of Baharlú, a hundred strong, had carried off several hundred sheep and attacked a village in the plain the night before; and a band of Kashkáis was said to be holding the pass to Sarvístán, the next village on our road.

The heat during the day was now becoming oppressive to man and beast, but I determined to wait for broad daylight before going on. Halfway to Sarvístán is a ruined caravanserai named Mián Jangal, and here a halt might be made, if the cattle seemed unable to get through the whole stage of twenty-seven miles. Here also I hoped to find some one to take a message to the Kashkáis, who, I was sure from experience, would not knowingly touch my property.

Accordingly, after getting a few matchlock-men from the village as a guard against minor pilferers, we started off our miscellaneous caravan of horses, asses, mules and camels, and rode on in front to Mián Jangal as an advanced guard. The caravanserai so swarmed with fleas and gad-flies that to stay there would have been misery to man and beast, and the donkeys coming up pretty fast, we made a push for Sarvístán. The path lay through a thick wood of the wild pistachio, hawthorn, and other trees below the high cliffs of the Kúh Kashkái, and rose rapidly for five miles, when the summit of the pass was reached, and we saw the plain of Sarvístán beneath us. Once there all danger was over, and leaving the caravan we rode on to the village.

Sarvístán is a large place with magnificent gardens of walnut and other trees, though the cypresses, which presumably gave it its name, have entirely disappeared[1]. It occupies nearly the same position at the south-eastern end of the Shíráz plain that the city does at the north-western, the lake lying intermediate between them.

We were now only fifty miles from Shíráz—so, leaving Muhammad Husain Beg to bring on the donkey part of the caravan as soon as he could find fresh beasts, we started the next afternoon, and camped for the night near a small village named Khairábád, going on to Mahálú the next morning. Mahálú, which gives its name to the lake, is a picturesque little village choked in between high limestone cliffs and the water, and reminding one a little, with its terraces, orange and pomegranate trees, of a place on the Italian lakes. Leaving Blanford to come on the next morning, I rode on the same afternoon. The path skirts the lake for twelve miles to the Pul-i-Fasá, a bridge across the main stream which fills it, whence a canter of as many miles more over smooth green turf brought me to Shíráz, 1200 miles from Gwádar, four months and a half after leaving that place.

Here I found that Sir Frederic Goldsmid and his party had just reached Tehrán, whither I was ordered to proceed at once. After a few days' halt at Shíráz I therefore rode post to Tehrán, leaving Blanford

---

[1] Sarvístán means 'the place of cypresses.'

to march up by the summer road, by which he reached Tehrán a month later, about the same time as the Sarhang, my coadjutor in Balúchistán, did by the Yazd road.

Thus ended a journey of 2500 miles, of which the most remarkable thing was its utter want of incident.

APPENDIX.

The longitude of Karmán.

As mentioned in the text, the Russian scientific expedition under M. Khanikoff to Eastern Persia in 1858–9 showed that the position of Karmán, given in our maps on the authority of Sir Henry Pottinger, was very incorrect. As also mentioned, I have found reason to diminish this correction considerably—an alteration which affects the longitude of all places on the high road from Karmán through Yazd to Isfahán, and from Karmán towards Sistán, as determined by the Russian expedition.

The following is a brief outline of the case, which I leave to the judgment of geographers.

M. Khanikoff had with him an astronomer, M. Lentz, and several topographers. The result of the labours of the latter have as yet been given to the world on a very minute scale only; but the observations of M. Lentz were published in a pamphlet of 158 pages at St. Petersburgh in 1868.

Being unfortunately in Russian, nothing but the results, and the bare data on which these are founded, are intelligible to a foreigner. From them, however, there is no difficulty in gathering that M. Lentz determined the positions of ninety-four stations, of which the principal, taking them in the order observed, are as follows: Astrabád; Mash-had; Herát; Tún; Birjand; Lásh; Neh; Karmán; Yazd; Isfahán; Káshán; Kúm; and Tehrán.

Of these, the first and last appear to have been assumed from the Caspian survey and from Lemm. Of the intermediate stations, the longitude of Mash-had given by M. Lentz is almost the exact mean of those determined by Fraser and Lemm respectively; and that of Herát agrees nearly with its position as fixed by English officers in 1839.

From Herát to Karmán was new ground or nearly so, and the first serious discrepancy with older authorities occurs in the last-named city, whose position had not been previously laid down from astronomical data.

It may be premised that M. Lentz fixed his longitude by chronometers, of which he appears to have had four. To correct them he took four sets of lunar distances at Mash-had, one at Ghorián, three at Herát, one at Tún, and two at Neh. Of the value to be placed on the last—on the correctness of which appear to depend all his longitudes between Neh and Tehrán, three and a half months' journey—geographers will be able to judge when I mention that they were taken on two successive days, and to the same star, which had an angular distance of 22° to 36° only from the moon, and that the results of the two are 1′ 21″ apart.

In my own journey from Gwádar to Shíráz I found, as stated in Chapter I, that little dependence was to be placed on chronometers, on a rapid land journey during which the same place was never twice visited; and I therefore trusted entirely to perambulating wheels and azimuths for longitude, fixing the latitude nightly by observation. On arriving at Shíráz, 1250 miles from Gwádar, I found my position ten miles east of that fixed by Captain Pierson and myself by telegraph. A careful revision of the sketch sheets enabled me to distribute this error without much doubt or difficulty, aided by sets of lunars, observed at Jálk and Bampúr, and reduced at Greenwich, which, though not enough to depend on, were useful in showing on which side my error at those places lay. In this way I laid down the longitude of Karmán at 59° 59′ 60″, being thirteen to fourteen miles nearer its old position on our maps than M. Lentz had placed it.

A superficial examination of that traveller's book with its formidable array of figures made me tremble for the correctness of my conclusions; but on going into it more carefully, and testing it in a manner now to be described, my confidence was restored, and I was emboldened to pin my faith on my own perambulators rather than on the chronometers and lunars of M. Lentz. I was fortified moreover in this resolve by a passage in M. Khanikoff's brief sketch of his expedition, which I have not at hand, and cannot therefore quote, but which shows that he himself had small faith in astronomical longitudes on land journeys, compared to carefully measured distances.

My test was as follows. In the spring of 1870, I made a compass survey along the line of telegraph from Tehrán to Isfahán, checked by latitudes at each halting-place. An easier road to survey accurately with little labour would be difficult to find, three azimuths, none inclined more than 25° to the meridian, covering the whole distance of 250 miles. The next winter Captain Pierson and I determined by telegraph the differences of longitude between Tehrán, Kúm, Káshán, and Isfahán; in each case by four independent sets of altitudes at either station. The results showed errors in the sketch sheets in no case amounting to more than a mile.

This gave me a method satisfactory to myself—whatever it may be to M. Khanikoff, who does not believe in the scientific accuracy of Indian officers—by which to measure the dependence to be placed on M. Lentz.

The following table shows the position of each halting-place between Isfahán and Tehrán according to my sketch sheets (corrected by longitudes fixed by telegraph), and according to M. Lentz's chronometers (uncorroborated by any topographical drawings). Ten seconds of time have been deducted from each of the Russian longitudes, on account of the correction for the longitude of Tehrán from Greenwich, ascertained by Col. Walker, Captain Pierson, and myself, in 1871:—

Locality.	Longitude from M. Lentz.		Longitude from Major St. John.	Difference.	
	Time.	Arc.			
	h. m. s.	° ′ ″	° ′ ″	′ ″	
Isfahán	3 26 53	51 43 15	51 39 2	+ 4 13	By telegraph.
Gaz	3 25 55	51 28 45	51 37 30	− 8 45	
Múrchikár	3 25 50	51 27 30	51 28 30	− 1 0	
Soh	3 24 58	51 14 30	51 26 15	−11 45	
Kohrúd	3 24 56	51 14 0	51 26 30	−12 30	
Fin (Káshán)	3 24 54	51 13 30	51 22 30	− 9 0	By telegraph.
Sin-sin	3 24 50	51 12 30	51 16 45	− 4 15	
Pasangán	3 23 52	50 58 0	51 4 30	− 6 30	
Kúm	3 22 57	50 44 15	50 54 0	− 9 45	By telegraph.
Kináragird	3 24 54	51 13 30	51 18 0	− 4 20	
Tehrán	3 25 40	51 25 0	51 25 0	0 0	

There are startling discrepancies. Taking the places first of which the longitudes were fixed by telegraph, it will be noticed M. Lentz and I agree as to the relative positions of Kúm and Káshán; but that he places them nearly ten miles further west than I do. Our agreement so far tends to corroborate my correctness, my longitude being independently fixed by telegraph from a common station, Tehrán. In the case of the intermediate stations I have no telegraph to rely on, but let it be observed that while M. Lentz and I are nearly in agreement as to the relative positions of Soh and Kohrúd, separated by a range of mountains and a winding pass, we differ as to those of Soh and Múrchikár by ten miles and three-quarters. Yet these two places are visible from each other, and an error of that magnitude seems impossible in a compass survey.

It may be objected that our points of observation may have been far apart. In Tehrán this is not the case, as the old Russian embassy, the station given by Lentz, and the telegraph office are on nearly the same meridian, and not more than a quarter of a mile apart.

In the other stations, with the exception of Kúm, where they might be a mile perhaps asunder, our points of observation must be practically identical. In Isfahán, no doubt, they were some distance apart, though certainly not more than half of 4′ 13″, the difference shown in the table. From my knowledge of the town and places where distinguished travellers are lodged, I am inclined to give about a mile and a quarter as the most probable distance apart. The discrepancies in the intermediate stations are, however, quite enough to make any English geographer doubt the accuracy of M. Lentz's work generally, and fully justify me, I contend, in adhering to my own longitude of Karmán. To a certain extent, moreover, I am able to corroborate the correctness of that longitude from M. Lentz's own work. The above table shows that his chronometers between Isfahán and Tehrán were misrated to the extent of two to three minutes of arc. Now he took twenty days to do this journey, and seventy days from the date of his first observation at Karmán till his arrival at Tehrán.

The error at the former place should therefore be three and a half times that between Isfahán and Tehrán, or from seven to ten and a half minutes of arc. Adding to this his error of two and a half minutes in the longitude of Tehrán, we obtain nine and a half to thirteen minutes, which, deducted from 60° 13′, gives a result closely approximating to mine, viz. 59° 59′ 60″.

In justice to M. Lentz I must add that I believe that his chronometric measurements between Isfahán and Tehrán are not a fair sample of his work generally.

Taking my own longitudes of Karmán and Isfahán as a base, I re-adjusted his positions of the intermediate stations, and found them with a single exception to agree closely with those on a careful compass survey made by the late Quarter-Master-Sergeant D. Bower, R.E., in 1870-71.

His Herát lunars also seem good, and the positions of places in Khúrasán, fixed on two expeditions, starting from and returning to that city, are probably trustworthy.

The error, if error there be, would seem to lie between Herát and Karmán. In constructing the map of Persia I assumed M. Lentz's position of Neh to be correct, and interpolated the whole error of 13′ 30″ between that place and Karmán. Subsequent examination of M. Lentz's work rather inclines me to distribute it throughout his whole route from Herát via Sabzwár, Lásh and Neh, to Karmán. Were this done, the position of Neh on the map would be shifted 5′ to the west and that of Lásh 3′ 30″ in the same direction.

O. St. John.

NARRATIVE

OF A

JOURNEY IN BALUCHISTAN.

BY

MAJOR BERESFORD LOVETT, R.E., C.S.I.

NARRATIVE

OF A

JOURNEY IN BALUCHISTAN.

BY

MAJOR BERESFORD LOVETT, R.E., C.S.I.

1. *Preliminary Remarks.*

THE tract of country in which lies the frontier line of delimitation between the territories of H. M. the Sháh and the Khán of Kalát may, I think, be best described in a general manner by reference to the river systems comprised within the limits of Bampúr to the west, Panjgúr to the east, Jálk to the north, and the shores of the Arabian Sea to the south, as it is by a study of the disposition and distribution of the watercourses that a just idea of the configuration of a country can be arrived at.

2. *River Systems.*

There is a mass of mountains lying east of Bampúr, of which the peak called the Kúh-i-Homand[1] is near the culminating point, from which stretch out three water-partings, dividing the country through which their ramifications extend into three large and distinct river basins. The basin which extends south of the Homand Peak is drained by various streams, all falling eventually into the Arabian Sea, at different points along the coast, and amongst the principal of these rivers are those which at their mouths are called the Hingol, the Dasht, the Báhú or Nigor, the Nam, and the Kir. There are, besides these, numerous smaller intermittent streams, comprised within the area of this southern river basin, which likewise make their exit into the waters of the Arabian Sea. The next or the north-west

[1] The spelling adopted by Major St. John in his Map of Western Baluchistan is here retained: but Baluch words are not always easily transliterated.—F. J. G.

river basin is drained by a stream of considerable size, which after collecting the waters of numerous tributaries, flows past the fort of Bampúr with a volume of water which, occasionally, is from 30 to 50 yards across and is forded by wading up to the knees. The ultimate course of this Bampúr river is not precisely known. It is supposed by some, and this is the generally received native opinion, to flow on westerly and issue into the Persian Gulf, near Mínáb, a port not far east of Bandar-Abbás. But as the whole of the tract of country lying between the sea and the limits indicated by the positions of Kasr-Kand, Bampúr, Bam, and Bandar-Abbás is unexplored, it is very doubtful if this supposed course of the Bampúr river will be borne out by future explorations. The third river basin, formed by the lines of elevation of the Balúch mountains, is that lying to the north-east. The rivers draining the districts of Magas and Dízak, as also perhaps the streams flowing from the still more elevated tracts of Sarhad, unite with the rivers coming from the east beyond Panjgúr and its outlying districts, and pour their united waters into the northern desert through a defile in the range of mountains called the Siáneh Kúh. The river thus formed goes by the name of the Máshkíd, the same which has been given to the stream flowing eastwards through the Dízak valley. The eventual course of this stream is problematical. According to the information I was enabled to collect at Panjgúr, the Máshkíd, after its passage through the Siáneh range, runs northerly for four stages or about sixty miles, and loses itself in a salt marsh, at a place called Hauz-i-Kaisr. This river was crossed by Sir A. Pottinger in 1809, and is represented on all maps published previous to our surveys as belonging to the southern river basin, that is, its course is represented as flowing south and eventually emptying itself into the Arabian Sea. That mistake is now rectified, and I think, from a consideration of the difference of elevation between the plateau in which lies the valley stretching from Dízak to Panjgúr and that of the lakes of Sistán, that the waters of the Máshkíd, at some seasons at least, eventually unite in the Sistán marshes with those of the streams flowing from the hills of Herát and Kábul. Should future exploration of the Persian frontier southwards from Sistán towards Jálk succeed in establishing this fact, the drainage area of the Sistán Lake will be found to be vastly larger than it is at present estimated.

3. *Mountain Systems.*

Having thus briefly given an outline of the Balúch river systems, our next consideration will be regarding the general direction and disposition of the mountains comprised within the limits of the districts we have visited.

The general direction of the ranges of hills in Makrán is east and west, in fact more or less parallel to the general line of the sea-coast. These ranges of hills have been elevated in chains parallel to each other, with valleys lying between them. Beginning with the level at the sea-shore, each valley inland is successively of a greater elevation than the preceding one; and thus it is that the valley in which are situated the villages of Dízak, Kúhak, and Panjgúr has a general elevation of 2500 feet above the sea-shore, from which it is not distant, in a straight line, more than 125 miles. The length of the valleys enclosed by these parallel ranges is in some instances considerable. We have an instance of one remarkable for its length in that, extending beyond the limits of Dízak to the west, to five stages east of Panjgúr to the east, where the barrier of the Kalát Hills running north and south closes it in. South of this valley, at the distance of about seventy miles from it, is another equally remarkable for its extent. Commencing at Kasr-Kand, it stretches to the east for about 250 miles, the important towns of Píshín, Mand, Mírí, &c. being situated in it. The other ranges of hills, parallel to those forming the northern and southern limits of these two long valleys, are generally so closely packed together that the intervening valleys are insignificant. There is, moreover, another axis of elevation which, cutting obliquely across these mountain ranges, closes them in on the west; as, for instance, at Kasr-Kand and near Magas. The country lying between these two points has consequently a very contorted mountain system—its ramifications run in some parts north-east and south-west, in others east and west—and peaks and masses of mountain of the most curious and fantastic appearance are frequent. It is undoubtedly the case, that should railway communication from Isfahán to India be undertaken hereafter, the construction of the line from the plain of the Bampúr valley, along the tortuous defiles that pierce this mass of mountain till the western extremities of either of the long valleys we have described be reached, will prove one of the most difficult tasks to be accomplished in the whole length of line. The route between Isfahán and Bampúr is so level that a coach can be driven without much difficulty between these two cities, and certainly no difficulty or obstacle exists for wheeled traffic from one end to the other of either of the two valleys we have mentioned, so that the selection of either of them as the line for a future railway is inevitable, and the importance of information regarding them is thus greatly increased.

4. *Mode of Travelling.*

Having thus in a brief manner sketched out the general conformation of the districts through which I passed, I will now proceed to describe with more detail the various routes I followed. I at first proceeded from Gwádar on the sea coast to Bampúr—reaching that place after a journey of twenty-six days; but as we were compelled to halt at various places owing to defective arrangements for carriage, this time must not be taken as the standard for marching. From Bampúr I returned to Píshín, on the road back to Gwádar, and striking off thence proceeded eastwards to Kej, and from that place northwards to Panjgúr, and then back to the coast. These wanderings enabled me to see a good deal of the country and of its inhabitants. Our mode of travelling was on horseback; servants, tents, and provisions being carried by camels. As I experienced considerable inconvenience from defective arrangements for carriage, a matter in that country of the utmost importance, it may be for the benefit of future explorers to embody the result of my experience in a few practical hints. My first recommendation is to bring your own horses, not to trust to the country to produce anything rideable, provide yourself with plenty of horse-shoes and shoeing apparatus, as also some one capable of shoeing horses, as a blacksmith possessing that art is very rarely met with in Balúchistán. If you desire to proceed at your own time, where and when you like; to avoid delay, disappointment, vexation, bargaining, and bother, it is by all means advisable to purchase your baggage camels; pay any price, in order that they may become actually your property. It is only fair to warn future explorers against the Balúch camel-driver, who partakes largely of the nature of the ungainly beast he tends. These men, for obstinacy and perverseness, are unequalled. Amongst other annoyances they will never stir from a halting-place till long after sunrise, and any stage over ten miles or any load over two hundredweight may be made a pretext for desertion or a general strike. If you can procure mules and dispense with the services of that much over-rated animal the camel, do so by all means, even though perhaps the former may require more elaborate arrangements for feeding them. There is fodder, however, to be obtained in most river-beds at a few miles from the coast, sufficient to sustain these useful animals.

5. *Gwádar to Chirak.*

When we set out from Gwádar on the 10th of January, 1871, we had to make three marches to the Dasht river, which flows into the Arabian Sea, near Gwatar. These marches began between nine or ten in the morning, and we reached our halting-places at about 2 p.m. Our halting-places between Gwádar and the Dasht river were Ankora and Faleri, the first thirteen miles and the latter twenty-six miles from Gwádar. The selection of these spots as halting places depended on the presence or absence of fresh water. As it had rained hard about fifteen days previous to our quitting Gwádar, the presence of a few pools of fresh water in the 'fiumara,' called as above, induced us to halt there; but when we set out from Gwádar we were prepared, if necessary, to make a continuous forty-mile march to the banks of the Dasht river. At the season of the year in which we journeyed this would not have been attended with any hardship beyond fatigue to man and beast, but later on in the year the passage from Gwádar to the Dasht river is a formidable undertaking, and much suffering from thirst is experienced. Our route up to the Dasht river lay along the telegraph line.

From the Dasht river, on whose right bank we halted several days, we proceeded westwards to Mírí Bazár. Our destination was Bampúr, and we might have selected the route *via* Píshín and Sarbáz, or Báhú and Sarbáz, but as Din Muhammad, the chief of Dashtiárí, represented to us that difficulties existed from want of water along these routes, we were induced to choose the route *via* Mírí Bazár and Kasr-Kand. Subsequent events proved there was no foundation for the representations Din Muhammad made, which were dictated entirely by interested motives. As a direct route from Gwádar to Bampúr there is no doubt the route *via* Píshín and Sarbáz is preferable. Sir Frederic Goldsmid, who arrived at Gwádar from Bampúr, performed this journey with a very numerous retinue in twelve days. I would observe here that were it not for the conveniences that exist at Gwádar for telegraphic and postal communication with India and Europe, and also from the fact that an established British authority is there resident, Gwatar would have been preferable as our 'point de départ,' and I think that, for military operations in Balúchistán, should necessity arise, troops landed there could advance along the banks of either the Dasht or Báhú river with greater facilities and less hardship, to the points in the interior where their presence might be required, than they could by proceeding from Gwádar.

We halted twice between the Dasht river and Mírí Bazár. Our first halting-place, Rimdán, was about eighteen miles from the banks of the Dasht; the road thereto lay over a perfectly flat plain, sparsely dotted with camel-thorn shrubs, which afforded pasturage to our camels as they marched along. The Balúchís do not attach their camels one behind the other by nose-tethers as in India, but they allow them to wander about, the drivers moving about in rear from flank to flank of the herd, urging them forwards with an occasional thwack, but mostly by a monotonous grunting, which seems as inherent to camel-men generally when driving their beasts, as the peculiar 'shishing' noise, when brushing down a horse, is to our grooms. The halting-place at Rimdán commended itself to our notice by a few pools of fresh water, otherwise it had no attractions, and the early part of our journey the next day was equally uninviting. Nothing was to be seen but the bare extent of plain all around, with arid-looking hills about eight miles to the north, and a singular mass of hills (the Darabol Kúh) lying about ten miles off to the south. The summit of the Khákhi Kúh to the west was visible, but all other objects to the east, and towards the sea, were distorted by the effects of the mirage which generally commenced to appear about two or three hours after sunrise. As we neared the village of Sísád, however, the dreary aspect of the country changed, and from this point, till we emerged a fortnight later upon the Bampúr desert, the country we passed through, whether plain or mountainous, was more or less interesting. The villages of Sísád, Náo, and a few very small hamlets, lay in our route to Mírí Bazár. They are situated on branches of the Báhú river, here much subdivided into small streams, which reunite south of a solitary rocky eminence in this neighbourhood, called Char-gul-ka-Dikri, and being joined also by the waters of the Kajú river, flow on in a broad stream to the sea, into which it disembogues near Gwatar. The banks of these streams, especially in the neighbourhood of the villages we passed by, were fringed with a thick belt of tamarisk bushes, as also graceful acacias and date-palms. The fields, fenced round by thorn hedges, were sown with barley and wheat, which were then green. There were numerous pools formed by the overflow of the Báhú, on which teal and wild duck were disporting themselves, whilst the adjacent copses afforded cover to numerous francolin, whose slaughter enabled us to effect a grateful change in our *menu*. We noticed too on the intervening plains lying between the streams sand-grouse and bustard, the 'ahubareh' of the Persians, a name which has been twisted into 'obára' by the Indians. We found Mírí Bazár an inconsiderable place, and to judge from the difficulty we experienced in obtaining provisions and fodder, as well as fuel, its resources might be supposed limited; but as our difficulties in that respect were entirely owing to the obstructive conduct of the local chief, Din Muhammad, such a deduction cannot be made. Our route towards the north lay in the direction of a lofty range of hills we could discern from Mírí Bazár, which is known as the Bagárband, on the further side of which we were informed lay Kasr-Kand, the chief town on our route to Bampúr. One day's march from Mírí Bazár brought us to Chirak, a village at the northern limit of the plain of Dashtiárí. We passed the village of Báji *en route* a few miles out of Mírí. Up to this place our route lay through well cultivated lands, irrigated by numerous canals, and plentifully studded with acacias, date-palm, tamarisk, and jujube trees. From Báji we had to cross a wide hot plain, irrigated by a system of reservoirs, representing considerable expenditure of time and labour—I will not say money, as the works were probably constructed by forced labour. We at last reached the village of Baila, and a couple of miles further on that of Chirak. As we had here attained the edge of the mountains, the leading characteristics of the districts we traversed may be thus summarised. From Gwádar to Rimdán we crossed the plain through which flows the Dasht river, and from Rimdán to Chirak our course lay through the districts of Sísád and Dashtiárí, which, as we have stated, are watered by the rivers Báhú and Kajú. The northern limit of these plains is the Bagárband range, and more to the east the Nigor Hills. On the west of the Dashtiárí plain a series of hills runs along the Kajú, and terminates south of Mírí Bazár, at the peak called Ripak. The hills lying east of the Dasht river, and south of Mírí in the Kej valley to the Talár Pass, indicate approximatively the eastern limits of the plains; and a chain of hills extending southwards from Píshín, and terminating in a very distinctive double-headed hill called Jambkí (near to which are the villages of Saman and Zirhan), separates the plains watered by the Kajú and Báhú, or Dashtiárí and Sísád, and from those irrigated by the Dasht river and its tributaries.

These plains are at a level above the sea, varying probably from 90 feet to 300. The soil is alluvial and very fertile, and its capabilities for produce under a systematic scheme of irrigation would be boundless. The other principal town in Dashtiárí, besides Mírí Bazár and Chirak, is Báhú, which I have not visited, but which I understand is of considerable size for Balúchistán. It would be more conducive to a distinct appreciation of the positive size of these places we mention could we give even an approximate estimate of the number of inhabitants. But though endeavours were made by our party to obtain such information, the results are little to be relied upon. I suppose, however, that Mírí Bazár may contain some 1200 souls, Chirak 800. This estimate I form from their size as compared with that of the village of Kalátak in the Kej valley, where I had an opportunity of taking a census with tolerable accuracy. I happened to be at that village on the Id-i-Kurbán, one of the great Islamic festivals, on which occasion all the adult males of the place were ranged, as is the custom for Musalmán congregations, in two rows in rear of the Pishnamáz, or Leader of Prayer. The total number inhabiting Kalátak I estimated, including women and children, to be about 1000. Assuming this as my standard of computation, I think the numbers I have stated pretty correct. Mírí Bazár therefore passes for a considerable place according to the Balúch standard of town populations, though in our eyes it appeared quite insignificant.

The inhabitants of Dashtiárí and Sísád originally came from Sind, and speak a degenerate Sindi, mixed with worse Persian. There are a great number of slaves, and traces of African descent are frequently encountered amongst the population. They live in badly-built mud huts, and are clothed in garments which are never changed except when discarded for new ones. The men wear their hair long, and are very proud of their locks, which they keep constantly moist with rancid butter. The characteristic red skull-cap of the Balúchís was not much worn by the Dashtiárís.

With regard to the aspect of these plains, nothing can be prettier than certain effects that the traveller meets with. For instance, just before and after sunset, under particular conditions of the atmosphere, the landscape is charming. The hills surrounding the Dashtiárí plain have very pronounced outlines: this, with the softening effect of distance, makes their arid sides display various blues and greys, forming a delightful background for the middle distance, composed of date-palm and jujube trees, and picturesque Balúch habitations. The wheels for raising water out of wells or canals, and the groupings of the inhabitants, variously occupied, as, for instance, women fetching water, have a very good effect. But like many Oriental scenes, a nearer inspection destroys the illusion.

6. *Chirak to Kasr-Kand.*

The next section of our march towards Bampúr was through a mountainous region, which occupied us a week of actual marching; but as we halted at Kasr-Kand several days, the time really employed from one place to the other was longer.

We ascended from the level of the Dashtiárí plain, that is about 300 feet, to the upland or plateau of Champ, which is about 3700 feet above the sea-level. We crossed two distinct chains of hills, the Bagárband range, north of which lies the town of Kasr-Kand, and a lesser range called the Nigoj Hills. The latter was stated to form the northern boundary of that part of Makrán where our route lay. In character both these chains resembled each other, both being sandstone with strata nearly vertical. On leaving the village of Chirak on the northern edge of the Dashtiárí plain, we followed the track of a dry watercourse up to its source westerly, and then, crossing a slightly elevated watershed, proceeded northwards along another watercourse, the watershed of which we reached in a gorge situated in the Bagárband mountains; and then we emerged into the Kasr-Kand valley. Both these ravines, along whose windings we were obliged from the steep and rugged nature of the banks to wend our way, were waterless, except at rare intervals, such as the spots where we encamped for the night. Their beds are covered with boulders of all sizes, and are studded profusely with plants, called in Balúchistán 'Písh,' and on the Indo-Afghan frontier 'Muzri.' This plant has been frequently described, but it is so generally met with in Balúchistán, and is so useful in various ways to its inhabitants, that no description of that country would be complete that did not contain some account of it. The 'Písh' grows wild along the river-beds and torrents in little clusters, its roots or rhizomes extending sometimes from ten to fifteen feet. I noticed few plants in flower, for as they belong to the aloe family, flowering is a rare occurrence. Like the Afghans, the Balúchís make great use of its leaves. Amongst the various usages, it serves for making matting, which, according to the coarseness or fineness of manufacture, is used for thatching, flooring, baskets, bags, bedding, caps, sword-belts, gun-slings, and even pocket-books. The leaf also, when steeped in water and beaten out so as to separate the fibres, is used in the same manner as hemp is, to make ropes, cordage, and string. The fibre also can be cleverly twisted and made up into sandals, which, however, will stand the wear and tear of a rough day's march but poorly. The Balúch wayfarers, whilst trudging along the rough torrent-beds and mountain-paths, are generally occupied in making up the sandals they will wear on the morrow, for as the day wanes the state of their *chaussure* gets visibly worse and worse. It is generally at night, whilst their dinner is being cooked, that they occupy themselves hammering out the stock of suitable leaves collected on the march, into fibre to be used in making sandals on the next day's march, accompanying this occupation either by singing, or listening to the vocalisation of some more gifted companions; but, however gratifying to Balúch ears, this singing sounds to the uninitiated merely a monotonous high falsetto note, alternated by deep bass grunts. The leaf, moreover, can be easily arranged to resemble a ladle, and as such is used by the thirsty traveller. The 'Písh' berries are threaded and then used as rosaries, and the young shoots are edible. I have also seen, but this was considered 'un objet d'art,' a water-pipe for smoking made out of the leaves of this universally useful plant.

7. *Kasr-Kand.*

After passing through the Bagárband range we reached the town of Kasr-Kand, situated at the western extremity of the long valley we have before described as stretching eastwards to the slopes of the Kalát hills, and close to where the Kajú stream issues from the hilly district to the north. Shortly below the village, the Parsuk stream joining the Kajú, the latter flows on past Búg and Heit, villages south and north of the river respectively. Kasr-Kand is a cluster of round wigwam-looking huts constructed of the stalks of palm-leaves and wattling. There are also surrounding the fort, which is the residence of the chief Shafi Muhammad (February 1871), a number of small square-built mud houses, with flat roofs. The village or town stands in the middle of an extensive grove of date-palms, interspersed amongst which are small fields, yielding crops of rice, barley, wheat and millet, also tobacco and beans. Near the village, standing on an eminence, are the remains of what used to be the fort in former days. There are also springs (seven in number) north-east of the village, which furnish the water-supply of the village. There were, besides date-palms, a few mango-trees. The route from Kasr-Kand eastwards along the valley is quite easy; and there are, so it would appear from the accounts we received, no obstacles to wheeled traffic, of much moment, between it and Píshín.

Leaving Kasr-Kand, where from deficiency of carriage we had to halt several days, we ascended the Káju stream, reaching its source at Champ on the third day. The march was a repetition of what we had experienced before, our course was confined to the meanderings of the river, the bed of which was covered with shingle and boulders. The banks were at intervals cultivated in small patches; a few barley fields fringed with date-palms constituting all that was to be seen in the way of agriculture or vegetation. We met very few nomads and no inhabitants till we arrived at Shurián and Champ.

The hills through which we passed are generally low, that is, not more than 400 or 500 feet high, except the Nigoj hills that are of considerable size and mostly composed of sandstone. The villages of Shurián and Champ are situated on a plateau, which is divided from the lower one of the Bampúr plain by a range of hills attaining considerable elevation, especially the peak called Ahu Ran. On the west the Lashar hills bound it, as on the south do the Nigoj hills we had passed through. To the east, it is not bounded by a distinct range; but by the blending together, as it were, of the hill-ranges to the north and south.

There was very little vegetation noticed on this plateau; there were a few plots of cultivation near Shurián and Champ, but nowhere else.

Champ itself is situated on the banks of a ravine, and boasts of a tower and a few mud houses. The inhabitants showed marked signs of negro blood, many amongst them indeed being pure Africans.

8. *From Champ to Bampúr.*

On leaving the village of Champ we proceeded northerly, and about a mile on we crossed the watershed separating the Champ plateau from the river-basin drained by the Bampúr river. Descending from the uplands along the rugged bed of a ravine that runs in a northerly direction, we suddenly emerged, after about three hours' marching, upon an immense wide plain, extending in a boundless horizon to the west. We camped for the night at the little village of Surmich, where we found the ruins of an old caravanserai, and two wells affording a supply of tolerably sweet water. The next morning, early, we recommenced our march towards Bampúr, enjoying the bracing air of the desert and admiring the perfect clearness of the atmosphere, which enabled us distinctly to see the tower of the fort at Bampúr, though distant forty miles from where we stood. The snow-capped Básmán Hill, about forty miles still further off, stood out in magnificent splendour against the bright blue sky, a marvellously grand and beautiful object. Seen from the southern edge of the Bampúr desert it has a sugar-loaf outline, and as there are no other mountains at all approaching it in height visible in that portion of the horizon, its appearance thus standing alone is rendered more imposing. The depth of the sands intervening between Surmich and Bampúr rendered a direct march to the latter impracticable for our laden camels. The appearance of the desert is curious: the sands have, by the action of the wind, been heaped up in great ridges or waves, running in a north-west and south-east direction, and attaining occasionally an altitude of forty feet. The average height from trough to crest is about sixteen to twenty feet; the crests of these veritable billows varying in distance apart from one hundred to three hundred feet. It is not precisely known what the limits of this sandy ocean are on the west, but eastwards they are distant about forty miles. From Surmich, on this account, we were obliged to pursue our march by skirting the scarp of the Champ uplands on our right hand, halting in one of the numerous ravines that intersected our route, where a small spring of water, called Morin Pisha, invited our camping for the night. Continuing our march for about five miles more along the foot of the hills, the lessened depth of sand enabled us again to resume our progress across the desert in a northerly direction. A small date-grove called Gwárpusht, where there was a well, furnishing a scanty supply of indifferent water, was our next halting-place; and here, on the following morning, our party was met by Sir F. Goldsmid's aide-de-camp, who, accompanied by several Persian officials and their following, proceeded with us into Bampúr, where we joined the Mission Camp.

9. *Bampúr to Píshín, viâ Sarbáz.*

As Bampúr and the surrounding country is described in other parts of this book, to avoid repetition I will now describe my route back from thence towards the coast, *viâ* Ispatki and Sarbáz.

Leaving camp late in the afternoon, I rode through the jungle along the north coast of the Bampúr river for about eight miles, and encamped at a weir in course of construction for irrigation purposes. I remarked several villages lay on my left hand, but none were to be seen on the south side of the stream. Crossing it next morning, and passing through a fringe of tamarisk scrub about a mile in depth that became thinner and scantier as we advanced, we found ourselves again in the desert, our steps directed towards a gap in the southern hills east of the Abu Ran Peak, as our path to Sarbáz lay through it. Wending our way slowly and wearily for many hot hours, we followed our guide, who, turning off slightly to the right of the direct route, was leading us to a halting-place near the hills where we had expected to find water in a tank. It, however, was empty, so we had therefore to do without water till about noon next day, for it happened that our third march out of Bampúr on the 17th of February lasted seven hours, and though our road lay entirely along a river-bed, at Ab Duzdán and Ab Sowárán, usual watering-places, there was no water to be had; mercifully, after proceeding on about four hours more, a little water was obtained by digging in the river-bed, otherwise our little party might have suffered severely. We encamped where the ravine or river-bed bifurcates, at a place called Kahíri. One route from hence is the easier but longer road to Sarbáz, and is practicable for guns; but the other, the more difficult one, *viâ* Ispatki, over a watershed of considerable altitude, was the one we pursued. The hills through which we passed were composed of clays, marls, and limestones, in vertical strata with occasional beds of sandstone. The vegetation was almost exclusively tamarisk and aloe.

We arrived at Sarbáz the next day, that is, in four marches from Bampúr. The road as hitherto was confined to the river-bed which at Sarbáz is of considerable width : water was found everywhere along this march, after we had descended about five miles below or south of Ispatki. We observed date-trees and cultivation commencing at about ten miles above Sarbáz, which consists of a mud castle on the summit of a rock overlooking and commanding the river, and surrounded by about fifty huts. It is situated at the junction of the rivers draining the Champ plateau to the west and the Nashkand district to the east— an area of considerable extent; so that occasionally, as happened in 1869, inundations occur, very destructive to the date-groves fringing their banks. I noticed the ruins of small breast-works of stone erected on the small hills surrounding and commanding the Sarbáz castle, indications of hostilities that had occurred here about the year 1860, when Saif-ud-din was ruler of Magas.

10. *Sarbáz to Píshín.*

Our march on the 20th of February was interesting, and lay chiefly through a long defile, piercing the continuation of the Nigoj hills to the west. Passing the village of Dipkhúr we halted at a village called Ghufar-Khan. The road as usual was the river-bed itself, in which was a full running stream all the way. The cliffs on both sides are of sandstone, and about 200 to 300 feet high and very steep. The banks on each side were thickly planted with date-trees, and every piece of ground capable of cultivation was covered with barley crops. We passed the small villages of Kuhmetah and Pirsan, on our way through the above defile.

The village of Dipkhúr, or the 'River mouth,' is situated at the confluence of the river flowing past Sarbáz and of another coming down from the north-west, called the Kásh.

We continued our course for two marches along the Sarbáz river to where it issues into the continuation of the Kasr-Kand valley which has been previously described. *En route* we passed the towns of Párúd, Fírúzábád, and Rask; the river as we advanced became much wider, and meandered through hills composed chiefly of conglomerate. At Rask, leaving the Sarbáz river, our route lay in an easterly direction at the foot of the Sardu or Rundu range, on the north side of which lies the village of Mortaneh, and south of our route lay the village of Baftán.

On issuing from the mountains we saw a wide plain stretching out to the south, bounded on the east by low hills, apparently connected by smaller ones to the Bagárband range. The Píshín and the Baftán valleys are drained by rivers which, uniting their waters to those of the Sarbáz river, have cut a deep river-bed through the clay and conglomerate soil as far as Báhú. The vegetation, consisting as usual of the aloe and tamarisk, was scanty until we reached nearly half way across the plain towards Píshín, where, owing to the presence of numerous streams (then dry), a thin fringing of mimosa thorn, tamarisk, madder, bushes, and jungle grass indicates the meanderings of these rivulets.

The village of Píshín has two forts, one called Múlla Chákar's tower, and the other belonging to Abd-ul-Rahím. Each of these towers is surrounded by a congeries of palm-leaf huts inhabited by a motley population of Balúchís and Africans. The date-groves attached seem to be of recent growth, and are extensive.

11. *Píshín to Kej.*

Another geographical feature we have to describe is the valley extending from Píshín to Kedj or Kej. This valley, as the reader will bear in mind, is but the continuation of the Kasr-Kand valley eastwards, though at a much lower level. The mountains on the north side of the valley, of which the peak called Kúh-i Shairas forms the most conspicuous object, have a lofty and bold outline. Those on the south are comparatively low. On our march from Píshín to Mand, the only place we found water at was a well about half way between these two places.

Mand is a place of considerable importance; it is inhabited by Rinds, a Balúch tribe, who can here turn out about 1500 fighting men. There are five towers to be seen, denoting as many villages at different points of the vast date-grove in which they are situated. This grove is irrigated by *kanáts*, or subterranean canals, leading from the foot of the hills on the north side of the valley.

The next town to the east, and distant about five hours' march, is Túmp. The road thereto lies on the south side of the valley: the Nihing river, issuing out of the northern range at about ten miles east of the Kúh-i-Shairas, makes a sweep to the south and east, and is fed by numerous tributaries, dry when we passed, but their courses from either side of the valley marked by bushes and trees. At about fifteen miles from Mand we passed a date-grove called Gumází, and farther on those belonging to the village of Túmp commence. They are extensive, and include within them small plots of ground under cultivation, that yield crops of barley, wheat, beans, clover, and tobacco. At the south side of these groves is a high mud-built castle situated in the midst of a quadrangular enclosure. Here, as also at the village where I halted the next day, viz. Nasírabád, we found that the inhabitants do not sow more than what just suffices for their immediate wants. We found their stores of wheat exhausted, and as no barley was to be obtained, our horses were obliged to be fed on millet grain and rice.

We crossed the Nihing at Asíabád, traversing from the south to the north side of the valley. The river at the time was about thirty feet wide and only a few inches deep; but it must be a magnificent stream when in flood, judging from the deep holes scoured out in its bed.

Nasírabád is the lowest point in this valley; here the Nihing meets the Kíl river, and the two uniting flow south under the name of the Dasht river. The defile through which it traverses the chain of southern hills is at the foot of a mountain called the Kúh-i-Mulla. The general character of the soil through which the Nihing flows is a conglomerate composed of *débris* washed down from the adjacent hills. The jungle growing on the banks is almost exclusively of camel-thorn trees, and east of Asíabád is very thick. Cultivation near the river is however abundant, and the number of *kanáts*, some in use and others abandoned, testify to former if not present prosperity.

Kedj or Kej is a small district comprising ten villages. Mírí is the chief village, though not the largest, that being Turbat. The fortress of Mírí looks very picturesque at a distance, as then it resembles a grim square four-towered castle, perched upon a rocky eminence overlooking the surrounding villages, fields, and dark-green date-groves. The distant background formed by the hills in the Kalwar direction has a fine effect, which, however, is rudely dispelled on a nearer approach. The grim mediæval-looking castle fades into the ugly reality of a paltry mud enclosure; the pretty villages are found to be but collections of miserable hovels of mud and thatch, and the soft blue hills are shown to be but arid bare rocks glistening and sweltering in the sun. Kej is reputed to be the hottest place in all Makrán, and this not unlikely is correct, as even so early as the month of March, whilst surveying in the neighbourhood, I observed the thermometer in the shade marked 125° Fahr.

12. *Kej to Panjgúr.*

The next portion of Balúchistán we have to describe is the Zámrán district, in which also lies the Bolida valley. This place had never been visited by any European before myself. The hills to the north of the Kej valley, which we have been describing, are traversed through to the Giruk Pass, which is about north of the village of Mírí. It is not very long, but impracticable for guns, though a few hours' labour bestowed on improving the road in the neighbourhood of the watershed of the hills would suffice to make the track passable. The pass is of course, as generally elsewhere amongst the hills in Balúchistán, the bed of a torrent; the surface at its mouth is very broken, being composed of large boulders, but the track improves as one ascends. The gradient is very easy.

On issuing out of the Giruk Pass, we reached the plateau of Bolida, which stands considerably higher than the Kej valley—in fact, it is on a level only slightly lower than the watershed of the hilly range through which we had passed. We marched for several hours over a plain dotted here and there with a few low hills, and having its surface sparsely studded with a scant vegetation of camel-thorn shrubs and other bushes. At last we arrived at the river Ghíshkhúr, on the banks of which is situated the Bolida date-grove. A description of Bolida must necessarily very much resemble that of other villages or clusters of villages, such as we have several times already described. In the midst of the grove are five villages, viz. Mináb, Salor, Chib, Bert, and Koshk. These villages are surrounded by a few fields yielding the usual crops of wheat, barley, millet, beans, &c., besides a few gardens in which I observed mango and lime trees. Each village has its castle or fort, built of mud-bricks, with its lookout tower and small gateway, and also its own chief or head man. Chib is supposed, at least when I was there, to be the chief village of this little district.

I will now describe the route from Bolida to Panjgúr *viá* Dís. There is an alternate route *viá* Isayáb, which I took when returning from Panjgúr. The route *viá* Dís lies for two long marches through the sandstone ridges of Zámrán. These ridges vary in breadth from a few yards to perhaps a quarter of a mile, and differ in height from 80 to 900 feet. The path along which we had to travel was the bed of a torrent, which was in a few places a narrow and deep channel not more than seven feet wide, so that a laden camel was with difficulty enabled to pass along. Owing also to the presence of strata of slaty clay alternating with the sandstone, portions of the torrent-bed were much water-worn, and so slippery as to be very hazardous footing for beasts of burden. We ascended a tributary of the Bolida river or Ghískhor, called the Mudí Khor, until we reached a watershed, crossing which we entered the bed of another torrent, which also eventually falls into the Ghíshkhúr. This stream, called the Shitáb, is ample, has many tributaries, and its clear sparkling waters course over a hard clayey bottom. The vegetation in the river-bed is more diversified than usual, consisting of aloe, jujube, wild almond, and tamarisk shrubs. Fodder of three different kinds of grass is also abundant. Leaving at last the Shitáb we accomplished a steep ascent, and gained a plateau, where the aneroid indicated an elevation of 2650 feet. This was the Parom plateau, and the next march brought us to the ruined fortress of Dís, situated on the Balúch frontier, not far from the source of the Nihing river. We observed evidence of former cultivation about this fort—the remains of artificial banks to collect rain-water abounding all over the district—but of actual cultivation we saw only a few patches near Dís. During our three marches from Bolida to Dís we came across only a few nomad Balúchís, and from all inquiries I could make, there exists no village between these two places, neither on nor off the direct route. It is a very desolate and wild country. The hills are peculiarly unattractive, even repulsive; but the river-beds, from more abounding vegetation, are pleasanter paths to travel than those, for instance, about Kasr-Kand or Champ. We noticed hardly any form of animated life, not even a bird.

West of the fort of Dís is the watershed dividing the Parom plateau from the valley along which the Nihing river flows. This spot is called Sar-i-Shum. It is about twenty-five miles distant from Dís. As now ascertained, the Nihing river rises there and flows in a south-westerly direction round the district of Zámrán, of which it forms the boundary. The reader will remember it entered the Kej valley, near the village of Mand. On the northern side of this river rises the lofty range of hills belonging to the Bampúsht district.

They present from Dís a striking appearance, and are said to be tolerably fertile on their northern slopes. The peaks reach an altitude of about 5000 feet above the sea-level.

The waters of the Parom plateau do not find an outlet into any stream of consequence, they are collected in a marsh lying east of Dís, spreading out about twelve miles in diameter. After heavy rains this area is flooded, but at the time of my visiting this locality, February 1871, all water had evaporated, and the area liable to inundation was unmistakably delineated by an expanse of dazzling whiteness, produced by salts left after the evaporisation of the waters.

The Bampúsht range just mentioned stretches in a thin broken line of hills almost up to Panjgúr. From the summit of one of these hills, called Pímpíska, I obtained a tolerably good idea of the aspect of the country lying to the north, which presents a spectacle of inconceivable desolation, aridity, and barrenness. In fact, since leaving the comparatively luxurious banks of the Shitáb stream, so desolate was the country we passed through, that our journeying was entirely dependent on the presence of water, and the length or shortness of the marches was regulated accordingly. As the supply of water at the spots we halted at is precarious, there was always some anxiety whether, on arrival at the well or pond our guides recommended, the necessary water for man and beast would be forthcoming. Thus, on leaving Dís, we halted eight miles further on near the Pímpíska peak at a well; and the next day we proceeded thirty miles towards Panjgúr, and halted late in the afternoon at the Sowárán tower, where the presence of a large pond of rain-water invited our remaining for the night. *En route* we crossed the bed of the Gwargo river, then perfectly dry, and from the absence of vegetation, such I should surmise is its usual state. However, the floods in this stream, when they do occur, are doubtless severe, if I may so infer from the deep scourings and other indications of the destructive force of the waters present in its bed. It drains the northern portion of Balgetta, a district still unexplored; and passes through another district called Dásht, the chief town of which is named 'Shabaz.' This tract of land must be more productive than the adjacent districts, as nearly all the wheat consumed in Panjgúr is obtained from Dásht. A short march the next day brought me to Panjgúr. I halted at a small outlying village called 'Kelug' (a generic Balúch term, it would appear, for a date-grove in which there is also cultivation), and was there met by some of the Panjgúr officials. Panjgúr is the name collectively applied to a cluster of villages situated on the Rakhshan stream. The names of these villages are as follows: on the right bank, commencing from the west, are situated Dúm and Tasp; then on the other side of a tributary called the Piskúl is Khudabandan, where the present governor resides; on the further side of Khudabandan flows the Newan tributary into the Rakhshan; and beyond that again, still on the right bank of the main stream, we have Grumkhan and Wajbôde. Opposite to these villages, on the left bank of the Rakhshan, is Sar Khuran and Sordu respectively. Returning westerly, we next pass a *ziárat* (shrine) situated between Sordu and the small village of Chíl Khan; and further on lies Dozanch, also a small village; and then, after a considerable interval, the villages of Mir Shing Khan, Esai, and Mírí, which, however, are so mixed up together that I could not ascertain their precise limits.

Of all these villages, Esai is the largest as regards population, and Tasp the village where most of the 'ancienne noblesse' reside. The date-groves surrounding it and the villages of Khudabandan and Sar Khuran are extensive.

No wheat is raised in Panjgúr itself, all being imported from the outlying districts of Parom, Dásht, and Gichki. Great attention is paid by the inhabitants to the cultivation of dates. These form the staple commodity of Panjgúr, and are exported to India *viâ* Kalát, and to the sea-coast, Gwádar being the principal port for exportation. The best description of dates grown at Panjgúr are of the kind known locally as 'masauti.' These dates are carefully packed in earthenware jars for exportation, and are highly prized, as much because the supply of this kind is limited as from their delicious flavour. As is well known, the fecundation of the female date-palm is effected artificially. When the spathe containing the male flowers, which resemble ears of corn, bursts, the flowers are culled and inserted amongst the flowers of the female tree. One or two of these ears of male flowers suffices to impregnate one female tree. There are about forty to fifty ears in each spathe, sufficient for about thirty female trees. The Balúchís use the pullen of the wild male date-palm trees found at a distance from any date-grove, as they say the produce thus obtained is finer. The palm-trees are raised from seed, and after the third season they bear fruit. The natives have to ascend the trees frequently for the purposes of artificial fecundation, gathering the fruit, and lopping off the dead branches. They perform the ascent by means of a rope passed round the tree, and also round the climber, who by alternately lifting the rope and then himself on the scars of the old branches, gradually gets to the top. The value of dates of all kinds annually exported from Panjgúr is said to be about £4500.

None of the villages at Panjgúr, with the exception of Esai, present any feature of peculiar interest: they resemble other villages in Balúchistán. Esai, however, contains two forts; one called Mírí, which was lately demolished by the Kalát Khán. Its premises cover over three acres of ground, consisting of a high enclosure wall of sun-dried bricks and a lofty interior keep. The architecture was readily recognisable as pure Persian, the remains of vaulting and groining being exactly similar to that seen amongst the ruins at Isfahán. The other fort, which is occupied, is called 'Thull.' Besides the Rakhshan, the water supply of Panjgúr is further increased by three *káriz* coming from the north, from the direction of the Kúh-i-Sabz. These mountains, the northern limits of the Kalát Khán's possessions near Panjgúr, are distant about sixteen to twenty miles north of this town. They form the eastern continuation of the chain that forms the northern boundary of the Dízak valley.

13. *Panjgúr to Mírí.*

The route from Panjgúr to Bolida, *viâ* Isayáb, and along the course of the Gazbastán river, occupied four days. The marches were long, and over very dreary country. Our first march out of Panjgúr led us over a plain covered with an efflorescence of saltpetre, which is collected and used for manufacturing gunpowder. We reached a well at a spot called Narain late in the evening. The next day we crossed the Dásht plain. We started at 7.30 A.M., and marched till 3 P.M. Shortly after beginning our march we passed a ruined fort, unoccupied, called 'Chib.' The plain was thickly covered with coarse grass, such as is used for thatching in Upper India; a few thorn bushes were also scattered about. Isayáb is at the head of one of the sources of the Gazbastán. This stream eventually falls into the Ghíshkhúr or Bolida river. Its course was westerly, and wound about considerably, being bounded on the north and south by lofty and precipitous hills, between which it meanders about. This stream has worn for itself a bed through a hard layer of pebbly conglomerate and alternating strata of indurated clay and sandstone, of the formation usual in Makrán. There is plenty of water in its bed, but in deep pools at short distances apart. Tamarisk, aloe, and oleander flourish in abundance, and the latter being in flower (March) presented a gay appearance in an otherwise desolate route. We at last left the Gazbastán, which trended away south, and crossing a watershed, arrived at the Shitáb stream, the upper portion of whose course it will be remembered we had partially ascended on our way from Bolida to Panjgúr. Here the stream was larger, and there were large deep pools of delicious water at frequent intervals. We crossed it; and after a march of twenty miles, through sandstone hills, very arid and bare, reached again the grateful shade of the palm groves of Bolida, at whose easternmost village of Koshk we halted.

14. *Mírí to Gwádar.*

We must now, to avoid repetition, pass over the route from Bolida to Mírí in the Kej valley, and, resuming our description from this latter place, relate our journey thence to Gwádar. We accomplished the distance in four marches. The first was to Amúlani. The road lay along the banks of the Kíl river for about eight miles. Our guide said that about twenty years ago (1851) a destructive flood had swept away completely an extensive date-grove that occupied the ground we were then traversing. As before mentioned, the rivers in Balúchistán, issuing into the Arabian Sea, are liable to very severe floods. The country through which our path lay was green with tamarisk jungle and *guwasir* thorn; and francolin or 'Black-breasts,' as the Balúchís called them, were numerous. After leaving the banks of the Kíl river, we turned southerly, and entered a series of ranges of low hills, pursuing our course through them for about ten miles. We then issued into a valley called the Amúlani Dumŭk. Water was very scarce during this march, and very muddy. The heat also amongst the low hills was most oppressive, the thermometer in the shade marked 125° Fahr. We halted for the night at a place where we found a few pools in which rain-water had collected, and where, accordingly, a few irregular patches of cultivation testified to the readiness of the inhabitants to utilise to the utmost the scanty rainfall. Sixteen miles over a plain of alluvial soil, intersected by the rivers Sháhid, Níluk, and Dádeh, brought us to a ridge of sandstone hills, crossing which we entered the bed of the Bírí river. Here we found water, and after a halt proceeded westerly and south for about five miles of very arid hills of sandstone alternating with clay. These hills are low, and form the northern outlying ridges of the lofty Saiji range, which extends from the Dásht river at Dradund for a long way to the east. Between these hills and the main range there is a narrow valley drained by rivers flowing from the east and from the west. These streams united form a considerable river, which flows south through the Talár Pass on its course to the ocean. The Talár Pass is about one mile long, and narrow. The defile, from the loftiness and steepness of its sides, presents a remarkably bold and rugged appearance. There is always ample water along the course of the stream, and judging from the marks left by former floods, which were fully 40′ above the level of the stream when we passed through, the roaring flood of water issuing through this defile must be a grand spectacle indeed. Shortly after leaving the Tálar Pass, the road to Gwádar may be followed either *viâ* Tonk and the Kolanch valley, or *viâ* the villages of Bán and Kapar. The latter was the route I adopted. At first we marched over a bare sterile plain, the only vegetation being jujube-trees at rare intervals. Bán is a small village lying on the right hand of the path. We eventually got amongst some low sandstone hills, very arid, and so glistening and glaring in the sun as to be painful to the eyes. When, however, we reached a position about west of Nolent, though yet invisible, we knew by the difference in the moisture of the air that we were approaching the ocean; and towards the evening the temperature was much lower than what we had previously felt for many days. Kapar has a few date-palms, and a little pasturage, with a few wretched hovels. However, I was rejoiced at reaching this place, as the line of telegraph passes through it, and that was tangible evidence of a return, after an absence of many weeks, to the outer confines of the civilised world.

The march into Gwádar the next day was along the sea-shore, and would have been uninteresting and monotonous, were it not for the curious spectacle presented by the Kúh Mehdí, which stands half way. Our route on leaving Kapar was through a labyrinth of 'fiumáre' for some miles. We then crossed the Kurwád river, and three miles more brought me to the sea-shore, along which I travelled right into

Gwádar. The Mehdí hill is a vast cliff of clay, perhaps 350 feet high. The rains of centuries have so furrowed and scooped it out, that at present it resembles, from some points of view, the ruins of some vast cathedral, or of a gigantic amphitheatre. The harder horizontal strata, comparatively unaffected by the rain which has furrowed the intervening softer clay, represent very strikingly tier upon tier of picturesquely dilapidated galleries, or of ruined pinnacles and buttresses. Altogether, the sight is one of the most impressive I have seen. I passed after leaving the Mehdí hill, near to the Daria Cham, a mud volcano, which has, however, been frequently before described; from this a canter along the hard sandy sea-shore, which swarmed with small crabs, for about eight miles, brought me back to the port of Gwádar.

BERESFORD LOVETT.

THE

PERSO-BALUCH FRONTIER MISSION,
1870, 1871,

AND THE

PERSO-AFGHAN MISSION,
1871, 1872,

BY

MAJOR EUAN SMITH, C.S.I.

THE PERSO-BALUCH FRONTIER MISSION, 1870, 1871.

BY

MAJOR EUAN SMITH, C.S.I.

Narrative of the Mission to Makrán.

THE Arbitration on the question of the Persian frontier in Sistán was undertaken by the English Government, under the provisions of Article 6 of the Treaty with Persia concluded at Paris on the 4th of March, 1857, which provided that the Shah should 'refer for adjustment to the friendly offices of England' any differences that might occur ' between Persia and Herát or Afghánistán.'

Persia was the first to signify her willingness to submit the question of Sistán sovereignty and boundary to British arbitration; and the Amir of Afghánistán also acceded to the proposal after some correspondence.

The officer selected by Her Majesty's Government to undertake this difficult and delicate duty was Colonel (now Major-General Sir) Frederic Goldsmid, C.B., who had had a long experience of Eastern peoples and Eastern countries, and who was, at the time of his being nominated the British arbitrator, filling the important post of Director-in-Chief of the Government section of the Indo-European Telegraph. His instructions were, to proceed with as little delay as possible to the province of Sistán, where he was to make a careful survey, and collect as much local evidence as was possible, in company with the delegates of the disputing powers of Persia and Afghánistán; and from whence he was to retire to Herát, or some other convenient town, deliver his arbitral decision, and there await the result of the reference that would necessarily be made thereon to head-quarters at Tehrán and Kábul.

Together with the Sistán arbitration, the settlement of a disputed frontier between Persia and Balúchistán was also entrusted to Colonel Goldsmid by Her Majesty's Government; but that officer was informed that it would not be advisable for him to proceed on this duty, pending an answer to the references on the first; and that it was purposed to address him thereon separately. It will be seen how greatly the line of procedure laid down at the outset had to be modified by force of circumstances[1].

Sir Frederic Goldsmid left England on his special mission on the 28th August, 1870. He was accompanied by Captain Euan Smith, who had been appointed his personal assistant and secretary; and he was empowered to engage the services of one of the Royal Engineer officers attached to the Indo-European Telegraph Department in Persia, to carry on the survey operations incidental to his task. Travelling by Hull, Gothenburg, and Stockholm, the Mission reached St. Petersburg on the 7th September, where Sir F. Goldsmid had an interview with M. Stremaïukoff, the Secretary to the Asiatic Department of the Russian Foreign Office, and after three days' stay left again for Moscow and Nijni-Novgorod, from whence a trip of six days in a very dirty steamer brought them to Astrakhán. At the time the Mission arrived at Nijni-Novgorod the annual fair had just finished, and the filthiness of the town had reached its climax. It is impossible to do even faint justice to so gigantic a subject: Nijni-Novgorod must be seen to be appreciated: the intensity of the dirt, the mud, the smells, the vermin, can only be brought home to one by bitter personal experience. At St. Petersburg we had been joined by Dr. Colville, returning to his appointment as Residing Surgeon at Baghdad. On our arrival at Nijni, we found, to our dismay, that the steamer did not start for Astrakhán till noon the next day, and we were consequently obliged to have recourse to such hospitality as the single hotel at Nijni could afford us. This building, already crowded to the utmost, had not even a dingy bedroom to place at our joint disposal, and we were beginning to meditate on the necessity of passing the night on the soft black mud of the so-called streets, when the cosmopolitan head-waiter suggested that we should jointly occupy

---

[1] For further details the reader is referred to the Introductory Chapter, the particulars given in which it is rather intended to illustrate than to repeat in the present narrative.

one of the dressing-rooms of the public hot baths attached to the hotel, where we passed a very steamy and uncomfortable night. The hotel was crowded with the queerest of characters, and with nationalities as numerous as the stars. A funeral party was carousing in one room: there was a Russian wedding party on the first floor; a Hungarian concert on the second: everywhere merchants were drinking, swearing, and spitting; while the air was permeated with a variety of smells so terrible as to defy analysis. Our steamer passage was not more comfortable. The decks and cabins were crowded with Persians, Armenians, and Jews, returning from the fair, the latter of whom spent their whole time in eating pickled cucumbers steeped in oil, of which they seemed to have an inexhaustible supply in the cavernous pockets of their baggy trowsers. On arrival at Astrakhán we had to go for 100 miles in a flat-bottomed boat to the Caspian steamer, for the mouths of the Volga are too shallow below Astrakhán to admit of navigation by vessels other than of exceptionally light draught. After a pleasant voyage of six days on this inland sea, during which time we had an opportunity of inspecting the famous everlasting fires at Bákú, described by so many writers, we landed at Enzeli, whence it is a five hours' journey to Resht, partly over a large inland lake, and partly over a very bad jungle road. At Resht we stayed for two days at the hospitable house of Messrs. Ralli and Co., and then, riding post for the 200 miles which intervene between that city and Tehrán, finally reached the capital without accident on the 3rd October, 1870. Here we became the guests of Mr. Alison, the British Minister, residing, for the season, in summer quarters at Gulahak.

At the time of our arrival in Tehrán, the Shah, accompanied by most of the principal officers of state, was absent on his pilgrimage to Karbala, having left the conduct of affairs at the capital in the hands of a high dignitary entitled 'Mustofi-ul-Mumálik' (Paymaster of the Kingdom). The Persian Commissioner for the Sistán arbitration had, however, been appointed, and was awaiting Major-General Goldsmid's arrival. Mirza Ma'súm Khán was a native of the province of Adarbaiján, very dark and swarthy, and with a sufficient knowledge of French to enable him to converse fluently in that language, though Turkish was his ordinary medium of communication with servants. He was a man of no family or position, and owed his present appointment to his being the nephew or cousin of Mirza Sa'íd Khán, the Persian Minister for Foreign Affairs, who at this time possessed much influence with the Shah. Mirza Ma'súm Khán's fitness for political employ had not as yet been put to the proof: he had hitherto filled but very subordinate offices, and had been attached to the Persian embassy at St. Petersburg as one of the smaller attachés, where he picked up his knowledge of colloquial French. He had no lack of general intelligence, and was possessed of a considerable fund of humour, which, when matters of duty were not on the *tapis*, made him a very pleasant travelling companion. But it is nevertheless probable that a more unfit man could not have been found for the work to be accomplished. Being possessed of no wealth of his own, he looked upon his present appointment as, above all, affording him the means of enriching himself by bribes and extortion, to which ruling idea the whole of his conduct was entirely subordinated. His want of social position, again, paralysed anything like free or independent action, through fear of responsibility; and his only notion of carrying on diplomatic work, evidently acquired in the Persian Foreign Office, found vent in endless carefully-worded letters, in which the sole object was so to distort the true sense of matters as to render it no longer recognisable. In this accomplishment he took especial pride, and showed great skill in using words which might bear two or three meanings different to that which they naturally at first sight conveyed. He was in utter ignorance of the nature of the work which lay before him, an ignorance which even extended to the geographical position of the province of Sistán; but it is fair to say that on this point he made no profession whatever of even superficial knowledge. Being a man of a singularly presuming nature, he was always striving for a little more than he had a rightful claim to; but the many and severe rebuffs to which he subjected himself by this line of conduct never served to ruffle his extraordinary good-nature. This wonderful good-humour certainly stood him in good stead; it made him a bearable companion, even when the knowledge of his endless petty wiles, deceits, and malversations of the truth was rankling very deeply in the mind—and possibly more than once saved matters from coming to a complete standstill; for it was evidently useless wasting anger upon a man who would not see or believe that you were angry with him. Mirza Ma'súm Khán was, in short, a deceitful friend, and a tricky and untrustworthy public servant; but he was ever and always a cheerful and good-humoured travelling companion.

The British Commissioner had only been in Tehrán a few days, and was busy making his preparations for an early start for Sistán, when he received instructions from the Government of India that completely altered his plan of operations. It was notified that owing to the difficulties in which the Amir of Afghánistán found himself involved with his son, Ya'kúb Khán, the question of the Sistán arbitration must be unavoidably postponed. Major-General Goldsmid immediately telegraphed to propose that in that case the question of the Perso-Kalát Boundary might be proceeded with at once, the Sistán arbitration being left to follow; and to this proposal the Government of India gave their assent. But here difficulties arose on the Persian side: the Shah's consent had been given to the Sistán arbitration on the understanding that it was to be immediately proceeded with; and there is no doubt that His Majesty felt considerable anxiety that, during his absence from Persia, his eastern frontier should be protected from all possibility of Afghan attack by the presence of the British Arbitrator. Now that this matter was postponed, none of the Persian authorities at the capital would take upon themselves the responsibility of ordering Mirza Ma'súm Khán to proceed with the Makrán question. A great deal of discussion and correspondence took place on the subject, and the utmost that could be obtained, in furtherance of the British Commissioner's wish to utilise the time at his disposal, was that the Persian Commissioner should march with the former in the direction of Karmán. Time was thus gained to make the necessary reference to the Shah; and there was also an understanding that, should affairs become sufficiently settled in Afghánistán to admit of the Sistán question being proceeded with by the time we reached Karmán, the Commissioners should branch off thence to Sistán and follow the procedure originally proposed. When it afterwards became evident that the chance of carrying into effect a Sistán arbitration during the year had quite passed away, there was much delay and difficulty in obtaining the Shah's consent to the immediate investigation of the Makrán Boundary. The non-receipt of orders gave the Persian Commissioner endless excuses for delaying at all the large towns through which we passed, where he had favourable opportunities of squeezing the Persian authorities: we were detained in this way four days at Káshán, and fourteen days at Isfahán; and it was not until the 27th November, and after Mr. Alison had been obliged to despatch his secretary to the camp of the Shah at Baghdad, that Major-General Goldsmid received official intimation of the consent of the Persian Government to the Makrán Boundary question taking precedence of the other. This consent was not conveyed to Mirza Ma'súm Khán by his own Government until the 26th December. We had then been halted five days at Karmán, and it would have been impossible to induce the Commissioner to advance a step further without official instructions.

While, however, all this preliminary correspondence was going on at Tehrán, preparations for an early start from the capital were being actively proceeded with. Sixteen good horses were bought at singularly low prices—for the approaching famine had already begun to make itself felt, and the keep of horses had become so expensive as to render owners generally anxious to part with them. The British Legation had furnished an ample supply of excellent Jabalpúr tents, and the necessary train of mules had been engaged. The strength of the Mission had been increased by Captain Beresford Lovett, of the Royal Engineers, who had ridden up post from Shíráz to take charge of the Survey department; and by Quartermaster-Sergeant Bower, of the same corps, who joined as Captain Lovett's assistant, and as a general and most efficient supervisor of camp arrangements and discipline. Mr. Alison had also kindly permitted three of the *ghuláms* (or couriers) attached to the Legation to accompany the Mission, and these men proved of the greatest use. One of them, named Ghafúr Beg, was appointed our Mírakhor, or master of the horse, and did his work right well. There can be no doubt that in this capacity he did not neglect the many favourable opportunities which occurred of feathering his nest by the acquisition of 'Mudákhil[1],' and in many other ways; but he was always active and energetic, and the horses and mules under his charge were, with few exceptions, unusually fit and in good condition.

It was on the 22nd October, 1870, that the camp finally started from Tehrán, and was pitched at a small village called Kala'h-nú, where the General was joined by the Persian Commissioner's party, consisting of Mirza Ma'súm Khán, his son, his step-son (a beautiful scribe always clothed in sky blue, and consequently known henceforth by the cognomen of the Blue Múnshi), and an engineer officer or 'Muhandis,' with a pronounced taste for spirituous liquors. At this

[1] 'Mudákhil' is a word of universal use and great significance in Persia, and is applicable to every sort of profit that is made, legally or illegally, justly or unjustly, by all classes, high and low. It is generally used with regard to profits in hard cash.

village there was a halt of three days to get everything into proper marching order, and to ascertain that no essentials had been forgotten. The weather was most delightful, and nothing could be finer or more delicious than the pure and bracing air. While we were at Tehrán a very remarkable aurora was visible to the north of the Albúrz Hills, presenting the appearance of the whole sky on fire. This occurrence was said by the natives to betoken a severe winter, a prophecy that was certainly borne out by facts.

It was arranged for the sake of convenience that the camps of the two Commissioners should always start at different times, one slightly in advance of the other; and it may be noticed here that at each halting-place the flagstaff with the Union Jack was invariably pitched in front of General Goldsmid's domicile or tent. No objection whatever was made to this arrangement during the whole period of the Makrán Mission; even though the Persian Commissioner had omitted to provide himself with a flag. The fact is mentioned here merely to mark the contrast between the course followed on this occasion, and what, as will be explained, happened later on during the progress of the Sistán Mission.

From Tehrán to Isfahán the road is so well known, and has been so often described by various travellers, that there is but little new to be said about it here. From Kala'h-nú we marched in seven marches to Káshán, passing in the second march through the desert known as 'The Valley of the Shadow of Death' to the magnificent caravanserai of Hauz-i-Súltán[1]. This caravanserai, one of the finest in all Persia, consists of three courts and a *hammám* or public bath. The principal and largest court was built by the Sadr Azim of the present Shah; the second largest by Shah Abbas the Great many years before; and the third by Shaikh Ali Khán, in the reign of Fath Ali Shah. It owes its greatest attraction, however, to its abundant supply of water brought from the neighbouring hills by underground canals six miles

---

[1] On our return to Hauz-i-Súltán in July 1871, as we marched back from Bushahr to Tehrán, we found the supply of water completely exhausted. The caravanserai was quite deserted, travellers being, of course, unable to stop there. The ground was strewed in every direction with the carcases of animals that had died from thirst; and as we left the post-house in the middle of the night, we passed two dead bodies of men who had also perished from thirst, within 50 miles of the capital. The persons in charge of the post-house told us they were often put to extreme straits, having to fetch water from many miles off; but there was not at that time, and probably will not be for some time, any effort on the part of the Persian Government to ameliorate this state of affairs.

long, which were executed at the expense of Hajji Ali, a rich merchant of Tehrán. The accommodation which this caravanserai affords to all travellers, rich and poor, is really on a magnificent scale; but such princely buildings are very common in Persia, being ordinarily erected as 'Sawáb,' or good work, by wealthy men, who have amassed large fortunes, sometimes perhaps in a dubious manner.

Between Hauz-i-Súltán and the holy city of Kúm we crossed the 'Kavir' or Great Salt Desert, which stretches away for hundreds of miles to the east towards Khúrasán. At this point it is 16 miles broad, perfectly level, and quite impassable in wet seasons, when travellers skirt round it along the base of a range of low hills which here terminate its encroachment to the west. The telegraph posts stretch across it in a perfectly unbroken straight line of 25 miles length, commencing from a little north of the Hauz-i-Súltán caravanserai and continuing a long way the other side of the desert. The scenery is of the most desolate description, and all the streams are salt—including the river at the station called Pul-i-Dalák, or the Barber's Bridge, situated 22 miles south of Hauz-i-Súltán, the surface of which was nevertheless covered with ducks and waterfowl of every description.

We halted for one day at the holy city of Kúm (where we received by telegraph the news of the capitulation of Metz with 170,000 men). This city, which is a very favourite spot for the interment of the Faithful, who are brought here from great distances, and of whose dead bodies carried upon mules we passed several caravans upon our way, contains one of the most holy shrines in Persia, in which is interred the body of Masúma Fatima, the sister of Imám Raza. The shrine, which presents at a distance very much the same appearance as one of the gilded domes in the Kremlin at Moscow, was originally erected by Shah Súltán Husain Nádir, the gilding of the dome being subsequently commenced by Fath Ali Shah, and completed by the present king. It is, as usual, a surface of gold on plates of copper. A handsome clock was afterwards added to the dome by the liberality of the Governor of Hamadán. The bodies of ten sovereigns, 444 saints and immediate members of royal families repose within the sacred precincts of the shrine, and the whole of the neighbouring ground outside the walls presents the appearance of one vast burying-ground. It is customary to make a pilgrimage to this shrine before proceeding to Mash-had or Karbala. A theological college was established here by Fath Ali Shah, which is now held in great repute, and is attended by more than 100 students.

Another curious feature at Kúm is presented in the number of conical buildings that rise above the level of the neighbouring houses. These are the shrines of saints of lesser note, but are more remarkable as being the favourite resort of an immense number of storks, which year after year have built their nests in a succession of layers on the top, and are looked upon as sacred. Notwithstanding the great repute in which the city is held on account of its shrine, it presents but a melancholy appearance, from the greater part of it being in ruins. Out of 20,000 houses which it originally possessed, only 4,000 are now habitable. Its streets and *bazárs*, except in the immediate vicinity of the shrine, are deserted and dangerous from the innumerable holes and pitfalls with which they abound; and its general condition provides an impressive commentary on the state of absolute stagnation which seems to be one of the chief characteristics of the Muhammadan religion. As might be expected, the mullas, or priests, form a large proportion of the population, which though extremely fanatic, are still much more civil and respectful in their bearing towards Europeans than in many other cities in Persia. A curious instance of fanaticism was, however, related by one of the European sergeants here in the employ of the Indo-European Telegraph, who, having lost his child, vainly endeavoured to purchase a plot of ground sufficient for its burial. The mullas, by asking an exorbitant price for the smallest allotment, practically refused the request, and the body had eventually to be interred in the sergeant's own compound. The principal manufactures of the place are pottery and shoes, the leather for the latter being tanned with the bark of the pomegranate, which abounds here and is excellent. Capital cotton is also grown in the vicinity, and the castor-oil plant appears to be largely cultivated. The Governor of the place, who visited Sir Frederic Goldsmid, expressed a most righteous horror of the telegraph, which he appeared to think exposed him to constant danger of capricious orders from Tehrán.

We reached Káshán on the 2nd November, and found our enforced halt there very welcome—especially for the horses, many of which were suffering greatly from severe chapped heels, occasioned by the unaccustomed exercise of regular and long marches at a foot pace, and by the excessive saltness of the soil, which irritated the open wounds and prevented their closing. Only the grey and white horses were affected in this manner. Horses with black or brown feet did not suffer at all.

While we were at Káshán the usual ceremonial visits were interchanged between Sir Frederic Goldsmid and the Prince Governor, a man of very unprepossessing appearance, who had the reputation of being excessively cruel. He was, however, very intelligent, and, strange to say, took a great interest in the Franco-Prussian war. His subjects in Káshán give him but little trouble, as they are famed for their industry; and especially for their love of peace at any price, which has caused them to be considered the greatest cowards in all Persia—a sweeping accusation. There are some 90,000 inhabitants in Káshán, of which town silk and copper pots are the chief produce. The latter, many of them beautifully inlaid and engraved, find their way to all parts of Persia; and the silk, of which the annual out-turn is about 1400 *manns*, is sent in a manufactured state to Russia. The *bazárs* in the city are very fine, and so extensive that it takes 25 minutes to ride through the main avenue. And there are no less than 24 caravanserais for the sale of goods, and 35 for the accommodation of strangers; in addition to which there are 34 *hammáms* or public baths, 18 large mosques, 90 lesser shrines, and a large college founded by the mother of Fath Ali Shah. The most interesting place in the neighbourhood is, however, the Palace of Fin, which has attained a melancholy notoriety in connection with the ill-fated Wazir, Mirza Taki Khán, to whom we shall shortly have occasion to revert. We rode over to see the village, situated about six miles west of Káshán, of which the principal attractions are its water and its garden. The former, which irrigates all the neighbourhood, is remarkable for its extreme purity, being clear as crystal, and is said to be possessed of wonderful curative properties for diseases of the skin. The villagers value its benefits at a *mann*, or seven pounds weight of pure gold a day, and gratefully compare their lot with that of other villages on the parched-up plains. The garden of Fin, surrounded by a high wall, was originally commenced by Shah Abbas, and finished by Fath Ali Shah, who beautified and enlarged it, and, finally, made it his favourite and almost constant place of summer residence. It is in the form of a large square, on three of the sides of which are dwelling-houses, while the fourth is occupied by the grand entrance—the centre being intersected by avenues of large cypress trees, between the rows of which flow streams of pure water in marble canals. Large marble tanks supply these canals, and the side walks are furnished with metal jets, by means of which, in an instant, the whole garden can be filled with playing fountains. In the middle of the garden is a large erection of Shah Abbas, called the 'Kulah-i-Faringi,' or the Faringi's hat, now much out of repair, from the top of which an extensive view may be obtained of the somewhat desolate Káshán plain. On the side opposite to the entrance gate is the principal building, which, though somewhat dilapidated, still shows many signs of former magnificence. It is filled with pictures of Fath Ali and his six principal sons, all amazingly alike, and all painted with an absolute ignorance of perspective. Some hunting and battle scenes are however rendered with wonderful life and spirit. An English gentleman and lady are also depicted on the walls, with the inevitable glass of wine in each hand. At the rear of this building are two tanks, one for male and one for female bathers, which are much frequented on account of their supposed curative properties. Many of the medallions painted on the ceilings are still remarkable for the taste and beauty of their colouring, and the whole place is made up of paltry pettiness and real magnificence. Whatever may have been the delights of the garden of Fin in former days, it is impossible to deny that now it has a most melancholy appearance—partly, perhaps, due to the gloom shed over the whole place by the huge cypress trees, whose deep shade throws everything into seeming darkness, partly to the deserted aspect of the buildings, and partly to associations connected with the locality, for it is only twelve years since Mirza Taki Khán, ex Prime Minister of Persia, was killed here by order of the present King. This unfortunate Minister appears, from all accounts, to have been one of those men whom Providence sometimes creates, as it were, to retrieve by their means the destinies of a fast sinking nation. Of low birth (for it is said that he was son of the King's cook), he contrived by his abilities and talents to gain the favour of the reigning Shah, while the latter was still only heir to the throne; and shortly after the Shah ascended the throne he made him Prime Minister, giving him at the same time his only sister in marriage. The conduct of the new Prime Minister was in no way affected by this sudden accession of fortune and power. Honest in purpose and able in action, he set himself to redress the abuses that he saw all around: he revised the code of laws; raised the politics of Persia from the low depths to which they had fallen; corrected with an unsparing hand the universal corruption that existed in all departments of the State, and, by himself setting the example in all the courses he initiated, speedily won an extraordinary popularity among the lower classes of the people. This popularity was his ruin. The numerous enemies his conduct had procured him among the corrupt *noblesse* were not long in filling the King's mind with doubts as to what might be the results of his fast-increasing influence; and while in the very midst of his career of well-doing, he was suddenly deposed from his office and sent to live in the Palace of Fin. Once having got him out of the way, his enemies had full play, and, forty days after his banishment, prevailed upon the King to issue orders for his execution, which the Shah had no sooner done than he was seized with remorse. It was too late, however. The executioners had arrived at Fin, and, seeing the ex-Minister, told him that they had been sent by the Shah to ask after his health. Mirza Taki Khán at once saw that his fate was sealed: he merely asked that instead of having his throat cut he might be allowed to die in his own way. The request was granted; he went into the *hammám*, where the King's barber opened the two principal arteries in each arm, and he quietly sat there and bled to death. We saw the stone on which this unfortunate man expired; and the gardener who showed us the place was one of those who had helped to remove the dead body. The remorse which the Shah suffered, on reviewing this cruel deed, has been lasting, as it was at first severe. He has not entered the garden since, excusing himself on the plea of the dust with which Káshán abounds. The two daughters of the deceased he married to his own two eldest sons, and his widow he married to the son of the unfortunate Premier's successor, while the corpse of the murdered ex-Minister was removed with all sanctity to Karbala for honourable interment. The fate of this able and upright Minister renders successful attempt at Reform in Persia somewhat problematical, though it is something to know that Mirza Taki Khán's uprightness and honesty were so appreciated by the lower classes, that his memory is revered and himself regretted to this day.

Káshán has one more notoriety, and that not of a pleasant nature. The town and neighbourhood are infested with black scorpions, considered to be of a very venomous kind. The Governor indeed told us that unless instantly treated with ammonia their bite was fatal; but this is probably somewhat of an exaggeration. There is a hill on the outskirts of the town which abounds with them; and the Káshánis make parties to this place for the purpose of having a regular massacre of the scorpions, which are driven out of their holes by the application of hot water, and instantly killed.

From Káshán to Isfahán there are six stages with an aggregate distance of about 106 miles, during which nothing of any consequence occurred. The marches at this time were most delightful, owing to the glorious climate and the weather, which, though very cold with hard frost at night and in the early morning, was most enjoyable during the day. We used to march generally about 7.30 or 8 a.m., breakfast by the roadside two or three hours afterwards, and get into camp early in the afternoon. The most excellent fruit was obtainable at every little village that we passed.

We reached Isfahán on the 10th November, and had our first experience of a real Persian *istikbál*—or deputation that is sent out by the Governor of a town to receive honoured guests, and the number and rank of the members of which are accurately laid down by rule and precedent. The cavalcade here was on a large scale, commanded by a 'Sartip' or Persian general, who was also accompanied by the Chief Commissioner of Customs, an enormously fat man, mounted on a magnificent grey horse. There was a crowd of cavalry as an escort; and as all the European inhabitants had also ridden out to meet Sir F. Goldsmid, by the time we reached the gates of the city the *cortège* was very large indeed. The heat, dust, flies, and, above all, the dense crowd of Jew beggars, made us very glad to get into the shade of the *bazárs*, where the importunities of the begging populace were kept at bay by the long wands of the *farashes* who preceded the procession; but the crush was very great, and our uniforms got much damaged. We rode right across the city; and, traversing the grand square or *máidán*, made our way by the Chhár Bagh across the river to the Haft Dast Palace, where excellent quarters had been prepared for us. This was a very handsome building built by the present Shah in the usual form of a quadrangle, with the rooms all looking inwards on to a fine marble tank of pure water situated in the centre. The Persian Commissioner and suite occupied one side of the quadrangle, and our party filled the other three: the rooms were unusually handsome and lofty, with beautiful stained glass in geometrical patterns, but it was so cold that we were compelled to have roaring fires all day long.

The day after our arrival at Isfahán, at 9 a.m., Sir Frederic Goldsmid, accompanied by his Staff and the British Agent, proceeded to call on the Governor of the town, who was by far the most gentlemanly Persian we had yet seen—an agreeable talker, and an amusing man. He was splendidly dressed in a Kashmír robe of honour, sent him by the King, which was ornamented with two magnificent diamond, ruby, and emerald brooches of great value. Our visit lasted some time, and was not at all tedious. Agreeable as we found the old gentleman, however, he was enormously unpopular in the city; and it was said that, owing to the representations of the populace on this head, the King had actually given orders for him to be killed, when his friends bought him off for 30,000 *tumáns*. Had he been executed, he would only have experienced in a milder form the fate of his ancestors, for his grandfather is stated to have been boiled alive in grease for oppressing the inhabitants of Yazd. One would have thought such a reminiscence calculated to make future generations more careful; but our particular Governor, quite conscious of how the people under his jurisdiction were starving, persisted in buying up every kind of grain that came to the city for 7 *tumáns* the *kharwar*, and selling it for 12. He was so hated for this, that a short time previously, when out walking, he had been attacked by a crowd of women, two of whom, brandishing swords, threatened to kill him. He ordered them to be seized and kept until they gave up the names of their husbands; but they persisted in saying that they were the wives of his two principal officers (already mentioned as having been sent out to welcome the General), and as they were veiled he, of course, could not discover who they were, and was obliged to let them go. It was generally believed that he paid 2000 *tumáns* or £800, monthly to the 'Mustofi,' or Regent, at Tehrán, to speak well of him to the King, but he could well afford this when screwing such enormous sums out of the populace. He showed himself especially desirous to be civil to the General and officers of his staff, and after he had returned the former's visit on the 14th November, sent an invitation to the whole Mission to dine at the Palace on the 15th. For this entertainment he had made preparations all the day, with the asked-for aid of our Názir, table servants and cook, so that he might have everything ready according to European notions. He had also sent many servants to search through Julfa for wine, brandy, and whatever other intoxicating liquors they could lay their hands on; and finally, as a last thought, an express came to our camp to borrow our English cheese. These preparations were thoroughly successful, and a better dinner has seldom been seen in the East. At 6.30 p.m. the General started from camp, preceded by bearers of many lanterns, the size and number of which articles are indicative of the rank of the individual they illuminate. When we reached the Governor's palace, we found that the guests had already assembled. The grandees were seated in an inner sort of room, very hot, while the smaller fry sat in an outside chamber, and could congratulate themselves on the greater purity of the atmosphere they enjoyed. Tea and pipes were, of course, brought in, and we were then invited to take a sort of 'zakouski,' or Russian relish, before dinner, which, in this case, consisted of sweetmeats and raw brandy. The room in which we dined was the Chamber of Mirrors, and from top to bottom the walls consisted of nothing but mirrors and fantastic patterns formed out of looking-glass. It was brilliantly lighted up, and looked very well. The table literally groaned under the enormous number of dishes of sweet-meats of every description placed on it, most of them good, and made by the women of the Governor's household: and the dinner itself was more than respectable. It was very good indeed; well cooked, and consisting of everything in the way of fish, flesh, and fowl procurable in Persia. The jellies caused much amusement; for the Governor, a very jolly old gentleman, discovering that they were flavoured with brandy, pressed them vehemently upon all his unsuspecting Musalmán guests, and then rallied them on their sin in having transgressed the law by tasting intoxicating liquors. During dinner we had plenty of music, which was not absolutely inharmonious, though the solos (vocal) by which it was accompanied were very trying. The principal performer on this occasion was a boy of about 14, with a falsetto voice on its last legs, which he pitched at the highest note it was capable of, and then continued in one long shake, accompanied by violent writhings and contortions of the body. Of melody and harmony there seemed to be no idea. The dulcimer, a stringed instrument, was, however, very soft and pleasing. The music was accompanied from time to time by dancing. The dancers consisted of four boys, of ages from 12 to 15, dressed alike, who danced in and out among the servants waiting round the table, accompanying their motions by constant jingling of castanets. Their gestures could not have much charm for English eyes; but the noise of the castanets was not unpleasant. These boys are, in purely Persian entertainments, generally dressed as women. There was abundance of wine and brandy handed round, of which none of the Persians partook, though some of them were very great drinkers in private; but a Persian thinks it is useless drinking wine except to get drunk, and this was not a favourable occasion for the latter exhibition. The musicians, however, had no scruple, and drank freely. We all dined with our forage-caps on, and the English clergyman, Mr. Bruce, and also Mr. Hoeltzer, sat at dinner with their wide-awakes, which presented a somewhat incongruous appearance. The Persian community ate little, but probably made up for their abstinence when we were gone. Some of the guests had their cousins and brothers there, who, not being invited to sit at table, came, during pauses in the banquet, and received on the ground portions of food from their more favoured relatives. Directly after dinner, the windows looking out on the courtyard were thrown open, and a grand display of fireworks took place, better and more artistic than we had been led to expect. This finished, a company of *lútís*, or players, came forward, and acted a species of farce. A few of the actors had some idea of dramatic treatment, and many of them had very good voices; but all these exhibitions are remarkable for the gross indecency which characterises both the language used and the accompanying pantomime, and this one was no exception to the rule. We heard afterwards, however, that, in deference to our insular prejudices, the Governor had desired that the more glaring objections should be subdued. The company rose and took their departure immediately this performance had been brought to a conclusion, and we reached home by 11 o'clock.

Prominent among our earlier and more interesting visitors was the Archbishop of the Armenian community at Julfa. He was a most noble-looking old man, of great stature, with a magnificent, long, snowy white beard; clad in purple velvet, covered with jewels; his mitre on his head, and his episcopal staff in his hand. Mounted on a gigantic mule, with jewelled trappings, he presented a gorgeous bit of colouring as he rode slowly along under the *chinár* trees—the very impersonation of priestly dignity and magnificence. The Armenian community are, however, much persecuted by the Persian authorities, and the Bishop has little real power. Their cathedral is a handsome building, with a fine dome, and many pictures, principally representing the torments of the damned, and more remarkable for prodigality of detail than artistic treatment. In the churchyard are several graves of Englishmen, among which are noticeable those of two young men, each aged 21, who both died of cholera on the same day at

Yazdikhást, and were buried the same day at Julfa. The Armenians make excellent wine, of which the monks, as is proper, keep a famous cellar. Through the Archbishop's kindness we were enabled to purchase some of their best samples, and attest their value.

There is one other of the lions of Isfahán that must be noticed, namely, the shaking minarets situated about six miles to the west of the city. The minarets themselves are about 70 or 80 feet high, and are built of strong brickwork; their circumference being just large enough to admit of one man inside them. They have a narrow flight of stairs that leads to the top, and which merely commences from a platform that divides the two. A man in either of them can shake both easily at the same time, and the vibration is distinctly felt all along the intervening platform, which has a width of some 12 feet. The top of the minaret when violently shaken diverges at least $1\frac{1}{2}$ or 2 inches from the perpendicular, and the whole tower moves with it. The platform, however, does not move, though it is sensible of the vibration in the towers at each side of it; but there is a large crack between the towers and the platform, into which a man could put his hand, and the idea is that there is a chain that communicates between the towers, concealed somewhere beneath the platform. The natives, of course, ascribe miraculous agency to the movement, and the place contains a shrine of a very holy man, a visit to which will, it is said, cure all present disorders and prevent possibility of future ailments: but this very easy way of getting rid of a doctor's bill does not seem to be much practised by the Persians themselves, though the keeper of the shrine evidently believes in it. The shrine and tower are said to be 782 years old, and are kept in wonderful repair. And the place is often visited by Persians as an agreeable rendezvous for a picnic.

For a general view of Isfahán the most advantageous resort is a summer-house on the slopes of Mount Sufia, which overlooks the Armenian burying-ground on the south of the city. From this point can be seen every part of the city, and the eye can trace, by following the line of ruins, the former boundaries of Isfahán. Owing, however, to the universal mud-colour of the buildings, it is difficult at this distance to distinguish either streets or bazaars. The Chhár Bagh and the great dome of the Masjid-i-Shah form the most conspicuous features in the landscape, which looks like a great mass of gardens interspersed with domes and minarets. No traveller, with a more intimate acquaintance with Isfahán, can avoid regretting that this is not the true capital. Of all the cities in Persia, it alone appears to possess any really princely buildings; and the ruins of former greatness, with which it abounds, show of what it would be capable were it taken in hand by a really intelligent and appreciative king. The pigeon-towers, which dot the landscape in every direction, are quite peculiar to Persia. They are large round towers, about 30 feet in height, and inside consist of numberless little brick cells, in which the pigeons lay and hatch their eggs and rear their young. The well in the middle collects all their dung, which supplies good manure for the melon-beds of Isfahán, and it is only for the purpose of collecting this manure that the towers are used. They are opened once a year. The Madrasah, or College of Isfahán, forms another landmark. This is, however, principally in ruins; but enormous silver gates testify to its former flourishing condition, while large patches of tin let into the gates prove that thieves have been at work, notwithstanding all precautions. The size to which the *chinár* tree grows here is very remarkable, and distinguishes Isfahán from all cities in Persia; indeed, it may be said that the chief features of this once famous city are *chinár* trees and ruins, for at least nine-tenths of the town is in ruins, and its ancient circumference must have been close on 20 miles.

As before stated, the Mission was detained in Isfahán during a fortnight, owing to the uncertainty on the part of the Persian Government as to the Makrán Enquiry taking place, should the Sistán Arbitration prove impracticable for that year. On the 22nd, Mr. Alison telegraphed that the Viceroy of India had informed him that nothing could be done for the present in Sistán; and that the Shah would consent to the Balúchistán Enquiry being commenced. This news having been confirmed two or three days after, Sir F. Goldsmid determined to move on to Karmán, thus giving time to the Persian Commissioner to receive his necessary instructions before arrival at that city. He accordingly left Isfahán on the 26th November; but the *personnel* of the Mission had by this time undergone one or two important changes. In view of the approaching Makrán question, Sir F. Goldsmid had directed Captain Beresford Lovett to proceed, *viá* Bushahr, to Gwádar, on the Balúchistán coast, and from thence to make his way up through Balúchistán and meet the Mission on the frontier, acquiring such useful information as he could gather on the march. That officer was accordingly left behind at Isfahán, from which place he started for the coast on the 28th instant. The strength of the Mission had been in the mean time increased by the presence of Dr. Cumming, of the Indo-European Telegraph Department, who was about to proceed to England on sick leave, and to whom the General gave authority to accompany the camp as far as Gwádar. Dr. Cumming joined the Mission on the 17th November. We had an agreeable surprise one morning, by Captain Campbell, of the Bengal Cavalry, riding in to breakfast. He had accompanied Major Champain, of the Royal Engineers, from England *viâ* Russia, and was then on his way to join his appointment in Madras, riding post. Captain Campbell is, it is believed, the first Indian officer who has returned to duty from furlough in this way. He found the life novel and pleasant; though riding post for any distance in Persia is beyond measure fatiguing.

The day before our departure for Karmán was the first day of Ramazán, and at early dawn a gun signified to the inhabitants the commencement of this great fast, which is very strictly observed in Persia. The hour at which the gun is fired is not fixed, but it is supposed to be when the day has dawned sufficiently to enable the inhabitants to distinguish between a white and a blue cord. All true believers observe a strict fast during the whole day, and are only released from their obligation as soon as the sun has disappeared below the horizon, when another gun gives the fasting populace the signal to 'fall to.' Everything is in readiness for the feasting that so soon succeeds the fast. The *kalián* is held ready to be lit, and probably not one man in fifty exists but has his mouth occupied in some way or other before the echoes of the gun have ceased reverberating among the surrounding hills. This trying ordeal—for trying, no doubt, it is—is of course escaped entirely by many people; but numbers get over it by sleeping during the greater part of the day, and feasting violently at night, especially toward the morning, when the time for firing the fatal gun draws near; but those who are actually *en voyage*, or about travelling, are excused this penance, having to make up for it at some other time in the year—as also all sick people. Our *ghuláms*, however, whose duty it is to be always on the march, do not hold themselves excused, and fast accordingly.

Between Isfahán and Karmán, *viâ* Yazd, whither we marched from Isfahán, there is a distance of 420 miles, Yazd being 191 miles from Isfahán and 229 miles from Karmán. The halting-stages are at easy intervals, and so generally level is the track that for the most part the journey might easily be performed on wheels.

The morning of Saturday, the 26th of November, was bright and cold. Having sent on our tents and baggage in good time, we left Isfahán at 1 p.m., and were accompanied for a certain distance by almost all the European community, inclusive of the Roman Catholic priest. The road was along the south bank of the Zaindarúd for some miles, and then crossed the river to pursue a twisting, deviating course up to some rising ground which passed by the left of a large hill easily visible from Isfahán. The many ruins observed show the former enormous extent of the city and, especially on this side, mark the epoch of the Afghan invasion, the quarter never having been inhabited since. A very high *minár* or tower was noticed on our left hand. The road, after rising as before mentioned, ran nearly due east for some miles, passing a great number of pigeon-towers and a large and seemingly prosperous village. After skirting the base of the hill, another village was passed to the right, and then the old mud caravanserai of Gulnabad (twelve miles) became plainly visible. The Katkhuda had sent out his son to meet us shortly before arrival, and was himself in waiting on foot, a singular spectacle, with a bright green coat and a bright red beard. A sheep had been also stationed on the road with its feet tied, all ready to have its throat cut directly the 'auspicious feet' of the General should approach. We saved its life, however, just in time. This barbarous custom of sacrificing an animal on the approach of an honoured stranger, so that its blood should actually flow under his feet, is somewhat too antiquated for modern ideas. We found the camp pitched outside the walls of the caravanserai, and fruit, with other orthodox minor presents, laid out in the General's tent. The night was very cold and bright; and the water froze hard in all the tents. The village, now principally in ruins—the inhabited part, about 100 families, being at some distance from the caravanserai— was the scene of a battle fought between the Afghans and Persians in the beginning of the last century, followed by the taking of Isfahán. We were told that no rain or snow, to speak of, had fallen here for three years. The water was excellent.

The day following, we marched at 10 a.m., after vainly pressing a present on the Katkhuda, who would neither accept one for himself or for the poor of the village. The road to Segzi was over a perfectly flat plain covered with *bhúta*, which, by its parched-up appearance and the universal salt excrescence on its surface, testified to the long and trying drought. About half way to Segzi we were overtaken by Captain Lovett, who had galloped out from Isfahán, bringing two telegrams for the General, one from the Bombay Government and the other from Mr. Alison. The last informed him that, in view of the impracticability of the Sistán question being settled this winter, the Persian Government had consented to their Commissioner accompanying the General straight to Makrán. This was good news, and relieved us from all uncertainty. Arriving at Segzi (fourteen miles) about two p.m., we found quarters in a small caravanserai of the time of Shah Abbas, still in excellent repair. Captain Smith was sent to the Persian Commissioner to apprise him of the contents of the telegram received by the General, at which he expressed himself much pleased. Segzi is a village of some size, with the usual fortifications in the shape of mud walls. The Katkhuda informed us, however, that there were but forty families, and that they were miserably poor. The effect of getting off the *chapar*, or post roads, and leaving the vicinity of the telegraph line, was here visibly apparent for the first time. So unfamiliar were the inhabitants with the sight of a European, that the whole village could do nothing but stare at us. Driven from one point of vantage to another they still persevered, and night found them scattered at every point round and in the caravanserai from which they could possibly hope to get a glimpse of the strange Faringís. They were, however, very civil and well behaved.

At sunrise on the 28th, we found all the inhabitants of the industrious and energetic village of Segzi seated in a body round the doors of the caravanserai, waiting for it to be opened, and evidently unwilling to lose a moment in pursuing their investigations into the personal appearance, habits, and customs of English officers. The inner square was soon filled, and there they sat until we made our appearance. When turned out by the departure of the mules, they calmly formed large groups outside, and considered themselves happy if rewarded for their patience by an occasional glimpse of us on the roof. This continued until our departure at 10 a.m. Captain Lovett left us early in the morning, returning to Isfahán, whence he was to receive instructions, by telegraph from the Bombay Government, as to the course he should pursue. The road to Kupa lay over a tract of desert and nearly flat country, covered with the usual *bhuta;* but there is little of interest to recall in this march. Some sand-grouse were seen: an excellent *áb-ambár* was passed, with really good water, and shortly after a smaller one; and the plain was dotted here and there with ruins of deserted villages. On arrival at Kupa (nineteen miles) at 2.30 p.m., we found the whole village turned out to see us; and the usual sheep, which was prepared for sacrifice, had its life saved at the critical moment. The Katkhuda, an *employé* of the Sahib-i-Diwan of Isfahán, and a schoolmaster, all three singularly intelligent men, paid the General a long visit in his tent on arrival, bringing the usual presents. They told us that the water of the Zaindarúd loses itself in a sort of quicksand about eight *farsakhs* to the south-west, near which the banks are from thirty to forty feet deep; but we had no means of testing the accuracy of the information. We found excellent quarters in a caravanserai of the time of Shah Abbas, and in capital repair. Kupa was represented to contain 500 families, most of whom were in great distress from want of rain. It is famous for its manufacture of camel's-hair cloth, said to be the best in Persia. We went to see it manufactured in a building where there were about ten looms of the ordinary description, on a level with the floor of the room, the workers sitting in holes conveniently deep to bring them on a level with the looms. The cloth is made of cotton and camel's-hair, the warp being cotton, the woof camel's-hair, and it is woven very close together, so as, in fact, to be quite impervious to rain. The camel's-hair, we were informed, is chiefly brought from Shíráz, where the camels are shorn once a year. The hair is carded in the same way as cotton, and spun into thread with the fingers. An ordinary coat made of this material costs about three and a half *tumáns,* but some better descriptions of cloth are made which are very much dearer. The glimpse we got of the village of Kupa gave the impression that it was clean and airy; though the inhabitants looked wretchedly poor; and indeed General Goldsmid remarked that he had never before seen so many beggars in Persia. They crowded round the doors of the caravanserai, and followed us for some distance on the road with their importunities. Kupa possesses four *hammáms,* and is surrounded by a strong mud wall with flanking towers.

The camp marched early the next morning, but the General and others remained until twelve o'clock, vainly awaiting the arrival of one of the *ghuláms* left behind to bring on the English mail expected at Isfahán. After twelve o'clock, however, as further waiting seemed useless, we started among a perfect crowd of mendicants, for whom General Goldsmid left five *tumáns* to be distributed by the Katkhuda. On leaving Kupa, the road continued over the same flat and desolate plain for about eleven miles, to the almost deserted village of Múshkinún, the inhabitants of which were engaged in making a coarse cotton cloth. Two or three flourishing-looking villages were observed on either side of the road. Three miles from Múshkinún, Tudeshk was reached, situated at the entrance of the hills, which apparently form a continuation of the Kohrúd range. We had passed numerous patches of cultivated land, generally surrounded by a wall, in the plain. Here, with our tents pitched on capital ground to the left of the road, we halted a day, in the hope of receiving the English mail; but the result was disappointment.

On the 1st December, we set out at 7.45 a.m. in tolerably bright but very cold weather. The Katkhuda of the village came to escort us on our way, dressed in a yellow skin-coat and mounted on a ridiculously small white donkey. Passing a white tower on a hill to our left outside the village, which our guide told us had been built as a precaution against robbers, we found the road gradually ascend, winding in and out in a narrow valley lying between hills of no great height. Numerous villages were observed on every side, with cultivated patches of land enclosed by walls. The inhabitants of these places seemed miserably poor, and a small landowner in one of them, who accompanied us for the first few miles, gave us a startling account, probably somewhat exaggerated, of the shifts to which they were put. He told us that his own family had so little clothing that his wife and daughters were unable ever to go out of doors; and spoke strongly of the screwing propensities of our friend the Governor of Isfahán, in whose jurisdiction all this country is, and who, he said, had just made him pay a yearly tax of four *tumáns* out of his miserable earnings. Ascents and descents in very gradual gradients succeeded each other as we moved onward; and the scenery was of a generally monotonous character till beyond Ishratabád, when the road, turning sharply to the left, sloped downwards to a continuation of the plain of Káshán which skirts the mountain range of Kohrúd. The large town of Nain was here visible on the left under isolated, and comparatively low hills. At about eleven miles from Tudeshk, the government of Yazd begins and that of Isfahán has attained its limit. We found all the villages strongly and well built, with excellent ponds of clear water: and all possessed respectable mud forts, in which to find shelter from the attacks of robbers. The houses, without exception, had dome-shaped roofs, probably adopted from the scarcity of wood or straight timber. No trees of any size were visible. After leaving Ishratabád, Allahabád (half a mile to the left), and then Pudár (the latter being the last village in the hills, and having an especially strong fort), the road turned to the right and made a more decided descent on Bambiz, which place we reached about half-past four, finding our tents already pitched. Its probable distance from Tudeshk is twenty-eight miles, of which three-sevenths of the road is through the hills. On arrival at Bambiz (a large village possessing eighty or 100 families, with little cultivation and no gardens or trees), the worthy old Hajji with whom the General and Major Smith had stayed on their journey in 1865 came to see the former. He literally was overjoyed at the meeting, and could for some time do nothing but utter ejaculations such as 'Praise be to God!' He stayed a very long time indeed talking to him, and telling him all about his travels. Well had he won the title of Hajji, for he had been five times to Mecca, having made his last journey only in 1869, when quite an old man. He had visited Damascus in the course of his travels. The General gave him a knife containing the usual saw, corkscrew, and accompaniments, with which he was much pleased. The air was here quite warm, and fires in tents became unnecessary: this difference in temperature on crossing the range of hills explains the meaning of the name *garmsír*, or warm region, applied to these parts as elsewhere under similar conditions. The inhabitants of Bambiz were mostly in a state of great destitution, and there may have been many deaths from starvation: for we were told that numbers had had nothing but turnips to eat for days, and there was no chance of improvement in this state of things before a heavy rain-fall. Bambiz had no caravanserai, and but little accommodation of any sort for travellers. The water was very good.

Our next day's short march of twelve miles brought us to Náugumbaz, where we found excellent quarters in a caravanserai of the time of Shah Abbas. The road, after leaving Bambiz, over a flat and perfectly desert plain, covered with scanty *bhúta*, is worthy of no remark. We joined here the direct *chapar* road to Yazd and Karmán from Tehrán *viâ* Káshán. Náugumbaz consists of merely a *chapar-khánah*, the caravanserai, and a walled enclosure containing from eight to ten families, all dreadfully poor. So bad and salt was the reputed water that we brought our whole supply with us. Gentle rain began to fall about 11 a.m., and continued without intermission all day, but it was hardly sufficient to do much good to the wretched and parched-up country. Our guide informed us that from this place Tehrán could be reached in three days across the desert by a determined and hardy pedestrian. There was some little cultivation in the neighbourhood of the caravanserai.

From Náugumbaz we marched twenty-six miles to Akda. The road was over the same flat and desert plain, with gravelly soil, and without any signs of population or cultivation: there were hills in the far distance right and left. Our guide stated that the several beds of water-courses which we traversed are impassable in the rainy season, when a fresh comes from the mountains. After twelve miles we reached a tank, or *áb-ambár*, with the inscription *Ya, Ali! aml-i-Husain Akdái*—i. e. "Oh Ali! Husain of Akda constructed this"—where we breakfasted. The water was good; but only about one foot and a half remained. Leaving the tank at noon, we continued our march over a monotonous tract. At three miles was a large caravanserai, in excellent repair, with a small walled village of twenty-five inhabitants, called Husainabád, where a large circular *áb-ambár* is being built at the expense of a benevolent merchant of Yazd. Five miles further was another tank of rude construction. The Persian Commissioner joined the General at Husainabád, and rode in with him to Akda. He had bought a horse on the road from a travelling merchant, for five *tumáns* or £2. Seven miles from Husainabád, at the cultivation of Shahrabád, we first saw young date trees, a sure sign of the *garmsír*. Three miles further on, over ground much broken and cut up by *kanáts*, we reached Akda at 3.30 p.m. Young date trees and wild myrtle bore witness to the general mildness of the climate; but we learnt that, sixteen years before, the whole of the date trees of this village were killed by severe frost; and those now standing were not allowed to grow to any height, their leaves being cut for brushes, sold for the benefit of the mosque. Akda is famous for the excellence of its pomegranates. It is a town of about 1,200 inhabitants, exclusively engaged in cultivation, as the extent of its gardens showed. The caravanserai where we found quarters was the finest we had seen in Persia, and was distinguishable afar off from the height of its *bádgir*, or tower for catching the wind in warm weather. There was also an excellent *áb-ambár*, with four *bádgirs*, built by a merchant of Resht, who had settled in Yazd and died there. It was about twenty-five years old, but still had every appearance of being quite new, the walls being of such immense strength and thickness to warrant the belief that it might last for centuries. Shortly after arrival, the General received a visit from five of the principal men of the place: four of these were Saiyids, of whom there is quite a colony here—100 men. The guide spoke of a possible attack of Bakhtiáris, but we saw no signs of them, and had every reason to believe his fears groundless.

On the 4th December we made a thirty-mile march to Máibút: road, as usual, over a perfectly flat and desert plain, in this instance very bad for our cattle, on account of the stones with which it was covered. A small village was met with on the left, about a mile from Akda, and after twelve miles the village of Chafta, with its good but deserted *chapar-khánah*, the horses having been removed on account of the dearness of grain. The only inhabitants were three men, two women, and four children, who inhabited a very strong mud round tower, lately put in repair. Breakfasting at Chafta, in the open plain, we resumed our march at 11 a.m. A very fine range of hills on our left, and a magnificent mountain range that appeared on our right front, with very high peaks, appear to be omitted in the generality of maps. But these hills, especially some to the westward, must be of great height and extent. The road, after leaving Chafta, pursues an easterly direction, and crossing a range of low clay hills reaches, at fourteen miles, a deserted walled village, built like a fort with towers at the four corners. For about four miles before reaching this point we had noticed some villages, evidently of large size and with extensive cultivated enclosures, lying at the foot of the hills to our left, and we now saw that those signs of habitation and cultivation continued, without intermission, right up to the walls of Máibút. From the deserted village above-mentioned to the caravanserai of Máibút is about four miles, and the road crosses over a peculiar white clayey soil, cut up in every direction by *kanáts*. Cultivation was visible to a very great extent. The entrance to Máibút lay through a narrow lane, with walled fields on each side, until it merged into the principal street of Máibút with its high two-storied houses on one side and cultivation on the other: then passing up a narrow ascent we reached the splendid caravanserai built by private munificence, with an excellent covered tank and spring of pure water situated in the centre of the open space inside. This caravanserai was quite as fine as the one we had seen on the day before, and we could not help being struck with admiration at the open-handed charity which builds these splendid resting-places for all travellers alike, rich and poor, and provides liberally for their wants and those of their horses, mules, and camels. The rooms in this building were very high and lofty, and the stables especially spacious, and every precaution appeared to be taken to make passing travellers comfortable, alike in winter and summer. On the opposite side of the narrow lane in which this caravanserai was situated rose an enormous *Yakh-chál*, or ice-house, which, constructed on high ground, formed a conspicuous landmark for many miles; we had noticed it for at least ten miles before arrival at Máibút. There were hardly any of the inhabitants visible on our approach, a circumstance explained by the fact that they had heard a Persian Ambassador was coming, and had bolted, to escape the inevitable and recognised extortion. Máibút is famous for its pottery manufacture, made out of the porous clay which surrounds the place. The goblets and other articles manufactured here did not appear to be as good as those of Kúm. The village, it may be remarked in conclusion, we found to be completely cut up by deep, dangerous, and precipitous ravines. The water, as at Akda, was very good. There were many villages seen or reported in the vicinity; and the large town of Ardagán was distinctly visible from the top of the caravanserai, lying about seven miles distant, north by west.

The day following we did not start till ten o'clock, owing to Dr. Cumming's illness. Our road was, for three miles, through a succession of cultivated villages and fields, and over ground much cut by *kanáts*, to Ruknabad, a village possessing a most remarkable cypress tree, presenting, at a distance, the exact appearance of a Persian, hat and all, in a standing position, previous to making his prostrations at evening prayer. This tree is visible fifteen miles on the other side of Máibút; and its resemblance to a human figure is quite unmistakeable. Four miles further on, over a flat road following the course of a *kanát*, we reached the village of Muhammadabád on the left, with a ruined fort, of which the walls were riddled with bullets, probably a memento of the attacks of the Bakhtiáris. Four miles further, we passed the village of Ibrahimabad on the right, and Shams-abad on the left,—the former noticeable from standing in a grove of Scotch fir trees, about thirty or forty in number, crowded with pigeons. In every direction the fields were alive with men, women, and children, busily engaged in preparing the ground for seed, and in sowing. About this point in the road the soil became excessively sandy, and proved very bad travelling for the horses and mules. The village of Shaftarabad was passed on the left, and, at the distance of six miles more, the *chapar* station and usual stage of Himmatabad was reached. We continued our march, however, through very bad roads, to the village of Ishkizar, where we had expected to find our camp, and good quarters in a caravanserai. On arrival there, failing to discover any trace of the domestics, we pushed on four miles further (in all thirty miles) to Gird-Firamurz, where our camp and people had taken up a position in a rude, small caravanserai. From this point the minarets and *bádgirs* of Yazd were visible. Gird-Firamurz, or, as some call it, 'Tifl-Omar,' six miles from Yazd, is a village of about 100 houses: its inhabitants are principally engaged in the culture of silk, of which it yields 100 *manns* per annum, sold at 150 *kráns* per *mann* of seven and a half pounds. Dates were obtainable here in abundance. The whole of the march from Máibút to Gird-Firamurz there was a really splendid view of the range of mountains lying due west of Yazd. Two of the highest were covered apparently many inches deep with fresh snow, and presented a beautiful spectacle against the clear blue sky. The highest is called the 'Shir-Kúh,' and the formation of its summit much resembles Mont Blanc. It must be between 11,000 and 12,000 feet high, and it is indeed astonishing that no notice of the existence of the two fine ranges of hills, which lie to the left and right of the road from Isfahán, should have been heretofore taken in the maps of Persia. The road for the last six miles into Gird-Firamurz, that is, for about two miles before Ishkizar, beggars description. It consisted of nothing but loose heaps and drifts of sand, and in muddy weather would be impassable. As it was, our horses sank over their fetlocks at every step, and the mules suffered so much that many of them did not arrive at the caravanserai till past midnight. Two miles an hour would be the utmost a well-mounted man could do on soil of this description, and that with extreme difficulty. But there are plenty of villages built in the neighbourhood, and Ishkizar is only approachable by wading through seas of this fine shifting sand. The drifts in some places were very high, and it would be easy for any traveller to lose his way and perish here on a dark and windy winter's night. The long-delayed mail came in, with our letters and papers, at a somewhat late hour.

About a mile after leaving Gird-Firamurz we came in full view of the town of Yazd, lying perfectly flat on the plain, in an amphitheatre of hills, quite unlike what it is represented to be on the maps. A fire-worshipper's temple was observed crowning a small hill to the extreme right front. Shortly after we had met the Persian Commissioner, a member of the Persian Foreign Office, resident at Yazd, and styled an 'Adjutant,' came galloping out to meet us, and begged our chief to delay his approach to the city as much as possible, as they were preparing an *istikbál*, which would take some little time. Accordingly, in about an hour's time, a number of horsemen, consisting of the principal men of the city, came out to escort the General, all dressed in uniform, and wearing whatever orders they might possess. They escorted us to our quarters, in a large and now somewhat dilapidated palace, called Daulatabád, at the entrance of the road going into the city on the left. Here we found our tents pitched in the enclosure, and also rooms prepared in the mansion itself. On the floor of the largest room, forty-eight plates of sweetmeats of various kinds were laid out, as a present to the General. The road from Gird-Firamurz to Yazd is very good, over a flat, hard plain. In the evening the Hindú residents in Yazd, five in number, with a *fakir*, came to visit us. The General had found seventeen of them here in 1866; but their number had now been reduced to five. These men, inhabitants of Sind, sent here only for the purposes of trade, seemed to have rather a bad time of it, and gave one a melancholy impression of their status. They were all dressed with very tall Persian hats, and told us they were much oppressed by the Musalmán population. They traded principally in indigo and silk, but did not seem to be doing much, and, of course, wanted the General to inquire into and redress their wrongs. They told us there were forty of their compatriots at Karmán, and also that two Hindú *fakirs* had lately left Yazd for the fires at Bákú on the Caspian, which they worship, and which we found deserted on our expedition thither in September last. It was strange to hear them talking Hindustáni.

We stayed for three whole days at Yazd, where the nights were so cold that fires became necessary. The city is large and comparatively populous: but it has few buildings, save one mosque, worthy of notice; and it is choked with ruins within and around. The new *bazár* looked handsome enough of its kind; but the older *bazárs* were very dark, ruined, and dirty; and we saw in them small signs of life or active trade. The second day of our stay, the General, accompanied by Captain Smith, proceeded at 2.30 to visit the Prince Governor of the place, a youth of about fourteen or fifteen years old, son of the Hisámú-s-Saltanah, and married to the Shah's daughter. Our way lay through the heart of the town and *bazárs*, to the *ark* or citadel, a walled enclosure inside the city, within which the Governor always resides. The latter official, a good-looking, fat-faced, and chubby youth, was clearly bewildered at the honour of the visit, and displayed a stolid indifference when informed of the war in Europe. He was handsomely dressed, and had nothing to say for himself, being evidently much relieved when we took our departure. It is difficult to understand the policy of placing these well-born puppets in such responsible positions, and thus leaving all the real power in the hands of the Wazírs of the towns, often unscrupulous and intriguing men. This boy of fifteen, we were informed, expected shortly to become a father! We found the Persian Commissioner here in full dress, quite different from the uniform which had attracted our attention at Káshán. On this occasion, his coat was covered with embroidery, and he had no less than five orders of the Lion and Sun, three Russian Eagles, and a large red and white ribbon over the right shoulder. He seemed somewhat embarrassed by such unusual magnificence: but he clearly reserved it for very special occasions, as he divested himself of his fine feathers when preparing to call with us upon the minister—a duty we performed soon after the visit to the young Prince. The Wazír, a very fine old man, with pleasant manners, possessed one of the best appointed and most comfortable houses we had seen in Persia, and his whole household seemed to be peculiarly well drilled and disciplined. Certainly the conspicuous bundles of bastinado-canes cooling in the tank in the enclosure, and the inevitable 'Felek' stick, pointed to that conclusion.

Our visit here was a short one, as the time for the believers to say their evening prayers was near. The Wazír expressed in courteous terms his regret that, owing to it being the month of Ramadhán, he would be precluded from showing hospitality to the Generals Our way home was again through the *bazárs*, crowded with masses of people anxious to see the Faringis, but generally civil and orderly. They all seemed to be very poor, and we heard that the destitution of the city was very great.

On the third morning, the General received a visit from two of the leading merchants of Yazd, most intelligent and gentlemanly men. The elder, Hajji Muhammad Taki, was very anxious to have a telegraph constructed from Yazd to Dehbid, and said that, were the work undertaken, the merchants of Yazd would gladly pay for it. This accomplished, Yazd would be at once connected by telegraph with London and India, and her trade would of course greatly benefit. This merchant had a brother resident at Hong-Kong. His principal business seemed to be in opium, of which he informed Captain Smith that 4,000 chests were exported last year. He complained much of the heavy duty levied at Bombay on the opium which touched there on its way to China, and which, he said, paid 600 rupees a chest for merely lying in harbour, it being taken on, as a rule, immediately. A handsome profit must, however, still be made on the drug, which is obtainable in Persia at comparatively little cost. For sale in the towns and villages here it is worked up into thin, dry, and brittle sticks, about a foot in length. In the afternoon the old Wazír returned General Goldsmid's visit early, and was much interested in looking at pictures of the war in the 'Illustrated London News,' which he took away with him. The Hindús paid us another visit. We learnt that in the time of the former Governor, Muhammad Khán, who greatly encouraged the silk trade, there were 1,800 silk manufactories in Yazd, employing probably 9,000 hands. Since his removal, and the governorship of the present boy and of his Wazír, only 300 were in work. The silk so extensively manufactured in these parts is considered by some persons to be the best in all Persia. There were in the city fifty mosques, sixty-five public baths, and eight public schools and colleges. The number of Gabrs in the government of Yazd was given at 3,800, and that of Jews 800. The revenue was stated to be 60,000 *tumáns* paid to the Shah's treasury, and 40,000 retained to defray the cost of government. The exports were sugar, opium, silk, rope, cotton, copper, and felt; and the imports—henna, wheat, and cotton goods. Yazd is celebrated for its sweetmeats.

On the 10th December we resumed our journey, moving out, on a bitterly cold morning, through a series of cultivated enclosures and villages, to Muhammadabád, a large village of silk manufacturers, boasting some 300 houses, planted in every direction with mulberry trees. A so-called temple of fire-worshippers, passed on our way, turned out to be a 'tower of silence,' or place where the Gabrs expose their dead on gratings till the bodies are devoured by birds. From Muhammadabád (ten miles) the road continued for fourteen miles over a deserted country to Sar-i-Yazd, where was a capital new caravanserai, built, as that of Máibút, by private munificence, with first-rate stabling. The old caravanserai, on the other side of the road, was utilised for mules and camels. The village had been an extensive one, but was for the most part in ruins at the time of our visit, and the inhabitants were, as usual, very poor. A fine view of the snow-capped hills to the west is obtained from the summit of the caravanserai. Water very good.

Hence our road lay for eighteen miles over a flat pebbly desert, with occasional undulations, to the caravanserai and *chapar-khánah* of Zain-u-din, situated in the midst of a very desolate landscape. The former edifice, of the time of Shah Abbas, must originally have been of great strength, being built with circular flanking towers of great thickness. Its ruined walls bore marks on all sides of having seen service, probably against the Bakhtiáris. We found a few musketeers stationed here for the protection of the road. They must have been useless for any real purposes of defence or protection, as, a few days before our arrival, two camel loads of opium had been stolen at the caravanserai or in the neighbourhood, and the victims of the fraud had not succeeded in obtaining assistance or redress. No provisions of any kind were to be had at Zain-u-din, and the water was salt. On the 12th we continued to move over the same pebbly desert, with no signs of habitation or life, to Karmánsháhán. For the first nine or ten miles we marched between two low ranges of hills, probably about three or four miles apart; then gradually ascended over a ridge of high ground, descending half a mile, to the halting-place (sixteen miles). The nearly new caravanserai at this place was an excellent one, with four or five good *bálákhánahs*, or upstair rooms. It was built by the old Wakíl-ul-Múlk, father of the present Governor of Karmán. There was also a good *chapar-khánah*, and a *kálah*, or walled enclosure, where the few inhabitants and musketeers resided. Some slight cultivation was observed; and there were sand-grouse in the vicinity.

Leaving Karmánsháhán, we found for the first seven miles a gentle ascent in the road, otherwise pursuing its course over the same stony desert as on the previous day. A spur of low hills was then crossed, and after another slight descent the road debouched again on to the desert plain. The entrance to this low range of hills was, we were told, a favourite place for the attacks of robbers, who, two or three days before our arrival, had carried away two camel-loads of opium, a valuable prize. Our first information was that it had been stolen from the caravanserai at Zain-u-din. The musket-men were principally employed in escorting caravans over this dangerous spot, which seemed certainly well adapted for the attacks of brigands, but as the guard always withdrew its protection at the same place, it would seem easy for the robbers to change their 'venue.' From this spur of hills the road continued for about eleven miles over an absolute desert to Shams, the name given to a deserted *chapar-khánah* and a ruined fort, inhabited by the few musket-men stationed there for the protection of the road. The water was very salt, and supplies should be brought from Karmánsháhán. The scene of desolation presented by the station of Shams, as it rises to our memory, could hardly be surpassed even in the desolate scenery of Persia. A stony unbroken desert, intersected here and there by low ranges of barren, bleak and rocky hills, stretches on every side, as far as the eye can reach; and neither beast, bird, shrub, tree, twig, nor human being breaks the impressive monotony. We had passed on our way hither a caravan of fifty or sixty camels, proceeding with dates and dried fruits from Karmán to Yazd.

The road to Anár was over a continuation of the same desolate and inhospitable country noticed in the previous march. It was stony, in some places very sandy, and no signs of animal or vegetable life were visible. At about fifteen miles from Shams we halted and breakfasted at a deep well of salt water dug in the desert, with a small mud hut adjoining. The wind was so high as to raise clouds of dust, and breakfast in the open air under these circumstances was not enjoyable. At this place we were met by an employé of the

Governor of Karmán, who had been sent to Anár, a distance of nearly 200 miles, to meet the General and conduct him to Karmán, seeing he wanted for nothing on the way. He had been waiting seventeen days at Anár, being unaware of the delay that had taken place at Isfahán. About seven miles further was the village of Anár, consisting of 300 houses, the old mud fort of which with double walls, situated on a hill, was visible for many miles. On arrival we were immediately conducted to the Governor's house, a new and extensive building with a large tank of fresh running water in the courtyard, where most hospitable preparations had been made for our reception, fires lit, rooms carpeted, and the invariable presents of fruit and sweetmeats spread out on the floor. The local Governor at the same time entertained the Persian Commissioner and his suite in another building. It need hardly be said that means were found of recompensing him for his open-handed hospitality. The fort here had the reputation of harbouring foxes. The caravanserai and *chapar-khánah* were good, and there was a fine mosque. The water supply was commendable.

From Anár the road, for the first few miles over a much cultivated plain, changed into the usual sandy desert until within three miles of Baiáz (eighteen miles), when the surface became covered with stones. We found Baiáz a small village, with a row of mulberry trees and a spring of running water; possessing a good caravanserai, the completed portion of which supplied us with excellent quarters.

The morning of the 17th December was bright and windy. With the exception of the last four miles into Kushkoh (eighteen miles), when it became very stony, the road was again over the sandy desert, here sparsely sprinkled with camel-thorn. Streams of pure water flowed along each side of the road for some distance before we reached the village, the country around which appeared to be well irrigated. Many cotton fields were observed covering a considerable tract of country, and cultivation of all sorts seemed abundant. The caravanserai here not being a good one, and the two large rooms on either side of the doorway being very dirty, General Goldsmid and Captain Smith camped in tents pitched outside. So short did the *farsakhs* on this side of Isfahán appear that we generally calculated them at three miles, instead of three and a half or four, as elsewhere in Persia.

The next morning commenced with a light misty rain, which

increased as the day advanced, and at last there was a heavy downpour, which with slight intermission continued till past midnight. This was a great blessing for the country in general, and the simple inhabitants of Bahramabád of course attributed it to the 'auspicious feet' of the General. Our baggage came up in good time, though most of the things were more or less wet, and the road, even in a very few hours, became slippery and difficult to traverse. A few days' rain would, it is to be supposed, make the roads in this part of the country quite impassable. For eighteen miles after leaving Kushkoh we traversed a plain of great extent, stretching as far as the eye could reach, and bounded apparently by hills on every side, at this season capped with snow, especially a range lying just behind Kushkoh. This plain was covered with earthy tumuli and the tamarind plant, and promised to afford excellent shooting. We saw a flock of thirteen or fourteen bustard feeding close to the road, but they were frightened by the dogs before we could get a shot at them: hares and deer were also said to be abundant. At about eighteen miles distance the large and flourishing village of Hormuzabad was reached, and in a quarter of a mile further another village named Daniabád. Hence to Bahramabád, about seven miles, the country wore a very desolate appearance, and was cut up and scored in every direction by *kanáts*, while occasional patches of green, though affording but little relief to the landscape, showed that cultivation had not been wholly neglected.

We halted on the 19th. Bahramabád, a large and flourishing village—almost a town—of recent and rapid growth, contained, at the period of our visit, a population of perhaps 5,700. It may be said to owe its success to the late Wakíl-ul-Múlk, father of the present Governor of Karmán, a man of energetic and enterprising character, by whom the greater part of the caravanserais and tanks contained within the provincial limits were directly or indirectly constructed. The mud caravanserai was of inferior kind: but we found quarters in an excellent house belonging to the Government. In the evening of our first day at Bahramabád, ten Hindús came to visit the General, one of whom remembered him when he had passed through five years before. These men, most of them natives of Shikarpúr, had come out from Karmán for the purpose of purchasing the raw cotton extensively grown in this neighbourhood. It is cleaned first by the natives here, and then exported to India *viâ*

Bandar-Abbas, whither they informed us there is a direct road from this place, doing away with the necessity of first transporting the cotton to Karmán. They seemed to be very happy and in good case, and presented a strong contrast to their miserable brethren at Yazd. They informed us that the yield of cotton in the Karmán district was about 4,000 *manns* yearly, or 28,000 lbs., and that its price was twenty-five shillings per eighty pounds. The imports for India appeared to be chiefly sugar, indigo, and cotton goods. There is no doubt that a good transit road from Karmán to the coast would work wonders in opening out the trade of this district, and in encouraging traffic with India from every part of Persia. Some few Parsis or Gabrs are to be noted among the residents of Bahramabád, which has a reputation for pottery. On our second day, the General received visits from the Naïb of the place, and the Yáwar or Major, who had been sent out to meet us from Karmán. The Hindús also paid him a second visit. The inhabitants here have a practice during the Ramazán of sounding a drum in the early morning, as a notice to the faithful that it is time to prepare their last meal before the rising of the sun compels them to commence their daily fast. The 'tattoo' was very loud, and awoke us regularly every morning about four o'clock.

On a bright, but cold and windy morning, after a night of hard frost, we quitted Bahramabád. The road for the first five miles led through a well-cultivated plain, cut up and scored in every direction by *kanáts*, until it reached the village of Abdulabád, when it passed for sixteen miles over a pebbly desert, and for about three miles more over soft sandy soil interspersed with patches of *bhuta*. We stopped and breakfasted at about fourteen miles, at a covered tank of excellent water, near a mud hovel situated on the side of the road. The hills on all sides of the plain we had crossed were covered with snow, and the snow-capped and lofty mountain range beyond Karmán was distinctly visible, forming a beautiful boundary to the landscape in our front. Kabútar-Khán, which takes its name from an old pigeon-tower in the vicinity, consists of two villages, one almost in ruins and the other new, containing about 150 inhabitants. A large number of these politely came out to meet the General, and the Katkhuda informed us he had orders from the Wakíl-ul-Múlk to supply all our wants both for men and animals free of charge. This, however, was an arrangement which was not allowed to have effect: we preferred paying for everything. It was impossible to prevent the villagers sacrificing a sheep by a rapid process of decapitation on the approach of our cavalcade. One man kept the bleeding carcase on the left of the road, while another ran across with the head; so that we had to pass between the two, which we understand to be the orthodox way of accepting a Persian welcome. They had endeavoured to sacrifice a sheep in a similar way at our every halting-stage, but we had, as a rule, hitherto managed to save its life. The caravanserai at Kabútar-Khán, in which we put up, was not in very good repair, besides being rather dark and dirty: but it had two pretty good *bálákhánahs*. Numerous pigeons were observable everywhere in the vicinity. The water here was good and abundant. Kabútar-Khán, as the private property of the Shah, paid no tribute, but had to supply certain articles of consumption on occasions. It had an arsenal with thirty guns.

There was more hard frost and much ice when we left Kabútar-Khán. The road, which had previously run over a hard sandy plain, after five miles entered an extensive marsh, which, owing to the heavy rains of two days previous, would have probably been impassable had it not been for the frost of the preceding night, which enabled us to get over the ground while it was yet hard. This tract is only difficult in wet weather; but, after any continuous rain, it would evidently be quite impassable, receiving, as it were in a basin of soft clayey soil, all the streams from the neighbouring high grounds. At thirteen miles we reached the flourishing village of Ribát, where we stayed and breakfasted at an excellent caravanserai, built by the late Wakíl-ul-Múlk, with a complete suite of good upper apartments, and with doors to all the downstair rooms—an unheard-of luxury in Persia. After leaving Ribát the valley became narrower, being bounded as before by the magnificent Jafar Kúh and range of snowy hills beyond Karmán in our front. The road from Ribát to Baghin was for fifteen miles over a stony desert, interspersed with patches of cultivation. The large village of Sadi was passed to the right, about eleven miles from Ribát. We were met at Baghin as usual by a deputation of the inhabitants, of whom there are about 1600. Baghin, we were told, paid no money revenue, but in kind, principally wheat and barley. The village was clean, and well supplied with excellent water. There was much cultivated land in the vicinity, extending to the foot of the hills bounding the plain on the right; and good shooting. The General and Captain Smith pitched tents outside the indifferent caravanserai. We halted here one day, and received a visit from the Zábit of the place, accompanied by the Yáwar and his son. All three were greatly surprised at and interested in a breech-loading gun, on the ordinary principle, with central-fire cartridges. They had never seen anything of the kind before, and their plaudits were long and loud.

From Baghin, which is really south of Karmán, the road, for several miles, winds about over sloping stony ground, until it has completely rounded the point of the Dawirán range, when it descends into the plain of Karmán (nineteen miles). At an old caravanserai, distant thirteen miles, the General was met about 12.30 by the *istikbál*, sent out to meet him by the Wakíl-ul-Múlk, consisting of from forty to fifty horsemen commanded by two Colonels, one of whom, Sarhang Ali Agha, spoke French very well, having been educated for three years at the École de St. Cyr, in Paris. A tame boar came out with the escort, and we were told that it invariably accompanied the horses when taken out. The Persians allow these wild boars (caught very young) to live in their stables, where they strike up a great friendship with the horses. This custom is the more curious, as the pig, being the uncleanest of animals in a Muhammadan's eyes, would hardly appear a fit object for admission to the stables, often considered a place of great sanctitude: the stables of the Shah and the British Minister at Tehrán are, for instance, privileged places where all criminals can securely take *bast* or refuge. We were escorted to the lodging assigned to the General by a great concourse of horsemen and *faráshes*. On arrival, however, the quarters and general arrangement were found to be so defective that Captain Smith was despatched to the Persian Commissioner to represent the state of affairs. The latter was found to be in a state of great discomfort and disquietude, as his abode was infinitely worse. The Governor, on learning the inferior character of the accommodation provided, directed the Bágh-i-Nishát to be placed at our disposal, and sent numerous apologies for not having selected it before, on the ground that there were no stables available there. Our habitat for the first day and night was situated on the east of Karmán outside the walls, and belonged to the chief of police; but was in a state of wretched repair. The *Múnshi báshi* of the Wakíl-ul-Múlk called in the afternoon to ask after the General's health, and the whole of the Hindús of the place, about forty in number, also came to pay their respects. We entered Karmán on the last day of the fast of Ramazán.

The next morning we made arrangements to move into the Bágh-i-Nishát, situated on the other side of the city. A man brought us a large and very fine wild goat as a present, he having shot it the day before in the Jufár-Kúh, which abounds with these animals. The General, accompanied by Captain Smith, paid a ceremonial visit to the Wakíl-ul-Múlk. Our way lay through the heart of the city, which was crowded with masses of people, in their best attire, at all places of vantage, to see the English envoy pass. The *bazárs* were filled with fruit, sweetmeats, and such like things, but shops that did not sell eatables were closed in honour of the feast following the expiration of the fast. We found the Governor's house situated inside the *ark* or citadel—practically a large square, with spacious huts inside the courtyard. The Wakíl-ul-Múlk received our chief with great cordiality, and spoke much concerning his friendship with his father the former Governor: alluding to the occasion of the General's visit in 1866, when he himself was only Colonel of a regiment. His rapid rise in fortune may be principally attributed to influence gained by the notably successful administration of his late father. After sitting for some time we took our leave, and proceeded to our new quarters on the opposite side of the city to those we had abandoned. The Bágh-i-Nishát, one of the nicest residences we had seen in Persia, was built by the present Governor, and is better adapted for summer than winter. The grounds are of great extent, partly laid out for fruit and partly for flowers. In the afternoon, the Nawáb of the Governor came again to see the General, and arranged about his return visit the next day. This gentleman spoke French fluently, and told us he had been seven years in Paris. He seemed to feel keenly his exile in this out-of-the-way part of the world, and longed to get back to Europe.

Our Christmas Day (Sunday) was bright and cold, with frost. We had visits from two Colonels in the morning; but the civility may have been prompted by a desire of consulting Dr. Cumming about their eyesight. At breakfast time, five large trays of sweetmeats arrived from the Wakíl-ul-Múlk, as a Christmas present. At one o'clock, the Governor, attended by the Deputy Governor, Persian Commissioner, Chief of Police (an enormously fat man), the French-speaking Colonel and the Nawáb, paid his return visit. He stayed nearly an hour, during which time the General presented him with a very handsome pair of gold eye-glasses, at which he was much pleased. He was also very anxious to consult Dr. Cumming about his eyes. The whole tribe of Hindús came about 6 P.M. to see the General. They said they had been trying ever since the morning to get access to him, but had been beaten away at three of the city gates: eventually, the Wakíl-ul-Múlk, hearing of their distress, had given orders for their admittance. These men generally have many complaints, either well or ill founded, to make against the Persian Government, and would naturally try to engage every passing Englishman in their favour; but General Goldsmid was, of course, unable to interfere directly in their behalf by any formal or adequate investigation.

On Monday, a very large present of oranges and dates arrived from the Wakíl-ul-Múlk, who had forbidden his servants to take any presents in return; and a deputation of Gabrs, succeeded shortly after by one of Hindús, made its appearance at our quarters. On Tuesday three Persian gentlemen called to see Dr. Cumming, and asked him to treat them for bad eyesight, a complaint which appears to be prevalent in Karmán. The Wakíl-ul-Múlk sent a present of deer that had just been shot, and a quantity of partridges and game, to the General. At two o'clock Captain Smith visited His Excellency, by desire, to present him with the translation of Malcolm's 'History of Persia,' done into Persian by order of the Bombay Government, and at the express wish of his late father, the old Wakíl-ul-Múlk, personally communicated to General (then Colonel) Goldsmid. The Governor was exceedingly pleased at the receipt of the book, and expressed his gratification and thanks in the most cordial manner. He read the preface, which set forth the circumstances under which the work had been translated, and said he felt strongly the kindness which had recollected and acted upon a wish of his father's expressed so many years ago. He was further very anxious to know when the second volume would be ready, and said that, when it was finished, he would have them both printed in Bombay. The book is beautifully written, and illustrated with copies of the engravings which accompany the original work. Captain Smith, on leaving the Governor's, proceeded to visit the Persian Commissioner, who had quitted his first place of residence, outside the walls, for one inside the city, and certainly had not made a change for the better. He stated that he had by yesterday's post received instructions from the Persian Government to proceed with the settlement of the Balúchistán frontier, should Sistán be found impracticable on arrival at Karmán; and that he was accordingly willing to proceed at once with this mission, if the General would inform him officially of the impossibility of going to Sistán. We were told that the hands and ears of two thieves had been cut off on the previous day in the public square[1]. In the evening a large dinner was provided for the servants of the Mission and those of the Governor employed about our domicile, which was kept up, with music and like accompaniments, until twelve o'clock.

Little of novelty occurred on Wednesday. The Yáwar called on the part of the Wakíl-ul-Múlk to tell the General that everything he, the Governor, possessed was at his disposal. The General called on the Persian Commissioner at his house in the town. There were no chairs, so we had all to sit on the ground. Mirza Ma'súm Khán expressed his willingness to accompany us to Balúchistán, on the understanding that the Sistán matter was impracticable for this year at least. The English mail arrived from Tehrán,

---

[1] Dr. Cumming relates a curious story in connexion with thieves. Three men had made an entry into a Persian's house at Isfahán, and, having secured a sufficiency of plunder, were on the point of making their way through a hole in the wall, when the victimised owner woke up, and arrived on the spot just in time to see the last of the party with his body half through the hole. He immediately caught hold of the burglar's legs, and held on, shouting in the meantime for assistance. The captive's comrades, on their side, tried with might and main to pull him through, but finding their efforts unsuccessful, and being, moreover, afraid of capture themselves, or recognition should they escape and their comrade be taken, they hastily cut off his head and decamped with it, thus leaving no trace by which they might be known, and doing away with all danger of their friend turning king's evidence. Bloodshed in any form seems to come natural to Persians. A slave boy in Shiráz, twelve years of age, shot his master's son, it was supposed by accident. The Governor, however, took a more serious view of the case, and ordered the wretched lad to be crucified. This was accordingly done, the victim being nailed up against the wall in the public square, with iron pegs through his hands and legs, and a stake driven through his back into the wall, to which he had his face turned. It is said that the sufferer actually lived in this position for some hours. At Shiraz, also, Quartermaster-Sergeant Bower saw the executioner cut the throats of eleven robbers in one morning. The wretched men stood all in a row, and smoked a *kalián*: the executioner walked up to them one by one, put their heads under his left arm, and cut their throats in much the same way as he would have killed sheep. All the shopkeepers had to pay a fee to the grim official.

having been brought by one of the servants we had sent back from Isfahán in the incredibly short time of seven days. His report was that he had started on the afternoon of the 20th, and had been sick one day at Yazd. By our route the distance would have exceeded 650 miles; by his it might have been about 600. On Thursday we continued our experience of the bright cold mornings of Karmán. The Nawáb of the Wakíl-ul-Múlk called to express his master's willingness to serve the General in any way. He brought with him as presents six or seven very ancient coins. In the afternoon, some of us proceeded to the town to visit the carpet and shawl manufactories. The Governor sent a man as escort from the Bágh-i-Nishát, and on arrival at the shawl manufactories, we were shown into a room where there was a variety of sweetmeats and fruits laid out for our acceptance, and where, while enjoying tea and the universal *kalián*, the owner of the factory showed us some of the best specimens of shawls manufactured, beautiful in texture, pattern, and make. An official of the Governor's household here presented himself, and said he had also been commissioned by His Excellency to take us round the workshops. This tall fine-looking Persian, with splendid black beard, turned out to be the individual who had been appointed *mihmándár* to the General when he and Major Murdoch Smith passed through Karmán in 1866. He had not known that the English Commissioner of to-day was the Colonel of five years ago, and was delighted when informed of the identity. The factory we were now at was, moreover, the same visited on the former occasion. After tea was finished we proceeded to the workshops, entering by a hole in the wall, just big enough to admit a man but certainly not large enough to pass a chair; and the first thing that struck us was the utter want of ventilation, there being absolutely no way of purifying the air, which was close and smelt most unwholesome. About sixty or seventy men and boys were seated in three rooms, working at looms placed horizontally before them. Each loom, worked by one man and two small boys, contained the fabric of one shawl. The man, always an experienced hand, sits in the middle, and the two boys on either side. They sit so close together that their arms actually interlace, but, nevertheless, their nimble fingers work away with great rapidity. They make the shawls with the right side downwards, so that their eyes can be of very little use in guiding them, and they learn the patterns by heart. Extraordinary as it seems, these intricate patterns are learnt by heart and rote, not from painted pictures with long written explanations, but entirely from manuscript. The pattern of a shawl is composed in the same way that another man would compose a piece of poetry, and the workers then learn the pattern by heart. This is certainly most marvellous, and must demand a constant and never-ceasing strain upon the memory. We were informed that it would take a clever lad six months or more to learn a pattern, but that when once learnt it was never forgotten. Some of the children we saw working there could not have been more than seven or eight years old, and children were by far the majority of workers. In one of the rooms the shawls in course of manufacture were of a very simple design, and adapted to beginners; a man was walking up and down reading out the patterns from a dirty and soiled manuscript. But the better shawls have all, as it were, to be learnt by heart. The threads of *kúrk*, or goat's-hair, dyed, are cut in short lengths, and these are woven in by the fingers into the web of the shawl stretched horizontally before the maker. The boys and men sit in holes with their feet under the web, which position brings their arms on a level with the shawl. That the work is unhealthy in the extreme, the pale sallow faces of the men and boys sufficiently testified; but it has also a serious effect in damaging the eyes; few of those whom we saw but had bleared and weak eyes, and many wore spectacles. The emaciated bodies of the children were especially noticeable and very pitiable, and their arms seemed to be almost withered away,—but there is no 'Factory Act' in Persia. We were informed by the proprietor that the hours allotted to sheer work averaged fourteen a day! A shawl of the best description, three yards in length, takes about a year to make, and should cost from forty to sixty *tumáns* (£16 or £24). The men are badly paid, the best workers averaging about 1s. a day, and the children about 2d. to 4d. It is impossible that, always being in such a position, with the body everlastingly bent over the same work, and the mind as well as fingers constantly strained, any of these poor creatures can live long. But the manufactures that spring from their nimble fingers are very beautiful. The Karmánís boast that their shawls are superior to those of Kashmír, to which place they export annually quantities of *kúrk* by way of Bandar-Abbas and Bombay. *Kúrk* is the fine wool found next to the skin of the goat. These shawls are entirely made from this material. The goats are shorn twice a year, in the spring and autumn. From the shawl manufactory we went some little distance to that of the no less celebrated carpets. These are manufactured in a way reminding one strongly of the gobelin tapestry made at present, or rather before the war, in Paris. The looms are arranged perpendicularly, and the workers sit behind the loom, but in this case, unlike the gobelins, they have the right side of the carpet towards them. The manufacture of carpets differs from that of the shawls also in this particular, that each carpet has a painted pattern, designed and drawn out by the master of the manufactory, which is pinned in the centre of the carpet, and which the workers can consult, if necessary, from time to time. Advantage, however, is rarely taken of this facility of reference, for the boy who sits nearest the pattern reads out in a monotonous voice any information required concerning it. The carpets are made entirely of cotton, woven in by the fingers into the upright web. Their manufacture is tedious and costly in the extreme, but they are beautifully soft and durable. The work is constantly hammered close together by a wooden hammer every few stitches. The man whose manufactory we visited was said to be without a rival in Persia, either for beauty of design or excellence of manufacture. We saw a beautiful carpet that he was making for the sacred shrine at Mash-had, which was to cost 500 *tumáns*, or £200, being eleven yards long by about two and a half broad; than which nothing could be more beautiful. But its manufacture would take at least two years from the commencement. The boys and men here did not look so unhealthy as in the shawl workshops. We were entertained here with the usual sweetmeats, fruits, and *sharbat*, laid out on a most beautiful rug that had just come from one of the looms. The doctor having left us to advise the Wakíl-ul-Múlk on the subject of his eyes, we went straight home through the *bazárs*. These are lofty and well built, owing their existence, as indeed do all the improvements in this town, to the energy of the late Governor; before whose promotion to high local administrative functions Karmán was, by all accounts, a wretched place. We noted that a great part of the city was in ruins; but the high wall by which it was surrounded, with its six large gates and flanking towers at regular intervals, gave it an air of neatness and solidity.

On Friday we were busy the whole day preparing the despatch of a Tehrán courier. In the evening the Persian Commissioner, with the Nawáb and the Colonel, Ali Agha, who had headed the *istikbál*, dined with the General. The conversation was carried on entirely in French, as these gentlemen had been in Europe, the two last having been chiefly educated in Paris. The next day, Saturday, the last day in the year, Captain Smith visited the Persian Commissioner, to ascertain what were his precise intentions as to future movements. Mirza Ma'súm Khán, evidently in great fear of the responsibility to be incurred by proceeding directly to Balúchistán, finally consented to go there, if informed in writing that the move to Sistán was impracticable.

On New Year's Day, the Nawáb of the Wakíl-ul-Múlk called in the morning with his verbal congratulations; and also brought some handsome presents from the Governor, consisting of a carpet and *namad* (felt) (worth about £60) for the General, a rug for Captain Smith, and a shawl for Dr. Cumming. The two former it was decided to send off at once to the India Office in England. After breakfast Captain Smith called on the Persian Commissioner, and announced to him the General's intention to march from Karmán on Wednesday at latest. He promised to be ready. The General received a letter from Sir W. Merewether in Sind, dated the 29th November, which had been brought up from Bandar-Abbas by the Wakíl-ul-Múlk's *kásid*, or messenger.

The day following, the Yáwar called early to inform the General that he had been ordered to accompany him all the way to Bampúr, and that he wanted leave to meet him at Ráyín, three stages on the way, as he was going to visit his family residing there. Permission was of course given. At 3 P.M. the General, attended by Captain Smith, Dr. Cumming, and Quartermaster-Sergeant Bower, called on the Wakíl-ul-Múlk to bid him good-bye. Mirza Ma'súm Khán was in attendance, as were the usual members of the Governor's suite. We were received very cordially, and the appearance of special refreshments prolonged the visit; but the ices were somewhat cold fare for a winter's afternoon. After the visit was over, the General returned to the Bágh-i-Nishát, while Captain Smith, Dr. Cumming, and Quartermaster-Sergeant Bower proceeded to the caravanserai in the city, which the Hindú traders are allowed to rent from the *mushtahid* at 120 *tumáns* per annum. It is a wretchedly dirty place, opening off one of the *bazárs*, crowded for the occasion; and throngs of people, principally women, blocked the entrance the whole time that we remained there. A more public visit was probably never paid; for our chairs were placed on a platform which runs outside and over the lower row of shops, and we had to sit here exposed to the full gaze of the population of the *bazárs* for a quarter of an hour, eating sweetmeats and otherwise engaged in scarcely dignified pursuits. One of the Hindús had been in Persia for thirty-five years, and another for twelve years; being unable to leave, so they informed us, on account of the bad debts they could not recover. Among them were agents for Shikarpúr merchants, who generally remain about five years at a time. There were also eight *fakirs*, professedly on the point of starting for the fires at Bákú, on the Caspian, a long and perilous journey amid a Muhammadan population. These Hindús would much like to have a British Consul at Karmán, whose presence would, no doubt, do much to encourage trade and commerce with India. They had asked General Goldsmid to pay them a personal visit at the caravanserai, in order that their social status might be enhanced in the eyes of the Muhammadans; but the officers of his suite, to whom the whole scene was comparatively new, had gone in his stead, and met with a warm reception. They showed us a little dirty room in the caravanserai, where they said a European, who could neither talk Hindustáni or Persian, had stayed for a fortnight about six or seven years before; and we were unable to determine who this might be[1]. We learnt that the Karmán shawls of the finer sort, made of *kúrk*, were not in great demand for exportation, they being principally made to order. Great quantities of the inferior kinds, however, made of lamb's-wool, were sent to the Turkish market. They paid a duty at every provincial town on the caravan route, and again an impost duty on the Turkish frontier. The local duty on the superior shawls was five per cent.

[1] When I was at Karmán in January, 1866, Muhammad Isma'íl Khán, the father of the present Governor, then Minister to the nominal Governor, a prince of the blood royal, told me that about fifteen years previously, a strange traveller, ostensibly an Englishman, had taken up his quarters at a summer-house belonging to himself. Some boys had assailed him there, probably with intent to dislodge him, and after a time he had been brought before the Minister. Finding the latter engaged in a question of carpets, he took an opportunity of entering into the conversation, asserting that the manufactures of Karmán were worth more money than the amounts commonly put upon them. Eventually, he got some carpets from the Khán, on the understanding that they were to be disposed of to the best advantage, and for a certain consideration; but after the stranger had departed, nothing further had been heard of him.—F. J. G.

The colours, bright when new, were very liable to fade if much exposed to the sun, especially yellow, green, and blue: the material, unlike Kashmír, shrinking slightly on being wet.

On Tuesday, the 3rd January, the Nawáb of the Governor came to breakfast; and shortly after the Persian Commissioner called on the General and sat for a long time. His visit was very satisfactory, as he made no further difficulties about starting, and arranged to accompany us on the Thursday. In the afternoon the General sent the *mírakhor* with two very handsome presents to the Wakíl-ul-Múlk, with which he was greatly pleased—an enamelled Paris opera-glass, and some beautiful silk for covering furniture. He also gave the Nawáb a silver watch. Dr. Cumming's reputation had become a *fait accompli* in Karmán; he had numerous patients every day, especially women. The people asked him to do strange things, and apparently thought he could work miracles.

On the 4th, Colonel Ali Agha and the Nawáb called to pay a farewell visit on the part of the Wakíl-ul-Múlk in the afternoon, and to convey his reiterated thanks for the presents sent him yesterday. The Hindús also called again. Large *douceurs* were issued to those servants of the Governor who had been detached for employment with the Mission during its stay in Karmán. Our old *faráshes* were also dismissed; new ones, carefully chosen by the Wakíl-ul-Múlk, being sent to supply their places. Karmán was reputed to contain 40,000 inhabitants: 40 Hindús; Gabrs, 180; Jews, 50: to possess *hammáms*, 32; caravanserais, 28, i.e. 12 for trade, and 16 for travellers; shawl manufactories, 120; cotton manufactories, 80; carpet manufactories, really good, 6. The revenue was stated at about 310,000 *tumáns*, or £124,000.

After a detention of nearly a fortnight, not wholly profitless if somewhat wearisome, we left Karmán on the morning of the 5th January; skirting the city walls up to the gate opposite the side by which we had entered. Our road passed through several miles of ruins and beside the Kala'h Dukhtar, or Virgin Fort, a high hill about two miles from Karmán, evidently strongly fortified in former times, but of late years in ruins. There were marks of a covered way that must have led to the outskirts of the city from the fort. On clearing the ruined suburbs the road ran over a sandy desert, much cut up and scored with old *kanáts*, until at about twenty-one miles distance from Karmán it rose to the village of Máhún, visible long before it was reached, lying on the sloping ground which bounded the view in front, and surrounded with most extensive gardens. The blue dome of the shrine stood out a conspicuous and effectual landmark. At about half way was a small mud caravanserai, where good water could be obtained. The Kúh-i-Jufár, to the right of the road, formed a beautiful object in the landscape. The village of Jufár itself might be just discerned lying at the end of the spur which terminated the hill to the west. At about five miles from Máhún we were met by a 'Yáwar,' with three gentlemen in scarlet, who had come out to meet the General; and as we entered the village we were received by some more *faráshes*: finally, at the entrance to the shrine, we found a guard of honour, drawn up in full dress, consisting of some twenty or thirty men. The whole village turned out to see us pass, and every advantageous place for beholders was occupied by staring crowds, amid which women decidedly had the preponderance. The shrine here is a famous one; it contains the body of Shah Niámat Ullah, a great saint or prophet of Indian extraction, who flourished in the fourteenth century, and is credited with much influence in bringing about the Indian mutiny, owing to his prophecy that the English power in India would be extinguished in 1857. Numerous devotees from all parts of the world flock to his tomb, and we saw several gifts there, entirely of Indian origin. The shrine, which lies to the left of the road, is very picturesque, with its large and beautiful *chinár* trees, in the midst of which the blue dome appears. On the opposite side of the road we observed a superior sort of caravanserai or dwelling-house, provided by the Wakíl-ul-Múlk, for the use of travellers. This building occupied three sides of a square, facing towards the shrine, with which it was connected by two graceful arches that bridged the road. It contained a very pretty garden, which should be beautiful in summer, with a broad stream of the purest water running through it. We found the shrine somewhat out of repair. The remains of the Shah lay underneath the dome in a large marble grave covered with *kráns*. A beautiful carpet adorned the floor of the room. Almost all the sovereigns of Persia had lent their assistance in beautifying and enriching the shrine from time to time, and the record of their good deeds was emblazoned on the walls. The garden surrounding was supplied with plenty of pure water—a most fortunate circumstance for travellers. Indeed the village abounded with purling streams and beautiful trees. The two *darvishes* who showed us over the shrine were singularly intelligent and free from fanaticism; they did not even request us to take off our boots, though of course we did not enter the sacred precincts where the remains of the prophet lay. Both these men well remembered the General's former visit in 1866, with Major Murdoch Smith, and were very glad to see him again. Máhún struck us as a particularly pleasant place, a good summer residence for the inhabitants of Karmán. The population of Máhún was estimated at about 5000 inhabitants; it had four *hammáms*.

Leaving a charming apartment which had been placed at our disposal under orders from Karmán, we marched after breakfast, at about 10 A.M.; having first paid a visit to the shrine of Máhún. The road ran over a pebbly desert, with camel-thorn, gradually ascending in a southerly direction till it entered the hills, when it followed the line of a watercourse till arrival at Hánakah (sixteen miles), a single caravanserai, built seven or eight years before by the deceased Wakíl-ul-Múlk. There was a brick-kiln here for making *kanát* pipes. In the rainy season the country about was said to abound with small game. The hills were covered with stones and the universal camel-thorn. Water was here good and abundant.

On the morning of the 7th, the Persian Commissioner started before us. We had shared the caravanserai together on the previous night. The road ran between hills until it reached a stone stable very strongly built, called Kala'h Shur, where we breakfasted, nine miles from Hánakah. At this point a strong and most unpleasant wind arose, which continued to blow with great force until we arrived at Ráyín. About four miles from Kala'h Shur the road had attained its highest point, and then we began to descend. Here we first got a sight of the beautiful snowy ranges of Sarvistan and Deh Bakri, with the lofty Kúh-i-Shah. After descending for some seven miles, over very stony ground and through a most desolate country, we made a *détour* to the right, and followed a course due south-west, for four miles across a barren plain, over which a strong wind blew, to the large village of Ráyín, situated on the sloping ground bounding the right of the level tract. Here we were received by an *istikbál* of the inhabitants, and conducted, amid crowds of curious villagers, to a comfortable and spacious house on the higher ground. The road we had traversed was not the usual road from Karmán in summer. There was another much more direct and shorter, which joined the Karmán road at Máhún, but being impassable in winter, ours was considered preferable. Ráyín could boast about 6000 inhabitants, a census having been taken in recent years. There were some beautiful *chinár* trees in the village; and the water was good and plentiful.

The weather had become perceptibly warmer; but the days were cloudy. For the first fifteen miles after leaving Ráyín we marched over a stony desert, with occasional cultivation, and covered with camel-thorn, at right angles to the road by which we had approached our stage on the previous day. Then, instead of going straight into Sarvistan, it made a further *détour* at right angles to the left, and followed this course for seventeen miles; forming three sides of a square, of which the fourth would have been the direct line from Hánakah to Khátunabad, had we followed that route. This distance of seventeen miles was for the greater part between the *bands* of a high and rocky ravine, along the bed of a river, no doubt high enough in rainy weather, but when we passed very sandy and stony. The course was winding in the extreme, and the march was especially tedious. Such water as there was in the pools in the bed of the river was very salt. No game was to be seen. The road then made another *détour* at right angles to the right, and leaving the bed of the river, which still ran parallel with it, continued for two miles over a richly-watered and well-cultivated plain to the small village of Khátunabad, or Khánah-Khátún, situated at the foot of a long and sombre black rock. There was another road from Ráyín joining this road at its last *détour*, and used when the river was full, but which was much longer. The reason of this one being used in preference to the more direct one from Hánakah and to Sarvistan was explained to be the utter desolation of the country in the latter case. We were received at Khánah-Khátún by the usual *istikbál* of the inhabitants, and found quarters in a very large and spacious mud caravanserai, built by the late Wakíl-ul-Múlk, where the Commissioner also found accommodation. The water here was very good.

About two miles after departure from Khánah-Khátún we saw a village to the right, apparently overhanging the bed of the river which gives the name of Tahrúd to the cluster of villages lying in this small district[1]. We soon entered a passage between hills following the course of a winding and clear stream for about three miles, when the road forked—the right branch leading to the ancient fort of Awárik, and the left debouching, after a short distance, on an extensive plain, covered with low tamarisk, and very stony, which apparently stretched in front up to the walls of Bam. To the right, built on a slight eminence about two miles from the road, the ancient fort of Awárik, though in ruins, presented a still remarkable construction. Quartermaster-Sergeant Bower rode off to inspect it; and came back in about two hours with the intelligence that the whole of the inhabitants living in the village below had turned out *en masse* to receive him at their stronghold. This building had not, it was stated, been inhabited since the commencement of the reign of the present Shah, having been deserted on account of the difficulty of transporting water to that height. Originally built, as were the whole of the similar group of forts in this district, for protection against the inroads of the Balúchís, there had not been a *chapáo* for sixty years. It is believed that the fort of Bam is the only one in the locality kept in a state of repair; and this state of things gives strong evidence of the present tranquillity of the district. Quartermaster-Sergeant Bower succeeded in getting two or three relics dug up from the ruins; a plate, a lamp, and an old silver coin, said to be 631 years old. There is no doubt that this fort is of great antiquity. Further away to the right front of Awárik lies the caravanserai of Sarvistan, situated on much higher ground, formed by the slope of the hills that bound the plain in that direction. At Darzin (twenty-five miles), where we arrived at 3 P.M., a new village was in course of erection, in the form of a square, with all the rooms facing inwards: two of these had been prepared for our reception. The caravanserai, a small mud one, was in a dilapidated state, but our horses found good quarters in it. The water here was abundant and good. Darzin had a ruined fort, similar to that of Awárik.

Hence the road traversed a partially cultivated and uneven plain, and at about eight miles crossed the bed of the Bam river, on the left bank of which, a mile further on, was the large village of Bahdiran, built of low houses with dome-shaped roofs; on the left bank, opposite to the village, was the caravanserai and settlement

---

[1] Tah-rúd clearly means the bottom of the river-bed.—*F. J. G.*

of Kwojah-Askir, where we breakfasted. This place was surrounded by date-palms, and near it, in the bed of the river, a marsh of high green flags reminded one strongly of India. The Persian Commissioner here joined forces with us, and we rode into Bam together. About five miles from the town we were met by the usual *istikbál*, headed by the Deputy Governor, Yáwar Suliman Khan, who was waiting on foot to receive the General, of whom he is an old acquaintance. He escorted him into the town (seventeen miles), where we found quarters prepared for us in a new and partially finished house in course of construction for the famous Ibrahim Khán, who had gone to Bampúr to await our arrival at that place. Bam at first sight is very like an Indian town. It covers a large space of ground, is very straggling, has large gardens, and there are no walls to mark a limit. The river appears to run through the centre of the town, or rather the centre of the houses and their adjoining gardens. The *bazár* is miserably small and insignificant, but the population seems fairly intelligent and well to do. The Commissioner called on the General in the evening, and arrangements were made for departure on the Thursday, if possible.

A letter received from the Persian Commissioner the next morning caused a change in the plans formed by the General, who had purposed detaching Dr. Cumming and Quartermaster-Sergeant Bower from Bam to the sea coast at Bandar-Abbas. Ma'súm Khán now notified his intentions of bringing to Bampúr the whole of his establishment, consisting of twenty servants, nineteen horses, nine mules, and fifteen camels. After some conversation with the Náib-ul-Hukumat, Suliman Khán, who called in the morning, and an interview between Captain Smith and the Persian Commissioner, we were rejoiced to find that there would be no real difficulty in procuring camels. Finally, therefore, it was decided that the whole camp should move on to Bampúr, merely leaving the *mírakhor* here with fifteen horses, three tents, and the necessary establishment, as originally contemplated. Three of our servants, considered superfluous, were to be dismissed, and our marching strength was to be the General and three Staff, twenty-three servants, ten horses, and forty-five camels. We had at once to take provisions for fifteen days for selves and servants; and grain for the animals was to be laid in at Regan, the frontier station of the desert, for nine days. The year was one of unusual drought and scarcity: and there were at Bam 500 camels waiting to proceed to Karmán with grain. We learnt to-day that there were only thirteen marches from here to Sekuha in Sistán, of which two were on our road to Bampúr. So that there would be little more trouble in organising an expedition to that quarter from this station, than there had been in making the arrangements for the Bampúr march.

Owing to failure in the supply of camels we were detained at Bam for two days longer; and it became necessary to modify our respective marching arrangements by the substitution of twelve mules for ten camels. Our disappointment was great at being refused admittance to the fort, the only object in Bam worth inspecting[1].

On the morning of the 10th January we left Bam. After getting clear of the town, the Persian Commissioner, accompanied by the Deputy Governor Suliman Khán, who was to accompany us to Regan, joined our cavalcade. The former told the General that he had received a letter from the Governor of Káïn, telling him that the commencement of the Sistán arbitration was anxiously expected there; as a firman had been received from the Shah, ordering the Persian authorities to remain perfectly quiescent and *in statu quo* until the arrival of the English Envoy. He further wished the General to telegraph to the Viceroy, asking him to restrain the Afghán authorities in like manner from taking any active steps on the frontier. The road at three miles from Bam passed through two large cultivated patches of ground, with houses and date-trees on each side of the road, and then crossed a perfectly flat plain till within a mile and a half of Wakilabad, a village fostered under the auspices of the Wakíl-ul-Múlk. The whole way it ran parallel with a bright, clear, and swift running stream, the banks of which were fringed with low tamarisk and thorn bushes. Near Wakilabad, it entered a low jungle with tamarisk-trees. Thence it traversed a country with plenty of low jungle, tamarisk-trees of a considerable growth, abundance of water, and constant cultivation, but very sparsely populated; a happy contrast and in general a great relief to the poor, dry, and stony districts of Persia. At two miles from Azizábád (28 miles) a deep descent led to the passage of the *rúd-khána*, about 100 yards broad,

[1] The Deputy Governor said he was unable to give the required permission without an order from the Wakíl-ul-Múlk at Karmán. On the occasion of my semi-official visit, when alone in 1866, this order had been spontaneously given to me, and I had been admitted to the interior of the fort and received most courteously by its Commandant.—F. J. G.

choked with rushes, and with about four or five feet of water, evidently abounding in wild fowl and pig. At our camping-ground was a small caravanserai or storehouse, but we slept in tents.

The next morning was unexpectedly cold, contrary to our preconceived notions of the Garmsír, or warm region we had reached; but the natives said this was the effect of the strong northerly wind blowing throughout the previous day and night. Our march was decidedly the most pleasant, so far as the country was concerned, that we had experienced since leaving Tehrán. At two miles from the encamping-ground, the road entered a belt of low jungle, which continued to Búrj-i-Maház (12 miles). This jungle was well supplied with running streams, and thickly studded with well-grown and peculiarly graceful tamarisk-trees, whose shade was most refreshing. The soil was very sandy, and the travelling consequently somewhat heavy. There should be quantities of small game here. Búrj-i-Maház, a small village situated on the borders of the jungle, is probably so called from the existence of a mud tower (*búrj*) in the centre of the village. Dr. Cumming recounted some strange anecdotes of the 34 patients he used daily to doctor at Bam. They had nothing in which to carry away their lotions and lineaments, and being told to procure some sort of vessel, many of them brought dishes, some broken bottles, some *kaliáns*, and some actually pieces of brick and old tiles. The weather was beautifully mild, and the sun very hot directly it had fairly risen.

Immediately after leaving Búrj-i-Maház, the road descended a hill covered with palm-trees on to a stony plain, after crossing which for about eight miles the country changed, and the same description of low jungle was entered as that through which we had passed on the previous day; when the track became sandy and heavy. Some of the Balúchís who formed part of the escort amused themselves and us by galloping all over the plain, firing their guns and performing various equestrian feats. Regan (19 miles) appeared to be a village of some twenty or thirty houses, of which the inhabitants were very poor. The women did not wear veils, and dressed in long blue cotton gowns, seemingly their only garment. They were all singularly plain. The Náib Suliman Khán informed us that this village was dreadfully hot in summer, and much infested with scorpions. It is visibly and unmistakably dirty. Some ruins we had passed just before entering Regan were the remains of the old village, deserted on account of the scorpions, by order of the late Wakíl-ul-Múlk, who built the fort here, a large walled mud enclosure, with one or two dwelling-places inside its walls. The camp was pitched near a running stream a little way from the village, with plenty of low jungle in the rear. Our horses found shelter inside the fort. Game was reported very plentiful in this neighbourhood, but two of the Mission who went out shooting saw nothing but a single partridge. Most of the inhabitants seemed to be engaged in dyeing. There was abundance of good water.

We halted at Regan on the 17th, in order to complete our preparations for crossing the Bampúr desert, a nine days' journey, during which we could obtain nothing on the road either for men or horses. The wind on the previous night had risen to a perfect gale, blowing down two of our tents and trying severely the stability of the remainder. In the morning the storm had increased, and continued with great violence until close on sunset, when it abated, and our camels were able to start. We learned that Ibrahim Khán had sent a letter to the Náib Suliman Khán, directing him to find out and refund the whole of the expenses to which the General and Mirza Ma'súm Khán had been put to since arrival at Darzin, when they entered his government. This offer of repayment of course the General was obliged to decline.

The story that the wind blows hard in these parts for seven consecutive days might well have been true, for we set off on our journey hence with a stiff breeze, which increased during the day, and blew with considerable force in the afternoon. Náib Suliman Khán came to take leave of the General before the latter had left his quarters. We had been much troubled with cockroaches during the night, a significant illustration of the change of climate. After leaving Regan, the road ran for about eight miles through a continuation of the same low jungle that we had passed on our march into the place, skirting a village with mud fort on the left. It then emerged into a very spacious and stony plain, covered with camel-thorn, crossing which at about 17 miles from Regan, it entered the chain of hills separating the Narmashír plains from Balúchistán. Four miles further was the stage of Ab-i-garm, so called from the existence there of a large spring of very pure water, quite hot, which issued from the side of the hill to the right of the road. All around and on the top of the hill was a marsh, of which the water was salt and cold. The water of the Ab-i-garm, though smelling strongly of sulphur, was sweet and tasteless when cool. Numbers of little fishes were observed in the pool immediately below the source of the spring, of which Dr. Cumming conjectured the temperature would be about 70 degrees. The natives bathed in this water, which they said was very good for skin diseases. Our camp was pitched in a valley between the hills, marshy, and covered with tall yellow reeds. The higher ground was very stony. There had evidently been much recent rain in these hills, for, two hours after our arrival in camp, a *rúd-khána* we had crossed on entering the hills was so swollen by torrents of water from the mountains, that we were obliged to send back guides and animals to help over some of our mules detained on the other side. The rain commenced in earnest in the evening, and at one time it was thought the Mission would have had to halt, but in communication with the Persian Commissioner it was decided to continue the march on the next morning, if possible.

We did march, as intended, but, contrary to our usual practice, not until 10 A.M., after breakfast. There had been violent wind the whole of the night, accompanied by heavy rain, but the weather had broken towards daybreak, and the camels were enabled to get off about 5 A.M. Fortunately the stage was a short one; for the clayey soil of the camping-ground at Ab-i-garm did not easily absorb the rainwater. In the morning a *jambáz sowár* (camel-rider) came in from Regan, bringing a packet with letters and papers from Major Ross and Captain Lovett, and a complimentary letter of welcome from Ibrahim Khán. The *kásid* had left Gwádar on the 26th December. On leaving Ab-i-garm, we ascended a very stony path on the hillside to the right; after which we descended to the valley, following it until we reached our camping-ground at Cháhi Kambar (10 miles) in an open space between the hills. We passed several impromptu streams with the water up to our horses' girths, occasioned by the rush of water from the heights. The afternoon was fine, but it commenced to rain heavily at sunset. The Commissioner, who had pitched his camp about 200 yards to our right, was divided from us suddenly by a regular river, which came down from the hills in front, several feet deep, and flowing with great force. We were unable to trace the well from which the place probably took its name in former times; and though water was generally to be found, the rain answered our purpose.

LEGEND OF FARHAD.

A stormy night with constant rain stopped our progress, and compelled us to halt on the 20th. The Commissioner despatched a *jambáz sowár* to Ibrahim Khán at Bampúr, requesting him to send out provisions three stages, in case we should be further detained by stress of weather. The river dividing our respective camps was so high as to be up to the horses' girths, when Captain Smith crossed on horseback. The rain continued all day, but towards evening slightly decreased, and the wind showed signs of shifting to the southward.

At sunrise the sky was quite clear. The wind had changed and blown away all the rain. Our camel train got off at about 6 A.M. The road after leaving Cháhi Kambar followed the course of the valley for about six miles, when it turned sharply to the left round a corner of the hills, and emerged on the plain of Saif-u-Dín, where Colonel Goldsmid had halted in 1866: this plain, impassable after continued wet weather, it crossed for about four miles, in an easterly direction, till it reached the foot of the Saif-u-Dín pass. We moved over it with difficulty, for the ground was so soft and yielding that the camels constantly lost, and could not readily regain, their footing. The pass of Saif-u-Dín is about 700 or 800 feet high, and is steep, stony, and rugged, but too short to be very difficult. From the summit a really magnificent view is obtained of the fine snowy range of the Deh Bakri hills, lying 80 miles away behind Regan. Our descent on the other side was very gradual, and led to a plain which must lie higher than the valley we had just left. In the centre of this hill-surrounded plain was an extensive lake of rain-water, of some depth and mud-coloured; skirting which for five miles, the road brought us to our camping-ground, Dag-i-Farhád, on the opposite border. We were told that water was procurable here till the Nauroz (21st March). The natives relate that the famous Farhád gave one puff with his breath which threw up the stones on the sides of the neighbouring hills so as to form a bed for the lake. All around, on high or low ground, were sharp black splinters of rock.

The next was a bright morning, and we marched early. But the cold was excessive, owing to the north wind which continued to blow with great violence. Thirteen of the camels were unable to move from cramp, until the sun rose, and one was reported to have died during the night. The road, six miles after leaving our camp, crossed the range of hills which marked the limit of the Narmashír district and our entrance into Bampúr. It then passed over a stony and most desolate country, winding in and out among the hills until it reached Girán Reg, the river of which name it crossed and recrossed. The scene of desolation presented by the high rocky mountains and bare black rocks of Girán Reg is not easily imagined or described. A very remarkable mountain, with perfectly flat top, called the *Takht-i-Nádir*, came in view just before we had met the river; and we had to pass to the further side of this by a circuitous route to find our encampment at Sar-i-Nárán (19 miles), situated on the banks of a broad *rúd-khánah* of unknown name. The ground selected was confined and very stony; in fact, the whole passage of these hills is difficult, from the large quantity of rugged stones with which the path is beset, to say nothing of stiff bits of ascent and descent. Just before diverging from the course of the Girán Reg river, the General received a report that a Balúch, wounded in a recent affray with some other Balúchís, was lying in the bed of the river. He rode back with Dr. Cumming to see the wounded man, and found him not far distant, with his leg badly broken above the ankle, by the blow of a heavy stone. In explanation of the affair, it was related that four of Ibrahim Khán's relatives, returning to Bam from Bampúr, had fallen in with a party of Balúch shepherds, who had refused to comply with their request to sell or provide them with a sheep; and that a quarrel had ensued, during which one of the four had got his leg completely smashed. Dr. Cumming, on examining the leg, found it had been primitively but fairly set in splints by the patient's comrades; but the man was in much pain, and the General had him brought into camp. His leg was afterwards reset and bandaged; and it was decided to take him on with us to Bampúr, so that he might have the advantage of good medical advice and attendance until arrival at that place. The patient and his associates had a peculiarly Negro-like cast of countenance. The bed of the Girán Reg river was plentifully fringed with well-grown tamarisks and date reeds, and had a considerable amount of pure and sweet water in deep pools. On this march we first observed signs of spring; as crocuses adorned each side of the road, and vegetation was so far advanced that a peculiar sort of prickly heath, yellow and pink, was in full flower. We observed many specimens of the wild oleander; an intensely bitter plant, said to be fatal both to horses and camels, who sometimes bite a piece of it unintentionally, when grazing. The water at our encamping-ground was very brackish.

The following day the weather was less cold, but a strong wind was blowing, and had continued to blow all night. The road passed over the same rock-strewn and desolate country as before, and through barren hills of most fantastic shapes and strange colours. At eight miles from Sar-i-Nárán it reached the bed of another river, probably the Girán Bega, and followed its course for five miles, emerging at last, through a somewhat difficult passage between high rocks, with very deep pools of water, on to a more open country. This pass, quite practicable in dry weather, was rendered difficult by the depth of the water in the pools, which rendered it necessary for us to dismount and scramble with our horses over the rocks at the side, the baggage animals having to make a long and difficult *détour*. After surmounting it and leaving the bed of the river above-mentioned on our right, a succession of ascents and descents over very rocky and utterly desolate country brought us to the outlet of the hills on the Bampúr side, and on to a wide plain with tamarisk and oleander, through which ran the *rúd-khánah* of Khúsrín. Crossing the plain for four miles, we arrived at our camping-ground (24 miles) to the right of the road, and at some distance from the water in the riverbed. Our mules and camels did not come up till late in the evening, the men declaring that the road by which they had come was a distance of nine *farsakhs*. The breakfast things did not arrive till 3 P.M., and we were glad to get some bread from the soldiers who had accompanied the camp in advance. The wind was still strong, but showed signs of decrease. Grouse, bustard, and partridge were observed in the rushes near the bed of the *rúd-khánah*. Sweet water was obtainable at a quarter of a mile distance.

From Khúsrín our route was across a river-bed; whence, making a slight ascent on to a very flat and stony plain, we gradually descended to the *rúd-khánah* of Sol, at seven miles distance. A slight but continued descent over a series of plains, more or less covered with stones, and divided from each other by dry beds of watercourses, led to the vast and extensive plain of Bampúr. For some distance the vegetation was sparse and scanty, but at fifteen miles the road entered a belt of jungle, principally consisting of wild caper and thorn. Five miles further we were at the camping-ground of Laddi, about a quarter of a mile to the right of the road, where our tents were pitched on a sandy soil covered with saline efflorescence. There were two wells here, both brackish, but the water of one was much better than that of the other.

The weather had become quite warm, the wind having dropped during the night. The top of the snow-covered hill of Básmán came into view about 10 miles from Khúsrín, from behind the hills skirting the left of the road, and bearing 40° from Laddi; and on looking back, the snowy summit of the Shah Koh hill was distinctly visible. To the right, the Bashkird hills appeared to bound the plain in an E. to W. direction. Our marching force was increased by the Balúchís who had wounded the sick soldier brought into camp. The Súltán had sent his *sarbáz* for these men that they might appear before Ibrahim Khán, at Bampúr, and they were secured on the previous night. They were very dark, with a Jewish cast of countenance, and woolly hair. Two or three pigs were observed in the jungle as we rode along.

The next morning was bright and cold until the sun rose, when the day became very warm. From Laddi to Kalanzáo (9 miles only) the road ran through the same low jungle as it had before entered. Five miles from Laddi the soil became much more sandy, and many thick tamarisk-groves were seen, as also some very fine specimens of the wild caper, which grows in these parts to a great size. One of the *ghuláms* shot a fine grey fox by the roadside. Our camp was pitched on a beautiful piece of open ground covered with low brushwood, to the left of the road, with a fine view of the Básmán Hill bearing 30°, at about 45 miles distance. We found a party of men here sent out from Regan and Bampúr, engaged in digging *kanáts*, as the Wakíl-ul-Múlk intended constructing a village in the locality, the soil being very favourable to cultivation. The men had built rude huts of mud and tamarisk, and seemed very comfortable.

The morning was cool, and we had a pleasant breeze, on starting for Cháh-i-Shúr (23 miles). The flat country was monotonous; but the jungle gradually lost its character of density, and the soil became heavy and sandy. At 13 miles we halted and breakfasted under the shade of a grove of thorn-trees. On arrival at Cháh-i-Shúr—or the 'brackish well,' a not inappropriate name—we found that no messenger had come out from Bampúr, and, as we had expected a supply of provender for our horses, the situation was somewhat disappointing. The Mirza of the Commissioner called in the evening to say that intimation had been received that a number of Balúch chiefs would receive the General to-morrow on his entrance into Kúch Girdan, and requested his instructions as to dress. We further heard that the wandering tribes of shepherds, generally encamped in the neighbourhood of the road we were travelling, had all removed themselves and flocks to a distance, to be out of reach of the numerous camp-followers and Persian authorities accompanying us.

Our camp was ready to start at 5.30 A.M., but as it did not get light until 6.10 A.M. by our watches (which, even if wrong, served to guide us), we somewhat delayed actual departure. The country and road presented little change, with the exception that the soil was more sandy, and the tamarisk-tree much more abundant, growing in large clumps. The sunrise was most beautiful. The morning was somewhat cold, but it was very hot at mid-day. We halted and breakfasted at 18 miles, under a grove of tamarisk-trees. Five miles further on we found the Persian Commissioner and suite waiting for us, in expectation of the reception by the Balúch chiefs, who, however, did not appear. At two miles from Kúch Girdan (26 miles) we were met by a messenger from Ibrahim Khán, with a letter for Mirza Ma'súm Khán, saying that he himself and a number of Balúch chiefs were waiting to receive the General at Bampúr. We found our camp pitched near a quantity of cultivated land, with the wheat well above the soil, which was irrigated by the water of the Bampúr river. We sighted this *rúd-khánah* at about eight miles distance from camp on the right of the road. The water was sweet and good. That near our camp was flowing in artificial channels. Ibrahim Khán had sent out two led horses to meet the General and Persian Commissioner about two miles from Kúch Girdan, and, on arrival in camp, we found that some sheep, a deer, and forage had also been sent for the General's acceptance. Heard that Major Ross was at Kasrkand on the 23rd, on his way to meet us at Bampúr. In the evening the General, attended by Captain Smith, called on the Persian Commissioner, when it was arranged, by express desire of the latter, that we should make our entry into Bampúr in full dress, as all the Balúch chiefs would be coming out to meet us.

During the night a messenger arrived with letters and papers from Major Ross, Major Harrison, and Captain Lovett. By these it appeared that, contrary to the General's first instructions, the whole of these officers were on their way to join the Mission at Bampúr, Captain Harrison being in attendance on the Kalát delegate, Fakir Muhammad Khán, with whom also were Darogha Ata Muhammad and the Chief of Túmp. Sir Henry Durand's sad death was communicated to us by this opportunity. The General and Staff left the camp in full dress, but half an hour after starting the rain commenced, and fell more and more heavily as the day wore on. At about six miles from Kúch Girdan we came again upon the Bampúr river, full of water, to the right of the road. At nine miles we found the Persian Commissioner and suite, wet through and having divested themselves of uniform, waiting for the General's arrival under some trees. At about four miles from Bampúr (16 miles) the *istikbál* was also in waiting, commanded by a nephew of Ibrahim Khán, about 17 years old, who held the rank of Major. There must have been about 500 men in all, principally wild-looking Balúchís, of whom some 200 perhaps were mounted on *jambáz* camels, and all armed with long guns. Albeit men of weird and strange aspect, they had a warlike and workmanlike demeanour. The *jambáz* in many cases carried two of these warriors. Formed up in two long lines on both sides of the road, they gravely saluted the General as he passed through them, closing in afterwards in the wake of the *cortége*. The rain at this time was very heavy, and somewhat spoilt what would otherwise have been a most singular spectacle. Shortly afterwards the fort of Bampúr appeared in view, a picturesque-looking object, apparently in good repair, with a handsome citadel and long lines of mud brick walls. It was situated on a rising ground in the midst of the clusters of mud huts, which formed the so-called town of Bampur—in truth little more than a large camp formed by the soldiers and their families, who composed a standing garrison. The women and children looked very poor, and excessively dirty and ugly. We found our camp pitched in a walled enclosure of cultivation with date-palms, and the Persian Commissioner in a similar enclosure close by. Everything here in the way of provisions, both for men and cattle, was supplied to us gratis by Ibrahim Khán, who had, moreover, forbidden any of the inhabitants of Bampúr to take money from the followers of the Mission. We ourselves found a sumptuous breakfast ready cooked and awaiting our arrival. The Persian Commissioner having sent over to say that Ibrahim Khán was greatly desirous of seeing the General as soon as possible, the latter expressed his willingness to receive him at once, and accordingly, attended by Ma'súm Khán, he soon appeared. This famous chief, quite a despot in these regions, was a little squat, stumpy man, very stout and round, with a good-natured face, a pair of piercing eyes, and an unusually long, handsome, and silky beard. Probably about 50 years of age, he looked much younger, owing to the jet black dye of his abundant hair. Though evidently full of vivacity, he did little to initiate conversation. His Persian was very difficult to understand, being mixed with Balúch, and he talked very quickly, clipping his words at the same time. The Commissioner professed inability to understand more than half of what our mutual host said. Expressing himself delighted to welcome the General a second time, he asked his more highly-trained countryman to pay on his behalf all the compliments befitting the occasion, as he himself was quite unversed in these matters. He stayed some time, but little or nothing was said on this occasion concerning the objects of the Mission. The weather cleared up towards evening, sufficient rain having fallen to do the country great good. The day's march was through much the same sort of country as we had experienced since leaving Laddi. The jungle was if anything thicker, the tamarisk-trees being larger, and the soil was very sandy and heavy. The jungle continued nearly up to the walls of the Bampúr fort, but was intersected by large and frequent patches of cultivation. The water at Bampúr was excellent, and the dates for which this place was especially famous were unquestionably fine.

Our first day's halt at Bampúr was on a Sunday. After morning service in tents the General, attended by the whole of his Staff, called on the Sartip Ibrahim Khán, the Persian Commissioner being also present. The chief received us in a long low room, roughly built, and as there was a scarcity of chairs, he and Mirza Ma'súm Khán sat on the ground. The conversation turned on general subjects, until the General happened to ask some question concerning Jálk and Sarbáz. These two names appeared to rouse Ibrahim Khán, who forthwith very rapidly and excitedly began to speak his mind. He said he considered this Mission quite useless, as it was well known that the disputed parts of the adjacent provinces in reality belonged to Persia, and had done so for many, many years, and that there could be no dispute whatever about them; and that as for Fakír Muhammad and the other chiefs coming up to Bampúr, it was well known they would never have dared to do so had they not been under the protection of the British authorities. Discussion could not, of course, be prolonged in this strain. The Sartip clearly laboured under a mistaken impression of our objects, and fancied that we proposed to take away much of the country from him for which he had been fighting for many years. The Persian Commissioner appeared much amused at his most undiplomatic outspokenness, and his manner may have rather encouraged him than otherwise. After the visit was over, however, he stated to Captain Smith his own impression that what had passed had been entirely through ignorance on the part of the speaker, and that he himself had, on the General's leaving, pointed out to him the absurdity and impropriety of such conduct.

In the afternoon of the 30th, Captain Smith called by order on the Persian Commissioner, and learnt from him that there had been a great reunion of chiefs, headed by Ibrahim Khán, at his camp in the morning. They were anxious to know the objects of the Mission, and apparently much disturbed at its presence, at the sight of the British flag, and also at the fact of Major Ross's party coming up to Bampúr with Fakir Muhammad and the Kalát people. They regarded the fact of the first meeting being held here as a sign that the district of Bampúr itself, and the immediately adjacent countries, were to be made a subject of arbitration, and were also somewhat nettled that their old enemy, Fakir Muhammad, should come in the midst of their territories without being able to touch him. The Persian Commissioner professed to have quieted their fears, and General Goldsmid, after receiving a visit from him during the day, wrote to him in the evening, requesting him to point out to Ibrahim Khán how groundless they really were. There was no doubt, however, from what we heard accidentally, that the presence of the Mission, under the circumstances, caused much alarm. Ibrahim Khán's conscience was perhaps not quite clear on the subject of acquired territory, and the poor Balúchís, the children of the soil, hated and feared him. Ibrahim Khán sent over some rope-dancers in the afternoon, but their performance was wretchedly bad. We had every reason to infer that the slave trade was not inactive in Balúchistán, and it was said that many of the natives at Bampúr were slaves in Tehrán. It should at least have been some consolation to them to escape from such a place as this.

The next day, after breakfast, Captain Smith again called on the Persian Commissioner, to consult him, with a view of decreasing the delay occasioned by the non-arrival of the Kalát party, on the propriety of sending out an express, requesting Major Harrison and Fakir Muhammad to push on in advance of the others as quickly as possible. He, however, thought it would be much more advisable to await the arrival of the whole camp, and he probably had reasons for thinking so which he did not state. He said that the receipt of the General's letter of the evening before had quite done away with Ibrahim Khán's misapprehensions. In the evening a special courier came in from Karmán, bringing official letters from Mr. Alison; with copies of telegrams addressed by the Ministry for Foreign Affairs to Mirza Ma'súm Khán, which authorised him fully and in any case to commence first with the Makrán inquiry. This intelligence was communicated to the Persian Commissioner, but he had received his full instructions by the same opportunity.

February commenced with an uneventful day. The General came across a sepoy belonging to one of our Balúch regiments in India, who was here on leave, being a native of Jálk. He spoke Hindustáni, but did not know Persian, and seemed to hold in little esteem the inhabitants of these districts. A man brought in two wild ducks that he had shot in the river. The tame ducks of Bampúr, so much lauded by Conolly, no longer exist, the breed being quite extinct.

On the 2nd February the weather, which had been gradually becoming warmer, was almost hot. Captain Smith called on the Persian Commissioner to inform him officially that news had been received from the Bombay Government, intimating to General Goldsmid the appointment by the Khán of Kalát of Fakir Muhammad as his commissioner. Mirza Ma'súm Khán stated he would be glad to have the same intimation in writing. He spoke a good deal concerning the advent of the party accompanying Majors Ross and Harrison, and said that Ibrahim Khán told him the 'whole face of Balúchistán' was changed by their march through the provinces. This was, of course, an exaggeration, but it is not to be doubted that the ignorant Balúch chiefs looked upon the presence of the English here, and of their enemy, Fakir Muhammad, under British protection, with apprehension; as, indeed, they would have regarded the presence of any stranger who came armed with authority to perform a, to them, incomprehensible duty. If the truth were known, Mirza Ma'súm Khán was probably also himself an object of distrust, as one sent from Tehrán to spy out the nakedness of the land. Ibrahim Khán's well-known unpopularity in these regions had, no doubt, something to do with the fear he expressed. The Persian Commissioner spoke again about the British flag, but frankly added he was quite incompetent, from ignorance, to express an opinion whether our Mission was justified or not in displaying it. He said he was convinced that the British Legation at Tehrán *paid* for the privilege of being allowed to fly it there! A messenger came in and reported that the Kalát party had slept last night at Sarmich, and would consequently be in here on Saturday morning. He said there were about 150 followers in all. We sent out a packet of letters in the afternoon to Majors Ross and Harrison and Captain Lovett.

On the following morning, Captain Smith called by order on the Persian Commissioner, and found him suffering very much indeed from fever and ague. The object was to arrange about an *istikbál* for the Kalát party, but Ma'súm Khán required a letter from General Goldsmid, informing him of the rank and titles of the persons expected. A messenger came in later, saying that the Kalátís were only at Sarmich the previous night, so that they would be at Gwárpúsht the following day, and at Bampúr on the Saturday. One of the Karmán *faráshes* got into a disturbance in the village, and was somewhat severely mauled. The villagers went to Ibrahim Khán with complaints against the *farásh*, whilst the latter came to our tribunal with counter complaints. The whole matter was referred to Ibrahim Khán for inquiry and disposal. Later in the day letters dated 2nd February came in from Majors Ross and Harrison. These officers were then at Chámp, four stages off, had great difficulty with their camels, and did not expect to arrive in Bampúr until the 6th at earliest. Hereupon it was proposed that, instead of waiting the arrival of the Kalát party, a move should at once be made in their direction; but the Persian Commissioner contending that such a move would lead the natives of these districts to believe that the Kalát party had not been allowed by Ibrahim Khán to come to Bampúr, the General abandoned the suggestion, and requested that Ibrahim Khán might be instructed to send out camels or otherwise assist the progress of the Kalátís. The Sartíp wrote in reply to say that camels might be collected, but time would be required.

Next day we despatched 15 mules with a guide to meet the Kalát party at the place, 14 *farsakhs* off, where they would probably pass the night—a help which might enable them to send back some camels for the things they had left behind at Chámp. We received another packet from them this morning, containing official letters for our chief, showing how completely agreeable the Shah had been some months before to have this Balúchistán question decided.

The General wrote officially to the Persian Commissioner, informing him of the rank and titles of the Kalát Commissioner and the officers accompanying him. In the evening a good many black partridges were seen in the jungle, not far from camp.

On Sunday, the 5th February, the Persian Commissioner was very unwell again with fever. We discharged one of the *faráshes* furnished to us by the Governor of Karmán, for inveterate gambling. Captain Smith and Quartermaster-Sergeant Bower, escorted by a Súltán and 10 *faráshes*, rode out at 10 o'clock to welcome Majors Ross and Harrison, and the Kalát Commissioner, who had arrived within 14 miles of Bampúr, accompanied by about 100 horse and 273 followers, but all most disciplined and orderly. Major Ross rode back into camp, and the remainder marched in the next morning. From this date to the 16th February the Mission remained at Bampúr, General Goldsmid endeavouring all that time to bring about the discussion of the frontier question. This, however, proving useless, owing to the attitude taken up by the Persian Commissioner and Ibrahim Khán, it was thought advisable to move down to the Coast Telegraph at Gwadur on the 16th February. Nothing of general interest occurred during the days omitted in this journal[1].

[1] It will, perhaps, be well to supply the gap here with the aid of my own diary. On Sunday afternoon, the 5th of February, 1871, Major (now Colonel) Ross joined us at Bampúr. He appeared in advance of the Brahúi camp, which had so inopportunely entered the territory of Ibrahím Khán; and the numbers and character of which had given to the Persians a means of repudiating the whole question of frontier settlement. Only those acquainted with the feelings of Balúch and Brahúi *at this particular juncture* could possibly understand the sensation caused by the march of some 250 clansmen of the one side into the territorial limits of the other side, under the sanction of the British power. And the British Commissioner at Bampúr, never having himself contemplated, and consequently not having prepared his Persian colleague for such procedure, was placed in the difficult position of accounting for it, as though he approved, but had been unconscious of the whole arrangement! That he was suspected of connivance—or rather, perhaps, that officially expressed suspicion of connivance was used against him—appears in the charge laid at his door in Tehrán by Mirza Ma'súm Khán, to which allusion has been made in the Introductory Chapter. On the 6th of February the whole party from the Kalát State arrived at Bampúr, and were received by General Goldsmid; to whom an official letter was, moreover, addressed by the Persian Commissioner, stating that he was not empowered to discuss the question of restoring lands already in possession of Persia. The newcomers called also on Mirza Ma'súm Khán; a reply was despatched to the latter's communication, and so far all was well. On the 7th February, the Persian Commissioner visited General Goldsmid, but rather to make objections on the actual situation than to progress towards a settlement; and up to a late hour of the night the British

Early in the afternoon of the 16th February we again broke ground, having been in Bampúr 19 days. Our mules had started very early in the morning, but there was some difficulty in managing the camel loads. The owners of most of our camels are Súltáns belonging to the regiments here, and they were very chary of admitting heavy loads. Mirza Ma'súm Khán and Ibrahim Khán called in the morning to take leave of the General, the former expressing his intention of soon following us. Ibrahim Khán did not seem to be in a good

Commissioner was engaged with his native scribe in putting to paper arguments to convince and mollify his colleague, who delighted in letters, and prided himself on epistolary style. The next day Ma'súm Khán's language to Captain Euan Smith caused General Goldsmid to take the decisive step of breaking up the camp of intended conference and requesting Major Harrison, the Kalát Khán's Political Agent, to prepare for departure as early as practicable. The next, a long correspondence was carried on between the British and Persian Commissioners, followed by a personal interview. The next, desertions of a suspicious nature took place from Major Harrison's camp; General Goldsmid visited the Persian Commissioner; and an attempt was made to effect a frontier inspection by means of the respective Engineer Officers, English and Persian. The next, there was more correspondence, and of an unsatisfactory kind, between the two Commissioners. The next, leave was taken of the Kalát Mission, which returned to its own side of the frontier after six apparently profitless days at Bampúr: the movement being followed by a visit to General Goldsmid of Mirza Ma'súm Khán and the Sartip Ibrahim Khán. Next day, the project of a joint survey by the Engineer Officers of either Commission fell through; and Mirza Ma'súm Khán declared that nothing could be done towards a frontier settlement, but through the respective governments concerned! On the 14th February, General Goldsmid visited the Persian Commissioner, and in a very long interview sought by fair argument and frankness to persuade him to agree to, at least, some practical course by which our ostensible object could still be attained. It was further essential to take every precaution, by letter as by word of mouth, to prevent any new aggression by Ibrahim Khán, pending receipt of instructions from Tehrán on our unprovided-for complications. On the 15th Captain Lovett was started to overtake Major Harrison and effect a personal survey (under Kalát protection as well as a letter from Ibrahim Khán) of so much of the actual frontier as he could visit in safety. Major Smith had two interviews with the Persian Commissioner; and more correspondence was carried on between the latter and General Goldsmid. The 16th February was the day fixed for striking the Mission tents; but letter-writing had been renewed, and General Goldsmid had to dispose of a long communication from his Persian colleague, which involved somewhat delicate questions not admitting of direct replies; he accomplished, moreover, another interview with the Commissioner and Ibrahim Khán, before taking leave of Bampúr. The feeling with which he mounted his horse on the occasion of departure was almost one of exhilaration. The nineteen days passed at the head-quarters of Persian Balúchistán might not show much progress in negotiations; but they had been days of no common anxiety, and of a peculiar responsibility scarcely intelligible to any but those versed in the details of the whole transaction.—*F. J. G.*

humour. Our escort consisted of the same Yáwar and Súltán who accompanied us here, 10 mounted *ghulám̀s*, 20 *sarbáz*, and 10 *jambáz sowárs*. The sun was very hot indeed when we left; and we were not sorry that the first march to Sar-i-band (8 miles) was a short one. The road ran through the same description of jungle as that by which Bampúr was closely surrounded, and presented no remarkable features. Our encamping-ground was on one side of the Bampúr river, where a dam had been constructed to force the water into an artificial channel, which conveyed it to the town. The river at this time was fairly filled, but the bottom and banks were very muddy and treacherous. Its source was about two miles further on, in an easterly direction, being obtained from large springs which, the natives said, sprang spontaneously out of the ground.

The next day we recommenced our early marches. During the night we had been disturbed by innumerable jackals, which spoilers stole the boots of the *názir* and *múnshi*. The road was much as before, with occasional cultivation, until, at seven miles, Pahra was reached, when the country became more open and the jungle gradually ceased. Pahra is a walled town, with a mud high fort and about 120 houses; situated in a perfect jungle of date-trees and with abundant water. Its fort was apparently valueless for defence against artillery. Hence the road turned to the right, and led over an open country, with occasional cultivation and most wretched huts inhabited by miserable-looking Balúchís, to the camping-ground situated in a plain called Sar Kohran (12 miles).

On the 18th our road was for nine miles over a stony desert plain to the hills in front, which it entered, and along a ravine of varying breadth. There were hills on either side of moderate height, which the Súltán stated we should not quit until arrival at Píshín. In about seven miles more we found our camp pitched to the right of and at some little distance off the road, where there was a large spring of excellent water. We passed a *band* about two miles before arriving at camp, which had been of some use in damming the water in the valley but had become dilapidated. All the trees and shrubs about were in full foliage, and many of them in full blossom. There were ferns on the adjacent hills.

For the first nine miles of the next day's march there was little variety of road, except that the ravine got wider and more open, and the *písh* palm increased at every step in quantity and growth. We then turned off to the right, in a south-westerly direction, and entering a narrow and winding ravine nearly choked with the said *pish*, followed it for about 11 miles, when we found our halting-place on the banks of a dry mountain torrent. The *faráshes*, however, with the greater part of our kit and all our tents, had taken the usual and more direct road to Sarbáz; and we had to borrow a tent from the Súltán, who was much put out by this miscarriage of the caravan more or less under his guidance. Luckily the provisions had reached our halting-place, so we were not so badly off as we might have been. Scouts were sent out all over the country; but returned saying that the missing camels had gone too far on the Sarbáz road to be recalled. The Súltán declared that the road we ourselves had taken was the regular and easier one for troops and ordnance; but we clearly understood the other to be the better and shorter; and if our road were really that selected for the passage of guns, such an operation must be no light or easy matter. There were constant and heavy showers during the night. Wood and water were here good and abundant.

Again for another day were we separated from our baggage. A mile and a half through a narrow *pish*-choked ravine brought us to the foot of the highest ridge in these hills dividing the watershed, which from hence is toward the sea. This ridge marks the end of the Bampúr, and commencement of the Sarbáz district. On crossing it the road follows the bed of the Sarbáz river, which it immediately enters; a track which narrows and widens, following the formation of the hills, and is sandy and pebbly. There was a quantity of water owing to the recent rain, but there were large deep pools at intervals collected under rocks, making it probable that water was obtainable here all the year round. Tamarisk-trees of considerable growth and the constant *pish* covered the banks, the hills on either side varying in height. The regular camping-place (Koláni, 17 miles), on the right of the stream, was found to be so infested with camel-ticks and bugs that we had to shift to the other side. Quartermaster-Sergeant Bower, who went out surveying among the hills, described with gusto the fear his presence caused among some nomads until it was known that he was a Faringí, when he was taken into their tents and welcomed. Having been observed by a scout on one of the hills, who had immediately made signs to the other hills—by the time he reached the encampment he found the flocks and herds driven in, and every preparation made for defence against the hated Persians. This was to us a significant commentary upon the popularity of Ibrahim Khán's rule. A *kásid* came in with letters from Major Harrison, reporting great anxiety on the part of the Kalát Commissioner from an anticipated attack of Ibrahim Khán on Túmp and Kej, and consequent preparation for defensive measures. The rain was continuous; wood and water abounded.

Leaving camp at Koláni, we proceeded along the bed of the Sarbáz river, and met at about six miles the generally used road from Bampúr, coming from N.W. by W. The bed of the river had become very broad and stony; and it increased in width up to Sarbáz (19 miles), where it formed a sort of amphitheatre, surrounded by rocks and fringed by palm-trees. The high mud fort of Sarbáz seemed to be in disrepair, but the tops of the hills all around showed signs of having been strongly fortified, and this had doubtless been at one time a very strong place. It contained about 60 huts, inhabited by a population miserably poor. Rice and dates were obtainable in limited supply, with excellent water. Tobacco was grown, and sold, woven into a sort of green rope. We found our missing party here in safety; some of them, with the mules, having come in last night. They described the road as followed very good, with the exception of the narrow gaps, where they had to unload. Two special *kásids* were despatched from this place, one to Major Harrison, with letters deprecating defensive or warlike action on the Kalát side, and one to Charbar, with telegrams for Tehrán and Calcutta.

We halted at Sarbáz a day to enable the camels to rest. The weather was deliciously cool with a slight breeze. Of the ruined fort here only one wall was standing, which faced towards the approach from Bampúr. Local information was to the effect that Sarbáz had paid tribute to Persia ever since the time of Fath Ali Shah, and to Ibrahim Khán personally for 30 years. The natives showed us the hill on the opposite side of the river on which had been placed the artillery that destroyed the fort and village, so far as we could learn, about 40 years ago; but we could gather no trustworthy statement of the real date of occurrence, or name of the Persian General in command. We reckoned there were about 50 huts in Sarbáz, built of reeds and leaves; but the people seemed very poor, and were decidedly plain and unprepossessing, at least two-thirds of the men squinting horribly. The women had large flat faces, with great blue beads strung through the cartilage of the nose, and wore the invariable long cloth gown, from the neck to the ankle. Dates and rice appeared to be the only provisions obtainable, and the latter in limited supply. The natives here confirmed what we heard everywhere, that Píshín was the farthest point east paying tribute to Persia, and they informed us that Mand was independent. They showed great willingness in parting with their spears, shields, and other specialities for money.

Our next march was an agreeable one. The hills on either side of the river changed character, and enormous masses of irregularly-shaped black rock bordered both sides of the river-bed, here fringed with groves of date-palm, the mango-tree, and the orange. The constant turnings and windings of the river created a succession of very picturesque bays, in which the black rocks at the side, the date-palms, fresh green cultivation, and the running water formed a pleasant and harmonious contrast. The cultivation, prolonged without intermission to Dipkhor (14 miles), was on raised artificial platforms, on the river banks, irrigated by artificial channels. The mango, orange-tree, and mulberry abounded and flourished. Beans and barley appeared to be the main crops, and were nearly ripe for the sickle. There was a continuous succession of small villages, of which the inhabitants, who lined the banks as we passed, were almost entirely engaged in cultivation. The head man of one of these informed us that the revenue paid annually by his village of some 30 huts to Ibrahim Khán was 14 *tumáns*, which cannot be considered excessive. The money was obtained by the sale of dates to travellers, who came from seaward, for the villagers themselves possess no ready coin. The year before our visit, a bad one for dates, the price was 100 *manns*, or 700 lbs., for four rupees; the year before, this amount went for two rupees; and in a good season the same quantity only fetched a rupee. We found the river-bed very stony and trying for horses, and water freely running or plenteously collected in deep pools. The bed opened out about a mile before reaching Dipkhor, situated in much the same kind of amphitheatre as Sarbáz, and possessing a ruined mud fort, and the usual number of mud huts. Major Ross considered this pass from Persia into Makrán to be very much easier than the one by Chámp, through which he had marched to Bampúr. The water here was good and abundant, and there were a few provisions obtainable. The revenue of Dipkhor was reputed to be 16 *tumáns* (£6 8s.)

The short march to Pá-rúd (12 miles) presented little change, but the bed of the river widened and became much more stony with less water. The hills on either side were not so high, and their bases sloped in a way to form a valley, in the centre of which wound the river-bed. The country in general, too, was much more open. The road shifted from one side of the river to the other, winding through patches of cultivation and groves of date-palms. About five or six villages dotted the banks. Some three miles from Pá-rúd the General was met by a large *istikbál*, consisting of Husain Khán, the hereditary chief of Sarbáz, who is the Persian Náib of all the districts, including Báhu and Dastiári, down to the Dasht; of Muhammad Khán, a sullen-looking warrior; of the Náib of Bampúr, and of the Chief of Kasarkand, with about 30 armed *jambáz sowárs*. Husain Khán was of prepossessing appearance, and his arms and accoutrements were profusely ornamented with silver. He had great power in these parts, and though probably otherwise at heart, was outwardly at least, and from necessity, a firm supporter of Persian rule. We received letters from Major Harrison reporting that all armed movements on the Persian side had been authoritatively stopped. Pá-rúd was a strange-looking place, consisting of the usual ruined mud fort and some 80 mud huts, with a poor population, and situated on a high bluff bank left of the river, which seemed here to terminate, as it made a *détour* at right angles to the left, and the two banks merged as it were in one to the eye of the downward passenger. It was probably from this appearance that the village received its name[1]. The road winding up through it from the river-bed led on to a stony and spacious plain beyond, where our camp was pitched. The people all about seemed to have a great fear of Ibrahim Khán, who was as much hated as feared, and whose rule was by no means firmly established. They stated that when their revenue was not made up he took a girl or two and sold her as a slave; and we heard that the price of a young man of about 25 in these parts was 12 *tumáns*. The revenue of Pá-rúd was given at 40 *tumáns* (£16). A broad river from Kasarkand joins the Sarbáz river just at the angle before described.

Next morning, moving over the stony plateau on which our camp had been pitched, we descended into the date-groves and cultivation on the left bank of the river, crossing at about two miles, and following the windings of the bed on the right side for some nine miles, when the path left the river-bed and turned off abruptly to the

---

[1] Pá-rúd, strictly Pái-rúd, the foot of the stream.—F. J. G.

right, through a narrow gorge in the hills on the bank. At less than two miles the gorge opened and the path forked, one branch leading to the village of Fírúzábád, plainly visible on the left bank of the river ahead, and the other winding among hills and groves on the left bank up to Rask (14 miles). By following the path we cut off a considerable bend in the river, which ran past Fírúzábád, and then made a circular sweep round to meet, as it were, the path to Rask. About five miles from Pá-rúd an old ruined square tower was observable on the left bank. Fírúzábád had a picturesque appearance, placed on a high site, and overlooking acres of fresh cultivation in the middle of green date-palms and very luxurious mango and orange trees. There was barley in the ear and there were beans in flower. The inhabitants in Balúchistán may be considered strict Musalmáns, very exact in the observance of all religious rites[1]. We had noticed in all the villages a high mud chimney, intended, as we learnt, to provide the means of calling the faithful to their devotions. The Balúchís were busy impregnating their date-trees, which are of two distinct sexes, male and female. Unless the female is impregnated with the flower of the male, the dates form, but neither ripen nor come to anything, and the dates of the male are worth nothing. The impregnation of the tree is produced by an incision in the top of the female tree and inserting the male flower. A very small quantity is sufficient to impregnate the whole tree, and they get quite different sorts of dates by mixing the species. Rask possessed about 100 huts, and was very similar to all other villages we had seen on the bank of the Sarbáz river.

We marched early on the 26th February, after a troublesome night among mosquitoes. We had made a short descent on leaving Rask, when our guide, who was taking us a quick way through the hills on the left bank of the river, suddenly stopped and said he was sure, by the absence of footmarks, that our camels had not passed along that road. Consequently we had to retrace our steps and return to the bed of the river, which we followed for about four miles, and then ascended by a steep little pass to the left bank, emerging into a wide and open plateau. The spacious plain, commencing at this point, continues between two lines of hills without intermission right up to the frontier of Sind; and the Persians, should they think fit, may march a large

---

[1] I do not hold this rule of general application.—F. J. G.

army across it in the direction of, and up to the Sind frontier, without any material obstacle, and finding water and provisions the whole way. The advance of Persia in this direction would seem therefore to present a question of grave consideration. On the right bank of the river was a similar plain, stretching back to Kasarkand and running as far as the eye could reach between two ranges of hills. On our right also, situated in a dense grove of date-trees, was the new village of Baftán, about five miles distant from Rask; while on the opposite side, and close to our road, we discerned the ruined fort and remains of the old village, taken and destroyed by the Persians 18 years before. The Yáwar informed us he had received his bullet wound in the cheek there. The Persians, he said, had invested the place (which was garrisoned by 100 men only) with 5000 men and 10 guns[1], and in the attack there were only two men killed and 10 wounded. Our road continued seven miles over the plain, and then, descending through a most steep and rocky pass into the river-bed, which it crossed, led through a thick low jungle of tamarisk and wild caper, very stony, four miles further to the camping-ground (Bugáni, 15 miles), reached round a bend in the river. Wood and water were abundant, and there was a deep pool available for bathing. There were no inhabitants or signs of cultivation.

Next morning, our road crossing the bed to a pass right opposite the camp, left the river for good, and ascended on to a high plain on the left bank; stony and quite flat. After four miles we entered a belt of low jungle, and at six miles further came upon the outlying cultivation and dense date-groves of Pishín. Our camp pitched west of the new village, on an open plain planted with date-trees. This, the last conquest of Persia towards the east, must be considered as one of the most important, for a footing has thus been obtained on the plain, within an easy marching distance of Kej and Túmp—districts from which Ibrahim Khán himself two years ago claimed tribute, a demand he might well have enforced had not his action been stopped by English interference. So long as Persia's conquests were limited to the places on the banks of the Sarbáz river, it did not much matter, but this advance into the plains and, so to speak, on to the high road to India, might have led to serious consequences if not stopped. Pishín resembled all other villages we had seen in Balúchistán, but it was more

---

[1] An unquestionable fiction.—F. J. G.

populous; the fort was in better repair and it wore the Persian yoke less easily. The *kásid* arrived with the English mail received at Gwádar on the 11th February, but did not bring a single official communication for the General. Provisions in moderation were here obtainable.

We halted a day at Píshín. In the morning 55 camels arrived from Túmp, sent to us with a quantity of provisions and grain by Major Harrison. Two representatives of Fakir Muhammad and Darogha Ata Muhammad also came with 20 *jambáz sowárs*, as the General's escort to the coast. The Balúchís were wild fellows in appearance, and required a great deal of coaxing to get them to work, but they seemed on the whole very desirous to please. We got rid to-day of the whole of our Persian escort and *faráshes* (with one exception), our *sarbáz* and *ghulúms*; in fact, of all the men who had been engaged to accompany us since Karmán. They appeared in a great hurry to get away, and would no doubt have been afraid to proceed further east than Píshín. We gave them all presents, but all were not satisfied. The weather had become very hot.

On leaving Píshín, our new Balúch escort of 20 *sowárs*, mounted on *jambáz* camels, accompanied us. The road, so soon as it had cleared the surrounding date-groves and cultivation, entered the hills and followed a winding narrow gorge, between low hills and very stony for about six miles, when it emerged on to a valley; and this gradually opened out. It was choked with *pish*-palm. We were surprised to find our tents pitched about two miles further on, but our progress was necessarily limited from scarcity of water. The water here, collected in pools, was good, and plenty of grass was obtainable for the horses. Our *názir*, cook, and *farásh-báshi* lost their way; not coming in at all, we sent out four *jambáz sowárs* to search for them. There were no signs of cultivation or inhabitants near our halting-ground, and the hills around were barren and stony. We were still (Kustug, 10 miles) in the Píshín district and in Persian territory.

Hot weather and mosquitoes had now fairly set in. Another short march brought us to Ghistan (ten miles): the road following the course of the valley, amid low jungle and wild caper, the latter in flower. About two miles from our halting-place the plain became very wide, and we passed to our left a small village of about twelve huts, probably a migratory one, as there were no traces of cultivation. The road here presents difficulties to the unattended traveller, for there are many divergent paths leading into the constant openings among the hills. The scenery was of the most desolate description. Our scouts having reported to us during the night how the missing servants had turned up at Mand, and been placed under an escort, we were not surprised to fall in with them on the march: they had been sent to rejoin our camp by a cross road. On the 3rd March, our road, after a mile over the plain, entered a wide gorge between precipitous masses of rock, and, pursuing its course along the bank of a mountain torrent full of water in pools, passed through a narrow gorge, after about eight miles, into a high plain situated on the right bank of a deep ravine. This ravine received various names according to the districts through which it passed, and was here called the Kustuk river. Crossing the plain for two miles the road descended into the ravine, in the bed of which we found our camp pitched, the camel-men having apparently refused to proceed beyond Gwár-Manzil, the boundary between Persian and Kalát territory. This disobedience of positive orders was not to be tolerated: so, dismounting for breakfast only and to mount again, we caused the camels to be brought in from grazing, the tents to be struck, and the whole camp to move on to the originally intended halting-place (Kulmarisúnt), about fourteen miles further. There was no cultivation or village to make the country valuable, but territory was principally desired on account of the grazing for flocks and herds. The road ascended the left bank of the river, crossed a flat stony plain, and then kept crossing and recrossing beds of mountain torrents until it arrived at a plain covered with low jungle, where the camp was pitched. Constant groups of graves were passed in this day's march, generally situated on eminences or tracks of ravines, which, in the absence of any neighbouring habitation, would seem to mark the scene of former conflicts. The water here was good, being obtained from pools formed by the rain; and firewood was plentiful. The season, we heard, had been an unexceptionably favourable one for rain in this part of Makrán, or the pools would not have been so full, and it is probable that a little later the water would all have disappeared.

On the 4th March, the road, after two miles, cleared the low jungle, and emerged on a spacious plain, which it crossed for some miles, and then descended to a shallow broad ravine, evidently under water in wet weather, with profuse vegetation and grass, and filled with black partridges. It then traversed a low spur of hills and led into the river Dasht, with its banks plentifully fringed with well-grown tamarisk-trees. The river-bed was of considerable breadth, but the water was low. On the other hand, in the wet seasons, the supply is so plentiful, that communication is sometimes stopped for weeks. The opposite side is covered with a low jungle, in which the camp was pitched, but the mosquitoes troubled us, and we moved a mile further on, to more open ground, near the village of Dardán (twelve miles), consisting of about 100 huts. The headman visited the General, and made a complaint of a raid by Persians some years ago. The English mail, with the Indian one, enclosing official letters and instructions for the General, came in at about twelve. In the evening a special *kásid* was despatched through Píshín to Mirza Ma'súm Khán, forwarding him a translation of a French telegram, which ordered him to act in concert with the General, and requesting him to lose no time in coming to Gwádar. There was a strong wind and something of a dust storm throughout the day.

We marched seventeen miles from Dardán to Gurrok. The road led for five miles through a dwarf jungle full of black partridge, and then crossing a white glaring plain, entered a passage between low, parched sandstone rocks. The surrounding country was of an unvarying ashen hue; everything looked burnt, and there was no vegetation to relieve the eye. Our camp was pitched in an amphitheatre between diminutive hills, where was no habitation or grass, and very little firewood or water. The last was thick but sweet, and only to be obtained when rain had fallen; consequently could not be depended on.

On the 6th we marched into Gwádar (twenty miles), winding along for about fourteen miles, over a perfectly flat plain, with low brushwood; then crossing a series of low undulating sand-hills covered with brushwood and scanty grass, something like the Lancashire moors at a distance. Gwádar Head was visible about fourteen miles off, but the sea could not be discerned until we had accomplished nearly a third of that distance. We cantered in the last six miles, and were all of us glad to see the blue ocean, after an inland march of 1293 miles. Our camp was pitched round Major Ross's pretty house. The climate was cool, and the breeze most refreshing.

The day after our arrival, the General received morning visits from the various classes of shopkeepers in the town, who seemed a contented race[1].

[1] The Mission remained at Gwádar up till the 30th April, having been joined there by Mírza Ma'súm Khán and the Brahúí chiefs, the latter of whom were summoned thither in the hope of re-opening negotiations. After vain attempts on the part of the British Commissioner to effect a *pro formâ* discussion, the mixed Commission was again broken up; and Ma'súm Khán having returned to Persian territory, and Fakir Muhammad, accompanied by other local chiefs, having moved into the interior, Major-General Goldsmid embarked for Karáchí. Here he remained from the 1st to the 15th May, when he re-embarked for the Persian Gulf. Touching and landing on the way at Gwádar and Maskat, and receiving a visit from the Governor while anchored at Bandar-Abbas, he reached Bushahr on the 28th May. Here the Mission disembarked, and stayed two days, to complete all arrangements for a march to Tehrán. Major-General Goldsmid and his officers were at Shíráz on the 9th June, and at Isfahán on the 1st July. From Kohrúd he and Major Euan Smith started on the afternoon of the 7th July, and reached Tehrán on the 10th. Owing to the famine and general scarcity of fodder and water, it was difficult to procure horses to accomplish this ride of 170 odd miles sooner. At Tehrán the Mission remained until the 4th September, on which date the Persian Government formally accepted the boundary-line in Makrán laid down by General Goldsmid, as notified by the late Mr. Alison to Her Majesty's Principal Secretary of State for Foreign Affairs, on the day following.—*F. J. G.*

THE PERSO-AFGHAN MISSION, 1871, 1872.

I. *Bandar-Abbas to Bam.*

THE successful solution of the long-vexed question of the boundary in Balúchistán, between Persia and Kalát, was ordered to be followed up without delay, by the prosecution of a similar settlement for the equally remote province of Sistán, which had long given rise to disputes between Persia and Afghánistán. As already explained [1], Sir Frederic Goldsmid had returned to England accompanied by Major Euan Smith, in September, 1871, having previously left full instructions to Major Beresford Lovett for his guidance should it be decided to commence upon the second question. When, therefore, he received orders at home to proceed to Sistán without delay, General Goldsmid had but to telegraph to Major Lovett to act on the instructions left with him, direct that a general rendezvous should be made at Bam in the early part of January, and start for Bandar-Abbas with as little delay as possible. He took his departure accordingly, on the 10th of November, 1871, after a stay of little more than five weeks in England. On this occasion, in addition to his personal assistant and private secretary, Major Euan Smith, he was accompanied by Mr. Gerard de Visme Thomas, of Magdalen College, Oxford, who joined the Mission as unpaid attaché. Mr. Rosario, the apothecary, was awaiting the Mission at Bandar-Abbas, and Major Lovett and Quartermaster-Sergeant Bower were to rendezvous at Bam, with the heavy baggage and general marching establishment—the Persian Commissioner having previously started from Tehrán *en route* to the same place. Colonel Pollock, C.S.I. (now Sir Richard Pollock, K.C.S.I.), who was to be associated with the Afghán Commissioner in Sistán,

---

[1] See Introductory Chapter, and note at the close of the last Section.

as agent for the Governor-General, also left England with Sir Frederic Goldsmid, and at Aden received orders to proceed at once to Calcutta, whence he would have to make his way as soon as possible, by the Bolan Pass and Kandahar (where he was to meet the Afghán Commissioner), to Sekuha. He was to be accompanied by the well-known Pashtu and scientific scholar, Dr. Bellew, who would act as his assistant.

It was expected that a special gun-boat would be in readiness at Aden, to convey the Mission direct to Bandar-Abbas, but owing to some mistake, this was not provided, and General Goldsmid and his staff had therefore to proceed by the mail steamer to Bombay, which they reached on the 3rd of December. Here he received a summons from the Viceroy to meet him at Calcutta, and leaving Bombay for that purpose on the 4th of December, he returned on the 10th of the same month, after a stay of just twenty hours in the former city. The Mission sailed for the Persian Gulf on the 11th of December in the steamship 'India,' and reached Bandar-Abbas early on the 21st idem. Here they found that camels and mules engaged for their use had been awaiting their arrival for a considerable time; as also several horses of the stud left behind at Bam in the previous year, which had been sent down by the Mírakhor in charge. Mr. Rosario, our medical adviser, at once came on board and reported himself: two Persian gentlemen, deputed by the Governor of the place to welcome the General, shortly followed; and at 3 P.M. the Mission, having landed under a salute of three guns, fired from a very old and rusty cannon on the beach, was conducted to quarters prepared for its reception in a house belonging to Hajji Ahmad, the *ci-devant* governor of the town, who was now deposed, and a prisoner, accused of embezzling some 30,000 *tumáns* of the public revenue. The apartments provided were far from clean, but they possessed the advantage of being at the top of the house, and consequently free from constant interruption: the furniture consisted principally of numberless mirrors, some in very handsome frames, but all dirty and dilapidated. Bandar-Abbas itself is one of the worst specimens of a Persian town: its low mud houses are half in ruins, its streets knee-deep in filth of every kind, without any drainage whatever, while its inhabitants appear as wretched as their dwellings. We were struck by the small number of persons to be seen in the streets; and were told that the population had been decimated by the ravages of cholera and famine, from which the town had lately suffered. Its revenues are however of considerable importance; large quantities of cotton, opium, asafœtida, and henna being exported hence, as it forms the chief outlet to the provinces of Karmán and Yazd. The custom-house duties are farmed by the British agent here, Nasr Rastonsi, for 25,000 *tumáns* (or £10,000) a year, and the remaining villages in the province pay a revenue of 5000 *tumáns* per annum.

The town presents but few attractions to Europeans, and consequently there are but four in the place,—the officer commanding the British India Steam Company's hulk, the Agent, an Italian doctor, and an Austrian photographer, with nothing to do. In summer the heat is fearful, the temperature on board the hulk at midnight being over $105°$[1].

At the time of our arrival the probable fate of the late Governor of the town, of whom we have already spoken, was causing much interest and excitement in the place. He had been already superseded by Ahmad Shah, the new Governor, and a Sartip, or general, from Shíráz had arrived to examine into the matter and report thereon to the head government. Hajji Ahmad of course protested his innocence; but the Sartip merely met these protestations by a demand for a good round sum, which increased daily the longer it remained unpaid; while thumbscrews and the bastinado were darkly hinted at, though as yet Hajji Ahmad had not suffered any ill-treatment. He was very popular with the few Europeans in the place; singularly liberal; ever in want of money, and unfortunately greatly addicted to the abuse of stimulants.

Shortly after landing, Sir Frederic Goldsmid received a visit of welcome from the son of the Governor, who was soon followed by a deputation of well-to-do Hindú merchants, one of whom had been to Samarkand, and was full of a report that the Russians had seized Bukhára; and these again had scarcely taken leave when the ex-Governor's son, a youth of about twelve years of age, came to crave an audience on behalf of his mother. Major Euan Smith was deputed to receive the last-mentioned lady and her daughter, who entered wearing the Arab mask, and at once claimed the General's protection for their husband and father on the ground that, being a British subject, he was exempt from any pains and penalties he might have incurred for his alleged offences. When it was clearly explained to them that

[1] The maximum heat during our stay in Bandar-Abbas was $78°$, the minimum $65°$.

this plea was untenable in the case of a man who for years past had exercised authority as Governor of a Persian town, the wife changing her ground, pleaded that were her husband but released for one week, he would be able to discharge in full all the claims urged against him. Official interference in the matter by the English Commissioner was of course impossible; but on his expressing a hope, both to the Sartip and the Governor, during the visits they paid him, that no severe measures would be resorted to, such as torture or the bastinado, he received from both functionaries an earnest denial of any such intention.

On the evening of the 22nd, after much trouble and difficulty, our camels were started off with the greater portion of the heavy baggage: and the same day we received a telegram from Colonel Pollock, saying that he was coming into Sistán by Jacobabad, the Bolan Pass, and Kandahar, and did not expect to reach Sekuha till the middle of February, or for nearly two months.

On the morning of the 23rd we set forth on our journey, and emerging from the town by the north gate, followed the road running parallel to the sea for about six miles, with the islands of Kishm and Ormúz standing out in bold outline to our right, while to our left the view was bounded by the lofty ranges of the Ghanú Hills. We were escorted by the secretaries of the Governor, Sartip, Consul and British Agent, for a considerable distance out of the town, and were also joined by the Postmaster of the place. The horse of this worthy bolted with him directly we had passed the gates; and we saw no more of the cavalier for several miles till we came upon him, dismounted, and with his horse tied to a tree. Our horses (especially that of Mr. Rosario, who, mounted on a tall chesnut, 'witched the world with noble horsemanship') were also extremely fresh, squealing and kicking, and taxing all our energies to prevent them having a battle royal with each other. The road lay over a sandy, marshy plain covered with low brushwood and camel-thorn, and studded here and there with date-plantations. Our first halting-place, Bágu, was reached by us at 6.30 P.M., lighted by a beautiful moon—no small boon, as in these parts at this season it gets quite dark at 5.30 P.M. Bágu is a humble village, situated under a high ledge of ground to the left of the road, and surrounded by extensive date-plantations, whose dark foliage forms a conspicuous landmark for miles around. The place belongs to Agha Muhammad Khán, of Bombay, who had issued orders to supply us with all we needed free of cost. Our camping-ground was very sandy, the water brackish, and firewood scarce. The island of Ormúz (i. e. its highest peak) bore nearly due south of this place, while the loftiest peak of the Naiyun Kúshkuh range in our front bore nearly north-east by east.

After one day's halt we resumed our march on Christmas Day at seven o'clock A.M., and traversing the same sandy plain, thickly covered with brushwood, camel-thorn and oleander, crossed a broad river, the Rúdkhánah-i-Shúr, whose waters were quite salt; then, turning nearly due north, we reached a higher tract of land with rich soil, bearing extensive fields of wheat. The view at the back of the Kúh-i-Ghanú, behind Bandar-Abbas, now opened out before us: the mountain stands alone, and between it and the range of rocky precipitous hills that rise at its back, lies the valley running nearly due east and west, in which is situated the village of Kala'h-i-Kázi, our second stage. This village consists of a series of very extensive date-plantations, and fields of wheat; the water is good, though rather muddy, and is obtained entirely from wells, called by the natives 'Ab-i-Rahmat.' The land is tilled by Ráiyats, who pay one-tenth of the produce to Government: and though there had been no rain here for two years, yet there were but few signs of the misery so prevalent to the westward; the inhabitants had, however, this year preferred keeping their grain for consumption, to sowing it and running the risk of losing it by its drying up in the parched ground. Our thermometers were set at 9.30 this night, and the next morning at 5.45 stood thus:—max. 61°, min. 38°, standard 45°. This exhibited a very marked change in the temperature, and the dew was excessively heavy, our tents being wet through during the night. From Kala'h-i-Kázi the road led us across a plain thickly strewn with stones, which caused great inconvenience to the horses: low brushwood, and the usual camel-thorn and mimosa covered the ground, and after five or six miles of most unpleasant riding, we came upon clusters of date-palms, and two or three swift clear streams, whose course might be traced by the trees and shrubs that clothed their banks. From this point the date-palms began to thicken till we reached the large village of Takht, standing in a forest of date-plantations, with extensive fields of wheat and henna. This was evidently the most populous place in the district, and a great storehouse of grain. The principal street was the dry bed of a watercourse, in a most filthy condition; the houses were neatly built of mud, thatched with, and in some instances entirely composed of, the leaf of the ever-useful date-palm. The inhabitants who flocked out to see us as we passed, presented features of abnormal ugliness, which the female portion did not think it necessary to conceal with the usual veil. The populous appearance of the village was to be ascribed to the excellence and abundance of the water supply; but in summer the heat and, above all, the musquitoes, bred in the date-trees and surrounding foliage, are described as maddening. After leaving Takht, though the same plain stretched before us, there was not a stone to be seen: all was rich, alluvial soil. The road now again entered extensive date-plantations, known by the name of Chástún; the ground became extremely marshy, and our attention was attracted by dense masses of tall reeds, which formed an apparently impassable barrier between the road and the sea, and which are largely used in the manufacture of pens and mats. The country was thickly wooded with well-grown trees of mimosa and the wild caper, interspersed with large fields of wheat, which belt of wood continued up to the village of Shámil, lying at the head of the valley we entered at Kala'h-i-Kázi. Winding through the jungle, we crossed from time to time many a deep and broad watercourse, whose intricate windings we never could have threaded without the aid of the guide: the easy and usual path for camels runs a little more to the north. These watercourses, though at this season dry, form the channels for conveying the torrents of Sig-i-Jandán to the sea. On arriving at 11 A.M. at the village of Shámil, we found that the caravan we had sent on the previous night had lost its way, and had only just reached camp. In a direct line this place is only three *farsakhs* from the sea-coast: it possesses a mud fort on a hill, about a quarter of a mile to the rear of the town, mounting two guns, and manned by thirty matchlock men; but for defensive purposes the building would be useless against any determined attack. Here and elsewhere, in these parts, we found the villagers quiet and unobtrusive. The village or town of Mináb lies to the south-west, about eight *farsakhs* from Shámil and two from the sea.

Our next day's march was very fatiguing. After crossing a river of sweet water which flows through the village, the road follows the bed of a watercourse, and for four miles winds in and out, when it leads across a hard stony plain, about two miles wide, lying at the foot of a range of barren hills. This plain, a great camping-ground for the Iliáts, appeared to be a network of watercourses that carry off the water from the hills beyond. The path which was very narrow, in some places only just wide enough for a mounted man, enters the hills by an opening which is known as the commencement of the Godar-i-Naürgún, and is the bed of a watercourse filled with a considerable amount of pure fresh water, and with many deep pools. For seven miles we rode along this rocky bed, till we ascended a higher plateau, from which we could still catch a glimpse of the Sig-i-Jandán in the far horizon to the north-west. The constant ascents and descents, added to the stony nature of the path, made this a most trying day's work for the horses. We met no human being *en route*, save four men whom we suddenly came upon, to our great surprise, perched at the top of a narrow pass, each with a guitar, waiting to sing the praises of the British Commissioner as he rode by; and of animal life there was none to be seen, save one large black eagle seated on a rocky crag. The camping-ground at Fariáb, the fourth stage, we found unusually good, dry and lofty, with excellent water and abundant firewood, and shaded by fine Jambul trees. It commands an extensive view of the plain of Rúdhán, a district of considerable importance, farmed by the consul at Bandar-Abbas, Mirza Abdullah.

The night we spent here was, however, anything but peaceful. To sleep was impossible, owing to the troops of jackals, who kept up the most melancholy howling all night through, and who were so numerous that we did not even venture to place our thermometers in the open air, lest the stand should be knocked over by them. Starting at 6 A.M., we again had to follow the bed of a watercourse, until by a sharp turn the road led us through a very steep and difficult pass (Godar-i-Shurún), to a high plateau on the summit of the hills whose base we had been traversing. This plateau stretches away for miles, bounded on all sides, as far as the eye can reach, by ranges of rocky hills; and the view from it presents a scene of utter lifelessness, solitude, and desolation, that it would be difficult to equal anywhere out of Persia, though in some of its features it reminded us strongly of the country between Bam and Bampúr, in Balúchistán. A flock of jungle sheep, scampering over the rocky cliffs to the left of the pass, were the only living things visible. From this point to our halting-place at Rúdkhánah-i-Dúzdi (sixteen miles) we traversed an undulating plain, clothed with the usual low brushwood: the surrounding hills being so shrouded in mist that we found it impossible to get any reliable observations.

About five miles from the Godar-i-Shurún we came upon an encampment of 200 donkeys, laden with Batavian sugar from Bandar-Abbas to Karmán, and a little further on we reached the small river known as the Rúdkhánah-i-Ghishkan, so called from the poisonous shrub (Ghish or oleander) which fringes its banks, and is said to be fatal to men, horses, and camels. Four miles beyond this river we came to a small *hauz* or tank, for the storage of rain-water, of great antiquity; and seven miles further brought us to our camp pitched on the north side of the Dúzdi river. The great date-plantations in the neighbourhood of this river are cultivated by the inhabitants of distant villages, who come here only in summer-time to tend the trees, leaving them to take their chance during the remainder of the year: and this is the case also with all the date-plantations through which we had been passing. We made a halt here till the morrow, to give our men and animals time for greatly-needed rest: the pass, or Godar, had doubtless tried them severely; and one camel had broken its leg in the ascent. The air now became very pure and bracing, and quite cold enough all day to make a great-coat very acceptable: in the morning, moreover, a reading of the thermometers had proved the temperature to have fallen during the night within four degrees of freezing-point. We walked up in the evening to visit a fort which, though in ruins, still mounted one rusty gun: it was situated on the left bank of the Rúdkhánah-i-Dúzdi, with the remains of a deep ditch surrounding it: from its walls was obtainable a very good view of the course of the river, the bed of which is here some 200 yards wide, with a shallow stream of water running rapidly to the east. At this point, its direction is east and west, but a mile further down, the river bends to the south, and flowing by Rúdhán and Mínáb, makes its way to the sea at a distance of about 130 miles. We were informed that it took its rise from springs, four miles to the N.N.W., and was supplemented by numerous rivulets. Fish are to be found in it, but of small size. The village of Rúdkhánah-i-Dúzdi, consisting of about 500 mud huts, lies in an amphitheatre bounded by hills, and is surrounded by thick date-plantations. It is part of the province of Rúdhán and, in conjunction with it, pays to the Laristan Government a yearly revenue of 10,000 *kráns*, principally drawn from its date-plantations. Each date-tree in the province (and there are about 10,000) is taxed at the rate of one *krán* for four trees; no tax is paid till the tree begins to bear, which it does generally when it is from about eight to ten years old. Date-palms live to a great age, and some were pointed out to us in full bearing that were over 150 years. In a good season a tree will produce from 30 to 40 *manns* of dates, i. e. from 250 to 400 lbs. The price of these was very high in the year preceding that of our mission, owing to the scarcity in other parts of Persia, but they ordinarily fetch about 2 *kráns* for 12 *manns* of 7 lbs. each; in English money about 1*s.* 4*d.* for 84 lbs.: but the dates are inferior to those of Panjgúr and Bampúr. Excellent oranges are grown here.

When the Khán of the village came to visit Sir Frederic, he proposed to him an alteration in our route, which, after much discussion, was accepted, as besides other advantages it possessed that of being quite new; for the road we had intended following was similar to that taken by Major Murdoch Smith six years ago[1]. We found that the inhabitants here had a lively and permanent recollection of that officer's visit.

As we had now entered the jurisdiction of the Karmán Government we learnt without surprise that a Mihmándár, named Yáwar Ghulám Husain, had been deputed by the Wakíl-ul-Múlk to receive the General, and had been awaiting his arrival for several weeks at Khánú. Hither we were escorted by Ja'far Khán, the headman of the district, who took us by a road which presented but few features of interest. At Ziárat, a miserable village of mud huts, the inhabitants came out to stare at us, and to implore the services of Mr. Rosario in curing the sore eyes from which they all suffered in a greater or less degree. They were dirty, ugly, and miserable in the extreme: we noticed, however, two of the younger girls, whose hair, hanging in uninviting plaits to the waist, was adorned with massive lumps of silver and beads. Many of the inhabitants had never seen an European before.

The general character of the country much resembles the neighbourhood of Bampúr, and is almost devoid of population—the soil, though rich, being cultivated only by the miserable inhabitants of a few small mud villages, who pay no tax for the land they thus occupy. The

---

[1] There are two roads to Bam from this place. One of these we followed, and of this we had not been able beforehand to ascertain the exact distance: of the other the following are the stages: Kalah Askir, 4 *farsakhs*; Khánú Panjir, 6; Asiáh Gangiabád, 7; Karimabad Jiruft, 4; Godar Makak, 8; Sagdir, 5; Godar Deh Bakri, 6; Miándasht, 6; Bam, 7, *viâ* Dárzin.

plain was covered with a yellow shrub called 'Salma,' edible for man and beast. The *kahur* tree affords abundant firewood; but the water, which is very good, is obtained almost entirely from wells. We passed a great number of graves, which, unlike those we saw in Balúchistán, were always surrounded by a stone wall two or three feet high. Large flocks of fine broad-tailed sheep were to be seen in every direction, but little human life. One man alone we met, transporting himself, his wife, and two children, with all his worldly goods, on the back of a fast-trotting camel. At a village called Ispid, twenty-two miles from Dúzdi, the valley narrows and passes between two ranges of hills, that on the right known as the Kúh-i-Garak, that on the left as the Devan-i-Murád, which is a somewhat lofty chain running N.W. and S.E. The road to Bam or Jírúft passes by the left of these hills; that we are following passes them on the right.

At two miles from Khánú the British Commissioner was met by a small *istikbál*, or deputation, headed by the Governor's brother; and just before we reached camp, a band of musicians placed themselves before us, preceded by an individual who walked into camp nearly the whole way on his head, while the mounted slaves meanwhile did astounding feats of horsemanship. We had scarcely arrived, when the Governor, a fine aristocratic old man with very dignified manners—and wearing, like all the dignitaries of the place, a coloured turban, instead of the usual Persian head-dress—came to visit the General, accompanied by his young son. He informed us of the defeat of Ibrahim Khán at Bampúr by the Balúchís, and was greatly interested in the fate of Hajji Ahmad at Bandar-Abbas.

For New Year's Day it was determined to halt here, and the place well merited close inspection, being one of the most singular we had seen. It is peopled entirely by a race of slaves. It appears that more than four hundred years ago, the ancestors of the present Governor migrated here from Khúrasán, accompanied by a train of slaves, whose descendants now people the town. The governorship has descended from father to son, in an unbroken line for more than four centuries, and is in fact a small hereditary kingdom. The Governor of Karmán, it is true, is the acknowledged superior, and receives tribute from the Governor of Khánú, but he would never dream of appointing any Governor, other than the acknowledged heir of the reigning family; and indeed were he to do so, his nominee would not be received. The population numbers about one thousand families of slaves, knowing no law but the will of their lord and master, the Governor of the town, who has absolute power over them, whether for life or death. They never leave the place except when in attendance on one of the reigning family, and are never sold by any chance, as they pass from father to son as so much entailed property. Having no thought or care for their livelihood, and ignorant of the sweets of a liberty they have never known, they lead a perfectly contented life, receiving their daily bread from the hands of their owner, and in return, serving him with a blind fidelity. They are chiefly occupied in tilling the ground, the proceeds of their labour being of course the property of their master. They intermarry exclusively amongst themselves, and thus this singular settlement is perpetuated from generation to generation, without break or change. Neither here nor elsewhere on this route did we find any want of suffering from famine. Many of the slaves resemble ordinary Persians, but others have the woolly hair and black skin of the negro. No guards were placed over our camp.

It was a strange feeling to realise that there was not a single free man in the town except the Governor's family and ourselves, for though there are about two thousand families of Ráiyats in the district of Khánú, they are quite distinct, and never settle in the town itself. The Governor, Núru-dín, and his brother, Chiragh Khán, visited the General several times; but we afterwards learned that he and all his family were such inveterate drunkards, that the state of sufficient sobriety to venture out of doors was entirely due to our presence in the town. As they left the tent the first time, a servant from each preferred a whispered request for a bottle of brandy, and Ja'far Khán, taking heart of grace, did the same on his own account. They had been much interested in a musical box which we showed them, and also a galvanic battery; insisting on experiments with the latter being made on the vile bodies of their unwilling retinue, and exhibiting great delight at the contortions thereby induced, until one son of Islam smashed the machine in his novel agonies. Mr. Rosario was busily employed all day doctoring the slaves; and every member of the Governor's family also petitioned for some sort of medicine.

The fort here, though built by the present man's father only thirty-five years ago, is entirely in ruins. We learned that from this place the plain runs east, in an unbroken level, right up to Bampúr; the district of Rúdbár, to which Khánú belongs, extending nearly over the whole distance. The Jamál Bárid mountain bears to the north-east, about sixty miles off. Excellent partridge shooting is to be had in the vicinity of the town, and two of our party shot thirteen brace in a very short time during our stay there.

From Khánú to Dusári, thirty-seven miles, the road runs over a fertile plain, and presents nothing worthy of remark, save, that before us lay the range of snow-capped hills, known equally by the name of the Dusári and Jamál Bárid range, which presented a truly magnificent appearance. Far away to the south-east lay the plain stretching to Bampúr. The climate was most enjoyable, and the supply of water excellent and abundant. At sixteen miles from Khánú the village of Sohrán is passed, and four miles further the river Halil, the banks of which are thickly fringed with tamarisk, affording shelter to immense numbers of partridge and sandgrouse. One of the ravines further on had obtained an unenviable notoriety, three years before our visit, as the haunt of a band of robbers, who were a terror to the district, till put down with a strong hand by the Governor of Khánú. Two miles from Dusári, we were met by the Governor's son with twelve *sowárs* bringing the unwelcome news that the Deh Bakri pass was closed. This, however, we afterwards found was a mistake [1].

Our arrival in camp, pitched close to the town of Dusári, caused the greatest excitement, and the Governor immediately came to pay the usual visit of ceremony, and was presented with a couple of watches for himself and his son, and also two shawls. He told us the

---

[1] There is another route from Khánú to Bam, which, though much longer, has perhaps the advantage of avoiding the hills, and in this way is good for heavily-laden camels: its stages are as follows:—

Bejánabád	5 farsakhs
Kúhistán	10 ,,
Togún	8 ,,
Mil-i-Farhád	6 ,,
Dehindarún	8 ,,
Kunar Nayi	5 ,,
Regán	8 ,,
Burj-i-Mahaz	5 ,,
Azizábád	3 ,,
Bam	8 ,,
Total	66 ,,

P.S.—With regard to these stages it should be remarked that the people here have no idea of actual *distance*, but calculate their stages by time.

name for Dusári is Jabl-i-Báriz (not Jamál-Bárid), and signifies the 'mountain of cold,'[1] so called because almost all its jurisdiction lies in the hills, adding that the country was formerly populated from Jirúft to Bampúr, but is now desolate. The town has a substantial wall of brick, with flanking towers and two lofty *bádgirs* or wind-towers: its inhabitants seemed very poor, chiefly cultivators of the ground, and possessed with such a love of medicine, that they thronged Mr. Rosario's tent all day, praying for pills and potions. The Governor and all his family also consulted our medico for their eyes, and his arrival was hailed as a godsend by the whole community. We were informed that the chief of Khánú is also the 'Bégi' of this place, and that his inordinate craving for brandy was shared by the local 'upper ten.' Travellers should hence take three days' supplies of forage and provisions for the journey to Bam, as there is only one thinly-peopled village on the road, and all necessaries are abundant here. Before starting, we despatched a messenger to Bam with letters for Major Lovett, telling him of our intended movements, and requesting him to communicate the same to the Persian Commissioner.

The route from hence again lay over the same plain—in this direction bounded by the hills which, running from Jirúft, join the Deh Bakri and Dusári chain. Four miles on our march, we passed a solitary hill rising abruptly from the level of the plain, called Khárpúsht (or the Porcupine), from whence we got a view of the snow-capped Ahmadi mountain, rearing its head to the south-west. We passed occasional patches of cultivation, with clusters of leaf-built huts, but the only objects of interest were the black partridges, which kept continually crossing our path in swarms. We had intended to push on that day to Dasht-i-Khúshk, but the guides had brought our *faráshes* and mules to a stop five miles nearer Dusári; and there we halted, the camp being in the Jirúft district. In the afternoon, arrived Yáwar Ghulám Husain Khán, who had been appointed Mihmándár to the General fully two months before. He was the son of the Diwan Bégi of Karmán, and was accompanied by Muhammad Hasan Khán. He confirmed the news of the defeat of Ibrahim Khán by the Balúchís of Chakhansur, at a place near Nasrabad in Sistán, about a month previously. He also informed us that Mirza Ma'súm Khán had reached Bam, and was there awaiting our arrival. The next day

[1] Perhaps rather the 'cold mountain;' if indeed the Persian genitive may be used with such purely Arabic words. The name refers to the district.—F. J. G.

we started under charge of the new Mihmándár; but though his anxiety to acquit himself of his duties caused him to furnish a led horse and some very unnecessary guards during the night, we benefited but little from his presence. We were much amused by the singular way in which these Persian sentinels performed their duty at night. General Goldsmid happened to leave his tent somewhat late in the evening, and was surprised to find a very lively sentry at the door with a drawn sword, porting, carrying and saluting, in the most approved fashion. On being questioned, the man replied that he was acting in accordance with the Yáwar's orders that the General's tent should be strictly guarded during the night. 'And pray how long do you stay here?' asked Sir Frederic. 'Oh! we wait until the Sardár (or General) is fast asleep, and then we all go home and sleep likewise!'

Our march the next day to the Deh Bakri pass came to rather an untoward ending. The Mihmándár had neglected to furnish us with guides, and so we wandered on and on, greatly surprised at the length of the stage, till we found that we had overshot the mark by several miles, and had left the camp far behind. We had passed early in the day the village of Dasht-i-Khúshk, which, as its name implies, marks the limit of cultivation on this side of Deh Bakri, and coming upon the stony, barren slope of the mountain range, had continued our ascent for ten miles, when we found ourselves at the entrance of the pass, from whence a very fine view of the Jírúft and Rúdbár plains is obtained. Our path then followed the course of a mountain torrent, between rocky cliffs, till we commenced the very difficult ascent known as the Godár of Sakhtdar. The summit of this pass, which is thirty-eight miles from Dusári, we reached with difficulty, and passing through a winding valley, came into the open plain of Sakhtdar, with the Rúdkhánah flowing through it. It was at this point we realised that we were far separated from our camp; but as it was raining hard, with a bitterly cold wind, and it was hopeless to turn back, we determined to push on to the caravanserai at Maskún—deluded with a false report that our camels were ahead of us. Eight miles from the river, we came upon the first snow we had seen, and pursued our course, cold and wretched, over steep and desolate hills, for about two miles, when one of the Yáwar's men who was leading, exclaimed that we had lost the way. It was now 3 P.M., and as we had not tasted food that day, a halt was ordered, and scouts were sent out to discover the right path. Shouts from a neighbouring hill soon caused us to hark back, and striking at last on the right track, we found ourselves, at 5 o'clock, at the desolate caravanserai of Maskún, situated in a hollow on the highest point of the pass, about 7300 feet above the level of the sea. The caravanserai, though nothing but a dark and miserable stable, was yet a most welcome harbour of refuge to our wearied men and animals from the bitter wind and driving rain. The hills and all around were deep in snow, and as none of the mules, camels, or servants were to be seen, all we could do was to make the best possible arrangements for the night. Luckily for us, the Abdár had with him a tin of sardines and another of jam, and we were thankful to dine as best we might off these. Our poor horses were in sorry plight, all their clothing and forage being with the missing mules: but in the midst of the general discomfort, we could only congratulate ourselves on having regained the right path, and thus being saved very unpleasant and serious consequences. Affairs looked gloomy enough when we awoke the next morning, after many comfortless hours passed huddled up together with the horses, mules, and men, all starving and wretched: for it had snowed heavily enough during the night to cut off all chance of our getting provisions for some time, the mountain paths being so slippery that neither mules nor camels would be able to ascend but with great difficulty. At 9 o'clock, however, the sun broke through the dense mists that enveloped us, revealing beautiful glimpses of the snow-capped ranges around, and cheering the spirits of all the party. Our missing servants and mules now came dropping in one after the other, full of the adventures and hair-breadth escapes of the preceding night; and mules were sent back to aid the camels and bring up loads of forage for the starving horses, and the sun soon dried all the soaking baggage.

In the evening all our numbers were complete, with the exception of four mules and their drivers, who were reported to be lost in the mountains, and in search of whom we despatched three *ghulāms* next day, with provisions and forage. This pass we shall long remember as one of the most dreary imaginable; for there was not a human being to be seen, nor provision of any kind to be found for man or beast. The hills, it is true, swarmed with black partridges, but these were so wild as to be quite unapproachable. In the course of the day, a messenger arrived from Jírúft with letters from Major Lovett, announcing his arrival with Sergeant Bower at Bam on the 25th of December.

The next morning broke bright, clear, and bitterly cold, as there had been a hard frost during the night. We found that two miles beyond the caravanserai, the road makes another steep ascent, to the extreme summit of the pass of Deh Bakri, for which the aneroid registered a height of 7800 feet. Descending by a steep and slippery path, we reached, a mile further on, the caravanserai of Deh Bakri, which closely resembled that at Maskún, and had been evidently built thus near it to afford certain shelter to travellers on either side this dangerous pass in severe weather. Entering a narrow valley with traces of summer cultivation, our road led into the stony bed of a watercourse, which is the outlet for the streams of the high land around; and after two miles of very rough ground, it forked off into two branches —one to the north-east, leading by Sarvastán to Karmán, and the other to the east, leading to Bam. Choosing the latter, we ascended some hills, from the summit of which we first saw the plain of Bam lying at our feet, with Dárzin to the north-east, and Bam east by south: the aneroid giving an altitude of 6400 feet. An easy and gradual descent to the plain soon brought us to the familiar ground we had traversed the year before, and we at once recognised the Tahrúd hills and the Dárzin road.

We breakfasted at the foot of the hills, the aneroid indicating a fall of 4300 feet from Deh Bakri, and then rode for eighteen miles to Behdirun, across a barren stony plain affording neither water nor firewood. Reaching Behdirun at 5.30 P.M., we hoped to find that Major Lovett had sent us out tents and provisions from Bam, but finding none, we again started in the fast fading light to ride the remaining six miles into that town. We had not, however, gone far, when we saw three figures approaching us in the dusk; and to our great delight, these proved to be Major Lovett, Quartermaster-Sergeant Bower, and the Mírakhor Ghafur Beg. It appeared that the messenger we had sent them from Dusári had never turned up; and it was by the merest chance they had heard of our expected arrival at Behdirun that evening. We all rode in together, and found excellent quarters prepared for us in a new house belonging to the Kalántar or Mayor of the place, with all our old servants and *faráshes* in waiting to welcome us. The establishment left at Bam the preceding year had profited much from their long rest, and both men and animals were looking sleek and well.

The Persian Commissioner was reported to be in excellent health and spirits, and our preparations for the somewhat difficult march into Sistán were declared to be in a forward state: for our servants, with that love of travelling so peculiar to Persians, were already beguiling one another with imaginary tales of the wonders and delights of the far away province, and were in high spirits and anxious for an early start. One difficult portion of our march from the sea-coast had already been accomplished most successfully, and this result was a good omen for future success. There was much to tell and to hear, between the two parties who had been separated for so many months, and night fell on a reunited and eagerly conversational community [1].

II. *Bam to Sistán.*

The Mission halted at Bam from the 7th till the 11th of January, 1872, in order that the necessary preparations might be completed for crossing the desert into Sistán. Thanks to the exertions of Captain Lovett and Sergeant Bower, these preparations were, as before said,

---

[1] The itinerary of the route followed by the Mission from Bandar-Abbas to Bam was as follows:—

Date. 1871.	Stage.	Distance in Miles.	Direction.
Dec. 24	Bágú	14	E.N.E.
,, 25	Kala'h-i-Kázi	12	N.E.
,, 26	Shámil	20	E. slightly N.
,, 27	Fariáb	19	7 miles E.N.E. / 8 miles E. / 4 miles S.E.
,, 28	Rúdkhánah-i-Dúzdi	23	N.N.E. by N.
,, 30	Ispid	22	E.N.E.
,, 31	Khánú	12	E.N.E.
1872.			
Jan. 2	Sohran	16	N.E. by N.
,, 3	Dusári	21	N. by E.
,, 4	Daulatabád	17	N.W.
,, 5	Maskún Caravanserai	36	14 miles N. by W. / 12 miles N. by E. / 10 miles N.E.
,, 7	Bam	36	10 miles N.E. / 2 miles E. by S. / 18 miles E. / 6 miles E. by S.

in a very forward state. The greater part of the transport animals had been engaged, and the horses that had been left behind last year under the charge of the Mírakhor were found to be in first-rate condition. The usual ceremonial visits were exchanged with the Persian Commissioner, who appeared in excellent spirits, seemed delighted to see the General, and prophesied smooth things and a style of procedure very different from that of last year. He had only one of his sons with him on this occasion, the other having been left behind to be married; and he had provided himself with a new engineer officer (Zulfakar Khán), resplendent in high knee boots and bright green gloves. He said that on this occasion he had been furnished with instructions that were quite clear and sufficient. The return visit of ceremony paid by Sir Frederic Goldsmid to the Persian Commissioner was chiefly memorable from the incidental misfortunes of the unpaid attaché. This gentleman had provided himself for the occasion with a gold-laced cap and a necessary pair of goloshes[1], both many sizes too large for him, and which could only be kept in their places by the strictest uprightness and rectitude of position. Consequently, whenever he had to make a slight jump over any one of the small water-courses intersecting our road, either the gold-laced cap or the goloshes, and often both these articles, would tumble into the water and float slowly away, leaving their bareheaded or half-shod owner mourning on the bank until such time as one of the laughing retinue would recapture and return them to him. The constant and unerring repetition of this incident somewhat impaired the dignity, though it added much to the hilarity, of the procession. At last, on the 11th, owing to every one having worked with right good-will, all was ready for a start. We had obtained an excellent guide, one Hajji Abdullah Khán, thin, tall, grey-bearded, dignified, and intensely loquacious, who boasted he knew every inch of Persia, and the possession of an immense Túrkman grey mare, displaying 'great symmetry of bone.' The missing mules and camels had been brought in safety from the Deh Bakri pass, having been found nine miles off the road with their drivers insensible from hunger; and on the morning of the 12th, after the distribution of numerous presents to all who had been

---

[1] Goloshes are always worn over the boots by Europeans in Persia when they visit Persians of rank. The discarding of the goloshes at the door is equivalent to the Persians invariably leaving their slippers at the door, and entering a carpeted room in their stocking feet.

instrumental in assisting us, the Mission finally started out of Bam on their way to Sistán[1].

Before leaving Bam, it may be interesting to compare briefly the present state of the city with the account given of it in Kinneir's Geographical Memoir. The town is no longer, as therein described, surrounded by walls and flanking towers. It lies quite open and unprotected on either side the river, which divides it into two very equal parts. This distribution, however, is of recent date, for it is only of late years that the country has been sufficiently quiet from the *chapáos* of the Afgháns and Balúchís to allow of the inhabitants dwelling elsewhere than in a circle of protecting walls. The present fort, situated about a quarter of a mile to the east, outside the town, was formerly the *ark* or citadel inside the city, which was surrounded by a high wall with towers. The prosperity of Bam seems to have reached its climax during the reign of Nádir Shah, who passed through it on his way to Afghánistán. Its position as a frontier town gave it much importance, for it was not only exposed to continual attacks from marauding Afgháns and Balúchís, but was also generally resorted to by rebellious chieftains or unsuccessful aspirants to power. As is well known, it witnessed the capture of the unfortunate Lutf Ali Khán, the last of the Zand dynasty, and more recently the rebellion of Agha Khán, now living in Bombay. The famous historical pile of skulls, raised by order of Agha Muhammad Shah to commemorate the defeat of the adherents of Lutf Ali Khán, no longer exists. Fath Ali Shah gave permission for it to be removed. Hajji Abdullah Khán was well up in the history of these parts, and he declared that his ancestors played an important part in the events that succeeded each other so rapidly during the rise of the

---

[1] The strength at leaving was as follows:—

Sir F. J. Goldsmid and Staff	6
Persian Government servants	32
Private servants	13
Guide	1
Mule drivers and camel men	21
Total	73

Animals.		Tents.	
Horses	24	Hill Tents	5
Mules	24	Bell Tents	7
Camels	90	Persian and other Tents	4
	138		16

Kajár dynasty. According to his account, his grandfather, Hajji Muhammad Husain Khán, was a most influential man here, and a Sardar of Persia. He had seven sons, of whom three, including the father of our guide, were induced by Fath Ali Shah, on his succeeding to the throne, to give him up the *ark* or citadel of Bam, on his swearing on the Kuran to receive them into favour. No sooner had he them in his power, however, then he took them to Tehrán, putting all their eyes out on the same day; but finding that, during their detention at Tehrán, the province and city of Bam were subjected to continued incursions from their adherents in Sistán and the neighbourhood, he at last received them again into favour, and sent them back, blind as they were, to quiet the province. Hajji Abdullah says that it was one of these blind uncles of his who, when a young man, had captured Lutf Ali Khán, by hamstringing his horse.

The population of Bam consists now of between eight and nine thousand inhabitants. Its principal trade is in the products of the Narmashír, cotton, henna, wheat, &c., &c., which pass through it *en route* to Bandar-Abbas. The water is good, though the natives say it is *sangin* or 'heavy.' The town is the residence of the famous Ibrahim Khán when he is not at Bampúr[1]. The fort is kept in good order, but they would not permit us to enter it. There was great suffering from the famine here last year, and many people kept themselves alive almost entirely on grass and herbs. Hence to Sistán there is a distance of about 280 miles, of eleven marches, which it took us nineteen days to accomplish, owing to a necessity for halting seven days at various places, to rest the animals and await the Persian Commissioner's arrangements for escort and provisioning.

The first fifty miles traverse the district of the Narmashír, famous for its excellent soil and abundant water supply. Wheat, henna, rice and indigo are grown in abundance, and black partridge, wild fowl, and wild pig are to be shot in great numbers. The principal large villages passed are Kruk, Azizábád, Na'imabád (which Pottinger visited in 1810, but which is no longer in the same flourishing condition), and Fahraj, a place of great antiquity, which passed into Persian possession in the reign of Fath Ali Shah. The last is situated on the right bank of the sluggish river rising, it is said, from some springs near Azizábád, and flowing up to this point through deep banks; finally releasing, spreading and losing itself in

---

[1] See mention of Bam also at page 85.

small streams in the plain beyond Fahraj, and at a much lower level (having no force to make a distinct bed) in the hard plain. The bed of the river, here two hundred yards wide, is choked with a reedy grass called 'Diránchu,' which gives excellent cover to all sorts of game. This place has been identified by Major St. John with Pahra, the ancient capital of Gedrosia, where Alexander met his heavy baggage and elephants after his march through Balúchistán. It now has about two thousand inhabitants, and its mud fort is in excellent preservation and in a commanding position. The village is surrounded by date-groves. Some little distance off are the scanty ruins of a very old fort, which tradition says was many hundred years ago occupied by Gabrs, and opposite the present village on the other side of the river are the ruins of a most remarkable fort of considerable extent, perched on a high hill. Time did not admit of our measuring the extent of the ruins, but they were evidently of great antiquity. The remains of a large village called Takiabád were also observed in the vicinity; the constant forays of the Afgháns and Balúchís having caused the spot to be deserted some sixty years ago. The inhabitants of the Narmashír, who came out to see us pass, seemed fairly well to do, though inexpressibly dirty. There appeared to have been but little acute distress from famine last year, but we heard that the paucity of rain had advanced the price of bread fivefold within the last two years.

It was remarkable how much the vegetation had advanced in the Narmashír compared with that in the immediate vicinity of Bam. The temperature was much warmer, there being a difference of some twenty degrees; the tamarisk-trees were in bloom, and the wheat was well above ground. The extensive belt of jungle which intervenes between Azizábád and Fahraj stretches right up to Rígán. Some very striking earth formations are to be noticed in the Narmashír, which at first sight have the appearance of an enormous city in ruins, with walls, gates, and bastions, but which on closer inspection prove to be masses of *kankar* and sand, worn into these fantastic shapes by the action of water. It is difficult to account for the uniform height at which these masses have been preserved above the clear level of the surrounding plain.

The last camping-ground before entering the desert that intervenes for the greater part of the distance between the Narmashír and Sistán, is at a place called Túm-i-Rig, or the 'hillocks of sand,' where there is good fresh water; and before leaving this point all preparations should be completed, even to the taking of men to dig wells in the rare spots where salt and brackish water is to be found. All drinking-water, at least for Europeans, should be provided as far as Nusratabád. The forage and provisions that we had to lay in had necessarily increased our transport train considerably, and the consequent number of camels and horses quite enlivened the dreary aspect of the desert. We had here an opportunity of learning by practical experience how utterly aggravating and maddening a servant the patient camel can become; and more especially the camel of Balúchistán. In other parts of Persia the camels are fed with flour at the end of the day's march; but here the only food they can get is that obtainable by browsing in the vicinity of the camping-grounds. Immediately on arrival in camp they are therefore turned quite loose to wander at their own sweet will all over the country until the evening, when the drivers go out and collect them : and this is often a work of considerable difficulty, for it sometimes occurs that camels are lost for days together. Another matter is that as the camel is an enormous feeder he requires the whole day to graze in. This necessitates his marching at night, or at some very early hour in the morning, to allow of his arrival at the next stage in good time; and the operation of loading the camels in the early evening for their midnight march is one that must be experienced to be appreciated. It is impossible to give even a faint idea of the gamut of inharmonious and heartbreaking sounds which this patient beast has at its command, and with which it 'protests' against being laden at all. Grumblings, rumblings, creakings, snortings, wailings, and groanings, interspersed with the guttural oaths of the drivers, and accompanied by the most villainous smells, continue in uninterrupted discord till the would-be sleeper in the tents around wishes that he might alike lose the sense of hearing and of smell until such sore trial be accomplished. And even when loaded and started these beasts are equally unmanageable, for here they are not, as in other parts, accustomed to follow each other in a long string, each attached to each, nose and tail, by a rope. Such restrictions would, say their Balúch drivers, infuriate and madden the free spirit of this child of the desert. Instead of this they must be allowed to follow one another scattered at intervals all over the country, browsing as they go along, continually dropping their loads, and giving sufficient work to a considerable body of men to keep them together at all; besides which, each isolated beast forms an easy prey for any chance marauder. They are, too, excessively timid, and frightened at the least unaccustomed sound, such as a European sneezing in their vicinity. We had a proof of this one night at midnight, when a horrible clattering and smashing sound woke us up, and we were informed that a young camel being loaded near Mr. Rosario's tent had been so startled by a more than usually earnest snore from that gentleman, that he had run straight away across country with a chest of drawers packed full of pills and potions of every description. The Jambáz or riding camel is of course a notable exception to the above remarks. His pace is pleasant for his rider when the latter has become accustomed to it, and his powers of endurance are most remarkable. Our guide told us a story, which was corroborated by other evidence, of a messenger having traversed the whole distance between Sistán and Karmán, with the news of the murder of Ali Khán by his nephew Taj Muhammad Khán, on one of those Jambáz camels in three days—a distance certainly not less than 360 miles. This was in 1861.

The temperature fell very low while we were encamped at Túm-i-Rig, on the edge of the desert, and it may be noticed here that it daily got much colder until we reached Sistán. Six inches below the surface of the ground, at Túm-i-Rig, there is a layer of pure salt, sufficiently hard to turn the tent pegs, and we found this the case at other places in the desert. The two camping-grounds so called between the Narmashír and Nusratabád (the latter place being a Persian settlement, and sort of half-way house to Sistán), are Shor-Gez, at twenty-two miles, and Gúrg, thirty-five miles further. The road for the greater part of the distance runs over a hard stony desert, somewhat undulating, but with no signs of life of any description. There are occasional sandy patches upon which *bháta*, stunted tamarisk, and small *kuhar* trees are found; but otherwise the desolation of these vast solitudes, which stretch away on the west right up to Tehrán, is complete and unbroken. Two most remarkable towers are passed which now serve entirely as landmarks, and which the natives declare were erected by the great Nádir Shah, to guide his army by night while traversing this desert *en route* to Afghánistán. The first of these is distant about nine miles from Túm-i-Rig, and is visible immediately on quitting that camping-ground. It is called the Mil-i-Nádiri, and we found its dimensions to be as follows:—height 55 feet; circumference at base 43 feet, slightly tapering to the top; thickness of wall 3½ feet; measurement of bricks 14 by 12 by 2 inches.

It is a strong structure of oven-burnt bricks (probably brought from Fahraj) standing quite by itself, with a spiral staircase of fifty steps ascending to the top, but with no interior rooms or place of protection. An extensive view of the surrounding desolation can be obtained from the summit. Though showing many proofs that it has suffered from the weather, this tower is still perfectly solid, and likely to last for many years. The other tower is eleven miles beyond Shor-Gez, but is now almost completely in ruins, having been destroyed by an earthquake about twenty-five years ago. It is said to have been twice the height of the former one. From appearances, the conclusion is warranted that Nádir Shah merely repaired these towers, which seem to be of a date far antecedent to his epoch.

Eleven miles beyond the second tower are situated the ruins of a considerable fort and caravanserai, called Ribát, which shows that the road must have been considerably used at one period. Both at Shor-Gez and Gúrg water was obtainable by digging wells five feet deep, but it was brackish and bad; and at the latter place there is a stream (Rúd-i-Máhi) so salt and bitter that none of our animals even would touch it: the wild ass being the only animal ever known to drink of it. Gúrg is situated at the foot of the range of hills which divide it from Nusratabád, in a valley running N.W. to S.E., along which the Balúchís used to raid from Balúchistán. The Rúd-i-Máhi, which is a brook of considerable size, was described as finding its way through the Nusratabád range and other hills right into Sistán, but it was impossible to trace its course from native description. The old road into Sistán used to follow the Gúrg valley to the east and turn the hills in front, but robbers caused its desertion. Remains of *kanáts* and mud-huts and a caravanserai afford proof that at one time a vain attempt was made to inhabit these inhospitable latitudes, which though so bitterly cold at the time we traversed them, are so hot in summer that the infrequent traveller has to wrap bandages round his stirrups to prevent his horse or camel being wounded from contact therewith.

The Persian settlement of Nusratabád, some sixteen years old, is situated in a valley about seven miles broad, and 37 miles N.E. of the camping-ground at Gúrg, from which it is divided by a range of utterly desolate and barren hills, of which the line of the watershed is crossed at an elevation of 4900 feet. This valley is bounded to the north also by a high range of hills, and consequently, receiving the watershed of the two ranges, is in wet seasons quite under water: in the dry seasons it is so thickly covered with saline efflorescence, that it has the appearance of being several feet deep in snow. The settlement is composed of a mud fort, strongly built, having walls about thirty feet high, square in form, with towers at the angles, each face 100 yards, affording accommodation at a pinch for 350 men. The garrison consists of fifty men, commanded by a *súltán* or captain; and there are, besides, some thirty wretched cultivators, who were brought here nine or ten years ago, and who have never been allowed to return. Neither these wretched creatures nor the soldiers are, for some unexplained reason, allowed to have their wives or female relatives with them; and no words could do justice to the extreme misery of their condition, thus shut off from all ties, and with no hope of a return to all that makes life bearable. The cultivators, especially, seemed to be half-witted; and, on the night of our arrival, came round the fire we had lit as a protection against the bitter cold, and thrust their bodies into the middle of the flames, looking more like brutes than human beings. Their exertions have reclaimed the salt swamp surrounding the fort, to the space of about a mile radius, and this affords sufficient grain for the wants of the scanty garrison. The water is very brackish, and there are two thermal sulphur springs[1] (temp. $75°$ at surface, $38°$ air) in the vicinity of the surrounding hills, which even here have a reputation for the cure of skin diseases. At one of these, eight miles from the fort, a small walled enclosure marks the grave of a Balúch, who committed suicide at this delectable place. No words can give an idea of the desolate appearance of Nusratabád; and here we were destined to halt from the 21st to the 26th of January, six days. The fort marked the limits of Karmán territory, and the escort that had hitherto accompanied us, under the command of the Governor of Bam, would consequently return hence to the Narmashír after handing us over, bag and baggage, to the escort that the Amir of Káin, Hashmat-ul-Mulk and Governor of Sistán, had some time since despatched to meet us, but which did not arrive at Nusratabád until the 25th of January. The halt thus rendered necessary was of great use to our baggage animals, who were quite knocked up by the unaccustomed cold, and it also afforded

[1] Or, perhaps three. They were visited by Mr. Thomas and Sergeant Bower, who described them as situated one above the other, in steps, and varying in temperature.—F. J. G.

opportunity for the members of the Mission to shoot deer and wildfowl, as well as to gain some experience of the intense suspicion entertained on their movements and objects, which later events led us to believe the Persian Commissioner commenced here to disseminate. Up to the present, this gentleman had been the impersonation of good-humour and *bonhomie* and he continued to play this part until arrival in Sistán; when, as will be seen hereafter, his conduct completely changed. But there were not wanting even here little signs to mark, as it were, the beginning of the end of those smooth things which while at Bam he had so gladly prophesied: even in this blank and dreary spot, it was almost impossible to get answers to the simplest questions: we were told that it was forbidden to give information; and remonstrance was unproductive of redress. It may be noticed that the march hither from Gúrg is a very trying one, being principally along the stony bed of the watercourse that drains the range of intervening contiguous hills. A curious ruin of a gate, situated in a very narrow gorge, about twenty-nine miles from Gúrg, is passed, and is said to be another remnant of Nádir Shah's passage, and to have been used as a toll-bar. The natives say that copper abounds in the hills around, and we heard the same thing wherever we halted on our march into Sistán. From Nusratabád, there is a little-used path to Bam which a determined man on a good *jambáz* could, it is said, traverse in twenty-four hours.

At noon, on the 25th of January, the long-expected escort from Sistán arrived. It consisted of fifty-five *sowárs* in all, some mounted on horses and some on camels, headed by two men specially deputed by the Amir of Káïn, named Abbás Khán and Muhammad Beg, the latter of whom was a Balúch chief in the service of the Amir. They brought us the news that the Amir was in Sistán, anxiously awaiting our arrival, and we accordingly moved thither at daybreak on the 27th. Between Nusratabád and Sekuha, in Sistán, there are three halting-places, called Kilágh-áb (water of the crow), Túrsh-áb (bitter water), and Túm-i-Mir-Dost. From Nusratabád, it is twenty-three miles to the first place, fifty-three to the second, and eighty-eight to the third; from whence again it is about thirty-four miles further to Sekuha. Túm-i-Mir-Dost is, however, literally in Sistán. It is situated in the Shilah tract; south of the more thickly populated portion of the above province, and at the same elevation—namely, about 1250 feet above the sea. The general character of the country between Nusratabád and Sistán comprises somewhat lofty ranges of hills, running parallel with each other from N.W. to S.E., and separated by intervening level and half-desert plateaus, which afford grazing ground for the flocks of the nomad Balúchís. The first elevated range crossed after leaving Nusratabád has a watershed-line of 5300 feet, and leads with gradual descent on to the plain of Kilágh-áb, at 4550 feet. Granite and white marble were met with in these hills. The second occurs on leaving Kilágh-áb, and has a watershed-line of 4800 feet, from which there is a gradual descent on to another broad, stony plateau; and the third, which has a watershed-line of 5100 feet, intervenes between this plain and the camping-ground, called Túrsh-áb, which lies at an elevation of 3700 feet, from which spot there is a gradual descent on to the alluvial plain of Sistán. The desolation of the country through which we passed was complete. Between Nusratabád and Sistán we did not meet one single human being: and the only living things we saw were some ibex and mountain sheep. The halting-places above mentioned are determined entirely from their supply of water; but there are no human habitations, and the escort sent to meet us from Sistán had buried the provisions that would be required at each place. On quitting Nusratabád, the Governor of Bam and his following rode out with us a short way to take leave, and then returned to the Narmashír, taking with them a large mail for England. They went away in good spirits, having all received handsome presents for the services rendered to the Mission. The Káïn escort, to whose tender mercies we were now consigned, were a far wilder-looking lot than their predecessors; and on the cold, misty morning on which we first made their acquaintance—with their faces muffled up to the eyes, armed to the teeth with every conceivable species of offensive and defensive weapons, and mounted on camels and ponies, as wild and rugged as their riders—presented a most singular appearance. There is a solitary well at Kilágh-áb, situated in the middle of the plain of that name, which, say the natives, never runs dry. It is cut through a substratum of white rock, and is in the centre of a system of *kanáts*, which stretch on every side to the base of the surrounding hills, said to have been dug, in days long gone by, by the Parsis. A remarkable solitary rock, crowning a hill in the vicinity, is also pointed out as a spot where they used to expose their dead. The weather experienced between Nusratabád and Sistán was most trying. Heavy rain, snow, frost, and biting winds predominated; and our servants, no less than ourselves, were surprised and disappointed at the severity of what we had been led to believe would prove a very mild climate.

The wind, hail, and snow, through which we pursued our march between Kilágh-áb and Túrsh-áb, were indeed so severe that several of our camels died, and many of our servants arrived in camp in a semi-moribund state. The Persian Commissioner was quite unhinged, and his wretched Engineer was so shrivelled by the cold that he rattled inside his bright green gloves and top-boots like a nut in its shell. Luckily there was plenty of firewood (tamarisk) at the wells of Túrsh-áb, and the European members of the Mission, having pushed far ahead of the main body, had exercised themselves with such a will in procuring firewood for the perished following, that a gigantic bonfire was ready to welcome and to thaw each starving member of our melancholy retinue on arrival. As night fell on our motley camp in this valley, the scene was really very picturesque. The beautiful silvery background afforded by the feathery and snow-covered tamarisk; the numerous camp-fires, which shed a lurid glow on to the strange costumes and wild faces of our Balúch attendants; the mists driving continually across the open, and causing all objects to loom out in abnormal magnitude; the queer sounds and echoes which came rolling in from the surrounding darkness; the uncouth conglomeration of tongues; and, over all, the serenity of a moonlit though cloudy sky: these were elements of an admirable picture, to which however, nobody, at that time and in the then state of the thermometer, felt inclined to do much justice. Persian servants on the march are in truth admirable. Though the majority of them had arrived in camp, literally perished from cold and half-frozen, no sooner had they been thawed at the big fire, than we found our tents pitched, an excellent dinner prepared, and every possible arrangement made for passing the night in comfort. A really good Persian servant never thinks at the end of a march, under whatsoever conditions, of attending to his own wants until he has first provided for every conceivable necessity of his master, and in this respect is unequalled by servants of any other race.

From Túrsh-áb the road into Sistán descends for ten miles along the broad, stony bed of a stream, which at times must contain a very considerable volume of water, for it has cut itself a channel in many places more than 100 feet deep. The path then leaves the bed of the river, and turning abruptly to the left, emerges through some low mud hills on to a *bhúta*-covered plain, sloping to the north, from which we first got a glimpse of the renowned Kúh-i-Khwájah, rising far away to the N.W. It was about three miles from this spot, or eighteen from Túrsh-áb, that we first saw Sistán lying low before us, and looking very barren and desolate: as far as the eye could reach, there was no sign of life: a dense cloud of smoke on the horizon marked the burning of the reeds that erewhile choked the body of the lake; and an extraordinary white radiating cloud seemed also to shoot up into the heavens from the far away horizon. A further advance of about eight miles from the point at which we had first sighted the province, brought us, by a gradual descent over shingly ground, to the tract known as the 'Shilah.' The entrance on to the alluvial soil of Sistán from the stony ground to the W. and S.W. is indicated by a clear and well-defined line. Stones and pebbles suddenly and entirely cease; and, instead of *bhúta* and camel-thorn, the soft earth is covered with a dried-up, yellowish-looking grass, called *bannu* by the natives, on which our horses commenced to feed vigorously. This grass, however, though excellent food for sheep and cattle, is too salt to be used as regular forage for horses without much previous washing. It grows in vast quantities, owing to the immense fertility of the soil formerly deposited after the overflowing waters of the lake had receded; and the excellent pasturage thus afforded makes this tract of country a regular resort for the nomad Nharui Balúchis, who are in the habit of coming here regularly to pasture their flocks, and who used to take refuge on the slopes of the surrounding hills when driven away by the waters of the lake. Now that there has been no inundation for five years, it is feared that the crop of *bannu*, getting less and less, may soon cease altogether. The dried grass is regularly fired about a month before the Nau-Roz, and a fresh crop of young green shoots soon appears in its place. The natives pointed to the fact of its having so long survived the absence of water, as a proof of the immense richness and fertility of the original soil deposited. This plain, called the Zamin-i-Shilah, is as flat as the palm of the hand, and, as already stated, was, until five years ago, regularly submerged during a certain season in the year. There were apparently no landmarks by which we could guide our course, and certainly no vestige of a path to follow. Our adventures were thus described at the time by one of the members of the Mission:—'Continuing our route over the plain, and trusting blindly to the so-called geographical knowledge of our wild Balúch guide, at eight miles we came to a low, shallow sort of ditch or canal, about thirty yards wide, quite dry, and which is known as the Shilah (the general term in Sistán for the bed of a small rivulet), and which gives its name to the surrounding country. This ditch, the guides say, used in former days to connect the two Hámúns or Lakes of Sistán and Zirráh; but it is difficult now to determine whether the canal was originally natural or artificial. It was now getting quite dark: a keen, cold wind commenced to blow from the N.E.; there was no firewood, or any prospect of obtaining any; tents, mules, and camels were far away in the rear; and it became more and more evident that our guide had lost his way. We marched on aimlessly for mile after mile, but halted on coming to a deserted sheep-pen, where hedges of cut *bhúta* afforded the wherewithal for a bonfire and beacon to our lost companions, and we sent out scouts to reconnoitre the surroundings of our position. The Persian Commissioner and suite soon came up, and after a long interval Major Lovett arrived: he had lost his way, and was making up his mind for a night of solitude on the bleak, unsheltered plain, when the gleam of our bonfire caught his eye. The scouts returned to say that water and firewood were to be obtained at an encampment of nomad Balúchís close by, and we accordingly remounted and pushed on to a small clump of stunted tamarisk-bushes, which afforded sufficient firewood for a blaze to guide our missing mules, laden with the very material tents and provisions. Night, however, wore on with hourly increasing cold, and though stragglers kept dropping in with varying accounts of the proximity of the caravan, it did not make its appearance, and we had to make up our minds to spend the night in the open. The Persian Commissioner and his Engineer, more fortunate than we, offered to share with us the shelter of two small tents, which they had with them; but we all, regardless of the bitter cold, preferred the purer atmosphere to be found under the open heaven. Indeed, our position, though sufficiently chill and forlorn, had its amusing concomitants: and the woe-begone countenances of our servants, who had expected that on arrival in Sistán all their "desert" troubles would be over, no less than the extraordinary and indescribable costumes which they extemporised to keep out the bleak air, provoked constant roars of laughter. We soon had a fire blazing in our midst, and after a hearty *al fresco* dinner, disposed ourselves in a circle around it, wrapped in blankets, rugs, and saddlecloths, and found forgetfulness from cold and all sublunary cares in deep and well-merited repose. This march has proved the error, as perpetuated in many of the existing maps, that the route to Sistán from the south was over a sandy and nearly impracticable flat desert[1]. As will have been seen, from Nusratabád the road runs almost entirely over a mountainous country, with water and firewood obtainable at moderate intervals, and with gradients that could be easily made practicable for artillery or any wheeled conveyance.'

III. *Sistán.*

The first morning that dawned upon us in Sistán found us in rather a distressing plight, and it was perhaps as well that the solitude of our position protected us from the inquisitiveness of the native inhabitants, who, prone to judge by the eye alone as are all Orientals, might have formed opinions somewhat averse to the dignity of the Mission, had they discovered its members reposing on the plain, beds and rugs thick with hoar frost, and without servants, tents, or necessaries of any sort. The missing caravan however made its appearance about 9 A.M., and we all moved on for four miles further to a place called Cháh-i-Khák-i-Muhammad Darwish, where a saintly Dervish had been buried many years ago, and where there were two wells furnishing an abundant

---

[1] The itinerary of the march from Bam to Sistán was as follows:—

Date.	Stage.	Distance in Miles.	Direction.
1872.			
Jan. 12	Krúk	24	S.S.E.
	(Off the direct road to Sistán)		
,, 13	Azizábád	18	E.N.E.
,, 17	Kúhar Manzil	18	E. by N.
,, 18	Túm-i-Rig	4	N.E.
,, 19	Shor Gez	22	E.N.E.
	(Desert)		
,, 20	Gúrg	35	N.E.
,, 21	Nusratabád	37	19 due N. / 18 E.N.E.
,, 27	Kilágh-áb	23	N.E. by E.
,, 29	Túrsh-áb	30	N.E. by E.
,, 30	Túm-i-Mir-Dost	35	E.N.E.

246

supply of excellent water. The plain we traversed was covered with thick low tamarisk, and was a continuation of the Zamin-i-Shilah. It was regularly flooded by the lake until about five years ago, and still showed signs of its submersion. The guides say that the tamarisk has taken the place of the vast quantity of reeds formerly choking this portion of the lake, and the roots of which, though the stalks have dried up, still cover the level ground. We halted one day at these wells, during which time the severest cold was registered. In the night of the 31st January the barometer fell to 5° above zero, or 27° of frost, and at 8 o'clock in the morning was still 20° below freezing-point. Such weather as this the natives tell us is quite abnormal, though hard frost is the rule at this season. We all suffered much from the extreme cold, having made no preparations for a temperature of this severity, and our horses especially felt the exposure. We used our bell-tents, finding them warmer and more cosy than the larger ones, but even then, with three or four tamarisk charcoal fires burning under the canvas, and covered with everything we could lay hands on, the cold was so searching that it kept us awake at nights.

From the Dervish's well to Sekuha, which may be taken as the commencement of the thickly populated portion of Sistán, there is a distance of some 30 miles, for the greater part of which the road runs over a vast desert plain of dry alluvial soil, and through some of the countless ruins that cover the province in every direction, bewildering and perplexing the traveller by their extent and the impossibility of obtaining any reliable information as to their former history or the epoch of their prosperity. The principal ruins in this tract of country through which we passed were those of Kundar, about 5 miles from the Dervish's well, and those of Hauz-i-dár, 4 miles further on. These ruins were of great extent, and the houses and walls, built of sun-dried brick, were still standing in a state of excellent preservation. Kundar is said to have been deserted about 90 years ago, but Hauz-i-dár is of much greater antiquity. It need hardly be said that Sistán is a land which teems with romance, every spot being more or less connected with the great hero Rústam, his family, his exploits, and his sufferings. Hauz-i-dár is said to be the spot where the dead body of Firamurz, the son of Rústam, was impaled upon a stake by his enemy Bahram, the son of Isfandiar; and about 10 miles to the east another group of ruins, still called the Shahr-i-Sokhta (or burnt city), is pointed out as the remains of the famous city of Rústam, destroyed by Bahram, who, anticipating in this respect the later reported feats of the Paris *pétroleuses*, had the walls smeared with naphtha and then burnt. Two small hills about a mile apart are also pointed out to the south-west of Hauz-i-dár, as marking the site of the stable of the famous horse of Rústam. They are called the Pá-band and Akhor-i-Rakhsh, and denote the place of his manger and the spot where his head was tied. This is, however, but one of many places which boast a traditional stable of this gigantic animal. Near Hauz-i-dár we passed a very remarkable graveyard of ancient date, in which all the graves were built above ground, every occupant having a small oblong brick building to himself. Years ago the natives say it was the custom to bury the dead thus with all their valuables upon them, but it was found that this system gave such unusual facilities and temptations for sacrilegious robbery that recourse was had to the safer mode of interment: some skulls were knocking about in the graveyard, which, as we reflected, might possibly have witnessed the passage of Alexander's army. About 9 miles from Sekuha the road makes a singular ascent of some 60 or 70 feet on to a desert plain with hard gravelly soil, stretching from east to west and here about 3 miles broad, called the Dasht-i-Sangbar, which it is said formerly limited the southern overflow of the lake in this direction to the north. We crossed this elevated barrier and again descended to the same level as the plain on the other side, and saw the three hills of Sekuha rising in front at about 6 miles distance. To the east were high detached masses of clayey soil, apparently severed from the Dasht-i-Sangbar by the action of water, and to the west was the Kúh-i-Khwájah, backed up in the distance by the mountains of the Neh-Bandan. At some distance from Sekuha an attempt was made by the authorities of that town, who came out to meet us, to direct us to a place called Viramad, some 7 miles to the west-north-west, on the ground that Sekuha was an inconvenient halting-place for a variety of reasons; but Sir F. Goldsmid decided on adhering to his original destination. The Náib or Zábit who headed the cavalcade, a fine-looking man of some 38 years of age, was mounted on a very fine chesnut Túrkman horse; and he and his attendants, some of whom wore buttons of the 4th Bengal Cavalry, performed marvels of horsemanship in jumping the numerous ditches and deep water-courses with which the country was completely scored: one rider, a most truculent ruffian, with bright red moustaches and whiskers, was pointed out to us as being literally a host in himself, being at any time considered equal to the somewhat formidable odds of 1000 to 1. This taste for jumping somewhat surprised us, as though the Persians are undeniably good, plucky, and firm horsemen, and will perform almost any *tour-de-force* on horseback, they generally have the strongest objection to riding over any ditch or wall, however small it may be. The ground in the neighbourhood of Sekuha is as bad as bad can be, cut up in every direction with water-courses, with banks which are completely rotten, owing it is said to the effect of the constant wind which hollows out the soil; so that it was with extreme difficulty that we found a place sufficiently hard and dry to render camping possible. We had, moreover, no sooner congratulated ourselves on having done so, than we discovered that the ground allotted to us had the cemetery on the one hand, and on the other a stream used for washing the dead, a ceremony which appeared, by the broken ice, to have been lately completed. This rendered necessary a speedy change of locality, and we were fortunate enough to find two enclosures with walls to protect us from the bitter wind, and still more from the obtrusive though natural curiosity of the populace. The Persian Commissioner rode off in triumph to comfortable quarters inside the fort. Our camels and mules got bogged in the broken ground, and had to remain out all night; and one of the baggage horses dropped down dead—presumably from the severe cold.

The town of Sekuha, which derives its name from three clay or mud hills in its midst, is built in an irregular circular form around the base of the two principal hills. The southernmost of these hills is surmounted by the *ark* or citadel, an ancient structure known as the citadel of Mir Kuchak Khán (the grandfather of Sardár Ali Khán); which is at present neither armed nor garrisoned, though kept in excellent repair. Adjoining this and connected with it, is the second hill called the Búrj-i-Falaksar, on which stands the present Governor's house; and about 150 yards to the west is the third hill, not so high as the other two, undefended and with no buildings on it but a mud caravanserai. The two principal hills thus completely command the town lying at their base, and are connected with one another by a covered way. Sekuha is quite independent of an extra-mural water supply, as water is always obtainable by digging a few feet below the surface anywhere inside the walls, which are twenty-five feet high, strongly built of mud and in good repair. The houses are half dome-shaped and half flat-roofed, and we noticed that in almost every courtyard were tethered two or more excellent donkeys. The population, which is somewhat migratory, numbers about 5000 all told, living in 1200 houses. The inhabitants are entirely engaged in agriculture, there being no manufactures of any kind, and are grossly ignorant of all matters unconnected with Sistán. In this ignorance they take a singular pride, and the Náib of the place told us that being a simple Sistání he knew nothing whatever; did not know his own age, the division of time, or the meaning of tables and chairs, rice and potatoes; but much of this blindness was doubtless simulated. The gardens outside the town, surrounded with high mud walls to protect them against the wind, produce excellent melons and grapes, with some mulberries and pomegranates; and we noticed several solitary trees of considerable growth, demonstrating, as it were, that times had changed since Conolly asserted that not a single tree was to be found in Sistán[1]. The people seemed darker in colour than their Persian neighbours, with a more decidedly Indian cast of countenance; their language is a species of debased Persian, somewhat similar to that spoken in Khúrasán. The climate of Sekuha is said to be the best in Sistán during the summer, and its distance from the bed of the lake renders it free from the countless myriads of mosquitoes bred therein. The town has no garrison of Persian soldiers, and pays no revenue; the ground belongs to the Chief for the time being, who takes one-third of the whole produce. Since Táj Muhammad Khán has been kept in Tehrán, they say however that the place has lost all its former importance, which has been transferred to the new city called Nasirabád lately founded by the Amir of Káin. The Governor's mansion on the Búrj-i-Falaksar is a very handsome building in the regular Tehrán style, quite worthy of a chieftain of rank. It was, indeed, built by Tehrán architects as a residence for the royal bride of Sardár Ali Khán, whom he brought here with him in 1859; but after the murder of the unfortunate Sardár in 1861 by his nephew Táj Muhammad Khán, the palace was left unfinished.

The Mission halted at Sekuha two days, during which time visits were interchanged between the Commissioners; and Mirza Ma'súm Khán here first commenced a repetition of his Balúchistán behaviour. Up to this point he had been a most agreeable and cheerful travelling

[1] In some part of the province, too, the tamarisk was found to have attained a very respectable size.

companion, prophesying that all would go well in Sistán, and that his influence would smooth away any difficulties that might arise. His good-humour during the march, and endeavours to secure our comfort and facilitate our marching arrangements, had somewhat lulled our suspicions to rest, and caused us to hope that, repenting him of his former trickeries, he had intended to act in as straightforward a manner as was possible to him. How absolutely and grossly we were deceived will appear in the latter course of this narrative. Nothing too severe can be said as to his conduct from the moment in which he first came within the immediate influence of the Amir of Káïn, whose power terrified him, and whose constant bribes excited his intense cupidity; and most keenly had we all to repent that this man, who in official matters displayed the low cunning and base trickery of the very worst class of petty attorneys, should have again been permitted to act as Commissioner on a mission of such importance. His very insignificance made him an easy tool in the hands of the Amir of Káïn, and the impunity with which he had escaped from all consequences of his Balúchistán conduct emboldened him to attempt an even more reprehensible course of action on this occasion. From the moment we reached Sekuha to the day when (six weeks later) we finally quitted the province, he never for one single instant ceased in his endeavours to thwart the entire proceedings of the Mission, to nullify the acts of the British Arbitrator, and to throw discredit and distrust upon the whole of the British officers and employés; and when after six weeks of this behaviour Sir Frederic Goldsmid had, with an extraordinary display of patience and forbearance and determination, all but succeeded in initiating some sort of formal enquiry, he suddenly left the province for Tehrán without even having once met the Afghán Commissioner, who had been deputed to confer with him. At Sekuha he commenced proceedings by bringing forward a trumped-up complaint against our old guide, Hájji Abdullah Khán, to the effect that he had openly said to the inhabitants of the town that all things were to be changed now the English had arrived in Sistán—for we were to burn their fathers, dishonour their households, and so forth. The charge was found, of course, utterly insusceptible of proof, but it was an earnest of what was to follow.

On February 4, we left Sekuha for our next stage, Chelling, the weather continuing bitterly cold. Chelling is but six miles in a direct line from Sekuha, but the constant *détours*, rendered necessary by the intervention of several irrigating canals and deep ditches, prolonged our march to ten miles at least. The bridges met with were of the most primitive and insecure nature, and the baggage animals experienced the greatest difficulty in the passage of the canals, which are very deep, with treacherous sides and muddy bottoms. We marched over a hard clayey ground alternated with patches of soft alluvial soil. Before reaching Chelling the large village of Sádiki is passed, containing some 300 houses, without walls or fort, and surrounded by extensive cultivation. Chelling is a large village of some 350 houses, with a square fort and one round tower in the middle, forming a capital landmark. The village is of very ancient date, but the fort was commenced by Muhammad Razá Khán and finished by Sardár Ali Khán. It is situated on the banks of the principal canal which draws off the waters of the Helmand for irrigating purposes, and which is at this point some thirty feet wide and six feet deep, with a current of about one mile an hour, supplying the whole of the surrounding district with water. This canal passes by Deshtak, and flows past Chelling in the direction of the Kúh-i-Khwájah, emptying eventually into the bed of the old lake whatever water may remain unexhausted. It was said to abound with fish, which the abnormal cold had driven to seek an asylum in the mud at the bottom. Much of the country traversed on this march was covered with *kirta,* a species of high yellow grass, which we were told, in contradiction of Conolly's account, formed most excellent food for horses and cattle. The air was alive with immense flocks of waterfowl, principally large grey geese, teal, wild duck, and plover; and a pair of very large owls were shot by one of our party, with plumage resembling that of a sparrow-hawk, and splendid yellow black eyes.

We were surprised to find encamped in the vicinity of the village nearly 1000 families of Barbaris, who stated that they had come here from the other side of Balkh, and were many of them hardly distinguishable from Chinese. Though apparently in the last stage of poverty, and supporting themselves entirely by begging, it was said that in their own country some of them were men of property and substance, but that the dangers incidental to travel in these little-known countries caused them to leave all behind and take to begging. They were Shia'hs like the rest of the Sistánís, and were on a pilgrimage to Mash-had, and thence to Karbala. Their women were all unveiled, and their language was the debased Persian spoken in Sistán, where they had already been three months when we saw them, subsisting on charity and awaiting the termination of the cold weather to make a start. We were again unsuccessful in finding any traces of Ferrier; but the natives here, as elsewhere, confessed to absolute ignorance on every conceivable subject, answered no questions, and would understand neither the nature of money nor the value or appearance of a *krán*. A solitary date-palm is noticeable at this place which bears no fruit, and the soil around the village is too salt for much cultivation.

From Chelling we marched thirteen miles to Nasírabád, the new capital of Sistán, after a night made hideous by the discordant row accompanying the passage of the camels over the neighbouring canals. Three got bogged, and as two others tumbled in bodily with all their loads, the screams and objurgations of the disconsolate drivers kept us awake all night. Before leaving camp, however, the Persian Commissioner commenced the discussion of what may be called the 'great flag question'—one destined to remain a 'burning' question during the whole of our stay in the province, to be the occasion of an endless and heartbreaking correspondence, and to remain unsettled as an ever open 'raw' until two days before the final departure of the Mission. It may be explained in a very few words. During the Balúchistán Mission of the previous year, and in the present Mission up to this date, Sir Frederic Goldsmid had always had the Union Jack flown from a portable flag-staff pitched in front of his tent or quarters. This had been done with the full knowledge and consent of the British Legation and the Persian authorities at Tehrán; and whereas last year the Persian Commissioner had not provided himself with a flag, this year, on our arrival at Bam, we found a Lion-and-Sun standard of the most approved and remarkable description flaunting in front of his quarters. In this tacit but friendly understanding, until the two Commissioners had entered Sistán, the flags were duly floated over their respective camps; though it may be remarked that the acute Persian Diplomatist had taken care to have his flag-staff made at least two or three feet higher than that of the English Commissioner. Now, however, all was to be changed. Very early on the morning of February 5, Mirza Ma'súm Khán sent us a letter requesting that the British flag might not be hoisted, as it gave rise to the most undesirable suspicions in the minds of the Sistánís with regard to our intentions in coming to Sistán. No proof whatever was adduced as to this, and the gross ignorance of the inhabitants on general matters rendered it extremely unlikely that they should have special information on the subject of the symbolic properties of a flag; but the matter was a convenient one with which to commence making difficulties, and as before said, the question was never allowed to drop during the remainder of our stay in the province.

The country over which we passed on this march was greatly cut up by canals, some of them long since out of use, and having in general a very desolate appearance. At two miles from Chelling extensive ruins, bearing the curious name of Chang-i-Múrghán[1], were noted; and seven miles further we observed the whole surface of the country covered with great heaps of blown sand, lining each side of the road up to the walls of Nasírabád. Our reception at Nasírabád was very peculiar. We had all put on undress uniform, expecting a somewhat ceremonious reception; and as we approached the walls a great body of horsemen that had lain concealed under their shadow came rapidly forward to our *rencontre*. These men were armed with every conceivable species of musket, rifle, spear, sword, shield, and known and unknown weapon of offence and defence. They came on, headed by Sardár Sharif Khán[2] and Sardár Khán Bábá

---

[1] *Changi-múrghán*—the talon of birds. I do not attempt to explain its application.—F. J. G.

[2] At the time of Dost Muhammad Khán's death, he left a young son, Darvish Khán, then ten years old, who in the ordinary course of things would have succeeded to the chieftainship. Sardár Sharif Khán, however, taking advantage of his nephew's youth, married his brother's widow, and himself usurped the power.

This Sardár Sharif Khán is a Nharui Balúch, son of Alam Khán (who was the son of Mirza Khán). Alam Khán was the chief who constructed the Burj-i-Alam Khán, which was situated on the banks of an extensive hollow, known as the Sabz-i-Kúm, yearly filled with water brought by a canal from the Helmand. Within the last thirty years or so (1872), the supply has dried up, and the ground thus left is now completely under cultivation, and is beyond measure rich and fertile, returning an ample profit to Sharif Khán. After this, Dost Muhammad Khán, Sharif Khán's brother, built another fort on a small hill called the Kala'h-i-Nau, about four miles distance. On his death, about 1857, Sharif Khán inherited the chiefdom and occupied this fort, which is now very populous, containing more than 1000 houses. He has also another fort called Kimak, containing about 300 houses and built on two hills. Sharif Khán is the only chief remaining who has any power in this part of Sistán, having about 3000 people of all tribes who obey his orders. He is however completely in the hands of the Persians, whose pretensions he favours, and he has married his daughter to the son of the Amir of Kúm. He is a very pleasant-looking old gentleman about fifty-five years old, with gold spectacles and a long beard. His power is as nothing compared with that

Khán—some of the number detaching themselves from the line, galloping furiously about, firing their muskets in the air, and uttering piercing shouts. They then halted as we approached, and, as both flanks wheeled inwards, we suddenly found ourselves in the centre of a yelling, squealing and kicking crowd of equally unmanageable horses and horsemen. There was no better course, however, than to take things calmly, and—though we were one and all in imminent danger of having our legs broken by the kicking brutes around us—to look as if we liked it. Thus we remained halted for a few minutes, while the Persian Commissioner, in a loud voice, read out the names and titles of the English Commissioner and his staff[1]. The cavalcade was then again put in motion, to conduct us to the city, about half a mile distant, and matters became worse and worse: the kicking, shouting, laughing crowd surrounded us on every side in a state of indescribable confusion, each man being desperately eager for a closer inspection of the strange Faringís. We soon became separated one from another, and had not Captain Lovett's horse luckily, from time to time, cleared a circle within his heels wherein we might reunite, we should have had to enter the city singly and at intervals. As it was, Mr. Rosario, the apothecary, resplendent in gold lace and stripes, with spurs, and perhaps a little too much of a magnificent pair of antigropelos, completely disappeared for some moments, and was next discovered on the extreme right flank, at the head of a number of laughing *sowárs*, whom, it might be conjectured, from his flourishes and gesticulations he was leading on to imaginary victory. He explained afterwards that he had gravitated to this point entirely by the force of circumstances. It is probable that the whole population had been turned out for our reception; for on entering the gates of the town, which were strongly guarded by *sarbáz*, or infantry, the streets were found to be nearly empty. We were conducted to the quarters prepared for the

of the Chakhansúr chief. The best but somewhat farcical description of Sharif Khán's present appearance would be, for Englishmen, that he exactly resembles the figure in the advertisement which recommends the excellences of the Nabob Pickle to the London Public.

The two principal sons of Sardár Sharif Khán are: Saíyid Khán, whose mother is the sister of Rustam Khán Sarbandi, and who occupies the fort of Nád Ali; and Muhammad Ali Khán, whose mother is the sister of Ibráhim Khán of Chakhansúr. This youth afterwards quarrelled with his father and went to Kábul.

[1] Before we arrived at the town, we were met by an old woman burning dried cowdung on an iron plate to avert the evil eye. Conolly mentions a practice similar to this.

Mission in a wretched mud house, inside a courtyard, with a tank in the centre, while the Persian Commissioner rode off to his quarters, which were infinitely superior and very comfortable; and we at once found that, owing to the question of the flag, we could obtain no allotment of ground on which to pitch our camp, though repeated messages were sent expressive of the General's wishes on this matter. These were replied to by a letter, enclosing one from the Amir of Káïn to the Persian Commissioner, in which he stated that the Múllas and Sáiyids were so fanatical in Sistán, that a general massacre would probably take place were the English flag to be hoisted, and for which he must hold the British Commissioner in that case responsible. No one was sent by the Amir to make the usual 'ahwál pûrsi,' or health enquiries, on this day, and other small evidences were not wanting to indicate the existence of hostile feelings: so that night fell on our first residence in the capital of Sistán, leaving a prevalent feeling that we were no longer in the country of friends.

We were halted in Nasírabád ten days in all, during the greater part of which time many little things were done by the Persian authorities with the evident intention of slighting the British Commissioner. The Sardár, Khán Bábá Khán, and Hájji Yáwar Khán, the Amir's factotum, called on the morning of the first day with the usual polite enquiries; and during the visit Sir F. Goldsmid took occasion to present the Sardár with a musical snuff-box, which he admired: but this was returned in the afternoon, with a note saying that the Sardár was sorry he had so far forgotten himself as to accept a present so unworthy of a warrior! Our quarters too were found, on closer inspection, to be utterly wretched and dirty, surrounded on every side by houses, which completely overlooked us, and rendered privacy impossible; while the Persian Commissioner's, on the other hand, were most spacious, airy, comfortable, clean, and perfectly private. Difficulties also arose about paying the first visit, and it was not until the 12th of February, or seven days after our arrival in Nasírabád, that General Goldsmid first met the Amir in his own house; but previously to this Captains Smith and Lovett had visited the Amir by the British Commissioner's order, and the Amir's son had called on the British Commissioner, who then himself paid a first visit to the Amir, which was returned the next day: but even here the Amir found means to be uncourteous. After having appointed an early hour for the visit, and having kept Sir F. Goldsmid and his staff waiting for him over an hour, he sent an excuse, postponing the visit until the afternoon, on the ground of sickness[1]. Again, our old guide, Hájji Abdullah Khán, was threatened that he would be killed if he did not instantly quit the province; and the men of his own tribe, the Shárikís, told him they were afraid to be seen speaking to him. Lastly, during the whole of this time, a constant correspondence (about ten letters a day) was going on about the Flag, and the reiterated demand for a place whereon we might pitch our camp was persistently declined. It was evident that the Persian Commissioner was playing a double game; decreasing the dignity of the British General to enhance his own; taking bribes from the Amir of Káïn to play into his hands; spreading distrust and suspicion broadcast among the inhabitants; thwarting all proposals for departure to inspect the province, or for the commencement of any sort of enquiry; attempting to establish unfriendly relations with the Amir, and all the while himself professing the most boundless devotion to the British Commissioner.

During the detention of the Mission in this species of prison, opportunity was taken to ride over the neighbouring country in the immediate vicinity of the town—though at no great distance from the walls, as a mounted escort was always sent by the Amir whenever any of the members ventured out. The weather was bitterly cold, and on the morning of the 8th February the ground was thickly covered with snow, a fact rarely observed in this province, and proving the abnormal severity of the winter.

The new Fort or Town of Nasírabád, simply called the 'Shahr,' or town, by the natives of the province, is built in the shape of a quadrangle, with very strong and high mud walls, having towers at regular intervals along its face, and surrounded on all sides by a deep wet ditch of considerable breadth, between which and the walls a covered way, some twelve feet broad, leads all round the fort. The present fort measures, according to a rough calculation, 400 by 500 yards, and is called by the natives the Shahr-i-Kadím (old city), in contradistinction to the Shahr-i-Nau (new city), which is gradually being built contiguous to it, and to mark the limits of which a mud wall has been

---

[1] It should here be added that in lieu of the Amir, Mirza Ma'súm Khán himself appeared full of arguments and explanations; and that when the Amir came in the afternoon, though the British Commissioner was personally disinclined to receive his visit, his manner was hardly that of a man giving intentional offence.—F. J. G.

raised, prolonging the sides of the Shahr-i-Kadím, and with a face to the north. The dimensions of this new fort will be about 1000 yards by 600 yards, and it will enclose an area of nearly half a square mile. Within this space the ancient Sistán village of Húsainabád has been enclosed; a fact which has apparently occasioned some confusion in India, for, in a report by Colonel Phayre, the Persians are described as strengthening a fort named Húsainabád, on the banks of the Helmand, near Traku, whereas the allusion is evidently to this rising city of Nasírabád. The new town is almost entirely populated by people from Káïn and Khúrasán, but the village of Húsainabád contains original Sistání inhabitants. Twenty-thousand people were driven by famine into the province last year, from Persia, and have of course received every possible inducement to settle down, and so propagate Persian influence; and all the necessaries of life are cheap and abundant. The quasi-modern capital, though quite close to the populous and fertile portion of the province, has been built in the middle of a most desolate tract of country. The bed of the old lake bounds it on the west side. At the time we were there no lake existed, and the road to the Kúh-i-Khwájah was quite dry. But though there was nowhere anything like a continuous expanse of water, all the lower ground was filled with muddy brackish water in which myriads of waterfowl assembled. Their abundance may be judged from the fact that fat wild ducks were selling at about 15 for the *krán*, or about three farthings each.

The Governor of Sistán, Amir of Káïn, Hashmat-ul-Múlk, and Amir-i-Túmán, is a tall fine-looking man, of some forty-five years old, rather dark, with a countenance principally noticeable for the immense size of the jaw bones, which project from his face like fins. He wears a thick moustache, is not unlike the Shah, and his expression—though somewhat stern and cruel, with a want of frankness in it—can at times be made very courteous and engaging. On the occasion of the first visit paid him by Captains Lovett and Smith, he was dressed in a magnificent Kashmír robe trimmed with sable, and seated in an upstairs room inside the inner citadel of the Shahr-i-Kadím, carpeted with unusually handsome rugs, and hung round with pistols and guns, the recesses of the mantel-piece being filled with bullets. On this occasion he expressed himself very jealous of the proceedings of the Mission, and especially suspicious as to Colonel Pollock's presence with the Afghán Commissioner, which he seemed to think intimated a foregone adverse conclusion on the part of the British Government. His views with regard to Sistán he expressed with much frankness. He intended to make it the garden of Persia. Men had been sent for to Tehrán to instruct the inhabitants in the cultivation of the potato, orange, date-palm, tobacco, and other plants—as he was of opinion that the soil of Sistán would produce every fruit or vegetable known to man; and excellent melons, grapes, mulberries and pomegranates had already been grown there. Artificers, he added, had been engaged to teach the ignorant people their various trades. The Amir confirmed the account of the deadly nature of the flies during the hot weather, when venomous insects and reptiles abound; but he said the report of the fatality of the climate as regards horses was exaggerated. They required careful looking after, and always to be covered up from head to tail, when they would live if they were kept in regular work and not allowed to be idle. He pointed to the presence of his 400 cavalry in proof of this, and we ourselves did not find our horses suffer either at this time or afterwards. He was anxious to know the meaning of the various military terms used in the English army, such as 'troop,' 'squadron,' 'battalion,' 'company,' and the like, and had one Sikh Havildar (sergeant), and probably some ancient *pandies* in his service. About the 'mitrailleuse' he also expressed great curiosity. He said his artillery was excellently served. He had four light brass pieces of field artillery mounted, and one unmounted. It being explained to him that the only map of Sistán extant was that drawn by Conolly, some thirty years ago, he said another Englishman had been there since, who had been murdered by Ibráhím Khán of Chakhansúr (alluding to Dr. Forbes), and he himself remembered a Faringí travelling in Afghánistán, who, from his description, must have been Ferrier.

On the 13th February, during the return visit paid by the Amir to the British Commissioner, it was arranged that Sir F. Goldsmid, accompanied by the Persian Commissioner, should go on a tour of inspection through the province, and up the Helmand, travelling in a very light marching order, and leaving all the heavy tents and *impedimenta* in Nasírabád; but, as we were not to start till the 15th, the Amir took the opportunity of inviting the Commissioner and his staff to a shooting party and breakfast, at a place about three miles distant, known as the Tapah-i-Rig, on the banks of the Húsainabád canal. We arrived at the *rendezvous* before the Amir, who came attended by a large mounted retinue, and with the sons of two Balúch chiefs, holding forts on the Helmand (which we afterwards visited), who had acknowledged allegiance to Persia, and who were this day evidently paraded with the purpose of declaring their love for Persian rule before the British arbitrator. A number of falcons were brought out to hawk the game, but on this occasion no game of any sort was to be seen; and, after wandering about in a desultory manner for an hour or so, we all returned to spacious silk tents pitched on the banks of the canal. The breakfast was not served till three hours after our return to the tents, but, when it did appear, came in extraordinary profusion. There were fifty-seven different sorts of eatables, to be washed down by twenty-seven various *sharbats* and sauces, and there were several lambs roasted whole, which were torn to pieces by the Persians with their fingers, though we were allowed to use knives and forks. Hungry as we were, our united effort made but little impression on the vast mass of victual, but, on our retiring into another tent for pipes and coffee, the servants came in and in a short time demolished it all, to the last crumb. It is almost incredible the amount a hale-bodied Persian servant will eat under these circumstances. After breakfast we sat on the banks of the canal, drinking coffee and inspecting each other's guns and pistols, while our india-rubber boat was also inflated and experimented upon. On this occasion the Amir, in a very pointed way, showed us a double-barrelled gun with the name of 'Sturman, London' engraved in gold letters on the barrel, which he assured us he valued very much, having obtained it from Kabúl, at great trouble and expense, and that it was the property of the English Lord (Sir W. Macnaghten) who had been murdered by Akbar Khán. This was probably not the case, but there can be no doubt that many relics of our unfortunate countrymen still find a ready sale in these regions. The Amir gave us some interesting particulars concerning Sher Ali's son, Muhammad Ya'kúb Khán, who had passed through the province the previous year, on his way to Herát. He was his guest at Nasírabád for two months, living inside the fort, while his 2000 followers were encamped outside the walls. He was described as excessively intelligent and sharp, but without much personal daring[1]. All the Persians present joined in saying that

---

[1] Allusion has been made to the breakfast with the Amir of Káin in the Introductory Chapter. *Vide* also Frontispiece to volume.

Herát had been delivered to him through the unpopularity of the then governor, whose Pish-Khidmat killed him and his son on the same day; and that the town, which they all said they infinitely preferred to Kabúl or Kándahár, could never be taken by force, but only fall through famine or treachery: and we found that this high opinion of Herát was universal. The Amir was on this occasion very curious on the subject of our opium traffic with China, which he said ought to be put down by the Chinese Government.

We left Nasírabád on the 15th February, heartily glad to get away from what so closely resembled an imprisonment within the confined limits of our wretched quarters. The only man of our party never allowed to rest was Mr. Rosario, who was eternally engaged in doctoring and patching up the too willing patients that flocked to him in great numbers. His knowledge was supposed to be as limitless as his good-nature, and questions on the most delicate subjects were confidently submitted for his decision. He was not even at a loss when asked in the most earnest manner whether riding with short or long stirrups was the more conducive to long life and happiness: but when, after some consideration, the verdict was given in favour of long stirrups, our excellent oracle, probably remembering the legal maxim, did not state any reasons for this important and thoughtful decision. Up to this time the question of our colours still remained unsettled, though a large document purporting to bear the seal of fourteen Múllas had been sent in to the Amir, protesting against the flag being hoisted. No news had been heard of Colonel Pollock and the Afghán Commissioner; and the season was getting so advanced that it was absolutely necessary to gain some idea of the geography of the province before the rapidly-increasing heat should render travelling impossible.

We started for our tour of inspection in the very lightest marching order—tents, baggage, and followers being reduced to a minimum—and so affording no ground for even simulated apprehension on the part of the Persian authorities or timid Sistán inhabitants. The entire party was in charge of the Yáwar Azád Khán, the confidant and factotum of the Amir, who was armed with the despotic powers of his master, and who certainly did not show any great desire to aid the British Commissioner in a thorough investigation of geographical or other evidence material to the success of the Mission. He travelled, as was natural, with the Persian Commissioner, whom he toadied to the top of his bent, and of course arranged in concert with him the plan of procedure. Under such auspices it was not strange that very much that should have been seen was left unseen : and the direction of our daily marches was practically dependent upon this gentleman's pleasure. At any time the whole of the cultivated part of the province of Sistán could have been submerged by cutting the network of the innumerable large and small canals, and progress of any sort thus rendered impossible ; and it was easy to plead that 'the floods were out' whenever Sir F. Goldsmid wished to go to any village or spot not deemed open to his inspection by the Persian authorities. Nevertheless, though our various camping-places and the line of our march were thus entirely under Persian superintendence; though our every action was jealously watched and scrutinised; and though it was quite impossible to obtain any trustworthy, oral, or documentary evidence bearing on the objects of the enquiry, and every peasant in the province was terrified to be seen talking to us; this march up the Helmand could not fail to be productive of much valuable information. By it we learnt how completely successful had been the able measures taken by the Amir of Káin to thoroughly Persianise the whole of the province on the west bank of the river; how thoroughly the old Balúch chiefs in the vicinity, with the exception of Chakhansúr and Lásh Juwain, were inclined to play into his hands, and how contented with the present state of affairs, or at least *insouciant* of change, were the general inhabitants. We were enabled too to gain some idea of the wonderful fertility of Sistán; and to appreciate the ease with which a very large body of Eastern troops could be kept here where supplies of all sorts are obtainable in profusion [1], and where water never fails. There was little doubt on our minds that under Persian rule the resources of Sistán had been wonderfully augmented, and that they were still capable, owing to the system of irrigation, of immense development; and the quantity of grain that could be grown in the province must be simply enormous. The climate during the summer would appear to be trying; and the Yáwar, a very thin spare man, endeavoured to give us

---

[1] Prices are as follows in Sistán :—

Wheat	.. .. ..	4 Tabrizi manns	..	1 krán.
Barley	.. .. ..	1 ditto ditto	..	4 shahis.
Chaff	.. .. ..	100 ditto ditto	..	5 kráns.
Roghan or Ghí	.. ..	1 ditto ditto	..	3 kráns.

N.B.—One Tabrizi mann equals about six and a half pounds.

some idea of the fact, by saying that whenever he sat down in that season, the parched-up earth around him became at once a small swamp of mud, owing to the excess of perspiration—a statement corroborated by his wasted appearance: but for the winter months of the year the climate is very pleasant, and the wind which, commencing two months after the Nau-Roz, blows for 120 days, renders that further period sufficiently bearable. It is only when this has ceased, and the heat and insects absolutely dominate the situation, that existence becomes a burden; and even the Sistánís themselves acknowledge that at such time there may possibly be pleasanter places in the world than their beloved province. A difficulty which some years ago might have been found, in the scarcity of firewood, to the retention of a large body of men, is now much lessened by the rapid spread of the tamarisk over the ground occupied by the old lake, so that we never experienced a deficiency in this respect; and, as we stated elsewhere, the fatality of the climate as regards horses and cattle is much less severe than described. The number of horses found all over the province, where in Conolly's time this animal was a rare creature indeed, sufficiently proves this assertion. Another extraordinary change in Sistán is the drying up of the lake, which can be no longer held to exist. It does not appear difficult to account for the circumstance. For some three years before our arrival the drought had been terrific: the smaller feeders of the lake, the Farah-rúd, the Adraskand, the Khásh-rúd, and their still smaller tributaries, had either not filled at all after the winter season, or in such a very moderate degree that their outflow into the lake was not sufficient to provide for the amount of water lost in the immense annual evaporation; while the Helmand, the principal feeder, instead of as in former years bursting after the winter through its *band,* and rushing northward into the lake by its proper bed above Chakhansúr, had been completely diverted into the great canal by the permanent *band* constructed by the Amir at Kúhak; and whatever overflow might escape over or through the *band* would not now probably arrive at the north-eastern bed of the old lake at all. The consequence is that, in time, the bed of the lake, which is to a great extent still covered with detached pools of stagnant water, will, if the present state of affairs continue, become completely dried up and a large area of immensely fertile soil be thus redeemed for cultivation; while the whole conditions of life in the province will undergo a very marked change—though it is difficult to imagine Sistán without its

SERPENTS AND BIRDS.

plague of insects and its countless myriads of snakes and water-fowl[1].

During our whole stay in the province, we found Conolly's journal

---

[1] The following is a literatim description given by inhabitants of some of the more common snakes and birds in Sistán. No pretension is made to scientific detail or arrangement. The record is, of course, a rough, hearsay statement.

SERPENTS IN SISTAN.

Shutar-már. One yard to two yards, Persian, in length. Ashy green colour. Not very venomous. Called the Camel Snake from its length; and about four inches in circumference.

Már-Kháni. Blood snake. Half-a-yard in length. Has a scarlet line from head to tail, on an ashy ground. White belly. If it sting any one, blood is said to issue from all the extremities. The poison is believed to be incurable, but not instantaneously fatal.

Már-Ja'fari. Flame colour with red. Spotted. Half-a-yard in length. Instantaneously fatal. Derives its name from its having been given an asylum in the sleeve of Imám Jafar Sadik (sixth Imám) when pursued by another snake. As soon as the pursuing snake was driven away the sheltered one bit the Prophet.

Parlah-már. Half-a-yard in length, very thick round the body. Dark green colour. Sits on its tail and springs ten or twelve yards at a time after its prey, men or animals. Its spring has force enough to knock a man down. Poison very fatal. (*sic.*)

Shikári-már. White ground with black spots. Lives in herbs and shrubs, and catches small birds. Not fatal to man. Half-a-yard long.

Khák-már. Short and thick, thick tail, instantaneously fatal, dark blue colour.

Dosák-már. Has two heads, one at each end, one larger than the other. Grey colour. Half-yard long. Acts with the larger head. Very rare. Not very poisonous. (*sic.*)

Sag-már. Thick body, half-a-yard in length, pursues men, white belly, grey back.

N.B.—Owing to the extreme cold we were able to procure but very few specimens of the Serpent tribe.

BIRDS IN SISTAN.

Kaftar-i-Sail. The Pigeon of the Rapids. White breast and back, grey wings, beak fine and white. Lives on the banks of canals and rivers, catches fish. Lays its eggs after the Nau-Roz (March 21st). When twenty or thirty collect together, it is a sure sign that rapids or floods are coming in two or three days. Generally comes to the province the month before the Nau-Roz.

The Saká, or Water Carrier. Sistán name, *Camao.* White body, very large, long legs, long beak, long neck. Under its throat is a large bag, which contains much water. Comes from Astrakhán. When flying it fills its bag with water and precedes all other birds, generally geese; supplying water from its store from time to time.

Murghábi Andak. Sistan, *Sabz-gardan.* The common wild duck.

Koh. Swan. Comes from Astrakhán, and remains in Sistán. Lays its eggs near the water. Somewhat rare. Feathers sell in Sistán for fifteen *kráns* the *mann*; at Tehrán for five *tumáns.*

Taghalak. The Grebe. Continually diving.

Teal. Wild Geese.

Chaór. Black. The common coot. To be seen in myriads.

Máhi Marwárid. The pearl or white fish.

of such incalculable advantage to us, in furnishing the kind of detailed information most useful to travellers in a quite unknown country, that it has been deemed advisable, in describing our halts and wanderings in Sistán subsequent to February 14 and up to March 12, when we finally quitted the province, to quote from the journal kept at the time by one of the members of the Mission. This will, it is believed, convey a correct idea of our daily life and experience, and also serve to indicate the sort of petty annoyances and small subterfuges by which the Persian authorities strove to render nugatory all attempts at straightforward enquiry:—

'Thursday, February 15, 1872. Marched to Deshtak, fourteen miles in a general south-south-east direction, passing by Bahrámabád. Morning bright, but the great heat of the sun[1], as the day advanced, made the shelter of our tents on arrival very agreeable. We take only our mules, horses, and small tents on with us, leaving our camels and heavy baggage under the charge of the Farásh Báshi and ten *faráshes*; and at Ma'súm Khán's request both flags remain behind: for we are supposed to be travelling *en chapari* or "post," without any state, and no "led horses." As soon as we cleared Nasírabád, some of our servants put up a hyena, and a number of them started off in pursuit, Captain Lovett eventually succeeding in running it through with his regulation sword. Once dead, its stomach was cut out by one of the younger of the servants, as being an infallible love-charm; while the whole of its hair was speedily cut off by one of the *jalwadárs* or grooms, as being an equally infallible remedy against retention of urine in a horse: in the latter case the hair is burnt under the belly of the animal afflicted, and the result is said to be marvellous. The road clears the outlying cultivation of Nasírabád at about a mile from the walls, and then crosses an absolutely unproductive desert with no water, and hard clayey soil with withered dead tamarisk, till at five miles it comes on an undulating deep sandy tract, bounded by high sand-billocks on every side: this desolate desert continues for four miles, when the path crosses a high sandy ridge, and emerges on to green fields, marking the commencement of Bahrámabád cultivation, which continues up to the village itself a mile further, or about ten miles from Nasírabád. The sandy tract mentioned above varies in its breadth and extent, the sand being blown hither and thither by the

---

[1] It was on the 10th February that the weather commenced to be palpably hotter.

constant high winds. It is fatal to cultivation wherever it encroaches. Bahrámabád is a small unwalled village, surrounding a square mud tower, with about 100 houses, of which the inhabitants seem very poor. It is situated on the banks of the great canal from the Helmand, here about thirty yards wide and six feet deep, but fordable in places. There is no bridge. Chelling is situated about six miles down the stream. There is considerable cultivation in the neighbourhood of the village. We halted here and breakfasted on the canal bank, but found the heat of the sun distressing. The water of the canal is most excellent. Leaving Bahrámabád we proceeded in a south-east direction, over dry sandy soil with *kirta* and tamarisk, and at three miles passed a considerable village called Kala'h-i-Khang (unwalled), and one mile further arrived at Deshtak, situated on the right bank of the same canal, where we were met by the Katkhudá and several inhabitants, and found that the Persian Commissioner had already arrived, having come from Nasírabád by a more direct road to the east, which is much shorter, and avoids Bahrámabád, but which we were told was impassable from water. The Katkhudá on meeting us made a set speech, in which he said that all the inhabitants of Deshtak were the happy subjects of Nasru-din Shah, with much more to the same purpose, which had been evidently learnt off by heart. Deshtak is a large walled town of some 500 houses, with a square mud fort in the middle, having towers at each of its angles. The inside of the town is filthily dirty, and the houses are of the poorest description. Ferrier makes a mistake when he says the Helmand is here 300 yards wide. He must have mistaken the canal for the river itself[1]. The main channel of the canal flows round the south corner of the walls of the town, and hugs the left bank; this channel is not more than twenty-five or thirty yards wide, and some six or seven feet deep, but it has overflowed its banks, and there is water now on three sides of the fort coming nearly up to the walls, but very shallow. The walls are in bad repair, but without any breaches, and it is evident that they are being gradually undermined by the canal. The canal is full of fish, some of which were caught twenty-one inches long, of the barbel species, but soft and not nice for the table; they say this is the only sort of fish

[1] Or more probably, I think, an inadvertency may have been committed in writing 300 for 30, and the mistake perpetuated by putting the figures into words; unless he is measuring the distance from bank to bank, which, even in the canal, may reach 100 if not 300 yards.—F. J. G.

obtainable. There are no reeds or rushes growing on the banks of the canal, which flows with a considerable current.

'February 16. Marched to Búrj-i-Alam Khán, four miles off in a south-east by east direction. Weather still continues to get perceptibly warmer. Before leaving Deshtak we rode through the filthy town, and were joined by the Commissioner outside, and by the Katkhudá, who kept galloping about on a mad Túrkman horse in the most insane manner, firing his gun and pistols into our very faces. Our road ran through continuous cultivation, in a strip of about a mile in breadth, for three miles, over very rich soil reaching up to the walls of a large village named Púlgi, which we passed to our left. Turning to our right we crossed a hard dry plain covered with *kirta* for one mile, skirting the right bank of the canal, and arrived on its bank just opposite the town of Búrj-i-Alam Khán, commonly called the Kala'h-i-Kadím, or Búrj-i-Kuhna. The Búrj, from which the place took its name, has long been in ruins, but the town is one of considerable importance, and has a populous and very prosperous appearance. The banks of the canal are at this point some 100 yards apart, though the deep channel is only about thirty-five yards wide, hugging the right bank, the water flowing with rapid current. We halted and breakfasted, and were about three hours getting the whole of our baggage and horses and mules across. The scene was one of great excitement and intense amusement to the inhabitants of the town, who lined the opposite bank in large crowds. Our small india-rubber boat proved most useful on this occasion, as we transported by its means all our tents and the greater part of the baggage, besides crossing in it ourselves. The mules swam across unaided, but our horses were conducted over two at a time, their heads being held by a man seated on a "tútí[1]," a species of reed raft accurately described by Conolly, and the construction of which has in no way altered since his time. There were but two of these "tútis," one of which was allotted to us and one to Mirza Ma'súm Khán; but our small india-rubber boat enabled us to

---

[1] 'Four or five bundles of reeds are fastened together by rushes or by the flexible tops of reeds, the cut edges forming a square stem, the upper ends being tied in a point for a prow. The passenger seats himself in the middle, one man pushes from behind and another pulls at the front. During the wet season the *tútis* are made of larger size so as to admit of as many as four men sitting in them, and are propelled by paddles and long poles, but are rarely taken into the deeper water, where the waves would wet and sink them. These boats last only a few days, for the wet reeds soon become rotten and heavy...'—*Conolly, Journal Bengal Asiatic Society*, vol. ix. page 717.

get over the passage sooner than he could. The distance for which we were obliged to use the boats was only some thirty-five yards over the deep channel. There was a mud bank in the middle of the whole channel on which the baggage was landed; thence it was transported through the shallower water on men's shoulders. Our camp was pitched in some sown fields at the back of the town. All our horses, mules, and baggage crossed without accident. The suspicion with which the presence of the Mission is regarded by the Persians in Sistán may be inferred from the fact that Ma'súm Khán assured us that the Katkhudá of Deshtak had come to him in the morning with a rude request that we might not be allowed to enter their town; alluding to an expressed intention of riding through it. This may not be true, but in any case it exhibits a disposition on the part of the Persians to make us believe that our presence here is most unwelcome. Búrj-i-Alam Khán is, as before remarked, a most prosperous village. It is situated on the left bank of the great canal, and on the borders of the "Sabz-i-Kúm," described in a former place as being the bed of a dried-up "hámun," formed here by the overflowing of the Helmand, and which gradually dried up on the Helmand changing its bed. This "Sabz-i-Kúm" stretches for miles in a south-east and southerly direction, and the former limits of the lake are still distinctly marked by a ledge of some thirty or forty feet high, which stopped the encroachment of the water, and which must indeed be a continuation of the "Dasht-i-Sangbar," noticed in the vicinity of Sekuha. The present chief of Búrj-i-Alam Khán is Sardár Shir Dil Khán, a brother of Sardár Sharif Khán, and who also possesses the fort of Kimak[1]. At the time of our visit he was suffering from chronic dyspepsia, and was consequently unable to come and visit the General; but he lost no time in asking for a visit from Mr. Rosario, who was thus enabled to do him some good, and also to prescribe for his wife. The lady, however, he did not see, as she favoured him with a written account of her ailments. Sardár Shir Dil Khán is a good-looking man of some fifty years of age, and of pleasing manners. He sent his son with some thirty *sowárs* to receive us about two miles on this side of Deshtak, and insisted on the Mission being considered as his guests during our stay at his village.

[1] He married a daughter of Muhammad Rizá Khán after the latter's death. He used formerly to inhabit the fort of Kimak, but has lately changed his residence at the request of his brother.

His son, Háidar Ali Khán, is a singularly intelligent and nice-looking lad of about twenty years of age, who had been at Tehrán, presumably as a hostage, for three years, and returned only last year. Some of the bread with which we were provided here was excellent, but another sort was mixed with asafœtida in large quantities, which makes it very unpalatable and nauseous, though the natives delight in it.

'February 17. Marched to Kala'h-Nau, two and a-half miles off, east by north. This place is also called Búrj-i-Dost Muhammad Khán. Cloudy weather. Road runs nearly parallel with the canal at some slight distance from its left bank over clayey soil with *kirta* and occasional cultivation. There was no *istiklál* or any attempt at one, either to receive the General or the Persian Commissioner, on our approaching the village; but we were informed that the chief and his son were away, at the new settlement of Sharifabad, which the former is making some miles to the north-east of this place, and that he was too occupied and unwell to be able to receive the Commissioners. Mirza Ma'súm Khán found lodgings in the town, but we encamped on the further side in some walled fields. Kala'h-Nau is one of the principal places in this quarter of Sistán, being the residence of Sardár Sharif Khán, the only one remaining of the old Balúch chiefs who still retains any power or influence before the rapidly-increasing authority of the Amir. The *ark* or citadel is built on a high clay cliff, with precipitous sides, and its walls are strong and well adapted for defence; it has a square tower at one of the angles, and contains the residence of the chief, his family, and immediate attendants. It is a very striking-looking object at a distance, but in the time of Dost Muhammad Khán, the original builder, it did not present the same appearance as now; the present chief having greatly enlarged and strengthened it. It towers high above the village disposed around its base and built on the undulating ground of which the highest part forms the foundation of the *ark*. A roughly-constructed mud wall surrounds the whole village and follows the undulations of the ground, being nowhere of uniform height. A few houses are however built outside the walls on the east face, and a strong species of mantled tower crowns the rising ground which lies beyond the town to the north. On a rough computation there may be about 1000 houses in the town, which presents no object whatever of interest or importance, and is very dirty. We were not allowed to enter the fort or citadel. There are not many Balúchís in this place, of which the inhabitants are mostly Shia'hs: Sardár Sharif Khán being himself a Shia'h. Our presence naturally gave rise to much curiosity and conjecture; but we were objects of less interest here than at the Fort of Kimak, situated at three miles distance to the north, on the right bank of the great canal, whither the General, with Captains Lovett and Smith, rode over in the afternoon on a visit of inspection, meeting the Persian Commissioner at the water-side. The said Kimak is a place of much more ancient date than either Búrj-i-Alam Khán or Kala'h-Nau, and has gradually increased from a small hamlet to a considerable town. It also is the property of Sardár Sharif Khán, who allows his brother, Shir Dil Khán, to hold it under him. It possesses a large square mud citadel, situated at the south corner of the town, which runs in straggling rows of houses for about 400 yards along the canal bank, surrounded by the usual mud walls, and with no outside habitations.

'In former times Kimak was a place of constant dispute between the Sharikis and Nharuis; and was occupied before the time of Sharif Khán by Sardár Muhbat Khán Nharui. Haídar Ali Khán, son of Shir Dil Khán, is the present governor. The fort has a high octagonal-shaped mud tower; but we were not allowed to go inside it, and indeed the crowds of people were so curious and pushing that it was with some difficulty we entered the town at all. Copious thrashing, however, by our rear and advanced guards, cleared and kept a way for us, until we gained the summit of the highest house in the place, whence Captain Lovett took the necessary survey observations. The inhabitants had never seen Europeans before, were not particularly civil, and certainly did not seem to pay much attention to the authority of the Persian Commissioner. The canal here is about sixty yards wide, counting the whole space between the banks, but of this not more than twenty-five yards from the right bank is the real deep channel, the remainder being so shallow that we could not use our india-rubber boat, and had to ride out to the deep water and then get on to one of two solitary *tútís*. The overflow of the canal has caused a marsh near the town, on which were vast quantities of ducks and wild-fowl, who were too wary to allow one to get within shot. Kimak and Kala'h-Nau are both situated on the edge of the high desert plateau, which places a limit alike to cultivation and irrigation on the south of Sistán, and which intervenes between the low rich country we have been traversing and the left bank of the Helmand. Large detached masses of clay, standing like outposts from the desert, dot the plain and testify to the action of long-past floods and rains, their bases being surrounded with shingle and water-worn pebbles. In the vicinity of Kala'h-Nau this continuous high ground is at some distance from the fort, but near Kimak it encroaches on the very banks of the canal, and our road from Kala'h-Nau was one of several ascents and descents. On the other side of Kimak a large hill of this clay is crowned with an ancient place of Parsi burial, and is still known as the Átash-Gáh. A further detached mass to the south of Kala'h-Nau is the site of the grave of Dost Muhammad Khán, the original builder of the town. A *kásid* came in to-day bringing the mail from Bandar-Abbas; he had been more than a month *en route*, but was very welcome. Our latest dates were December 15 from England, and January 8 from India. We were all glad to hear that the Prince of Wales was out of danger. By this mail the General heard of the serious trouble in Kalát and of the consequent suspension of proceedings in Major St. John's survey. Supplies of all kinds are cheap and plentiful, but grain, which sells at thirty-four *kráns* the hundred Tabriz *manns*, is slightly dearer than at Nasírabád.

'February 18. Marched at 8.30 A.M. to Kúhak or Sar-i-band, nine miles east by south. Morning bright with very cold north wind. For the first mile our road ran over cultivated land which was interspersed with the masses of detached clay above mentioned, and then mounted about sixty feet on to an undulating plateau covered with shingle, and absolutely barren. At five miles we descended on to a wide valley, of which we were surprised to see the bed on our left hand covered with a lake of some miles in extent with water of a pale green colour: the strong wind that was blowing had raised miniature waves upon its surface, and gave it the appearance of a small inland sea. This lake owes its existence to the overflow of the great canal which escapes into this reservoir by a passage some miles above Kimak. In the summer the waters dry up and the poor Balúchís then come and cultivate the rich deposit which they leave behind. A short distance past this lake, another expanse of muddy-coloured water on the right hand is visible; the two lakes are divided from one another by a small clay ridge, but it is probable that they both owe their original existence to the same cause. The valley in which the first lake is situated is known as the "Gôd-i-Kúrkúrin." Crossing this valley for two miles, the road then rises again on to the desert, and passing by some clay mounds descends gradually into the narrow tamarisk-covered valley which borders the left bank of the Helmand. In this valley we encamped just in a line with the Great "Band," having the fort of Kúhak on our left front, with the village of Khojah Ahmad some distance beyond. The Great "Band" across the Helmand, near Kúhak, has existed for more than fifty years, but it is only within the last six or seven years that it has been so constructed by the Amir of Káïn as to completely turn the course of the river and transvert its waters into those districts of Sistán which own Persian rule. Practically speaking, except when its waters are at flood, the natural course of the river ends at this "Band," from which point it is made to follow the artificial channel of the canal. In former years the "Band" used regularly to be swept away by the river every year, and a new "Band" constructed. The Amir, however, on his arrival in Sistán, gave his attention to this point, and has expended so much care on its construction that the present "Band" has now held for six years, and will probably prove permanent. The banks of the river at this point are very low, the stream itself being about 172 yards broad with deep water. The dimensions of the "Band" are as follows: entire length, 720 feet; length across original bed of river, 520 feet; breadth at broadest part, 110 feet; depth, 18 feet on river side. It is formed of fascines of tamarisk branches closely interwoven together with stakes driven into them at intervals: the branches used for this purpose are green and fresh, but of no great size; while the interlacing of them is very close. The Amir initiated the practice of filling up the interstices between the branches with loose earth and stones brought from a distance, and the natives ascribe the stability of the present "Band" to this process; one which had never before been tried in Sistán, the ancient "Bands" affording a free passage for a considerable quantity of water. The present "Band" was constructed by 2000 men in three months, all classes in Sistán giving their aid to a work on which their own prosperity was so much dependent. The great part of the labour was in bringing from a distance the enormous quantity of tamarisk required; but it is said that when once the branches were collected, the actual construction was performed in a short time by one man, a native of Banjár, the sole possessor of this art, and who refuses to impart his knowledge to any one but his own son. The "Band" still requires a small yearly repair when the spring floods are over, and its face towards the river is annually increased by a yard or more, but these repairs are now easily accomplished by fifty or sixty men. When the river is at flood its waters escape over the summit of the "Band" and flow in the original channel north up to the Hámún, near Chakhansúr, where they are lost; and a passage, some sixty feet wide, is also cut in the "Band" itself, by which much of the violence of the pressure is mitigated. The canal is, at the point it receives the waters of the Helmand, 150 feet wide, flowing with considerable current; but half its contents are drawn off by supplementary canals by the time it reaches Kimak. On the left bank of the river, at some 400 yards distant, there is a small canal cut above the "Band" which was commenced by Táj Muhammad, and intended to convey water to Sekuha. The work was however abandoned, and this canal now joins the great canal some quarter of a mile below the "Band." On the right bank and about a mile above the "Band," a broad canal is cut which supplies Nád Ali with water. At the time of our visit, a considerable quantity of water was flowing through the upper part of the "Band," and the original bed of the river on the northern side also contained a fair quantity. When the floods come down at the flowering of the tamarisk in the spring, the river overflows both its banks, and rushes with great velocity over the "Band" into its natural bed: and when the waters subside the natives say that great fish come to the foot of the "Band," and attempt to leap over it into the deeper water beyond, but being of course unable to do so, are staked in the tamarisk branches, and great numbers are caught in this way. In the dry season the "Band" is found to harbour great quantities of snakes who breed inside it. They say that several men are always bitten when they commence to remove the branches for the annual repairs[1].

'In every other direction there was nothing to be seen but what Ferrier calls the "silent and sterile deserts of Sistán." In the

---

[1] They say that the original course of the Helmand turned from a point higher than the present *band*, and, flowing for some distance in the valley to the left of its present bed, close to the *band*, pursued its course in the channel which is now the great canal. This ancient bed was connected with the *band* of Kúhak (on the river changing its bed and flowing towards Chakhansúr and the north) by Sardár Ali Khán, who collected the people of Sistán and dug the canal required to join the old and new beds.

The neighbourhood of the *band* harbours a great number of waterfowl which, it is said, generally leave Sistán about the first of March.

afternoon we crossed the "Band," inspected the small mud tower which was built for its protection on the opposite bank, and then, accompanied by the Yáwar Azád Khán, who wished much to do the honours of the place, Captains Lovett and Smith with Quartermaster-Sergeant Bower started off to take observations from the top of the Kúhak fort, which is situated about one and a-half mile below the "Band" on the left bank of the original bed of the Helmand, in a sort of delta enclosed by the Helmand on one side and the great canal on the other[1]. Their expedition, however, was unsuccessful. Arrived at the fort, which is a square strong mud enclosure of 40 paces square built on a high clay mound, from which it takes its name, they found the garrison all assembled on the walls with the gate fast locked, and a red-bearded Náib looking down like a second Roderick Dhu from the ramparts and absolutely refusing admission. In vain did the honey-tongued Yáwar try to persuade him that our coming in would do no harm, nay, that it was absolutely necessary to complete the map which was being prepared by order of the Shah. "By your head, by the head of the Shah, and by the beard of the Prophet," swore the Náib, "neither your noble self, nor any of the others, not even the Sartip or General himself can come in unless a written authority is produced to me from the Amir to open the door." And from this position he would not depart. The Yáwar feigned intense chagrin, but we had nothing for it than to take the requisite observations outside the fort and then to depart, leaving the triumphant Náib to the enjoyment of his victory. This refusal, however, furnishes a significant commentary on the way in which the Persian authorities here interpret the Shah's order that the Commissioners are to go any where and to inspect whatever places they please. Kúhak Fort has a garrison of some forty *sarbáz*, but is without other inhabitants and has no cultivated land. The soldiers find occupation in shooting and

---

[1] From the "Band" to Kimak the following larger canals drain the great canal on its right bank, commencing from Kohak downwards:—
1. Húsainki Canal supplies Banjár, Kot Iskil, Záhidún, Nasírabád, &c.
2. Jalálabad Canal supplies that town and vicinity.
3. Kadang and Kasimabád Canal.
4. Sharifabád-Tiflak Canal.
5. Jahánabad Canal.
6. Wasilán Canal.
7. Kimak.
8. Khamak-Gauri Canal.

fishing. We got a view of Sharifabad and Shahristan, but the rest of the country was desert. In the morning a *kásid* came in from Colonel Pollock with a letter, informing us that he was coming by the Kala'h-i-Bist and Garm-sail route, and that he hoped to be at Sekuha in about eleven days from this date. Captain Smith was directed to give the necessary information to the Persian Commissioner, and also to impress upon him that in proceeding with him beyond this point it was to be clearly understood that Sir Frederic Goldsmid did so merely for the purposes of inspection and survey, and that the action could in no wise be held to have any bearing at all on the question of territorial possession. The Commissioner said he quite understood this. The Yáwar informed us to-day that there were no less than ten Persian regiments of infantry still in Sistán. Bright moonlight night with cold air.

'February 19. Marched at 9 A.M. to Dak-i-Dehli, twenty-eight miles south by east. Hard frost last night. Weather this morning bright and cold, but it got very hot towards mid-day. Despatched a return *kásid* to Colonel Pollock with a note, saying we hoped to meet him at Rúdbár. The Yáwar said yesterday, in reply to a question from Mirza Ma'súm Khán, that the Afghán Commissioner would not be allowed to enter Rúdbár unless the Amir issued orders for him to do so. Our march to-day was tedious and uninteresting in the extreme. Quitting the narrow valley in which we had been encamped, the road almost at once rises to the shingly barren desert on the left bank of the river, and continues its dreary course over it for fifteen miles, when it descends to the former bed of the river, the light alluvial soil of which rose in clouds of dust under our horses' hoofs: this strip of land is covered with tamarisk jungle, very thick in places, and continues for thirteen miles more until it arrives at the halting-ground of Dak-i-Dehli. At four miles from our starting-point we passed an old *kanát* which formerly carried water from the bed of the river to irrigate some low land on the other side of the desert; and at five miles there is a bend in the river where it is fordable, and to which there is a well-beaten road from Búrj-i-Alam Khán, which we crossed. The river, from the "Band" to Dak-i-Dehli, pursues a somewhat winding and deviating course; and the stream flows contiguous to the right or higher bank, except in places, where, having cut for itself an arbitrary channel, the deserted land becomes choked with thick tamarisk jungle. So far as we could judge, it flows over a sandy bed with many shoals and shallows, and would be very difficult of navigation. It has a considerable current, and the breadth of the water varies from 100 to 200 yards. The opposite side appeared to us nothing but desert, thick tamarisk jungle near the bank, and innumerable ruins in every direction. On the left bank, however, we passed no signs of human habitation, and the only human beings we saw were some Toki Balúchis, engaged in cultivating small strips of ground on the river bank, who drew up at the side of the road to see us pass. The water is unusually low for this particular season of the year, and has been so for the last two years. The floods come down at the time of the tamarisk flowering, and the low land on the banks is then inundated to a considerable extent. We were much struck with the lifeless appearance of the stream—no villages or cultivation on its banks, no boats or rafts, few birds, no jumping fish, and even the vegetation in its vicinity dried up and parched[1]. There are great numbers of wild hog on both banks, and we saw traces of their burrowing in every direction. The road we followed often leaves the river for a considerable distance, and the traveller then loses sight of the only object capable of giving interest to the unspeakably dreary and fatiguing desert route. It is surprising that no efforts have been made to utilise this noble river all along its course, but until one actually catches sight of the stream itself there are no signs whatever by which one could suspect its existence. Our camp at Dak-i-Dehli was pleasantly situated on the very banks of the stream, which is here very low, and with half-shut eyes one could imagine that it was the Thames and not the Helmand that was stealing by so quietly; though in the former case the surrounding atmosphere would hardly have been so still and undisturbed. Dak-i-Dehli derives its name from a Sistáni word "Dak," which signifies mound or hill. There is a high clay hill on the left bank crowned by the ruins of an old fort, and this hill still marks the spot where, in years gone by, existed one of the many "Bands" across the river known by the name of Dehli, or the Band-i-Yakáb, supplying Kala'h-i-Fath. It was formed of tamarisk interlaced, but without earth; so that the greater part of the water escaped through the

[1] Pottinger, in one of his chapters, remarks that there are no magpies in Central Asia. On the banks of the Helmand they abound, as also in Sistán, and are called Kilágh-i-ablak, or the 'piebald crow.'

interstices of the branches, and the construction served merely to check the stream sufficiently to force a good supply of water into the canals which had been dug above it. The natives ascribe an almost antediluvian date to the erection of this "Band," all traces of which, and of the canals, have now disappeared. On the opposite side are some high mounds crowned by the remains of ancient tombs and burial towers. The principal ruins passed on the right bank in to-day's march from Kúhak here, are as follows, in order: Dam Dewáli, absolute ruins; at eighteen miles from Kúhak, Kala'h-i-Fath, principally in ruins; then a ruined Masjid without name; and then the tombs opposite to Dak-i-Dehli. Bright moonlight, with temperature very cold.

'February 20th. Marched at 8 A.M. to Bandar-i-Kamál Khán, twelve miles south-south-east. Cold wind blowing. Road leads over the desert close to the left bank of the river for six miles, and then descends on to the deserted bed near the bank, which it traverses, for five miles among tamarisk jungle, when it again ascends on to the desert plateau, and after a short distance passes some domed tombs and graves, making a gradual descent on to the cultivation and fort of Kamál Khán. We were met at a short distance by the Sardár's son, Sarfaráz Khán, whose brother, Muhammad Rizá Khán, we had seen with the Amir at the breakfast at Nasírabád. The fort of Kamál Bandar[1] is situated about three-quarters of a mile from the left bank of the Helmand, in a valley which must be nearly eight miles across, which on this side the river and near the fort is very highly cultivated, and which when the river is full is almost entirely under water. The fort is an irregular-shaped walled enclosure, with the Sardár's[2] house standing in a square citadel in the centre and with a

[1] In pre-historic ages, the Helmand is reported to have flowed hence in a south-west direction to the lake of Zirah, and tradition has it that Kai Khúsrú had sailed down it in a vessel. This Helmand merely contained the overflow of the water, and what escaped through the great *band* made by Gurshasp at Múlla Khán, which accurately partitioned off the water, and which was destroyed by Sháhrúkh, the son of Taimúr. There are still the distinct remains and banks of the canal to Tráku, Kundar, and Hauz-i-Dár from this point, which dried up long ago on the bursting of the Balba Khún Band.

N.B.—The above information was afforded by Sardár Kamál Khán and was traditionary with the inhabitants.

[2] Sardár Kamál Khán is a Sanjaráni Balúch, and is a cousin to Ibráhim Khán of Chakhansúr and Imám Khán of Rúdbár. They had the same grandfather, Ján Beg.

Sardár Kamál Khán has eight sons, of whom the principal are, Umar Khán, Muhammad Rizá Khán, and Sarfáraz Khán. His authority is principally over the wandering Balúchís between this and Rúdbár, on the left bank of the river. Rúdbár is divided between him

few mud huts scattered around it. There are but few houses at Kamál Bandar, the greater part of this chief's subjects being Toki Balúchís, who dwell in tents, and tend their flocks and cultivate the ground on the banks of the river. The Sardár is in the pay of the Persian Government and receives a pension of 500 *tumáns* a year, in return for which he acknowledges the authority of the Shah, obeys such orders as he may receive and as may chime in with his own ideas, and sends a few sheep and camels yearly as a present or tribute to the Amir. We were informed, on arrival, that he was ill, and began to suspect that he was suffering from the same illness that had attacked Shir Dil Khán and Sharif Khán on the approach of the Mission, and which was probably simulated in pursuance of orders; but in the morning he called on the General. He is an old man of very pleasant manners, but quite infirm and suffering much from asthma. He talked away on various subjects, and told us that the whole country up to Múlla Khán belonged to the Shah. He said there was a route across the country from Rúdbár to Jálk of twelve days, with water in wells at intervals, but no *abádi* or cultivation. He also informed us that the river had been very low indeed for the last two years; that the flies here were most troublesome, but not so bad as in Sistán, though the heat was worse; that the *bad-i-bistróz* commenced to blow about two months after the Nau-Roz, and blew with great violence, being very hot for the first three or four days, but cooling down afterwards; and that horses suffered from the flies in the way so often described, but only after they commenced to eat grass towards the autumn. We were the first Europeans who had ever come here, and he knew nothing of Ferrier. The weather is getting perceptibly hotter, and the crops are much more advanced here than at Búrj-i-Nau and Alam Khán. The houses here are not built of mud entirely, but have a light framework of tamarisk branches with mud cakes plastered upon them. We were visited by two Hindús who had been here twenty-five years.

and Sardár Imám Khán, and they each have a fort there, held by a son or dependent to see that the proceeds of the land are fairly divided. Kamál is somewhat more powerful than his neighbour Imám Khán. Sardár Ján Beg's descendants are as follows:—

Ján Beg		
Khán Ján	Aslam Khán	Nawáb Khán
Ibráhim Khán (Chakhansúr)	Imám Khán (Húsainabád)	Kamál Khán (Bandar).

These men gain a livelihood by importing dates and sugar from Kandahár and other places; but they struck us as quite wanting in the usual intelligence of their people. They had their wives and children with them, but had left Shikárpúr when quite young. The Sardár informed us that the date-tree would not grow here owing to the high winds that prevail; he also mentioned the fact that though the river was full of fish no Balúchís ever knew how to catch them.

'February 21st. Marched at 8.15 A.M., ten miles east by south to Chahár Búrjak—also called Já-i-Imám Khán and Húsainabád. Cloudy morning with cold wind. The thermometer fell one degree below freezing-point last night. Our road ran through cultivated fields for two miles to the banks of the river, when we crossed it by a ford to the right bank, the water being up to our horses' girths. We breakfasted on the right bank, and then resumed our course for six miles over a shingly dry desert, passing a small ruined fort on the right, called the fort of the Mir. At six miles we made a slight descent on to some low land which had been deserted by the river, and which is very highly cultivated, the fields continuing for two miles further to the walls of the fort of Imám Khán. At a short distance from the town we were met by Sardár Imám Khán's son, Shir Muhammad Khán, a youth of some twenty years of age, greatly resembling his brother, Dost Muhammad Khán, whom we had seen at Nasírabád; he was riding a very fine blood bay Túrkman horse, blind of one eye. An old man who was with him took occasion to tell us that Sardár Imám Khán, and all he possessed, were the property of the Shah. This chief is also in the pay of the Persian Government on similar terms to Sardár Kamál Khán; he used to receive 500 *tumáns* a year, but the visit of his son Dost Muhammad Khán to Tehrán has been the means of getting his pay raised to 600 *tumáns*. From Kamál Bandar the Helmand river, which had flowed from nearly due east, takes a northerly course. The land on each side of it is low, but bounded beyond by the higher plateau of the desert, which in former ages probably formed its banks at this season. It runs over a sandy bed with very low banks opposite the fort of Imám Khán, which is known by the three names given above. The fort is the ordinary mud walled enclosure, and immediately overhangs the right bank, here about thirty feet high. In the spring the overflow of the water covers the land on either side, but the stream is now very low. We encamped in the deserted bed of the river immediately under the bank. Three Hindús, who have been residents at this place for some years, did not present to us a very flourishing appearance. In the afternoon Sardár Imám Khán and his son called on Sir Frederic Goldsmid. The Sardár is a younger man than his cousin Kamál Khán, of pleasing, gentlemanly manners, and possessed of much general information. He suffers much from chronic asthma. We are not the first English he has seen, as he says he perfectly remembers Pattinson who stayed with him some thirty years ago in Rúdbár, and he seemed proud of having had him as his guest. Sardár Imám Khán, in the course of conversation, took the opportunity of saying that all the country from here to Rúdbár, with Rúdbár itself, was the property of the Shah. This complete acknowledgment of Persian sovereignty and influence on the right bank of the Helmand cannot be generally known, and proves the way the Persians have been working while the Afgháns have been quarrelling. The Yáwar said, however, to-day, that at present the Amir's orders are not obeyed beyond Rúdbár. The Sardár said that Jálk was twelve marches from this by Rúdbár, over a long and difficult road, and that few caravans traversed it except after the date season in Balúchistán, when they bring up the supplies for Sistán. The fort here resembles that at Kamál Bandar: there are, inside it, a large mud citadel containing the Sardár's house, and a few straggling houses in which his personal retainers live; but the greater part of his subjects are nomadic Balúchís living in tents, and there are some hundred mud houses outside the walls. This place has only been lately called Húsainabád, and is now termed Húsainabád-i-Nau in contradistinction to the ruins of the old village of the single name, which are some few miles further up the river [1].

'Halt, February 22. The whole of this day was taken up in correspondence with the Persian Commissioner, and in endeavouring to get him to come on to Rúdbár; or, if he would not come himself, to make arrangements that we might go. The Commissioner however is equally unwilling to go himself or to assist us to go. For the former his ostensible reasons are that he will not proceed further unless

---

[1] About twelve miles higher up the river, on the right bank, is a tract called Ashkinak, which was colonised and cultivated in the time of the English occupation of Kandahár by a chief named Jabar, who obtained pecuniary assistance from the English for that purpose. This Jabar brought with him some Mamasani Balúchís, who still hold the tract, which is of small extent.

the General acknowledges now that all the country is in possession of Persia: his real one being that he does not wish to meet the Afghán Commissioner in his present light marching order, without establishment or servants wherewith to make impression—for he says he intends to act 'bien pompeusement' towards him; that he has now come as far as he wanted, and having seen the Chief to whom Rúdbár is said to belong, does not wish the trouble of going to see Rúdbár itself; and that at the outset he never intended to come further. The way he has effectually put a stop to our own progress is by issuing orders that no grain or supplies be sold to us; sending the Yáwar to make personal report that this place is quite destitute of supplies, that it is altogether impossible to get sufficient grain to take us from here to Rúdbár and back, that no supplies of any kind are obtainable at Rúdbár, and that this station has to be itself fed from Nasírabád. The latter assertion may possibly be true, but none of the former are. In the first place, on our arrival here, a man was sent into our camp from Sardár Imám Khán, saying that supplies of all sorts were at our disposal; and on the day of our arrival we could purchase anything. Secondly, all to-day we had been able to purchase grain and chaff, until late in the evening, when the General still announced his intention of going to Rúdbár; and although orders came to the poor Balúchís that nothing was to be sold to us, they said we might buy from them plenty to-morrow morning very early, before the authorities were awake: in addition to this, the place is surrounded by cultivation on every side. But so it is; and it shows the way in which our arbitration is assisted by the Persian Commissioner. He could not have more effectually barred our further progress in this direction with troops and artillery than he has by this stoppage of supplies. Orders are issued in every direction that no information is to be given to us, and the peasants and Balúchís we question beg us not to address them, as they know nothing, and will be punished if they are seen speaking to us. And when we make protestations against this treatment, nothing is tendered in reply but honeyed words and sugared disavowals. It is impossible to believe that the Sardár Imám Khán, who is a gentleman according to his lights, would act so; but we are helpless, and for the present the Commissioner has the game in his hands. He has got his wish this time—for the Yáwar came late at night to say that, unfortunately, want of supplies would quite prevent the General going as far as Rúdbár, and proposed that we should leave to-morrow with Mirza Ma'súm Khán, who resolutely declines to halt another day. Sir Frederic Goldsmid, however, has determined to halt long enough to enable Captain Lovett to survey as far as he can towards Rúdbár, and also, if possible, to gain some news of Colonel Pollock of whom we hear nothing.

'Halt, February 23. Weather much warmer. The Persian Commissioner left this morning for Nád Ali, after sending over his Mirza to ask the General what his plans were, and to report the issue of orders that we were to be supplied with whatever the place afforded—a message soon followed by the appearance of the Sardár's own Názir with two lean sheep, for which he wanted no less a sum than 50 *kráns*, five times the proper price. The way in which they fleece us may be gathered from the fact that for fowls and eggs, which we are permitted to buy, we pay nearly as much as in London; and the absolute falsehood of the pretence that we could not go to Rúdbár for scarcity of provisions was proved by the Mírakhor purchasing from the Balúchís around, before the sun was up, three days' fodder and barley for the horses. Captain Lovett went out surveying in the direction of Rúdbár with four Balúch *sowárs*, and got out about fifteen miles. In the evening Captain Smith returned the visit that Sardár Imám Khán had paid the General. The chief was seated in open "majlis" on a piece of ground inside the fort, with some hundred Balúchís and servants around. Of these a few were permitted to be seated, and all took a part in the conversation when they had anything to say. Imám Khán was curious as to the extent of our rule in India, was aware that Sind and the Panjáb were wholly in our hands, and wanted to know when we were going to take Kashmír and Jamu. He remembered our occupation of Afghánistán perfectly well, and said it was from Kandahár that Mr. Pattinson had come to see him in Rúdbár. He also asked many questions about China; and the whole assembly were greatly amused at hearing that the Chinese Emperor only pays his physicians when he is well, the force of which arrangement they quickly appreciated. The Sardár was anxious for information, but did not seem to have much to impart: it may be, if he had any, that he was prevented from expressing his feelings by the presence of the Yáwar Azád Khán, who assisted at the interview. He spoke of the gross ignorance of the Balúchís, and said they had never learnt to catch the fish of the Helmand, or to make boats or rafts, and probably never would; but that they lived from hand to mouth like wolves. The present fort of Húsainabád had only been built by himself twenty years ago. In reply to a request preferred that he would send a messenger with letters to Colonel Pollock, he said he could do so as far as his authority extended—a little way beyond Rúdbár, but that his tribe had a blood feud with the Balúchís beyond. The Helmand at this season of the year is easily fordable opposite Húsainabád. The Sardár said that the heat in summer was so great here that, were it not for the violent wind which blows, human life could not support it. The people seem miserably poor, but very idle, as they spend all day seated in crowds on the bank, looking at ourselves and our tents, objects which cause them great amusement. They bring numbers of small red stones like garnets for sale, with a few old illegible coins which they state are procurable in some neighbouring ruins. Sent off a messenger with letter to Rúdbár for Colonel Pollock.

'February 24. Marched at 6.30 A. M. on our return to Kúhak in a north-west direction to Kala'h-i-Fath, twenty-five miles distant. We were disturbed in the night by an alarm of thieves; and it was found that they had carried off the old bony, white, unprepossessing-looking Túrkman horse belonging to the Hájji, which the old man said had been presented to him by the Shah, and which was his constant companion, confidant, and friend. These two have been such inseparables that it is difficult to imagine one without the other. The thieves had got clear away with it; and though Sardár Imám Khán was informed of the theft as soon as day broke, and sent out *sowárs* in pursuit, there is small chance of seeing it again. The Hájji is naturally very wroth, swears that the theft has been committed purposely by order of Mirza Ma'súm Khán, which is very probable, and in the meantime consoles himself by putting upon his horse a fabulous price, which he is going to charge as compensation. We had slight rain last night and this morning at starting; and it did not get fairly light till 6.30 A.M. Our road ran over stony barren desert, keeping away from the river, and skirting the high ground which must formerly have been its right bank, for seven miles in a west-north-west direction. It then ascends on to the high ground (about seventy or eighty feet), and continues north-west by west for the remaining eighteen miles, twelve of which are over shingly, barren, and absolutely unproductive desert, without water; then, at nineteen miles from our starting-point, descends on to the low ground on the right bank of the river, the high ground receding by degrees and gradually trending further eastward. Two miles before this descent we passed Dak-i-Dehli, our halting-place on the opposite bank. At the end of the plateau, on the left hand, is a well-built brick tomb in capital repair, reputed to be the burial-place of one of the Kaiáni kings. The last six miles over the low ground is through very thick jungle composed of tamarisk and a plant called "shúr," both now dry and withered owing to the river having not overflown its banks for two years, but which, were they supplied with water, would grow so rapidly as to be almost impassable. We reached the ruins of Kala'h-i-Fath at 1.15 P.M., and pitched our camp in one of the many ruined mud enclosures. The ruins of Kala'h-i-Fath are situated on the right bank of and close to the Helmand, about twenty miles above the "Band" of Kúhak. Ferrier describes them: and in a foot-note in his book they are said to be the most extensive in Sistán. This, however, is either inaccurate or gives a very exaggerated idea of their extent, for the whole circumference of the city walls cannot be more than two or two-and-a-half miles. With the exception of a large caravanserai outside the walls, the ruins and citadel are composed entirely of mud sun-dried brick, with a foundation of baked brick. The citadel is probably the oldest building, and the town must have been an after-growth round its base. It is built on a very high clay mound, which was scarped to the foundation of the walls, the summit of which from the ground is about seventy feet: the circumference of the *ark* is considerable, and from the outside we observed some ruins of fine arched buildings within; but the town, which lies at its base, has nothing remarkable. Spacious court-yards, remains of reservoirs, caravanserais, large houses, etc., etc. abound, but there are no vestiges of remarkable structures, nor of anything in the least approaching to magnificence, or even above mediocrity. The only object really worthy of notice is a spacious caravanserai outside the walls, to the south-west, built throughout of large baked bricks, eleven inches square, and displaying a nicety of construction and design foreign to Sistán. The building consists of a large domed centre court-yard, with wings on each side containing several rooms, and from the right wing a continuation at right-angles for stables. The dome is really fine, but the building has the appearance of never having been finished; the stables for the left wing are altogether wanting, while the top of the dome also is incomplete. Adjoining this is a huge "yakh-chál" or ice-house, built of mud bricks; and opposite, a grave-yard with fragments of alabaster and tiles scattered about. After an inspection of Kala'h-i-Fath it is impossible to believe it to have been a very ancient city. The conditions of the country preclude the notion of permanent stone buildings; but these mud-constructed remains would naturally succumb to the action of weather in a moderate space of time. The edges of the bricks in the caravanserai are sharp, and the lines of the building well-defined, with the mortar complete, and showing no signs of great age; and the walls around the city, divided by towers, and built of mud six feet at the base and tapering to one foot at the top, are nearly perfect, except where the river has carried away a large portion at the north-west angle. It is the same with the ruins of the houses, which are built in streets running from east to west: such parts as still remain have the appearance of quite recent construction. Local tradition, and apparently with reason, represents this place to have been the last capital of the Kaiáni kings, deserted by them when, attacked by Nadir Shah, they took refuge in the Kúh-i-Khwájah—and never inhabited since. There is nothing to reward a search among the ruins but pieces of tile, which do not appear to be very old. The oven in which the bricks for the caravanserai were baked is still in perfect repair. The whole of the ruins with which, at this point, this side of the Helmand is covered are of a similar description. There are no traces of wood anywhere in the construction of the houses, which are nearly all arched, and the city walls are always supported by thick mud buttresses some six yards apart. The interior of the ruins of Kala'h-i-Fath is choked with tamarisk; and abounds with jackals, as evidenced by a fearful howling all night. The Persians have a garrison here of sixty *sarbáz*, some of whom came and talked to us, assuring us they had been in the place for two years, and were engaged in keeping this part of the river quiet. Many things however caused us to doubt the accuracy of this statement, and to institute careful enquiries among the Balúchís around—the result of which is to place it almost beyond a doubt that these men have not been here a month, and indeed were only sent over on the arrival of the Mission in Sistán, to throw dust in the eyes of the British Commissioner, and induce a belief that this part of the right bank of the Helmand had been in the unquestioned possession of Persia for a long period. To prove the fact there is the testimony of the disinterested Balúch shepherds: there is no sign of cultivation or of recent human habitation anywhere round the station: we were strictly prevented not only from entering but from going near the fort, notwithstanding which Quartermaster-Sergeant Bower got near enough to see that the door in the old gate was quite new, and the plaster of the surrounding bricks still fresh and wet: in truth, there are all the signs of fresh occupancy, and none of long residence. Moreover, unless we had come here, what would have been the conceivable reason for the presence of a detachment of soldiers—for there are no villages, roads, or settlements in the vicinity to guard; and the garrison will probably be withdrawn as soon as we have left, and it has served its purpose? Some wandering Balúchís we met on the road to-day took the opportunity of telling us that Ibráhim Khán's son had arrived in Chakhansúr from Kandahár, bringing with him the Afghán Commissioner and Colonel Pollock. If this be true we shall soon meet. The Persian Commissioner encamped here last night, and told the *sarbáz* that he was a very great man; and would do this year as he did last, when he took fifty countries from the hands of the infidel Faringís, and gave them to the Persian government; a statement clearly intended as his exposition of the Makrán boundary settlement! We had a proof to-day, however, that the Persian rule on this bank is not so popular as they would wish us to believe. One of our *faráshes* had lost his way, and got off the road into the jungle, when he was suddenly surrounded by five armed Balúchís, who asked him with many threats and curses if he was a detested "Kajár." The man, an Isfahání bred and born, naturally asseverated that he was not, and, indeed, that if there was one thing he hated more than another in this world it was a "Kajár." The Balúchís, not satisfied with this, still kept threatening him, and it was not till he told them he was a servant of the English Sáhib that they let him go, which they then did at once—one of them guiding him to our camp, and telling him if it had been as they had suspected, they would have cut him into pieces. The man arrived in camp much terrified, but thankful for his lucky escape. Caught a peculiar snake in the ruins to-day: flies and gnats are also beginning to fill the air: all signs of the approach of warm weather. The Persian surveyor, Sarhang Zúlfakar Khán, has just turned up on his way from Nád Ali to Húsainabád, very unwell and as dilapidated as ever. Sardár Imám Khán sent in a wretched pony for the Hájji, as a remplaçant *pro tem.* of his own horse, but the Hájji rejected the beast with scorn, and already talks of 300 *tumáns* compensation. Heavy rain in the afternoon.

'February 25. Marched at 7.30 A.M. to Kúhak or Sar-i-Band, on the right bank of the Helmand, twenty miles north-north-west. Weather cloudy, with slight rain. Road ran the whole way over the level valley on the right bank of the river, densely covered with dry tamarisk and *shúr* jungle, except for the last few miles, when the jungle is less thick and is replaced by camel-thorn and *kirta*. For the first six miles our path was almost entirely through ruins (principally on our right hand, and some two or three miles from the river), of so extensive and wide-spread a nature as to impress us strongly with a belief in the stories so prevalent in Sistán of the extraordinary former populousness of the province. There is nothing particularly interesting about these ruins, built as they are of sun-dried mud brick; but the present desolation of cities that must have formerly been teeming with life and energy is very impressive, even to the passing traveller. Dry water-courses from the river, scoring the plain in every direction, show that for many years this part of the Helmand must have flowed in its present bed. We encamped on the right bank of the river, close to it and the "Band," just under the Búrj, and many of us had a pleasant swim. The water is here very deep, and abounding with fish. Heavy rain in the afternoon, and magnificent thunder and lightning, sheet and forked, unlike anything of the sort one ever sees in England, lighting up the heavens in a sheet of dazzling flame. We heard to-day that Colonel Pollock and the Afghán Commissioner still intend coming *viâ* Rúdbár, and that Ibráhim Khán's son parted from them at Girishk; it is impossible however to trust any news in the atmosphere of intentional deceit and mendacity in which we live. There are many Balúchís in the neighbourhood with flocks and herds; and a number of people have been sent here to repair the Amir's "Band."

'Halt, February 26. Beautiful clear day after the rain of last night, and our camping-ground on the banks of the river most enjoyable. All our servants are amusing themselves with taking pot shots at a water bird, which is a species of diver, with long legs, body as large as a duck, beautiful silvery breast, long neck and very small black wings: it sits very deep in the water, and is very difficult to shoot, as it dives the moment it sees the flash of the gun, and the shot in general passes harmlessly over the place where it has been; on an average it took about ten shots to kill one, but a domestic managed to bag six, and the Yáwar immortalised himself by shooting one through the head with a ball. The *sarbáz*, too, caught some fish who were entangled in the branches of the "Band," but they proved to be all of the same barbel species we caught at Deshtak. We sent in one of our *ghuláms* to-day to Nasírabád for more supplies: he will get into the town this evening, and should meet us at Nád Áli to-morrow.

'February 27. Marched at 7 A.M. to village of Aghá Ján Sarbandi and the ruins of Bina-i-Kai or Nád Ali, 17 miles north-north-east. Morning cloudy with cold north wind. Crossing the actual bed of the Helmand, 200 yards north of the "Band," where the water was up to our horses' bellies, and ascending on the opposite bank, we crossed the small canal which supplies Khwájah Ahmad with water, and passing the fort of Kúhak immediately on our left, continued our way over a flat tamarisk-covered plain to the wretched village bearing the former name, situated on the summit of a clay mound some two miles from the "Band." The village has no fort and is in a most tumble-down and dilapidated condition. Leaving this on our right, and having the new settlement of Sharifabád on our left front, we continued for some six miles further over a very highly cultivated country, with the green crops well grown; and then entered a dense tamarisk jungle, which we traversed for two miles, again coming on cultivated land in the neighbourhood of a village called Gorjak. At thirteen miles, finding that the path returned to the river, we kept along the bank for four miles, finally pitching our camp on the left bank close to the water, in front of a small village called Agha Ján, the property of Muhammad Sharif Khán. The first four or five miles we traversed from Kúhak must form the flat country separating the left bank of the Helmand river from the high desert plateau which lays immediately to the east of Búrj-i-Nau; this belt of cultivated land gradually widening out into the delta of Sistán. The general characteristics of this plain are alternate strips of tamarisk jungle and cultivation, with numerous small deep canals cut from the river itself as well as from the great canal for the purposes of irrigation. The land swarms with game; and partridges, sand-grouse, quail, teal, duck, geese, and pigeon were to be seen in every direction. All along the last four miles of the left bank of the river we observed a high artificial embankment, which seemed to have been raised there more for the purpose of keeping the water of the canals from escaping into the river-bed, than of confining the water of the river itself. The banks of the river below the "Band" are from 100 to 120 yards apart, and the river-bed is fringed on both sides with dense tamarisk jungle. Even at this time of the year it contained a considerable amount of water which had escaped through the "Band," but it is fordable at any point, and has no perceptible current. In the spring, however, when the floods come down, it runs with considerable force and volume, and empties itself into the Hámún, some 15 or 20 miles to the north-west of Chakhansúr. The bed of the Hámún used to be much nearer, but the recent dry weather has caused it to recede considerably; and a Balúch informed us that it would take at least fourteen hours' marching to reach its shores from the spot where we were now encamped. The inhabitants of this village were civil, but very poor. They informed us, much to our chagrin, that a Hindú had visited them some short time before our arrival and purchased a number of old coins they had found in the ruins at Nád Ali, and taken them away to Kandahár. In the afternoon, leaving the camp pitched, we forded the river just opposite, and, crossing to the right bank, made our way through one-and-a-half miles of dense tamarisk jungle to the fort of Nád Ali, the ruins of which we inspected. The road was very bad, and we had to cross one deep canal with rotten banks, where many of us nearly came to grief, the Mírakhor getting a heavy fall by his horse putting his foot in a hole. The fort of Nád Ali is in the hands of the Persians, who have a garrison there, under the command of a son of Sardár Sharíf Khán. We were not permitted to go inside. There is no cultivation of any sort around the walls, from the summit of which we got a clear view of Chakhansúr, Jahánabád, Kásimabád, Shahristán, and other posts. The neighbouring country appeared nothing but uncultivated jungle. The ruins of Nád Ali are situated about one mile and a-half from the right bank of the present actual bed of the Helmand river, north of the "Band," and the garrison is supplied with water from a deep canal, opened at about 100 yards above the "Band" of Kúhak. The present fort is situated on a very high hill (between 150 or 200 feet high) formed of clay, and which is said to be even higher than the famous Kúh-i-Khwájah. It is a small square enclosure built of the bricks of the former ruins. No one inspecting Nád Ali can have a doubt as to its immense antiquity, and the natives claim for it a date long prior to the days of the fabulous Rústam, alleging that the city formerly extended from here as far as Kala'h-i-Fath. The remains of the buildings of the old city are now completely submerged under the mountains of sand which the winds of centuries have raised over them; but from the summit of the mound the extent and shape of the walls can still be distinctly traced, forming an enormous rectangle, of which the mound, which must have contained the *ark* or citadel, would be the north-east corner. The surface of the earth comprised within this rectangle is quite covered with pieces of ancient brick, glazed tiles, glass bangles, &c., &c., and it is not to be doubted that a diligent search and excavation would disclose many far more valuable antiquarian treasures; for the ruins have certainly not been touched or submitted to intelligent inspection since their first decay. The remains of the *kala'h* show that there were an outer and an inner fort, built of baked brick, with walls and foundations of great thickness, and there are still the traces of two very deep wells by which the garrison would be supplied with water. The mound itself, which is of considerable extent, is surrounded by a wet and deep ditch. The view from the summit is very extensive. The most interesting ruin still standing is that of a very massive brick-built, octagonal-shaped tower, with excellent mortar, situated at the south-west corner of the town walls, in the neighbourhood of which are the remains of a reservoir with enormous bricks, and a very spacious gateway. This tower has a spiral vaulted staircase of forty steps, about four feet broad with an average height of six feet, by which we ascended to the top. It was probably designed for the Múazzin, and has two rooms inside it. To the east of the walls are two lofty mounds, from which they say that the *ark* was at last, and in more recent times, enfiladed and commanded by artillery: these are universally known as the "Dam-Damah." The ancient name of this place, the Yáwar informs us, was Bina-i-Káí[1], signifying that it was the work of the first of the Kaiáni kings. The architecture of the tower is certainly more Hindú than Muhammadan. The circumference of the city walls, so far as they can be traced, must be about four miles. The fort, now held by some sixty *sarbáz* of the Amir, was only in late years taken from the chief of Chakhansúr.

'Returning to camp we found a messenger from Colonel Pollock, bringing letters of the 20th from his camp at Hazárjúft, and an-

---

[1] *Bina-i-Káí*, or 'construction of Káí'; *damdamah*, a 'mound.'—F. J. G.

nouncing his intention of coming to Rúdbár. He also informed us that he had been promoted to the rank of Major-General, a fact which greatly aroused the suspicions of the Amir of Káïn. Later on in the evening a messenger brought in a mail from Bandar-Abbas, which place he had left on the 22nd instant, with Indian dates of the 22nd January, and English news of the 29th December. We are all thankful to hear of the Prince of Wales' complete recovery. Late at night our *ghulám* returned with supplies from Nasírabád, and with the news that Ma'súm Khán had already returned there. Weather colder towards the evening.

'February 28. Marched at 7.30 A.M. to Tiflak, or Jahánabád, seven miles—three miles north-west, four west-south-west. Weather cold, the thermometer having fallen to 36° last night. Sent off letters to the Persian Commissioner and to General Pollock before starting. Our road ran for three miles through cultivation and tamarisk jungle over quite level country to the fort of Jahánabád [1], the usual square mud-walled enclosure with unusually high walls. The gates were shut, and the garrison crowding the walls resolutely declined to allow any of us to enter, threatening all who came near with their matchlocks; a queer way of carrying out the commands of the Shah that perfect freedom should be accorded to the Arbitrator to inspect all places. But the worst is that this procedure damages the survey. Jahánabád is a solitary fort standing in the midst of jungle, with no cultivation or houses in its vicinity, and surrounded by a wet ditch: it is utterly uninteresting. Four miles further, terminating amid well-irrigated cultivation, brought us to the ruined fort of Tiflak, around which are to be seen the remains of the city in embryo, which the Persian authorities

[1] Jalálabád, Kadang, Tiflak, Jahánabád, Deh-i-Dád Shah, Deh-i-Aghá Ján, and Sharifabád were all in the hands of Ibráhim Khán of Chakhansúr until one year before the arrival of the late Wakil-ul-Múlk in Sistán. On Táj Muhammad Khán having a dispute with Ibráhim Khán somewhere about 1866, the Persian government sent the Múzaffarúd-Daulah to the assistance of the former, but before he arrived Jalálabád had already fallen into Táj Muhammad's hands, and naturally fell into Persian possession on that chief submitting to Persia. The cause of this dispute was as follows. When Ibráhim Khán succeeded his brother Ali Khán (Toki Balúch), Jahánabád and its dependencies were the only possessions he had on the left bank of the Helmand. The places named above, with the exception of Jalálabád, were taken by him on the expulsion of Jaláludín Kaiáni; and he took Jalálabád on the death of Sardár Ali Khán of Sekuha. It was this circumstance that led to the dispute between him and Táj Muhammad Khán, Ali Khán's murderer and successor. The whole of the former property of the Sharikis and Sarbandis is now in possession of the Amir of Káïn.

intended to be the capital of Sistán before Nasírabád was under contemplation. A great number of houses were built, the ruins of which still remain, when it was found that the high wind here prevalent covered them with sand almost as fast as erected. This incident alone afforded a sufficient reason for abandoning the site; but questions of irrigation and cultivation had also their due weight. It was here that the forces which entered Sistán about 1866 under the late Wakíl-ul-Múlk, the Amir, and the Múzaffarú-d-Daulah, were united, and the house of the latter official still remains. There are some one or two hundred inhabitants still living here. In the afternoon two Brahúi Balúchís brought in a letter from General Pollock, written so far back as January 17th, from Kalát. It is wonderful how they reached us in safety. One of the *sarbáz* caught one of the *kásids* outside our camp, and gave him a severe beating for "bringing letters to the Faringís," as he said. A complaint, instantly made to the Yáwar and vigorously pressed, had the effect of bringing to the front the guilty soldier, to undergo a richly-merited thrashing in the evening. We had however to smuggle the Balúchís out of camp at night after they were paid; or they would have inevitably been followed, plundered, and severely beaten. We closed a mail for England this night, and sent it off by the men who brought up the first despatches from Bandar-Abbas. Evening very cold, though in the middle of the day the weather is very hot.

'February 29. Marched at 7.15 A.M. to Zahidún, south-west, five miles: then five miles north-north-west to ruined Pillar of Kásimabád: then one mile west-north-west to Kásimabád village. Weather bright, but morning cold, the thermometer having fallen to 33° during the night. We sent our tents and mules straight into Kásimabád, only six miles off by the direct road; but made, ourselves, a slight *détour* to inspect the ruins of Zahidún [1] and its chief lion, which Conolly calls

[1] The ruins of Zahidún, both from local tradition and external signs, may be set down as of a much more recent period than those of Nád Ali. They give no real evidence of a date much before the time of Taimúr, to whose armies are ascribed the destruction of this city, and the ruin of the whole of Sistán. The ruins at the present day are utterly uninteresting. They are principally of mud sun-dried brick, and cover a vast space of ground, of which the northernmost point from the old ruined fort is that marked by the standing tower; but there is nothing whatever to repay inspection, and the natives say few relics of any kind are found in them. Remains of glass bangles, tiles, and brick mark the extent of the city. The remains of the citadel are still inhabited. The citadel is built on a high clay mound, is square in form, and had no less than four towers on each face. Built of mud, it resembles any other mud fort or citadel in the interior of Persia.

the Pillar of Kásimábád, but which is here known by the name of the "Míl-i-Zahidún." Our road ran over a level plain intersected by ridges of sand, and amid hollows where the water, collected in small lakes from the overflowing of the Hasanki canal, was quite black with ducks and geese[1]. These lakes or pools contain from three to four feet of water, and the ground around them is very treacherous, especially for horses. Mr. Thomas got a heavy fall with his horse in cantering over it. We arrived at Zahidún at about half-past eight, and breakfasted there; first going up into the ruins of the old fort, the dilapidated houses of which contain the few families of tillers of the neighbouring land. From Zahidún to the Pillar are sandy ridges and clay desert, but for the whole way the earth is covered with *débris*, ruins and bits of tile, brick, etc., etc. showing the remains of a city. The Pillar of Zahidún is hollowed into a spiral staircase, but has no spiral column in its centre. Built of kiln-baked brick, no mortar whatever has been used in its construction, the plastering having been effected with the common clay or *kankar* of the surrounding desert. It is very extraordinary how this mud or clay can have held together for so long. The staircase is also worthy of notice, being formed entirely of bricks which lap over one another, cemented by this *kankar*, the first brick, as it were, being built out from the wall, and the other bricks overlapping. The sweep of the staircase is very good, but the centre of it has given way, so that the upper part of the tower has been rendered inaccessible. Around the top is a floral scroll, exactly resembling that so much used for the ornamentation of railings in England, and not unlike a fleur-de-lis. Two inscriptions in Kufic, probably texts from the Koran, are built in brick set on end into the tower, one about thirty feet from the ground, the other at the summit; but they are both illegible. The dimensions of the tower are as follows: fifty-five feet in circumference at the base, which is built on a square foundation, and twenty-five feet at the summit; it is now eighty feet high, but has lost some of its original height. The bricks are of the same description as those now used in Persia, and of the dimensions of ten inches square by two thick. The tower, which must formerly have been a station for the Múazzin, now stands quite by itself with no ruins near it, though the neighbouring ground is covered with brick and tile fragments. From this Pillar to

[1] At Zahidún we saw some tamed wild ducks and geese which are used for decoy purposes, and which the inhabitants resolutely refused to sell.

CONTINUED DISCOURTESY.

Kásimabád we reckoned the distance only a mile. Kásimabád is a small but prosperous-looking village of some 50 or 60 houses, surrounded by cultivation, and with a canal which supplies it with pure water. With Iskil and Banjár it belonged of quite late years to the tribe of the Kalántars, who in bygone ages were the masters of the whole of Sistán: and the Katkhudas of these three places, though chosen by the Amir, are still of this tribe.

'Friday, March 1. Marched at 7.15 A.M. eight miles due north to Jalálabád, and five miles further north to Búrj-i-Afghán. Bright weather but somewhat cold. The thermometer during night 33°. The road the whole way was over a flat plain, principally consisting of hard baked clay, with extensive ruins on the right hand, stretching as far as the eye could reach, and cultivated land on the left. We were obliged to make a considerable *détour* from the direct road to Jalálabád[1] as the country is much flooded. We arrived at 9 A.M.: and shortly after our arrival, on Captain Lovett wishing to go and inspect four very large tamarisk-trees outside the town, he was stopped by some men who were stationed about fifty yards from camp, and told he could not proceed unless he had express permission from the Yáwar Azád Khán—moreover, that, under orders issued, none of our servants were to be admitted either into or near the town. The Yáwar, who was at once summoned, made some false excuses, saying he would find out the reason; and a short time afterwards sent word that the place was in the hands of Abbas Malik Khán, who declared that he could not permit the General, his staff, or any of his servants to enter. On hearing this the General sent the Mirakhor to say that he could not stop here any longer, but would move off in the evening towards Búrj-i-Afghán[2]. Tents were accordingly

---

[1] Jalálabád was built by Bahrám Khán, the last of the Kaiáni kings, for his eldest son Jaláludin. Jaláludin quarrelled with his aged father and went off to Herát; his father remaining in the village of Kachiun. Shah Kámrán assisted him, and after the death of Bahrám Khán, invaded Sistán with Jaláludin and a large force. The whole of Sistán resisted the aggression, but were defeated, and Kámrán departed leaving Jaláludin on the throne. On his departure the Sistánis rose and expelled Jaláludin, and Kaiáni rule ceased from that date. Muhammad Rizá Khán and Háshim Khán then divided the power; and Ibráhim Khán Balúch seized the opportunity of increasing his territory on this side of the Helmand, by taking the places in the vicinity of Jahánabád, which latter had been given him by Bahrám Khán, and of which, with the rest of his conquests, he was deprived by Táj Muhammad Khán later on.

[2] Búrj-i-Afghán was originally a settlement given by Bahrám Khán to Muhammad Khán, son of Azam Khán, Ghilzái, who came with a number of Afghans from Khabis,

struck, and we arrived at the latter place at about 4 A. M. The excuse that Malik Abbas Khán had refused us entrance is of course a farce; we owe this opposition, as indeed all our other *désagrémens*, to Mirza Ma'súm Khán, who sends orders as to our treatment through the Amir; and we know that the Yáwar despatched two men from Kásimabád to Jalálabád this morning with a message to the Katkhuda. Some Afghán residents of the Búrj-i-Afghán whom Captain Lovett met, told him they were certain to be punished for speaking to him; and indeed during the whole of our tour we have been absolutely unable to gain any information whatever from the inhabitants. At this place our camp has been quite tabooed, and our servants have been prevented from entering the town by a chain of sentries: we have in short been treated as prisoners within a circumscribed space. Jalálabád is a town of about 400 houses, with a low, useless mud wall; it has a mosque among the trees outside the walls. The march to the Búrj-i-Afghán was over a clay plain covered with ruins. There is considerable cultivation around this village, which much resembles that of Chelling, having the same octagonal-shaped tower in the centre. The place contains no less than 200 Afghán families, but we were not allowed to have any intercourse whatever with them, and the inhabitants resolutely refused to let us have anything on purchase until permission to sell was received from the Yáwar. Captain Lovett rode out in the afternoon, straight from Jalálabád about ten miles due north, and came to the "Náizár," or borders of the Hámún, now dry. A letter came in during the evening from the Persian Commissioner, objecting to the proposition from the General that the Commissioners should meet at Búrj-i-Alam Khán, for the discussion of evidence; and shortly afterwards two Afgháns arrived from General Pollock's camp with letters stating that he would reach Rúdbár on February 28. In the morning, before leaving Kásimabád, we saw a Balúch who had taken an active part in the disputes that used formerly to rage in Sistán between Ibráhim Khán and Sharif Khán Balúch on the one side, and Táj Muhammad Khán of Sekuha on the other. This man's neck was nearly cut through with a sword, and the scar is so wide now that you can put your finger in it lengthways. To aggravate his case he is all over scars,

near Karmán, on being turned out by Fath Ali Shah. These men were the descendants of the old Afghán conquerors of Isfahán. Bahrám Khán married the daughter of Muhammad Khán; and *their* descendants still inhabit the place.

and has lost some part of most of his fingers. The whole of the neighbouring country here is covered with ruins, among which are two or three large villages. They say that from Jalálabád northward till the territory of Lásh Juwain the country is a desert where neither food or water are obtainable.

'March 2. Marched at 8 A.M. five miles south-south-west to Banjár. Bright clear morning. Road ran over clay desert, crossing three small canals. The village of Banjár, lying about eight miles east of Nasírabád, the towers of which are visible from it, is one of the largest and most populous in Sistán, and is surrounded by a great extent of cultivation. It is one of the group of villages which formerly were the especial property of the Kalántars, of whom the head man, Mir Wáris Kalántar, is now the Katkhuda of Banjár. Here, as usual, all communication with the village was prevented. There is a small lake of water in the vicinity of Banjár, formed in a hollow from the overflow of the numerous canals which abound in the neighbourhood. This lake is temporary only, and is quite covered with wild fowl, which are very difficult to get near. Ma'súm Khán sent out a letter to say that, as he understood the Afghán Commissioner was coming into Sistán with an army of 500 men, he thought it his duty to return to Tehrán. This, coupled with the fact that the Yáwar wrote to the General asking for a testimonial and leave to quit the camp for the purpose of seeing the Amir, may be taken as a sign that some new move of annoyance and obstruction is about to be attempted. The Mírakhor and some of the servants who went into the town to-day saw both the Persian Commissioner and the Amir, and gave them a short account of the way in which we had been treated, which was of course met with protestations of regret and ignorance. Ma'súm Khán will probably accept this as a fitting place for discussion, but he pretends to feel personal fear at meeting the Afghán Commissioner so far from the town of Nasírabád. He told the Mírakhor that the Hájji's horse had been found at Túrsháb, but on its way here died at Sekuha from exhaustion. While telling this precious story, our informant said, the Commissioner himself could not help laughing.

'The gnats, flies, hornets, and other insects peculiar to the place, are already beginning to make their appearance. On the morning of March 3 messages came in from General Pollock with letters saying that his camp had arrived opposite Chahár Búrjak, on the left bank of the Helmand; that Kamál Khán had refused them supplies, but that

Imám Khán had sent them a polite invitation; and that he hoped to reach Búrj-i-Alam Khán about the 5th instant, having with him 100 *sowárs* and fifty beasts of burden. Return messengers were despatched without delay, asking him to join our camp at Banjár. The Yáwar, on the other hand, informed us that Mirza Ma'súm Khán had sent off the whole of his tents and baggage, and intended to leave himself the next day for Khúrasán. This rumour, though hardly credible concerning his personal movements, was so far corroborated by our muleteers, that they had been in town and helped their brother muleteers to pack his tents and baggage. The evenings are becoming intensely close, the temperature at 9 P.M. being higher than at 9 A.M.

'March 4. Halt. Weather cloudy. In the morning Captain Smith was sent into the town to visit Mirza Ma'súm Khán and the Amir. The object of his visit was to settle the question of the visits to be paid, to find out about the reception that had been ordered for the Afghán Mission, and, now that tents were to be pitched as heretofore, to bring the objections that had been raised concerning the flag to an issue. The Commissioner assured Captain Smith that all necessary arrangements had been made for the honourable and fitting reception of General Pollock and the Afghán Mission, and that Sardár Sharif Khán's son had been ordered to receive them on their entrance into his father's territory: he also said that Kamál Khán's conduct was quite contrary to orders. With regard to the visits he said that General Pollock and the Afghán Commissioner should, according to etiquette, first call on himself and the Amir, and that the visit would be at once returned. He added that if the General would write two lines to the Amir, the latter would see the Mullas on the subject of the flag, and endeavour to explain matters to them. The Amir has given a number of horses and camels to the Commissioner, who sent off the whole of his baggage to Káïn on Monday evening, but who did not say anything in this visit about his own departure, save that he had already been kept waiting for the Afghán Commissioner for a month, and did not know whether he could wait much longer, certainly not more than a week or fortnight.

'Wednesday, March 6. Halt. Weather cloudy and much cooler. In the morning letters from General Pollock came in, saying that he was at Búrj-i-Alam Khán, had been well received by Sardár Sharif Khán, whose son had come out to meet them, and who had himself called on them; and that the Afghán Mission hoped to cross to Deshtak this day. Captain Lovett returned from a surveying expedition to the Kúh-i-Khwájah, and describes the hill itself as being very uninteresting, with a few ruins on its undulating crest, and those quite unworthy of notice. At 2 P.M. Captain Smith was sent into town, on his way to General Pollock's camp, to visit the Persian Commissioner, and see that everything was settled for the reception and *istikbál* of the Afghán Mission. To go to Deshtak from Banjár it is necessary to pass by Nasírabád, as the whole of the intervening country is under water. Matters having been arranged for the *istikbál*, Captain Smith rode out towards Deshtak, but on arriving at Jásinák learnt that the Afghán Mission had gone to Wásilán, to which place he accordingly followed, arriving in their camp about 6 P.M. He found the camp without a single person in it to represent either the Amir or any Persian authority, and the inhabitants of Wásilán absolutely refusing to sell them provisions; but through an official of the Amir, who was with him, of course the latter difficulty was soon put right. Accompanying Sáiyid Núr Muhammad Sháh was Ahmad Khán, chief of Lásh Juwain, and some 120 *sowárs*, the number of followers all told being probably about 300. Ibráhim Khán of Chakhansúr, with his son, had crossed the Helmand, and held an interview at Dak-i-Dehli with General Pollock and the Afghán Commissioner. Startling stories had been told to the new-comers concerning General Goldsmid's Mission, and they had even heard that the Amir had given orders for the people to rise and kill us all. Sardár Imám Khán had met the Afghán party at Chahár Búrjak, and informed them that all he had done with regard to ourselves was under Persian compulsion.

'Our larger camp was pitched this day, and the Mission moved into it during the afternoon, with the flag flying as in the first instance. Letters had been received from the Persian Commissioner and Amir in the morning, stating that the General's letter to the Amir, explaining the real meaning of the flag, had enabled him with infinite trouble to silence all religious objections! Yet, in the afternoon, the Yáwar Azád Khán wrote a letter to Sir Frederic from the village, saying that the minds of the people were most uneasy at the sight of the flag, and requesting an explanation, for which the General referred him to the Amir. It was found that the Persian Commissioner had pitched his flagstaff that morning on the very summit of his house, from which the flag could be seen for miles.

'General Pollock and the Afghán Mission arrived at Nasírabád on the 7th inst., and were received at about one mile from the town by an *istikbál* of some seventy *sowárs*, headed by Hájji Azád Khán, an *employé* of the Hisám-u-saltanah, who had been sent here from Mash-had to find out what was going on. It was noticeable that, in return for the usual polite enquiries, the Sáiyid Núr Muhammad Shah omitted altogether asking after the Amir's health, and only asked after the Hisám-u-saltanah. The camp for the Afghán Mission was pitched at the east corner of the town, right beneath the Amir's house. Shortly after arrival, Sardár Khán Bábá Khán and Mirza Mússa were sent by the Amir and Mirza Ma'súm Khán to make the usual health enquiries, which were duly returned. A phase in Persian diplomacy was exhibited to-day. No sooner had the Sáiyid alighted at his tent, than he received a message secretly, saying that all the Sarbandis and Sharikis were ready to rise and kill the Amir and take his fort, if he the Sáiyid would give the signal; and Khán Bábá Khán, on calling on him, told him he was discontented with the Amir's treatment, and intended to go to Herát. It is needless to say to what source these messages owed their existence.

'On the morning of March 8, the whole of Sir F. Goldsmid's staff, with servants and led horses, rode out at 8 A.M., accompanied by the Yáwar and fifteen *sowárs*, for the *istikbál* of Major-General Pollock and Sáiyid Núr Muhammad Shah, who, with Dr. Bellew and an escort of some 100 or 150 *sowárs*, arrived at head-quarters camp at Banjár about 9.30 A.M. In the afternoon the Mírakhor was sent into Nasirabad, to say that General Pollock and Dr. Bellew would call on the Amir and the Persian Commissioner the next day, on the understanding that the call should be returned in Banjár on the Monday following. To this message the Commissioner returned answer that he would write his reply, but none had arrived by 11 P.M. The Afghán Commissioner resolutely declines to call first on the Persian Commissioner and the Amir on the following grounds: that it would be very displeasing to the Amir Shir Ali Khán; that it would seriously damage his cause with the people around in Afghán interest, who would be told that he had gone to make his "arz" or petition to the Amir; that he had been treated with such gross incivility as to render his calling first impossible; and that it was the duty of the Amir and Mirza Ma'súm Khán to call first on him, as he was a greater official and higher dignitary than either of them.

'Sáiyid Núr Muhammad Shah, the Afghán Commissioner, is a tall, well-built, fine-looking man, of some fifty years of age, with prominent nose, and a somewhat Jewish cast of countenance. He is frank and outspoken to a degree, very determined on what he considers to be the rights of his cause, and to press them to the utmost. He is represented as being the most powerful man in Afghánistán next to Shir Ali Khán himself, and to be the latter's principal and most trusted adviser. The absence of all pomp or affectation of show which marks his procedure is very noticeable; his own dress and the trappings of his horse being of the plainest and commonest description. He walks about the camp unattended by any following whatever, and is equally without affectation in his conversation. He gives one the idea of a shrewd clever man, sure of himself, whose every action would be based on some good grounds. He professes, and it is to be believed, feels a sincere friendship for the English, to whom he owes gratitude for many acts of kindness. He accompanied the Amir as his chief adviser on the occasion of the late visit to Ambála, and was sent by Sardár Kohandil Khán as ambassador to Tehrán in 1857, when he remained at the Persian capital for thirteen months.

'March 9. In the early morning a letter came in from Mirza Ma'súm Khán demanding the reason of the number of followers who accompanied the Afghán Commissioner; stating that with regard to General Pollock's visit to the Amir, the latter did not consider it advisable to return it; and that, for his own part, he could not say how he should act until he had received an answer to his present letter. The Persians here display a great deal of ill-feeling towards the Afgháns, punishing in some sort every one who has anything to do with them, and the Afgháns are naturally eager to resent this discourteous and unseemly treatment.

'March 10. The high winds with violent dust storms, which prevail at this season of the year, have set in with unusual severity, and make camp life miserable. In the early morning two letters came in from Ma'súm Khán, declining to return General Pollock's visit at Banjár and requesting that the Afghán Commissioner should send him in a statement of his claims in writing, when he would receive a "silencing" answer. He also in another letter threatened "most undesirable consequences" if Ahmad Shah, the Lásh Juwain chief, did not leave the camp. Sir Frederic Goldsmid, after consultation with General Pollock, therefore wrote to the Persian Commissioner, and informed him that as his actions and correspondence both pointed to the fact that he was bent on not meeting the British arbitrator's wishes in any way, he had no course left but to withdraw from Sistán. He should accordingly leave the next day for Lásh Juwain, sending Captain Lovett to complete the survey of Chakhansúr and that district. No answer to this letter came till late at night, when Ma'súm Khán wrote to say he had done everything to meet the General's wishes, but that the fault of non-success did not lay with him: he enclosed letters of safe-conduct for Captain Lovett as well as for the Mission, and was evidently very pleased to hear we were going. He said that as the next day was the first of Muharam, and it was considered very unlucky to move out of a town on that day, he had already made a garden just outside the walls, his *nakal makán*, or "stage of first setting out." There is a report that a Faráhi who had accompanied Sardár Ahmad Shah, and had gone on to Banjár to see his relations, has been severely beaten, has had all his arms taken from him, and has been missing for two days. The portmanteau which Sir F. Goldsmid lost in Italy on the way here, arrived in camp to-day from Bandar-Abbas, having all its contents untouched and safe. It had been brought by a Balúch on a camel, sent by the Governor of Karmán.

' March 11. Winds higher than ever, and weather most unpleasant. Captain Smith rode into Nasírabád this morning and had an interview with the Persian Commissioner, who was encamped in a garden just outside the walls of the town. The Commissioner endeavoured to explain his past conduct, but was informed that all that had taken place would now have to be discussed at Tehrán. He was very anxious to find out the reasons why Sáiyid Núr Muhammad Shah had not called upon him, and was apparently much enraged that the Amir and himself should have been guilty of any civility whatever towards the Afghán Commissioner; as he kept saying that the *istikbál* and "áhwál pursi" had been intended entirely for the honour of General Pollock; and that for 'Amir Shir Ali Khán without "vous autres" the English,' the Persian Government did not care at all. He kept repeating that all would be well at Tehrán; and towards the end of the visit begged Captain Smith to give his especial compliments to Sir Frederic Goldsmid, General Pollock, and the Afghán Commissioner, and to tell the two latter that he hoped to meet them in General Goldsmid's tent at Birjand or Mash-had. Report has it that he has been very highly bribed by the Amir to break off matters without a conference, and to act in the way the Amir told him; certainly the treatment that the British and Afghán Missions have received at the hands of the Persian authorities is without parallel. Illustrations of discourtesy might be added in respect to the supply of baggage animals, cash payments, and other pressing matters for the treatment and disposal of which we were, at the last moment, necessarily dependent on the local officials. Suffice it to say, we were detained by these harassing negotiations until late in the day; though General Pollock and the Afghán Commissioner started at noon. Captain Lovett left in good time with a Persian escort for Chakhansúr for survey purposes, but it was not until evening that the head-quarters camp marched for Bolah, a small village only seven miles distant. Its position was due north, over a dry clay plain, scored into furrows by the wind, which is so strong in this part of the neighbourhood that all the plants grow horizontally along the ground like creepers. The Yáwar left us at Banjár, and we have now no escort with our camp; but orders have been sent to Jalálabád for forty *sowárs* to join us. A report has reached camp that the missing Farúhi was killed in Nasírabád this morning, but it is not supported. They say also that on the approach of the Afghán Commissioner two regiments had been ordered here from Khaff.

'March 12. We were obliged to halt at this place (Bolah) to-day, as our camels stuck at the ditch in the night, and could not get in here till the morning, and now the men are making great difficulties about going further. The animus displayed by the Amir of Káin towards the Mission naturally affects the general behaviour of his subordinates. We notice here a great anxiety on the part of all the Persians with us to leave our camp at this point, much in the same way as they were anxious last year to get away when we had reached Pishín. The probabilities are that they do not care to go farther north, and that the Amir's authority does not extend much beyond this village. We dismissed all our late Persian *sowárs* in the evening and received six *sowárs* from Jalálabád to escort the Amir's camels, but the forty that we were informed had been ordered for our escort from the same village did not make their appearance.

'On the 13th March we finally quitted Sistán, after a stay of six weeks' duration. As has been recounted, all the British Commissioner's efforts to bring about a meeting between the delegates of Persia and Afghánistán had been frustrated by the Persian authorities,

It had been found impossible to procure any species of evidence affecting the enquiry at issue, and the results of our sojourn in the province might be summed up in the excellent survey that had been prepared by Captain Beresford Lovett, and in the *primâ facie* evidence as to the present condition of Sistán that we had been able to collect by the evidence of our senses. The Amir had certainly been successful in stifling on the spot an enquiry which might, if once commenced, have caused considerable agitation in the minds of the various members of the ancient deposed families who were so carefully kept out of the way of the British Commissioner. As far as he dared, he had endeavoured to lower the dignity of the representative of the British Government, and to slight in a marked manner the Commissioner of Shir Ali Khán and General Pollock who accompanied him. But after all, the decision on the whole matter would have to be pronounced in Tehrán. One inevitable conclusion forced upon the mind after our Sistán experiences was, that the Persian Government had most signally and culpably failed in the commonest courtesy, not taking even the most ordinary precautions to ensure that the dignity and safety of a Mission it had itself solicited should be suitably upheld and regarded. With the exception of the superficial and empty courtesies shown to the British Commissioner on his first arrival, no single opportunity was neglected of placing slights upon the Mission, and of rendering independence of action practically impossible. Instead of being furnished at the outset with a suitable escort, and accompanied by a responsible Persian official of high rank who would have eventually had to answer for his conduct to the Shah on every detail, we were dependent upon a hostile Governor (who in these far-off regions is absolutely despotic) not only for the means of locomotion, for guards and sentries over our camp, but for the supply of the very necessaries of life. Anything like free action was therefore hopelessly crippled; and instead of the British Commissioner being able to move about the province wherever he thought proper, and in a style and manner commensurate to his dignity, his sphere of action was practically limited by and dependent on the wishes of the Amir. Had the Persian Commissioner been a man of another stamp, matters might of course have worn a very different complexion. But poor and needy and with nothing to lose, he was only too ready to play into the Amir's hands, and he probably took away with him recognition of his tractability sufficiently solid to make him regardless of the suspension of one year from public employ—which was the punishment eventually awarded him at Tehrán, in deference to the representations of the British Legation[1].'

IV. *Sistán to Mash-had.*

'Leaving Bolah at 7.30 on the morning of the 13th March, we marched north-north-west twenty-eight miles to the ruins of Pesháwarán, camping in their vicinity at a spot called Salián. At four miles from Bolah we passed the villages of Rindán on the right and Kala'h-i-Nau[2] on the left, which are the last inhabited places in this direction towards the bed of the Hámún; and for the first ten miles our road ran over a desert plain of alluvial soil baked hard and covered with heaps of sand, but furrowed in every direction from the action of wind and water. At ten miles we reached a belt of thick tamarisk jungle, and at twelve miles halted and breakfasted in the bed of a dry canal, some thirty feet wide, which runs through the jungle,

[1] The following itinerary in Sistán may be useful:—

Date, 1872.	Stage.	Distance in Miles.	Direction.
January 31	Cháh-i-Khak-i-Muhammad Darvish		
February 1	Sekuha	30	N.
,, 4	Chelling	10	N.N.W.
,, 5	Nasirabád	13	N.
,, 15	Deshtak	14	S.S.E.
,, 16	Búrj-i-Alam Khán	4	S.E. by E.
,, 17	Kala'h-i-Nau	2½	E. by N.
,, 17	Kimak	3	N.
,, 18	Kúbak	9	E. by S.
,, 19	Dak-i-Dehli	28	S. by E.
,, 20	Bandar-i-Kamál Khán	12	S.S.E.
,, 21	Húsainabád	10	E. by S.
,, 24	Kala'h-i-Fath	25	N.W.
,, 25	Sar-i-Band	20	N.N.W.
,, 27	Nád-Ali	17	N.N.E.
,, 27	Village of Aghá Ján		
,, 28	Jahánabád	7	3 N.W.
,, 28	Tiflak		4 W.S.W.
,, 29	Záhidun-Kásimabád	11	5 S.W. / 6 N.N.W.
March 1	Jalálabád	8	N.
,, 1	Búrj-i-Afghán	5	W.
,, 2	Ranjár	5	S.S.W.

[2] From this tract north the desert is liable to inundation from the Hámún, and is known as the Shilah-i-Kala'h-i-Nau.

and where were some wells of brackish and uninviting water. This canal is said to have come from Jahánabád, but there were no signs of cultivation in its vicinity. At a mile beyond our breakfasting-place, we reached the Náizár, which forms the neck connecting the east and west portions of the old lake. The Náizár is a tract of about five miles in width and varying in length, covered with high yellow reeds and bulrushes, the former very thick and strong. The way through it is by a path about six feet wide, originally cut for the passage of rafts or *tútís*. On first viewing the Náizár it was easy to realise Conolly's description of the Hámún, as seen from the summit of Kúh-i-Khwájah—minus the water. As far as the eye could reach, on every side were to be seen the tops of a waving sea of yellow reeds, with nothing to break the view, save where dense black columns of smoke rising to the sky marked the spots where the wandering tribes were burning the reeds, in order that, later on, the young green shoots which replace them might afford pasturage for their flocks and herds. It is only within the last four or five years that this tract (and much further to the south) has at this time of the year been passable by any other method than in *tútís*. The water, however, would never be much deeper than three or four feet. Two or three mounds, one called Kuha, the other Ab Kand, similar to those on the plains to the south of Sistán, form landmarks to guide the traveller amid the dreary waste of reeds. Leaving the "Náizár," the road then runs over a saline desert plain, thickly covered with tamarisk, *bhuta*, *trat*, and camel-thorn—of a clayey substance, and with deep hoof-marks showing that it had lately been under water. We encamped a short distance to the east of the ruins of Pesháwarán, but amid other large ruins, by the side of a small and new canal of water brought from the Farah-Rúd last year by Sardár Ahmad Khán. We are now in Lásh territory, and several well-known points of view can be seen from our camp. The wind dropped in the afternoon, but began to blow again at sunset. We hear that the Amir of Káïn has given out that if we had not gone when we did, he had made up his mind to have us turned out by force[1].

'On the afternoon of March 14 we all went to see the ruins of Pesháwarán[2], which we found as disappointing as have been the

[1] Such reports may or may not have been true: I do not credit them; and it is very certain that those who brought them were rather inclined to stimulate than to allay our irritation at the Amir's behaviour.—*F. J. G.*

[2] The ruins of Pesháwarán are divided into several groups known by different names,

ruins of Sistán in general. They are of great extent and are strongly built, many of them of alternate layers of sun-burnt and baked brick, but there is nothing that tells of their date or nature. The remains of a *madrasah* or mosque, with a *mihráb*, were among the most extensive, and had traces of ornamentation and a Kufic inscription. The walls of the *ark*, or citadel, are still in good repair. This was of a circular form, somewhat irregular in shape, with a diameter of from two to three hundred yards. The walls are about fifty feet high, built strongly of baked brick, with a species of arched covered gallery, five feet wide and five feet high, running round the summit of the ramparts. Two massive round towers guard the gateway, which is approached up a narrow steep ascent. In the centre of the fort is a mound, on which are the ruins of a house of superior character, probably the residence of the governor. To the south dense drifts of sand run to the summit of the ramparts. The usual remains of tile, brick, vases, &c. strew the surface of the ground, but we could discover nothing novel. The great characteristic of these ruins is the number of accurately constructed arches which still remain, and which are seen in almost every house, and the remains of very strongly built windmills, with a vertical axis, as is usually the case in Sistán.

'March 15th. Marched at 7.30 A.M., nineteen miles north to Lásh Juwain. We went out of our way some three or four miles to the west, on account of the ruins, in the endeavour to discover an ancient inscription, which directs the traveller to turn to the left hand and dig, when he will be rewarded by discovering seven jars of gold. We, however, were not successful in attaining the desired object, as our guide could not verify his clues: he showed us, instead, the ruins of what was most probably some place of worship, with a *mihráb*, and above the *mihráb*, in the wall, the masonic star of five points surrounded by a circle, and with a round cup between each of the points, and another in the centre: we also saw the tomb of Sáiyid Ikbál, mentioned by

---

such as Kol-Márút, Salián, Khúshabád, Kala'h-i-Mallahún, Nikára-Khanah, and more. Eight miles west-north-west from the ruins is a flat-topped irregularly-shaped hill, called the Kúh-i-Kúchah; somewhat smaller than, but resembling, the Kúh-i-Khwájah. To its east flows the Farah Rúd, to its west the Hárút Rúd, and near it are four villages, named Ghonah, Kuhga, Damboli, and Gárgúri, the latter deriving its name from the gurgling caused by the waters rushing through a narrow passage near the village. Slag is said to be found all over this hill. We could find no trace of the name Lukh mentioned in Conolly's map.

Christie, lying about three miles to the north-north-east. Leaving the ruins and pursuing our course to the north over a hard plain of alluvial soil with plentiful tamarisk and camel-thorn, we arrived, in two and a-half hours from starting-point, at the village of Khairábád, a portion of Sardár Ahmad Khán's territory, wretched in construction and numbering 120 inhabitants. The inhabitants of Khairábád came out to talk to us, and inveighed bitterly against the Amir of Káïn, who, they said, had last year sent a number of *sowárs* and cattle to graze on and destroy their crops, headed by a son of Sardár Sharif Khán. These villagers are Popalzái-Afgháns. They had only just commenced to plough and sow, whereas the crops in Sistán are nearly full grown. This they accounted for by the fact that the season had been quite abnormal, and that the Farah-Rúd had only just come down and furnished them with the required water for irrigation, conveyed by a small canal from the river. Hence to our camp in Lásh Juwain, ten miles further, the road was over a flat plain, desert for the first five miles, but afterwards thickly covered with *kirta*. Extensive detached plateaux, of a clayey formation with shingle on the top, stand out in all directions, and most probably mark the former level of the valley, which, if it only enjoyed security, might be most fertile and productive. We found the camp pitched in the valley, underneath the fort of Lásh, and about a quarter of a mile from it, with the river intervening. On arrival, Sardár Ahmad Khán paid Sir F. Goldsmid a visit in his tent. The Sardár is a pleasant but somewhat foxy-looking man of probably fifty-five or sixty years of age, but his dyed beard and whiskers and painted eyes make him appear much younger. He is the grandson of the famous Shah Pasand Khán of this place, son of Abdúl Rasúl Khán, and nephew of Ibráhim Khán of Chakhansúr. He remembers quite well Conolly's visit to his grandfather, thirty years ago, and speaks of Conolly (Khán Ali) as having been his great friend, saying that he accompanied him as far as the Kúh-i-Khwájah, and that he had received from him a telescope, which was sent from Kábúl, and which he had given to his Chakhansúr uncle. He also perfectly recollects Khánikoff and his mission, who, he says, were afraid to go into Sistán, but went off to Neh and Bandan. The Sardár is at present greatly exasperated against the Amir of Káïn. He represents that last year his subjects have been reduced by more than two-thirds, through the tricks of the Amir, who used to send emissaries at night, and tell his people that if they would join him they would be well fed and taken care of. In this way more than 2000 families were enticed away, and the majority of the land is in consequence left uncultivated this year, while numerous villages are completely deserted: for he estimates the whole of his subjects now remaining as not more than 1000 families at the outside. The runaways would be certain to return, he thinks, if only there was any chance of their being secured against the attacks of their ambitious and cruel neighbour. He also bears testimony to the lateness of the period at which the Farah-Rúd is filled. The waters of this river apparently remain for about sixty days longer; when it gradually dries up. Poor as he must be, the Sardár insists upon providing everything for our camp gratis, saying he is not like Mir Alam Khán. He is married to a daughter of Ibráhim Khán of Chakhansúr, for whom the natives in these localities seem to have at once the greatest respect and awe. This latter chief is described as a great warrior and great hunter, but not a man who could take his place in a *majlis* or assembly. He has no powers of conversation, is thoroughly wild in speech, manner and appearance, and is addicted to the use of *charas*, *bang*, opium, and other stimulants, under the influence of which he becomes completely mad. From constant enquiries made since we have been in Sistán, there can be no doubt whatever that he was the murderer of Dr. Forbes, and that Ferrier's account of Sardár Ali Khán's commission of the crime, and subsequent treatment of Dr. Forbes' body, is at variance with facts. The natives, moreover, all assert that Ali Khán had been dead many years when Sardár Ibráhim Khán shot Dr. Forbes. Concerning the details of the murder, we have ascertained that Khánikoff's relation of the incident is nearly correct: and there can be little doubt that Ibráhim Khán was under the influence of *bang* when he fired the fatal shot. From information collected at Lásh, it appears that Sháh Pasand Khán implored Forbes not to trust himself in Chakhansúr, telling him that Ibráhim Khán was a drunkard and a madman, and would certainly kill him. As Forbes persisted in going, Sháh Pasand Khán made him, before he left, write a paper saying that he did so against advice and on his own responsibility: and he then dismissed him, telling him his blood must be upon his own head. How Ferrier came to connect Sardár Ali Khán's name with the deed it is impossible to conceive, for here no doubt or concealment of the fact of Sardár Ibráhim Khán's guilt is attempted. It is talked of quite commonly and openly. For many years Sardár Ibráhim Khán almost entirely discontinued intercourse with his fellow men—either shutting himself up in his fort surrounded by numbers of large, powerful and savage dogs, who permitted no one to approach him save a negro boy slave, who brought him his meals—or else living in the jungle, engaged in hunting the wild boar, of which sport he is passionately fond. Captain Lovett however, who visited him, gives a better account of his ways: but he is quite incapable of managing business, which is done for him by his wife and her favourite son Khán Jahán. Ibráhim Khán has six sons :—Malik Khán, a youth addicted to *bang* and opium, who has quarrelled with his father and is living under the protection of the Amir of Káïn at Sharifabád; 2. Khán Jahán, heir to the chieftainship, clever and sharp, and fond of English dress; 3. Muhammad Ali Khán; 4. Sarfaráz Khán, who has been at Tehrán for some years; 5. Muhammad Khán, and one other.

'Saturday, March 16. Halt. The weather is getting much warmer, and the maximum of this day's thermometer reaches 98°. While at breakfast in the morning we were astonished to hear a general firing in camp, and on going outside the tent found the *sowárs* discharging their rifles at an enormous flock of pelicans flying over head, in several long lines, in a north-west direction. There must have been at the least 500 or 600 of these birds. They kept close together, flew very high, and were probably migrating on the approach of the hot weather. There is another report in camp that the Amir has killed the Faráhi who was detained at Nasirabád, but it is impossible to ascertain its truth. At 5 P.M. Sardár Ahmad Khan, accompanied by Mardán Khán, the Akhúnd-zádah of the Sardár, Mústafá Khán, and the chief of Púlálak called on Sir Frederic Goldsmid. It was most interesting to hear these men talk of Conolly and his Sergeant, Cameron, and Múnshi Karámat Khán. In Lásh Juwain Conolly's name is known as well as the Sardár's, and all people talk of him with affection. The Sardár and the remainder of the chiefs were very anxious to know what was going to be the upshot of the Mission. They said that they had suffered unheard-of things at the hands of the Amir of Káïn, but that their own hands had been tied by the influence of the English Government with the Amir Shir Ali Khán, and that they could not retaliate. Sardár Ahmad Khán repeated he had already lost more than two-thirds of his subjects, who had been enticed into Sistán by the

Amir of Káin; adding that he himself had received two or three letters from the Hisám-i-Saltanah, offering him 5000 *tumáns* a year if he would obey the Persians, which he had hitherto refused; and that unless he was speedily enabled to maintain his position, he would have no resource but to join the Amir, the other chiefs up to Farrah following his example, Ibráhim Khán of Chakhansúr included. Mústáfá Khan told us that he had been sent to ask the meaning of the army that some years previously entered Sistán under the orders of Muhammad Salah Khán, Kúrd-bacha; and that he had received no less than two written letters, addressed by the father of the present Amir of Káin to Dost Muhammad Khán, who sent him from Herát, saying that the Persians had nothing to do with Sistán, but that Muhammad Salah Khán had merely come down with a small force as escort, in order to pay the annual subsidy to Sardár Ibráhim Khán and other Balúch chiefs, for keeping open the roads to Persia by Afghánistán, such as the Haftád Ráh and others. Mardán Khán, who is a tremendous warrior, breathed nothing but fire, blood and devastation, and spoke with contempt of the Amir of Káin, who, he said, had been with him formerly and under his thumb, and was at that time a Súnni. The Sardárs did not leave till the last moment at which they could say their evening prayers, when they went just outside the tent and performed their devotions, led by the Akhúnd Zadah. After dinner our Shia'h servants made a great noise,—wailing, weeping, and beating their bosoms for Husain and Ali.

'On the morning of the 17th we rode over and inspected the fortress of Juwain, a rectangular building, 400 yards by 300 yards, with towers at each face, and two large towers on either side of the gate, situated about two miles east-north-east of Lásh. It is the largest place in Hokát, and is surrounded by a covered way and wet ditch with a breadth of fifteen feet. Its east and west faces have six bastions each, its south face three, and the north two. The walls are about sixty feet in height, very thick and strong, and scored all over with the marks of the cannon-shot which Yár Muhammad fired against them. The only gate to the place is in the north face, and about 600 yards from it are the remains of an artificial mound of earth which the Wazír erected as a good site for his artillery. The fortress has never been taken, though it could not stand for a moment against heavy guns or shells. It is constructed on a high mound, and therefore towers above the plain. The wet ditch, which is of no depth, is dependent for its water supply on the Farah Rúd, with which it is connected by a canal. We were received in the most friendly way by Sardár Samad Khán, the governor of the place, and a brother of Sardár Ahmad Khán; and here again we found that Conolly was perfectly well remembered, for we were taken to the room where he had sat, when he called on Gulzár Khán, who after Conolly's departure went off to Herát and died there. The description of Juwain given by Conolly, that it was one of the most populous places he had seen since leaving Kandahár, does not apply now. The numerous houses around the walls are all deserted and ruined, and the Sardár assured us that out of 400 families who used to live inside the walls, no less than 250 had been enticed away into Sistán[1]. It appears that the year before last the Farah-Rúd did not fill at all, and the inhabitants were in consequence unable to sow their crops: last year their crops had come above ground, when the Persians came and destroyed them all; and it is owing to the scarcity which these two events have produced that the Amir has been enabled to entice over so many of the starving people. The Katkhuda of the place, a very old man, who as a boy remembers Yár Muhammad's siege, assured us that three years ago grain was so plentiful that fifteen *manns* sold for a *krán*, whereas only one is obtainable now for the same money. He represented the soil as being extraordinarily rich, a statement borne out by the fact that though the ground has only been sown seven days the crops are already appearing. They seemed especially proud of their melons, which they say are the finest in the world. From the summit of the walls an excellent view is obtained of the plain of Hokát lying below[2], bounded on every side, except to the south-west, by the higher plateau of the desert. There are three or four windmills inside the ditch and one outside, all with vertical axles, and sails of a coarse tamarisk-made canvas. All the houses in the fort, even the smallest, have little *bádgírs* or wind-towers of their own, and we were

---

[1] The names of the inhabited villages at present in the district of Lásh Juwain are as follows:—Juwain, Deh-Nau, and Khairabád, on the left bank of the river; Lásh, Panj-Deh, Sámár, Dirg, on the right bank. The following villages have been recently deserted all on the right bank:—Damboli, Kúchah, Kúhga, Jah-i-Dirg, Khúshabád.

[2] As is mentioned in Conolly, the name of this district is known as Hokát. The Sardár claims to the south all the Pesháwarán country as his own up to the Náizár. The valley is also called the *júlgah* of Laftán, from a village near, which is now in ruins. Farah is distant about sixty miles, and between it and this place there is said to be a pillar similar to those we had seen in the deserts between the Narmashír and Sistán.

assured that of late years the flies and mosquitoes had become as bad as in Sistán, though formerly there were hardly any : the heat here is very great. Many of the inhabitants came to Mr. Rosario for medical advice, and the Sardár accompanied us back to camp to get some medicine for his eyes. He told us that only five villages remained inhabited now in the whole of his brother's territory, and the country was consequently quite uncultivated. The plain from the summit of the fort appears to be almost entirely covered with *kirta*. That portion below Lásh still bears the name of Laftán Juwain, as it did in Conolly's time, from a new canal dug by Shah Pasand Khán[1]. The village of Laftán is in ruins, but the canal remains. On our return we visited an ancient *ziárat-gah*, said to have been constructed by the Uzbeks. A well-built arch is still standing, covered with ornamentation and Kufic inscriptions. We were accompanied by Muhammad Hasan Khán, son of Shah Pasand Khán, a fine-looking bearded man of about forty-five. This is the " pet child " of whom Conolly speaks. Shah Pasand Khán survived his son Rasúl Khán three years ; and was himself succeeded, as chief, by Sardár Ahmad Khán, of whom he was very fond. Shah Pasand Khán's body was taken on his death to Herát for burial. His uncle, Gulzár Khán, the chief of Juwain, who also died at Herát, is said to have reached the age of 110 years ; and when he died to have all his teeth perfect in his head.

'March 17th. Halt. More large flocks of birds were observed flying over head to-day. This plain seems to swarm with venomous reptiles ; for while we were at breakfast, our servants brought in a large snake, two black scorpions, a yellow scorpion, and a sand snake. Weather much hotter. In the afternoon Captain Lovett returned from his survey expedition to Chakhansúr, and at the same time the eldest son of Ibráhim Khán of Chakhansúr, Khán Jahán Khán, came in—accompanied by the eldest son of Sardár Sharif Khán, who said he had quarrelled with his father and wished to join the Afgháns. Captain Lovett has succeeded in getting a good survey of the country. He reports Chakhansúr as being about sixty miles from this place, and says the country between is very desert. He found Ibráhim Khán encamped with 300 men close to the fort of Nád Ali, intent on hostile measures, but Captain Lovett persuaded him to return to the fort of

[1] The word Juwain seems to me a likely contraction from *Jái-nau*, the new stream.—F. J. G.

Chakhansúr, where he himself stayed for two days. He describes the Sardár, the murderer of Dr. Forbes, as a pleasant enough old man; believing, from all he heard and saw, that the famous dogs which used to form his only guard have been dispersed, and that he lives more among his fellow-men. At 5 P.M. Sir Frederic Goldsmid, accompanied by General Pollock, Dr. Bellew, and Captain Smith, returned the visit of Sardár Ahmad Khán in the fortress of Lásh. Sardárs Mardán Khán, Samad Khán, and the eldest son of Ahmad Khán, a fine-looking youth of some twenty-five years old, named Shamsudin, accompanied us to the fort. We forded the Farah-Rúd about a quarter of a mile below the fort, with the water above our saddle-girths, and the river running with a very strong current over a pebbly bottom. It had increased since the morning, and when we returned an hour later, the water in that short space of time had again risen perceptibly. Conolly's description of the fort of Lásh is so true, that it would be impossible to improve on it. It is a very striking-looking place, and is divided into three *arks* or citadels, each one higher than the other, and each provided with its own supply of water from deep wells sunk below the bed of the river. The east face of the cliff is at least 400 feet high, and Conolly's prediction that some portion of the fort would come down, from the undermining of the water, has not been fulfilled; but the crack he observed in the cliff became so large as to render necessary the evacuation of a *hammám* above, whose walls were split by it. The river has however of late years hugged its left bank, and now makes a nearly circular swoop to the east of the fort, at about 300 yards from it. It is very rare, only once in five or six years, that the waters actually touch the cliff on which it is built, but about five years ago they were so high as to render impossible all communication with the fort for five or six days. We were informed that the year before last a man had fallen from the top of the cliff on to the ground below without further injury than breaking two of his ribs. Winding our way up the nearly perpendicular ascent to the highest room of all, we were met at the second gate by the youngest son of the Sardár, a remarkably handsome, clever-looking child of twelve or thirteen years, dressed in clean and becoming garments, and who came and welcomed us all with a very pleasant politeness. At the entrance to his house the Sardár himself met us, and conducting us through several dark and narrow passages, led us into the highest room in the castle, long, lofty, and well-proportioned, and with two windows to the east and south that commanded the view of which we can well imagine that Conolly never got tired. The broad expanse of plain and river, the numerous villages (the greater part now deserted) dotting the plain, the bright green of the fresh crops, the distant mountains, all seen in the gorgeous hues of sunset, made up a picture that was very pleasant to look upon. In the more prosperous days of the province, the whole of this plain was one mass of cultivation, but now the greater part of it is covered with *kirta*, the cultivation merely lying in patches round such villages as are still inhabited. The Sardár received us very pleasantly and politely, and we had the usual *sharbat*, tea, and sweetmeats. The room we were in was that in which Shah Pasand Khán used to receive Conolly, and lower down was the chamber Conolly himself occupied. The Sardár said that unless affairs in Sistán changed for the better, he would leave his province altogether, come over to India, and take service with the Indian Government; but this was of course mere talk. They were all very anxious to find out how the Arbitration was likely to go, and persisted that the Faráhi left behind at Nasírabád had been killed by the Amír of Káin. We stayed for about three-quarters of an hour, chatting on various subjects, the room being quite filled with the Sardár's retainers. When we took our leave, the Sardár accompanied us to the lowest part of the castle, where we mounted our horses, much pleased with the visit. It is impossible to imagine a place more suited by nature to be the residence of a chieftain of rank, for from its summit the Sardár has an uninterrupted view to the furthest corner of his territories. Sardár Ahmad Khán has three sons, each by a different mother. The eldest, Shamsudin Khán, the future chief, is quite a European-looking youth; he wears trousers and straps with a waistcoat and species of overcoat, all profusely ornamented with English gilt military buttons. He accompanied the Amír Shir Ali Khán to Ambála, sat in the same carriage with him, and is one of the figures represented in the historical picture painted on that occasion. He is naturally impressed with a sense of the power and greatness of England. The other two sons are still boys, both remarkably handsome, named Sultan Ján and Muhammad Háidar respectively. The three forts are provisioned and watered, each independently of the other.

'March 18th, 1872. Marched two and a-half miles north-northwest to Panj-Deh. The wind, which has been so unpleasant for the last week, seems to have ceased. In the afternoon General Pollock's *dák* came in from Kandahár, bringing the terrible news of the assassination of Lord Mayo by a life convict at the Andamán Islands on the 8th February. It would be useless to attempt a description of the shock and grief caused by this intelligence throughout the camp; it is but a repetition of the profound sorrow and sensation with which the news was received throughout the length and breadth of the Indian Empire. The Afghán Commissioner, Sáiyid Núr Muhammad Shah, is much moved by it, and sees in it a cause of serious distress as well as personal loss to his master, the Amir Shir Ali Khán. He admits that the English Empire has many men at command capable of filling the place thus cruelly made vacant by an assassin's hand, but thinks it improbable that any one of them will take such immediate interest in the affairs of the Amir, and feel such friendship for him as were engendered by the famous conference at Ambála. General Pollock knows the assassin well. For three years he was his personal orderly at Peshawar, and used to ride behind his carriage; and while he was in his service he committed a murder close to the gate of his compound. General Pollock tried, convicted, and sentenced the man to death, but in consequence of his previous good character, and especially owing to excellent service he had rendered during the Ambaila campaign, his sentence was commuted to one of transportation for life to the Andamán Islands. Banished thus, as it were, to a remote corner of the world, he was enabled, in after years, to take the life of the Indian Viceroy. In the morning we sent all our baggage on to Panj-Deh. The river was so high that it had to be transported across on camels, the mules being useless for that purpose. At 4 P.M. we mounted, and fording the river about half a mile below the fort of Lásh, with the water considerably higher than the horses' girths and a very strong current, we passed over some high desert ground to the west of the fort for one mile, and then descended on to the plain, encamping close to the village of Panj-Deh, surrounded by cultivation and situated about one mile from the right bank of the Farah-Rúd. Panj-Deh is a walled village, containing thirty families; and was formerly the chief of a group of five other villages, whose ruins still dot the plain. The village lands are irrigated by a canal from the Farah-Rúd. On this side of the river the desert recedes more to the west, and leaves a broad strip of land level and fertile, varying from one to two miles in width and about five miles in length. The course of the stream through this tract is winding and irregular. More to the south, however, the desert runs right up to the river bank, and it is on a cliff at this extremity that the fortress of Lásh is built. As mentioned by Conolly, the east face of the fort is impregnable: the north and west, being separated from the adjacent desert by a deep ravine, are difficult of approach; but the south side, when once the river is crossed, offers little obstruction to an attacking force. The caves which Conolly noticed still abound in the adjoining cliffs. The climate is getting very much warmer, and this evening the atmosphere was very close and oppressive.

'March 19. Marched at 6.15 A.M. to the Khúsh-Rúdak, or rather Khúshk-Rúd[1], eighteen miles north-north-west. Bright clear morning, with slight breeze. Our road for the first five miles crossed the level plain lying between the desert plateau and the Farah-Rúd, and then ascending on to an arm of the desert, crossed it for half a mile, and descended into another valley, covered with tamarisk, willow, and *kirta*, which is known as the Karawán Rig, and is marked on Conolly's map. The Farah Rúd runs through it quite close to the road, over a gravelly bed. This valley is about half a mile broad: after leaving it the road again ascends on to a stony desert, similar to that on the banks of the Helmand, and at seventeen miles from Panj-Deh descends some forty or fifty feet into a broad and deep ravine, running north and south, the bed of which is covered with abundant *kirta*, and through the centre of which runs the "Khúsh-Rúdak," a small stream with brackish water. This is the river marked on Conolly's map as the "Khashek Rood." Its actual stream now is not more than ten or twelve feet broad, but the breadth of the ravine, some 200 yards, probably marks the extent of the river's surface when at its greatest flood. The earth around is thickly covered with salt. There is capital grazing for cattle here, but water for drinking purposes should be brought from the Farah-Rúd. This stream joins the Hárut river further to the south. From our

[1] The left bank of the Khúshk-Rúd marks the end of Lásh Juwain territory to the north; from the right bank the Afghán territory commences with the district of Farah. Though such of the uneducated Afgháns as we have met call this river the Khúsh-Rúd, there is little doubt that its real name is Khúshk-Rúd, or dry river, in consequence of the little water it possesses in the winter and spring drying up directly the summer heats commence.

Rúdak is the diminutive form of *rúd*, a river.—F. J. G.

camping-ground the Farah Hill bore N.N.E., and the range of hills called the "Kúh-i-Kala'h-i-Kah" N.N.W. The evening of this day marks the commencement of the Persian new year, which falls on our 20th instead of the 21st of March, owing to leap-year[1].'

Starting at 6 A.M., on account of the increasing heat of the weather, which necessitated an early move, we ascended a desert plateau continuing right up to the cultivated district of Kala'h-i-Kah and, though covered with shingle, affording good grazing for camels. We passed several flocks of grouse, with a few young bustard; and some of our party caught a young fox alive. The Chief of the district complained much of the extortions the villagers of Do Kala'h had suffered, first at the hands of Sardár Muhammad Ya'kúb Khán, who passed through here last year *en route* to take Herát; and secondly from Sardárs Muhammad Aslam Khán and Farámurz Khán, who were sent in his pursuit by Amir Shir Ali Khán. They had so eaten up the whole place that we could not even obtain chaff for our horses. In the afternoon Sardár Ahmad Khán of Lásh Jowain called on General Pollock to enquire again whether the English Government would be prepared to make him an absolute chief, independent alike of Afghánistán and Persia. And as he and his companions were to take leave on the following day, General Goldsmid sent over for themselves and their relatives a variety of gifts, among which were pistols and telescopes. March 21st being New Year's Day and a great feast of the Persians, all the servants came in a body to congratulate the General; and in return were promised a handsome *douceur* on arrival at Mashhad, to enable them to celebrate their feast at that place.

Kala'h-i-Kah is the name given to a tract of land about twelve miles in length and eight to nine miles broad, lying at the foot of a range of hills bearing the same name, and running due west and east. They are from 800 to 1000 feet high, quite barren, and of a sandstone formation. In the district there are eight villages, of which the principal is Do Kala'h, where we pitched our camp. This place is divided into two parts, Shib-Deh and Deh-i-Paīn, or the 'sloping' and 'lower village.' The land is irrigated partly by canals brought from the Farah-Rúd, 36 miles distant, and, when they fail, by *kanáts* dug from the neighbouring hills. The population is principally pure Tájik, with an intermixture of Afgháns. The revenue is paid to the

---

[1] The selections from the journal seem to terminate here, rather than on the 12th March, as implied by the writer on commencing to extract, at page 274 *ante*.—F. J. G.

Governor of Herát, and the district has nothing to do with Farah, which belongs to Muhammad Afzal Khán. To the west, the jurisdiction of Kala'h-i-Kah terminates at Cháh Sagak, which is six *farsakhs* beyond the Hárút-Rúd; the Afgháns have the right of pasturage up to that point, but there is no cultivation. The heat in summer is very great. A considerable quantity of cotton is grown here, which is sold in Sistán.

From Kala'h-i-Kah to the Hárút-Rud there is a distance of sixteen miles in a due westerly direction, and at the fifth mile the famous Ziárat of Imám Záid is passed on the right of the road. This Ziárat, which is called the Rig-i-rawán, or moving sand, is most remarkable and singular. At the extreme west of the range of hills which has been described as lying in a straight line due north of the Kala'h-i-Kah district, is a hill some 600 feet high and half a mile long. The southern face of this hill, to the very summit, is covered with a drift of fine and very deep sand—which has evidently been there for ages, as testified by the number of large plants growing on its surface. None of the adjacent hills have any traces whatever of sand-drift, and the surface of the surrounding desert is hard and pebbly. The westernmost portion of this elevated ground contains the Ziárat, and the natives say, and with reason and truth, that at times the hill gives out a strange startling noise, which they compare to the rolling of drums. Captain Lovett, who was fortunate enough to hear it, describes its effect upon him as like the wailing of an Æolian harp, or the sound occasioned by the vibration of several telegraph wires—very fine at first, but increasing every moment in volume and intensity; and the secret strain is said sometimes to last as long as an hour at a time. The face of the hill is concave, its cavity is filled with the sand, and underneath there appears to be a hard limestone surface. It would be useless, after a summary inspection, to hazard an opinion as to the cause of the remarkable sounds that proceed from the hill; but it is noticeable that they may be produced by any large number of men, at the top, putting the sand in motion. It should be remarked at the same time that the noise is often heard in perfectly still weather, and when nobody is near the hill; and it is singular also that the limit of the sand at the bottom seems never to be encroached upon by falling sand from the summit, though the face of the hill and sand-drift is very steep. On watching the sand this morning at the time he heard the sound, Captain Lovett observed that its vibrations and the movements of the pilgrims who had gone to the summit of the drift, occurred at the same moment. The natives, of course, ascribe miraculous properties to the hill. It is believed to be the grave of the Imám Záïd, the grandson of Husain, the son of Ali. Tradition says that, being pursued by his enemies, he came to this hill for refuge, was covered one night by the miraculous sand-drift, and has never been seen again. They say that the sand, thus miraculously brought by Heavenly aid, could be removed by no earthly power, and that were any one impious enough to try it, the sand would return of its own accord. They believe the hill, like the ancient oracles, to give out warning when anything important is going to happen in the district. Thus, in the time when the Túrkmans used to make their forays as far south as this, the hill always gave warning the night before their arrival; and we are assured that the arrival of our Mission was heralded by the same sounds. The head of the district told us that the noise could be heard in still weather at a distance of ten miles; and Sáiyid Núr Muhammad Shah declares he heard it distinctly last night at our camp five miles off. Shia'hs and Súnnis alike, unable to contend against the evidence of their ears, come to worship at this miraculous spot, and here find a common ground on which they can meet in amity. Obese Muhammadans do not generally subject themselves to so severe a trial of faith as that of visiting this particular *Ziárat-gáh*. It is a very steep climb for them to the commencement of the band of sand, about 200 feet broad and nearly perpendicular; and as they sink up to the thighs in this at every step, often must they regret that the Imám could not have hid himself in a more accessible spot. The tomb is situated at the top of the sand ridge, and it is in their descent that the faithful are generally rewarded for the trouble they have voluntarily undergone by hearing the miraculous noise. Sardár Ahmad Khán, all his attendants, and a great number of stalwart Afgháns, went up the hill, and we observed that they were more than half-an-hour getting across the sand: our more effeminate Tehrán servants did not seem to care to make the attempt. The base of the hill is surrounded by graves of the faithful, who, it is to be hoped, are not disturbed in their last sleep by the unearthly warnings of the object of their devotion. It is probable, after all, that science could give a very simple explanation of the phenomena; but he would be a bold man who tried to explain the same by natural causes within 100 miles of its influence.

After this Ziárat is passed the range of the Kala'h-i-Kah hills falls back to the northward, but the view is bounded in every direction, on the north and west, by other ranges of mountains. Twelve miles from the Do Kala'h we passed a small conical hill to the left, and plunged into the ravine known as the Shilah-i-Zahák, which collects the watershed of the hilly ranges to the north, but never contains any great amount of water. Its bed was, as usual, covered with *kirta* and brushwood. Four miles further over the desert brought us to the left bank of the Hárút-Rúd. To our disappointment we found the river-bed, which at this point is 100 yards wide with a gravel bottom, quite dry; but we soon obtained a plentiful supply of good water by digging three or four feet below the surface. The river is here known as the Hárút, and higher up it is called the Adraskand; but we could not discover where the change of name occurred. From our halting-place to its fall into the Sistán lake its waters are not utilised in any way whatever. At times it is so full as to be impassable. Sardárs Ahmad Khán and Mardán Khán accompanied us for about two miles on this day's march, and then departed, the former for Lásh, the latter for Farah.

Five o'clock the next morning (March 22nd) saw us in the saddle; all our heavy tents and baggage having been sent on the night before under a strong guard, owing to reports that the road was unsafe. Our route for sixteen miles was a constant ascent and descent over stony desert and rocky slopes, till we reached the well of Damdam, situated at the foot of a small hill of the same name on the right of the road. The water, though uninviting in appearance, was drinkable, and we halted here for breakfast, and then rounding a hill to the right found ourselves in a desert valley, nearly six miles wide, called the Dasht-i-Atashkhánah, covered with asafœtida[1]. Deserted as the whole country was, not a single human creature being visible, it yet lost much of its desolate appearance owing to the abundant verdure which clothed the ground and the numerous thorn-bushes now in full bloom. The most remarkable feature of the plain of the Cháh-i-Damdam was found in the numerous fragments of variegated marble of all colours which strewed its surface, some of which were really beautiful. The

---

[1] The Afghán Commissioner informed us that further to the north the Dasht-i-Atashkhánah (or 'Waste of the Fire-house,' so called from the fact that the natives find flints for their muskets on a hill situated therein) changes its name to the 'Waste of Despair;' and further north still stretches away until it joins the great desert of Merv.

rock of Damdam itself is a beautiful pink granite, and its south face is covered with a sand-drift similar to that of the Rig-i-rawán at the Ziárat of Imám Záïd. From the peasants who accompanied the camp we learnt that in olden times this road was most unsafe, but since the advent of the Amir of Káïn highway robberies had ceased. We saw a few deer and sand-grouse during our march, and were struck with the increasing coldness of the temperature caused by the ascent we had made. Two miles beyond the Dasht-i-Atashkhánah we found our camp pitched at the entrance to a range of barren hills, and by the side of a well called Cháh-i-Sagak, 24 miles W. from the Hárút river. The water in the well was stinking and undrinkable.

From Cháh-i-Sagak to Duruh, twenty-eight miles north-west, we had a fatiguing march. Leaving the camp at the former place the road rises through hills, with a gradual ascent for four miles to the line of the watershed and top of the pass, called here the 'Godar-i-Lard-i-Zárd,' owing to the yellowness of the rocks in the vicinity. This pass is 600 feet above the level of the Dasht-i-Atashkhánah, and from it a fine view can be obtained of the mountainous and desolate country around, which appears to be bounded, in every direction but the south, by barren and rocky ranges of serrated hills. The descent from the top of the pass is very gradual, through hilly and utterly desolate scenery, the severity of which was however somewhat mitigated by a number of beautiful orchids, and other wild flowers, which manage in some unaccountable manner to flourish in this sterile region. At a mile from the summit of the 'Godar,' two springs called 'Garnish' are passed on the right hand with fairly good water. At eight miles from the pass the road again ascends and crosses another line of watershed, not of the same elevation, and then makes a more decided descent on to a valley some three miles broad, affording excellent camel pasturage, and known as the Rúd-i-Míl. This valley runs nearly north and south, and has a high hill to the west called the Kala'h-i-Kúh. The road then follows this valley which winds along the base of the hills, and, passing two good springs of fresh water at twenty-six miles, finally emerges through the narrow bed of a mountain torrent into the spacious plain, called Tag-i-Duruh, on the east side of which is situated the village of Duruh. Apparently enclosed in every direction by hills, the area possesses an outlet in the south-west which carries off the drainage to Neh-Bandán. The village is built immediately under the range of rocky hills which forms the eastern boundary of the village, having to its south-west a high mountain, still streaked with snow at the time of our visit, called the Kúh-i-Shah. It contains 300 houses and almost 2000 inhabitants, and has extensive cultivation and some gardens surrounding it. The hill which more particularly overlooks it is crowned by a very old and ruined fort, which they say dates from the time of the first Kaiáni kings. It is matter of tradition that this was one of two forts (the other being near the Kala'h-i-Kúh), which were occupied by two brothers, of whom the name of one, Sikandar Pashi Khán, alone remains, and who used to plunder and rob all travellers on this road, they themselves owning obedience to no one. The fort of Duruh is said to have come into the possession of Khwájah Ali Kázi almost 150 years ago: this personage acknowledged the Shah of Persia, and from that time it has descended in his family—the present Katkhuda, whose name is also Khwájah Ali Kázi, being the great-grandson of the original possessor. It possesses six small springs of excellent water, and two *kanáts*. Its climate is good all the year round, but cold in winter.

Duruh was so destitute of supplies, that though we had intended halting there for two days, we were obliged to push on the next morning to obtain forage for the horses. Our march was but a continuous ascent and descent over the same rocky mountain ranges. For the first fourteen miles the road runs straight over the plain of Duruh in a west-north-west direction, when it reaches the mountain range on the western side, and turning the corner of some low granite hills to the right, arrives at the 'Cháh-i-Bermeh,' a good well with good water, which is situated in a narrow valley between the granite hills aforesaid and a lofty hill called the 'Kúh-i-Zilzila[1].' On the plain were some few tents of shepherds and large flocks; but the grazing here was much more scanty than that obtained in the neighbourhood of the Hárút river. We dismounted and breakfasted at this well; and remounting at 10.15 A.M. pursued our way along the bed of a watercourse, which, ascending gradually for three miles, reached the summit of the range of the Zilzila hills and the line of the watershed, at an elevation of 500 feet above the level of the Duruh plain, or about 4800 feet above the level of the sea. This pass is known as the 'Godar-i-Meshum,' and from its summit the road gradually descends for three miles through hills, which it clears at the twentieth mile

[1] Anglicè, 'Hill of the earthquake.'—*F. J. G.*

from Duruh, and emerges into the spacious hill-locked valley of Húsainabád, reaching the village at four miles distance from the hills. Basaltic and granite formations were noticeable in the hill ranges, and rhubarb and asafœtida were also observed growing on their sides. Húsainabád, which is only of eight years' standing, owes its existence to the energy of Mir Alam Khán of Káïn, who built it of neatly-constructed houses, surrounded it with a wall flanked at the corners by four towers, and induced immigrants from Káïn and Sar Bíshah to settle in it. The soil though gravelly is very productive, yielding excellent crops of wheat and barley; and the water is good and plentiful, though somewhat brackish. About thirty-six families constitute the population, of whom half are Shía'hs and half Súnnis. A broad line down the centre of the village divides the rival sects, and though the Súnnis are not allowed to call the 'Azán,' there is no quarrelling, as the Amir has placed over all an Akhúnd, Mullah Haidar Muhammad, to see that peace is preserved. On entering the village we came upon an old crone burning incense to keep off the evil eye; and shortly after our arrival the Mihmándár who had been sent from Birjand, by name Sáiyid Mir Asad Ullah Beg, a fine old man with a long black beard, came in from Sar Bíshah (of which place he was the Naïb) to pay his respects to the General. From him we learnt that the Persian Commissioner was still at Birjand, having passed through this village ten days previously. The climate in the valley of Husainabád was delightfully pure and invigorating; and the rosy, healthy children we saw on all sides, testified to its excellence. A great deal of snow falls here during the winter, and the inhabitants told us that this year they had seen it on the ground fully three feet deep for twenty-four days. Our new Mihmándár we found was a man of great power and authority in these parts, and much dreaded, as he had the right to cut off the ears, noses, and hands of all who offended against law. There had once been many struggles for power between him and the reigning governor of Mash-had, but their differences had been amicably arranged for some years past.

We halted at this village for two days to give the men and animals a rest, and on the 26th March marched to the large village of Sar Bíshah, twenty-nine miles west-north-west. For seventeen miles the road runs in a general west-north-west direction, with gradual ascent over the valley in which Húsainabád is situated, and then enters the hilly range which forms its western boundary, popularly known as the range of the 'Gonda-kúh.' At the eighteenth mile from our starting-point is a spring of fresh water, where there had formerly been a small village and some cultivation now abandoned, and where we halted and breakfasted amid a shower of rain. We found that at this point we had already ascended nearly 1100 feet from Húsainabád. A great number of Iliáts' black tents with flocks and herds were observed in the neighbourhood of the entrance to the Gonda-kúh, and a shepherd informed us that the valley afforded excellent pasturage for the flocks, tended by 400 families. This winter, however, the snow was so severe, and remained so long upon the ground, that numbers of the sheep were lost. From here we found that the road continued to ascend for four miles further to the summit of the pass and line of the watershed, 1840 feet above the level of Húsainabád, and 740 above the spring at which we breakfasted. The ascent to this pass was somewhat steep. From the summit the road descends very gradually on to another spacious plain, similar to the three we have traversed in succession since leaving Kala'h-i-Kah, and bounded on all sides by mountains. It is noticeable that as we have advanced west, each of these steppes has been higher than the last, and this is especially the case with the valley of Sar Bíshah, the level of which is not more than 600 feet below the level of the summit of the pass, and consequently about 1200 feet higher than the Húsainabád plateau. The village of Sar Bíshah is situated seven miles west of the summit of the Godar-i-Gonda Kúh, on the western side of the valley, and at the foot of a range of barren hills. It consists of 500 domed-roofed mud houses with about 2000 inhabitants, and has the remains of a strong *ark* or citadel, which was destroyed at the time of the quarrels between the father of the present Amir of Káin and our Mihmándár's father. There are also the remains of an Uzbek watch-tower in the vicinity. Bread is very cheap here, the ordinary price being eight *manns* for the *krán;* and water is also good and abundant. We were detained two days at Sar Bíshah by heavy rain, with frost, ice and snow, but marched on the 28th March for a village called Múd, twenty-one miles distant, north-west by west. The general character of the intervening country was gravelly level plain with scanty vegetation: there were few inhabitants, and cultivation was only seen at the base of the hills. At sixteen miles the line of watershed of another range of hills is crossed by a pass called the Godar-i-Rig, 6500 feet above the level of the sea, and 300 feet above Sar Bíshah, from which there is a gradual descent through low hills on to the valley in which Múd is situated, and which is about four miles broad.

From Múd a march of twenty-three miles west-north-west brought us into the capital city of Birjand, from which there was a distance of about 400 miles further to Mash-had. The march from Múd to Birjand exhibited quite a change in the scenery. The road ran over a fertile valley some ten or twelve miles broad, bounded on either side by a range of barren hills, and beyond those on the right hand again was another valley of which we caught occasional glimpses through openings in the hills, the summits of which were streaked with snow. At every two or three miles we passed *ábambárs* or water-tanks, some of them dry and ruined, but the generality in good repair, with an excellent supply of fresh cold water—furnishing another proof of the excellence of the Amir of Káïn's rule in his own province : wherever we have been we have noticed that he seems generally popular, and the flourishing condition of the villages bears testimony to the security the inhabitants feel under his government. Our road made a gradual and very slight ascent for the first ten miles, and then commenced an equally slight descent. Four miles from Múd is situated the flourishing village of Yek-Darakht (or ' one tree '), and at sixteen miles we passed the large village of Bojd on the right hand, situated at the extremity of the range of hills which divided the valley we were traversing and the plain we had noticed lying beyond. Bojd is a village of considerable size, and is built on the surface of the hills, being surmounted by a ruined fort. It is surrounded by gardens and cultivation. Half a mile further on is the pretty little village of Hajjiabad, standing in a perfect grove of orchards, and also surrounded by cultivation ; while five and a-half miles further is Birjand, situated at the end of the valley, with surrounding country and scenery much resembling the neighbourhood of the Alburz at Tehrán. At one mile and a-half from the town we were met by an *istikbál* with two led horses, headed by the youngest son of the Amir, a very little fellow of some eight or nine years old, who had already made a visit to Tehrán : he was an exact representation on a small scale of his father the Amir, riding a very large horse that he could barely straddle in a very plucky manner ; and whenever he could bring the horse within speaking distance, was most anxious to engage in conversation.

We found that the Persian Commissioner had left for Mash-had five or six days previously, having from all accounts bled the authorities considerably, not alone in respect of money, but of the carpets for which this place is famous. He had also given out that he had received a 'sanad' or document from the British Commissioner, to the effect that Sistán was the inalienable property of the Persians; and had further informed the authorities here that we meant to proceed to Tehrán *viâ* Herát. This latter invention caused us much trouble, both in obtaining money and camels. On our march this day we met a Persian official on his way to Sistán with a letter from the Hisámu-s-Saltanah— probably on a mission of enquiry as to what was doing in the province, for it is said there is no great friendliness between the two governors; but we hear that a sword of honour is on its way to Sistán as a present to the Amir from the Shah.

We were detained three days in Birjand by the impossibility of getting beasts of burden, and eventually had to leave all our heavy tents and baggage behind to be forwarded on by the camels, which were hourly promised; while we marched with the bell-tents and such baggage as could be carried on our own mules. During this time the usual ceremonial visits were paid and received without the occurrence of anything of note. The Amir's eldest son was a singularly-stupid wooden-headed youth, wanting manners and conversation, and was entirely in the hands of the Mustofi or manager of affairs, who was remarkably intelligent. While the Amir himself is away in Sistán, it is said that his mother, a very rigorous old lady, rules the province of Káin, and that it was principally to her obstinacy that we owed so much difficulty in obtaining camels. The *ark* or citadel of Birjand, in which the Amir's palace is situated, is a handsome mud-brick building with two very large square towers, and five or six mud ones connected by high walls. The reception-room—ceiling, walls, and all—is composed entirely of mirrors of various sizes dovetailed one into the other, with many tawdry pictures let into the glass. While we were at Birjand a great distribution of alms took place in the town on account of the close of the Múharam, during which time the Amir had at his own expense no less than seventy Tázias, or representations of the death of Ali, &c., &c., continually exhibited in various parts of the province: thus keeping up his popularity both with priest and people. Mr. Rosario's tent was crowded the whole time of our stay here by applicants for advice and medicine; sore eyes and cutaneous diseases being the principal maladies. He was also sent for on an emergent summons to the

Amir's harem, but found he was merely expected to re-beautify a freckled face. Birjand, the capital city of the province of Káïn, is situated under a range of low hills on the northernmost side of a fertile valley running east and west, and of which the southern boundary is the lofty range of barren hills known as the Kúh-Bákrán[1]: from which the principal supply of water is obtained for the city by four large *kanáts*. The city at the present time consists of about 3,000 dome-roofed mud-built houses, erected on the sloping ground of the hills above mentioned: it faces to the south and has a frontage of about three-quarters of a mile; is not surrounded by a wall; and has no *ark* or citadel or means of defence, except such as may be afforded by the walled enclosure in which is situated the residence of the Amir, built on the lowest ground. The old citadel, built on rising ground at the north-west corner of the town, is in ruins; and the town itself is completely commanded from any of the low hills to its rear: it has no buildings of any importance, but possesses six caravanserais and some 200 shops, and the Amir has already commenced the construction of a grand *bazár*. The city numbers at the present moment some 15,000 inhabitants, and has within its jurisdiction seventy to eighty villages: these villages, however, being principally situated near natural springs, are dependent for their existence on a very precarious supply of water: in seasons of drought these springs very often dry up, and the villagers then come into the town, deserting their villages until such times as water may be more plentiful. Villages in the district are called 'Kilat.' The town is divided into two unequal portions by the broad and generally dry bed of a water-course which drains the hills to the north. The carpets for which the locality has long been famous are almost entirely fabricated in the village of Darakhsh, about fifty miles to the north-east of Birjand. The principal products of the province of Káïn are saffron, carpets, a cloth called *bark*, *kirbás*, unmanufactured silk, *zirishk*, nuts of all sorts, dried fruits, almonds, and a small quantity of cotton. These are exported to Karmán, Yazd,

---

[1] Behind the hills of Bákrán to the south-east, about 22 miles distant, the natives told us that an enormous *chinár* tree was to be found near a place called Gúl-fánz. This tree measures about 68 English yards in circumference, according to the native account, and has 5 or 6 species of stables built in its trunk, capable, so it is said, of containing 1000 sheep. Some of its branches still bear leaves. Query? Can this be the 'Arbre Sec' of Marco Polo?

Mash-had, Tehrán, Herát, Bandar-Abbas, &c., &c.; and the province receives in exchange from Karmán the coarser species of shawl manufactures, turbans, *abas* or cloaks, and *kúrk*: from Herát, rice: from Yazd, manufactured silk, turbans called Imámas, a substance known as *kadak*, and native sugar: from Khabis, oranges, lemons, dates, and other fruits: from Sistán, grain of all sorts; and from Bandar-Abbas, tea, spices, sugar, and European manufactures generally. From Birjand to Karmán by Khabis is ten stages: to Yazd by Karmán twenty-two stages: to Herát by Sunnistan and Tabas (Shia'h Tabas), nine stages. The Amir[1] of Káin pays no fixed revenue to the Shah, but supports the whole expenditure of troops and government servants located in his province, as well as that incurred in the government of Sistán: he, moreover, transmits from time to time presents or 'ta'arufs,' in money and kind, to Tehrán.

We quitted Birjand on April 2nd, having previously sent off a courier with a heavy mail for Tehrán, *viâ* Mash-had. It was long since we had received any news from England; and some members of the Mission may remember the cruel disappointment occasioned by the conduct of one of their unsympathetic brethren who, on April 1st, called out loudly in the middle of the camp that the English courier had arrived at last! The woe-begone faces of the deluded ones, when, rushing from their tents, they were informed that they were merely so many 'poissons d'Avril,' gave to the joke, however, a somewhat melancholy character. Breaking up camp at 1 P.M. amid a crowd of spectators, we left all our big tents and heavy baggage behind under charge of the Farash Báshi and Farash Khanah. Crossing low hills at the back of the camp, and leaving the town on the left, the road turns abruptly to the right, and for five miles runs in an east-north-east direction, skirting the water-course that divides the town of Birjand, and passing at every two miles an *âbambár* or water-tank of excellent pure cold water. It then changes direction to the north-north-east, and crosses a stony plain which bends to the east and joins the Sar Bíshah valley, having on the right a remarkable conical hill known

---

[1] The Amir has three sons:
 1. Sarhang Ali Akbar Khán, now at Birjand. His mother was the daughter of a son of Saiyid Khán, governor of Darakhsh.
 2. Sarhang Mír Ismáíl Khán, at Karbala. His mother was the daughter of a son of Lutf Ali Khán, governor of Neh Bandán.
 3. Háidar Kuli Khán, came to the *istikbál*.

as the 'Már-Kúh,' or Hill of Serpents, at the foot of which is a large village called Kala't-i-Bújdi. Rising again over a rocky ridge and passing nine *ábambárs* and the village of Ishkambarabád to the left, the road pursues its course over another wide stony plain, with small hamlets and patches of cultivation dotting its surface here and there, and then, changing direction to north-north-west, reaches at the tenth mile the little village and garden (with water-tank) of Máhi-abad. From this point the road runs nearly north, and a mile afterwards enters the range of the Samand-i-Shah hills, running, so far as we could judge, nearly east and west. At twelve miles we passed the picturesque-looking fort and village of Pisukh; then, ascending gradually through wild and desolate scenery, we traversed the *tang* or defile of the same name, and in the face of a bitterly cold north wind reached, at the sixteenth mile, the summit of the pass and line of the watershed, at an elevation of 1,900 feet above the level of Birjand. From this point a good road, with a gradual descent of 450 feet in two miles, took us to the village of Ghiuk, charmingly situated among the hills. At Ghiuk [1] we were induced to halt for one day owing to the unusually heavy rain. The village was exceedingly picturesque, being built stage upon stage on the side of the hills, and embosomed in orchards and fruit trees. The wind here is however so high that all the gardens are surrounded by high stone walls for protection, especially for the grape-vine which is extensively grown. The whole scene strikingly recalled the charming village of Kohrúd on the Isfahán road, familiar to every Persian traveller. The place had suffered severely from the famine, losing more than half its population.

Our start for Seh-Deh, the next halting-place, was made very early on the 4th, in bright, clear, bracing weather. The road, as usual, led us through range after range of hills, interspersed with narrow valleys,

---

[1] It may be noticed that there is another and a shorter route from Birjand to Turbat-i-Háidari, whither we were proceeding, of which the stages are as follows:—

Birjand to Ribát	4 farsakhs.	(Brought forward)	30 farsakhs.
Cháhak	4 ,,	Ribát-i-Imrani	4 ,,
Muhammadabád	4 ,,	Mehneh	6 ,,
Nokáb	4 ,,	Sikandarabad	4 ,,
Nim Balúch	4 ,,	Ribát-i-Beli	4 ,,
Kahkh	4 ,,	Turbat-i-Háidari	8 ,,
Kuzhd	6 ,,		
	30	Total	56 farsakhs.

most of them under cultivation, with good springs of water, while the mountain slopes offered unusually good pasturage for large herds of cattle. The hills were mostly of sandstone, limestone, slate, clay, or trap formation. Wild rhubarb and tulips grew in abundance on all sides, and we noticed that when the trap ceased, so did the wild rhubarb. In spite of the increasing fertility of the country, it was still desolate to a degree: not a single human being was met with on this day's march, and the villages in the valleys had been almost depopulated by famine and emigration. We reached Seh-Deh in a tremendous storm of wind, hail and rain, and our camp was soon invaded by a crowd of its inhabitants, who came to stare at the strangers and offer them carpets similar to those of Birjand, only much dearer, and made by two emigrants from Darakhsh, who are settled here. The Túrkmans sometimes sweep down the valley in which Seh-Deh lies, and over the hills into the Káin district[1]. The village itself is like the ordinary run of Persian villages, and the majority of its mud-built dome-roofed houses are in ruins, owing to the distress of the famine year. The chief of both the village and the valley is a man named Mirza Husain, possessed of great wealth and influence and a local reputation for hospitality. He keeps, it is said, a granary for charitable distribution, which he never allows to become empty. He, with thirty of the villagers, is a follower of Agha Khán, at Bombay.

As we were anxiously expecting news of our camels from Birjand, it was decided to make a short march of ten miles hence to Rúm, a village lying to the west of a lofty hill called Angarin, in the hope of receiving news of them there, and instead of going in at once to Káin. The only incident of the march worth mentioning was the sudden appearance, during our halt for breakfast, of a dumb man, who seemed most anxious to make us understand some story he tried to explain, by various signs, such as firing with a gun, striking with a sword, tying his hands behind his back, etc. He was not deaf, but he could give no quite intelligible answer to the questions put to him; and we came to the conclusion that he was probably the victim of some *chapáo* or raid. Rúm is an uninteresting little village, with about thirty families now dwelling in it. It had the same tale to tell of the sufferings caused by

[1] Beyond the range of hills which bound the Seh-Deh valley to the east is the continuation of the desert plain which we passed near Cháh-Sagak and which stretches nigh up to Merv.

the famine, having lost seventy of its inhabitants through death and emigration. Some more Khwojah disciples of Agha Khán are to be found here, who remit a portion of their scanty savings to him from time to time. The villagers have but a hard life of it, with their recent severe sufferings from the famine and their constant dread of the Túrkmans, against whom they have no defence or protection whatever, save, it may be, their extreme poverty. The march from Rúm to Káïn, a distance of about twenty miles, led us through an extensive elevated area of cultivated land, which surprised us, as we could see no means whatever of artificial irrigation. The hill sides were ploughed, and ready for sowing: the upturned soil appeared to be of unusual richness; and the mulberry-tree was extensively cultivated for silk in the villages through which we passed, and of which there were a great many nestling in the sheltered nooks of the ranges of hills that bounded the plateau. These hills were still streaked with snow, and our ears were pleasantly greeted with the familiar note of the cuckoo on all sides. Ascending the pass, or *godar*, of Khanak, 730 feet above, and at a distance of seven miles from Rúm, we made a sharp descent to the valley in which lay the villages of Khanak and Kharwaj—the latter now deserted by all but thirty families, chiefly Sáiyids. From the *godar* itself we obtained a very fine view of the town of Káïn, lying at our feet in a valley commanded by the hill Abúzir, and surrounded by a deep belt of cultivation and gardens. The charm of the scene, however, was completely dispelled on nearer acquaintance; for we found the gardens deserted and dried up, and the town itself a mass of ruin, desolation, and confusion. The inhabitants crowded out to see us, causing us a good deal of inconvenience by their uncivil curiosity; but, to our surprise, there was no *istikbál* sent to greet the General. This, however, was explained by the Mihmándár, who attributed the omission to the fact that there were scarcely any horses to be had in the place; and also to the absence of the Governor and his Deputy in Birjand. He was confirmed in this statement by a deputation of twelve of the principal inhabitants of the town, who waited on the General the day after our arrival, to apologise for the apparent neglect, and to explain to him the state of ruin and depression from which Káïn was then suffering. Setting aside losses from death, so many families had emigrated to Sistán (which they described as a 'hell full of bread'), that the place was bereft of almost all its inhabitants, excepting the

Sáiyids and Múllas. The town of Káïn[1] is situated on the eastern side of a broad valley stretching north and south at the base of a lofty hill called Abúzir, and is said to be very ancient, dating back to the time of the Gabrs (Guébres); but it is now represented by ruins, which lie scattered over the valley to a very considerable extent: its walls are broken down, and it is without any citadel. It now contains only about 2500 inhabitants: and it was most melancholy to see the hundreds of empty houses and deserted gardens that met us at every turn. In happier days the district could show large yields of silk and saffron; but the three terrible years of drought that have passed over it have so blighted the mulberry-trees, that last year's yield of silk was not more than one-fourth of the average, while the cultivation of wheat has everywhere superseded that of saffron. The whole province suffered; the rich became poor, and the poor died, so that the misery was universal. The valley surrounding the town contains some twelve to fifteen villages, which are well supplied with water by ten *kanáts*: and there are about 200 villages in the whole district. The town itself possesses from seventy to eighty wretched shops, three *hammáms*, and two ruined caravanserais: it further boasts an ancient mosque, which forms a conspicuous object in the landscape, and is interesting, not from any architectural beauty, but from its antiquity. By an inscription let into its walls, engraved on stone, the name and date of its original founder

---

[1] After the fall of the Safavian dynasty, Nadir Shah took the province of Káïn and gave it to Mir Ismáíl Khán, whose descendants are as follows:—

Mir Ismáíl Khán.
|
Mir Alam Khán.
|
Mir Ma'sum Khán.
|
Mir Ali Khán.
|
Mir Alam Khán.
|
Mir Asadullah Khán.
|
The present Mir Alam Khán of Káïn.

It is from the days of Mir Ismáíl Khán that Birjand began to supplant Káïn as the capital of the province. It had been ruined by Sultán Husain Mirza Bákirah, and Birjand was preferred to it on account of its greater proximity to Sistán and the Afghán frontier.

are given as 'Karin-i-Ibn-i-Jamshid. A.H. 796,' and it was repaired by Yusúf, the son of Dáulatyár; who also erected the large wooden 'minbar,' or pulpit, which it contains. The mosque was much injured some years ago by an earthquake, which cracked the rear wall to such an extent that it became necessary to prop it up with buttresses.

On the summit of the hill Abúzir[1], which completely commands the town, are the ruins of strong and extensive fortifications said to have been built by the Gabrs as a protection against the Túrkmans, who were a scourge even in those days; and behind the hill is a natural reservoir in the rock, filled with water to the depth of some twelve feet, in which bodies of deer and other wild animals are constantly found drowned, having slipped in while drinking. To add to all the other woes of the wretched city we heard that a band of Tekeh Túrkmans, variously estimated at from 400 to 1000, had swept down from Merv a day or two before our visit, and carried off no less than 180 human beings with sheep and oxen. For fifteen years the district had been free from such raids, and this outburst had completely paralysed the inhabitants.

We found these latter unpleasantly inquisitive and importunate, thronging our camp to beg for alms and medicine; and so depressing was the place in every way that we should have been glad to turn our backs on it at once, had not the Mihmándár urgently requested a halt for a couple of days, to give time for the arrival of our camels from Birjand, and also to allow of his mustering a guard of fifty matchlock men who were to escort us over the two stages beyond Káïn which were deemed peculiarly exposed to the Túrkman raids.

During our stay in the town the General received a visit from a Sáiyid, named Abú-l-Kásim, who was well acquainted with Colonel Farrant and Sir Justin Sheil, and who had been saved from death many years ago by the former. He had been sent by the late

---

[1] These fortifications, as above stated, are said to have been constructed by the Gabrs (whose towers of silence still crown the neighbouring hills) before the era of Jangiz Khán. But behind the present town are the ruins of a still older city called the Shahr-i-Gabri, which, in common with the Hill Fort, is said to have been destroyed by Súltán Husain Mirza Bákirah, the grandson of Amir Taimúr, and to have remained for 300 years in the hands of the Uzbegs, who were eventually expelled by Shah Abbas. The latter monarch then appointed Mirza Araf Súltán as governor of the family of Sáiyid Muhammad Núr Bakoh, who had come with 2000 people from Arabistán and had settled in the Káïn province during the reign of Shah Sulaiman. The descendants of this Sáiyid still form the majority of the population.

Asafú-d-Dáulah with letters from Karbala to Colonel Farrant, then in Tehrán, begging the latter to advise Muhammad Shah to stop proceedings against the Sipah Salár who was in rebellion at Mashhad. The Shah was at once informed of this, and told also that the Sáiyid had secret instructions to stir up discontent in Tehrán: upon which the unfortunate man was first condemned to death, but afterwards to imprisonment in the state fortress of Ardabil. When the news of his fate reached Colonel Farrant, he remonstrated so strongly that the prisoner was released, but secret orders were given to kill him on his way back by Hamadán. Colonel Farrant therefore sent him the whole way from Tehrán to Baghdad under the charge of British employés, receiving a formal receipt for him from the then British Resident at Baghdad, Sir Henry Rawlinson. The Sáiyid now delights to tell the story of his escape and to call himself a British subject.

Another Súnni Sáiyid of Káin called on the Afghán Commissioner and interested him much by the stories he related respecting our mission in Sistán. He said that Hájji Azád Khán, who had been sent by the Hisámú-s-Saltanat to watch proceedings in Sistán, had been much annoyed by the conduct of the Amir of Káin; and that the latter had planned an attack on our camp at Deshtak, which was only averted by the report that the Afghán Commissioner was coming down with a large force. If this be true, the flag question may possibly have been the intended forerunner of more hostile measures. The same Sáiyid also warned the Afghán Commissioner to place no trust whatever in the natives of this district, and specially to guard against poisoned food. Whether these warnings had real foundation, we had of course no means of discovering.

We finally left Káin[1] on the 9th of April: our stay had been a very unpleasant one; the pushing inquisitiveness of the wretched inhabitants had allowed us no species of privacy, and the high winds had made tent life extremely uncomfortable, so that we were all glad when we turned our backs upon the deserted and famine-stricken city. On the previous night matchlock men had been sent out to see if the pass was clear from Túrkmans; and at seven o'clock we mustered all our band for the start, a motley crew indeed. Our servants were

[1] It should be specially noticed that Káin is situated forty-eight miles north of Birjand. All previously existing maps have hitherto placed it fifty miles to the south of the last-mentioned city. Firewood here was very dear and scarce.

armed with any weapon they could lay hands on, and the cook looked very valiant with a large spit; but when our much vaunted guard did make its appearance from the town, it certainly was not calculated to inspire great confidence, though nothing could exceed the eagerness with which each man breathed out threats of blood and vengeance, declaring that his one and sole object was to win the reward of twenty *tumáns* offered by the Amir for every Túrkman's head. Perhaps the most really anxious individual of our party was, however, the old Hájji Abdullah Khán, whose natural dread of falling into the hands of the Túrkmans was heightened by the knowledge that they give no quarter to aged prisoners, as they do not care to keep them for slaves.

For the first few miles we proceeded in a north-westerly direction across the valley, which, though stony, wore a brilliant carpet of red tulips, wild geraniums, and numberless other flowers; but we had not gone more than six miles on our road when we were pursued by angry parties of men from Káïn, from whom it appeared that our Mihmándár had in some high-handed way taken five or six donkeys for our use. They caught up the caravan at Shir Múrg, a village some six miles distant, vowing vengeance against the Mihmándár, and a row ensued which baffles description, our own servants being only with great difficulty prevented from taking part in the fray. Guns and pistols were grasped, the air resounded with the foulest abuse showered freely on the remotest ancestors of the combatants, and it was a toss up how it would end, when our Mírakhor suddenly rushed to the front as peace-maker, kissed the perspiring cheeks of the leading malcontents five or six times over, and by degrees softened them down sufficiently to hear reason. Hardly had he accomplished this, with infinite pains, when another furious party arrived from Káïn, and the whole quarrel burst out afresh as fiercely as before. The end of it was that our Mihmándár had to make a bolt of it over the hills for his life, and that two donkeys were ceded as a peace-offering to the men of Káïn, who then returned home, having gained but little by their twelve-miles walk. The delicious silence that ensued, after the frantic cries and cursing that had rent the air, was most soothing.

Traversing an undulating country we reached the base of the Behúd mountains, at the foot of the Godar-i-Gúd, 800 feet above and 12 miles distant from the town of Káïn. We ascended with very little difficulty to the pass, as the weather was dry and the road easy.

The hills are composed of sandstone, with great mounds of clay on their sides, and would be impassable for laden beasts in wet weather. At six miles from the summit of the pass we crossed the Rúd-khánah-i-Miánbiáz, which was now well filled from the melting snows, and entered the extensive valley of Nim-balúk, also called Miánbiáz. When we arrived at the prosperous little village of Giri-manj, we found its inhabitants in a state of great excitement and terror. The Túrkmans had been seen on the hills that very morning, and had plundered a village on the other side of the hills only the day before. We accordingly mustered our guard, spoke encouragingly to them, presented forty-two of their number with a *krán* apiece, and started the next day at seven, expecting every moment to see something of the dreaded robbers—but in vain. This valley is dotted over with curious round mud towers, into which the peasants rush for protection if attacked. The Túrkmans, who rarely dismount unless in great force, swoop down on horseback, seizing whatever they can as they dash by, so that these towers usually afford as good a shelter from them as from a storm of driving rain. The stage from Girimanj to Kisri and Dasht-i-Biáz was considered the critical one of our march; but with the open plain on one hand and lofty hills on the other, it seemed difficult to imagine how any considerable body of men could be taken by surprise. We learnt that the Túrkmans always came across the plain by one of four passes from the north, where are four watch-towers, named Balághar, Rejang, Meh Kahnú, and Kam-Nasir, occupied by men stationed to give notice of their approach. Probably the noise of their frantic cries, and the dust caused by their furious riding, so terrify their victims that they lose their heads, separate, and thus fall into their hands an easy prey. The best way to receive a Túrkman attack, we were told by the Afghán Commissioner, is to form up in a square and fire a volley at them; they never stop to return it, or to pick up any of their number who may be wounded unless they are in great force.

The important village of Dasht-i-Biáz, or the White Plain, lies at the north of the Nim-balúk valley, thirty-four miles from Káin, surrounded by extensive gardens, its chief products being opium, silk, wheat, cotton, barley, and vegetables. It numbers now three hundred houses, and has four *kanáts* (one of which, built by the Gabrs, never runs dry), the remains of an ancient mosque, with ruins of other large buildings, and a very old *hammám* with curious encaustic tiles. The mosque is said to have been built by the Wazír of Shah Abbas. With Káïn this village fell under the yoke of the Uzbegs. Its ancient name was Shahr-i-Farsi. We were compelled to remain a day longer than we intended in the place, to satisfy the entreaties of the Zábit Agha Ján Khán, who was so terrified by the report that a band of four hundred Túrkmans had been seen the previous evening close to the village, that he declared he would not allow us to start till he had obtained more correct information of their movements, as he felt himself responsible for our safety. Meanwhile we amused ourselves visiting a group of black-tented Iliáts, who were about two miles from our own camp, and who received us very civilly, boasting loudly, and we fear without any grounds, of their scorn of the Túrkmans, and declaring that they always took the initiative themselves and attacked them whenever they had a chance. These Iliáts had two large spring steel traps set for wolves and baited with a kid.

In compliance with the wishes of the Zábit, our start for the march to Kákhk, *viâ* Kala't-i-Múlla, was not made till the sun was well up, and we had light at least to see the Túrkmáns should we cross their path. Terrible rumours of their having attacked the town of Káïn itself during the night were rife, but we pursued our way, with a guard of fifty matchlock men, in peace and safety, never even catching a glimpse of our much dreaded foes. At nine miles from Dasht-i-Biáz the road crosses the watershed of the Laki range by a pass called the Godar-i-Darakht-i-Benar, or the pass of the Benar-trees, so called from two large withered trees on its northern side, 1200 feet above the village of Biáz. This pass, till very lately, was famous as a haunt of robbers, but these have now disappeared. It forms the boundary between the provinces of Káïn and Tún-wa-Tabas, and here too the ranges of the Laki[1] and Siah-Kúh hills meet. At the thirteenth mile from Biáz the village of Kala't-i-Múlla situated on the northern skirt of these hills is reached, and one mile further the road finally clears the hills and emerges on the extensive plain of Gúnábad. All the villages were completely deserted through fear of the Túrkmans.

The town of Kákhk, also called the 'Happy Village,' is situated immediately under the range of lofty hills bounding the valley of Gúnabád to the south and west, which, according to local report, are rich in minerals. Its population at the time of our visit consisted of some 500 families, but it had suffered greatly from the famine of the preceding year (of which the traces daily became more and

---

[1] These hills are said to abound in copper.

more strongly marked as we journeyed westwards), during which 20,000 people are said to have perished in the district of Tún-wa-Tabas alone. Its water-supply from four *kanáts* and fifty natural springs is excellent; and the quantity of opium grown is very considerable. Kákhk is however specially famous for an Imámzádah or tomb which contains the remains of Shahzádah Sultán Muhammad Ali, brother of the holy Imám Riza of Mash-had. This tomb, built on a stone platform and embosomed in gardens, has a splendid dome covered with beautiful and many-coloured encaustic tiles, which was constructed by order of Shah Sufi. Formerly the whole of the produce of Kákhk was devoted to the service, or 'Maukufát,' of this tomb, but the practice has been lately modified, and it now only receives sufficient to keep it in good repair. Múllas and Sáiyids of course abound in the town, where there is also a Madrasah or college, and two Masjids, one built by the Uzbegs and one by Shah Tamasp, A. H. 921. At the present day, the shrine is used only by the inhabitants of Tún-wa-Tabas. Two ancient citadels, constructed one within the other, form another remarkable feature in the town. They are built on an elevation, with high walls and flanking towers, are connected by a drawbridge, and each has an independent supply of water. The outer of these forts is still kept in an efficient state, and has a small garrison.

Iron agricultural implements are largely manufactured in the town, and we counted as many as forty ironworkers' shops. We were also much struck with the silk embroidery for which the place used to be so famous, called *kashedah*. It is worked on common cloth in beautifully-variegated colours and designs, and in former days was almost exclusively used for ladies' trousers. In those halcyon times the women used to sit in assemblies with their legs before them, and a display of elegant nether garments was a *sine quâ non*; now, however, it is the fashion to sit on the legs, and this renders useless and unnecessary the once gorgeous pantaloons that were the chief glory of a Persian lady's costume in these parts. Struck with the beauty of the design and colouring of this work, we bought up all the pieces of new and unmade-up embroidery we could find, and no sooner was it noised abroad that we had a fancy for such articles, than, to our intense astonishment, the unmade stock being exhausted, native after native came rushing into camp with various pairs of 'inexpressibles' flaunting in the air like so many banners, which they had ruthlessly wrested from their wives, mothers, and daughters, to sell to the 'infidels,' who manifested such a strong fancy for these garments[1]. We could not help reflecting on the possibly uncomfortable consequences of this arbitrary and wholesale spoliation: but this reflection did not prevent the members of the Mission eagerly availing themselves of the opportunity of becoming possessors of so strange a memento of Eastern travel.

From Kákhk our direct road to Túrbat, whither we were bound, would have been by Gúnábad, straight across the plain to the north; but fear of the Túrkmans compelled us to keep close within the shadow of the hills to the south, amidst which was descried many a picturesque village surrounded by extensive cultivation. The most charming of these was the village of Kala't, built on a high hill, nine miles from Kákhk, and lying in a semicircle of lovely gardens, which were now in full leaf and flower, and alive with the music of countless birds and the rippling of numerous streams flowing down from the heights above. It was a picture which called forth our especial admiration from its great rarity in Persia, and from its contrast to the sterile scenery we had hitherto traversed. Most unwittingly, however, our approach to this paradise caused the greatest terror to the inhabitants, who, mistaking us for Túrkmans, fled to the neighbouring hills for refuge, carrying off any valuables they could take with them. It was a long time before they could be convinced of our peaceful intentions and induced to venture back. The stampede over, we halted to breakfast under the shade of some very fine English-looking walnut-trees, while around us grew the mulberry, peach, apricot, pomegranate, vine, etc., in rich luxuriance. Opium for the market at Yazd is extensively cultivated in the neighbouring valley, as well as cotton.

At Zibad, the next village of importance, we found the people in a state of great excitement, owing to the discovery of the long-missing body of an officer named Mirza Jahán, who had disappeared suddenly, and over whose suspected murder a veil of mystery had hitherto hung. This unfortunate man had been sent from Mash-had by the Hisámú-s-Saltanah to settle some revenue question in the district, and was returning to Mash-had, having finished his task, when he was attacked at night, in a small village, by a gang of twenty-one robbers, murdered, and buried, in one grave with five of his servants, in the desert. Nothing having been heard of him at Mash-had, the Hisámú-s-

---

[1] A pair of these embroidered squares were sent by Major Euan Smith to the South Kensington Museum, and were considered such valuable specimens of 'raiment of needlework,' that they were purchased by the Directors for £25 the pair.

Saltanah sent to the Governor of Tabas, to whose district he had been *en route*, to demand him dead or alive, or a sum of 30,000 *tumáns*. It so happened that at that very time the Governor had seized a man who was accused of stealing some donkeys, and who, being put to the torture, denied any dealings with the donkeys, but confessed himself one of the gang[1] who had murdered the Mirza Jahán. The discovery of the six bodies at the spot he indicated was corroboration sufficient of his statement, and he and the bodies of his victims were forwarded at once to Mash-had. We did not learn the sequel of this story.

Between Zibad and Begistán[2], the next important village on the road, a distance of about twenty-eight miles, we passed undisturbed by Túrkmans; though our opium-eating Mihmándár raised many a false alarm, by declaring that he saw in the distance clouds of dust, the certain forerunners of their approach. The villages scattered over the country were all extremely prosperous in appearance, surrounded by extensive gardens, and well supplied with water. A low range of hills is passed at fifteen miles from Zibad, forming the western boundary of the Gúnábad plain: leaving these, the road gradually descends till it reaches, at thirteen miles further, the town of Begistán, situated on the borders of the great salt desert, extending from Herát and Ghórian, to Káshán and Hauz-i-Súltán. We were now 600 feet below the level of Zibad; the difference in the temperature became very marked, and the weather was so oppressive that a severe thunderstorm the next morning gave a welcome relief in clearing the air. As we neared the desert, the springs and wells became more and more rare, till for twelve miles before reaching Begistán there was no water to be seen anywhere. Wild flowers, however, carpeted the hills on all sides, the rhubarb ceasing with the trap formation, as before noticed.

To our surprise and pleasure we were greeted at Begistán by our Káin Mihmándár, Mir Asadullah Beg, who gave us the welcome news that our camels and heavy baggage from Birjand were close at hand. It had taken them eleven days to march from Birjand, as the camels were always bolting, and they had had the greatest difficulty in keeping the caravan together. Another piece of good news we learnt from the *istikbál*, sent out to welcome the Mission, was, that our courier, Muhammad Ismail Beg, had passed through Begistán in safety some days previously.

[1] This was a gang of twenty-one robbers of the Táimúri tribe of Herát, who frequented some hills near Túrshíz.

[2] I prefer 'Bájistán;' as 'Dasht-i-piáz,' instead of 'Dasht-i-biáz,' in page 345.—*F. J. G.*

This town has a population of some 4000 souls, with a ruined fort, two good caravanserais, four *hammáms*, fifty mosques, and seventy shops: it is famous for the manufacture of a very costly species of cloth made of goat's wool, and called *barak*, and of a cheap silk material, called *chádar-i-shahi*. It is also celebrated for its excellent water-melons and abundant fruit. Three *kanáts* supply it with water, and there are still to be seen the remains of an ancient *kanát*, of which the tradition is that it was built in the time of the Safavian kings, and that whoever drank of its waters became mad. The story goes, that when Shah Abbas visited the place, he ordered his Wazír to test the truth of the tale by drinking of the water himself, and that no sooner had he tasted it, than he took off his trousers, wound them round his head, and returned to the presence of his master thus attired. The Shah, convinced beyond doubt, ordered the *kanát* to be closed at once, and its mouths sealed up with tar. Another ancient tradition common among the natives is that the whole of the country around Begistán was once covered by the sea, and that the place derives its name from باج, which signifies a toll, and ستودن to take, alluding to the toll at the ferry paid by travellers for boat hire when the waters had partly receded.

At Begistán we parted with Mir Asadullah Beg, Mir Ali Beg, and the opium-eating Náib Muhammad Ali Beg, who left us well satisfied with the handsome presents they received as farewell gifts. Passing through a barren valley after leaving the town, we descended into a wide plain, in which lies the village of Yúnsi, marked by local traditions as the spot on which the prophet Jonah was cast by the whale, and where he lay for many days concealed under a pumpkin plant. His grave is, however, at Mosul, between Baghdad and Diarbekir. Yúnsi itself is an insignificant village, very dilapidated and miserable-looking, with about 100 families; it suffered grievously during the famine, and lost a great number of its inhabitants. Nevertheless, it sent out a numerous *istiklál* to greet the Mission, headed by the Katkhuda, a stalwart individual in blue attire, who, after the usual salutations, stated that he was a 'Pahluwan,' or wrestler, and, craving leave to display his powers, immediately threw off his cerulean garments, and seizing two powerful clubs, performed wonderful feats, walking backwards before the General the whole way. Nothing could exceed the wonder and delight with which this exhibition was watched by the admiring subjects of the performer. As we entered the village, rue was burned before our horses' feet, to avert the evil eye—the custom being as universal in this province as it was in that of Káin. The wind and dust storms rage here from sunrise to sunset.

On reaching camp the General received a letter from the Hisámú-s-Saltanah, Governor of Mash-had, bidding him welcome to Khúrasán, and another from the British agent at Mash-had, saying that every possible arrangement had been made for the courteous reception both of the British and Afghán Missions, not only at Mash-had, but at all the stages on the way.

We now found ourselves in a country where the regular track of the last great famine was even more marked than in any of our previous marches. At Begistán we had relieved eighty persons with bread; and the crowd of beggars was becoming most importunate. At this village, 120 of the inhabitants perished from the famine, and the survivors complain bitterly of the cruelty of the Governor of Tabas[1], who refused to remit one jot or tittle of the usual taxes, notwithstanding their sufferings.

The morning after our halt at Yúnsi was made very pleasant to us all by the arrival of a courier from Tehrán, bringing English letters of the 18th of January. The man declared he had been stopped on his way by robbers, who had stolen his shoes but left his mail-bags intact. Immediately on leaving Yúnsi the road passes over a brick bridge of nine arches, which is a boundary mark between the districts of Tabas and Túrbat, and then crosses a desert stony plain[2] for thirteen miles, till it leads to Miándeh, a village so named from its position midway *(mián)* between Mash-had and Tabas. Beyond this the interminable expanse of sandy stony desert again intervenes, till the large and prosperous village of Faizabad is reached at the 27th mile from Yúnsi, and three miles further, Abdúlábad, our halting-place. Here we found excellent quarters prepared for us in the house and garden of the Governor, and every possible arrangement made for our comfort; iced *sharbat* and fruits, with other refreshments, standing ready for our acceptance. Seven miles from the town we were met by an *istikbál*, consisting of Hájji Agha Beg (the Mihmándár sent by

---

[1] The Governor of the Tún and Tabas district is Hájji Mirza Bákir Khán, whose family have been dominant from ancient days. The present seat of government is at Tabas; but before the visit of Shah Abbas, Tún was the capital, once, undoubtedly, a very large and influential city, possessing twelve gates, a thousand mosques, two thousand water reservoirs, and a fortress of great size and strength.

[2] This plain skirts the great salt desert of Khúrasán.

the Prince of Mash-had), Governor of the district, and twenty or thirty well-mounted *sowárs*. And later in the day a hundred *sowárs* arrived in the town with a standard to escort Sir Frederic Goldsmid into Mash-had. At every village on the road the inhabitants turned out *en masse* to make their *saláms*; and sheep, in accordance with the barbarous national custom, were killed at every halting-place, that their blood might sprinkle our path: in fact, we were treated with every honor, and the Afghán Mission met with the same courteous welcome as ourselves. The only *contretemps* was that sixteen of our camels disappeared in the night before leaving, and we had difficulty in meeting with donkeys at Yúnsi to supply their place. Abdúlabád is one of a group of four villages, which go by the name of Mahwilát, the other three being Faizabad, Dughabád, and Mehnah, with numerous small villages as dependencies. It contains about 400 families, and is renowned for its gardens and fruit, and, above all, for its silk—which in a good year yields 30,000 *tumáns*, and is sent in its raw state to Mash-had, to be worked up there. The neighbourhood has many traditions connected with the renowned Rústam: several spots are pointed out as the scenes of his battles; at one he is said to have killed his son Zohráb; at another is shown the site of Zohráb's grave; at another the graves of the Shahzádahs, sons of Afrasiáb.

A band of 400 Túrkmans attacked the plain about six months previous to our visit, and carried off 200 prisoners and 600 camels from a tribe of nomadic Balúchís who had brought their flocks into the 'Mahwilát.'

We remained a couple of days here to give the camels a rest, and started again at 4 A.M. on the 18th of April, passing through a dense belt of flourishing gardens which encircles the town. After a gradual ascent of ten miles, we entered a range of low marl and clay hills, and, passing the caravanserai of Ribát-i-Bibi and the deserted villages of Zirábád and Aliabád, cleared the hills at the fifteenth mile and emerged on the wide plain of Túrbat—the villages scattered over which nestled amongst gardens, that were now gay with luxuriant blossoms and the fresh bright green of the early spring. Seven miles further we were met by the Wazír of the Governor of Túrbat, with four led horses, and a numerous body of *sowárs*, armed with huge blunderbusses known by the name of *shamkal*. At the twenty-sixth mile from Abdúlabád the Governor himself awaited us with a still larger escort of *sowárs*. From this point we rode through miles of flourishing gardens and cultivated land, watered by clear running streams, till we reached the town of Túrbat-i-Haidari, the houses of which were scarcely visible from the dense masses of foliage in which they lay hidden. Nothing could exceed the courtesy of the welcome that awaited both Missions. A large body of *sarbáz* and *faráshes* were drawn up at the entrance of the town, armed with long green wands, and by them we were conducted through the town and *bazárs*, all the people standing up and saluting while our cavalcade, headed by the Governor, went by: sheep, as before, being killed at our entrance into and exit from each *bazár*—where also incense was burnt, and sweetmeats were offered at constant intervals. It was, in fact, a very different reception to any experienced in Sistán; and on arrival at the quarters set apart for us, we found them situated in a beautiful garden, the house in which, belonging to the Governor himself, and thoroughly cleaned and newly carpeted for our reception, was sufficiently large to afford ample room, not only for Sir Frederic Goldsmid and his staff, but also for General Pollock and Dr. Bellew. Tea and iced *sharbat* had been prepared, and trays of sweetmeats of every kind spread out on the floor, the Governor himself doing the honours, and welcoming us in true Persian style[1].

Túrbat-i-Haidari takes its name from a member of the kings of Balkh, named Kútbu'-d-din-Haidar, who came here some seven centuries back, and who lies buried under the dome (*túrbat*) outside the town. The latter is more appropriately called Túrbat-i-Isa-Khán, from the ruler of that name (so fully described by Conolly), who reigned here about 100 years ago—and whose grandson still lives in the place, and is sometimes Wazír, sometimes Náib. In favourable years the town pays 3000 *tumáns* of revenue, with a large quantity of grain, but in 1872 this was remitted on account of the famine. Silk and cotton are largely grown in the principality, to the amount of 100,000 *tumáns* annually. The *bazárs* of the town are unusually fine, built of burnt brick, with good roofs, and contain over 200 shops. They were erected about ten years ago by Asadullah Mirza, now Governor of Bushahr. Before the disastrous famine, Túrbat could boast 1500 families; there are now not over 200. It possesses a garrison of 200 *sowárs*, and 100 *shamkalchis* or mounted matchlock-men.

[1] News arrived, before our start from Abdúlabád, of a great victory gained by the Persians over the Túrkmans, near the upper hill tracts: they had taken 600 prisoners, 800 horses, and 300 heads. [Round numbers of course mean hyperbole.—*F. J. G.*]

We remained here three days, detained partly by heavy rain, partly by our camels; and then determined to make one long march of it to Asadabád, a distance of twenty miles, so as to avoid stopping at Kamih, where provisions were scarcely procurable. Before leaving, Sir Frederic sent a watch and chain, a horse and other gifts, to the Governor, and a handsome *douceur* in money to all the servants. For three miles after leaving the town our road traversed gardens and luxuriant cultivation, and then struck over a desert stony plain to the foot of a range of low rocky hills, which it entered by the pass Godar-i-Khir-Sang, 300 feet above the level of Túrbat. Three miles from the summit of this pass is the substantial caravanserai of Kiskat, built near the village of the same name, where we were glad to breakfast and dry our wetted garments before commencing the steep ascent to the Godar-i-Baidar. In three miles, we rose 2250 feet above the level of Túrbat to the summit of this pass, from which, in fine weather, there is a splendid view; but the driving mist and rain-clouds hid all from our sight. Here the ranges of the Kúh-i-Nasar to the west and the Kúh-i-Bars to the east join. The descent is as difficult and fatiguing as the ascent, and is impracticable for camels in bad weather, though the road is fairly broad and levelled. The descent from the Godar-i-Baidar to the plain of Dasht-i-Rukh on the northern side is about 1200 feet. The ranges of hills which bounded the valley were covered with snow, presenting a very picturesque contrast to the fresh, green grass which clothed their lower slopes. We halted for the night at Asadabád, a small village, thirty miles from Túrbat, just struggling into existence, whose only object of interest was its curious door. This is used as a protection against the Túrkmans, and is formed of one immense circular stone, sliding into a groove into the wall, and of enormous thickness. Once closed, it is proof against any native attacks; but it requires so many men to move it, that it is never used except in cases of dire necessity. On the other side of Asadabád, at about eleven miles' distance, we entered the Tang, or defile of Muhammad Mirza, a most picturesque valley, winding through rocks of green serpentine, down which trickled numberless clear streams of water. Tradition points to the ruins of an old citadel crowning the rocks to the left, which is known as the Kala'h-i-Dukhtar (virgin's fort), having been built by the daughter of an ancient Persian king, to whom a Dervish had dared to raise his eyes in ardent admiration. As the king would not sanction a marriage between the pair, the damsel, followed by numerous adherents, fled to this spot, and built this castle, where she lived by the plunder of the travellers who passed by, while her Dervish lover built himself a small house, immediately under her windows, from whence he could watch his lady's movements. The ruins of the Ka'lah-i-Dukhtar, and the Khánah-i-Darwish, are still pointed out by the peasants as proofs of the truth of the legend.

This defile passed, we entered a fertile valley, in which lay the village of Kala'h-i-Bagalun and the caravanserai of Ribát-i-Safid, a tract peculiarly exposed to the attacks of the Túrkmans, on whose account watch-towers are built on the crests of the surrounding hills, and *ghulâms* and troops are always stationed in its villages. Vast flocks are pastured on the hills, and form no doubt the chief object of attraction to the Túrkmans. The valley passed, we emerged, seven miles further, on to the small plateau on which stand Kafir-Kala'h, a strong mud fort—and Sar Zar, a village surrounded by gardens and trees, presenting, in the distance, an appearance of great prosperity. The latter, however, was found on inspection to be utterly deserted, half the population having perished by famine during 1871, while the survivors were carried off for slaves by the Túrkmans during the present year. Watch-towers, in which, every night, guards are stationed to watch the movements of the dreaded Túrkmans, crown the hills that surround this plateau. If the foe be visible, a fire is lit in the early morning, the smoke of which at once warns the villagers on the plateau not to send out their flocks to pasture. The hills here are curiously honey-combed by the burrowing of a species of marmot or prairie-dog, two specimens of which were shot for preservation. Near the village of Kafir Kala'h is a range of hills affording excellent salt, sold in large quantities at Mash-had and the neighbouring towns. General Pollock saw in these an exact resemblance to hills forming the salt ranges of the Trans-Indus country. The plateau of Kafir Kala'h was succeeded by another plain of far greater extent, with an undulating surface, over which lay scattered numerous forts and villages. To the west lies the far-famed city of Nishapur; and to the south-east a splendid view of the snowy mountains behind Herát burst upon our sight. Crossing this plain at thirty miles from Asadabád, we reached a ruined watch-tower and tank, which is the meeting-place of all the roads to Mash-had from different parts of Persia; and one mile beyond this *carrefour* lay the village of

Sharifabád, where we halted for the night—resuming our march next day through a hilly country affording excellent pasturage, but now destitute of flocks or herds, which had all perished in the general famine. The road over the hills hence to Mash-had has an unusually broad track, with very fair gradients; and is the work of the late Sipah Sálár, who constructed it on the occasion of the Shah's visit to Khúrasán in 1867. The most difficult part of it is carried over solid rock across the Godár-i-Sipah Sálár, and stone pillars erected at each end of the pass commemorate the fact. Nine miles from Sharifabád is the Kúh-i-Salám, or hill of Salutation, from which pilgrims to Mash-had generally catch the first glimpse of the golden shrine of the Imám Riza; but unfortunately the day was so misty we could not appreciate the much-lauded prospect. Descending the hills, said to be rich in unworked mines of various minerals, we traversed the plain which runs up to the walls of Mash-had, and reached this far-famed city on the 25th of April, having traversed 328 miles between it and Birjand[1].

[1] Itinerary from Sistán to Mash-had:—

Date.	Stage.	Distance in Miles.	Direction.
March 11	Bolah	7	N.
,, 13	Ruins of Pesháwarán	28	W.N.W.
,, 15	Lásh-Juwain (including circuit)	19	N.
,, 18	Panj-Deh	2½	N.N.W.
,, 19	Khúsh-Rudak	18	N.N.W.
,, 20	Kala'h-i-Kah	15	N.W.
,, 21	Hárúd	16	W.
,, 22	Cháh Sagak	24	W. by N.
,, 23	Duruh	28	N.W.
,, 24	Húsainabád	24	W.N.W.
,, 26	Sar-Bíshah	29	W.N.W. Half N.
,, 28	Múd	21	N.W. by W.
,, 29	Birjand	23	W.N.W.
April 2	Ghiuk	18	N.
,, 4	Seh-Deh	18	N. by W.
,, 5	Rúm	10	N. by W.
,, 6	Káin	20	N.
,, 9	Girimanj	21	W.N.W.
,, 10	Dasht-i-Biaz	13	W.N.W.
,, 13	Kakhk	16	N.W.
,, 14	Zibad	15	N.W.
,, 15	Bajistan	28	N.W.
,, 17	Yúnsi	25	N. by E.
,, 18	Abdúlabád	30	N.E.
,, 20	Túrbat-i-Haidari	32	E.N.E.
,, 23	Asadabád	30	N.
,, 24	Sharifabád	31	N.
,, 25	Mash-had	21	N.

When within seven or eight miles of the town we were met by an *istikbál* of unusual size and magnificence. This consisted of a body of 200 mounted *sowárs* commanded by a Sartip, eight led horses with trappings of gold and jewels; and a carriage drawn by six horses, for the use of the British Commissioner should he prefer to drive—but which however was so dilapidated, and its outward appearance so uninviting, that Sir F. Goldsmid did not care to venture inside it. Two Colonels, each with half a troop of cavalry, were sent to escort General Pollock and the Afghán Commissioner; and we were also preceded and followed by an immense body of officials in full dress, sent from the Prince's household and mounted on enormous Túrkman horses, *pishkhidmats*, falconers, huntsmen, spearmen, standard-bearers, and orderlies, to the number of 2000 at least—and by them were conducted, according to the strict rules of Persian etiquette, at a foot's pace to the walls of the town. To a European nothing can exceed the weariness of such a progress, but to an Eastern the pageant would be shorn of all its dignity were it conducted at any pace quicker than this slow deliberate movement.

On entering the town, we found guards of honour, with drum and fife bands, stationed at intervals, who presented arms as the *cortége* passed, while a multitude of *faráshes* and runners, armed with silver sticks, ran before to clear the way: all the proceedings being arranged and controlled by an official clad in the uniform of a French general, who was known as the 'Adjutant Bashi.' We proceeded for a considerable distance up the chief street, which is a remarkably fine avenue known as the Khyabán, and which traverses the city from one gate to the other, leading from either gate up to the shrine and mosque of the Imám Riza, the particular glory of Mash-had. The Khyabán is bordered on each side by splendid *chinár* trees, and is lined with shops; while down its centre runs a canal which, though it serves to keep it cool, does but little towards cleansing it. The quarters allotted to us were in a spacious garden looking out on to the Khyabán, but as they were on the western side of the shrine we were compelled to turn off from the direct road and make a great *détour* before reaching them, in order to avoid passing on horseback before the venerated spot, within a quarter of a mile of which no one, not even the Shah himself, is allowed to ride. The interdicted space is walled off by an arched barrier of brick, built right across the street; and inside this no rider, it is believed, has ever dared to encroach.

Turning therefore off the main road, we were led with much solemnity, by many evil-smelling lanes and back slums, through an enormous graveyard, where slept thousands of the faithful, brought dead or alive from all parts of Persia, to rest under the shadow of the Imám's shrine—for the saint is supposed to take special care of such during their last long sleep. At last, to our great relief, the wearisome procession was over, and we were permitted to rest awhile in the rooms prepared for us in the garden already mentioned, and found that every possible arrangement had been made for our comfort. The Afghán Commissioner was also conducted with conventional ceremony to his quarters close to ours, while exactly opposite was the house allotted to the Persian Commissioner, from the summit of which the Persian flag floated in the air. We had not been many hours in the place when the General received a message from Mirza Ma'súm Khán, through his son, making the usual 'Ahwál Púrsi[1],' and desiring to know when he might visit him. It was evident that the Persian Commissioner was now anxious to place matters between himself and the English Commissioner on a friendly footing, but the memory of his recent acts in Sistán was too fresh to allow of the past being condoned in this manner: he was therefore given to understand, that though no objection would be made to receive a visit from him, it would not be returned until the whole transactions in Sistán had been laid before the British Minister at Tehrán.

The Persian Commissioner's son was succeeded by the head chamberlain of the Prince, sent to make the usual polite enquiries, and to fix the time for the official visit of the Mission to the palace; and next day a message was sent from the Prince Governor to ask whether General Goldsmid would object to the presence of Mirza Ma'súm Khán at the official visit to His Royal Highness, fixed for three o'clock that afternoon. To this a reply was sent to the effect that no exception would be taken to the Prince's ceremonial arrangements; so at the appointed hour, General Goldsmid, accompanied by his staff, with General Pollock and Dr. Bellew, started in full dress (goloshes being *de rigueur*) for the palace: the two Generals being mounted on really magnificent Túrkman horses (each 16½ hands high, with jewelled trappings of gold and silver), sent for their use, by the hands of many attendants, from the Prince; beside which the travel-worn animals ridden by the rest of the staff made but a sorry appearance.

[1] Or enquiry after health or condition. The expression has been already used in this narrative.

A great body of *faráshes* and orderlies preceded the *cortége*, which proceeded at a snail's pace through narrow and extremely filthy lanes shut in on each side by high walls, till after a monotonous ride we reached the *ark* or citadel in which dwelt Súltán Murád Mirza, Prince of Mash-had, Sword of the Empire, and the highest dignitary in the land except the Shah, than whom he acknowledges no other superior. He is the brother of the late and uncle of the present Shah, and is possessed of vast wealth and influence: and the ceremonial observed at his Court is nearly the same as that of the Imperial Court at Tehrán. On arrival at the Palace, of which the exterior was by no means imposing, we were led through various arched passages and across courtyards swarming with the usual retainers and hangers-on of an Eastern prince's Court, until we reached a point at which all our personal followers and servants were commanded to halt. The Prince's chamberlain then met us and conducted us through an open court planted with roses and jessamine, to a building at the end, into the centre room of which we were ushered, after having divested ourselves of our goloshes at the entrance; and the Prince himself entered from an inner chamber at the same moment as ourselves, and motioned us all to be seated. The chamberlain, however, remained standing outside in the court-yard, with his head on a level with the Prince's chair, while we sat in chairs on either side of the room. The only persons present besides ourselves were the Persian Commissioner, in full uniform, who had received permission to be seated in the presence of the Prince for this occasion only, and a Prince of the blood royal, whose name we could not catch. The visit lasted two hours, and was far more interesting than Persian visits generally are.

The Prince is a man of about sixty years of age, aristocratic alike in appearance and manners: he has played so important a part in the history of his country that his remarks were well worth listening to; and he talked as one born in the purple, who from his youth up had been a ruler of men. His dress was very simple, much resembling that of an English gentleman; nor was this resemblance in one respect only: he discoursed on all subjects with an ease and fluency which denoted not only extensive reading, but the readiness of a complete man of the world: appearing fairly well versed in European politics (a rare thing in Persia), and displaying some knowledge of the details of the English Constitution. We had heard much of his powers as a conversationalist, and were not disappointed;

for he led the conversation with such ease that it never flagged for a moment during the whole of our long visit. He is a man with a great thirst for knowledge, ever eager to obtain information from every available source. His manners are peculiarly pleasant and conciliatory, though he can be very stern on occasion; and the mingled affection and awe with which he is regarded by the whole Persian community, prove that his rule has been both salutary and beneficial. Having filled many arduous public offices during his career, he now looks somewhat fatigued and weather-worn, but the use of the dyes and other artifices which all Persians employ takes off at least ten years from his age: he is decidedly plain, though his singularly-shaped nose forms the redeeming feature in his face. During our visit, in addition to the usual tea, coffee, and pipes, the most delicious ices and *sharbat* were handed round, the work of a Persian cook who has studied in Paris. Every article of the equipage in which the refreshments were served was of pure gold: and some of the pipes and cups must have been worth a fortune, so encrusted were they with pearls, diamonds, emeralds, rubies, and other jewels. The room too was covered with carpets of great price. The Prince is, however, said to be extremely avaricious; and report has it that he knows where every fraction of his immense wealth is placed, and can tell to a farthing the value of every tea-spoon in his establishment. The very cooking-pots in his kitchen are said to be of gold, and he wisely enjoys his treasures himself, using them every day and not keeping them merely for State occasions. The visit over, we were conducted back to our quarters by the same attendants, and with the same rather tedious ceremony.

During our stay in Mash-had, which lasted exactly a week, we paid three visits to the Court, the first of which, just described, was strictly official, but the second was more friendly and less ceremonious. It took place in the Prince's garden near the citadel, where he received us in an open tent, and talked freely on all matters connected with our mission to Sistán, and also discussed the progress the Russians were making in Central Asia, which he considered most detrimental to English interests in India. In the gardens we were particularly struck by a Túrkman tent, which for space, warmth, lightness, and portability was a perfect marvel. The third visit took place the day before our departure from Mash-had: the Prince was anxious that all the members of the Mission should be photographed in a group with himself, by a member of his Court who was himself a prince, and rejoiced in the imposing title of A'kásh Báshi. We accordingly presented ourselves at eight o'clock on the 2nd of May, and were received by the Hisámú-s-Saltanah, in one of the inner court-yards of the palace, where the photographer of the blood royal also awaited us. Several groups were taken with greater or less success; the photographer informing us that the air of Mash-had was peculiarly unfavourable to his art. A conversation took place on this occasion which lasted fully two hours: among other subjects the late French revolution coming on the tapis, the Prince declared, speaking of the Communists, that in many points the French people greatly resembled the Persians. Before leaving, His Highness sent two Túrkman horses as presents to Generals Goldsmid and Pollock, which though fairly good were by no means first-rate animals; and indeed, in spite of his great wealth, he is said to give few presents of any great value. Túrkman horses are generally very tall, standing quite as high as English carriage horses, unmistakably handsome, with great bone and sinew: they all, however, fall off behind. They have one peculiarity which mars their beauty in English eyes, which is that they have no mane, this being cut off as soon as they are foaled and the place seared with hot iron, so that the hair never grows again. Such a custom renders the mounting of a Túrkman horse of seventeen hands high a somewhat difficult undertaking for a European; but the Persians place silver bands around the horses' necks, by which they help themselves into the saddle. The various visits which Sir Frederic Goldsmid paid to the Prince were returned by the uncle of His Highness, a pleasant, well-informed man, who was well up in European politics, having travelled in Egypt and Italy, and had spent some time in France, especially Paris, during the reign of Louis Philippe. He is entitled the Náïbu-l-Aiálah, or Personage next in rank and power to the Hisámú-s-Saltanah. He spoke much of the extreme misery caused in the province of Khúrasán by the famine which still prevailed. Mash-had alone, he said, had lost 24,000 inhabitants, while in the province 100,000 had perished; and he assured us that numerous cases of children being devoured by their own parents had come within his own personal knowledge. Every horse, mule, donkey, cat, or rat in the town had been devoured: the consequence was that the few Túrkman horses brought to us for sale were so exceedingly dear that we declined to select any for purchase; the general price asked, from £80 to £100, representing a very high figure for Persia. Our own horses had carried us well and bravely hitherto; but the fatiguing and trying marches they had made since we left Bandar-Abbas were naturally telling on them, and to our great regret they began to show signs of breaking down. Our servants also gave us a great deal of trouble during our stay in Mash-had: they had not been able to spend any of their wages for months, while passing through the long and dreary deserts of our march; and once arrived here, they found themselves in the possession of so much money that they became quite demoralised. Many of them, for very good reasons of their own, preferred remaining at Mash-had to returning with us to Tehrán; and others, hearing that the famine was still severe in the capital, feared to face it, and decided to stay in Khúrasán till the harvest was reaped. Insubordination to their superiors and quarrels amongst themselves became so incessant that we began to long for the time when we could get them away from the evil influences that surrounded them in the holy city. Our quarters also grew very wearisome, as we scarcely ever could stir out except escorted by a wholly superfluous but ever-provided crowd of *faráshes* and attendants; and the garden itself, though delightful during the first warm days of our stay, now became most unhealthily damp, owing to heavy and frequent rains; while many of our party began to suffer in health. Innumerable nightingales filled the air with their song, and though we thought this very charming at first, yet, after a time, their clamour at night positively prevented our sleeping, and they were voted a nuisance. Cooped up in a secluded garden, we saw but too little of the city, as we were always engaged either in making or receiving ceremonial visits, and we chafed much at this forced inaction. The Persian Commissioner called on the General, as arranged, the second morning after our arrival; but nothing of any consequence transpired during the interview, though he tried hard, if in vain, to explain away much of the unpleasantness that arose in Sistán, throwing all the blame of course on the Amir of Káin. Through him we heard much of the scarcity still existing in the country lying between Mash-had and Tehrán, and learnt with regret that at least 250 miles of our march lay through districts desolated by want and misery. In the evening of the 28th Sir F. Goldsmid called on the Sartip Húsain Ali Khán, who had headed the *istikbál* sent to greet us on our arrival. This officer is so like the Shah that he is known far and wide as the 'Shabah-i-Shah' (image or likeness of the king), and is a great favourite with his sovereign, whom he is constantly sent to personate in places where the royal presence is necessary and at the same time attended with danger. He received the General and his Staff in full dress, wearing his numerous orders. We found him singularly intelligent and amusing, possessing a more than ordinary acquaintance with the geography and manners of Europe: he told us he could formerly speak English well, having learnt it in Urúmia from the American missionaries stationed there, especially from one lady, a Mrs. Perkins. His house was superior to any of the private dwellings we had seen in Mash-had, being remarkably clean, handsome, and well arranged. This visit was returned the following evening, when the Sartip spent a long time in conversation on various subjects, displaying curiosity on matters connected with Europe, and especially with England.

Courteous and pleasant as were all the great personages in Mash-had, they yet had no power to obtain permission for us to visit the Mosque and gilded shrine, the only objects of real interest in the town, but which to us, as infidels, were strictly closed. We heard from the Afghán Commissioner and our servants that the shrine was of surpassing magnificence and beauty, but we had to content ourselves with viewing it from a distance. Mash-had, after Makka and Karbala, is the holiest city in the world to Musalmáns, for in its midst reposes, under a magnificent gilded dome, the body of their most cherished saint, the Imám Riza. The shrine is visited annually by more than 100,000 pilgrims, who flock to it from all parts of the world. We have already mentioned the fact that no rider is allowed to pass before it, within certain limits marked off by an arched barrier and chains: neither is horse, cow, or quadruped of any kind allowed to enter these limits, all waifs or strays being at once forfeit to the shrine. We nearly lost our best horse in this way, for being led out for exercise one morning, he broke away from his groom, jumped the chain, and would have been confiscated had not the man been quick enough to catch him before he could be taken prisoner. This iron chain marks also the commencement of the 'bast,' or sanctuary, within which all criminals are safe from the arm of the law, and which is amply provided with shops, baths, and everything a man can require; so that, provided he has only money, a criminal can laugh all authority to scorn, and stay there as long as he cares to do so. Within the 'bast,' however, there is a prison belonging to the Imám Riza, where thieves can be locked up and bastinadoed till they restore their booty. If a criminal were guilty of any very heinous crime, the authorities would probably starve him out by forbidding the shops to sell him anything, but such extreme measures are seldom put in force. We ourselves had some experience of this refuge; for on arrival at Mash-had, we found that a number of articles stolen from various members of the Mission were exposed for sale in one of the pawnbroker's shops of the town. The theft was traced to one of our own servants, but before he could be seized he stepped across the chain and was safe—refusing to give up any of the stolen property, but offering on payment of a certain sum to tell us where it could all be found. It was aggravating to be unable to punish this man according to his deserts. Through a strong representation made to the Prince, he was confined in the sanctuary prison: but we left Mash-had two days after, and he probably got off scot-free as soon as our backs were turned. The Imám Riza, who for so many centuries has slept beneath his gorgeous tomb, is still to all intents and purposes treated exactly as if he were living. His shrine is enormously rich, possessing land and property in all parts of Persia, and attached to it is a large establishment of officials and servants complete in every respect, and exactly such as would attend a powerful reigning prince. Questions are asked at the shrine and oracular answers given by the officials appointed for that purpose. Five hundred dinners are cooked daily for distribution to the pilgrims who flock to the place, each one of whom dines as it were with the Imám Riza for one night; and any pilgrim who is sick or disabled has his dinner sent to him. The Saint has also a Prime Minister, who is himself a Prince, and reigns over a considerable portion of the city lying within the sacred limits, administering justice and punishing all offences that come within his jurisdiction. Holy as Mash-had is said to be, we were struck with the great amount of drunkenness prevalent there amongst the followers of the Prophet. They were continually to be seen reeling and shouting up the Khyabán, while rows and brawls were occurring every hour. On the last day of our stay one of our *faráshes*, who was in the Khyabán, had bought some bread and was drying it in the sun, when a drunken *sarbáz*, who passed by, attempted to snatch it from him. A fight ensued, in which other *sarbáz* joined; knives were drawn, and our *farásh* was brought in with his arm half cut through at the elbow. Reference being made to the Prince, he sent down his 'Adjutant Báshi' to settle the affair. This judge's decision was unique. The wounded *farásh* was to be kept at the expense of the *sarbáz* till his wound was healed, and his assailant was to be beaten in his presence until he (the *farásh*) gave the signal to stop.

Mash-had was so famous in past days for its beautiful carpets, shawls, and turquoises, that we were anxious to procure specimens of each: but we soon ascertained that no articles of value or beauty could be obtained in the city, as all such had been sold during the terrible dearth. The workmen remained, it is true, but they had sold stock, tools, and all they possessed, and now would not even take orders for execution unless paid in advance. After remaining a week, as before mentioned, we became most anxious to get off, but the difficulty we experienced in getting camels and baggage animals for the march was untold; and it must be confessed we were rather badly used in the matter. Not only were we delayed two days unnecessarily, but we had to pay double the usual price, viz. three *kráns* a day, for each camel, and to advance, besides, the whole hire of the animals from Mash-had to Tehrán, an unheard-of thing. In vain we appealed to the Prince and the Náïbu-l-Aiálah: we could get no redress whatever: very probably their own servants had arranged the exorbitant price, and the superiors winked at it, while throwing the blame of the transaction on the British agent. The Prince is said, indeed, to have no objection to his people being paid by any *mudákhil*[1] or perquisites they can pick up, and strangers like ourselves are therefore doubly exposed to exactions of this nature. It may be mentioned that the Hisámú-s-Saltanah had three interviews with the Afghán Commissioner during our stay, in which Sistán matters were fully discussed. The former was most anxious to find out the full extent of the Afghán claims, but it was a case of 'diamond cut diamond,' and he could extract nothing out of the astute Afghán which the latter did not choose him to know.

At last, after infinite trouble and annoyance with the servants and the camels, matters were sufficiently arranged to allow of settling our departure for the 2nd of May, and, on the 1st, our camels were despatched in advance by the Sharifabád and Kadamgáh road, with

---

[1] For the meaning of this expression see note in page 150, where an explanation has been attempted. Perhaps the word should be *madákhil*, the plural of *madkhal*, which Freytag translates *ratio vivendi.*—F. J. G.

orders to join us at Nishápúr, as we had decided to go by the more hilly route, viá Já-i-Gharak. Before leaving, Sir Frederic Goldsmid gave a present in money, for distribution amongst those of the prince's household and attendants who had rendered us any service; while to the prince he sent a pair of gold revolvers, a very handsome photographic album and a silver-gilt centre-piece for the table, with other things, with all of which his Royal Highness expressed himself highly delighted. The Persian Commissioner was to leave the day after ourselves for Tehrán: he had sold off all his horses and broken up his establishment, having decided to travel 'chapar' or post. From all sides we heard the famine was still very severe at Tehrán, the roads having been so blocked up with ice and snow that it had been impossible to get supplies into the city: but providentially the harvest throughout the country was unusually abundant and just ready for reaping, so that we hoped that by the time we had journeyed over the 500 miles that lay between us and Tehrán, the scarcity in the capital would have passed away.

We left Mash-had on the morning of the 3rd of May by the Kúchán[1] gate and pursued our way across a flat plain for 10 miles; the ground being so scored with *kanáts* as to make it very unsafe riding. The plain was dotted with villages here and there, and covered with innumerable towers for safety, which told their own tale of the terror caused by the Túrkmans, who, to the disgrace of a powerful government like that of Persia, are allowed to carry their raids unchecked right up to the gates of Mash-had itself. Clearing the plain, we reached the lofty range of hills by which it is bounded on the south, south-west, and north-west, and after a short and steep ascent, entered the plateau beyond, by the pass called the Kothal-i-Páchinár. From this pass the first glimpse of Mash-had and its shrine is caught by the pilgrims travelling thither by the Dehrúd road, and its summit is crowned with tall cairns formed of the stones piled up by them to commemorate the event. We now crossed the river Chashmah-i-Gilásh, which flows on through Mash-had and, at about two miles above the summit of the pass, is confined at a narrow point in its bed by a strongly-built dam of brick, causing it to form a lake of some dimensions at the entrance of the lovely valley of Já-i-Gharak. A little beyond the *band* lies the populous village of Gu-

---

[1] Darwáza-i-Bála-i-Khyábán. Anglicé, 'the upper gate of the avenue.' The name of the town, the road to which is reached by the gate, is often added to the strictly local designation.—F. J. G.

listán, with two-storied houses, surrounded by beautiful trees, gardens, and cultivated fields, whence a pleasant avenue of mulberries led us into a valley of such beauty that we congratulated ourselves on having chosen this the Dehrúd route in preference to that by Sharifabád. It would be difficult to do justice to the beauty of the picture here presented: we compared it by turns to one of the far-famed Swiss valleys, without its background of snowy peaks; to a Kashmír glen; an Italian scene near the lake of Como; or a Devonshire glade. It was so entirely unexpected that it came upon us like a glimpse into paradise; and after months of marching over waste and howling deserts, to find ourselves riding for miles through scenes of a beauty so rare in Persia, made us feel at times inclined to rub our eyes and wonder whether we were not the victims of some illusion. For eighteen miles we rode through this valley, between hills whose slopes were a carpet of green turf, and flowers whose perfume filled the air, under glorious trees and past shady orchards, while bubbling brooks and tiny waterfalls threaded the mountain sides with silver, and filled the air with their music, telling of a plentiful harvest near, and a merciful close to the reign of famine and of death. The delight of riding for nearly two days over green turf, by the side of a brawling watercourse, catching nothing but glimpses of the blue sky through the lofty trees above us, was a luxury that could indeed only be thoroughly appreciated by those whose eyes, like ours, had been starved so long for the sight of green leaves and running streams. We reached the village of Já-i-Gharak, at twenty miles from Mash-had, and halted for the night in rooms prepared for us in the village, as there was no ground suitable for pitching the tents. The name of this village is derived from an old tradition that the country here was once covered by the sea, and that a ship foundered here— 'Já-i-Gharak' meaning literally 'the place of drowning.' In its surroundings and construction it much resembles a hamlet in Switzerland: in height it is 1200 feet above Mash-had. In its prosperous days it yielded a revenue of 1200 *tumáns*, fruit and wood being its chief products, and felled poplar-trees sell here usually for a *krán* apiece. The Katkhuda of the place informed us that although he had kept numerous families alive by borrowing money from Mash-had and doling it out in small sums, just enough to keep body and soul together till the crisis had passed by, 400 out of 700 families had perished during the recent famine.

Four miles after leaving Já-i-Gharak the lovely landscape has disappeared: slate hills take the place of the turf-covered slopes, and the road ascends gradually to the caravanserai Pa-Godar, eleven miles distant, a strong well-built place, standing amid scenery of the most desolate description imaginable. From this spot we rode three and a-half miles to the pass Godar-i-Dehrúd, over snow and stones, till the path became so difficult that we had to dismount and lead our horses. The summit[1] of the pass and line of the watershed is reached at the fifteenth mile from Já-i-Gharak, and here in fine weather a magnificent view may be obtained of the plain of Mash-had and the holy city on the one hand, and the plain of Nishápúr on the other to the south. Unfortunately the atmosphere on the occasion of our ascent was so misty, that all was indistinct and shadowy, though the golden dome was just dimly visible in the distance. Numerous pyramids of stone, the work of the pilgrims, again testified that they who had passed by this way had from this spot caught the first glimpse of the goal of their pilgrimage. The descent of the pass is even more trying than the ascent; at all seasons of the year it is a difficult undertaking, and should never be attempted with heavily-laden mules; it is quite impracticable for camels, and in severe winters entirely impassable. As it was, our mules stuck in the snow and did not arrive in camp till very late in the evening. The summit of the pass forms the boundary between the districts of Nishápúr and Mash-had, and the great quantity of snow, still found here and on the neighbouring mountains, gave promise of an abundant supply of water, for that year at least, to the scorched and thirsty provinces that lay below. In our descent on the southern side we passed a stone caravanserai about eleven and a-half miles from the summit, and then entered upon wild and magnificent scenery, with enormous limestone bluffs and precipices, down which roared innumerable waterfalls; and at seven miles from the summit vegetation again recommenced and continued till the ravine opened out into a fertile valley, in which lay the village of Dehrúd reposing in a perfect forest of gardens and fruit-trees. The southern slopes of these mountains were almost free from snow, and the increased warmth of the temperature became very perceptible. Dehrúd from a distance looked a perfect picture of prosperity and fertility, but we soon found it to be in reality a very charnel-house,

[1] All the aneroid barometers fell beyond scale on the summit of the pass. The height was estimated by Captain Lovett at about 10,000 feet above the sea-level.

in ruins, and for the most part deserted, while the pinched, diseased, and listless countenances of the inhabitants we met in the streets, were sufficient to tell us of their past sufferings and to point them out as the survivors of the fearful famine, which seemed to have visited this charming spot with unusual severity, and had swept off 1500 inhabitants out of 3000. An odour of disease and death pervaded the place, and the streets were literally strewn with dead men's bones. On taking possession of the rooms that had been prepared for us we found children's skulls lying scattered on the roof, while at our door lay the living skeleton of another child, so sunk in stupor that not even the money put into its hand could rouse it to any signs of life. Providentially, however, there were tokens of an abundant harvest on all sides, giving hope that plenty would soon again revisit the stricken village. We did what we could to relieve the present misery, by feeding the crowds of beggars who flocked to ask for charity, and who received the instalment given with gratitude; but we were struck with the great contrast they presented to the inhabitants of the Já-i-Gharak valley over whom the same famine had passed, but without leaving the same terrible traces. The revenue of the village had been reduced for one year to 900 *tumáns*, but even this the unhappy villagers were utterly unable to pay, having sold all they possessed to meet the taxes of the previous year. We were not sorry to leave the miserable village early next morning, though we could not forget the sad and pitiful sights we had witnessed in it. From Dehrúd we descended the southern slope of the mountains and entered the plain of Nishápúr, reaching the town of the same name after a march of twenty-three miles. The appearance of this plain with its innumerable gardens and villages, and its streams of water running down from the hills from every nook and cranny, fully bore out the character of extraordinary richness and fertility ascribed to it by Ferrier and other writers, but the famine had depopulated half the villages, which on closer inspection presented a most miserable and deserted aspect. At this time, however, the whole country appeared to be teeming with an abundant harvest, and bread was already much cheaper than it had been, though still at one *krán* the *mann*. The account given by the villagers of the number of deaths that had taken place amongst them was appalling, but it was impossible to obtain any very accurate statistics from them on the subject. Several miles from Nishápúr itself we were met by an *istikbál* sent out by the Prince Governor, who is the nephew of the Hisámú-s-

Saltanah; and as we neared the town, crowds of beggars, men, women, and children, flocked out to meet us, and surrounded us with cries for help. Sulaiman Mirza declined the General's offer to distribute food to the poor of the city, on the ground that such relief was no longer necessary; but there could be no doubt that the local destitution was still very serious and widespread. So much has already been written on the subject of Nishápúr and its ancient history, by Khanikoff, Ferrier, and other travellers, that we will not touch upon it here. We found the town in a most distressing state; and out of 600 shops that were occupied three years before, only 150 managed to eke out a bare subsistence by a peddling trade in the commonest necessaries of life. It usually pays an annual revenue of 40,000 *tumáns* to the Shah, and 20,000 *tumáns* for the expenses of government; but 12,000 had been remitted on account of the famine. The famous turquoise mines are situated at the base of the hill of Súlaimániah lying to the north of Zamánabád, a village about 16 miles from the city, and are farmed by Government for 8000 *tumáns* per annum. To our great regret we were not able to visit them, and we were still more disappointed to find that it was impossible to buy any turquoises in the place, as all are sent to Mash-had and Tehrán as soon as found. The morning after we reached Nishápúr our camels came in, having made five stages from Mash-had, and were soon followed by the Afghán Commissioner and his train. The Governor called on the General in the evening of our arrival, and spent more than two hours conversing on every subject that was started, with an ease and intelligence that reminded us strongly of his shrewd uncle: he was a man of about five and twenty, with peculiarly aristocratic manners and appearance; and we were much amused by the pride he took in his boots, which we judged to be of Paris manufacture, but which he told us with national pride had been made for him by a Persian in Shahrúd.

From Nishápúr the road ran across a well-cultivated plain, with the lofty range of the Albúrz hills to the north, the country studded with villages and gardens, and green with the fresh crops of the year, though the mortality of 1871 had stopped three-fourths of the usual cultivation. For ten miles this road was excellent, but the soil then changed, and the remaining six miles to Zamánabád proved to be most unpleasant travelling, our horses sinking over their fetlocks in the soft salt-covered earth, called 'Zamin-i-Kavir.' We entered Zamánabád over a strongly-built brick bridge thrown over the salt river Shúráb. The weather had hitherto been delicious, but here a tremendous wind blew all day, making tent-life a simple misery. The plain below was covered with the usual round towers for safety from the Túrkmans; and it may be mentioned that we were accompanied in our journey by two Persians, travelling with their wives to Shahrúd, who took advantage of our escort. They said that they had been prisoners at Bukhára for thirteen years, and had been released, with thousands of other captives, by the 'Russ,' who gave them money to return to their own country. They got as far as Kabúl, but here their funds failed, and the Amir, Shir Ali Khán, then gave them sixty *kráns*, which brought them on to Mash-had, where they besought aid from the Prince, but obtained in return nothing but advice. They were quite penniless, so we fed them daily till they reached their journey's end. At Shúráb, a small village, nine miles beyond Zamánabád, half ruined by the famine (thirty houses only standing out of seventy), we noticed the foundations of a magnificent caravanserai commenced by the Mústasharu-l-Múlk, Wazír of Khúrasán. Though stopped suddenly by the ordinary occurrence of deposition from office, it was hoped he would finish it eventually. Being extremely wealthy, this man was at one time condemned by the Hısámú-s-Saltanah to a fine of 150,000 *tumáns*, which he actually paid; and this fact will give some idea of his riches. On the road to Shúráb we noticed many human skulls lying by the path, relics of the past famine. Eight miles beyond the village we arrived at the excellent new caravanserai of Sang Kala'h-dár, situated near the village of the same name, with about sixty inhabitants. We had now entered on the district of Sabzawár, and, passing the *ábambár* of Zafarúni, reached, five miles further on, the magnificent Zafarúni caravanserai, which, however, we carefully avoided, as it had the reputation of being infested by a peculiarly poisonous species of bug. This caravanserai was built partly on the ruins of the old one by Sadr Azim Mirza Agha Khán during the present Shah's reign, with money left by a wealthy man named Khúsru Khán Kajár, the bulk of whose fortune was employed in public works of charity. Only thirty families were left in this village out of seventy before the famine. The severe illness of one of our party (Mr. Thomas) compelled us to halt here for a day, in order to give him rest, while an express was sent on to Sabzawár to obtain a proper litter for him. This was, however, not to be found, so we had to make shift with *kajáwas* or travelling panniers.

We left Zafarúni at 4 P.M. the next morning, in cool pleasant weather, but the sun became very powerful before nine o'clock in the morning. A good road over a desert plain, bounded on either side by hilly ranges, brought us, after a march of ten miles, to the caravanserai of Sar Poshida, and from this point we passed through a succession of flourishing villages, well supplied with water and surrounded by cultivation, till fifteen miles further we reached the city of Sabzawár—apparently much sooner than the good people had expected us, for the *istikbál* was barely ready in all its details. When, however, its members were all properly mustered, the welcoming *cortége* proved a handsome one, and we were escorted by it with the usual ceremony to our quarters, through extensive *bazárs* teeming with life and occupation, the towns-people presenting a remarkable and very pleasing contrast to the miserable creatures we had hitherto seen in our marches from Mash-had. We were located in the Governor's own house, which he had courteously vacated for us, and were most comfortably lodged, our rooms opening on to a courtyard planted with roses and jessamine, in full blossom. Finding, to our astonishment, on entering this courtyard, the Governor of the town seated there with Mirza Ma'súm Khán, we at first imagined there had been some mistake as to our quarters; but it became clear that the Governor had merely come to certify that his orders for our reception had been properly carried out, and had been joined by the Persian Commissioner—both being taken by surprise at our arrival, which was much sooner than had been expected. We sat talking together for some time, while coffee was served with a most delicious *sharbat* made from the wild rhubarb. In the evening the Governor paid a long visit to the General, accompanied by the Kázi of the place. He is a relative of the Hisámú-s-Saltanah, and his wife is the sister of Súlaimán Mirza of Nishápúr. We noted him to be a stout little man, quite as broad as long, very chatty, and very proud of a smattering of French picked up at the Court at Tehrán. He gave us most distressing accounts of the ravages of the famine in his district; and said that much misery and suffering still existed in the town and neighbourhood, though in prosperous years Sabzawár is considered the cheapest town in Northern Persia. Being asked what gift would be most acceptable to him, he replied with many protestations that he expected nothing, but that a breech-loading rifle was what he specially coveted. Sabzawár was at one time a very extensive city;

and a *minár* or column, situated five miles to the west on the Tehrán road, is said to have been included within its walls, which in the days of the sainted Ali, the nephew of the Prophet, extended to the village of Mazinán. At present it only contains 3000 houses with about 10,000 inhabitants, out of 9000 houses and 30,000 inhabitants before the famine; many of the people having died from excessive eating of grass, and from cold. The *bazárs* had ample space for 2000 shops, but only 200 were occupied when we visited the town. There are six caravanserais for merchants, and four for travellers. Its mosque is 800 years old, dating from the time of Taimur Shah, Ghúrikáni. Silk, cotton, and a small supply of opium are the products of the province—containing nine *balúks* or districts, many of the villages in which have lost three-fourths of their population. Sabzawár exports wheat to Astrabád, with dried fruits, cotton, and sheep-skins, receiving cooking utensils, etc. in return; and there is a rich copper mine in the neighbouring hills of which, during the famine, the ore was sold for its weight in bread.

We remained here for a whole day, to give rest to Mr. Thomas, and to arrange a proper litter or *takhti rawan* for his use. During this halt we discovered an Armenian merchant, who sold bad wine in small quantities as a great favour, and who informed us that wine and spirits were to be obtained from a Russian at Shahrúd—a piece of information hailed by us all with much satisfaction. We had been unwilling tea-totalers for some time past, our supplies of wine and spirits having been exhausted just after leaving Sistán. We marched from Sabzawár on the 13th of May, at half-past four in the morning, for we had a very long stage before us—of seven *farsakhs*, according to the Persians, but according to Ferrier, nine at the least, or over thirty-two miles. The camp was astir at three, but the usual difficulties in getting the servants together, and loading the baggage animals in the narrow streets, did not allow of our starting as soon as we wished, so that we rode through the *bazárs* and cleared the gates of the town at half-past four, just as the latter were opened. Five miles from Sabzawár stands the Minár of Khusru Gird, already alluded to, a very remarkable solitary round tower, about 120 feet high, built of baked brick, with a flight of interior steps leading to the summit, only wide enough to admit one man. Round its exterior the bricks are arranged at intervals so as to form a Kufic inscription. It is in excellent repair, though of considerable antiquity, and stands on a square foundation, still perfectly sound, and which is now exposed to the depth of about six feet. The bricks of which it is constructed are joined together with *gach* (mortar), and in appearance it reminded us much of the tower we had seen at Kásimabád, in Sistán. A belt of cultivated land and occasional villages extends beyond Sabzawár for eleven miles, but at that distance vegetation ceases, and our road ran over a hard gravelly desert till we reached Rivad, twenty miles from Sabzawár, and about twelve from Mehr, our halting-place for the night. The sun was so powerful that it became necessary to halt for several hours during the extreme heat, and we did not therefore reach Mehr till the evening, when, eschewing the very stuffy and inodorous quarters our Mihmándár had secured for us in the village, we pitched our tents in a field outside. Like all villages on this route, Mehr had suffered terribly from the famine, only sixty families remaining out of 100 of the former population. The first crop of barley had been already reaped; but the sight of a large crowd of starving women and children, craving alms, induced the General to attempt the grant of at least temporary relief, by forwarding to the Kázi of the place a sum of money for distribution. We noticed that fifteen miles from Sabzawár the ranges of hills and detached hillocks to the south, which for many miles had been gradually diminishing, entirely ceased, and the salt waste of the great desert of Khúrasán was visible in the distance, gleaming white through a misty haze. The temperature was greatly affected by the proximity of the desert, and became extremely hot and close: and the inhabitants of the neighbouring villages suffer much from the wind that, constantly blowing from that quarter, injures their crops by desiccation and diminishing the yield. The hills on the north, on the contrary, are well watered, with prosperous villages nestling in the fertile valleys between them. Numerous round mud towers testified as usual to the constant dread of the Túrkmans. From Mehr a march of twenty miles brought us to Mazinán, a village standing in the midst of scanty cultivation and extensive ruins, amongst which is to be found the tomb of the father of the saint Imám Riza. It possesses a very fine caravanserai, but we preferred passing the night in our tents. During the day we suffered great inconvenience from the wind, which enveloped us in clouds of dust, strongly impregnated with saline matter and affecting the eyes most painfully. Mazinán is so peculiarly exposed to Túrkman attacks, that in lieu of taxes to the Shah it is bound to support 150 *túfangchis* (matchlock-men) and twelve artillery-men, with their horses; and from this point the road for the next four stages is considered so unsafe that we were compelled to travel with an escort of eighty *túfangchis* and between 150 and 200 mounted *sowárs* and a piece of artillery, drawn by six horses: it was a four-and-a-half pounder, of Turkish construction, and bearing the Sultan's monogram. The artillery and *sowárs* struck us as being soldierlike and well up to their work. Though this escort was probably increased on account of the Mission, yet the presence of an armed party of considerable strength is held so necessary in crossing the perilous district, that a body of *sowárs* with one gun leaves Mazinán and Shahrúd regularly twice a month, on the 3rd and the 17th, for the protection of all travellers journeying that way. The respective parties meet at Mian-Dasht, half-way between the two places, relieve one another, and return each to its starting-point. We made a very large *cortége* with our own camp and that of the Afghán and Persian Commissioners, but though there is always a great concourse of people waiting for the guns, we were accompanied by few actual pilgrims. One great trial of our patience was the inconvenient but necessary order of the day to travel at the same pace as the camels and baggage-mules; but we felt that stragglers might have shared the fate of the French photographer who, some time before, had lingered behind the escort to complete a picture, and was swept off by the Túrkmans, and kept a prisoner till ransomed by the Persian Government for £3000. Our Mihmándár from Mash-had left us at Mazinán, taking back handsome presents for himself, and the coveted breech-loading rifle for the Governor of Sabzawár.

We started from Mazinán at half-past four the next morning, and as no particular danger was anticipated for the first fourteen miles of the stage, which ran over the desert skirting the hills, were only too glad to shake ourselves clear of the crowd of travellers, and ride on ahead to the fort and fine caravanserai of Sadrabád, where we breakfasted. This fort is inhabited by three families in the pay of Government, whose lot appeared to us most unenviable, as, not to speak of the loneliness of their abode, they live in constant dread of falling into the clutches of the Túrkmans. Beyond this fort the dangers of the road were considered so imminent that we were compelled to wait till the main body came up; when with horse, foot, artillery, pilgrims, and outsiders, we formed a long line stretching across the desert, which here became sandy, treacherous, and covered with salt. Two miles beyond the caravanserai is the Pul-i-Abrisham, a bridge, now nearly ruined, which crosses a narrow rivulet of salt water. This is the dreaded spot of the stage, for four miles beyond the bridge is an oäsis of green turf watered by a fresh-water spring called the 'Chashmah-i-Gez,' concealed by a dip in the road, which affords a convenient halting-place for the Túrkmans, who here await at their ease the approach of the caravan they intend to rob. Rather to the disappointment of some of our party, however, nothing was to be seen this day of the robbers; and the spring once passed the danger for that stage was considered over, and we pushed on without the wonted escort to Abbásabád, the station reached at noon. This village is peopled by the descendants of Georgians brought by Shah Abbás from the neighbourhood of Tiflis, who are now all Musalmáns. Originally there were sixteen families placed here to look after the very fine caravanserai, and the *kanát*, constructed at the same time, as also to help the pilgrims to Mash-had: for this service an annuity of 100 *tumáns* and 100 *kharwars* of wheat was settled on the villages, which is continued to this day. The women are said to be surpassingly beautiful; but of this we were of course not permitted to judge: as the Shah took one to wife some three years ago, we may reasonably conclude that such reputation has been well founded. There was but little cultivation round the village, the inhabitants living principally by what they can make in attending to the wants of the numerous pilgrims who pass through *en route* to Mash-had. Some excitement was caused by a report that fourteen of our camels and one man had been carried off by the Túrkmans in the middle of the night; and though we had intended to march at three in the morning, we were compelled to await the daybreak and result of a mission in quest of the missing driver and animals. It turned out, however, that the former having fallen asleep his camels had strayed; and after much delay, and of course many conflicting reports, they were all brought in safely, and we started with our number complete. Half-way over a range of low hills that crossed the desert plain, we met the caravan coming from Shahrúd, with one gun and a few *túfangchis*, whose small numbers showed that the people, from Shahrúd at least, anticipated but little danger from the Túrkmans at this season of the year. There was a considerable number of pilgrims with this caravan. At Alhak, a ruined fort and deserted village about eight miles from Abbásabád, we changed escorts, the gun from

Mazinán being relieved by the one from Shahrúd. Our courier from Tehrán, Mahomed Ismáil Beg, was with this caravan, and to our great delight brought us English letters up to the 17th March, and the good news that the famine was gradually passing away at the capital. Our pleasure, however, was marred by receiving tidings of the death of Mr. Alison, H. B. M. Minister in Persia.

From Alhak we made a gradual descent of twelve miles to Mian Dasht, through a tremendous storm of dust, wind, thunder and rain. Mian Dasht is nothing but a cluster of ruined mud huts, a partially ruined burnt brick fort, and a new caravanserai in course of construction. This last promised to be very large and handsome, and its half-finished rooms were at once occupied by the members of the caravan; but we preferred the quiet of our own tents, pitched outside on the open plain, on which rhubarb and wormwood were growing. Mian Dasht stands 1000 feet above Abbásabád. The fort was garrisoned by about forty or fifty matchlock-men, who received the unusually good pay of 100 *tumáns* per annum. The old caravanserai dates from the reign of Shah Abbás: the new one was commenced three years ago by the Amir-i-Tumán, Hájji Húsain Khán. Beyond Mian Dasht lay the noted valley of Ja-i-Jirm, studded with villages and forts, the inhabitants of which lead the most insecure life imaginable, being constantly exposed to the attacks of the Túrkmáns, who enter the valley from the north by a pass in the low hills called the 'Dahnah-i-Zaidar,' and scour the roads right and left. Six miles further we passed the village of Zaidar, a small hamlet with good trees and running water, situated on the eastern slope of the lofty hill of Miámái; and skirting this hill on the left, and the snow-capped Siah Kúh on the right, we reached the pleasant tree-sheltered village of Ibrahimabad, whence we pushed on to Miámái, the last recognised halting-place on this road to Shahrúd. The village was surrounded by fields of wheat and barley ready for the sickle, and our camp was pitched in two fields that had been already reaped. Grain was, however, still almost at famine prices. A truly fatiguing march of forty-one miles lay between us and Shahrúd, and the heat of the noonday sun being now very great, we started at 3 A.M., in order to get over as much ground as we could during the cool of the early morning. The utterly desert road was most uninteresting, presenting no features worthy of notice, nor did anything occur to relieve the monotony of the march. We arrived at Shahrúd at six o'clock in the evening dead beat, both animals and men. To our surprise no *istikbál* was sent out to receive us, and we at once attributed this fact to the action of Mirza Ma'súm Khán, who had arrived at Shahrúd three hours before ourselves. When the Náib of the place was spoken to on the subject, he tacitly admitted that in neglecting to give the usual welcome to the English Mission he had acted under the instructions of the Persian Commissioner. The Prince Governor here, Jánsoz Mirza by name, an impoverished *roué*, seemed a mere non-entity, the real Governor being the Náib, who resides at Shahrúd while the Prince lives at Bostán—a place about three miles and a-half from Shahrúd, seated at the foot of a lofty range of hills, and embosomed in trees and gardens. We were glad that the circumstances of the Prince's residence at Bostán made it unnecessary for the General to pay him any visit of ceremony, for he was a man of an evil reputation, an unusually bad specimen even of a Persian Governor, and so *criblé de dettes*, that he could scarcely leave Tehrán to take up his appointment as Governor of Shahrúd. There is good reason to believe that he made the wretched artillery-men, *ghulámns*, and *sowárs*, who had escorted us from Mian Dasht, disgorge all the money they had received in fair recompense for their services.

Shahrúd is situated at the foot of a spur of hills branching off from the lofty Shah Kúh. It was formerly the capital of the province, but Bostán is gradually usurping that position, and Shahrúd sinking into the character of suburb to the younger city. The Prince Governor as before mentioned resides at Bostán, and here the troops and artillery are quartered. It also contains the grave of a famous Shaikh named Báyazíd, who it is said refused to have any dome raised over his grave, and whose only monument is a heap of stones. Near the grave, however, is a *minár*, to which is attached a stick : those of the faithful who wish to consult the deceased prophet grasp the stick, and the saint is said to answer them by causing the *minár* to vibrate with such violence, that were any one to stand at its summit he would be precipitated to the ground. Shahrúd contains about 1000 houses. It entirely escaped the horrors of the famine, as supplies were easily to be had from Astrabád. It has 200 shops, of which twenty are exclusively devoted to the sale of boots and shoes, for which the place is famous : the Shah and all the nobles of Persia being supplied by the shoemakers of this town. Four caravanserais for merchants and sixteen for pilgrims are to be found here. The chief products of the district are wheat, cotton, fruits, and tobacco. The town is infested with the poisonous bug already mentioned, called the *shabgaz*, and we therefore kept to our own tents outside the walls, pitched in the midst of gardens surrounded by fine trees. We halted here for six days, viz. from May 18 to May 23, and experienced the most remarkable changes in the weather during that time. The mornings were delicious, the air quite soft and pleasant, reminding those of our party who knew Kashmír of the climate there; but towards three o'clock in the afternoon a storm invariably came on, sometimes of wind only, but oftener of thunder, lightning, and heavy rain, which quickly swelled the numerous mountain torrents in the vicinity. Our servants were completely knocked up by the trying march from Miámái, as were also the horses, so that the camp for the first day was unusually quiet; but a good deal of excitement was infused into it the third day of our stay by the report that 400 Túrkmans had made their appearance at a spot between Miámái and Shahrúd, having come down with the intention of intercepting the Mission. This news was brought down by our Mirákhór, who had gone up to the Prince at Bostán with the usual polite messages from Sir Frederic Goldsmid, in return for enquiries sent by him through the Náib; and who reported that a large body of *sowárs* had been sent in pursuit of the robbers. One of the servants of Mr. Hoeltzer of the Telegraph Office met us and told us he had obtained leave to visit his family living in one of the villages of the Ja-i-Jirm valley, but on arrival there found that all the members had been swept off by the Túrkmans.

Two Russian residents in the town called on the General, natives of Moscow, apparently upper class 'mujiks;' they seemed perfectly contented with their life here, and spoke good Persian. We tasted some of the wine made from grapes grown in the neighbourhood, and found it very like Shíráz wine; and we also obtained a good supply of excellent oranges, brought from Mazandarán. The Telegraph Station here, supposed to keep up communication both with Tehrán and Astrabád, appears to be of little use, as the line is almost always broken down: during the time we were at Shahrúd no message had been interchanged with either place, and the clerk in charge declared he had no idea where the break was to be found.

On May 22 the Persian Commissioner left for Tehrán. On the 23rd we were all busily employed preparing budgets for home, which were to be entrusted to Quartermaster-Sergeant Bower, who was to leave the Mission at Shahrúd for Europe, carrying despatches from Sir Frederic Goldsmid to the Foreign Office. The mail was closed at sunset, and early the next morning Bower left the camp, to the great regret of all our party. He was to go down to Astrabád in four days, over a very bad hilly road of fifty miles, and from thence might expect to reach London in twenty days, taking the train at Tsaritsin, on the Volga. The road from Shahrúd to Deh Múlla is for the most part desert and stony, at times skirting the hills to the right, at others the eternal salt wastes of the Khúrasán desert to the left. Up to Deh Múlla the telegraph wires, which are supported on poplar poles, were in good repair, and it was curious to find with what feelings of pleasure we regarded them, as an earnest of the civilisation to which we were returning after our six months' travel in the deserts of Persia and Sistán. We passed five or six villages on the road, none of which presented any features of interest, and halted for the night at Deh Múlla, a small village 700 feet below Shahrúd, with about seventy families left of the one hundred of its population previous to the famine. It possesses a ruined fort, originally built for protection from the Túrkmans, and a large caravanserai. The latter, however, had such a reputation for the *shabgaz*, or bug, that we avoided it carefully, and were glad to find quarters had been prepared for us in an excellent two-storied house, quite new, standing in a large garden, in which was a particularly beautiful species of Iris. Here the Mihmándár appointed by the Prince of Shahrúd to attend us, left, as the jurisdiction of his master ceased at this place, and that of the Governor of Damghán commenced. For the next few stages we started at half-past three in the morning, in order to get over the march before the great heat of the day: the moonlight was brilliant in the extreme, and these rides in the quiet and cool of the hours preceding dawn were most enjoyable. Between Deh Múlla and Damghán we passed two villages, Mominabád and Kádirabád, both built by Mirza Mahdi Khán, the Wazír of the great Nádir Shah, who left them in perpetuity to his heirs male. Then came Mihmandost, the special property of the Shah, and behind it Imámabád, formerly belonging to the late Sipah Salar. Finally we passed through the ruins of Bostajan and reached, somewhat further, ancient Damghán, twenty-seven miles from Deh Múlla. These remains mark the site of the once populous town, said to have been destroyed two centuries since by the Afgháns, who in one day slew 70,000 of its inhabitants; but so vast was its population then, that this wholesale slaughter, so the legend goes, made no perceptible difference in its numbers. Before that time also 40,000 had perished in an earthquake. Since these two calamities the town has been steadily on the decline, and is now a heap of melancholy ruins, among which are the remains of fine mosques and shrines, an ancient citadel, claiming to be 3000 years old, and a *minár* with a surface of ornamental brick-work, and Kufic inscriptions dating from the commencement of the Muhammadan era. Another ancient monument is called the *minár* of Harúnu-r-Raschid. We rode straight through the town, or its ruins, and out at the western gate to our camp, which was pitched beside an excellent caravanserai; but the inimical *shabgaz* had fairly closed its doors to European travellers. We had ridden so fast that we reached the place before the *istikbál* was ready for us, and came upon the members one by one, each and all profuse in their apologies and regrets. Ferrier has written of the high wind so prevalent here. The Persians say that it is occasioned by a mystic spring in the mountains about two *farsakhs* off, which, the moment anything dirty is thrown into it, causes a tremendous gale to blow, which lasts several days, till the spring is purified; and a sentry is always kept at the well to prevent tampering with its waters. It is said that when the Shah passed through Damghán *en route* for Mash-had, being incredulous of the story, he ordered some of his suite to throw dirt into the spring, when immediately such a wind arose that the royal camp was rolled up like so much paper, and the Shah was compelled to have the cistern completely cleaned out and purified before the wind would cease! There are three inámzádahs in Damghán, one of which is that of the Forty Virgins. We found the telegraph lines in working order from here to Tehrán, but messages could only be sent in Persian and through a native clerk.

Gúchah, lying about twenty-three miles beyond Damghán, was our next halting-place; and we reached it by a good road through uninteresting country, with three or four large villages *en route*, standing amongst luxuriant fields of wheat and barley. Ferrier describes one of these, Dáulatabad, as one of the most flourishing villages of Persia, but this did not seem to us to be borne out by facts; its walls were very dilapidated, and could never have covered any great extent of ground, two of the triple lines scarcely deserving the name of walls: the chief beauty of the place consisted in its trees, which were remarkably fine. It is watered by numerous streams of water, which accounted for the extreme fertility of the soil; nowhere had we seen finer crops than those of Dáulatabad. It had however suffered severely during the famine, many of the villages and forts near being entirely deserted, while the many 'Túrkman protection' towers told of the ever-dreaded visits of those detested men-stealers. A cluster of villages of some importance lay beyond, the chief of which, Amirabád, was built by the late Sipah Salar, who spared no pains or expense to make it successful. He brought architects and builders from Tehrán, and erected many handsome houses, baths, etc., besides ensuring for it at a great outlay an abundant supply of water, the beneficial effects of which are visible in the great extent of cultivation which surrounds the village. Between Amirabád and Gúchah lay a desert road, traced out by the telegraph poles and wires. Gúchah itself consists merely of a very dirty caravanserai, a water-tank, and a *chapar khánah* or post-house. Bread and water were obtainable here, but nothing else, and travellers should take care to bring sufficient supplies from Damghán. The insecurity of the road, owing to the Túrkman attacks, and the ravages of the famine, had of late caused a great diminution in the numbers of travellers and pilgrims passing through Gúchah, a fact bewailed bitterly by the keeper of the caravanserai, who lived by selling bread at exorbitant prices to all passers-by.

At Gúchah we received a complimentary message from the Persian head of the telegraph at Tehrán, which cost us £1; but our Mirza, more fortunate than ourselves, knew a clerk in the Tehrán office, who sent him a beautiful message of welcome in poetry, and charged nothing for it! The air in these early morning marches was most deliciously cool, and we felt no inconvenience from the sun till about nine o'clock, when it became so powerful that we generally arranged to halt then, and remain in camp for the rest of the day.

Ahúan, the stage beyond Gúchah, is a village of no interest, possessing two caravanserais, one very ancient, built by Náushirwán, and in ruins, the other erected by Shah Sulaimán Safavi, somewhere about the time of our Queen Elizabeth. We were surprised to find the country between this place and Gúchah swarming with an insect unknown to us previously, with the body of a large beetle and the legs of a grasshopper. The natives call it 'locust,' but it certainly was not the locust of Egypt and Syria. We were told by the keeper of the Gúchah caravanserai that the great Khúrasán desert to the south of Gúchah was covered for many miles by an inland salt sea, so deep as to be impassable except in one place, where a passage can be effected with infinite difficulty and labour, but where many have been drowned in making the attempt. We could observe something in the far distance much resembling a sheet of water, but whether this was really water, or merely a mirage, it was impossible for us to decide. It is quite possible, however, that the drainage from the southern slopes of the Albúrz may collect on the lowest level of the great desert, but it is strange that the sea, if existent, should never have been mentioned by any previous travellers. Former writers relate that at one time a herd of tame deer was to be found at Ahúan, whose presence was accounted for by the following legend. The sainted Muhammad Riza, passing through the village one day, met a huntsman who had just caught a deer. At sight of the saint the animal became gifted with speech, and besought him to allow her to return to her young ones at home, who would perish for want of nourishment if she were kept a prisoner. Thereupon the saint ordered the huntsman to let her go, promising to go bail for its re-appearance. The huntsman obeyed, but as the deer never returned, he complained to the saint, who then, by force of prayer, summoned back the animal to its captor, and it was kept sacred by him ever after.

After a march of about twenty miles from Ahúan we reached the plain of Samnán, which lay stretched out like a map before us, with a few scattered villages and scanty cultivation. The town itself stands in a belt of gardens, at about 2100 feet below Ahúan, a difference which was at once perceptible in the increased warmth of the temperature. We got into our camp, which was pitched under fine mulberry trees, close to a watermill, so early (at 8.45) that the preparations for our reception were not completed. Two hundred yards from the town, however, we were met by a cavalcade headed by the cousin of the Governor, who was the Náib of the place, sent out to meet the General, accompanied by a very rickety tumble-down carriage, apparently of Russian origin, and drawn by two horses without blinkers. The Náib informed us that Mirza Ma'súm Khán was now at Samnán detained by illness, and that it was very doubtful when he would be able to resume his journey. We found a good supply of apricots in this place, of excellent flavour, though not large, and this at once showed the great difference between the climate here and that of the spur of hills we had lately traversed to the north-east. A violent wind blew all day, which caused us great discomfort from the clouds of dust it raised from the neighbouring plain. It was probably owing to this wind that so many of the telegraph posts along this stage were on the ground, with the wires nearly touching the earth. We were, however, much surprised to learn that notwithstanding this, the line was reported to be in good working order. No visit was received by Sir F. Goldsmid from the Governor of Samnán himself, the usual civilities being offered by his Wazír as his proxy, and we learnt afterwards that he had been specially excused by the Shah from paying first visits. We halted a day here to give the men and animals a rest, and during this time received from the Governor presents of a kind of bread or rusk for which the place is celebrated, but which, as it had been baked the year before, we did not appreciate. Samnán is a tolerably thriving place, trading chiefly in the rusks above-mentioned and horse-shoes, of both of which it sends large supplies to Tehrán. It suffered but slightly during the famine, owing to its proximity to Mazandarán, from which it obtained supplies; its population consisted of 2500 families.

At the time of our visit it was governed by one Muhammad Húsain Khán, a personage of high descent and titles. Its walls and citadel we found in a very dilapidated condition, but it possesses twelve caravanserais, excellent *bazárs*, with 700 shops, four *hammáms*, and three mosques, one of which last is of great antiquity, and reputed to be of the epoch of Náushirwán. Unfortunately time has obliterated the date from the inscription on the ancient stones over its portal. The other two mosques were erected, one by Shah Abbas, the other by the late Fath Ali Shah, forty-six years ago. The more modern structure is very handsome. Four colleges have also been built by the inhabitants themselves in the town, which possesses besides a *minár* similar to the one at Damghán, standing in front of the ancient mosque. The town itself is surrounded on the west by a belt of gardens quite two miles wide, and these past, the stony desert again commences, and continues up to the remarkable village of Lásh-gird, twenty-two miles distant, of which the fort and houses are built in tiers, like a gigantic pigeon-roost. The ancient name of this hamlet was Boklu-Kala'h, or 'the filthy fort,' and it fully deserves that title still. A more evil-smelling, uncleanly spot it would be difficult to find, and it was so infested with mosquitoes, that we found it quite impossible to sleep in our tents: had we ventured into the village we should have encountered still worse enemies of the insect tribe. The old village consists of two ranges of houses, built one above the other, in an irregular circular shape, to construct balconies to which poles have been driven into the walls, and a species of basket-work has been superposed for flooring. This primitive projection is without protection of any kind, and it may be imagined how many children are killed by rolling over it on to the ground beneath, either in play or sleep. The inhabitants, however, are quite accustomed to such accidents, and spend the greater part of their day on these balconies, which, filthily dirty themselves, look down upon a village yet dirtier, the receptacle of all the refuse thrown from the houses above. The new village surrounds the old, and is embedded in gardens and cultivation. The place is 'Wakf,' or sacred to the shrine of the Imám Riza at Mashhad, to which it pays an annual tribute of 400 tománs. The old fort is said to have been built 1600 years ago. Lásh-gird suffered much during the famine, losing a third of its population. It is famed all over Persia for melons and pomegranates. For ourselves, only too glad to get clear of its untempting vicinity, we started at half-past one the morning after arrival, in a storm of violent wind and clouds of dust, the Náib of the place being courteous enough to see us off notwithstanding the hour, and to accompany us on our way for some distance. This proved to be one of the most trying marches of our journey: the road skirts the desert of Kúhrasán to the south, and being utterly without water, is so hot and fatiguing, that few Persians ever attempt to traverse it except at night. Twelve miles from our starting-point we passed the large deserted village and post station of Abdúlabád, standing in the midst of the wild waste, a melancholy picture of ruin and decay, want of water having driven away all its inhabitants more than thirty years back. Further on, the road ascends gradually to Deh Namak, or 'the salt village,' through a plain covered with camelthorn and scanty pasturage, which increased as we neared the station. This stands in the midst of a wind-swept clay plain, and is a collection of miserable mud huts with a post-house and caravanserai. We reached it in the very teeth of a gale of wind, steadily gaining strength till it became a perfect hurricane. On arrival the caravanserai was found to be so full of dirty pilgrims, that we ordered our tents to be pitched on the open plain, where with great difficulty three were raised by 8 A.M. As the day advanced, however, the ripening gale whirled against us such clouds of dust and small stones that the canvas housing, fairly succumbing to the influence, was beaten down and finally torn to ribbons. At 2 P.M. our party, after an endurance rather stoical than heroic, wearied out with the struggle and discomfort, was driven to take refuge within the walls of the dirty and already overcrowded caravanserai. But the ills of this, perhaps the most unpleasant day we had passed since leaving Bandar-Abbas, did not end here. The wind continued to beat with a fury that searched out every crack and cranny in the walls of our new refuge, causing eddies of dust to sweep through the rooms: our ears and noses were assailed with sounds and smells that defy description; and we were devoured by fleas, mosquitoes, and sandflies. Our practical consolation was in the abundant supply of ice we could obtain in the village. With feelings of intense relief we left the next morning at 1.30 A.M.; attended, however, by the same tremendous gale, which continued for hours. Passing the half-ruined villages of Pá-deh and Ala Kharába, we reached the large walled hamlet of Aradán at the thirteenth mile from Deh Namak; and from this point the desert gave place to cultivated lands, rich pasturage, and numerous villages, the country being abundantly watered both by *kanáts* and streams of water flowing from the hills to the north. Eighteen villages lay in the plain between Pá-deh and Kishlák, ten miles further, our next halting-place, all apparently enjoying a plentiful supply of water. Warned by the unpleasant experiences of the previous day we did not attempt to pitch tents at Kishlák, but took up our quarters in a well-built Mihmán-Khanah, or caravanserai, which had two excellent upper rooms capable of holding us all seven, servants and horses occupying the rooms below. At night the plague of sandflies recommenced, and made sleep an impossibility: these are even more tormenting than the mosquitoes. This village is called *khálsa*, or the 'special property of the Shah,' and supplies the royal stables with grain and fodder. It is well watered by springs, coming down from the Firuz-Kúh, which the natives call 'the water of the Jájrúd river.'

For the last few nights we had heard large flocks of geese passing overhead, though it was too dark to distinguish them. They were probably taking their flight from Sistán for Russia and the cooler regions of the north; their departure having been delayed much later than usual, owing to the exceptional severity of the winter. To the same cause might be traced also the well-stocked condition of all the ice-pits to be found in every village on our route through this district.

Between Kishlák and Aiwáni Káif, the next stage, twenty-two miles distant, is a defile known as the Tang-i-Sardári, passing through some low hills at about eight miles distance from Kishlák, for which it is usual to take an escort of matchlock-men as a protection against Túrkmans and robbers. We however dispensed with this precaution, and neither here nor at any other time saw anything of these *bêtes noires* of Persian travellers. Two ruined caravanserais guard the entrance and outlet of the pass, but are in too dilapidated a state to be of any use. The country on which we emerged after clearing the defile was an extensive plain, well watered, partially cultivated, and surrounded by hills. In its midst stood the large and prosperous village of Aiwáni Káif, or, literally translated, the 'abode of pleasure.' It also is *khálsa*, like Kishlák, and furnishes annually a certain proportion of the grain and chaff used in the royal stables. It is celebrated for its figs and pomegranates, and a particular species of pottery made from very fine clay. Our camp was pitched beyond the village on some high ground, where, again, the wind blew with such violence that, as in many parts of Persia, tent life was the reverse of pleasant; and when the gale abated towards sunset, the sandflies and mosquitoes recommenced their attacks, and made the night long and weary. From this spot we first saw the snowy peak of the Kuh-i-Shamrán, with the still loftier summit of the Damávand, towering above a low range of hills to the right. We were surprised to find the fruit and grain crops here far behind those of Samnán. Neither had yet ripened, and on this account provisions were still at famine prices; and the villagers complained much of the losses they had sustained in their fruit crops from the high wind. At Aiwáni Káif we halted for a day, and sent in a *ghulám*, who had brought us letters to Lásh-gird, to Tehrán, to enquire respecting the fate of a courier by whom Sir F. Goldsmid had sent important despatches from Shahrúd: we had as yet heard nothing of him and were beginning to fear the man had been tempted from his fidelity. The morning however after the *ghulám's* departure, a courier arrived from Tehrán with the news that the messenger from Shahrúd had lingered sixteen days on the road and had only just delivered his letters. We further learnt that the famine was still very severe in the capital, though a magnificent harvest was ready for reaping. On the morning of the 3rd of June, Sir Frederic Goldsmid rode straight into Tehrán, relays of horses having been sent out for him from the city, on the day before, to Náugumbaz, the regular post-stage. The remainder of the Mission followed more slowly by an excellent road over the fertile plain of Verámin, at this time literally covered with flourishing villages and fields of waving corn. It owes its fertility to the numerous rills of water which flow through its length and breadth, coming down with great force from the Jájrúd river. It belongs chiefly to the nobles of Persia, and is considered the most valuable landed property in the country. We halted for our last night at the splendid caravanserai of Khátúnábád, about thirty-two miles from Tehrán, and at 1 A.M. on the 5th June started for the capital, much tormented by our old enemies the sandflies and mosquitoes. Our servants all turned out in their best attire; but the news we had received of the mortality, sickness, and famine still reigning in the city made our return a much less joyous affair to us all than it would have been in happier times. Pursuing our way in the dark we skirted a range of hills, and traversing a highly cultivated plain reached the village of Shah Abdul-Azim at 5 A.M., where we made a short halt. A few hours later we were met by a courier from Sir Frederic Goldsmid, with the intelligence that an *istikbál* would be sent out to meet the Afghán Commissioner, and every arrangement made for his courteous reception at the capital. The road from the village of Shah Abdul-Azim to Tehrán is too well-known to need description here. We reached the gates of the city at 7 A.M., and traversed the whole length of its *bazárs*. Even at this early hour, when but a fourth of the shops were opened, we were struck with the deserted aspect of the streets and listless appearance of the passers-by, presenting such a contrast to the busy scene usual in the *bazárs* of an Eastern capital when it has just thoroughly awaked into daily life. We passed numbers of dead bodies and many living skeletons, all telling of the misery still existent, and found also that a very bad kind of typhus fever was prevalent, owing to the system of intramural interment by which thousands of bodies had been buried during the winter under a few inches of earth: it was feared that, as the summer advanced, the air would by this means become so poisoned that fever and contagious diseases would be rife in Tehrán.

Clearing the city we reached the summer quarters of the British Legation at the village of Gulahak, 7 miles from Tehrán, at 9.30 A.M.[1]

---

[1] At the time of our arrival the Shah was absent on a shooting excursion in the hills, but was expected back very shortly; and it was evident that but little would be done in

THE MISSION ENDED.

The members of the Mission were not sorry to reach the end of their wanderings, and were all very thankful that so long and trying a journey, with constant vicissitudes of climate, had been free from disease, accident, or any casualty. With the exception of the somewhat severe illness of Mr. Thomas, the camp had throughout our long journey enjoyed singular immunity from sickness[1], a privilege which had extended to the horses and beasts of burden in the camp. The former reached Tehrán in excellent condition, and with but few exceptions were sold for more than their original price.

Sir Frederic Goldsmid, Majors Euan Smith and Lovett, together with General Pollock and the Afghán Commissioner, remained at Gulahak for more than two months endeavouring to come to a settlement of the points at issue[2]. During this time a great mass of irrelevant documentary evidence was produced by the Persian Foreign Office in support of their claim to the whole of Sistán, further pressed upon General Goldsmid by Mirza Melkam Khán, who now fills the office of Persian Ambassador in London. This very capable and accomplished official had been at once appointed to supersede Mirza Ma'súm Khán on our arrival in Tehrán; and from that period our friend the Persian Commissioner may be said to have completely disappeared from our ken. He took no subsequent part in the proceedings, and the last we heard of him was in the announcement that he had been suspended from all official employment for one year in consequence of his conduct in Sistán. It is probable,

---

the matter of the Sistán Arbitration until His Majesty had returned: though on his arrival after a fortnight, Sir F. Goldsmid and the members of the Mission were received by His Majesty at once.

[1] It is with the greatest regret that we have to record here that Quartermaster-Sergeant Bower, of the Royal Engineers, who had been for many years resident in Persia, and who had accompanied this Mission to Balúchistán and Sistán, fell a victim to typhoid fever very shortly after his return to Persia from the special duty on which he had been detached to England by Sir Frederic Goldsmid. Quartermaster-Sergeant Bower had been several times recommended for his commission, which doubtless would have been soon bestowed on him, and his immediate superiors had on repeated occasions testified their appreciation of his many excellent qualities. It would be therefore out of place here to enlarge on this subject; but we would nevertheless here express our deep regret for the loss of a most active, willing, cheerful, and thoroughly competent and trustworthy friend and travelling companion.

[2] Dr. Bellew and Mr. Rosario left for India viâ Baghdad almost immediately after arrival at Tehrán, and Mr. Thomas returned to England under medical advice a few weeks later.

however, that the spoils which he had brought away from that province more than compensated him for any loss sustained by temporary degradation.

The Afghán Commissioner also submitted his case in writing: indeed he had, in this respect, been earlier than his colleague in the field; and Sir Frederic Goldsmid finally delivered his Arbitral decision on the 19th August, 1872. This decision was at once rejected by the Commissioners of both the Persian and Afghán Governments, who gave notice of appeal to the Secretary of State for Foreign Affairs in London, in accordance with the terms under which the Mission of Arbitration had been initiated. The Afghán Commissioner left almost immediately for Kábul, whither he was directed to proceed by Isfahán,

Itinerary of Stages from Mash-had to Tehrán:—

Date, 1872.	Stage.	Distance in Miles.	Direction.
May 3	Já-i-Gharak	20	{10 W.N.W. {10 W.S.W.
,, 4	Dehrud	24	S.W.
,, 5	Nishapúr	23	W.
,, 7	Zamánabad	16	W.S.W.
,, 8	Shúráb	9	W.
,, 9	Zafaruni	17	W.
,, 11	Sabzawár	25	W.
,, 13	Mehr	32	W.N.W.
,, 14	Mazinán	20	W.
,, 15	Abbásabád	23	W.N.W.
,, 16	Mián-Dasht	20	W.
,, 17	Miámái	24	W.S.W.
,, 18	Shahrúd	41	W.
,, 24	Deh-Mulla	16	S.W.
,, 25	Damghán	27	W.S.W.
,, 26	Gúchah	23	S.W. by W.
,, 27	Ahúwán	24	S.W.
,, 28	Semnán	23	S.W.
,, 30	Lásh-gird	22	S.W.
,, 31	Deh Namak	25	S.W.
June 1	Kishlák	23	W. by S.
,, 2	Aiwán-i-Káif	22	8 N.W. {6 N.W. by N. {8 W.N.W. by N.
,, 4	Khátúnabad	27	W.N.W.
,, 5	Tehrán	32	N.W.

Total distance, 558 miles.

Bushahr, Bombay, and India. Major Lovett remained in the Persian capital to await orders from the Indian Government as to his movements; and on the 25th August, Sir Frederic Goldsmid, accompanied by General Pollock and Major Euan Smith, taking final leave of Tehrán, proceeded, by Resht, the Caspian and Astrakhán, to the railway terminus at Tsaritsin on the right bank of the Volga. Hence, with the exception of a few hours' incidental respite, and a brief rest at Berlin, they travelled incessantly without stopping day or night to Charing Cross, by Smolensk, Orel, Eydt Kuhnen, Königsberg, Cologne, and Brussels. London was reached on September 13, 1872, or in less than a fortnight from embarkation at Enzali, the port of Resht; the shortest time, it is believed, on record for such a journey.

No cause for reversal of proceedings in the Sistán Arbitration was shown on Appeal. In the summer of 1873, the Shah's visit to England enabled Her Majesty's Government to obtain the Imperial assent to Sir Frederic Goldsmid's award, though not without difficulty; and the Amir of Afghánistán had also signified unwillingly, as it is believed, his acceptance. The boundary between the two countries is therefore now that which is delineated in the accompanying map.

C. B. EUAN SMITH.

"MIHRÁB," OR SPECIAL PLACE OF PRAYER, WITH WALL "TÁKCHAHS" (NICHES); ON ONE SIDE OF AN OLD OBLONG ROOM AT KOLMÁRUT NORTH OF SISTÁN.—(*See page* 315.)

APPENDICES.

APPENDIX A.

The Sistán Arbitration.

Summary of evidence formally produced on either side; of conclusions drawn from personal observation or enquiry on the spot of litigation; and of oral or other information gathered by the Arbitrator in the general exercise of his functions. Dated Tehrán, 17th August, 1872.

Discussion on this question having been formally opened at Tehrán, the following statement of proceedings is placed on record. I summarise the original papers received.

Persian original statement.

Persia sets forward her claim to Sistán under 15 heads:

Of these, the 1st is an assertion of principle, as the last is of general right, the 2nd, 3rd, 5th, 6th, 10th, 12th are inferences drawn from diplomatic treaties and writings; the 11th and 4th are arguments on the general character and condition of the country under dispute and its inhabitants; the 7th, 8th, and 9th point to the Arbitrator's own opinions on the question at issue, the 13th recites an individual instance of procedure tantamount to written admission of sovereignty; the 14th is a positive assertion that, while Persia has of old been the recognised sovereign power in Sistán, the name of an Afghán Governor there is unknown to history.

Afghán original statement.

Afghánistán, on the other hand, commencing from a distinct period, claims Sistán as an integral portion of the monarchy founded by Ahmad Shah. Names of particular Governors of the day, as well as specific acts of allegiance, are adduced in illustration.

APPENDIX A.

The Commissioner carries on the history to the present day, with the view of showing that, up to recent years, the chiefs of the country have acknowledged the same ruling power by supplying troops when required on particular occasions, sometimes even against Persia herself. He adds that, in the collection of grain as revenue to Afghánistán, his own agent had been employed; while in the recovery of stolen property from the people of Sistán he himself had been the medium of communication with the Persian Government. He sums up his case under 11 heads.

Of these, the 1st is a general assertion of accuracy; the 3rd, 4th, 5th, 7th, 10th, and 11th indicate particular witnesses in support of his allegations; the 6th, 8th, and 9th are inferences in favour of his claims deducible from facts, and the 2nd quotes a particular document, which can be produced in evidence.

Although consideration of these statements in detail is essential to the due formation of an arbitral opinion on the issue to which they relate, few of the component parts have sufficient importance for separate discussion.

The 13th and 14th on the Persian, and the 2nd on the Afghán side, are recorded last for readier reference, as their practical character has seemed provocative of oral enquiry. Their purport has, moreover, been put before a special meeting of Commissioners, when an original letter of Sardár Kohandil Khán was produced in support of the written statement, and the question of particular Afghán Governors of Sistán freely argued. The agreement of Muhammad Rizá Khán (anno Hijrah 1260), quoted by the Afghán Commissioner, was also exhibited.

But the cases themselves were exchanged, and a copy of the original Persian statement was furnished to the Afghán Commissioner, and *vice versâ*. I analyse the replies which have been received in both instances.

Persian reply, or second statement.

Persia has four grounds on which to base the Sistán claim—

  1st.—Because the country is an integral part of Persia, and no revolutions or changes can make it otherwise.

  2nd.—Because temporary dispossession does not invalidate a natural and universally-acknowledged right: otherwise she would herself urge claims to countries of which she had for a time held possession.

3rd.—Because she has taken possession of the country in pursuance of her rightful claim.

4th.—Because the *British* Government letter of the 5th November 1863 authorised her to resort to arms, and she is now in possession of Sistán under that authorisation.

Afghán reply, or second statement.

Afghánistán makes a more direct answer to her opponent, taking certain of the heads just as they occur in the Persian original, and others more generally, thus:

To the first or general assertions of Persian sovereignty in Sistán, an appeal is made to history in favour of an opposite view, and a Persian historian is cited to prove Afghán possession in the reign of Fath Ali Shah.

To the assertions under the second head, that during the war between Persia and Afghánistán there were Sistánís in the Persian ranks, it is replied that, if such were the case, they must have been following Afghán leaders hostile to their own Government.

To the argument that Mr. Ellis's disapproval of the Wazír Yar Muhammad's invasion of Sistán recognised the rights of Persia to that province, it is contended that the attack was not upon a Persian Governor, but by Herat on Kandahár. Divisions among the Afgháns are admitted, and intrigues on the part of Governors, such as Ali Khán Sarbandi; but they are not held to affect the question of sovereign rights to the country. And as to the difference of language and habits, it is urged that the same exists with many subjects of Afghánistán besides the Sistánís, such as Badakhshánís, Uzbegs, Turkistánís, Hazárahs, Siáhposh Káfirs, and others.

Documentary evidence.

In addition to the writings heretofore alluded to, produced at a meeting of Commissioners, copies of *sanads* (deeds) and other documents, compared with the originals in Her Britannic Majesty's Legation, have been forwarded by the Persian Government. Those bearing upon the tenure in Sistán of the Káiyání Maliks, governing under the Safavi Kings, are interesting and valuable records ante-dating for periods from some 150 to 300 years ago.

A second letter from Kohandil Khán, though without date or address, indicates the time of writing by a detailed account of the recovery of Kandahár from the Saduzáis.

There are also fifteen more sealed papers received on a later occasion, professedly in original. These are from Sardárs Kohandil, Mehrdil, and Rahmdil Khán of Kandahár, and from the Wazír Yar Muhammad and his son, Saiyid Muhammad of Herat; one is from Mír Afzal Khán; they bear no date, but the period may be traced in many of them from the particular occurrences to which they relate. The general sense of these papers is expressive of dependence on Persia.

Local enquiry.

The direct evidence gathered in Sistán was not such as had been contemplated. Neither the Amir of Káin nor the Persian Commissioner assisted the Arbitrator to carry out the professed objects of the Governments of England and Persia in the manner which he himself judged proper; and admission was denied to the British officers at Jahánábad, Nad Ali, Kuhak, and (with exception, under pressure, in favour of the Engineer Major) at Jalálabád.

At some places, such as Burj-i-Afghán and Bolah, supplies could not be purchased without an order, and free communication with the chiefs or inhabitants was, as a rule, restricted and difficult. The Arbitrator, nevertheless, using his best endeavours to meet the wishes of the two Governments, and referring the subject of these impediments to ordinary diplomatic discussion, has applied himself to his task with such means as have been at his disposal, and now proceeds to set forward the result of his enquiries.

It is not his fault if the action of the Persian officers concerned invoked at any time in his mind natural doubts and misgivings in the cause which they had to sustain.

Ancient right[1].

Having been instructed to pay special regard to the two heads of ancient right and of present possession, I shall consider the question in each of these respects separately. As regards the former, there will be no occasion to go into any minute investigation of sovereignty over the province before the days of Nadir Shah. But I will glance

[1] From this point the first person is resumed as more appropriate.

at the familiar local traditions as well as more popular histories treating of the subject, premising that such statements as are not susceptible of proof need not affect the gist of arbitration.

We are told that Jamshid married the daughter of the Prince of Sistán, and had a son named Ahut, whose son was Gurshasp, whose son was Nariman, whose son was Sám, the father of Zál, and grandfather of Rústam. Sám is called 'hereditary prince' of Sistán, and had been nominated Governor thereof, as also of Kábul and countries north of the Indus, by Manuchahr. Sistán claims to be the scene of battle between Kai Khusrú and Afrasiab; to have been invaded by Bahman; to have been recovered by the family of Rústam by Azarbazin.

We need not advert to the 'Maluk-i-Túáif,' or Princes of the Ashkári dynasty. The stories of these remote and uncertain periods rather point out old associations than supply missing links to history; and if such associations be conceded in a national sense, as I think they should be to Persia, they can only afford a vague and very general testimony in a practical question of present boundary.

During the 425 years of the Sásáni Kings, from Ardashir Bábakán to Yazdijird, I find that Sistán was included with Khúrasán and Karmán in one of the four great Governments of Náushirwan, and that Yazdijird fled there after the battle of Naháwand (A. H. 21). Subsequently to the days of the Pishdádi, Káiyáni and Sásáni monarchs, Sistán fell under the rule of the Khalifs, and Ya'kub bin Láis, passing his boyhood there, made it the seat of his power when conquering the greater part of Persia. Before his accession it had been seized by Salah-ibn Nasir, whose successor was Dirham bin Nasir. Amr bin Láis succeeded his brother Ya'kub, at one time acknowledging the authority of the Khalif, at another in arms against him (A. H. 264). Finally, he was conquered by Ismáíl Samáni, brother of Nasr, Governor of Máwaráu-n-nahár, a distinguished prince, who is said to have had his palace in Sistán. During the interval of 100 years, from this epoch to that of Muhammad of Ghazni, the Samánís held power over Khúrasán, Sistán, Balkh and other neighbouring countries, and among the names of governors of Sistán are recorded Badi'u-z-Zamán Mirza, son of Súltán Husain Mirza of Khúrasán, Súltán Ali, brother of Zulnun, and some princes of the family of Bin Láis, one of whom, Khalif, a protegé of Mansur Samáni, was deposed and imprisoned by Súltán Muhammad.

After the Ghaznavi dynasty, which in the time of Madad lost all its Persian possessions, Alp Arslan, Malik Shah, and the Saljukis became masters of Khúrasán, their first leader, Toghrul, having set up sovereign claims at Nishápur in the Hijrah year 429 (A. D. 1037).

Súltán Sanjar (A. H. 511–552) and others of the tribe were successively paramount in Persia, and may be considered as sovereign princes until the conquest of Jangiz Khán, to whose son, Tuli Khán, were assigned Persia, Khúrasán, and Kábul. It was, however, to his son (A. H. 651), Halaku, that history accords the consolidation of power in Persia. He was succeeded by Abaka (A. H. 663), and he by others of the same dynasty, of whom Abu Sáiyid is said to be the last who enjoyed any power. But there is special mention in history that Sistán was subdued by an invasion of Jaghatái Mughals in A. H. 700, at which time Gházan Khán held sovereign sway in Persia. This was somewhat prior to the accession of Abu Sáiyid (A. H. 716), within fifty years of whose decease Táimur Lang (A. H. 736–785) added Sistán and Mazandarán to his numerous conquests.

In the former province the terror of the name and devastations of the renowned Tartar Amir has supplied an unfailing topic of conversation among all classes of people up to the present day. By some he is said to have destroyed Zuranj, the capital, sending its Prince, Kutbu-d-dín, into captivity; but it is impossible at this distant period to determine whether the capture of Zaidán many years later by his son Shah Rukh, and dispersion of the inhabitants, is a different version of one and the same event, or a separate occurrence altogether.

On the death of Shah Rukh, Sistán must have shared in the troubles (853), in which were involved Mirza Ulagh Beg, Abu Sáiyid (873), and other of the descendants and successors of Taimur. But after a series of revolutions extending over sixty years, Shah Ismáil Safavi conquered Khúrasán (914) and adjacent countries, and founded a dynasty of powerful kings which held dominion for more than 260 years, or up to the Hijrah year 1135 (A. D. 1722). During this period it may be admitted that Sistán remained more or less a dependency of Persia; nor do I find any proof that the province was actually seized by the Afgháns when they had advanced from Kandahár through the Sistán desert, and Karmán to Isfahán, at the close of Shah Husain's reign. On the other hand, the conduct of its chief on this last noted occasion was certainly not that of a loyal vassal to Persia.

But we have reached the days of Nádir Shah, and from this date the history of the province may be investigated apart from fable and tradition, and more in detail.

The government of Sistán, at least under the Safavi dynasty of Persia, appears to have been vested in the Káiyáni Maliks, who claim descent from the royal house of Kái. Malik Muhammad Káiyáni was the reigning prince at the time of the Afghán invasion of Mir Muhammad; and by league with the invader, or other intrigue, he secured for himself not only his accustomed principality, but Mash-had also, and a great part of Khúrasán. There is good evidence to infer that when Prince Thamasp applied to him for armed assistance, he was sufficiently strong to afford it, but turned the successful result of his intervention to his own personal advantage[1]. Finally, it is related that he was slain by Nadir Kuli Khán, the general of Shah Thamasp, who, however, allowed his relative, Malik Husain Káiyáni, to succeed to the Sistán Government. History states that the province of Sistán was formally confirmed to Nadir Kuli Khán, afterwards Nadir Shah, by Shah Thamasp, together with Khúrasán, Mazandarán, and Karmán.—(A. H. 1143.) It is certain that on Nadir's subsequent accession to the throne and conquests, Sistán formed part of the conqueror's vast dominions.

But it is also stated that the Káiyánis for some time resisted the authority both of Nadir and his nephew, Ali, afterwards Adil Shah. The names of Fath Ali and Lutf Ali, and their prowess in these early contests, are not forgotten in their native land; and the retreat of the Káiyáni chiefs from the right bank of the Helmand to Kuh-i-Khwájah is a well-established local narrative. On the death of Nadir and Adil Shah, Sistán passed, together with other provinces, into the dominion of Ahmad Shah Abdali. This change occurred about 125 years ago, when Afghánistán became first a defined and consolidated kingdom[2]. It is from this epoch that the Afghán Commissioner takes his stand. He considers that Sistán is essentially part of the one kingdom of Afghánistán, created by Ahmad Shah, and that it has remained so till within a few years, when circumstances transpired, which are reserved for later consideration.

His arguments are much as follows:

Under Ahmad Shah, Sulaiman Káiyáni was governor of Sistán.

[1] Krusinski, vol. 2, page 182.   [2] A. H. 1162-1165 (A. D. 1751).

He gave his daughter in marriage to the King, furnished troops, and paid revenue [1].

Under Taimur Shah, Zamán Khán Populzái was the Governor. He rebelled, but his rebellion was put down [2].

Under Shah Mahmud, Bahram Káiyáni was Governor, and gave his daughter in marriage to Shah Kamran, the King's son. Shah Mahmud was attended by the Sistán chiefs when he proceeded to take Kandahár. Hajji Firuzu-d-din, another son of Taimur Shah, captured Farah by the aid of the Sistánis. Shah Kamran, putting down a revolution in Sistán, confirmed his authority by giving the daughter of Muhammad Rizá to the son of his Wazír Yár Muhammad [3].

The Bárakzáis have similar claims on their side; the Sistán Chief assisted Wazír Fath Khán at Káfir Kala'h; Kohandil Khán obtained an agreement in proof of allegiance from Muhammad Rizá, was aided by his troops and revenues, and at a later period Ali Khán Sarbandi was his own *protégé* and nominee. It was only on the death of Kohandil Khán, and owing to the weakness caused by internal dissension among the Bárakzái chiefs, that part of Sistán fell into the possession of another power.

Persia does not accept or deny the above statement. But, as already shown, she puts in a general claim to Sistán on the score of ancient rights; protests against former occupations of the country by Afghán chiefs as unwarrantable aggression, and points to possession as now obtained.

The Saduzáis are disavowed as a dynasty of kings: the Bárakzáis are considered as Persian subjects—in revolt, or submissive, as the case may be. In proof of the latter theory are produced letters from Kohandil Khán, addressed to Muhammad Shah as a liege lord: and as regards Ali Khán Sarbandi, Taj Muhammad, and brother chiefs, written evidence is given in of acknowledged allegiance to Persia.

I have paid great attention to these points, for upon their true appreciation the question of ancient right must be determined.

The reign of Ahmad Shah began in the English year 1747, or 125 years ago, and the death of Sardár Kohandil Khán occurred in 1855. If, then, up to seventeen years from the present period (1872), a continuous Afghán sovereignty of more than one hundred years be established, an important aid is obtained, because we very nearly reach

[1] A.H. 1160–1187. [2] A.H. 1187–1207. [3] A.H. 1216–1218.

the time when the Sistán question was specially brought into discussion by the representative of the British Government at Tehrán.

Now I find the circumstances to have been these during the specified limit of 108 years:

Sistán was certainly part of Afghánistán when Afghánistán was a consolidated kingdom. It was afterwards dependent on Herát or Kandahár, according to circumstances, or, it may be, independent of either if occasion offered.

I am unable to divide these periods with confidence according to dates, but the nearest approach to truth must be sought in local history. From the accession of Ahmad Shah to that of Mahmúd Shah there is an interval of fifty-four English years, and from the accession of Mahmúd Shah to the death of Kohandil Khán there is another of precisely the same duration.

I am of opinion that these two periods will meet the two phases of Sistán history here described. The termination of the first portends a struggle for possession of the province between two members of one and the same sovereign house. The second closes on the appearance of a third claimant, who would set aside not only the two litigants, but the household of which they are members. No good purpose would be served were I to examine the circumstances under which the Káiyánis were contented to give their allegiance to Ahmad Shah and his successors until the one kingdom of Afghánistán was broken up into separate chiefdoms. I have good independent historical evidence to show that, while events were in progress leading to the last-named result, Malik Bahram Káiyáni was ready to take an active part with Shah Mahmúd against his brother Zamán Shah; and Bahram's son Jalálu-d-din had no supporter so strong and earnest as Prince Kamran[1], son of Shah Mahmúd. Nor need I explain minutely how the Sarbandis, Shahrakis, and Balúchis established themselves in joint possession of the country and became sharers in its fortunes. Whatever the origin of the two first,—whether they were settlers in, or aboriginal inhabitants of, Sistán,—it is tolerably certain that they did, at one time in their history, migrate from Western Persia (Hamadán, Gulpáigan, or some say nearer Shiráz) to Sistán, and that in comparatively recent times Mír Khán, Sarbandi, and Hashim Khán, Shahraki, were distinguished among Sistánis, as

[1] A. H. 1207-1216.

Alam Khán, Nharúi, and Khán Jahán Khán, Sanjaráni, were the most noted of the Balúchis who settled in the province.

I have said that the second period which has been selected in illustration of the status of Sistán was one of shifting and uncertain dependence. In proof of this I may cite the published testimony of travellers and historians, as well as evidence more directly bearing on the present arbitration.

Allusion has already been made to the assistance given by the Sistánis to Shah Mahmúd or his son. Nearly forty years ago the latter overran the country and reinstated Jalálu-d-din, the Káiyáni Chief, whose cousin he had married.

Muhammad Riza Sarbandi had then succeeded his father, Mír Khán, and Ali Khán Sanjaráni had succeeded *his* father, Khán Jahan Khán, in authority over their respective tribes. The first, in concert with Hashim Khán and the Balúchis, had been mainly instrumental in expelling Jalálu-d-din; and, notwithstanding the favour shown to him by Kamran, the conspiracy was renewed on return to power of the rejected Káiyáni, and a second expulsion effected. On this occasion the investment of Herát by Persian troops (A. H. 1254) prevented further armed intervention from that quarter, and Muhammad Rizá, Hashim Khán and the Balúchis divided the possessions of the Káiyáni chiefs. Dost Muhammad Balúch became head of the Nharúis in Sistán on the death of his father Alam Khán.

In the spring of 1839 (A. H. 1255) Sardár Kohandil Khán passed through Sistán on his way to Persia. Returning there from Shahr Babak two or three years later, he was accompanied by some of the chiefs to Kandahár. On the death of Muhammad Rizá Khán, Shah Kamran supported the claims of Lútf Ali, son of the deceased; but the brother's succession found favour at Kandahár. Lútf Ali was deposed and blinded, and Ali Khán, his uncle, installed at Sekuha by Sardár Mehrdil Khán, acting under orders from his brother Kohandil Khán. The Wazir Yar Muhammad died before he could carry out a new invasion, and four years afterwards Sardár Kohandil Khán died also.

There is no evidence before me to prove acknowledgment of Persian sovereignty by the local chiefs of Sistán during the whole period sketched; certainly not for more than one hundred years. But there is evidence that certain Afghán chiefs, who nominally or really held the country, were driven or tempted by circumstances to seek aid from Persia, and make admissions of *quasi*-allegiance. The question is, in what light are such admissions to be regarded with reference to the present enquiry? I confess that I do not attach to them weight or importance even though in the form of sealed writings.

Whatever force such documents may have, they can only apply to particular short-lived conditions and circumstances; and I do not consider they can affect the validity of Afghán sovereignty over the province in respect of the period under review. The allegiance of Sistán was of a feudal nature which could not be transferred to suit the personal convenience of a temporary ruler. I have no hesitation in affirming that had I been honoured with a call to arbitrate in an appeal from Persia against Yar Muhammad Khán for supporting Lútf Ali, Sarbandi, or against Kohandil Khán for blinding Lútf Ali and installing Ali Khán, I must have decided that, whatever the merits of the case, no other country but Afghánistán had the right of exercising interference: and both occurrences are of comparatively recent date.

But the enquiry does not end here, far from it; at this epoch dates the commencement of a new state of things.

More than twenty years have elapsed since the occurrences last named, and it is seventeen years since the death of Sardár Kohandil Khán. At that time Ali Khán remained in undisturbed possession of Muhammad Rizá's share of Sistán, and his brother chiefs were Hashim Khán, Shahraki, Dost Muhammad, and Ibrahim Khán, Balúchis. The last had become sole representative of his family on the death of his brother Ali Khán, Sanjaráni.

It is not necessary to analyse motives or inducements; the fact is patent that before long the Sarbandi Chief had entered into negotiations with responsible Persian authorities closely affecting the interests of the country under his charge. Two and a half years after the death of his Barakzái patron, he came to Tehrán, was received with distinction, and returned in three or four months to his government, married to a princess of the Persian royal family. His acts would bear record of his intentions were there no written evidence to adduce; and there is no doubt that personally he had transferred his old allegiance, or sacrificed his precarious independence by constituting himself a vassal of Persia. His reception in Sistán was not, however, that of a chief acknowledged and approved by those whom he had come to govern; and five months had not passed after his departure from Tehrán, when the news of his assassination reached that capital.

The particulars are well known:—Sardár Ali Khán had been murdered in his own castle at Sekuha; and it was said that his wife, the princess, was present and had been wounded on the occasion. Taj Muhammad, son of the old chief Muhammad Rizá, and nephew of Ali Khán, had either himself done the deed, or was one of the assaulting party.

A special envoy was despatched from Tehrán to bring the widowed lady back, but no attempt to displace Taj Muhammad appears to have been made in any quarter; and he continued to exercise the control he had usurped. There is evidence to prove that he also professed allegiance and submission to the Persian Government, accepting pay and honours in return; that about seven years ago, Persian troops entered Sistán from Khúrasán with the avowed object of retaliating upon one Azád Khán, who had plundered the district of Káïn; that the late Governor of Karmán went there under special orders of his Government in 1866, when one or more regiments under the Muzaffaru-d-Daulah were brought in from the Neh side of the Hámún; that later still the Amír of Káïn occupied the province with a considerable force; in short that, for the last six or seven years, the more esteemed part of Sistán may be said to have been in military occupation by Persia[1]. Moreover, certain of the sons or other relatives of Sistán chiefs were sent to Tehrán; and on the occasion of the visit of His Majesty the Shah to Mash-had, Taj Muhammad himself, who had been specially summoned thither, was made a prisoner, and deported with his brother Kohandil to the capital.

The question of right remains to be applied to the events of which an outline has been here recorded.

Persia holding to the theory that original possession constitutes a continuous claim, and disavowing the authority of Afghánistán over Sistán, has of late years entered into direct correspondence with the local chiefs of that province, and actually pushed forward troops to garrison its forts and towns. She further quotes Lord Russell's letter of the 5th November, 1863, in support of her action.

Afghánistán, admitting that a brief period of trouble and revolution called off the attention of its chiefs from Sistán, and gave Persia the desired opportunity of active interference, adds that she has refrained from taking any steps at the close of that period to regain lost

---

[1] A. H. 1282.

territory, because the British Government proposed to effect an amical adjustment of the difficulty.

I have given it as my opinion that the Persian claim to Sistán on the score of ancient right is not such as to warrant revival after the lapse of a hundred years, during which it has virtually been in abeyance; and I do not think that the English ministerial letter quoted alters the position in this respect. It left the litigants to settle their quarrel together, but gave no right to Persia which she did not possess irrespectively. Therefore, in an arbitration on right, an unjust conquest cannot be considered just by virtue of this letter.

If Sistán were in no way subject to Afghánistán, when brought under the ægis of Persia and subsequently garrisoned by Persian troops, then has her independence been assailed; and I cannot say that the acts of Ali Khán and Taj Muhammad, Sarbandis, have satisfied me that their allegiance to Persia was the general desire of the inhabitants.

Possession.

I will now turn to the question of present possession.

It is not easy to define what, in the present day, is meant by the term 'Sistán.' The expression is very vague, for ancient limits have long since become obsolete, and modern signification practically comprehends the Peninsula of the Helmand and Hámún only.

I see no better way to illustrate the case than by supposing two territories,—one compact and concentrated, which I will call 'Sistán Proper;' the other, detached and irregular, which may be designated 'Outer Sistán.'

The first is bounded, on the north and west, by the Hámún, which divides it from the Lásh Juwain and Neh Bandán districts, respectively; on the south generally by the Hámún, but immediately by the Dasht-i-Sangbar and barren tracts south of Sekuha and Búrj-i-Alam Khán; and on the east by the main branch of the Helmand below the *band* at the mouth of the great canal.

The second is composed of the country on the right bank of the Helmand, and extends to a distance of about 120 English miles in length, or from the vicinity of the Charboli and Khuspas River north, to Rúdbár south. Its breadth is variable, but trifling compared to the length, the actual boundaries being assumed as the limit of river cultivation on the east. To this may be added the Sistán Desert, comprising Zirah and the 'Shilah.'

Sistán Proper is now, under certain reservations, to be hereafter noted, in possession of Persia, whose Governor is Mir Alam Khán of Káïn. Outer Sistán, on the other hand, irrespective of the Desert, Shilah and uninhabited tracts, is in possession of Balúch chiefs who profess to acknowledge Persian sovereignty, or disclaim allegiance to any sovereign power but Afghánistán.

A study of the territorial history of Sistán Proper leads to the conclusion that in the days of Shah Kamrán, Jalálu-d-din, son of Bahram, Káiyáni, held Jalálabád, Banjár, and other places to the north and west of this tract; Muhammad Rizá, Sarbandi, held Sekuha, Chilling, and other places west and south-west; Háshim Khán, Shahraki, held Dashtak, Pulgi, and other places in a central position and near the main canal; the Nharui Balúchis under Dost Muhammad Khán held Burj-i-Alam Khán and the south-eastern corner; and Ali Khán or Ibrahim Khán, Sanjaráni, whatever his claims on this side the Helmand by inheritance from his father Khán Jahán, was restricted to Chakhansúr and the opposite bank. Ali Khán had at one time to recover Chakhansúr from an Afghán nominee of Shah Kamran; but fighting and dispossession were not uncommon in Sistán, and the above distribution seems to illustrate with sufficient accuracy the condition of things at a particular epoch.

On the expulsion of Jalálu-d-din, Muhammad Rizá took Jalálabád and other places to the north. It is probable that his associates shared in the spoil, and that, before his demise, Ibrahim Khán had crossed to the left bank of the Helmand; but it is evident that, if, during his life-time, there was any *one* acknowledged Chief of Sistán at all, that one was Muhammad Rizá. Lutf Ali succeeded his father Muhammad Rizá, but was removed by his uncle Ali Khán; and he again was killed and succeeded by Táj Muhammad, a younger brother of Lutf Ali. The latter, before the arrival of the Governor of Karmán in Sistán, appears to have availed himself of Persian soldiers to oust Ibrahim Khán from Jahánabád and other places seized and held by him in Sistán Proper; and the subsequent arrival of strong reinforcements from Persia prevented the return of the Balúchis.

Mir Alam Khán, of Káïn, then possessed himself of the whole country of 'Sistán Proper.' Sharif Khán, brother of Dost Muhammad, whose succession to that Chief on his death in 1857 (A. H. 1273) was acknowledged to the prejudice of Darwish Khán, son of the deceased, is associated with him to some extent in administration, but in a subordinate capacity. Few traces of the old feudal or independent Sistán chiefdoms now remain. Of the Káiyánis, two grandsons of Malik Bahram have some kind of nominal status,—one at Jalálabád and one at Bahrámabád. Of the Sarbandis, the recognised head, Táj Muhammad, has been removed to Tehrán. The representative of the Shahrakis, Muhammad Ali Khán, resides in the same capital.

Briefly, being unable to justify the recent action of Persia in Sistán on the score of ancient right to that province, I am bound to state my opinion that as regards her possession of 'Sistán Proper,' the *fact* is established; although the action of the authorities before described has unquestionably caused me to entertain misgivings on the attitude or sentiments of the population in certain instances.

As regards 'Outer Sistán,' the professed allegiance of Kamál and Imám Khán, the Balúch chiefs, residing on the banks of the Helmand, does not to my mind constitute a case of absolute possession similar to that of 'Sistán Proper;' nor do I find that any arguments bearing upon these particular lands have been used by the Persian Government, except that my own request for the recovery of a stolen horse, made on the right bank of the Helmand to a Persian Yáwar, is cited in favour of Persia's claim. As it is unusual for an arbitrator to express his opinion on the merits of a dispute while actually in process of investigation, or to supply at such time evidence on either side, I am bound to explain that my reference was simply to the head of an escort accompanying me for ordinary protection, and had no bearing whatever on the matter of territorial possession. Had the Yáwar chosen to decline the responsibility as being in a foreign country, I might not perhaps have demurred. But the horse was never recovered at all, nor compensation given for the neglect of the Persian soldiers.

The garrison in Kaleh-i-Futh, I regret to consider as brought there in contravention of the terms of the arbitration; therefore the fact of its existence can have no value, nor can its discussion be appropriate in the present paper.

Chakhansúr is not in Persian possession, but held by Ibrahim Khán on the Afghán side.

(Signed) F. J. GOLDSMID, *Major-General,*
On Special Mission.

APPENDIX B.

The Sistán Arbitration.

*General Summary and Arbitral Opinion; dated Tehrán,
the 19th August 1872.*

Preamble.

The Arbitral opinion which I am required to deliver has been formed after perusal of the several histories of Sistán of more general note; after examination of much oral and written evidence; and after a stay of forty-one days within the localities under dispute. Naturally the more immediate argument with which I have to deal is contained in the statement authoritatively given in by the Persian Government (through the Foreign Office, or Mirza Melkam Khán), and Afghán Commissioners. These have been carefully considered together with the documentary evidence with which they are supported.

I now proceed to summarise my views on the whole Sistán question, and to carry out the instructions with which I have been honoured.

Summary.

I. Sistán was undoubtedly in ancient times part of Persia, and it appears to have been so especially under the Safavian Kings: but under Ahmad Shah it formed part of the Duráni Empire. Further it had not been recovered to Persia until at a very recent date; and *that* only partially, and under circumstances the nature of which materially affect the present enquiry.

II. Ancient associations, together with the religion, language, and perhaps habits of the people of Sistán Proper, render the annexation of that tract to Persia by no means a strange or unnatural measure. But Persia has no valid claim to possess it on abstract right, whether the country be taken from Afghánistán, or whether it be simply deprived of independence. The period referred to for former connection is too remote. A century of disconnection cannot fail to be a bar to validity.

III. The possession of the Afgháns for the second half-century may have been more nominal than real, and more spasmodic than sustained. It may have been asserted by raids and invasions, or mere temporary tenure: but it has nevertheless a certain number of facts in support; and these are most material in an enquiry of this nature. General principles and theories are always important, but they cannot produce facts: whereas facts have a more practical tendency—for they support and establish general principles and theories. Neither ancient associations nor national sympathy are strong enough to nullify the force of circumstances, and circumstances show that Persia has exercised no interference in the internal administration of Sistán from the days of Nadir Shah until a very recent date.

IV. Geographically, Sistán is clearly part of Afghánistán, and the intrusion of Káin into that province is prejudicial to the delineation of a good natural frontier.

It has been commonly considered part of Herát and Lásh Juwain; though its dependence on the Helmand for irrigation may cause it to be included by some in the general valley of that river. The Neh Bandan Hills manifestly separate Sistán from Persia. I cannot but believe such would have been found to be the *status* had an illustrative map accompanied the sixth article of the Paris treaty.

V. But while, in my opinion, Afghánistán has the advantage in claims on the score of an intermediate tenure, superseding that of Nadir Shah or the Safavian Kings, it cannot be denied that from year to year she has been relaxing her hold over Sistán; and this has been evinced in a marked manner since the death of the Wazír Yar Muhammad. It would be absurd to contend that the second half-century of Afghán connection with the province has been a period of continuous possession. That Sistán has now fallen into the hands of the Amir of Káin can only be attributed to the helplessness of its independence and the personal action of its ruler. It was for a time at least out of the hands of Afghánistán. I do not admit that the manner in which Sistán was occupied by Persian troops corresponds with an appeal to arms such as contemplated by Lord Russell's letter quoted—There was no fair fighting at all. Nor can it be admitted that allegiance was obtained by the single means of military movements or open procedure of any kind. On the other hand, I cannot see that the Afghāns took any measures to counteract the proceedings of Persia when treating with Ali Khán, Taj Muhammad, or other Sistán chiefs.

VI. As the Sistán of the present day is not the separate principality of the past, and it is essential to a due appreciation of claims, that the parts in possession of either side should be intelligibly defined, I revert to a territorial division which has appeared to me convenient and approximate. By this arrangement the rich tract of country, which, the Hámún on three of its sides and the Helmand on the fourth, cause to resemble an island, is designated 'Sistán Proper,' whereas the district of Chakhansúr and lands of the Helmand above the Bank, and Sistán desert, are known as 'Outer Sistán.'

The first may be considered in absolute possession of Persia, and has a comparatively large and mixed population.

The second is either without population or inhabited chiefly by Balúchis, some of whom acknowledge Persian, some Afghán sovereignty. The professions of Kamal Khán and Imam Khán do not to my mind prove a possession to Persia, similar to that of Sistán Proper. Chakhansúr on the right bank of the Helmand is under the Afghāns. But the fort of Nad Ali on the same bank has been lately taken by the Persians.

VII. I have to consider ancient right and present possession, and report briefly my opinion on both these heads: 1st. That Sistán was incorporated in the Persia of ancient days: but the Afghánistán of Ahmad Shah, which also comprised Sistán, had not then come into existence; and it is impossible to set aside the fact that this kingdom *did* exist, any more than that Ahmad Shah was an independent monarch. 2nd. That the possession of Sistán obtained in recent days by Persia cannot affect the question of right as regards Afghánistán. If admitted at all under the circumstances, it can only be so subject to certain restrictions, and with reference to the particular people brought under control.

Arbitral opinion.

Weighing therefore the merits of the case on either side as gathered from evidence of many kinds, and with especial regard to the great advantages of a clearly defined frontier, I submit an opinion that the tract which I have called 'Sistán Proper' should be hereafter included by a special boundary line within the limits of Persia, to be restored to independence under Persian protection, or governed by duly appointed governors. This opinion is accompanied by an expression of the sincere and earnest hope that the Persian rule will prove beneficial to a people whose nominal state has been from time immemorial one of terror, suspense, and suffering.

But I am thoroughly convinced that, by all rules of justice and equity, if Persia be allowed to hold possession of a country which has fallen to her control under such circumstances as these detailed, her possession should be circumscribed to the limits of her actual possession in Sistán Proper, as far as consistent with geographical and political requirements. She should not possess land on the right bank of the Helmand.

If in a question of ancient right and present possession, a military occupation of six or seven years and the previous action of a local chief be suffered to outweigh rights and associations extending more or less over a whole country, and Arbitration award the most coveted, populous, and richer part of the Sistán province, it is manifestly fair that some compensating benefit should accrue to the losing side.

It appears therefore beyond doubt indispensable that Nád Ali should be evacuated by Persian garrisons, and both banks of the Helmand above the Kohak Band be given up to Afghánistán. And this arrangement becomes doubly just and proper when the character of the inhabitants along the banks of the river is compared with that of the Sistánis of Sekuha, Deshtak, and Sistán Proper.

The main bed of the Helmand therefore below Kohak should be the eastern boundary of Persian Sistán, and the line of frontier from Kohak to the hills south of the Sistán desert should be so drawn as to include within the Afghán limits all cultivation on the banks of the river from the Band upwards.

The Malik Siáh Koh on the chain of hills separating the Sistán from the Karmán desert, appears a fitting point.

North of Sistán the southern limit of the Naizár should be the frontier towards Lásh Juwain. Persia should not cross the Hámún in that direction. A line drawn from the Naizár to the "Kuh Siáh" (black hill) near Bandan, would clearly define her possessions.

It is moreover to be well understood that no works are to be carried out on either side calculated to interfere with the requisite supply of water for irrigation on the banks of the Helmand.

F. J. GOLDSMID, *Major-General,*
On Special Mission.

Postscript.

A Map, showing the boundaries claimed as well as those of possession, has been prepared to lay before the final meeting. A smaller Map, illustrating the country awarded by Arbitral opinion, will be given with a copy of the said opinion to each Commissioner.

APPENDIX C.

GENEALOGICAL TREES, WITH NOTES, FOR THE SISTAN CHIEFS OF THE KAIYANI, SARBANDI, AND SHAHRAKI FAMILIES; AS ALSO THE NHARUI AND SANJARANI (TOKI) BALUCHIS OF SISTAN.

Compiled from various sources and information gathered on the spot by Major-General Sir F. J. Goldsmid, on Special Mission.

Memorandum.

The accompanying Trees and notes may be useful in illustrating the position and claims of the principal families or tribes of Sistán as represented by individuals at the present hour. The only notable names under recent Persian encroachment and occupation are those of

    Lutf Ali, No. XIII.   } Tree No. 2. Sarbandi Sistánis.
    Taj Muhammad, No. XVI.

The first of these is said to be still living at or near Sekuha, blind; the second is a prisoner at large in Tehrán:

Sharif Khán No. III. Tree No. 4. Balúchis, Nharúi, a Shia'h, and connected by marriage with the Persian Governor Mir Alam Khán, whose lieutenant he may be considered to be in the general administration of the province of Sistán:

    Ibrahim Khán, No. VII.
    Imám Khán, No. XI.   } Tree No. 5. Balúchis Sanjaráni.
    Kamál Khán, No. X.

The first of these acknowledges Afghán sovereignty in Chakhansúr, while the other two profess allegiance to the Shah in the Kamál Bandar and Rudbar districts of the Upper Helmand.

19th August, 1872.

APPENDIX C.

TREE No. I. KAIYÁNIS.

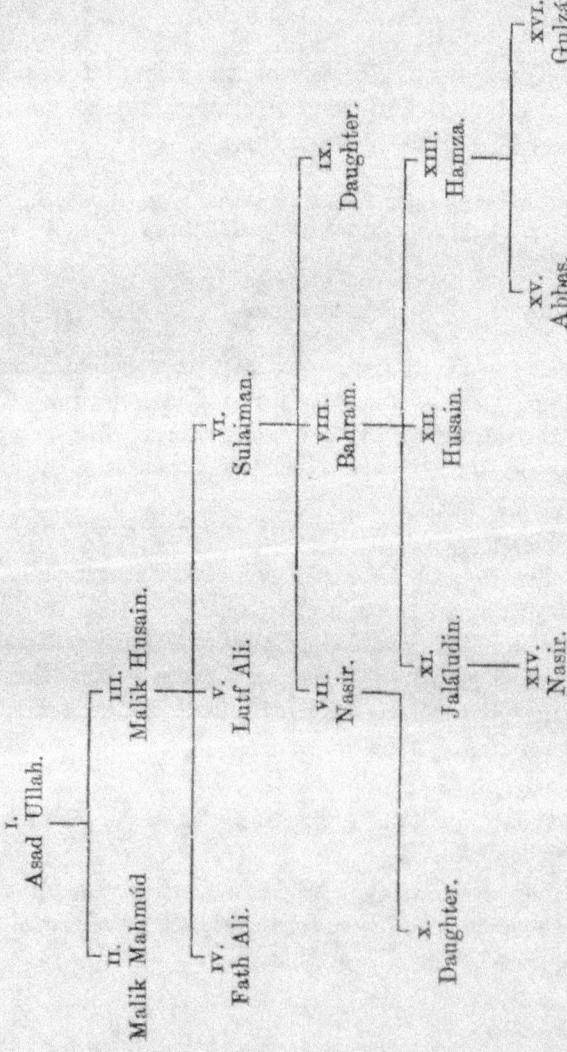

N.B. The Malik Mahmúd here mentioned flourished in the reign of Shah Husain (abdicated A.D. 1722); but a *sanad* produced at Tehrán shows that there was a Malik Mahmúd also in the time of Shah Abbas. It is dated 995 Hijrah (A.D. 1586), and is important in solving a doubtful point as to whether Abbas was actually raised to power before 1587. *Vide* Note in Malcolm's *History of Persia*, vol. i, p. 523. Other *sanads* of Shah Abbas show a Malik Jalálludin and his son Shuja u-d-din, the latter of whom is succeeded in the Sistán Government by Malik Fazl Ali (A.D. 1606-1608).

TREE No. I. KAIYANIS.

I. Asad Ullah, mentioned by Khanikoff as the father of Malik Husain, flourished probably about A.D. 1700. There appears to have been a Malik Ja'far about the same period, but his omission from the tree does not affect the general question.

II. Malik Mahmúd, called 'Shah of Mash-had,' whose name is still well known in Sistan and parts adjacent. According to Malcolm he made terms with the Afghans when they besieged Isfahan in 1722; and retired from the neighbourhood of that city with 10,000 men to take possession of Khurasán, awarded to him, in addition to his hereditary province of Sistan, by his new allies. Later on, Malcolm says he proclaimed himself king, and gained possession of almost all Khurasán, except Herat. Put to death by Nadir.

III. Malik Husain, called the younger brother of Malik Mahmúd by Mr. Wynne, quoting Conolly. He is also mentioned by Khanikoff as the son of Asad Ullah; and evidence locally obtained is to the same effect. As he is said to have been invested with the government of Sistan by, and to have rebelled against Nadir, he must have flourished between A.D. 1730 and 1747.

IV. V. VI. Mr. Wynne, quoting still, I apprehend, from Conolly, says: 'The Káiyáni brothers Fath Ali and Lutf Ali were succeeded in Sistan by their brother Sulaiman.' I have endeavoured to test the truth of the statement by local evidence and have obtained at least negative corroboration of the conclusions exhibited. Khanikoff, moreover, makes Sulaiman the son of Husain. Flourished certainly between 1740 and 1780.

VII. Malik Nasir, called the elder brother of Bahram by Khanikoff, and mentioned by Leech as the deceased uncle of Jaláludin.

VIII. Malik Bahram, mentioned by Elphinstone, Malcolm, Christie, Conolly, Leech, and Khanikoff. His position as chief in Sistan is corroborated, moreover, by all local evidence. The date of his decease is undetermined, but I take it to have been at an advanced age in about 1833.

IX. Daughter of Malik Sulaiman, married to Ahmed Shah Abdali, who reigned in Afghanistan from 1747 to 1773.

X. Daughter of Malik Nasir, married to Shah Kamran, who was killed in 1842.

XI. Jaláludin, eldest son of Malik Bahram, whose history is told by Leech and Taj Muhammad, and summarised by Mr. Wynne. Although the exact period of his rebellion is doubtful, as well as of his first expulsion, I gather from local enquiries that the first event took place shortly before his father's decease, and probably between 1832 and 1835, and the second in the latter year, or 'about four years before' Lieutenant Leech wrote his Report on Sistan. That he was reinstated in 1836 and 1837, and re-expelled in 1838, is tolerably well ascertained from a report of Major Todd to Government, dated 2nd October, 1839. He writes that Jaláludin was *then* a refugee in Herat, having been driven from his country 'twelve months before.' As in November, 1837, Mahmud Shah's army arrived before Herat, and the siege was not raised until September, 1838, so the last insurrection against Jaláludin was most probably at some time between these two dates, when the Herátis were engaged in resisting the Persian aggression. He is said to have died ten years ago, a powerless prince in Sistan.

XII. Husain, of whom no particulars are given, beyond the fact that he never obtained any high position.

XIII. Malik Hamza, mentioned by Leech, and local evidence of the present day.

XIV. Nasir, mentioned by Leech, but no particulars given by local evidence.

XV. Malik Abbas, as he is still called, is now nominal governor of Jalálabad; in reality an inferior kind of mayor, or burgomaster. Attended the 'istikbal' which met the Mission on arrival at Nasirabád this year.

XVI. Gulzár, Katkhuda, a local functionary like his brother Abbas, but in a less important place, Bahramabad.

F. J. G.

GENEALOGICAL TREES.

TREE No. II. SARBANDIS.

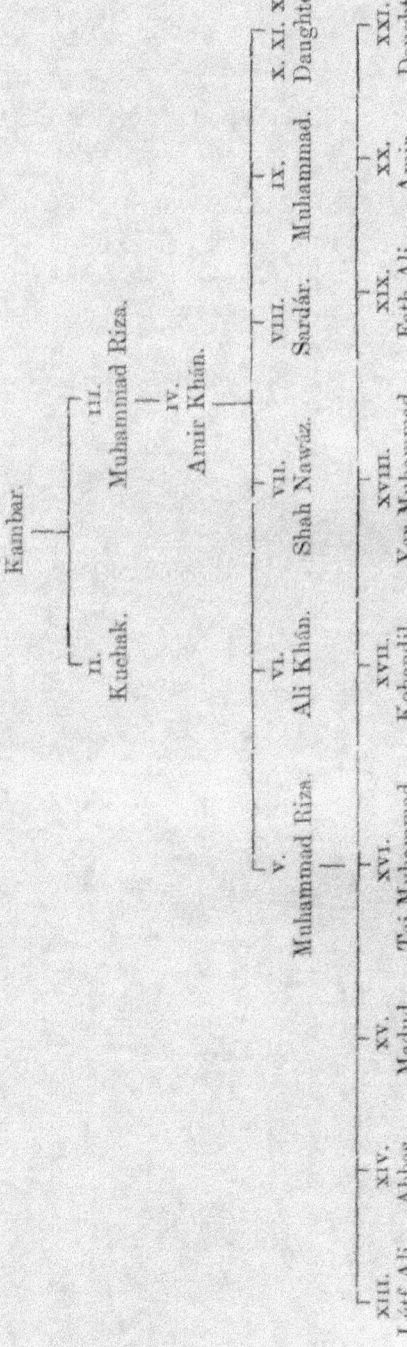

TREE No. II. SARBANDIS.

I. Kambar, or Mir Kambar, said to have been chief of Sekuha in the time of Nadir Shah, A.D. 1730-47.

II. Kúchak, or Mír Kúchak. On local evidence I am informed that Adil Shah, Nadir's nephew and successor, conferred upon him Karman in *jágir*—i.e. free from state levies. Shah Rúkh Afghan, then governor there, would not, however, surrender the place. They fought, and Kúchak was killed.

III. Muhammad Riza. Khanikoff makes him the *son* of Kúchak, and I should have accepted this arrangement as more consistent with the chronology of the Tree; but local evidence was opposed to the change. The above-named writer states that Mir Kambar, 'chief of the Sarbandis from Shiráz,' was sent to Sistan by Nadir Shah for purposes of cultivation, and settled at Sekuha as *Kalántar;* and that the title descended to his successors. Probably A.D. 1780-90.

IV. Amir Khan. Khanikoff calls him 'Mir Khan' and says that in Fath Ali Shah's time he became nearly independent, 'encroaching on the lands of the Káiyánis.' He is one of the persons mentioned in Mr. Wheeler's Memorandum of the 17th February, 1868, as the three independent chiefs of Sistan.

V. Muhammad Riza: eldest of five sons and his father's successor in power. Joined Háshim Khan Shahraki and Ali Khan Sanjaráni Baluch against Jaláludin Káiyáni, whom they succeeded in expelling. He was reinstated by Shah Kamrán, but again driven out of Sistan, Muhammad Riza becoming possessed of much of the Káiyáni territory. He was found by Ferrier in 1845, perhaps at the zenith of his power; but he is wrongly described by that author as a 'Sharegi' (page 415, Caravan journeys), and Baluch chief (page 417). Died, it is believed, in the same year as Muhammad Shah of Persia, or A.D. 1848.

VI. Ali Khan; having been passed over in the succession on the death of his brother Muhammad Riza, took up arms against him, and eventually obtained the assistance of Sardár Kohandil Khan of

Kandahar. Sardár Mihr Dil Khan, bringing an Afghan force to Sistan, seized and blinded Lutf Ali Khan, the son and successor of Muhammad Riza, and deposed him from the chiefdom in favour of his uncle, Ali Khan. The last-named looking to Persia for support, in his ill-gotten authority, was induced to proceed to Tehran and accept in marriage the hand of a royal princess. On his return to Sekuha with his bride he was assassinated.

VII. VIII. IX. Need no separate mention.

X. XI. XII. Daughters of Amir Khan: one married to Dost Muhammad Nharui Baluch; one to Hamza Khan Káiyáni.

XIII. Lutf Ali: now living in Sistan, blinded and deposed as stated under No. VI.

XIV. XV. Need no separate mention.

XVI. Táj Muhammad. If not the actual assassin, was present at and instigated the murder of his uncle, Ali Khan, whom he succeeded at Sekuha. Acknowledged allegiance to Persia; visited the Shah at Mash-had; is now at Tehran.

XVII. Kohandil Khan. Died at Tehran, whither he had proceeded on more than one occasion from Sistan. Date of casualty comparitively recent.

XVIII. XIX. XX. XXI. Need no separate mention, one daughter of Muhammad Riza given by Shah Kamran to the son of his Wazir, Yar Muhammad.

F. J. G.

422 APPENDIX C.

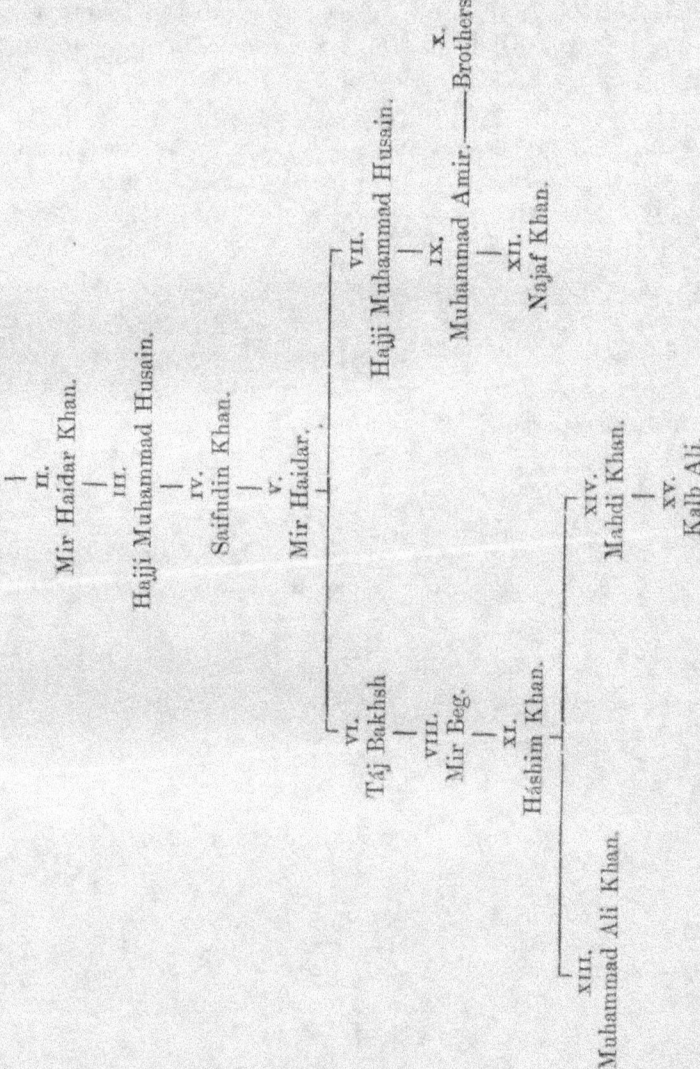

TREE No. III. SHAHRAKIS.

I. Mir Sáifudín Khan.
II. Mir Haidar Khan.
III. Hajji Muhammad Husain.
IV. Saifudín Khan.
V. Mir Haidar.
VI. Táj Bakhsh.
VII. Hajji Muhammad Husain.
VIII. Mir Beg.
IX. Muhammad Amir.——Brothers.
X.
XI. Hásbim Khan.
XII. Najaf Khan.
XIII. Muhammad Ali Khan.
XIV. Mahdí Khan.
XV. Kalb Ali.

TREE No. III. SHAHRAKIS.

An old Shahraki, Hajji Abdullah, guide to the Sistan Mission, states that he and his clansmen can in no way be considered Balúchis, or indeed anything but Sistánis, as they were residents in Sistan centuries ago together with the Káiyánis and Sarbandis. They were originally 'Nakháis.' After Taimur's death, his son Shah Rúkh came to Sistan, destroyed the *band* of Gurshasp across the Helmand at Malakhán, and captured the city of Záïdán, driving out and scattering its inhabitants. The Sistánis spread here and there, the Nakháis and others going towards Hamadan and Gulpäigan in Irak, and acquiring a grant of land there. Years afterwards the Nakháis returned to Sistan as 'Shahrakis' from their Persian settlement of Shahrwan; and some of their companions took the name of Sarbandi from their abode in the 'Sarband' of Silakhor.

VI. Háshim Khan. Perhaps the most noted in modern times of the Shahrakis. He joined with Muhammad Riza Sarbandi in effecting the expulsion of Jaláludin Káiyáni. But though he shared in the distribution of Káiyáni territory consequent on this revolution, it does not appear that the Shahraki chiefs had the same influence as, or divided the ruling power in Sistan with the Sarbandis.

XIII. Muhammad Ali Khan. In 1867 accompanied Táj Muhammad, Sarbandi, of Sekuha, to Mash-had, to meet the Shah of Persia. Thence they were sent, as *quasi* prisoners, to Tehran. Had been deputed before to Tehran, some three years after the death of Ali Khan Sarbandi.

Other numbers need here no separate mention.

F. J. G.

424   APPENDIX C.

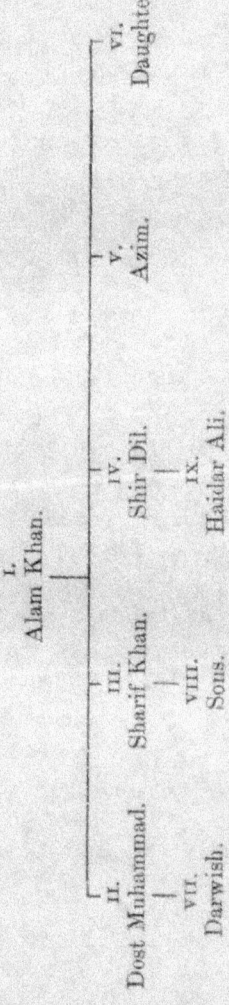

TREE No. IV.   BALUCHIS (NHARUI).

TREE No. IV. BALUCHIS (NHARUI).

I. Alam Khan. Said to be first cousin of Shah Mihrab, Khan of Bampur in Pottinger's time. Settled in Sistan, under the auspices of Malik Bahram Káiyáni, on the borders of the little Hámun in the lands called 'Sabz Kim.'

II. Dost Muhammad. A powerful chief, died 1857. Leech, writing probably in about 1838–39, mentions that he married the sister of Riza Khan, and gave his own sister to Ali Khan Baluch, adding 'He is under Kámrán.' His tomb is shown close to Kala'h-i-Náu, or, as sometimes called, 'Kala'h-i-Dost Muhammad Khan,' near Burj-i-Alam Khan, the capital town of the Nharui Baluchis in Sistan.

III. Sharif Khan. The principal Baluch chief in Sistan, whose devotion to Persian interests, whether assumed or real, has no doubt greatly tended to consolidate the power of the Amir of Káin. The son of the latter is, it is believed, married to Sharif Khan's daughter. Sharif Khan has many sons, of whom one has expressed openly allegiance to the Amir Shir Ali Khan of Afghanistan. Others are in Persian pay or service.

IV. Shir Dil Khan, of Kimak and Burj-i-Alam Khan. Has local influence, but is ostensibly in Persian interests.

V. Azim Khan, of Deh Sharif Khan.

VI. Needs no separate mention.

VII. Darwish, passed over in the succession to his father's chiefdom in favour of his uncle Sharif Khan.

VIII. One of them is in charge of Nád Ali, the recently acquired Persian fort on the right bank of the Helmand.

IX. Haidar Ali: a well-mannered youth educated in Tehran, but now at Burj-i-Alam Khan.

F. J. G.

TREE No. V. BALUCHIS TOKI (SANJARANI).

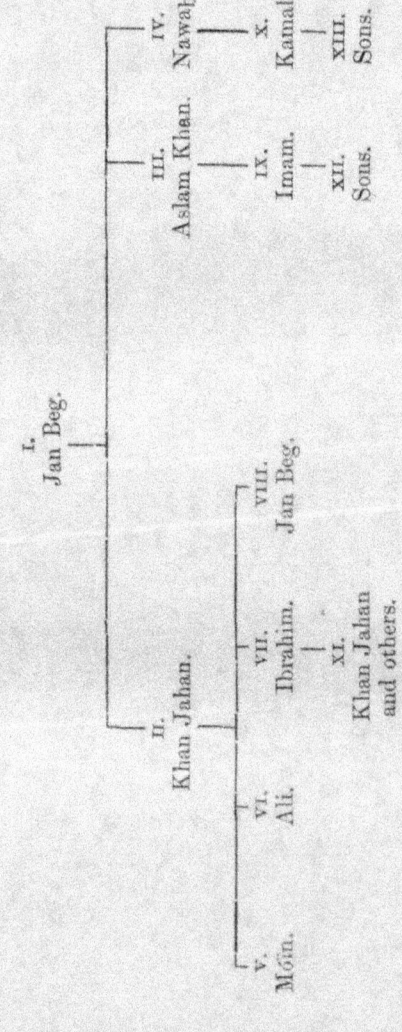

TREE No. V. BALUCHIS TOKI (SANJARANI).

The story is, that in the days of Malik Bahram Káiyáni, the Toki Baluchis, of whom the Sanjaránis may represent the ruling branch, under their chief Khan Jahán, had wandered some time on the left bank of the Helmand, when Jaláludin, son of Bahram, fell in love with the chief's daughter and married her. The consequence was the gift of a fortress, whence sprung the settlement of Jahánabad, and a considerable increase of the influence of Khán Jahán.

I. Ján Beg. The first of any note of whom mention is made in Sistan history, among these particular Baluchis.

II. Khán Jahán. Spoken of by Christie, Khanikoff, Leech, and other writers on Sistan. He seems to have held Chakhansúr in gift from the Wazír Fath Khán Barakzái.

III. IV. Need no separate mention.

V. Móin: murdered by his brother Ali Khan, after the death of their father Khán Jahán.

VI. Ali Khan. Succeeded to the chiefdom of the Sanjaránis in Sistan on the assassination of his elder brother. Is supposed to have died in 1840.

VII. Ibrahim; now chief of Chakhansúr. Shared power with his brother Ali Khan during his lifetime.

VIII. Besides Jan Beg there may have been two other brothers; but there is little worthy of record regarding them to be here noted.

IX. Imám Khan, now residing at Chahár Burjak on the right bank of the Helmand. Shares control over Rudbar, and other places bordering on the river, with his brother,

X. Kamál Khan. Both these chiefs profess themselves to be subjects of Persia.

XI. XII. XIII. Need no separate mention. One or more of the sons educated at Tehran.

F. J. G.

APPENDIX D.

1. *Itinerary from Tehrán to Karmán.*

Date.	Name of Stage.	Approximate Distance in Miles.	General Direction.
1870.			
October 20..	Kala'h-Nú or Náu	7	S.
,, 26..	Kináragird	20	S.
,, 27..	Hauz-i-Sultán	25	S. by W.
,, 28..	Púl-i-Dalák	22	S. by W.
,, 29..	Kúm	13	S. by W.
,, 31..	Langarúd	8	S.E.
November 1..	Sin-Sin	27	S.E.
,, 2..	Káshán	20	S.E by S.
,, 6..	Kohrúd	26	S. by S.W.
,, 7..	Sáu	21	S.E. by S.
,, 8..	Murchakár	24	S. by W.
,, 9..	Gaz	20	S. by E.
,, 10..	Isfahán	12	S. by W.
,, 26..	Gulnabad	12	E. by N.
,, 27..	Segzi	14	E.N.E.
,, 28..	Kupa	19	E.N.E.
,, 29..	Tudashk	14	E. by N.
December 1..	Bambiz	28	{ 9 E. by N. 7 E.S.E. 5 E.N.E. 7 E.by S.
,, 2..	Nángumbaz	12	E.S.E.
,, 3..	Akda	26	S.E.
,, 4..	Máibút	30	{ 13 E.S.E. 17 S.E. by S
,, 5..	Gird-Firamurz	30	{ 20 S.E. 10 E. by S.
,, 6..	Yazd	6	S.E.
,, 10..	Sar-i-Yazd	24	S.E. by S.
,, 12..	Záinu-d-din	18	S.E. by S.
,, 13..	Karmánshahán	16	S.E.
,, 14..	Shams	17	S.E. by S.
,, 15..	Anár	22	S.E.
,, 16..	Báiyáz	18	E. by S.
,, 17..	Kush-Kuh	18	S.E.
,, 18..	Bahrámabád	25	S.E.
,, 20..	Kabútar Khán	24	E.
,, 21..	Bághin	18	E. by S.
,, 23..	Karmán	19	E.N.E.

665 miles to Karmán.

2. Karmán to Gwádar.

Date.	Name of Stage.	Approximate Distance in Miles.	General Direction.
1871.			
January 5..	Máhún	22	S.E.
„ 6..	Hánakah	16	S.S.E.
„ 7..	Ráyín	24	{17 S. by E. / 7 S.W. by S.
„ 8..	Khánah Khátun	32	{15 E.S.E. / 2 N.N.E. / 15 S.E. by S.
„ 9..	Dárzín	25	S.E.
„ 10..	Bam	17	E.S.E.
„ 14..	Azízábád	28	E.S.E.
„ 15..	Búrj-i-Maház	12	E.S.E.
„ 16..	Rigán	19	{10 E.S.E. / 9 S.E.
„ 18..	Ab-i-garm	21	{11 S.S.E. / 10 S.E.
„ 19..	Cháh-i-Kambar	10	S.E. by S.
„ 21..	Dag-i-Farhád	15	{6 S.E. by E. / 4 E. by N. / 5 S.S.E.
„ 22..	Sar-i-Nárán	19	S.
„ 23..	Khúsrín	24	S.S.E.
„ 24..	Ladí	20	S.S.E.
„ 25..	Kalánzao	9	S.S.E.
„ 26..	Cháh-i-Shúr	23	E. by S.
„ 27..	Kúch Gardán	26	S.E.
„ 28..	Bampúr	16	E.
February 16..	Sar-i-Band	8	E.
„ 17..	Sar Kohrun	12	S.E. by E.
„ 18..	Ab-sowárán	17	S.E. by S.
„ 19..	Pa-Godár	20	E.
„ 20..	Koláni	17	S.S.E.
„ 21..	Sarbáz	19	S.
„ 23..	Dipkhaur	14	S.S.W.
„ 24..	Pá-rúd	12	S.E. by E.
„ 25..	Rask	14	S. by E.
„ 26..	Búganí	15	E.S.E.
„ 27..	Pishín	10	E. by S.
March 1..	Kastag	10	S.
„ 2..	Ghistán	10	S.S.E.
„ 3..	Kulmarisunt	23	S.E. by E.
„ 4..	Dardán	12	S.S.E.
„ 5..	Gúrrok	17	S.E.
„ 6..	Gwádar	20	S.E.

Karmán to Gwádar, 628 miles.

TOTAL.

Tehrán to Karmán	.. ..	665 miles.
Karmán to Gwádar	.. ..	628 „
Total	.. ..	1,293 „

430   APPENDIX D.

3. *From Bandar-Abbas to Nasírabád in Sistán:*—

See page 241 of Major Smith's Narrative to Bam ..   .. 248 miles.
 „   255   „   „   Túm-i-Mir Dost 246 „
 „   313   „   „   Nasírabád   .. 57[1] „

                                    Total 551

4. *From Nasírabád in Sistán to Chahár Búrjak, on the right bank of the Helmand, and back to Banjár:*—

Page 313, Major Smith's Narrative   ..   ..   .. 180½ miles.

5. *From Banjár in Sistán to Mash-had:*—

Page 356, Major Smith's Narrative   ..   ..   .. 582⅔ miles.

6. *From Mash-had to Tehrán:*—

Page 391, Major Smith's Narrative   ..   ..   .. 558 miles.

N.B.—The road from Mash-had to Tehrán is well known. My note-book makes it 544 miles. Ferrier reckons it at a less figure (or 141 *farsakhs*), unless he allows nearly four miles a *farsakh* for the long measurements of Khúrasán. It should be noted, with reference to Table No. 2, that Major St. John makes the distance between Bam and Bampúr less, by 12 miles, than Major Smith. A difference of actual route followed, between Bam and Rigán, would only in part account for the discrepancy. My own computation recorded in 1866 is in favour of the higher figures; but it was roughly effected, and Major St. John's measurements are doubtless more accurate.—F. J. G.

[1] Inclusive of four miles from Túm-i-Mir Dost to Cháh-i-Khak-i-Muhammad Darvish.

INDEX.

Abaka, 400.
Abárík, 86 (Awárik, post).
A'bás, 99.
Ab-band, 75.
Abbásabád, 376; inhabitants, ib.
Abbás Khán, 250.
— Malik Khán, 303.
Abbott, Keith, 12, 87, 92.
Abdúlabád, 180, 351, 385.
Abd-ul-Rahím tower, 133.
Abdúl Rasúl Khán, 316.
Ab Duzdán, 131.
Ab-i-garm, 82, 199.
Ab-i-Rahmat, 229.
Abivard, 8.
Ab-patán, 70.
Ab Sowárán, 131.
Abú-l-Kásim, 342.
Abu Sáiyid, 400.
Acacias, 125.
Adarbaiján, 2.
Aden, 226.
Adil Shah, 401.
'Adjutant Bashi,' 357.
Afghán Commissioner, see Sáiyid Nur Muhammad Shah.
— Mission, see Perso-Afghán.
Afghánistán, Amir of, 145, 149.
Afrasiáb, sons of, 352, 399.
Aghá Beg, 351.
— Ján Khán, 346.
— — Sarbandí, 297; camp at, ib.
— Muhammad Khán, 92.
— — of Bombay, 228, 243.
Ahmad Khán, 307, 316, 321, 322.
— Shah, 227, 309, 395, 402.
Ahnan, 382.
'Ahubareh,' 125.
Ahut, 399.
'Ahwál pársi,' 265, 358.
Aibí, 60, 66.
Aiwáni Kaif, 387.

A'kásh Báshí, 361.
Akbar Khán, 269.
Akda, 169; tank on road to, ib.; cultivation, ib.; the caravanserai, 170.
Akhúnd Zadah, 319.
Ala Kharába, 386.
Alam Khán, 404, 408.
Alexander, march of, 74, 245.
Albak, 376.
Ali's horse, hoof-prints of, 63.
Ali Agha, 182, 189.
— Khán, assassination of, 406.
— — Sarbandí, 397, 402.
Aliabád, 352.
Alison, Mr., 147, 149, 162, 165, 209; death of, 377.
Aliahabád, 168.
Almond, wild, 57, 104.
Aloe, 136, 140.
Alp Arslan, 399.
Ambála conference, 324.
Amir of Afghánistán, 145.
Amirabád, 382.
Ammo-Perdix Bonhami, 24.
Amr bin Lais, 399.
Amúlani, 140.
— Dumúk, 140.
Anár, 177.
Ankora, 123.
Appendices, 395.
Apricots, 383.
Arabs, 53; robbery and murder by chief, 98.
Aradán, 386.
'Arbábís,' 59; districts inhabited by, 59, 71; Pottinger's account of, 59.
Ardabil, 343.
Ardagán, 171.
Ardashir Bábakán, 399.
Arján, 104.
Armenian Archbishop, 160.
Arsinján, 50, 94.
Asadabád, 354.
Asadullah Mirza, 353.

Asafœtida, 57, 72, 329.
Asafú-d-Daulah, 343.
Ashkinak, 289 note.
Asiabád, 134.
Asparagus, wild, 104.
Aspich, 67.
Asses, wild, 107.
Astrabád, 373.
Astrakhán, 147.
Atak, 5, 17.
Átash-Gáh, 280.
Atash Kadah, 109.
Aurora, 151.
Awárik fort, 195; relics from, ib.
Azád Khán, 56, 62, 283, 291, 303, 406.
Azarbazin, 399.
Azizábád, 197, 244.

Bábism, head-quarters of, 108.
Bádbíní, breakfast at, 105.
Bádgirs, or wind-towers, 237.
Badí'u-z-Zamán Mirza, 399.
Báft, 104.
Baftán, 132; valley, 133, 219; old village, 219.
Bághin, 102, 104, 181.
Bágu, 228.
Baharlú, reiving part of, 109.
Bahdirán, 195.
Bahman, 399.
Bahram, 256.
— Káiyáni, 402.
Bahrámabád, 179; cotton cultivation, ib.; the Náíb, 180, 274, 409.
Báhú, 123, 126, 133.
— Kalát, 22, 27; temperature, 29.
Baiáz, 178.
Baila, 125.
Báji, 125.
Baker, Colonel Valentine, 8.
— Dr., 18.

INDEX.

Bákú, everlasting fires at, 147.
Balá Kalát, 60.
Balághar watch-tower, 345.
Balgetta, 137.
'Balúch,' 47; plateau, 11; camel drivers, 21; mode of driving, 124; origin of, 46; a wounded, 202.
— Khán, 55.
Balúchis, Rígí, 62; camp of, 82.
— (Nharui), genealogical tree of the, 424.
— Toki (Sanjaráni), genealogical tree of the, 426.
Balúchistán, orders to survey, 18; plateau, 25; fauna, 27; forts, 34; Pottinger's journey, 51; land tax, 67; Major Lovett's journey, 119–142; river systems, 119; mountain systems, 121.
Bam, 50; fort, 86, 195, 197; extent of town, 196; route to, 233 note, 236; plain, 240; halt at, 241; Kinneir's account of, 243; population and trade, 244.
Bam-Narmashír, 28.
Bambiz, 168; the Hajji, ib.
Bampúr, plain, 9, 199, 203; thermometer at, 76; fort and garrison, 76; 112, 130, 206; British flag at, 209; Náib of, 217.
Bampúsht, highlands, 23, 53, 62.
Bán, 141.
Bandar-Abbás, 6, 19, 120; exports, 227; temperature, ib.
Bandar-i-Kamál Khán, 286 and note.
Banjár, 303.
Bannu, 253.
Barak, 350.
Bárakzáis, the, 402.
Barbaris, camp of, at Chelling, 261.
Barúi, 53, 56.
Basmán, 50, 68.
'Bast,' or sanctuary, 363.
Báyazíd, grave of, 378.
Begistán, or Bájistán, 349; population, 350; tradition of an ancient kanát, ib.
Behdirun, 240; kalántar or mayor of, ib.

Bellew, Dr., 226, 308, 389 note.
Bert, 135.
Beshná, 107.
Bezoar-stone, 100; as a talisman, 101.
Bídarán, halt at, 86 (Behdirun).
Bína-i-kál, 297, 299.
Birds—
 Black-breasts, 140.
 Bustard, 'houbareh,' 37, 125, 179, 203, 326.
 Cháór, 273.
 Cuckoo, 340.
 Duck, wild, 125, 152, 261, 267.
 Eagle, 231.
 Geese, 297.
 Grouse, Sand, 125, 177, 203, 297.
 Kaftar-i-Sail, or Pigeon of the Rapids, 273.
 Koh, Swan, 273.
 Magpie, or Kilágh-i-ablak, 285.
 Máhi Marwárid, 273.
 Murgháhi Andak, Sabzgardan, or wild duck, 273.
 Nightingale, 361.
 Partridge, 203; black, 211, 244, 297.
 Pigeon, 297.
 Quail, 297.
 Saká, Water Carrier, or Camao, 273.
 Sístán, of, 273.
 Stork, 153.
 Taghalak, 273.
 Teal, 125, 261, 273, 297.
 Water-fowl, 152, 261.
Birjand, 334; population, 336; route from, to Turbat-i-Háidari, 338 note.
Blanford, Mr., 1, 13, 19, 33, 52, 94, 110.
Blue Múnshi, 150.
Bog, creation of, 14.
Bojd, 334.
Boklu-Kala'h, 384.
Bolah, 311.
Bolida valley, 135.
Bostajan, 380.
Bostán, 378.
Bower, Quartermaster-Sergeant, 77, 115; appointed to Perso-Balúch Mission, 150; 195, 214, 225, 240; leaves Mission for England with despatches, 380; his death, 389 note.
British Flag question, at

Bampúr, 209, 262, 265; settlement of, 307.
Bruce, Mr., 160.
Búdúr, 51.
Búg, 128.
Bugáni, 219.
Búhsé, Dr., 15.
Bújnúrd, 8.
Bukhára, prisoners of, 371.
Búrj, 198.
Búrj-i-Afghán, 303.
Búrj-i-Alam Khán, 276, 284, 304, 408.
Búrj-i-Falaksar, 258.
Búrj-i-Maház, 198.
Búrj-i-Muhammad Khán, 84.
Bushahr, 6, 18, 95.
Búz-míjí, 83.

Camel, lifting, 28; supply, 30; killed by change of climate, 31; thorn, 71, 134; drivers, 70, 122; owners, 212; obstinacy, 246; anecdote, 247.
Camels, trouble with, 103, 105; — hair cloth, 166.
Cameron, Sergeant, 318.
Campbell, Captain, 163.
Cannibalism, 361.
Caper, wild, 204.
Capra ægagrus, 100.
Caravan, our, 22.
Carp, 105, 109.
Carpet manufactories, 101, 187.
Carrefour, 355.
Carunas, tribe of, 90.
Caspian Survey, 111.
Castor-oil plant, 153.
Cats, 16, 84; Angora, 84.
Cave-dwelling, 105.
Central Persia, area of, 5.
Chádar-i-shahi, 350.
Chafta, 170.
Chahár Búrjak, or Já-i-Imám Khán, 288.
Cháhbár, attack on, 75.
Cháh-i-Bermeh, 331.
Cháh-i-Damdam, 329.
Cháh-i-Khák-i-Muhammad Darwish, 255.
Cháh-i-Shúr, 79, 204.
Cháh Kambar, 82, 200.
Cháh Sagak, 327, 330.
Chakhansúr, 271, 282, 298, 408.
Champ, plateau, 127; village, 129; inhabitants, ib.
Champain, Major, 95, 163.
Chang-i-Múrghán, 263 and note.

Chapáo, 72.
'Chapar,' or post, 366.
Chapar khánah, 382.
'Chashmah-i-Gez,' 376.
Chástún, 230.
Chelling, 260; canal at, 261; 275.
Chib, 135; fort, 139.
Chíl Khan, 138.
Chinár-tree, 103, 108, 162; at Ráyín, 194.
Chíragh Khán, 235.
Chirak, 125; probable population, 126.
Christie, Captain, 12, 50, 316, 417.
Chronometers, difficulties with, 26.
Clark, 15.
Colville, Dr., 146.
Conolly, Edward, 209; journal, 273; 316, 318, 320, 322, 417.
Copper, at Karmán, 100, 250.
Corn, &c., price of, in Sistán, 271 note.
Cotton, in the vicinity of Kúm, 153; cultivation at Bahrámábád, 179; yield of the Karmán district, 180, 327.
Crocuses, 202.
Cumming, Dr., 163, 171, 184, 185 note, 191, 196; patients at Bam, 198; 202.
Cypress-tree at Ruknabad, 171.

Daena, 13.
Dag-i-Farhád, 82, 201; legend of, 201.
Daharzin, 86 (see Dárzin).
Dak-i-Dehli, 284; tombs, 286.
'Dam-Damah,' 299.
Dam Dewáli, 286.
Dánghán, 15, 380; ruins, 381.
Daniabád, 179.
D'Anville, 74.
Darah-gaz, 8.
Darákhsh, 336.
Dardán, 222.
Dariá-i-Kabir, 81.
Darogha Ata Muhammad, 205.
Darvishes, 84.
Darwísh Khán, 409.
Dárzin, 195; fort, ib.; 240.
Dasht, 137; plain, 139.
Dashtiári, chief of, 123, 125; inhabitants, 126.

Dasht-i-Atashkhánah, 329.
Dasht-i-Biáz, or Shahr-i-Farsi, 345; mosque, 346.
Dasht-i-Khúshk, 238.
Dasht-i-Kuweer, or Daria-i-Kabir, 15.
Dasht-i-Rukh, plain of, 354.
Dasht-i-Sangbar plain, 257.
Date, trade, 55; groves, 63, 66, 72, 125, 169, 215; cultivation, 138; impregnation, 218; tax, 232.
Dáulatabad, 381.
Dáulatyár, 342.
De Blocqueville, M., 375.
Deer, 179; legend, 383.
Dehak, 67.
Dehgwar marsh, 63.
Deh Mulla, 380.
— Namak, 385.
Deh-i-Pain, 326.
Dehrúd, 368; effect of famine, 369.
Delta of Persian Arabistan, 8.
Dervish's well, 256; barometer at, ib.
Deshtak, 261, 274, 408.
Diláwar Khán, 33, 61, 68.
Dín Muhammad, 123, 125.
Dipkhor, 216; revenue, ib.
Dipkhúr, 132.
'Diránchu,' 245.
Dirham bin Nasir, 399.
Dís, 135.
Diz, 47.
Dizak, 50, 68, 120; valley, 139.
Do Kala'h, 326.
Donkey encampment, 232.
Dost Muhammad Khán, 263 note, 278, 280.
— Balúch, 404.
Dozaneh, 138.
Dradund, 141.
'Drík,' 87.
Dughabád, 352.
Dúm, 138.
Durand, Sir Henry, 205.
Dúrmáná plateau, 91.
Duruh, 331.
Dusári (Jabl-i-Báriz), 237.

Echis viper, experiment with, 80.
Elizabeth, Queen, 382.
Ellis, Mr., 397.
Elphinstone, 417.
Enzeli, 147.
Esai, 138.
'Evil eye,' the, superstition, 264 note, 332, 350.
Executions, 185 note.

Fahraj (ruins) 74, 84, 244; or Pahra, 245.
Faizabad, 351.
Falari, 22, 123.
Famine, 94; feeble attempts to check, 96; deaths through, 98; cannibalism during, 361.
Farámurz Khán, 326.
Fariáb, 231.
Farrant, Colonel, 342, 343.
Fars, 69; disturbed state of, 99.
Fasá, 109.
Fath Ali, 401.
— Shah, 152; college established at Kum by, 153; 154, 243, 384.
— Khán, 402.
'Felek' stick, 175.
Fern, Maiden-hair, 57, 65.
Ferrier, J. P., 262, 268, 275, 282, 287, 293, 370, 373, 381.
Figs, 387.
Fin (Káshán), longitude, 113.
Firamurz, 256.
Fir-trees, Scotch, 171.
Fírúzábád, 132, 218.
Fog, 90.
Forbes, Dr., 268; murder of, 317.
Fort, ancient ruined, 86.
Fox, grey, shot, 204.
Fraser, J. B., 112.

Gach, 374.
Gadrosia, 74.
Game, see Birds.
Garambigáh, 81.
Garmsíl, 48.
Garmsír, 109, 198.
Gávkhánah swamp, 10, 15.
Gaz, longitude, 113.
Gazella fuscifrons, male, 65.
Gazelle, 37.
Geh, 67, 80.
Géroft, 74 (see Jírúft).
Ghafúr Beg, 150.
Ghazan Khán, 400.
Ghazni, Muhammad of, 399.
Ghistan, 220.
Ghiuk, 338.
Ghorián, 112.
Ghufar-Khan, 132.
Ghuláms, 88, 103.
Gibbons, Sarjeant, 107.
Gichki, 138.
Gill, Lieutenant, R.E., 8.
Girán Reg, 202.
Giranrig, 81.

VOL. I.   F f

Gird-Firamurz, 172; silk culture, ib.
Girimanj, 345.
Gishtigán, 39, 41; fort of, 44, 46; 47.
Goat, wild, 100.
Gôd-i-Kúrkúrin valley, 280.
Goldsmid, Major-General Sir Frederic, 20, 28, 31, 62, 74, 83, 87, 92, 110, 123; as arbitrator of the Sistán frontier question, 145; interview with M. Stremaïukoff, 146; at Astrakhán, 147; at Tehrán, ib.; at Isfahán, 159; at Karmán, 183; visit to the Wakíl-ul-Múlk, ib.; reception of Hindús, 184; interview with Persian Commissioner, 185; at Bam fort, 197 note; 201, 205; reception of Ibrahim Khán, 206, 211 note; at Gwádar, 223 and note; ordered to Sistán, 225; at Calcutta, 226, 242, 265; at Kinak, 279; interview with Sardár Imám Khán, 289; visit to Sardár Ahmad Khán, 322; the Mashhad escort, 352; interview with Súltán Murád Mirza, 359, and Sartip Húsain Ali Khán, 362; presents to the Prince of Mash-had, 366; 379; enters Tehrán, 387; 389; arbitral decision, 390; in London, ib.
Gorjak, 297.
Grant, Captain, 51.
Great Salt Desert, 16.
Greyhounds, 61.
Grumkhan, 138.
Gúchah, 381.
Gulahak, 388.
Gulistán, 367.
Gulnabad, 164.
Gulpáigán, 105.
Gulzár Khán, 320; death at the age of 110, 321.
Gumbokí, 84.
Gúnabad, plain, 346, 348.
Gúrg, 247.
Gurrok, 222.
Gurshasp, 399.
Gwádar, 19, 112, 138, 141, 223.
Gwám-i-Talab Kháni, 81.
Gwár-Manzil, 221.
Gwárpusht, 130.
Gwatar, 123.

Gypseous strata, 10.

Haftád Rāh, 319.
Haftar, 73.
Haidar Ali Khán, 278.
Hájji Abdullah Khán, 242, 266.
— Abdun Nabi, 69.
— Ahmad, 226; Major Euan Smith's interview regarding, 227.
— Ali, 152.
— Firuzu-d-din, 402.
— Muhammad Húsain Khán, 244, 377.
— — Taki, 175.
Hajjiabad, 334.
Hadaku, 400.
Hamadán, 15.
Hánaka, 89, 193.
Hares, 179.
Harrison, Major, 31, 205, 215.
Harún-ar-Raschid, minar of, 381.
Hasanki canal, 302.
Hashim Khán, 404.
Hashmat-ul-Mulk, 249; visit to, 267.
Hauz-i-dár, 256; graveyard near, 257.
Hauz-i-Kaisr, 120.
Hauz-i-Súltán caravanserai, 151 and note.
Heath, prickly, 202.
Heit, 128.
Helmand robbers and the Korán, 54.
Henna manufactory, 86.
Herát, 50, 112, 115, 270, 355.
Himmatabad, 172.
Hindú, in Jálk, 62.
Hisámú-s-Saltanah, 174, 308, 319, 335, 348, 361.
Hoeltzer, Mr., 160; servant to, 379.
Hokát plain, 320.
Hormuzabad, 179.
Húng plateau, 40, 53.
Húsain Ali Khán, Sartip, 362.
— Khán, 217.
Húsainabad, 169, 267, 332; valley, 332.
Húsainabad-i-Nau, 289.
Hydrography of Persia, 1–10.
Hyena hunt, 274.

Ibex, 37, 251.
Ibrahimabad, 172; Scotch firs at, ib.

Ibráhím Khán, 22; administration of, 28; 60, 66, 71, 76, 85, 196, 199, 205; defeat of, by Balúchis, 234; 259, 304, 307; the murderer of Dr. Forbes, 317; his sons, 318; at Nád Ali fort, 321; 334, 398, 405, 409.
— Súltán, 33, 54, 77.
'Ichthyophagi,' 69.
Id-i-Kurbán, 126.
Iliáts, 89, 96, 98, 231.
'Illustrated London News,' 175.
Imám Juma, the, 97.
— Khán, Sardár, 288, 409; visit to, 291; 306.
— Riza, 347; shrine of, 356, 363; father of, 374.
Imámabad, 380.
Imámzádah, 85; of Shah-zádah Sultán Muhammad Ali, 347; of the Forty Virgins, 381.
'India,' the, 19, 226.
Indian servants, 64, 70.
Irafshán, 40, 67, 68.
Iranian plateau, 2; area, height above sea-level, and drainage, 3; heated stratum of air, 6.
Irij, ancient fort, 109.
Iris, fine species, 380.
Iron at Karmán, 100; Parpá mine, 107.
Irrigation, 7, 9, 104.
Isayáb, 135.
Isfahán, 10, 18, 50, 98, 106, 122; longitude, 113; 149, 157; Haft Dast Palace, 157; the governor, ib.; banquet, 159; the drama at, 160; the shaking minarets, 161; view from Mount Sufia, ib.; the Madrasah, 162; 164.
Isfandak, 55, 57, 60, 66.
Isfandiar, 256.
Ishkambarabád, 338.
Ishkizar, 172.
Iskil, 303.
Ismáíl Samáni, 399.
Ispatki, 131.
Ispid, 234.
Isratabád, 167.
Istabonat, or Savonát, 109.
Istikbál, 75, 91; at Níris, 108; at Isfahán, 157; Yazd, 173; Karmán, 182; Ráyín, 193; Bam, 196; Bampúr, 206; Pá-rúd,

INDEX. 435

217; Khánú, 234; Banjár, 308; Birjand, 334; Yúnsi, 350; Abdúlábad, 351; Mash-had, 357; Nishápúr, 369.
Itinerary of route, Sistán to Mash-had, 356; Mash-had to Tehrán, 391; Tehrán to Karmán, 428; Karmán to Gwadár, 429.

Jackals, 213.
Ja'far Khán, 233, 235.
Jaghatái Mughals, 400.
Jahánabád, 300 and *note*.
Já-i-Gharak, 366, 368.
Ja-i-Jirm valley, 377.
Jalálabád, 303 and *note*, 409.
Jalálu-d-dín, 404.
Jálk, 56, 61, 112.
Jamáli, 84.
Jambáz sowar, 200, 217.
Jambul trees, 231.
Jamshid, 399.
Jangíz Khán, 400.
Jánson Mirza, 378.
Jásinák, 307.
Jaz-morián, 79.
Jester, a Nírís, 108.
Jirúft, 74, 79; plain, 106.
Jonah, the prophet, 350; his grave at Mosul, *ib.*
Jordan willow-trees, 107.
Jufár, 192.
Juma Khán, 60.
Jungle of tamarisk and acacia, 22.
Juwain fortress, 319.

Kábul, 399.
Kábulí pilgrim, 62.
Kabúshán, 8.
Kabútar-Khán, 180.
Kabútarkhána, 104.
Kádirabád, 380.
'Kafsh,' salt swamp, 106.
Káfir-Kala'h, 355, 402.
Kahírí, 131.
Kái, royal house of, 401.
Kai Khusrú, 399.
Kaiáni kings, burial-place of, 293.
Kainagár, 72.
Káin, escort, 251; products and exports, 336; imports, 337; town, 341 and *note*; mosque, 341, 343 *note*; Amír of, 406 (Mir Alam Khán), 408; Amír's sons, 337 *note*.

Káiyáni Maliks, 401.
Káiyánis, genealogical tree of the, 416.
Kajár dynasty, 244.
Kajúrs, 27, 103.
Kajáwas, 371.
Kákhk, 346; tomb at, 347; ancient citadels, *ib.*
Kalag, 63.
Kalagán, 48, 50; ravine, 58, 59, 61; valley, halt in, 64.
Kala'h, 67.
Kal'ah-ad-dín, 65.
Kala'h-i-Aspikán fort, 39.
Kala'h-i-Bagalun, 355.
Kala'h-i-Dukhtar, or virgin's fort, 191, 354; legend of, 354.
Kala'h-i-Fath, 292; camp at, 293; garrison, 294, 409; fort, 295.
Kala'h-i-Kah, 326.
Kala'h-i-Kázi, 229; temperature, *ib.*
Kala'h-i-Khang, 275.
Kala'h-Nau, 278, 313.
— Shur, 193.
Kalaki, march to, 37; character of country, 38, 70.
Kalánzao, 80, 204.
Kala't, 348.
Kalát, 50; one of the defenders of, 53.
Kalátak, 126; Islamic festival at, 126; population, *ib.*
Kala't-i-Bájdí, 338.
Kala't-i-Mulla, 346.
Kalpúrakán, fort of, 66, 67.
Kamál Bandar, 286.
— Khán, 305, 409.
Kamih, 354.
Kam-Nasir, 345.
Kamran, Prince, 403.
Kanát, 61; superstition regarding, 103; diggers, 204.
Kandahár, 288.
Kapar, 141.
Karáchí, 6, 50.
Karaen-ul-Mélk, 107.
Karawán Rig, 325.
Karbala, 147.
Karin-i-Ibn-i-Jamshid, 342.
Káriz, 61.
Karmán, desert of, 12, 16; governor of, 21; ruins of fort, 93; copper at, 100, 150; position given by Pottinger incorrect, 111, 163; *istikbál*, 182; the Bágh-i-Nishát, 182; Wa-

kil-ul-Mulk, 183; the Nawáb, *ib.*; Christmas presents, 183; arrival of English mail, 185; carpet and shawl manufactories, 102; shawls superior to Kashmir, 187; visit to, *ib.*; presents from the Wakil-ul-Mulk, 189; farewell to, *ib.*; visit to Hindús, 190; parting gifts, 191; population and revenue, *ib.*
Karmán-Bandar-Abbas road, 9.
Karmánsháhán, 176.
Kasarkand, Chief of, 217, 219.
Káshán, 94, 149, 156; governor and inhabitants, 154; produce, *ib.*; importance and extent, *ib.*; palace of Fin, *ib.*; plain, 155.
Kashalah, 347.
Kashit, 86.
Kashkái tribe, 109.
Kashmir, 379; shawls, 102.
Kásimabád, ruined pillar of, 301.
Kasr-Kand, 120, 123; springs, 129; valley, 132.
Kastag, 33.
'Katkhuda,' 83.
'Kavir,' or Great Salt Desert, 152.
Kavira, 13.
Kázrún, failure of water at, 96.
Kedj, or Kej, disturbances at, 20; 122, 134; thermometer at, 135.
Kelag, 137.
Kh, pronunciation of, 69.
Khabis, 91, 93.
Kháf, plateau, 5, 15.
Khairabád, 316; swamp, 106; village, 107, 110.
Khalíf, 399.
Khálsa, 386.
Khán Bábá Khán, 263, 308.
Khán of Dizak, 40.
Khán-i-Khátún, 87.
Khán-i-Surkh, 104.
Khán Jahán Khán, 318, 321.
— —— (Sanjarání), 404.
— of Kalát, 38, 44, 54, 119, 139.
— Muhammad, 46.
Khánah-i-Darwish, 355.
Khanak, 340.
Khanikoff, M., 11, 15, 49, 81, 92, 111, 316, 370, 417.

INDEX.

Khánú, 234; governor of, ib.; slave inhabitants, ib.; route from, to Bam, 236 note.
Khárán, desert, 5, 48, 51, 68.
— Núshírwánís, 67; reported raid of, 83.
Kharwaj, 340.
Khátúnábád, 388.
— (Khánah Khátún), 194.
Khir, 108.
Khojah Ahmad, 281.
Khúdadád of Kalát, 78.
Khudabandan, 138.
Khúrasán, plateau, 81, 98; Wazír of, 371, 374.
Khúsrín, 80, 203.
Khúsru Khán Kajár, 371.
Khúzistán, plain of, 8, 14.
Khwájah Ahmad, 297.
— Ali Kázi, 331.
Kilágh-áb, 250; plain, 251; well at, ib.
Kimak, 279.
Kináragird, longitude, 113.
Kinneir, 243.
Kirta, 261.
Kishlák, 386.
Kishm island, 228.
Kiskat, 354.
Kisri, 345.
Kogán, 9.
Kohandil Khán, 309, 396, 398, 402.
Kohrúd, 81; longitude, 113.
Kolanch valley, 141.
Koláni, 214.
Kolmárut, 'Mihráb' at, 391.
Kolvár, 109.
Koshán, 71.
Koshk, 135; halt at, 140.
Kruk, 244.
Kúch Girdan, 204.
Kúcháhgardán, halt at, 79.
Kúchán, 366 and note.
Kúh, 85.
Kúhak, or Sar-i-Band, 44, 53; capture of, 60; 121, 280; fort, 283.
Kúh-Banán, 12.
Kuhmetah, 132.
Kúhpá, 81.
'Kulah-i-Faringi,' 155.
Kulmarisúnt, 221.
Kúm, Kavir, 16; sacred city of, 81, 152; shrines. 153; present state of, ib.; fanaticism of priests, ib.; manufactures, ib.
Kunár-bastah, 60.
Kundar ruins, 256.

Kúnúkúh, 103.
Kupa, 165; its manufacture, 166 (Kúhpá, ante).
Kúrds, 53.
Kúren Dágh, 8.
Kúrk, 187.
Kúrúk, 84.
Kushkoh, 178.
Kustug, 220.
Kutbu-d-dín, 400.
Kútbu'-d-din-Haidar, 353.
Kútrú, 15, 107.
Kwojah-Askir, 196.

Laddi, 80, 203.
Ladgasht, 63.
Laftán Juwain, 321.
Lají, 60.
Lár plain, 106.
Las Baila, 50.
Lásh, 115; fort, 316, 322.
Lásh-gird, 384.
Lásh Juwain, 271, 307, 315, 320 note.
Leach, Major, 69.
Lead at Karmán, 100.
Leech, Lieutenant, 417.
Lemm, 112.
Lentz, M., 92; published observations, 111.
Liquorice, wild, 109.
Locust, 382.
Loories, 69.
Louis Philippe, 361.
Lovett, Major Beresford, 12, 31, 47, 73, 79, 94; route through Beshná, 107; journey in Balúchistán, 119; hints to explorers, 122; Gwádar to Chirak, 123; to Kasr-Kand, 127; Champ to Bampúr, 130; joins Mission-camp, 131; Bampúr to Píshín, ib.; at Sarbáz, ib.; Píshín to Kej, 133; to Panjgúr, 135; Panjgúr to Mírí, 139; Mírí to Gwádar, 140; 150, 162, 165, 200, 205, 225, 240, 274, 283, 291, 303, 307, 310, 321, 368 note, 389.
Lút, 63.
Lút, or Lot, desert of, 16, 81.
'Lútís,' or players, 160.
Lutf Ali Khán, 243, 401.

Macnaghten, Sir W., 269.
Madder, 133.
Madrasah of Isfahán, 162.
— at Kákhk, 347.
Magas, 51, 67, 72; murder of the chief of, 69; 120, 121.
Magpies, 89.
Mahálú, 110.
Máhi-abad, 338.
'Máhi-Khorán,' 69.
Mahomed Ismáíl Beg, 377.
Máhún, 90, 192; shrine, ib.; population, 193.
Mahwilát, village group, 352.
Máibút, 170; potteries of, 171.
Makrán, 6; coast scenery, 22, 68.
Malcolm's 'History of Persia,' 184, 417.
Malik Husain Káiyáni, 401.
— Muhammad Káiyáni, 401.
— Shah, 400.
'Maluk-i-Túáif,' 399.
Mamasanís, 54; attack caravan, 56.
Mand, 121; importance of, 133; 216.
Mango-tree, 216.
Mansur Samáni, 399.
Manuchahr, 399.
Marco Polo, 89.
Mardán Khán, 319, 321.
Marmot, or prairie-dog, 355.
Mash-had, 98, 357; the Prince of, 359; loss of inhabitants by famine, 361; shrine, 363.
Mashísh, 81, 103.
Máshkíd, 51, 53; report of enemy at, 54.
Maskat, 6, 19.
Maskún, 239.
Masonic star, the, 315.
Ma'súm Khán, 196, 205.
Ma'súma Fatima, 152.
'Maukufát,' 347.
Máwará-un-nahár, governor of, 399.
Mayo, Lord, 324.
Mazandarán, 379.
Mazinán, 373; escort, 375.
'Mazra'hs.' 37.
Meh Kahnú, 345.
Mehnah, 352.
Mehr, 374.
Mehrdil Khán, 398, 404.
Merewether, Sir W., 189.
Merv, 342.
Metz, news of capitulation of, 152.
Miánaú, 377.
Mian-Dasht, 375, 377.
Miándeh, 351.
Mián Jangal, 109.
Mihmándár, the, 22.

INDEX.

Mihmandost, 380.
Mihmán-Khanah, or caravanserai, 386.
'Mihráb' at Kolmárut, 392.
Mihráb Khán, 68.
Miles, Captain, 19, 22, 70.
Míl-i-Nádiri, 247.
Míl-i-Záhidún, 302.
Mimosa thorn, 133.
Mináb, 120, 135, 230.
Minár of Khusru Gird, 373.
Minarets, the shaking, 161.
Minstrels, 231.
Mir, fort of the, 288.
Mír Afzal Khán, 398.
— Akhirdád, assistance of, 39; breach of contract, 40; quarrel with, 42.
Mirage 124.
Mírakhor, 75.
Mírakhor Ghafur Beg, 240.
Mir Alam Khán, 317.
— Asadullah Beg, 349.
— Kuchak Khán, citadel of, 258.
— Muhammad, 401.
— Múrád, 44, 59, 60.
— Shing Khán, 138.
— Wárís Kahántar, 305.
Mirheim, 91.
Mirí Bazár, 121, 123, 125; probable population, 126; 134, 138.
Mirza Abdullah, 231.
— Ashraf Ali Khán, 20, 54, 72, 111.
— Husain, 339.
— Jahán, murder of, 348.
— Khán, 60.
— Mahdi Khán, 380.
— Ma'súm Khán, 147; unfitness as arbitrator, 148; 150, 185, 189, 199, 209, 237, 242, 250; treachery of, 260; 289, 304, 309; suspension of, 313; 334, 358, 378, 383, 389.
— Melkam Khán, 389.
— Taki Khán, 154; his popularity, 155; his death, 156.
— Ulagh Beg, 400.
Mominabád, 380.
Mortaneh, 132.
Mosquitoes, 218.
Mountains, uniform direction of ranges, 10; exceptions, 12; same phenomenon probable in Arabia, 13; surveyed portions, 11; minor ridges, 12; absence of prominent spurs, 13; general elevation, *ib.*;

gravel slopes, *ib.*; highest continuous range, *ib.*
Ab Kand mound, 314.
Abúzir hill, 340, 342 *note*, 370.
Ahmadi, 237.
Ahu Ran, 129.
Akhor-i-Rakhsh, 257.
Albúrz chain, 5, 10, 13, 15, 81.
Angarin hill, 339.
Askarúh hills, 89.
Badamán hills, 102.
Bagárband range, 35, 125, 127.
Balkan, Lesser, 5.
Balúchistán system, 5.
Bampúsht hills, 44, 47, 57, 137.
Báshakird hills, 79, 204, (or Búshkúrd), 9.
Básmán hill, 73, 79, 130, 204.
Behúd, 344.
Caucasus, 2, 11.
Chahár Gúmbaz, 93.
Char-gul-ka-Dikri, 124.
Dahnah-i-Níris, 107.
'Dahnah-i-zaidar,' 377.
Damavánd, Mount, 7, 10, 13, 79, 387.
Damdam rock, 330.
Darabol Kúh, 124.
Daria Cham, mud volcano, 142.
Dawirán range, 182.
Deh Bakri, pass, 87, 93, 238; range, 193, 201.
Devan-i-Murád hills, 234.
Dízak hills, 6, 57, 66, 70.
Dúrmán, 93.
Fanoch pass, 80.
Farah hill, 326.
Firuz-Kúh, 387.
Ghanú hills, 228.
Giruk Pass, 135.
Godar-i-Baidar, 354.
Godar-i-Bonsir, 57.
Godár-i-Brinjinán, 66; or Bringinán, 73.
Godar-i-Darakht-i-Benar, 346.
Godar-i-Dehrúd, 368.
Godar-i-Dukhtar pass, 103.
Godar-i-Gúd, 344.
Godar-i-Khir-Sang pass, 354.
Godar-i-Lard-i-Zárd pass, 330.
Godar-i-Meshun pass, 331.
Godar-i-Rig pass, 333.
Godar-i-Shurún, 231.
Gonda-Kúh range, 333.

Gwánkúh ridge, 67.
Hindú Kúsh, 11.
Hindúwán pass, 47, 535 view from summit, 48.
Jafar Kúh, 181, (spelt Jufár), 192.
Jamál Bárid, 236.
Jamal-Báriz range, 13, 82.
Jambkí range, 23, 25, 32, 126.
Jhal, 38.
Jupá, 89, 90, 102.
Kala'h-i-Kúh, 330.
Kalát hills, 121, 128.
Khákhi Kúh, 124.
Khán-i-Surkh pass, 81.
Khárpúsht, or the Porcupine, 237.
Khúrasán hills, 6, 11, 13, 73, 104.
Kohrúd range, 81, 93, 104, 167.
Kopet, 2, 4.
Kothal-i-Páchinár pass, 366.
Kuha mound, 314.
Kúh Bákrán, 336.
— Dinar, 13.
— Dúm-ba-Lár, 107.
— Hazár, 13, 85, 88, 103.
— Kafút, 86.
— Kal-i-gav, 103.
— Kashkai, 110.
— Mehdí, 141.
— Salai, 41.
— Túdah, 109.
Kúh-i-Bars, range of, 354.
Kúh-i-Basmán, 12.
Kúh-i-Birg, 51; altitude of, 72.
Kúh-i-Garak hills, 231.
Kúh-i-Ghanú, 229.
Kúh-i-Guebre, 51.
Kúh-i-Hemand, 73, 119.
Kúh-i-Ispidán, 73.
Kúh-i-Kala'h-i-Kah range, 326.
Kúh-i-Khwájah, 253, 257, 267, 307.
Kúh-i-Mazampúsht, 47.
Kúh-i-Mulla, 134.
Kúh-i-Nasar, range of, 354.
Kúh-i-Naushádá, or Salammoniae, 12, 79.
Kúh-i-Panj, 104.
Kúh-i-Sabz, 48, 139.
Kúh-i-Sagurkand, 47.
Kúh-i-Salám, or Hill of Salutation, 356.
Kúh-i-Shah, 193, 330.
Kúh-i-Shairas peak, 133.
Kúh-i-Shararán, 387.
Kúh-i-Zilzila, 331.
Kúrdish, 7.

Kúrdistán, of, 8, 13.
Kúren, 2, 4.
Kúrú range, 13.
Laki range, 346.
Lashar hills, 129.
Már-Kúh, 338.
Meh-Kúh, 79.
Naiyun Kúshkuh, 229.
Ná-kúh, 38.
Neh-Bandan, 257.
Nigoj hills, 127, 129.
Nigor hills, 125.
Nusratabád range, 248.
Pá-band hill, 257.
Persian hills, 80.
Petteh hills, 32.
Pímpíska, 137.
Ripak peak, 125.
Rúndú hills, 35.
Saifu-d-dín pass, 82, 201.
Saiji range, 141.
Sanaud-i-Shah Múlk, 338.
Sarawán hills, 48.
Sardu or Rundu range, 132.
Sarhad hills, 6, 12.
Sarvistan range, 193.
Savalán, Mount, 13.
Shah Koh hill, 203.
Shah-Sowárán range, 82.
Shairas peaks, 36, 39.
Shír-Kúh, 172.
Siáh-Kúh, 32, 346.
Siáneh Kúh range, 12, 48, 57, 66, 73, 120.
Sig-i-Jandún, 231.
Sufia mount, 161.
Súlaimáníah, hill of, 370.
Súrok hills, 41.
Tahrúd cliff, 86; hills, 240.
Takht-i-Nádir, 82, 202.
Talár range, 36; pass, 126, 141.
Tang-i-Karím pass, 109.
Tang-i-Sardári pass, 387.
Taurus, 11.
Zágros, slopes of the, 8.
Múd, 333.
Mudákhil, 150 *note*, 365.
Muhammad of Ghazni, 399.
— Afzal Khán, 327.
— Aslam Khán, 326.
— Beg, 250.
— Háidar, 323.
— Husain Beg, 102.
— Húsain Khán, 384.
— Hasan Khán, 237, 321.
— Ismail Beg, 349.
— Khán, 205, 217.
— Razá Khán, 261.
— Riza (Imám Riza), 383.
— Rizá Khán, 396, 402.

Muhammad Ya'kúb Khán, 326.
Muhammadabád, 88, 171; silk factories, 176.
Muhammadi, 67.
'Muhandis,' 150.
Muhbat Khán Nharui, 279.
Mulberry-tree, 340.
Mules, 99.
Múlla Chákar's tower, 133.
— Khán, 287.
Mullah Haidar Muhammad, 332.
Múnshi báshi, 182.
Múnshi Karámat Khán, 318.
Múrchikár, longitude, 113.
Múrgháb, 107.
Múrti, 39, 41, 53, 54, 56.
Múshkinún, 167.
Mústafa Khán, 33, 36, 44, 45, 53, 57.
Mústasharu-l-Múlk, 371.
'Mustofi,' the, 158.
'Mustofi-ul-Mumálik,' 147.
Múzaffarú-d-Daulah, 301, 406.
Muzri, 127.
Myrtle, wild, 169.

Nád Ali, 282; fort, 298; ruins, 299.
Nadir Kuli Khán, 401.
— Shah, 243, 250, 401.
Naháwand, battle of, 399.
Náib Suliman Khán, 199.
Náibs, 106.
Náibu-l-Aiálah, the, 361.
Na'imabád, 244.
Nain, 167.
'Náizár,' the, 304, 314.
Nakal makán, 310.
Nál, 56.
Náo, 124.
Naraín, 139.
Nariman, 399.
Narmashír, 50, 74, 80; plains, 199, 245.
Nasírabád, 134, 259; reception at, 263; fort, 266, 275.
Nasr, 399.
— Rastonsi, 227.
Nasru-din-Shah, 275.
Náu-Gúnbaz, 168, 388.
Nau-Roz, 201, 253, 272, 287.
Nánshírwán, 382.
'Nawáb,' the, 101 and *note*.
Nectarinia, the new, 32.
Neh, 112, 115.
Neh-Bandán, 330.
Nharúi, 404.
Nharúis, the, 404.

Nijni-Novgorod, 146; hotel at, *ib.*
Nim-balúk, or Miánbiáz, 345; valley, *ib.*
Nirís, 107; head-quarters of Bábism, 108.
Nishapur, 355, 366, 370.
Nolent, 141.
Núru-dín, 235.
Núshírwání, 46, 55, 60.
Núshki, 51.
Nusratabád, 246, 248; garrison, 249.

Oleander, 140, 202.
Opium, 102; trade, 175, 347.
Orange-tree, 216.
Oreography of Persia, 10-17.
Ormúz Island, 228.
Owls, 261.

Pá-deh, 386.
Pa-Godar, 368.
'Pahluwan,' or wrestler, a, 350.
Pahra, 213.
Pahúrá, 58.
Palm group, 67, 70.
Panj-Deh, 323, 324.
Panjgúr, 53, 122, 135; date cultivation, 138.
Paris, *pétroleuses*, 257; treaty of 1837, 145.
Parom plateau, 136.
Parpá iron-mine, 107.
Partridge, francolin, 70.
Pá-rúd, 132, 216; revenue, 217; ruined tower near, 218.
Pasand Khán, 72.
Pasangán, longitude, 113.
Paskúh, 67.
Pattinson, Lieut., 289.
Perkins, Mrs., 363.
Persepolis, 105.
Persia, the famine, 94; physical geography of, 1, see Physical; population, 98.
Persian, Commissioner, see Mirza Ma'súm Khán; service, pay in, 106; sentinels, 238; New Year, 326; lady's costume, 347; statement of claims to Sistán, 395, 396.
Perso-Afghán Mission, 225; the Sistán question, *ib.*; Sir Frederic Goldsmid leaves England, *ib.*; from Aden to Bombay, 226; sail for Persian Gulf, *ib.*; at Bandar-Abbas, 226; leave, 228; halt at Bágu, *ib.*;

INDEX 439

Takht, 229; camp at the Rúdkhánah-i-Dúzdi, 231; at Khánú, 234; communicate with Major Lovett, 237; at the Deh Bakri pass, 239; Major Lovett and Sergeant Bower at Bam, 239; joined by Major Lovett at Behdírun, 240; preparations for march into Sistán, 241; itinerary of route, Bandar-Abbas to Bam, 241 *note*; halt at Bam, 241; misfortunes of the unpaid attaché, 242; leave Bam, *ib.*; strength of Mission, *ib. note*; camp at Túm-i-Rig, 247; halt at Nusratabád, 249; arrival of the Sistán escort, 250; camp at Túrsh-áb, 252; sight Sistán, 253; on the Zamin-i-Shílah, *ib.*; itinerary of march, Bam to Sistán, 255 *note*; halt at the Dervish's well, 256; at Sekuha, 259; Chelling, 261; reception at Nasírabád, 263; evidence of hostile feeling, 265; the Persian Commissioner's treachery, 266; visit to the Governor of Sistán, 267; breakfast at Tapah-i-Rig, 269; leave Nasírabád, 270; march up the Helmand, 271; at Kala'h-Nau, 278; Kimak, 279; the Sistán 'Band,' 281; camp at Dak-i-Dehli, 285; march to Chahár Búrjak, 288; further trouble with Persian Commissioner, 290; at Kala'h-i-Fath, 293; Aghá Ján Sarbandi, 297; Jahánábad fort, 300; Zahidún, 302; refused admission to Jalálabád, 303; at Búrj-i-Afghán, 304; opposition to meeting of Commissioners at Búrj-i-Alam Khán, 304; at Banjár, 305; Ma'sum Khán, 305; preparations to receive General Pollock and the Afghán Mission at Banjár, 306; leave Banjár, 311; quit Sistán, *ib.*; object of Mission frustrated by Persian authorities, *ib.*; visitors at Lásh Juwain, 318; Captain Lovett's return from survey of Chakhansúr, 321; Lásh fort, 322; Panj-Deh, 323; receive news of assassination of Lord Mayo, 324; camp at Dokala'h, 326; Duruh, 331; detained at Sar-Bishah, 333; march from Múd to Birjand, 334; April 1st in Birjand camp, 337; at Seh Deh, 339; Kám, 341; Dasht-i-Biáz, 345; Kákhk, 347; memento of travel, 348; Begistán, 349; *istikbál* at Yúnsi, 350; the Tehrán courier robbed, 351; halt at Abdúlábad, *ib.*; welcome at Túrbat-i-Haidari, 353; in the Tang of Muhammad Mirza, 354; Sharifábád, 356; reach Mashhad, *ib.*; reception by Sultán Murád Mirza, 359; officers not admitted to the shrine of Mash-had, 363; leave Mash-had, 366; beauty of the Dehrúd route, 367; halt at Já-i-Gharak, *ib.*; at Dehrúd, 369; halt at Zafarúni, 371; at Sabzawár, 373; Mehr, 374; Mazinán escort, 375; meet the Shahrúd escort, 376; Miánái, 377; arrive at Shahrúd, *ib.*; Quartermaster-Sergeant Bower leaves for England, *ib.*; halt at Deh Múlla, *ib.*; Damghán, *ib.*; Gúchah, 381; Ahúan, 382; Samnán, 383; march from Lásh-gird, 385; pass Abdúlabád, *ib.*; wind and sand-storm at Deh Namak, 386; Kishlák, *ib.*; camp at Aiwáni Káif, 387; Sir Fred. Goldsmid rides into Tehrán, *ib.*; halt at Khátúnábád, 388; enter Tehrán, *ib.*; rejection of Arbitral decision by Persian and Afghán Commissioners, 390; Sir Frederic Goldsmid, General Pollock, and Major Euan Smith quit Persia for London, 390. Perso-Balúch Mission, 145; Sir Frederic Goldsmid as Arbitrator, *ib.*; Sistán question postponed, 149; Makrán question proceeded with, 150; leave Tehrán, *ib.*; at Kala'h nú, *ib.*; at Kúm, 153; reach Káshán, *ib.*; route from Káshán to Isfahán, 157; leave Isfahán, 164; at Bambiz, 168; joined by Persian Commissioner at Husainabád, 169; at Akda, 170; reception at Yazd, 173; Bahramabád, 179; halt at Baghín, 182; reception at Karmán, 183; instructions to Persian Commissioner, 185; quit Karmán, 191; Ráyín, 193; Bam, 196; arrangements for march to Bampúr, 197, 199; detained by storm at Cháhi Kambar, 201; on the Bampúr plain, 203; preparations to meet Balúch chiefs, 205; reception at Bampúr, 206; Ibrahim Khán and arbitration question, 207; advent of Major Ross and party, 210; unlooked-for complications, 211 *note*; leave Bampúr, 212; anticipated attack of Ibrahim Khán on Túmp and Kej, 215; at Sarbáz, *ib.*; Pá-rúd, 217; Píshín, 220; dismissal of Persian escort, *ib.*; at the Persian and Kalát boundary, 221; arrival at Gwádar, 222; acceptation of the boundary-line in Makrán by the Persian Government, 223 *note*.

Peshawarán, 313; ruins, 315.
Phayre, Colonel, 267.
Photographer, a Royal, 361.
Physical Geography of Persia, 1; Iranian plateau, 2; boundaries, *ib.*; drainage, 3; rainfall, 5, 7; prevailing winds, 6; heated stratum of air, *ib.*; rivers and streams, see Rivers; uniform direction of mountain ranges, 10, see also Mountains; valleys and plains, 14; salt-swamp, *ib.*
Pierson, Captain, 112.
Pigeon-towers, 162.
Pigs, 204, 244.
Pirikasr, 63.
Pirsan, 132.
Píshín, camp at, 34; dress of natives, *ib.*; forts, 35, 121,

INDEX.

133; valley, 133; inhabitants, 34, 216, 219.
Písh-palm, 21, 25, 40, 127; uses, 128; 213.
Pistachio, wild, 57; nuts, 106.
Pisukh, 338.
Plane-trees, 89, 107.
Plover, 261.
Poet, a Níris, 108.
Pogí, 70.
Pollock, Colonel (now Sir Richard), 225; route to Sistán, 228, 267, 292, 295, 305, 355, 389; knowledge of antecedents of Lord Mayo's assassin, 324.
Pomegranates as an article of commerce, 106, 169, 387.
Popalzái-Afgháns, 316.
Poplar-willow, or Pádárbid, 65.
Population of Persia, 98.
Potatoes, 106.
Pottery, 387.
Pottinger, Sir Henry, 12, 48; his journey, 50–52, 58, 66, 83, 89, 92, 94, 106, 120, 244, 285 note.
Prince of Wales, the, news of, 280.
Pudár, 168.
Púhrá, 74.
Púlgi, 276, 408.
Pul-i-Abrisham, 376.
Pul-i-Dalák, 152.
Pul-i-Fasá, 110.

Rahím Khán, 97.
Rahmdil Khán, 398.
Rainfall on Oceanic and Caspian watersheds, 5; Gílán and Mazandarán, 6; average, 7, 14; at Súnan, 24.
Ráiyats, 229.
Ralli and Co., Messrs., 147.
Ramazán, fast of the, 163, 180, 183.
Rás-al-Hadd, 6.
Rask, 132, 218.
Rasúl Khán, 321.
Rawlinson, Sir Henry, 343.
Ráyín, 86, 88; population, 193.
Regán, ruined village of, 48, 197; inhabitants, 198; halt at, 199; storm, ib.
Rejang watch-tower, 345.
Resht, 147.
Rhages, 14.
Rhubarb, 72, 103, 339.

Ribát, 181, 248.
Ribát-i-Bibi, 352.
Ribát-i-Safid, 355.
Rice, 32, 215.
Rígán, 50, 79, 83; costume of inhabitants, 83, 245.
Rindán, 124.
Rindán, 313.
Rinds, tribe of, 20, 34, 46.
Rivad, 374.
Rivers and streams:—
Abrisham, 15.
Adraskand, 272, 329.
Aimini, 9.
Aji-Chái, 10.
Araxes, 2, 7.
Askán, 53.
Atrak, 8.
Báhú, or Nigor, 35, 119, 124, 126.
Bam, 195.
Bampúr, uncertainty of outlet, 4, 120.
Bandani, 109.
Bendameer, 10.
Bírí bed, 141.
Búdúr, 56.
Chasmah-i-Gilásh, 366.
Dádeh, 141.
Dasht, 9, 22, 32, 119, 123, 126, 134, 223.
Dashtiárí, 9, 22, 32, 126.
Dasht-i-Sangbar, 277.
Diála, 8.
Diz, 8.
Euphrates, 4.
Farah-rúd, 272, 314, 317, 322.
Firúzábád, 9.
Garnish, springs, 330.
Gazbastán, 139.
Germeh Khaneh, or Germe Rúd, 8.
Ghíshkhúr, 135.
Girán Bega, 203.
— Reg, 202.
Godar-i-Naúrgún, 231.
Gúrgán, 8.
Gwargo bed, 137.
Halil, 236.
Hamadán Rúd, or Kárasu, 10.
Hámún, 298.
Hamzai, 39, 40.
Hari-Rúd, 5.
Hárut, 5, 325.
Helmand, 3, 5, 48, 272, 282 note, 283 note, 286 note, 288.
Hingol, the, 119.
Húng, 40.
Indus, 2, 8.

Jaghatú, 10.
Jajrúd, 386.
Jaráhi, 8.
Jirúft, 9.
Káju, 124, 126, 128; source, 129.
Kalagán torrent-bed, 65.
Kalaki, 24.
Kár-agach, 9.
Kárasú, 15.
Karkhah, 8.
Kárún, or Kúrán, 8.
Kásh, 132.
Kavír, 15.
Khásh-rúd, 272.
Khaur-i-chahár-rúkán, 71.
Khúsh-Rúdak, or Khúshk-Rúd, 325.
Kíl, 134, 140.
Kir, 9, 119.
Kizil-Uzún, or Safid-Rúd, source of, 3; 7.
Kodání, 53.
Konar-nái, 82.
Kúr, 2, 7; source of, 3; 10.
Kurwád, 141.
Kustuk, 221.
Lár, source of, 7.
Mashísh, 104.
Máshkíd, or Boodoor, 5, 9, 48, 57, 63, 120.
Minab, 9.
Morin Pisha, spring, 130.
Mudí Khor, 136.
Nam, 119.
Newan, 138.
Níhing, 9; course, 23; camp in bed of, 39; journey up bed, 43; 48, 133; source, 136.
Níluk, 141.
Parsuk, 128.
Piskúl, 138.
Rakhshán, 9, 48, 138.
Rúdbár, 9, 79.
Rúd-i-Máhí, 248.
Rúd-khána, 197.
Rúdkhánah-i-Dúzdí, 232.
Rúdkhánah-i-Ghishkan, 232.
Rúdkhánah-i-Miánbiáz, 345.
Rúdkhánah-i-Shúr, 229.
Salt, tainted, 10.
Sarbáz, 132, 215.
Sháhid, 141.
Sháhrí, 42, 49.
Shaitáb, 56.
Shatt-ul-Arab, 8.
Shitáb, 136, 140.
Shúráb, 10, 15, 371.
Sol, 203.
Táb, 8.
Tahrúd, 86.

INDEX.

Tajand, 5.
Tigris, 2, 8.
Volga, 147.
Zaindarúd, 10, 104, 106, 164.
Roane, Mr., 19.
Rohnis, start for, 109.
Rosario, Dr., 225, 233, 235, 270, 335, 389.
Roses, a happy omen, 67; briar, 104.
Ross, Major, 200, 205, 222.
Rúdhán plain, 231.
Rúd-i-Míl valley, 330.
Rúdkhánah-i-Dúzdí, 233.
Rú-hilleh, 9.
Ruknabad, 171; cypress-tree at, ib.
Rúm, 339.
Russell, Lord, 406.
Russian Caspian Survey, 13.
— Scientific Expedition, 111.
Rústam, 256; horse of, 257; 298, 352, 399.
— Khán, 69.

Saadatábád, 105.
'Sabz-i Kúm,' 277.
Sabzawár, 371, 372; governor of, ib.; exports, 373.
Sabzwár, 115.
Sadí, 181.
Sádiki, 261.
Sadr Azim Mirza Agha Khán, 371.
Sadrabád, 375.
Sadnzáis, the, 402.
Saidábád, 81.
Saif-ud-din, 132.
Saint, Prime Minister to a, 364.
St. John, Major Oliver B., Physical Geography of Persia, 1; journey with Mr. Blanford, ib.; surveys, 12; journey through Balúchistán and Southern Persia, 18; lands in Gwádar Bay, 19; difficulties with the 'Sarbang,' 21; at Siroki, 22; camp at Báhú Kalát, 27; interview with Yár Muhammad, 29; at Pishin, 34; reaches Kalakí, 38; Gishtigán, 47; at the Hindúwán pass, 48; attack on date-caravan by Balúch Khán, 55; at Jálk, 61; starts for Dízak, 64; leaves Dízak for Bampúr, 70; camp at Bampúr, 75; Jamálí, 84; at Bam, 85;

halt at Ráyín, 89; Karmán, 92, 101; crosses the Kohrúd range, 104; reception at Níris, 108; Sarvistán, 110; reaches Shíráz, ib.; 245; joins Sir Frederic Goldsmid at Tehrán, 108, 110, 280.
Sáiyid Ikbál, tomb of, 315.
— Mir Asad Ullah Beg, 332.
— Muhammad, 398.
— Núr Muhammad Shah, 295, 308, 324; and the Hisámú-s-Saltanah, 365; see Afghán Commissioner.
Saiyidabád, 103; arrive at, 105; governor of, ib.
Salah-ibn Nasir, 399.
— Khán, 319.
Salián, 313.
'Salma,' 234.
Salor, 135.
Salt, layer at Túm-i-Rig, 247; plain, 106.
Sám, 399.
Samad Khán, 320, 322.
Saman, 23, 126.
Samnán, 15, 383; mosques and colleges, 384.
Sandstone, 43.
Sang Kala'h-dár, 371.
Sangábád, 84.
Sanjaráni, 404.
Sarakhs, 5, 16.
Sarawán, 50, 69.
Sarbandís, genealogical tree of the, 419.
Sarbáz, 78.
Sarbáz, 67, 68, 123, 131, 215.
Sar Bíshah, 332; population, ib.; valley, 337.
Sarbistán, 86, 109.
Sardár Ali Khán, 258, 261.
— Kohandíl Khán, 396.
Sarfaráz Khán, 286.
Sarhang, 106.
'Sarbang,' see Mirza Ashraf Ali.
Sar-i-band, 213.
Sar-i-Fahraj, 72.
Sar-i-Nárán, 202.
Sar-i-Sham, plateau, 47.
Sar-i-Shum, 136.
Sar-i-Yazd, 176.
Sarján, 94.
Sarjo, 69, 70.
Sar Khuran, 138.
— Khuran plain, 213.
— Poshida, 372.
Sartip, the, 76; see Ibráhím Khán.
Sarvistán, 110, 194.

Sar Zar, 355.
Scorpions, 78, 156.
Seas, Lakes, &c. :—
Arabian Sea, 2.
Bakhtegán Lake, 10.
Caspian Sea, 2; watershed of, 4, 7.
Gokcha Lake, 4.
Hámún, or Lake of Sistán, 3, 5.
Kazrán Lake, 10.
Níris Lake, 10, 14.
Persian Gulf, 2, 7.
Shíráz Lake, 10.
Urmía or Urúmíyah Lake, 4; basin, 7, 10, 14.
Van Lake, 14.
Segestán, 74.
Segzi, 165; curiosity of inhabitants, ib.
Seh-Deh, 338.
Sekuba, 197, 250, 256; population, 259.
Serpents, in Sistán, 273.
'Shabah-i-Shah,' 363.
Shabaz, 137.
Shabgaz, 379.
Shafi Muhammad, 129.
Shaftarabad, 172.
Sháh, H. M. the, representative of, 20; 44, 119; pilgrimage to Karbala, 147; and a mystic spring, 381, 388 *note*; visit to England and consent to Arbitral decision of Perso-Afghán Mission, 390.
Sháh Abbas, 154, 376, 384.
— Abdul-Azim, 388.
— Ismáil Safaví, 400.
— Kamran, 402.
— Mamud, 402.
— námah, 47.
— nawáz Khán, 60.
— Niámat Ullah, 192.
— Pasand Khán, 316, 321.
— Rukh, 400.
— Sulaimán Safaví, 382.
— Sufi, 347.
— Sultán Husain Nadir, 152.
— Tamasp, 347.
Shahraki, 405; genealogical tree of the, 423.
Shahr-i-Bábak, 50, 94, 106.
Shahr-i-Kadim, 266.
Shahr-i-Nau, 266.
Shahr-i-Sokhta, ruins, 256.
Shahristan, 284.
Shahrúd, 377; manufacture and produce, 378; Russian residents, 379; telegraph line at, ib.

INDEX

Shahzádah Sultán Muhammad Ali, 347.
Shál, 102.
Shámil, 230.
Shams, 177.
Shams-abad, 172.
Shamsudin Khán, 322.
Sharif Khán, 263 and note; his likeness in London, 264 note; 304, 408.
Sharifabád, 284, 297, 356.
Shawl manufactories, 101; of Karmán, 187.
Sheep, wild, 41, 88; sacrifice of, 164, 181, 234.
Sheil, Sir Justin, 342.
Shib-Deh, 326.
Shikárpúr, 288.
'Shilah' tract, 253.
Shilah-i-Zahák, 329.
Shír Ali Khán. 308, 371.
— Dil Khán, 277, 279.
— Muhammad Khán, 288.
Shíráz, 9, 11, 12, 27, 50, 94, 96, 110.
Shíráz-Firúzábád road, 9.
Shírpachár, 39.
Shírván, 8.
Shor-Gez, 247.
Shúráb, 371.
Shurián, 129.
Siánch Kúh, 25.
Sib, 67, 71.
Sikandar Pashi Khán, 331.
Sikh Havildar, 268.
Silk, culture, 172; trade at Yazd, 175.
Sind frontier, 219.
Sin-sin, longitude, 113.
Sipah Sálár, 343, 356, 380, 382.
Siroki, 22.
Sísid, 22, 124; inhabitants of, 126.
Sistán, 51; lake, 120; arbitration, 145; postponement of, 149; 253; price of corn, &c., 271; snakes and birds of, 273; the 'Band,' 281; 311; itinerary of route in, 313; summary of Arbitration evidence, 395; Persian claim, ib.; Afghán claim, ib.; Persian second statement, 396; Afghán second statement, 397; documents connected with, ib.; difficulty of collecting evidence, 398; Sir Frederic Goldsmid's statement, ib.; ancient right and government, 399; a dependency of Persia, 400; basis of Afghán claims, 401; as a part of Afghánistán, 403; present possession, 407; Arbitral opinion, 410; part of Persia under the Safavian kings, ib.; 'Sistán Proper' and 'Outer Sistán,' 412.
Smith, Major Euan, 83, 145, 147, 149, 184, 196, 205, 208, 211, 225, 283, 306, 389; see Perso-Afghán and Perso-Balúch Missions.
Smith, Major Murdoch, 87, 92, 186, 233.
Snake poison, bezoar as remedy for, 100.
— Typhlops, 105.
Snow-fall, 72.
Soh, longitude, 113.
Sohrán, 236.
Sonmiání, 50.
Sordu, 138.
Sowáráu tower, 137.
Spring, 104; a mystic, 381.
Stables as places of refuge, 182.
Steppes:—
  Bukhára, 2.
  Khiva, 2.
  South Russia, 2.
Stork, sacredness of, 153.
Stremáiukoff, M., 146.
Sulaiman Mirza, 370.
Sulimán Khan, 85.
Sulphur springs, 249.
Sultán Ali, 399.
— Husain Mirza, 399.
— Ján, 323.
— Muhammad, 399.
— Murád Mirza, 359; interview with, ib.
— Sanjar, 400.
Súltáns, 106.
Súrún, 70.
Surmich, 130.

Tabas, 15; Governor of, and the famine, 351.
Tag-i-Duruh, 330.
Tahrúd, 194.
Taimur Lang, 400.
— Shah, 373.
Táj Muhammad Khán, 259, 282, 304, 402, 421.
Tájiks, 105.
Takht, 229.
Takht-i-rawán, 18, 373.
Takiabád, 245.
Tamarisk, 71, 125, 133, 136, 197.
Tang, or defile of Muhammad Mirza, 354.
Tapah-i-Rig, 268.
Tarábád, 106.
Taradár-i-narm, 39.
Tarantulas, 78, 80.
Tartar Amir, 400.
Tashkúk, 53.
Tasp, 138.
Tehrán, 11, 18, 50, 98, 110; longitude, 113, 147.
Telegraph, Anglo-Persian, 18, 95; line on the 'Kavir,' 152; at Shahrúd, 379; at Deh Múlla, 380; at Damghán, 381; at Gúchah, 382.
Thamasp, Prince, 401.
Thomas, Mr. Gerard de Visme, 225, 371, 389.
Thull fort, 139.
Tiflak, 300.
Tobacco, cultivation, 134, 215.
Todd, Major, 418.
Toghrul, 400.
Tonk, 141.
'Tower of Silence,' 176.
Trees, tamarisk, 197.
Trézel, 15.
Trullhier, travels of, 12, 16.
Tudeshk, 167.
Túfangchis, 374.
Tuli Khán, 400.
Tulips, 339.
Tumáns, 106.
Túm-i-Mir-Dost, 250.
Túm-i-Rig, 245; temperature, 247.
Túmp, 38, 133; chief of, 205.
Tún, 112.
Tún-wa-Tabas, 346.
Turbat, 353.
Turbat, 134, 348; Governor of, 352.
Turbat-i-Haidari, 353; garrison, ib.
Turbat-i-Isa-Khán, 353.
Túrkman horses, 361.
Túrkmans, Russian expedition against, 5, 17; raids, 339, 342, 345, 352; unchecked by the government, 366, 379.
Turquoise mines, 370.
Túrsh-áb, 250; camp at, 252.
Túrshíz, 15.
'Tátís,' 276 note.

Umbelliferous plant, 104.
Uromastix lizard, 82.

INDEX.

Uzbeg watch-tower, 333.
Uzbegs, 346.

Valleys, plains, &c.:—
　Adarbaiján, Valley of, 14.
　Araxes, Valley of the, 2.
　Bampúr Valley, 67.
　Ghistan Valley, 220.
　Indus Valley, 2, 23.
　Isfahán Plain, 14.
　Karmán Plain, 14.
　Kavír, or Kafeh, swamp, 14.
　Kej Valley, 68, 75.
　Kúhak Plain, 25.
　Kur, Valley of the, 2.
　Lar Plain, 106.
　Mand Valley, 23, 38.
　Mogán Plain, 14.
　Paskúh Valley, 84.
　Persepolis Plain, 14.
　Rainfall, effect of, on valleys, 2.
　Roghán Ravine, 24.
　Safíd Rúd, Plain of the, 14.
　Sarján, or Saidábád Plain, 15.
　'Shadow of Death, Valley of the,' 151.
　Shíráz Plain, 14.
　Sultániah table-land, 14, 15.
　Tigris Valley, 2.
　Tump Valley, 23.
　Verámín, Plain of, 388.
　Zaindarúd Valley, 14.
Vincent's, Dean, 'Voyage of Nearchus,' 69, 74.
Viramal, 257.
Volcanoes, extinct, 12.

Wádí, 71.
Wajbőde, 138.

'Wakf,' 385.
Wakilabad, 197.
Wakíl-ul-Mulk, 36, 86; his police, 88; action during the famine, 94; supply of mules from, 99; ride with Blanford, 100; payments to the Sháh, ib.; exchange of presents with, 101; 177, 181, 183, 189, 197.
Washt, 67.
Wásilán, 307.
Water-hen, 71.
'Westminster Review,' 66.
Wheat, 102.
Willows, Jordan, 107.
Winds, causes of prevailing, 6; rain-bearing, 7; destructive, 386.
Wolf-traps, 346.
Wool exporting, 99.
Wynne, Mr., 417.

Yahia Khán, 105.
'Yakhchal,' at Maibút, 171, 293.
Ya'kub bin Láis, 399.
—— Khán, 149.
Yár Muhammad, 46, 47.
—— the Wazír, 398, 402.
—— Khán, 28; interview with, 29.
Yáwar, 106.
Yáwar, the, 36, 54, 76, 85.
—— Ghulám Husain Khán, 233, 237.
—— Suliman Khán, 196.
Yazd, 12, 50, 98; trade with India, 100, 173; Hindú residents, ib.; the Prince-Governor, 174; the Wazír,

ib.; opium trade, 175; silk trade, ib.; revenue, ib.; exports and imports, 176.
Yazdijird, 399.
Yazdikhást, 13.
Yek-Darakht, 334.
Yule's, Colonel, 'Marco Polo,' 87.
Yúnsi, 350; traces of famine, 351.
Yusúf, 342.
—— Khán, 54, 56.

Zafarúni, 371.
Zahidún, 301; ruins, ib. note.
Zaidan, 400.
Zaidar, 377.
Zain-u-din, 176.
Zál, 399.
Zamán Khán Populzái, 402.
—— Sháh, 403.
Zemánabád, 370.
'Zamin-i-Kavir,' 370.
Zamin-i-Shilah plain, 253.
Zamirán, highlands, 23, 44.
Zámrán, 135.
Zand, 103.
'Ziárat,' 67, 133, 233; ancient, 321; of Imam Zaíd, 327.
Zibad, 348.
Zirábád, 352.
Zirhan, 126.
Zirreh, swamp, 5, 75.
Zodiacal light, 29.
Zorháb, 352; his grave, ib.
—— Khán, 105.
Zúlfakar Khán, 242, 295.
Zulnun, 399.
Zuranj, 400.

www.ingramcontent.com/pod-product-compliance
Lightning Source LLC
Chambersburg PA
CBHW080918180426
43192CB00040B/2450